The Practice of System and Network Administration

The Practice of System and Network Administration

Thomas A. Limoncelli
and
Christine Hogan

ADDISON–WESLEY

Boston • San Francisco • New York • Toronto • Montreal
London • Munich • Paris • Madrid
Capetown • Sydney • Tokyo • Singapore • Mexico City

The publisher offers discounts on this book when ordered in quantity for special sales. For more information, please contact:

Pearson Education Corporate Sales Division
One Lake Street
Upper Saddle River, NJ 07458
(800) 382-3419
corpsales@pearsontechgroup.com

Visit us on the Web at *www.awl.com/cseng/*

Library of Congress Cataloging-in-Publication Data

Limoncelli, Tom.
      The practice of system and network administration/Tom Limoncelli, Christine Hogan.
            p. cm.
      Includes bibliographical references and index.
      ISBN 0-201-70271-1
            1. Computer networks—Management.   2. Computer systems   I. Hogan, Christine. II. Title.
      TK5105.5 .L53 2001
      004.6--dc21   2001041266

ISBN 0-201-70271-1

Text printed on recycled paper.
1 2 3 4 5 6 7 8 9 10 – CRS – 0504030201
First printing, August 2001

Contents

Preface

The goal of this book is to write down all the things that we've learned from our mentors and our real-world experiences. These are the things that are beyond what the manuals and the usual system administration books teach.

System administrators (SAs) often find themselves swamped with work, struggling to keep the site running, and faced with requests for new technologies from their customers. Servers are overloaded or unreliable, but fixing the problem requires weeks of planning and painstakingly untangling a mess of services so that they can be moved to new machines. Hidden dependencies are lurking around every corner, and getting bitten by one can be catastrophic. In the meantime, repetitive day-to-day tasks still need to be done. The challenges seem insurmountable.

Most sites grow organically, with little thought given to the big picture as each little change is implemented. Haphazardly, SAs learn about the fundamentals of good site design and support practices. They are taught by mentors, if at all, about the importance of simplicity, clarity, generality, automation, communication, and doing the basics first. These six principles are recurring themes in this book.

- *Simplicity* means that the smallest solution that solves the entire problem is the best solution. It keeps the systems easy to understand and reduces complex interactions between components that can cause debugging nightmares.

- *Clarity* means that the solution is not convoluted. It can be easily explained to someone on the project or even outside the project. Clarity makes it easier to change the system, as well as to maintain and debug it.

- *Generality* means that the solution solves many problems at once. Sometimes the most general solution is the simplest. It also means using vendor-independent open standard protocols that make systems more flexible and make it easier to link software packages together for better services.

- *Automation* is critical. Manual processes cannot be repeated accurately nor do they scale as well as automated processes. Automation is key to easing the system administration burden, and it eliminates tedious repetitive tasks and gives SAs more time to improve services.

- *Communication* between the right people can solve more problems than hardware or software. You need to communicate well with other SAs and with your customers. It is your responsibility to initiate communication. Communication ensures that everyone is working toward the same goals. Lack of communication leaves people concerned and annoyed. Communication also includes documentation: document customers' needs to make sure you agree on them, document design decisions you make, document maintenance procedures. Documentation makes systems easier to maintain and upgrade. Good communication and proper documentation also make it easier to hand off projects and maintenance when you leave or take on a new role.

- Doing the *basics first* means that you build the site on strong foundations by identifying and solving the basic problems before trying to attack more advanced ones. Doing the basics first makes adding advanced features considerably easier, and it makes services more robust. A good basic infrastructure can be repeatedly leveraged to improve the site with relatively little effort. Sometimes we see SAs at other sites making a huge effort to solve a problem that wouldn't exist, or would be a simple enhancement, if the site had a basic infrastructure in place. This book will help you identify what the basics are and show you how the other five principles apply. Each chapter looks at the basics of a given area. Get the fundamentals right, and everything else will fall into place.

These principles are universal. They apply at all levels of the system. They apply to physical networks and to computer hardware. They apply to all operating systems running at the site, all protocols used, all software, and all services provided. They apply at universities, non-profit institutions, government sites, businesses, and Internet service sites.

What Is an SA?

It's difficult to define what a system administrator is. Every company calls SAs something different. Sometimes they are called network administrators, system architects, or operators. Maybe the name isn't important—a rose by any other name . . .

Explaining What System Administration Entails

It's difficult to define system administration, but trying to explain it to a nontechnical person is even more difficult, especially if that person is your mom. Moms have the right to know how their offspring are paying their rent. A friend of Christine's always had trouble explaining to his mother what he did for a living and ended up giving a different answer every time she asked. Therefore she kept repeating the question every couple of months, waiting for an answer that would be meaningful to her. Then he started working for WebTV. When the product became available, he bought one for his Mom. From then on, he told her that he made sure that her WebTV service was working and was as fast as possible. She was very happy that she could now show her friends something and say, "That's what my son does!"

System administrators do many things. They look after computers, networks, and the people who use them. An SA may look after hardware, operating systems, software, configurations, applications, or security. A system administrator is someone who influences how effectively other people can use their computers and networks.

System Administration Matters

System administration matters because computers and networks matter. Computers are a lot more important than they were years ago. What happened?

First of all, the technology has changed. Corporate computers used to be independent, now they are connected. Business processes used to have a component that involved using a computer, now entire processes are done online and come to a halt if any part of the system is broken.

The widespread use of the Internet, intranets, and the move to a dot com world has redefined the way companies depend on computers. The Internet is a 24×7 operation, and sloppy operations can no longer be tolerated. A paper purchase order can be processed any time, anywhere; therefore there is an expectation that the computer system that automates the process will be available all the time, from anywhere. Nightly maintenance windows have become an unheard of luxury. That unreliable power system in the machine room that caused occasional but bearable problems now prevents sales from being recorded.

The biggest change, however, is due to CEOs[1] putting a new importance on computing. In business, nothing is important unless the CEO feels it is important. The CEO controls funding and sets priorities. Now CEOs have become dependent on email. They notice when an outage or an overloaded system slows down their email. The massive preparations for Y2K also brought home to CEOs how dependent their organizations have become on computers.

Management now has a more realistic view of computers. Previously people had unrealistic ideas of what computers could do; seeing them as portrayed in film: big, all-knowing, self-sufficient, miracle machines. This has changed. Even the need for SAs is now portrayed in films. In 1993, *Jurassic Park* (Crichton 1993) was the first mainstream movie to portray computers as needing system administration, leading to a better public understanding of what it is.

Computers matter more than ever. If computers are to work and work well, then system administration matters. We matter.

About the Book

This book was born from our experiences as SAs in a variety of companies. We have helped sites to grow. We have worked at small start-ups and universities, where lack of funding was an issue. We have worked at mid-size and large multinationals, where mergers and spin-offs give rise to more challenges. We've worked at fast-paced companies that do business on the Internet and have high-availability, high-performance, and rapid scaling issues. On the surface, these are very different environments with diverse challenges. But underneath, they all need the same building blocks, and the same fundamental principles apply.

This book gives you a framework—a way of thinking about system administration problems—rather than a narrow how-to solution to a particular problem. Given a solid framework, you can solve problems every time they appear, no matter what operating system (OS), brand of computer, or type of environment. This book is unique because it looks at system administration from this point of view, whereas most books for SAs focus on how to maintain one particular type of OS. With experience, however, all SAs learn that the big-picture problems and solutions are largely independent of the platform. This book will change the way you approach your work as an SA and the way you view the site you maintain.

---

[1]We use the term chief executive officer (CEO) loosely to mean the top person in an organization. Educational institutions have CEOs, they're just referred to as president, provost, proctor, or head. Governments have CEOs—they're just referred to as mayor, governor, Prime Minister, leader, or President.

The principles in this book apply to all environments. The approaches described may need to be scaled up or down, depending on your environment, but the basic principles still apply. In chapters where we felt that how to apply the information to other environments might not be obvious, we have included a section that illustrates how to apply the principles at different companies.

This book is not about how to configure or debug a particular OS. It will not tell you how to recover the shared libraries or DLLs when someone accidentally moves them. There are some excellent books that do cover those topics, and we will refer you to many of them throughout the book. What we *will* discuss here are the principles of good system administration, both basic and advanced, that we have learned through our own and others' experiences. These principles apply to all OSs. Following them *well* can make your life a lot easier. If you improve the way you approach problems, the benefit will be multiplied. Get the fundamentals right, and everything else falls into place. If they aren't done well, you will waste time repeatedly fixing the same things, and your customers[2] will be unhappy because they can't work effectively with broken machines.

We believe that SAs of all levels will benefit from reading this book. It gives junior SAs insight into the bigger picture of how sites work, their roles in the organizations, and how their careers can progress. Intermediate SAs will learn how to approach more complex problems and how to improve the sites, making their jobs easier and more interesting and their customers happier. It will help you to understand what is behind your day-to-day work, to learn the things that you can do now to save time in the future, to decide policy, to be architects and designers, to plan far into the future, to negotiate with vendors, and to interface with management. These are the things that concern senior SAs. None of them are listed in an OS's manual. Even senior SAs and systems architects can learn from our experiences and the experiences of our colleagues that are captured in these pages, as we have learned from each other in writing this book. We also cover several management topics, both for SA managers and for SAs who aspire to move into management.

The easiest way to learn usually is by example, particularly in the case of practical areas like system administration. Throughout the book, we use examples to illustrate the points we are making. The examples are mostly from medium or large sites, where scale adds its own problems. Typically, the examples are generic rather than specific to a particular OS, although some are OS-specific, usually UNIX or Windows. One of the strongest motivations we

---

[2]Throughout the book we refer to the end-user of our systems as "customers" rather than "users." A detailed explanation of why we do this is in Section 26.1.2.

had for writing this book is the understanding that the problems SAs face are the same across all OSs. A new OS that is significantly different from what we are used to can seem like a black box, a nuisance, or even a threat. However, despite the unfamiliar interface, as we get used to the new technology, eventually we realize that we face the same set of problems in deploying, scaling, and maintaining the new OS. Recognizing that fact, knowing what problems need solving, and understanding how to approach the solutions by building on experience with other OSs let us master the new challenges more easily.

We want this book to be something that changes your career. We want you to become so successful that if you see us on the street you'll give us a great big hug.

Organization

This book has four major parts:

- Part I, *The Principles,* discusses the most basic issues SAs deal with, but we view them from the perspective of the frameworks that will lead you to doing them well.
- Part II, *The Processes,* deals with change and the frameworks for making changes in ways that ensure success.
- Part III, *The Practices,* collects our thoughts on what makes a great system, a great email service, a great print service, a great helpdesk, and so on.
- Part IV, *Management,* comes next. Don't be afraid—it won't bite you. Actually, it will bite you, and we want you to be prepared. This part should help you understand your organization, your customers, yourself, and your managers. It ends with an exciting chapter on how to fire other SAs—a very delicate situation indeed.

The book ends with several *appendices.*

- Appendix A discusses the roles that you and others play. It's a catalog of the various people we've met or worked with and the value they bring to an organization.
- Appendix B connects the dots. It covers many situations you may experience and points you to the various places in the book that should be helpful. Please don't look at it now because you may find it so interesting that you won't return to finish reading this preface.
- Appendix C contains a list of acronyms used in the text.

Each chapter discusses a different topic, and the topics vary from the technical to the nontechnical. If one chapter doesn't apply to you, feel free to skip it. The chapters are linked to each other, so you may find yourself returning to a chapter that you previously thought was boring. We won't be offended.

There are two halves to each chapter: The Basics and The Icing. *The Basics* discusses the essentials that you just plain have to get right. Skipping any of these items will simply create more work for you in the future. Consider them investments that pay off in efficiency later on. *The Icing* deals with the cool things that you can do to be spectacular. Don't spend your time with these things until you are done with The Basics. We have made an attempt to drive the points home through anecdotes and case studies from personal experience. We hope that this makes the advice here more real for you. Never trust salespeople who don't use their own products.

What's Next?
Each chapter stands on its own. Feel free to jump around. However, we have carefully ordered the chapters so that they make the most sense if you read the book from start to finish. Either way, we hope you enjoy the book. We have learned a lot and had a lot of fun writing it. Let's begin.

Thomas A. Limoncelli
Lumeta Corporation
`tom@limoncelli.org`

Christine Hogan
Independent Consultant
`chogan@chogan.com`

P.S. Books, like software, always have bugs. We intend to maintain a list of updates to this book on its web site: `http://www.awl.com/cseng/0201702711` or our website, `http://www.EverythingSysAdmin.com`. Please visit!

Acknowledgments

We can't possibly thank everyone that helped us in some way or another, but that isn't going to stop us from trying.

Much of this book was inspired by Kernighan and Pike's *The Practice of Programming* (Kernighan and Pike 1999) and John Bentley's second edition of *Programming Pearls* (Bentley 1999).

We are grateful to Global Networking and Computing, Inc. (GNAC, pronounced Gee-Nack), Synopsys, and Eircom for permitting us to use photographs of their data center facilities to illustrate real-life examples of the good practices that we talk about.

We are indebted to the following people for their helpful editing: Valerie Natale, Ann Marie Quint, Josh Simon, and Amara Willey.

The people we have met through USENIX and SAGE and the LISA conferences have been major influences in our lives and careers. We would not be qualified to write this book if we hadn't met the people we did and learned so much from them.

Dozens of people helped us as we wrote this book—some by supplying anecdotes, some by reviewing parts of or the entire book, others by mentoring us during our careers. The only fair way to thank them all is alphabetically and to apologize in advance to anyone that we left out: Rajeev Agrawala, Al Aho, Jeff Allen, Eric Anderson, Ann Benninger, Eric Berglund, Melissa Binde, Steven Branigan, Sheila Brown-Klinger, Strata Rose Chalup, Brent Chapman, Bill Cheswick, Lee Damon, Tina Darmohray, Bach Thuoc (Daisy) Davis, R. Drew Davis, Ingo Dean, Arnold de Leon, Barbara Dijker, Viktor Dukhovni, Chelle-Marie Ehlers, Michael Erlinger, Paul Evans, Rémy Evard, Lookman Fazal, Robert Fulmer, Carson Gaspar, Paul Glick, David "Zonker" Harris, Katherine "Cappy" Harrison, Sandra Henry-Stocker, Mark Horton, Tim Hunter, Jeff Jensen, Jennifer Joy, Alan Judge, Christophe Kalt, Scott C. Kennedy, Brian Kernighan, Jim Lambert, Eliot Lear, Steven Levine, Les Lloyd, Ralph Loura, Bryan MacDonald, Sherry McBride, Mark Mellis,

Cliff Miller, Hal Miller, Ruth Milner, D. Toby Morrill, Joe Morris, Timothy Murphy, Ravi Narayan, Nils-Peter Nelson, Evi Nemeth, William Ninke, Cat Okita, Jim Paradis, Pat Parseghian, David Parter, Rob Pike, Hal Pomeranz, David Presotto, Doug Reimer, Tommy Reingold, Mike Richichi, Matthew F. Ringel, Dennis Ritchie, Paul D. Rohrigstamper, Ben Rosengart, David Ross, Peter Salus, Scott Schultz, Darren Shaw, Glenn Sieb, Karl Siil, Cicely Smith, Bryan Stansell, Hal Stern, Jay Stiles, Kim Supsinkas, Ken Thompson, Greg Tusar, Kim Wallace, Rabbit Warren, Dr. Geri Weitzman, PhD, Glen Wiley, Pat Wilson, Jim Witthoff, Frank Wojcik, Jay Yu, and Elizabeth Zwicky.

Thanks also to Lumeta Corporation and Lucent Technologies/Bell Labs for their support in writing this book.

Last but not least, the people at Addison-Wesley made this a particularly great experience for us. In particular, our gratitude extends to Karen Gettman, Mary Hart, and Emily Frey.

About the Authors

Tom and Christine know each other through attending USENIX conferences and being actively involved in the system administration community. It was at one of these conferences that they first spoke about collaborating on this book.

Thomas A. Limoncelli

Tom is Director of Operations at Lumeta Corporation, a venture start-up in New Jersey that focuses on enterprise network and security management. Most of Tom's experience comes from his seven years at AT&T and Lucent Bell Labs, where he supported the network used by the researchers and scientists. He led the effort to separate the Holmdel Bell Labs network among AT&T, Lucent, and NCR when the company split into three.

He learned his fundamentals from his three years at Mentor Graphics, Corp. Before that, he was at Drew University in Madison, New Jersey, where he received his B.A. in Computer Science.

Outside of work, Tom is a grass-roots civil-rights activist, who is recognized on both state and national levels. Tom's first published paper (Limoncelli 1997) extolled the lessons SAs can learn from activists. Tom doesn't see much difference between his work and activism careers—both are about helping people.

Christine Hogan

Christine's system administration career started at the Department of Mathematics in Trinity College, Dublin, where she worked for almost five years. After that, she went in search of sunshine and moved to Sicily, working for a year in a research company, and followed that with five years in California.

She was the security architect at Synopsys for a couple of years before joining some friends at GNAC, Inc., a few months after it was founded. While there, she worked with start-ups, e-commerce sites, bio-tech companies, and large, multinational hardware and software companies. On the technical side, she focused on security and networking, working with customers and helping GNAC, Inc., establish its data center and Internet connectivity. She also became involved with project management, customer management, and people management. After almost three years at GNAC, she went out on her own as an independent security consultant, working primarily at e-commerce sites for a few months, before returning to a colder climate.

She has recently returned to university and is studying for a Ph.D. in Imperial College, London. Christine also has a B.A. in mathematics and an M.Sc. in computer science from Trinity College, Dublin, and a Diploma in Legal Studies from the Dublin Institute of Technology.

Introduction

The manuals that came with your computer and network equipment do a
great job of telling you what commands to type and what buttons to click—
but they omit the principles that let you build an infrastructure that makes
it all run smoothly. They don't describe the human side of the processes
that make it all happen. They describe how to install various services, but
they don't reveal to you the insights other system administrators (SAs) have
gained through experience and what they have established as best practices.
Finally, the manuals don't advise you on the management practices that
system administration organization needs to have to keep it running; things
like how to structure the organization; size it; and manage it, yourself, your
team, and your boss. They also never discuss the one thing SAs always talk
about: negotiating salary.

That's why we wrote this book. This is where the computer manuals
left off.[1]

The chapters of this book are divided into two primary sections: (1) identifying the "The Basics" and (2) the "The Icing" for each topic. The Basics
sections are the things that you should be doing, and The Icing sections
are the things you should aspire to do when you have everything else under control. Senior SAs need to be able to say, "This is enough for now,
but in the future we will try to accomplish these other things." That is the
premise behind the way the chapters are organized. First, deal with the Basics and ignore the Icing sections. When you have finished with the Basics
in each chapter, look at the Icing—what's described there will seem more
attainable.

---

[1] We know what you're wondering, and the answer is on page 592. Come back here when you're
done.

However, don't completely skip the Icing section if you feel you are still mired in getting the Basics right. Reading the Icing will give you a vision of the ultimate direction in which you will want to go. Ever wonder how those older SAs seem to knowingly leave hooks in just the right places so that future growth "just happens"? That's because they know the things that are in the Icing sections.

I.1 Do These Now!

We tried to order the chapters logically. There are, however a couple issues that are so critical that we want to discuss them first. If you aren't doing these things you're in for a heap of trouble elsewhere. Do the following things right now.

I.1.1 Use a Trouble-Ticket System

SAs receive too many requests to remember them all in their heads. You need software to track the flood of requests you receive. Whether you call this software "request management" or "trouble-ticket tracking" you need it. If you are the only SA, at least you need a personal digital assistant (PDA) to track your to-do list.

Without such a system, we are certain that you are forgetting people's requests or not doing a task because you thought your coworker was working on it. Our customers get really upset when they feel their requests are being ignored.

Fixing the Lack of Follow-Through

Tom started working at a site that didn't have a request tracking system. On his first day, his coworkers complained that the customers didn't like them and did nothing but complain. The next day Tom had lunch with some of the customers. They were very appreciative of the work that the SAs did, *when* they completed their requests! However, they felt that most of their requests were flat out ignored.

Tom spent the next couple days installing a request tracking system. Ironically, this required putting off requests he got from customers, but it wasn't like they weren't used to service delays already. A month later he visited the same customers and they were much happier. They felt they were being heard; their requests were being assigned an ID number and they could see when the request was completed. If something wasn't completed, they had an audit trail to show to management to prove their point—there was less finger pointing. It wasn't a cure-all, but the tracking system got rid of an entire class of complaints and put the focus on the tasks at hand, rather than not managing the complaints. It unstuck the processes from the no-win situations they were in.

The SAs were happier also. It had been frustrating to have to deal with claims that a request was dropped when there was no proof whether it was dropped or whether a request was ever received. Now the complaints were about things that SAs could control—Are tasks getting done? Are reported problems being fixed? There was accountability for their actions. The SAs discovered other benefits too. They now had the ability to report to management how many requests were being handled each week, and to change the debate from "who messed up" (which is rarely productive) to "how many SAs are needed to fulfill all the requests" (which turned out to be the core problem).

There is a more complete discussion of request tracking software in Section 15.1.7. Until you get there, install a simple system right now. If you use UNIX, we recommend "Request Tracker."

Chapter 16 discusses how to process a single request, with advice for collecting requests, qualifying them, and getting the requested work done. Chapter 15 contains a complete discussion of managing a helpdesk. Maybe you will want to give that chapter to your boss to read.

I.1.2 Manage Quick Requests Right

Ever notice how difficult it is to get anything done when people keep interrupting you? Too many distractions make it impossible to finish any long-term projects. To fix this, organize your SA team so that one person handles the day-to-day interruptions, thereby letting everyone else work on their projects uninterrupted. This person is your shield.

If the interruption is a simple request, the "shield" should process it. If it is a more complicated request, she should delegate it (or "assign" it, in your helpdesk software) or, if possible, start working on it between all the interruptions.

If there are only two SAs, take turns. One person can handle interruptions in the morning and the other can take the afternoon shift. If you have a large SA team that handles dozens or hundreds of requests each day, you can reorganize your team so that some people handle interruptions and others deal with long-term projects.

Many sites are still stuck in the "every SA should be equally trained in everything" mentality. Remember, specialization is a good thing. Try it. You'll like it. Amazingly enough, your customers will like it too. You see, customers generally do have a perception of how long something should take to be completed. If you match that expectation, they will be much happier.

For example, people expect password resets to happen right away and new machines to be installed in a day or so. If the SA handling interruptions resets passwords quickly, customers won't mind if you let the installation of new machines slip for a couple hours. If, however, someone has to wait for a password reset because none of the SAs can be found, he will be unhappy.

In the course of a week, you'll still do the same amount of work, but by being smart about the order in which you do the tasks, your customers will be much happier with your response time. It's as simple as aligning your priorities with customer expectations.

You can use this technique to manage your time even if you are a solo SA. Train your customers to know that you prefer interruptions in the morning, and that afternoons are reserved for long-term projects. Of course, it is important to assure them that emergencies will always be dealt with right away. You can say it like this:

> First of all, let me state that if there is an emergency, that will be my top priority. However, for nonemergencies, I will try to be interrupt-driven in the morning and work on projects in the afternoon. Always feel free to stop by in the morning with a request. In the afternoon, if it isn't an emergency, please send me an email and I'll get to it in a timely manner.

Yeah, maybe your boss won't go for it, but do it anyway. He'll come around.

We expand on this technique in Section 26.1.3. Chapter 25 discusses how to structure your organization in general. Chapter 27 has a lot of advice on time-management skills for SAs.

I.1.3 Start Every New Host in a Known State

Finally, we're surprised by how many sites do not have a consistent method for loading the operating system (OS) of the hosts they deploy. (Solving this problem is the main focus of Chapter 1.) This anecdote highlights the issues.

Lack of Infrastructure Becomes Very Expensive

A large e-commerce site suffered a huge break-in. Most, if not all, of their machines were compromised and/or being hijacked to run everything from FTP servers loaded with pirated software to network chat systems. The site brought in security consultants to deal with the situation.

Nearly every host in the e-commerce platform had to be reloaded. With the advice of the consultants, the SAs started reloading the machines. After a few weeks, they had rebuilt less than a quarter of the machines because they were rebuilding them by hand. The security consultants advised the SAs that this approach was wrong. Building every machine by hand is error-prone and time-consuming. Even with a checklist for the SAs to use for securing the machines, steps would be missed because of mistakes and time pressures.

The problem was that the site had very little infrastructure and all the machines were built by hand using the same manual techniques that got them in trouble in the first place. What the site needed was an automated way to install the OS, software, and configuration onto the e-commerce servers. Normally, building such an automated system is done by an infrastructure group or a senior SA, not the security staff. However, no one else in the company could find the time to do it, so the security consultants did.

The security consultants had realized that it was their job to change the company's way of doing things. Before they could secure the site, the consultants knew that essential infrastructure would need to be built. The most essential part of security is a strong infrastructure to build on. Once the build process was automated, the SAs, who had been spending most of their time building new machines, could spend time addressing other problems.

The security consultants had to put several other basic infrastructure pieces in place to create the security infrastructure they had been chartered to build. The overall cost of "securing the site" was much higher than it would have been had the site already had good infrastructure in place. However, the new infrastructure had the added benefit of reducing the SAs' workloads.

Why didn't the original SAs know enough to build this infrastructure in the first place? The manual explains how to automate an OS installation, but knowing how important it is comes from experience. These SAs hadn't any mentors to learn from. Sure there were other excuses—not enough time, too difficult, not worth it, we'll do it next time—but the company would not have had the expense, bad press, and stock price drop if they had taken the time to do things right from the beginning.

Inconsistent OS configuration doesn't just affect security; it makes customer support difficult when every machine is full of trips and traps. It is confusing for customers when they see things set up differently on different computers. It breaks software compiled to expect files in particular locations.

If your site doesn't have an automated way to load new machines, set up such a system right now. Chapter 1 provides complete coverage of this topic.

I.2 Conclusion

Now that we've warmed you up with some high-impact changes you should make to your environment, there are still 32 chapters and three appendices left to go.

Part I of the book, Principles, deals with the *basic infrastructure* items that sites need to have.

Part II covers the *basic processes* that sites need to be able to handle well.

Part III discusses what we've learned from building various systems; it's our *best practices* for designing email systems, networks, backup and restore systems, and so on.

Part IV changes gears and discusses the organizational and *management* issues that concern SAs. We find that most senior SAs slowly get pushed into management. First, an SA becomes the senior SA, then the "team leader." Then, she becomes a "technical manager." Soon she realizes she is managing larger and larger groups of people. This is why we've included advice, based on our experience, about creating organizations; managing your group's visibility; managing yourself, your team, and your boss; and issues such as hiring and firing.

The final part of the book contains a Conclusion and Appendices. Appendix B, which brings it all together, proposes various situations and lists what parts of the book will be most useful to deal with each one. Some of you may want to start there, but the rest of us will want to begin at the beginning.

PART 1

The Principles

Chapter 1

Desktops

Managing operating systems on desktop workstations boils down to three basic tasks: loading the system software and applications initially, updating the system software and applications, and configuring network parameters. We call these "the big three."

If you don't get all three things right, if they don't happen uniformly across all systems, or if you skip them altogether, everything else you do will be harder. If you don't load the operating system (OS) *consistently* on all hosts, you'll find yourself with a support nightmare. And if you can't update and patch systems *quickly,* you will not be able to deploy patches and updates efficiently. If your network configurations are not administered from a centralized place such as a Dynamic Host Configuration Protocol (DHCP) server, then making the smallest network change will be painful.

Automating these tasks makes a world of difference.

Automating NT Installation Reduces Frustration
Before Windows NT installation was automated at Bell Labs, Tom found that personal computer (PC) system administrators (SAs) spent about 25 percent of their time fixing installation problems. Customers usually weren't

productive on new machines until they had gone back and forth with the
helpdesk on numerous issues. This often took a week. This was frustrating
to the SAs and the customers as well. This made a bad first impression:
every new employee's first encounter with an SA happened because his or
her machine didn't work properly from the start.

Obviously the SAs needed to find a way to reduce their installation
problems, and automation was the answer. The installation process was
automated using a homegrown system named *AutoLoad* (Fulmer and Levine
1998), which loaded the OS, as well as all applications and drivers.

Once the installations were automated, the SAs were a lot happier.
The boring process of performing the installation was now quick and easy.
The new process avoided all the mistakes that can happen during manual
installation. Less of the SAs' time was spent debugging their own mistakes.
Most importantly, the customers were a lot happier too.

Desktop workstations are usually deployed in large quantities and have
long life cycles. As a result, if you need to make a change on all of them,
doing it right becomes as complicated as it is critical. If something goes
wrong, you'll probably find yourself working late nights, blearily struggling
to fix a big mess, only to face grumpy users in the morning.

Case Study: A New Printing System

An SA was hired by a site that needed a new print system. The new system was
specified, designed, and tested very quickly. However, the consultant spent weeks
on the menial task of installing the new client software on each workstation because
the site had no automated method for rolling out software updates. Later the
consultant was hired to install a similar system at another site. This site had an
excellent (and documented!) software update system. Changes could be made *en
masse* very easily. The client software was packaged and distributed very quickly.
At the first site, the cost of building a new print system was mostly deploying to
desktops. At the second site, the main cost was the same as the main focus: the
new print service. The first site "saved money" by not implementing a method to
automate software rollouts and instead spent large amounts of money every time
new software needed to be deployed. They didn't have the foresight to realize
that in the future they would have other software to rollout. The second site saved
money by investing some money up front.

Desktops also have an interesting life cycle. Rémy Evard produced an
excellent treatment of an OS's life cycle in his paper "An Analysis of UNIX

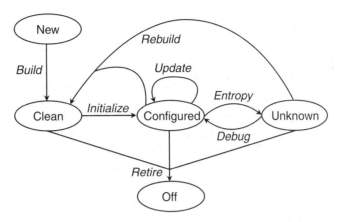

Figure 1.1: Evard's life cycle of a machine

System Configuration" (Evard 1997). Although his focus was UNIX hosts, it can be extrapolated to other OSs. He has developed the model shown in Figure 1.1 for thinking about the life span of an OS.

The diagram depicts five states: New, Clean, Configured, Unknown, and Off. "New" refers to a completely new machine. "Clean" refers to a machine on which the OS has been installed, but no localizations have been performed. "Configured" means a correctly configured and operational environment. The computer is in "Unknown" state when it has been misconfigured or has become out of date. "Off" refers to the machine being retired and powered off.

There are many ways to get from one of those states to another. The machine "build" and "initialize" processes are usually one step at most sites; they result in the OS being loaded and brought into a usable state. "Entropy" is deterioration that we don't want that leaves the computer in an "unknown" state, which is fixed by a "debug" process. Sometimes, either as a result of severe entropy or the need to recreate the system for a new purpose, the "rebuild" process happens and the machine is wiped and reloaded to bring it back to the "configured" state. These processes repeat as the months and years roll on. Finally, the machine becomes obsolete and is retired. It dies a tragic death or, as the model describes, is put into the "off" state.

What can we learn from this diagram? First, it is important to acknowledge that the various states and transitions exist. We plan for installation time, accept that things will break and require repair, and so on. All of these things require planning, staffing, and other resources.

Second, we notice that although there are many states, the computer is usable only in the configured state. We want to maximize the amount of time spent in that state. Most of the other processes deal with bringing the computer to the configured state or returning it to the configured state.

Therefore these setup and recovery processes should be fast, efficient, and, hopefully, automated.

To extend the time spent in the configured state, we must ensure that the OS degrades as slowly as possible. Design decisions of the OS vendor have the biggest impact here. Some OSs require new applications to be installed by loading files into various system directories, making it difficult to discern which files are part of which package. Others permit add-ons to be located nearly anywhere. Microsoft's Windows series is known for problems in this area. UNIX, on the other hand, provides strict permissions on directories and, as a result, user-installed applications can't degrade the integrity of the OS. However, architectural decisions made by the SA can weaken that protection. Is there a well-defined place for third-party applications to be installed outside of the system areas (see Chapter 23)? Has the user been given `root` or "Administrator" access and thus increased the entropy? Has the SA developed a way for users to do certain administrative tasks without having the supreme power of root?[1] SAs must find a balance between giving users full access and restricting them from anything but the access a normal user receives. This decision affects the rate at which the OS will decay.

If installation is completely automated, new hosts can start out identical to each other before they start to degrade. Manual installation is error-prone. When mistakes are made during installation, the host will begin life with a head start into the decay cycle.

Reinstallation ("Rebuild") is similar to installation, except one may potentially have to carry forward old data and applications (see Chapter 11). The decisions the SA makes early on affect how easy or difficult this process can be.

Finally, this model acknowledges that machines are eventually retired. We shouldn't be surprised: Machines don't last forever. However, there are tasks associated with retiring a machine. As in the case of reinstallation, some data and applications must be carried forward to the replacement machine or stored on tape for future reference, or else they will be lost in the sands of time.

In this chapter, we will use the term *platform* to mean a particular vendor/OS combination. Some examples are a PC running Windows 2000, a Sun Sparc Ultra60 running Solaris 7, and a Sun Enterprise 10000 running Solaris 8. Some sites might consider the same OS on different hardware to be different platforms, for example, Windows 2000 running on a desktop PC and a laptop PC might be two different platforms. Usually, different versions of the same OS are considered to be distinct platforms if their support requirements are significantly different.

---

[1] "To err is human; to really screw up requires the root password."—Anonymous

1.1 The Basics

The following are the basics of managing the OS on desktop workstations.

- Loading the system software and applications initially
- Updating the system software and applications
- Configuring network parameters

If your site is to be run in a cost-effective manner these three tasks should be automated for any platform that is widely used at your site. With these things done well, many other tasks become easier.

If your site has only a few hosts that are using a particular platform, it is difficult to justify creating extensive automation. However, with growth, you may wish you had the extensive automation you should have invested in earlier. It is important to recognize when you are getting near that point, whether by intuition, using business plan growth objectives, or monitoring customer demand.

First-Class Citizens
When Tom was at Bell Labs, his group was asked to support just about every kind of computer and OS one could imagine. Because it would be impossible to meet such a demand, it was established that some platforms would receive better support than others based on the needs of the business. "First-class citizens" were the platforms that would receive full support. SAs would receive training in hardware and software for these systems, documentation would be provided for users of such systems, and all three major tasks (loading, updating, and network configuration) would be automated. This permitted these hosts to be maintained in a cost-effective manner. Equally important, investing in automation for these hosts would reduce tedium, which would help retain employees (see Section 30.1.11).

All other platforms received very little support, which usually was in the form of providing an Internet Protocol (IP) address, security guidelines, and "best-effort support." Customers were supposed to be on their own. An SA couldn't spend more than an hour on a particular issue providing "best-effort support" to such systems. It was found that it was best to gently remind the customer of this time limit before work began, rather than to surprise the customer when the time limit was up.

A platform could be promoted to first-class citizen for many reasons. Customers would request it and demonstrate that certain projects would bring a large influx of a particular platform. SAs would sometimes take the initiative if they saw the trend before the customers did. For example, they tried not to support more than three versions of Solaris at a time, and they would promote the newest release as part of their process to eliminate the oldest release.

Sometimes it was cheaper to promote a platform rather than deal with the headaches caused by customers' own botched installations. One platform could take down the network by speaking the 802.3 Spanning Tree Protocol (the network would think it was a bridge). This was normally disabled, unless someone rebuilt the kernel and enabled "all features." ("It sounded like a good idea at the time!") After numerous disruptions as a result of this feature being enabled, the platform was promoted to take the installation process away from customers. Also, it is sometimes cheaper to promote OSs that have insecure default configurations than to deal with the security problems they create. Universities and organizations that live without firewalls often find themselves in this situation.

Creating such automation often requires a large investment of resources and therefore needs management action. Over the years, the Bell Labs management was educated about the importance of making such investments when new platforms were promoted to "first-class" status. They learned that making such investments paid off by providing superior service.

It isn't always easy to automate some of these processes. In some cases, Bell Labs had to invent them from scratch (Fulmer and Levine 1998) or build large layers of software on top of the vendor-provided solution to make it manageable (Heiss 1999). Sometimes, one must sacrifice other projects or sacrifice response time to other requests to dedicate time to building such systems. It is worth it in the long run.

When vendors try to sell us new products, we always ask them if and how these processes can be automated. We reject vendors that have no appreciation for deployment issues. Increasingly, vendors understand that the inability to rapidly deploy their products affects the customers' ability to rapidly purchase the products.

1.1.1 Loading the System Software and Applications Initially

Automation[2] solves a huge number of problems, and not all of them are technical. First, it saves money. Obviously, the time saved by replacing a manual process with an automated one is a big gain. Also, automation obviates two hidden costs.

---

[2]Every vendor has a different name for their systems for automated OS loading: Solaris has JumpStart, RedHat Linux has KickStart, SGI IRIX has RoboInst, HP-UX has Ignite-UX, and Microsoft Windows has AutoLoad (Fulmer and Levine 1998).

The first one relates to *mistakes:* Manual processes are subject to human error. A workstation has thousands of potential settings, sometimes in a single application. A small misconfiguration can cause a big failure. Sometimes, fixing this problem is easy: If someone accesses a problem application right after the workstation is delivered and reports it immediately, the SA will easily conclude the machine has a configuration problem. However, these problems often lurk unnoticed for months or years before the user accesses the particular application. At that point, why would the SA think to ask "Are you using this application for the first time?" In this situation, the SA often spends a lot of time searching for a problem that wouldn't have existed if installation had been automated.

The second hidden cost relates to *nonuniformity:* If you load manually, you'll never get the same configuration on all your machines, ever. When we loaded applications manually on PCs, we discovered that no amount of SA training would result in all our applications being configured the same way on every machine. Sometimes, the installer would forget one or two settings; other times, he just felt he had a better way. The result was that users often discovered that their new workstations weren't properly configured, or a user moving from one workstation to the next didn't have the exact same configuration and applications failed. Automation solves this problem.

Be Sure Your Automated System Is Truly Automated

Setting up an automated installation system takes a lot of effort. However, in the end, the effort will pay off by saving you more time than you spent initially. Remember this fact when you're frustrated in the thick of setup. Also remember that if you're going to set up an automated system, do it properly; otherwise it can cause you twice the trouble later.

The most important aspect of automation is that it must be *completely* automated. This statement sounds obvious, but implementing it can be another story. We feel it is worth the extra effort to not have to return to the machine time and time again to answer another prompt or start the next phase. This means prompts won't be answered incorrectly and phases won't be forgotten or skipped. It also improves time management for the SA, who can stay focused on the next task rather than having to remember to return to a machine to start the next phase.

Machine Says "I'm done!"

One SA modified his JumpStart system to send email to the helpdesk when the installation is complete. The email is sent from the newly installed machine, thereby testing that the machine is operational. The email that is generated notes the hostname, type of hardware, and other information that the helpdesk needs in order to add the machine to their inventory. On a busy day, it can be difficult to remember to return to a host to make sure that the installation completed successfully. With this system, the SA did not have to waste time checking on the machine. Instead the SA could make a note in their to-do list to check on the machine if email hadn't been received by a certain time.

The best installation systems do all of their human interaction at the beginning and then work to completion unattended. Some systems require zero input, because the automation "knows" what to do based on the host's Ethernet media access control (MAC) address. The installer should be able to walk away from the machine, confident that the procedure will complete on its own. If the procedure requires someone to return halfway through the installation to answer a question or two, it isn't truly automated and you'll lose efficiency. For example, if the SA forgets about the installation and goes to lunch or a meeting, the machine will hang there, doing nothing, until the SA returns. If she's out of the office, and she's the only one who can take care of the stuff halfway through, everyone who needs that machine will have to wait until she gets back.

Solaris' JumpStart is an excellent example of a truly automated installer. A program on the JumpStart server asks which template to use for a new client. This template can be set up by a senior SA in advance. When the time comes to actually install the OS, the installer—who can even be a clerk sent to start the process—need only type 'boot net - install.' The clerk waits to make sure the process has begun and then walks away. The machine is loaded, configured, and ready to run in 30 to 90 minutes, depending on the network speed.

Remove All Manual Steps

Tom was mentoring a new SA who was setting up JumpStart. The SA gave him a demo, which showed the OS load happening just as expected. After it was done, the SA showed how executing a simple script finished the configuration. Tom congratulated him on the achievement, but politely asked the SA to integrate that last step into the JumpStart process. Only after four rounds of this procedure was the new JumpStart system completely automated.

An important lesson here is that the SA hadn't actually made a mistake. First, it's easy to forget that executing that simple script at the end of the installation is actually detracting from your automation process. Next, it's also important to remember that when you're automating something, especially for the first time, you often need to fiddle with things to get it right.

When you think you've finished automating something, have someone unfamiliar with your work attempt to use it. Start him off with one sentence of instruction, but otherwise refuse to help him. If he gets to a point where he can't continue, you've found an area for improvement. Repeat this process until your cat could use the system.

Partial Automation

Partial automation is better than no automation at all. Until an installation system is perfected, one must create stop-gap measures.

A lack of automation can be justified when there are only a few of a particular platform, when the cost of complete automation is larger than the time savings, or if the vendor has done the world a disservice by making it impossible (or unsupported) to automate the procedure.

The most basic stop-gap measure is to have a well-documented process, so that it can be repeated the same way every time.[3] The documentation can be in the form of notes taken when building the first system, so that the various prompts can be answered the same way.

One can automate parts of the installation. Certain parts of the installation lend themselves to automation particularly well. For example, the "initialize" process in Figure 1.1 configures the OS for the local environment after being loaded to the vendor default. Usually this involves installing particular files, setting permissions, and rebooting. A script that copies a fixed set of files to their proper place can be a lifesaver. One can even build a `tar` or `zip` file of the files that changed during customization and extract them onto machines after using the vendor's install procedure.

Other stop-gap measures can be a little more creative.

Case Study: *Handling Partially Completed Installations*

Early versions of Microsoft Windows NT 4.0 AutoLoad (Fulmer and Levine 1998) were unable to install third-party drivers automatically. In particular, the sound card driver had to be installed manually. If the installation was being done in the person's office, the machine would be left with a note telling the owner that when they received a log-on prompt, the system would be usable except for the fact that audio wouldn't work. It then listed what time the SA would return to fix that one problem. Although a completely automated installation procedure would be preferred, this was a workable stop-gap solution.

---

[3] This is not to imply that automation removes the need for documentation.

Cloning and Other Methods

Some sites use cloned hard disks to create new machines. *Cloning hard disks* means setting up a host with the exact software configuration that is desired for all hosts that are going to be deployed. The hard disk of this host is then "cloned," or copied, to all new computers as they are installed. The original machine is usually known as a *golden host*. Rather than copying the hard disk over and over, usually the contents of the hard disk are copied onto a CD-ROM, tape, or network file server, which is used for the actual installation. A small industry is devoted to helping companies with this process and can help with specialized cloning hardware and software.

We prefer automating the loading process to cloning disks. If the hardware of the new machine is significantly different from that of the old machine, you have to make a separate master image. You don't need much imagination to envision ending up with lots of master images. Then, to complicate matters, if you want to make even a single change to something, you have to apply it to each master image.

Some OS vendors won't support cloned disks because their installation process makes decisions at load time based on what hardware is detected or other reasons. Windows NT generated a unique security ID (SID) for each machine. Initial cloning software for Windows NT wasn't able to generate unique SIDs for each host, causing many problems. This was eventually solved.

You can strike a balance here. Some sites clone disks to establish a minimal OS install and then use an automated software distribution system to layer all applications and patches on top.

Finally, some OS vendors don't provide ways to automate installation. However, there are "home-grown" options. SunOS 4.x didn't include anything like Solaris' JumpStart, so many sites loaded the OS from a CD-ROM and then ran a script that completed the process. The CD-ROM gave the machine a known state, and the script did the rest.

PARIS: Automated SunOS 4.x Installation

Given enough time and money, anything is possible. You can even build your own install system. Everyone knows that SunOS 4.x installations can't be automated. Everyone except Viktor Dukhovni. Dukhovni created Programmable Automatic Remote Installation Service (PARIS) in 1992, while working for Lehman Brothers. PARIS automated the process of loading SunOS 4.x on many hosts in parallel over the network long before Sun Solaris JumpStart was released.

At the time, the state of the art required walking a CD-ROM drive to each host in order to load the OS. PARIS allowed an SA in New York to remotely initiate an OS upgrade of all the machines at a branch office. The SA would then go home or out to dinner and some time later find that all the machines installed successfully. The ability to schedule unattended installs of groups of machines is a feature of PARIS still not found in most vendor-supplied installation systems.

Should You Trust the Vendor's Installation?

Computers usually come with the OS preloaded. Knowing this fact, you might think that you don't need to bother with reloading an OS that someone has already loaded for you. We disagree. In fact, we think that reloading the OS makes your life easier in the long run.

Reloading the OS from scratch yourself is better for several reasons. First, you probably would have to deal with loading other applications and localizations on top of a vendor-loaded OS before the machine would work at your site. Automating the entire loading process from scratch often is easier than layering applications and configurations on top of the vendor's OS install. Second, vendors can change their preloaded OS configurations, unknown to you, but loading from scratch gives you a *known state* on every machine. Using the preinstalled OS leads to deviation from your standard configuration. Eventually, such deviation can lead to problems.

Another reason to avoid using preloaded OSs is that eventually hosts have to have their OSs reloaded. For example, the hard disk might crash and be replaced by a blank one, or you might have a policy of zapping a desktop workstation and reloading its OS whenever it moves from one owner to another. When some of your machines are running preloaded OSs and others are running locally installed OSs, you have two platforms to support. There will be differences between them. You *don't* want to discover, smack in the middle of an emergency, that you can't load and install a host without the vendor's help.

The Tale of an OS That Had to Be Vendor-loaded

Once upon a time, Tom was experimenting with a UNIX system from a Japanese company that was just getting into the workstation business. The vendor shipped the unit preloaded with a customized version of UNIX. Unfortunately, the machine got irrecoverably mangled while the SAs were porting applications to it. Tom contacted the vendor, whose response was to send a new hard disk preloaded with the OS—all the way from Japan! Even though the old hard disk was fine and could be reformatted and reused, the vendor hadn't established a method for users to reload the OS, even from backup tapes.

Luckily for Tom, this workstation wasn't used for critical services. Imagine if it had been, though, and Tom suddenly found his network unusable—or, worse yet, payroll couldn't be processed until the machine was working! Those grumpy customers would not have been amused if they'd had to live without their paychecks until a hard drive arrived from Japan and had been recustomized.

If this machine had been a critical one, keeping a preloaded replacement hard disk on hand would have been prudent. A set of written directions on how to physically install it and bring the system back to a usable state would also have been a good idea.

The moral of this story is that if you *must* use a vendor-loaded OS, it's better to find out if you can load it from scratch right after it arrives, rather than during a disaster.

This anecdote describes an OS from long ago. However, history repeats itself. PC vendors preload OSs and often include special applications, add-ons, and drivers. Always verify that add-ons are included in the OS reload disks provided with the system. Sometimes the applications won't be missed, because they are "free" tools that aren't worth what is paid for them. However, they may be critical device drivers. This is particularly important for laptops, which often require drivers that do not come with the basic version of the OS. Tom ran into this problem while writing this book. After reloading Windows NT on his laptop, he had to add drivers to enable his PCMCIA slots. The drivers couldn't be brought to the laptop via modem or Ethernet because those were PCMCIA devices. They had to be downloaded to floppies using a different computer. Without a second computer, there would have been a difficult catch-22 situation.

Some vendors will preload a specific disk image that you provide. This combines the benefit of saving you from having to load the systems yourself with the advantage that you know exactly what is being loaded. However, you still have the burden of needing to update the master image as hardware and models change.

1.1.2   Updating the System Software and Applications

Wouldn't it be nice if an SA's job was finished once the OS and applications were loaded? But, as time goes by, people identify new bugs and new security holes, all of which need to be fixed. Also, people find cool new applications that need to be deployed. All of these tasks are *software updates*. Someone has to take care of them, and that someone is you. Don't worry though; you don't have to spend all of your time doing updates. Just like installation, updates can be automated, saving time and effort.

Software update systems[4] should be general enough to be able to deploy new applications, to update applications and to patch the OS. If a system can only distribute patches, new applications can be packaged as if they were patches. These systems can also be used for small changes that must be made to many hosts. A small file, such as `/etc/ntp.conf`, can be packaged into a "patch" and deployed by AutoPatch for Solaris. Most systems have the ability to include postinstall scripts—programs that are run to complete any changes required to install the package. One can even create a package that contains *only* a postinstall script as a way of deploying a complicated change.

Updates Are Different from the Initial Load

Automating software updates is similar to automating the initial load, but it is also different in many important ways.

The host is in usable state: Updates are done to machines that are in good running condition, whereas the initial load process has extra work to do— disks have to be partitioned, network parameters have to be deduced, and so on. In fact, initial loading must work on a host that is in a disabled state, such as with a completely blank hard drive.

The host is in an office: Update systems must be able to perform the job on the native network of the host. They cannot flood the network or disturb the other hosts on the network. An initial load process may be done in a laboratory where special equipment may be available. For example, it is common in large sites to have a special "install room" with a high-capacity network, where machines are prepared before delivery to the new owner's office.

No physical access: Updates shouldn't require a physical visit, which are disruptive to customers; plus coordinating them is expensive. Missed appointments, customers on vacation, and machines in locked offices all lead to the rescheduling-appointments nightmare. Physical visits can't be automated.

The host is already in use: Updates involve a machine that has been in use for a while; therefore the owner assumes it will be usable when the update is done. You can't mess up the machine! If the initial load process fails, you can wipe the disk and start from scratch.

The host may not be in "known state": As a result, the automation must be more careful, because the OS may have decayed since its initial

---

[4]Every vendor has a different name for its system for automating software updates: Solaris has AutoPatch, Microsoft Windows has SMS, and various people have written layers on top of Red Hat Linux's RPMs, SGI IRIX's RoboInst, and HP-UX's Software Distributor (SD-UX). Others are multiplatform solutions (Ressman and Valdés 2000).

installation. During the initial load, the state of the machine is much more controlled.

The host may have "live" users: Some updates can't be installed while a machine is in use. Microsoft's System Management Service (SMS) solves this problem by installing packages after a user has entered her user name and password to log in but before she gets access to the machine. The AutoPatch system used at Bell Labs sends email to a machine's owner two days before and lets her postpone the update a few days by creating a file with a particular name in /tmp.

The host may be gone: In this age of laptops, it is increasingly more likely that a host may not always be on the network when the update system is running. Update systems can no longer assume that hosts are alive, but must either chase after hosts until they reappear or be initiated by the host itself on a schedule plus any time it discovers that it has rejoined its home network.

The host may be dual-boot: In this age of dual-boot hosts, update systems that reach out to desktops must be careful to verify that they have reached the OS that they expected to reach. A dual-boot PC with Windows on one partition and Linux on another may run for months in Linux, missing out on updates for the Windows partition. Update systems for both the Linux and Windows systems must be smart enough to handle this situation.

One, Some, Many

A failed patch process has different ramifications than a failed OS load. A user probably won't even know if an OS failed to load because the host usually hasn't been delivered yet. However, a host that is being patched is usually at the person's desk, and if the patch fails and leaves the machine in an unusable condition, it is much more visible and frustrating.

You can reduce the risk of a failed patch by using the *one, some, many* technique. The technique works as follows:

One: First, patch one machine. This machine may belong to you, so there is incentive to get it right. If the patch fails, improve the process until it works for a single machine without fail.

Some: Next, try the patch on a few other machines. These machines may belong to the people in the cubicles next to yours. However, if possible, you should test your automated patch process on all the other SAs' desktops before you inflict it on users. SAs are a little more understanding.

Many: As you test your system and gain confidence that it won't melt someone's hard drive, slowly, slowly, move to larger and larger groups of users who are more and more risk-averse.

An automated update system has potential to cause massive damage. You *must* have a well-documented process around it to make sure risk is managed. The process needs to be well defined and repeatable, and you *must* attempt to improve it after each use. You can avoid disasters if you follow this system. Every time you distribute something, you're taking a risk. Don't take unnecessary risks.

Think of an automated patch system as being like a clinical trial of a experimental new anti-influenza drug. You wouldn't give an untested drug to thousands of people before you'd tested it on small groups of informed volunteers; likewise, you shouldn't implement an automated patch system until you're sure it won't do serious damage. Remember those grumpy customers? Think about how grumpy they'd get if your patch killed their machines and they hadn't even noticed the problem the patch was meant to fix!

Here are a few tips for your first steps in the update process.

- Create a well-defined update that will be distributed to all hosts. Nominate it for distribution. The nomination begins a buy-in phase to get it approved by all stake-holders. This practice prevents overly enthusiastic SAs from distributing trivial software packages that are not business critical.
- Establish a communication plan so that those affected don't feel surprised by updates. Execute the plan the same way *every time,* because users find comfort in consistency.
- When you're ready to implement your "Some" phase, think about using a metric such as *If there are no failures, each succeeding group is about 50 percent larger than the previous group. If there is a single failure, the group size returns to a single host and starts growing again.*
- Finally, you need a way for customers to stop the deployment process if things go disastrously wrong. The process document should indicate who has the authority to request a halt, how to request it, who has the authority to approve the request, and what happens next.

1.1.3 Network Configuration

The third component you need for a large desktop environment is an automated way to update network parameters. Network parameters are tiny bits of information that are often related to booting a computer and getting it onto the network. The information in them is highly customized for a particular subnet or even for a particular host. This characteristic is in contrast to a system such as application deployment, in which the same application is deployed to all hosts in the same configuration. As a result, your automated system for updating network parameters is usually separate from the other systems.

The most common system for automating this process is DHCP, the younger brother of the Boot Protocol (BOOTP). Some vendors have DHCP servers that can be set up in seconds; others take considerably longer. However, creating a global DNS/DHCP architecture with dozens or hundreds of sites requires a lot of planning and special knowledge. Some DHCP vendors have professional service organizations that will help you through the process, which can be particularly valuable for a global enterprise.

A small company may not see the value in letting you spend a day or more learning something that will, apparently, only save you from what seems like a minute or two of work whenever you set up a machine. Entering an IP address manually is no big deal, right? And for that matter, neither is manually entering a netmask and a couple of other parameters. Right?

Wrong. Sure, you'll save a day or two by not setting up a DHCP server. But there's a problem: Remember those hidden costs we mentioned at the beginning of this chapter? If you don't use DHCP, they'll rear their ugly heads sooner or later. Eventually, you'll have to renumber the IP subnet or change the subnet netmask, DNS server IP address, or some network parameter. If you don't have DHCP, you'll spend weeks or months making a single change, because you'll have to orchestrate teams of people to touch every host in the network. The small investment of using DHCP makes all future changes down the line nearly free.

Some customers complain that they don't like DHCP because they feel it gives away control of their machines to the SAs. This is misdirected anger. However, having a DHCP server is a good thing. DHCP balances centralized control with individual needs. A customer does not have to determine what netmask he will use or select his own IP address. If the complaint is that the DHCP server that you run is unreliable, then fix that problem, rather than lose the benefits of DHCP.

Anything worth doing is worth doing well. DHCP has its own best and worst practices. The following section discusses what we've learned.

Use Templates Rather Than Per-Host Configuration

DHCP systems should provide a templating system. Some DHCP systems store the particular parameters given to each individual host. Others store templates that describe what parameters are given to various classes of hosts. The benefit of templates is that if you have to make the same change to many hosts, you simply have to change the template. This is much better than scrolling through a long list of hosts trying to find which hosts require the change. Another benefit is that it is much more difficult to introduce a syntax error into a configuration file if a program is generating the file. Assuming your templates are syntactically correct, the configuration will be too.

Such a system does not need to be complicated. Many SAs write small programs to create their own template systems. They store a list of hosts in a database (or even a simple text file), and the program uses this data to program the DHCP server's configuration. Rather than putting the individual host information in a new file or creating a complicated database, it can be embedded into your current inventory database or file. For example UNIX sites can simply embed it into the `/etc/ethers` file that is already being maintained. This file is then used by a program that automatically generates the DHCP configuration. Sample lines from such a file are as follows:

```
8:0:20:1d:36:3a    adagio       #DHCP=sun
0:a0:c9:e1:af:2f   talpc        #DHCP=nt
0:60:b0:97:3d:77   sec4         #DHCP=hp4
0:a0:cc:55:5d:a2   bloop        #DHCP=any
0:0:a7:14:99:24    ostenato     #DHCP=ncd-barney
0:10:4b:52:de:c9   tallt        #DHCP=nt
0:10:4b:52:de:c9   tallt-home   #DHCP=nt
0:10:4b:52:de:c9   tallt-lab4   #DHCP=nt
0:10:4b:52:de:c9   tallt-lab5   #DHCP=nt
```

The token '`#DHCP=`' would be treated as a comment by any legacy program that looks at this file. However, the program that generates the DHCP server's configuration uses those codes to determine what to generate for that host. Hosts `adagio`, `talpc`, and `sec4` receive whatever configuration was proper for a Sun workstation, a Windows NT host, and a HP LaserJet 4 printer respectively. Host `ostenato` is an NCD X-Terminal that boots off a Trivial File Transfer Protocol (TFTP) server called `barney`. The NCD template takes a parameter, thus making it general enough for all of the hosts that need to read a configuration file from a TFTP server. The last four lines indicate that Tom's laptop should get a different IP address based on the four subnets to which it may be connected (his office, at home, or the fourth- or fifth-floor labs). Notice that even though we are using static assignments, it is still possible for a host to hop networks.

By embedding this information into an `/etc/ethers` file, we reduced the potential for typos. If it were in a separate file, the data could become inconsistent.

One site put this information in the comments of their `/etc/hosts` file, along with other tokens that indicated JumpStart and other parameters. The scripts that extracted this information into the JumpStart configuration files, DHCP configuration files, and other systems were integrated into a `Makefile`. By editing the `/etc/hosts` file and typing `make`, an SA was able to perform huge amounts of work!

When to Use Dynamic Leases

DHCP has many options and features. Don't feel obligated to use all of them. One feature that you may not need is the one that hands out IP addresses dynamically from a pool. Many people think that DHCP has to assign addresses in this way. In fact, it doesn't. Instead, it is often better to lock a particular host to a particular IP address. This is particularly true for servers whose IP address is in other configuration files, such as Domain Name Service (DNS) servers and firewalls. This technique is termed *static assignment* by the RFCs, or *permanent lease* by Microsoft DHCP servers.

The right time to use a dynamic pool is when you have many hosts chasing a small number of IP addresses. For example, say you have a Remote Access Server (RAS) with 200 modems for thousands of hosts that might dial into it. In that situation, it would be reasonable to have a dynamic pool of 220 addresses.[5] Another example would be a network with a high turnover of temporary hosts, such as a laboratory testbed, a computer installation room, or a network for visitor laptops. In these cases, there may only be enough physical room or ports for a certain number of computers. The IP address pool can be sized slightly larger than this maximum.

Typical office local area networks (LANs) are better suited to statically assigned leases. A typical office LAN will have a relatively fixed number of hosts. It would be silly to assign a pool of addresses that is smaller than the number of hosts; when they are all powered on, some would not receive addresses. If the addresses outnumber the hosts, you'd be wasting address space. Another benefit of static leases is that unknown hosts will not receive IP addresses. Although a rogue machine could simply hardcode an IP address and be functional, this does add a certain amount of nuisance to the intruder's task. One should remember that not receiving an IP address via DHCP does not prevent someone from plugging a rogue host into an LAN.

DHCP and Public Networks

DHCP can be integrated into systems that let one manage public networks. Office LANs tend to be tightly controlled, but there are many LANs that are not: LANs in university labs or dorms, sites with unprotected network jacks, hotel rooms, and wireless LANs (IEEE 802.11b) are some examples. In these situations, SAs would like the plug-in-and-go ease of an address pool, while being able to authenticate that users have permission to use corporate, university, or hotel resources. Tools and techniques for dealing with this problem are discussed by Beck (1999) and Valian (1999). Both systems

---

[5]Although you only need a pool of 200 IP addresses, a slightly larger pool has benefits. For example, if a host disconnects without releasing the lease, the IP address will be tied up until its lease period has ended. Allocating 10 percent additional IP addresses to abate this situation is reasonable.

permit unregistered hosts to register themselves. The system associates that person with the unknown host. The host is permitted to use the network because its behavior can be traced back to a responsible party. In the case of hotels, such systems are integrated with the billing system.

1.1.4 Dynamic DNS with DHCP

We're unimpressed by DHCP systems that update Dynamic DNS servers. This adds unnecessary complexity and security risk in return for a flashy feature.

In systems with Dynamic DNS, a client host tells the DHCP server what its hostname should be, and the DHCP server sends updates to the DNS server. (The client host can also send updates directly to the DNS server.) No matter what network the machine is plugged into, the DNS information for that host is consistent with the name of the host.

Without these Dynamic DNS updates, hosts with static leases will always have the same name in DNS because it always receives the same IP address. When using dynamic leases, the host's IP address is from a pool of addresses, each of which usually has a formulaic name such as `dhcp-pool-10`, `dhcp-pool-11`, `dhcp-pool-12`. No matter which host receives the tenth address in the pool, it's name in DNS will be `dhcp-pool-10`, which will most certainly be inconsistent with the hostname stored in its local configuration.

This inconsistency is unimportant unless the machine is a server. That is, if a host isn't running any services, nobody needs to refer to it by name and it doesn't matter what name is listed for it in DNS.[6] If the host is running services, the machine should receive a permanent DHCP lease and always have the same fixed name. Clients rarely deal well with a server that changes IP address during a reboot, and how often do servers just hop from one network to the other? Possibly only in heavy earthquake zones, or when using IPv6.

Letting a host determine its own hostname is a security risk. Hostnames should be controlled by a centralized authority, not the user of the host. What if someone configures his host to have the same name as a critical server? Which should the DNS/DHCP system believe is the real server? Most dynamic DNS/DHCP systems let you "lock down" names of critical servers, which means the list of "critical servers" is a new namespace that must be maintained and audited. If you accidentally omit a new server, you have a disaster waiting to occur.

---

[6]Some services are designed to run on hosts that change IP addresses. At each IP address change, they register their new location with a central registry that uses a fixed name and/or IP address. H.323 communication tools such as Microsoft Netmeeting use this technique.

Avoid situations in which customers are put in a position that allows their simple mistakes to disrupt others. LAN architects learned this a long time ago with respect to letting customers configure their own IP address. We should not repeat this mistake by letting customers set their own host-name. Before DHCP, customers would often take down an LAN by accidentally setting their host's IP address to the same as the router. They're handed a list of IP addresses to use to configure their PC. "Was the first one for 'default gateway' or was it the second one? Aw heck, I've got a 50/50 chance of getting it right." If they guess wrong, communication with the router essentially stops. The use of DHCP greatly reduced the chance of this happening. Permitting customers to pick their own hostname sounds like a variation on this theme that is destined to have similar results. We fear a rash of new problems related to customers setting their host's name to the name that was given to them to use as their email server, or their domain name, or another string.

Another issue relates to how these DNS updates are authenticated. The secure protocols for doing these updates ensure that the host that inserted records into DNS is the same host that requests that they are deleted or replaced. The protocols do little to prevent the initial insertion of data and have little control over the format or lexicon of permitted names. We foresee situations in which people configure their PCs with misleading names in an attempt to confuse or defraud others (a scam that commonly happens on the Internet[7]) coming soon to an intranet near you.

So many risks to gain one flashy feature!

Advocates of such systems would point out that all of these risks can be managed or mitigated, often through additional features and controls that can be configured. We reply that adding layers of additional complicated databases to manage risk sounds like a lot of work that can be avoided by simply not using this feature.

Some would argue that this feature increases accountability, because logs will always reflect the same host name. We, on the other hand, argue that there are other ways to gain better accountability. If you need to be able to trace illegal behavior of a host to a particular person, it is best to use a registration and tracking system as described in Section 1.1.3.

Dynamic DNS with DHCP only creates a system that is more complicated, more difficult to manage, more prone to failure, and less secure in exchange for a small amount of aesthetic pleasantness. It's not worth it.

Despite these arguments, OS vendors have started building systems that refuse to work unless dynamic DNS updates are enabled. Companies are put in the difficult position of having to choose between adopting new technology

---

[7]`http://www.whitehouse.com` is not the same as `http://www.whitehouse.gov`.

or reducing their security standards. Luckily, the security industry has a useful concept: containment. *Containment* means limiting a security risk so that it can only affect a well-defined area.

Therefore we recommend that Dynamic DNS should be limited to specific DNS zones that only contain information that is dynamically entered from a limited set of machines. This is known as building a "jail" for dynamic DNS information. For example, all hosts that use dynamic DNS might have names such as `myhost.dhcp.corp.example.com`. Hostnames in the (`dhcp.corp.example.com`) zone might have collisions and other problems, but those problems are isolated to that one zone. This technique can be extended to the entire range of Dynamic DNS updates that are required by Domain Controllers in Microsoft ActiveDirectory. One creates many jail DNS zones with funny looking names such as `_tcp.corp.example.com` and `_udp.corp.example.com` (Liu 2001).

Managing DHCP Lease Times

Lease times can be managed to aid in propagating updates. DHCP client hosts are given a set of parameters that they are expected to use for a certain amount of time, after which they must renew their leases. Changes to the parameters are seen at renewal time.

Suppose the lease time for a particular subnet is two weeks. Suppose you are going to change the netmask for that subnet. Normally, one can expect a two-week wait before all the hosts have this new netmask.

On the other hand, if you know the change is coming, you can set the lease time to be short during the time leading up to the change. Then change the netmask in the DHCP server's configuration, and the update will propagate quickly. Once you have verified that the change has created no ill effects, you can increase the lease time to the original value (two weeks).

Using this technique you can rollout a change much faster than without DHCP.

DHCP Also Assists in Moving Clients Away from Resources

At Bell Labs, Tom needed to change the IP address of the primary DNS server. Such a change would take a moment, but it would take weeks to propagate the change to all clients via DHCP. Clients wouldn't have functioned properly until they had received their update. It could have been a major outage.

He temporarily configured the DHCP server to direct all clients to use a completely different DNS server. It wasn't the optimal DNS server for those clients to use, but it was one that worked. Once the original DNS server had stopped receiving requests, he could renumber it and test it without worry.

Later, he changed the DHCP server to direct clients to the new IP address of the primary DNS server.

Although hosts were using a slower DNS server for a while, they never felt the pain of a complete outage.

The optimal length for default leases is a philosophical battle that is beyond the scope of this book. For discussions on the topic, we recommend, *The DHCP Handbook* (Lemon and Droms 1999) and *DHCP: A Guide to Dynamic TCP/IP Network Configuration* (Kercheval 1999).

Case Study: Bell Labs Laptop Net

The Computer Science Research group at Bell Labs has a subnet in its famous "UNIX Room" with a five-minute lease. Laptops can plug into the subnet in this room for short periods. The lease is only five minutes because the SAs observed that users require about five minutes to walk their laptops back to their offices from the UNIX Room. By that time, the lease has expired.

1.2   The Icing

Up to this point, this chapter has dealt with technical details that are basic to getting desktop deployment right. These issues are so fundamental that doing them well will affect nearly every other possible task. This section will help you fine-tune things a bit.

Also, once you have the basics in place, keep an eye open for new technologies that help to automate other aspects of desktop support (Miller and Donnini 2000a). Desktops are the most numerous machines in the company. Every small gain in reducing desktop support overhead has a massive impact.

1.2.1   High Confidence in Completion

There are automated processes, and then there are automated processes. When we have exceptionally high confidence in a process, our mind is liberated from worry of failure and we start to see new ways to use the process. Christophe Kalt had extremely high confidence that a JumpStart at Bell Labs would run to completion without fail or without the system unexpectedly stopping to ask for user input. He would use "**at**" to schedule hosts to be JumpStarted[8] at times when neither he nor the customer would be awake. This changed the way he could offer service to customers. This was only possible because there was high confidence that the installation would complete without error.

1.2.2 Involve Customers in the Standardization Process

If a standard configuration is going to be inflicted on customers, you should involve them in specifications and design. In a perfect world, customers would be included in the design process from the very beginning. Designated delegates or interested managers would choose applications to include in the configuration. Every application would have a service level agreement detailing the level of support expected from the SAs. New releases of OSs and applications would be tracked and approved, with controlled introductions similar to those described in the section on automated patching.

However, real-world platforms tend to be controlled either by management, with excruciating exactness, or by the SA team, which is responsible for providing a basic platform that users can customize. In the former case, one might imagine a telesales office where the operators see a particular set of applications. Here the SAs work with management to determine exactly what will be loaded, when to schedule upgrades, and so on.

The latter environment is more common. At one site, the standard platform for a PC is its OS, the most commonly required applications, the applications inflicted on everyone by the parent company, and utilities that customers commonly request and that can be licensed economically in bulk. The environment is very open, and there are no formal committee meetings. SAs do, however, have close relationships with many customers and therefore are in touch with the customers' needs.

For certain applications, there are more formal processes. For example, a particular group of developers requires a particular toolset. Every software release that they develop has a toolset that is defined, tested, approved, and deployed. SAs should be part of the process so that they can match resources with the deployment schedule.

1.2.3 A Variety of Standard Configurations

Having multiple standard configurations can be a thing of beauty or a nightmare, and the SA is the person who determines which category applies. The more "standard configurations" a site has, the more difficult it is to maintain

---

[8]The Solaris command `reboot -- 'net - install'` eliminates the need for a human to type on the console to start the process. It can be done remotely if necessary.

them all. One way to make a large variety of configurations scale well is to be sure that every configuration uses the same server and mechanisms rather than having one server for each standard. However, if you invest time into making a single generalized system that can produce multiple configurations and scale, you'll create something that will be a joy forever.

The general concept of managed, standardized configurations is often referred to as Software Configuration Management (SCM). This is a process that applies to servers, as well as desktops.

We don't discuss servers until the next chapter, but it should be noted that special configurations can be developed for server installations. Although servers run particularly unique applications, they always have some kind of base installation that can be specified as one of these custom configurations. When redundant servers are being rolled out to add capacity, having the complete installation automated can be a big win. For example, many Internet sites have redundant servers for providing static pages, Common Gateway Interface (CGI) (dynamic) pages, or other services. If these various configurations are produced through an automated mechanism, rolling out additional capacity in any area is a simple matter.

They can also take some of the pain out of OS upgrades. If you're able to completely wipe your disk and reinstall, OS upgrades become trivial. This requires more diligence in areas such as segregating user data and handling host-specific system data.

1.3   Conclusion

In this chapter, we have reviewed the processes involved in maintaining the OSs of desktop computers.

Desktops are different from servers in that they are usually deployed in large quantities, each with nearly the same configuration. All computers have a life cycle that begins with the OS being loaded and ends when the machine is powered off for the last time. During that time, the software on the system degrades as a result of entropy, is upgraded, and is reloaded from scratch as the cycle begins again. Ideally, all hosts of a particular platform begin with the same configuration and should be upgraded in parallel. Some phases of the life cycle are more useful to users than others. We seek to increase the time spent in the more usable phases and shorten the time spent in the less usable phases.

Three processes create the basis for everything else in this chapter: the initial loading of the OS should be automated, software updates should be automated, and network configuration should be centrally administered through a system such as DHCP. These three objectives are critical to economical management. Doing those basics right makes everything that follows run smoothly.

Exercises

1. What constitutes a "platform," as used in Section 1.1? List all the platforms used in your environment, and group them based on which can be considered the same for the purpose of support. Explain how you made your decision.

2. An anecdote in Section 1 describes a site that repeatedly spent money deploying software manually rather than investing once in deployment automation. It might be difficult to understand why a site would be so foolish. Examine your own site or a site you recently visited and list at least three instances in which similar investments had not been made. For each, list why the investment hadn't been made. What do your answers tell you?

3. Select a type of host or OS in your environment that is not, as the example in Section 1.1 described, a "first-class citizen." How would you make this a "first-class citizen" if it was determined that demand soon would increase? How would platforms in your environment be promoted to "first-class citizen"?

4. In one of the examples, Tom mentored a new SA who was installing Solaris JumpStart. The script that needed to be run at the end simply copied certain files into place. How could the script (whether run automatically or manually) be eliminated?

5. DHCP presupposes IP-style networking. This book is very IP-centric. What would you do if you're in an all-Novell shop using IPX/SPX? OSI-net (X.25 PAD)? DECnet environment?

Chapter 2

Servers

This chapter is about servers. A server is different from a desktop because more (people and computers) depends on a server. This makes reliability and up-time a higher priority. Therefore we invest effort in making a server reliable, we look for features that will make repair time shorter, we give it a better working environment, and we configure it with special care.

A server may have hundreds, thousands, or possibly millions of clients relying on it. Every effort to increase performance or reliability is amortized over many clients. Servers are often expected to last longer than clients, which also justifies the additional cost. Purchasing a server with spare capacity becomes an investment in extending its life span.

2.1   The Basics

Hardware sold as a server is qualitatively different from hardware sold as a desktop machine. Such hardware has different features and is engineered to a different economic model. Special steps are taken when installing servers. They typically have maintenance contracts, disk backup systems, different OS configurations, and better remote access, and they reside in the data center. Understanding these differences will help you make better purchasing decisions.

2.1.1   Buy Server Hardware for Servers

Systems sold as servers are different from systems sold to be clients or desktops. It is often tempting to "save money" by purchasing desktop hardware and loading it with server software. This usually works in the short-term, but it is not the best choice for the long-term or in a large installation. You would be building a house of cards. Server hardware usually costs more, but it has additional features that justify the cost. Some of the features include

More internal space: Servers usually have more physical space inside for devices such as hard drives and slots for cards and CPUs.

More CPU performance: Servers often have multiple CPUs or a single fast CPU. The same CPU may be available in various speeds, each linearly priced with respect to speed. However the fastest revision of a CPU tends to be disproportionately expensive. One may think of this as a surcharge for being on the cutting edge. Such an extra cost can be more easily justified on a server that is supporting multiple people. Because a server is expected to last longer, it is often reasonable to get a faster CPU that will not become obsolete as quickly. Note that CPU speed on a server does not always determine performance, because many applications are Input/Output (I/O)-bound, not CPU-bound.

High performance I/O: Servers usually do more I/O than clients. The quantity of I/O is often proportional to the number of clients. This justifies a faster I/O subsystem. That might mean SCSI or FC-AL disk drives instead of IDE, higher-speed internal buses, Redundant Array of Independent Disks (RAID) standard, or network interfaces that are orders of magnitude faster than the clients.

More upgrade options: Servers usually have more upgrade options than hardware sold for the desktop. They are designed for growth. They often have the ability to add CPUs or replace individual CPUs with faster ones. For example, the CPUs of large servers from SGI and Sun can be replaced without replacing the motherboard.

Rack mounts: Servers should be rack-mountable. In Chapter 17, we discuss the importance of rack-mounting servers rather than stacking them. Although nonrackable servers can be put on shelves in racks, this wastes space and is inconvenient. Whereas desktop hardware may have a pretty, molded plastic case in the shape of a gumdrop, a server should be rectangular and designed for efficient space utilization in a rack. Any covers that need to be removed to do repairs should be removable while the host is still rack-mounted. Having the word "server" included in a product name is not sufficient; care must be taken to make sure that it fits in the space allocated.

No side-access needs: A rack-mounted host is easier to repair or perform maintenance on if tasks can be done while it remains in the rack. Such tasks must be performed without access to the sides of the machine. All cables should be on the back, and all drive bays should be on the front. We have seen CD-ROM bays that opened on the side, indicating that the host wasn't designed with racks in mind. Some systems, often network equipment, require access only on one side. This means the device can be placed "butt-in" in a cramped closet and still be serviceable. Some hosts require that the external plastic case (or portions of it) be removed to successfully mount the device in a standard rack. Be sure to verify that this does not interfere with cooling or functionality. Power switches should be accessible but not easy to accidentally bump.

2.1.2 Vendors Known for Reliable Products

It is important to pick vendors that are known for reliability. Some vendors cut corners by using "consumer grade" parts, whereas others use parts that meet MIL-SPEC[1] requirements. Some have years of experience designing servers. Vendors with more experience will include the features listed above, plus other little extras that one can only learn from years of market experience. Vendors with little or no server experience will not offer maintenance service except for exchanging hosts that arrive dead. It can be useful to talk with other SAs to find out which vendors they use and whom they avoid.

Environments can be homogeneous (all the same vendor or product line) or heterogeneous (many different vendors and/or product lines). Homogeneous environments are the easiest to maintain because training is reduced, maintenance and repairs are easier (one set of spares), and there is less finger-pointing when problems arise. However, heterogeneous environments have the benefit that you are not "locked" into one vendor, and the competition between the vendors will result in better service to you. This is discussed further in Chapter 3.

---

[1] *MIL-SPEC* refers to the U.S. military specifications for electronic parts and equipment. Its intent is to specify a specific level of quality to produce more repeatable results. The MIL-SPEC standard usually specifies higher quality than civilian average, but not always. This exacting specification generally results in significantly higher costs.

2.1.3   Does Server Hardware Really Cost More?

To understand the additional cost of servers, you must understand how machines are priced and how "server features" add to the cost of the machine.

Most vendors have three[2] different product lines: home, business, and server.

The home line usually focuses on being the absolute cheapest initial purchase price, because consumers tend to make purchasing decisions based on the advertised price. Add-ons and future expandability are available at a higher cost. Components are specified in general terms, such as video resolution, rather than particular video card vendor and model, because maintaining the lowest possible purchase price requires them to change original equipment manufacturer (OEM) vendors on a daily or weekly basis. These machines tend to have more "game" features such as joysticks, high-performance graphics, and audio.

The business desktop line tends to focus on total cost of ownership. The initial purchase price will be higher than a home machine, but it should take longer to become obsolete. It is expensive for companies to maintain large pools of spare components, not to mention the cost of training repair technicians on each model. Therefore the business line tends to adopt new components such as video cards and hard drive controllers infrequently.

The server line tends to focus on having the lowest cost per performance metric. For example, a file server may be designed with a focus on lowering the cost of the SPEC SFS97 (formerly LADDIS) performance divided by the purchase price of the machine. Similar benchmarks exist for Web traffic, On-Line Transaction Processing (OLTP), aggregate multi-CPU performance, and so on. Many of the "server" features described previously add to the purchase price of a machine.

Servers cost more for other reasons, too. A chassis that is easier to service can be more expensive to manufacture. Restricting the drive bays and other access panels to certain sides means not positioning them solely to minimize material costs. However, the small increase in initial purchase price saves money in the long term in mean time to repair (MTTR) and ease of service.

Therefore it is inaccurate to state that a server costs "more" than a desktop computer because it is not an apples-to-apples comparison. Understanding these different pricing models helps one frame the discussion when asked to justify the superficially higher cost of server hardware. It is common to hear someone complain of a $50,000 price tag for a server when a high-performance PC can be purchased for one tenth as much. If the server

---

[2]Sometimes more, sometimes less. Vendors often have specialty product lines for vertical markets such as high-end graphics, numerically intensive computing, and so on.

is capable of serving millions of transactions per day, or it will serve the CPU needs of dozens of users, the cost is justified.

A more valid argument against such a purchasing decision might be that the performance being purchased is more than the service requires. Performance is often proportional to cost, and purchasing unneeded performance is wasteful. This is when capacity planning predictions and utilization trends become useful, as will be discussed in Chapter 24.

2.1.4   Maintenance Contracts and Spare Parts

When purchasing a server, one should also consider how repairs will be handled. All machines eventually break.[3] Vendors tend to have a variety of maintenance contract options. For example, one form of maintenance contract provides on-site service with a 4-hour response time, 12-hour response time, or next-day options. Other options include having the customer purchase a kit of spare parts and receive replacements when a spare part gets used.

Some reasonable scenarios for picking the appropriate maintenance contracts are:

Low/medium critical host: Some hosts are not critical, such as a CPU server that is one of many. In that situation, a maintenance contract with next-day or two-day response time is reasonable. Or, no contract may be needed at all if the default repair options are sufficient.

Large groups of similar hosts: Sometimes, a site has many of the same type of machine, possibly offering different kinds of services. In this case, it may be reasonable to purchase a spares kit so that repairs can be done by local staff. The cost of the spares kit is divided over the many hosts. These hosts may now require a lower-cost maintenance contract that simply replaces parts from the spares kit.

Controlled model selection: Technology improves over time, and sites described in the previous paragraph soon need to upgrade to newer models, which may be out of scope for the spares kit. In this case, you might standardize for a set amount of time on a particular model or set of models that share a spares kit. When the period is over, you might approve a new model and purchase the appropriate spares kit. At any given time, you would only have, for example, two spares kits. To introduce a third

---

[3]Desktops break, too, but we decided to cover maintenance contracts in this chapter rather than in Chapter 1. In our experience, desktop repairs tend to be less time-critical than server repairs. Desktops are more generic and therefore more interchangeable. These factors make it reasonable not to have a maintenance contract, but instead have a locally maintained set of spares and the technical know-how to do repairs internally or via contract with a local repair depot.

model, you would first decommission all the hosts that rely on the spares kit that is being retired. This controls costs.

Critical host: Sometimes it is too expensive to have a fully stocked spares kit. It may be reasonable to stock spares for parts that commonly fail and otherwise pay for a maintenance contract with same-day response. Hard drives and power supplies commonly fail and are often interchangeable among a number of products.

Large variety of models from same vendor: A very large site may adopt a maintenance contract that includes having an on-site technician. This is usually only justified at a site that has an extremely large number of hosts. However, medium-size sites can sometimes negotiate to have the regional spares kit stored on their site, with the benefit that the technician is more likely to "hang out" near your building. Sometimes, it is possible to negotiate direct access to the spares kit on an emergency basis. Usually, this is done without the knowledge of the technician's management. An SA can ensure that the technician will spend all her spare time at your site by providing a minor amount of office space and use of a telephone as her base of operations. In exchange, a discount on maintenance contract fees can sometimes be negotiated. At one site that had this arrangement, the technician would unbox and rack-mount new equipment for the SAs if she didn't have anything else to do.

Highly critical host: Some vendors offer a maintenance contract that provides an on-site technician and a duplicate machine ready to be swapped into place. This is often as expensive as paying for a redundant server, but it may make sense for some companies, especially ones that are not highly technical.

There is a trade-off between stocking spares and having a service contract. Stocking your own spares may be too expensive for a small site. A maintenance contract includes diagnostic services, even if over the phone. On the other hand, sometimes the easiest way to diagnose something is to swap in spare parts until the problem goes away. It is difficult to keep staff trained on the full range of diagnostic and repair methodologies for all the models used in-house. This is especially true for nontechnology companies, which may find such an endeavor to be distracting. Such "out-sourcing" is discussed in Section 14.2.2 and Section 25.1.8.

Sometimes an SA discovers that a critical host is not on the service contract. This discovery tends to happen at a critical time, such as when it needs to be repaired. The solution usually involves talking to a salesperson who will have the machine repaired on good faith that it will be added to the contract immediately or retroactively. It is good practice to write purchase orders for service contracts for 10 percent more than the quoted price of the contract, so that the vendor can grow the monthly charges as new machines are added to the contract.

There are three easy ways to prevent hosts from being missed from the contract. The first is to have a good inventory system and use it to cross-reference the service contract. However, good inventory systems are hard to find, and even the best can miss some hosts. The second is to have the person responsible for processing purchases be the person who is responsible for adding new machines to the contract. The person should know who to contact to determine the appropriate service level. If there is no single point of purchasing, it may be possible to find some other "choke point" in the process at which time the new host can be added to the contract. Third, you should fix a common problem caused by warranties. Most computers have "free" service for the first 12 months because of their warranty and do not need to be listed on the service contract during those months. However, it is difficult to remember to add the host to the contract so many months later, and the service level is different during the warranty period. To remedy these issues, the SA should see if the vendor can list the machine on the contract immediately, but show a zero dollar charge for the first 12 monthly statements. Most will do this because it locks in revenue for that host.

Service contracts are reactive repairs, rather than proactive solutions, such as having multiple, redundant servers for a given service, which is discussed in the next chapter.

2.1.5   Data Backups

Servers have critical data and unique configurations that must be backed up. This is the topic of Chapter 21.

Clients often are not backed-up. Clients are usually mass-produced with the same configuration on each host, and users are required to store their data on servers. This eliminates the need for backups. If a client's disk fails, the configuration should be identical to its multiple cousins, unmodified from its initial state, and therefore can be recreated from an automated install procedure. That is the theory. However, people will always store some data on their local machines, software will be installed locally, and OSs will store some configuration data locally. It is impossible to prevent this on Windows platforms. Roaming profiles store the users' settings to the server every time they log out, but do not protect the locally installed software and registry settings of the machine. UNIX systems are guilty to a lesser degree, because a well-configured system, with no "root" access for the user, can prevent all but crontabs (scheduled tasks) and a few other small services from being stored locally.

2.1.6   Servers Live in the Data Center

Servers should live in an environment with proper power, fire protection, networking, and so on. This is discussed more in Chapter 3. It is a good idea to allocate the physical space of a server at the same time as it is being purchased. Marking the space by taping a paper sign in the appropriate rack can safeguard against having space double-booked.

After assembling the hardware, it is best to mount it in the rack immediately before installing the OS and other software. We have observed the following phenomenon: A new server is assembled in someone's office and before moving it into the machine room, the OS and applications are loaded onto it. As the applications are brought up, some trial users are made aware of the service. Soon the server is in heavy use before it is intended to be, and it is still in someone's office without the proper protections of a machine room (uninterruptible power supply (UPS), air-conditioning, and so on). Now the people using the server will be disturbed by an outage when it is moved into the machine room. The way to prevent this is to mount it in its final location as soon as it is assembled.

Field offices aren't always large enough to have data centers. Some entire companies aren't large enough to have data centers. However everyone should have a designated room or closet with the bare minimums: physical security, UPS (many small ones if not one large one), and proper cooling. A telecom closet with good ventilation is better than having your company's payroll on a server sitting under someone's desk.

2.1.7   Same, Different, or a Stripped-down
OS on Clients

Servers don't have to run the same OS as their clients. They can be completely different, completely the same, or the same basic OS but with a different configuration to account for the difference in intended usage. Each is appropriate at different times.

A web server, for example, does not need to run the same OS as its clients. The client and server only need to agree on a protocol. Single-function network appliances often have a mini-OS that contains just enough software to do the one function required, such as being a file server, a web server, or a mail server.

Sometimes a server is required to have all the same software as the clients. Consider the case of a UNIX environment with many UNIX desktops and a series of general-purpose UNIX central processing unit (CPU) servers. The clients should have similar cookie-cutter OS loads, as discussed in Chapter 1. The CPU servers should have the same OS load, though it may be tuned differently for a larger number of processes, pseudo-terminals, buffers, and other parameters.

It is interesting to note that what is appropriate for a "server OS" is a matter of perspective. When loading Solaris 2.x, you can indicate this host is a server, which means all the software packages are loaded, because diskless clients (or clients with small hard disks) may NFS-mount certain packages from the server. On the other hand, when loading Red Hat Linux, the "server" configuration is a minimal set of packages, because it is assumed that you simply want the base installation on top of which you will load the specific software packages that will be used to create the service.

2.1.8   Remote Administration Access

Servers need to be maintained remotely. In the old days, every server in the machine room had its own console: a keyboard, video monitor (or hardcopy console), and possibly a mouse. As SAs packed more into their machine rooms, many started consolidating these consoles. For example, ASCII terminals were eliminated by attaching the serial consoles of servers to terminal servers or hosts with many serial ports. These are known as "console servers" or "serial concentrators." To do a task from a machine's console, you simply log in to the console server and from there connect to the appropriate serial port. Software that performed this "console consolidation" grew increasingly sophisticated by logging output from the console, providing better secured access, and so on.

Eliminating the terminals saved space; however, the biggest benefit was that now all the tasks that had to be done at the console could be done remotely. Tasks that often require physical presence typically include forcing a reboot when the system is hung. In this kind of emergency situation, you do not want to drive an hour to get to the machine. Remote console software lets you simulate the funny key sequences that have special significance when typed at the console.

Sometimes a machine has crashed "hard" and must be power cycled (powered off, then powered on again) to be brought back up. This is rare enough that it is reasonable for an SA working remotely to call some-one in the building and ask them to "be my eyes and hands" to power cycle the system. Security implications of doing this include the possibil-ity of revealing access codes that let the person into the data center or other passwords and secrets. Remote locations can benefit from power sys-tems that have the capability to remotely cycle the power on particular hosts.

PCs and other systems without serial port consoles have similar console consolidators, albeit more complicated and often with distance limitations.

For example, PCs require KVM[4] switches that consolidate all the PC consoles to a single keyboard, video monitor, and mouse. These have the downside that remote access is not provided except in the most expensive systems. Some BIOS chips permit serial access to servers for simple operations, which is certainly an improvement. Software solutions for PCs exist in both commercial and freely available forms. However, they do not work when a system has crashed hard or isn't booting properly. Remote-control power switches can be somewhat useful in these situations.

When purchasing server hardware, a major consideration should be what kind of remote access to the console is possible, and to determine which tasks require such access. In an emergency, it isn't reasonable or timely to expect SAs to travel to the physical device to perform their work. In nonemergency situations, an SA should be able to fix at least minor problems from home or on the road and optimally be fully productive remotely when telecommuting. There are obvious limits to this, because certain tasks, such as inserting media or replacing faulty hardware, require a person at the machine. These issues require physical presence, either an on-site operator or the previously mentioned process of finding a person who is on-site to perform these tasks. However, replacing hardware should be left to trained professionals.

Remote access to consoles provides cost savings and improves safety factors for SAs. Machine rooms are optimized for machines, not humans. They are cold, cramped, and more expensive per square foot than office space. It is wasteful to fill expensive rack space with monitors and keyboards rather than additional hosts. It can be inconvenient, if not dangerous, to have a machine room full of chairs.

SAs should never be expected to spend their typical day working inside the machine room. Filling a machine room with SAs is a formula for disaster. Rarely does working directly in the machine room meet ergonomic requirements for keyboard and mouse positioning or environmental requirements such as noise level. Working in a cold machine room is not healthy for people. SAs need to work in an environment that maximizes their productivity, which can best be achieved in their offices. Unlike a machine room, an office can be easily stocked with important SA tools such as reference materials, ergonomic keyboards, telephones, refrigerators, and stereo equipment.

Having a lot of people in the machine room is not healthy for equipment either. Having people in a machine room increases the load put on the heating, ventilation, and air-conditioning (HVAC) systems. Body heat and loss of cooling from a door that opens and closes often will add to cooling costs.

---

[4]This is short for keyboard, video, and mouse.

❖ **Monitor Room Temperature to Detect Traffic**   You should
monitor room temperature not just for emergency situations such as
HVAC failures and fires but also to prevent the development of bad
habits. A manager wasn't concerned that his SAs were leaving a machine
room door open occasionally until he noticed that sometimes when he
entered the room it was nearly normal room temperature and the HVAC
system was running on high trying to compete with the open door. At a
staff meeting, he was assured by everyone that nobody was leaving the
door open. He configured Cricket (an SNMP monitoring tool) to collect
temperature data from the routers in this and other machine rooms. At
the next staff meeting, he presented graphs of the data that demonstrated
that the temperature rose 10° during the day but was just fine during
weekends and holidays. More revealing was that the other machine rooms
did not have such variations in temperature. At the next staff meeting, he
presented graphs that demonstrated that the problem had disappeared
and thanked everyone for being more mindful of the door.

Security implications must be considered when you have a remote console. Often, host security strategies depend on the console being behind a
locked door. Remote access breaks this strategy. Therefore console systems
should have properly considered authentication and privacy systems. For
example, you might permit access to the console system only via an encrypted channel, such as a secure shell (SSH), and insist on authentication
by a one-time password system such as a handheld authenticator.

When purchasing a server, you should expect remote console access.
If the vendor is not responsive to this need, you should look elsewhere for
equipment. Remote console access is discussed further in Section 17.1.10.

2.1.9   Mirrored Root Disks

When purchasing a server it is often useful to consider RAID solutions to
maintain data integrity. Disk drives fail. A simple fix is to mirror the main
system disk. This is often the most difficult disk to replace if it gets damaged,
so a mirror can be extremely valuable. The cost of disks has dropped considerably over the years, making this once luxurious option more commonplace.
Some form of software RAID comes with most server OSs "for free," and
hardware RAID systems are rapidly becoming less expensive. Data integrity
is further discussed in Chapter 8.

The two ways to mirror a system disk both have trade-offs. The simple
approach uses two disks—the working disk and a clone that is updated at
regular intervals, such as once a night. If disaster strikes (a physical problem

or human error), one can return to the previously known-good state. The benefit of this technique is that you can select the time that the clone is made, for example, right before a major system change. A drawback is that if the mirror becomes seriously out of date, it is useless.

The more modern technique is to use software or hardware mirroring, otherwise known as *RAID Level 1.* This is built into all serious server OSs and provides a constantly updated mirror of the system disk on a second disk. Some systems gain a performance benefit by dividing disk reads across the two spindles. Writes are somewhat slower because twice as many disk writes are required, though they are usually done in parallel. This is less of a concern on systems that have write-behind caches, such as UNIX.

Always remember that a RAID protects against hardware failure. It does not protect against software or human errors. Erroneous changes made on the primary disk are immediately duplicated onto the second one making it impossible to recover from the mistake by just using the second disk.

Even Mirrored Disks Need Backups

A large e-commerce site used RAID 1 to duplicate the system disk in its primary database server. Database corruption problems started to appear during peak usage times. The database vendor and the OS vendor were pointing fingers at each other. The SAs ultimately needed to get a memory dump from the system as the corruption was happening to track down who was truly to blame. Unknown to the SAs, the OS was using a signed integer rather than an unsigned one for a memory pointer. When the memory dump started, it reached the point at which the memory pointer became negative and started overwriting other partitions on the system disk. The RAID system faithfully copied the corruption onto the mirror, making it useless. This software error caused a very long, expensive, and well-publicized outage, which cost the company millions in lost transactions and dramatically lowered the price of their stock. The lesson learned here is that mirroring is quite useful, but never underestimate the utility of a good backup for getting back to a known-good state.

Deciding which technique is most appropriate depends on the situation. Whether you are more concerned about human error or physical problems, and whether you want near manual or automatic control are both at issue. For some particularly critical machines, you may want to try a hybrid approach or even triple-mirrored disks.

It should be noted that some software-only RAID systems can't be used for the boot disk. Check with the vendor.

2.2   The Icing

With the basics in place, we now look at what can be done to go one step further in reliability and serviceability. We also take time to summarize an opposing view.

2.2.1   Server Appliances

A server appliance brings years of experience together in one box. Designing a server is difficult. The physical hardware for a server has all the requirements listed earlier in this chapter, plus the system engineering and performance tuning that only a highly experienced expert can plan. The software often involves assembling various packages, gluing them together, and providing a single, unified administration system for it all. It's a lot of work! Appliances do all this for you.

An appliance is a device designed specifically for a particular task. Toasters make toast. Blenders blend. One could do these things using general-purpose devices, but there are benefits to using a device designed to do one purpose very well.

The computer world has appliances too. There are file server appliances (such as NetApp and Auspex), web server appliances, email appliances, DNS appliances, and so on. The first appliance was the dedicated network router. Some scoffed, "Who would spend all that money on a device that just sits there and pushes packets when we can easily add extra interfaces to our VAX and do the same thing?" It turned out that quite a lot of people would. It became obvious that a box dedicated to a single task, and doing it well, was more valuable than a general-purpose computer that could do many tasks.

Although a senior SA can engineer a system dedicated to file service or email out of a general-purpose server, purchasing an appliance can free her to focus on other tasks. Every appliance purchased results in one less system to engineer from scratch. Appliances also let organizations without that particular expertise gain access to well-designed systems.

The other benefit of appliances is that they often have features that can't be found elsewhere. Competition drives the vendors to add new features, increase performance, and improve reliability. For example, NetApp Filers have tunable snapshots of the filesystem that permit the end-users to "cd back in time," thus eliminating many requests for file restores.

2.2.2   Redundant Power Supplies

After hard drives, the next most failure-prone component of a system is the power supply. So, ideally, servers should have redundant power supplies.

Having a redundant power supply does not simply mean two such devices are in the chassis. It means that the system can be operational if one power supply is not functioning. This is called $n + 1$ redundancy. Sometimes, a fully loaded system requires two power supplies to receive enough power. In this case, *redundant* means having three power supplies. This is an important question to ask vendors when purchasing servers and network equipment.[5]

Each power supply should have a separate power cord for three reasons. First, operationally speaking, the most common power problem is a power cord being accidentally kicked out of its socket.[6] A single power cord for everything won't help you in this situation! Any vendor that provides a single power cord for multiple power supplies is demonstrating ignorance of this basic operational issue.

The second reason for separate power cords is that they permit the following trick. Sometimes a device must be moved to a different power strip, UPS, or circuit. In this situation, separate power cords allow the device to move to the new power source one cord at a time, eliminating downtime.

Finally, for very-high-availability systems, each power supply should draw power from a different source, such as separate UPSs. If one UPS fails, the system keeps going. Some data centers lay out their power with this in mind.

Benefit of Separate Power Cords

Once Tom had a planned power outage for a UPS that powered an entire machine room. However, there was one router that absolutely could not lose power because it was critical for projects that would otherwise be unaffected by the outage. That router had redundant power supplies that had separate power cords. Tom moved one power cord to a non-UPS outlet in the room that had been installed for lights and other devices that did not require UPS support. During the outage, the router only lost UPS power, but it continued running on normal power. The router was able to function during the entire outage.

---

[5] Network equipment is particularly prone to this problem. Sometimes, when a large network device is fully loaded with power-hungry fiber interfaces, dual power supplies are a minimum, not a redundancy. Vendors often do not admit this up-front.

[6] Formal studies of power reliability often overlook such problems because they are studying utility power.

2.2.3 Full and $n + 1$ Redundancy

As mentioned before, $n + 1$ redundancy refers to systems that have been engineered such that one of any particular component can fail, yet the system is still functional. Some examples include disk RAID configurations that can provide full service even when a single disk has failed, or an Ethernet switch with additional switch fabric components so that traffic can still be routed if one portion of the switch fabric fails.

This is different from full redundancy. Full redundancy is when two complete sets of hardware are set up and some kind of "fail-over" is configured. Often the first system is running, and the second system sits idle waiting to take over in case the first one fails. This "fail-over" might happen manually (someone notices that the first system failed and activates the second system) or automatically (the second system monitors the first system and activates itself if it has determined that the first one is dead). Other fully redundant systems are "load-sharing." In load-sharing, both systems are fully operational and perform about half the workload, but have enough capacity to spare to handle the workload of the other. When one system fails, the other detects this and takes on its failed counterpart's workload.

$n + 1$ is cheaper than full redundancy when n is two or more. Customers often prefer it for the economical advantage.

Usually, only specific subsystems are $n + 1$ redundant, not the entire box. Always pay particular attention when a vendor tries to sell you on $n + 1$ redundancy, but only parts of the system are redundant: a car with five tires isn't useful if its engine is dead, and likewise a car with two engines isn't useful if one of its tires is flat.

2.2.4 Hot-swap Components

Redundant components should be hot-swappable. *Hot-swap* refers to the ability to remove and replace a component while the system is running. Normally, parts should be removed and replaced only when the system is powered off. Being able to hot-swap components is like being able to change a tire while the car is driving down a highway. It's great to not have to stop to fix common problems.

The first benefit of hot-swap components is that new components can be installed while the system is running. You don't have to schedule a reboot to install the part. However, installing a new part is a planned event and can usually be scheduled for the next maintenance period. The real benefit of hot-swap parts is during a failure.

In $n + 1$ redundancy, the system can tolerate a single component failure, at which time it becomes critical to replace that part as soon as possible or risk a "double component failure." The longer you wait, the larger the risk. Without hot-swap parts, an SA will have to wait until a reboot can be scheduled to get back into the safety of $n + 1$ computing. With hot-swap parts, an SA can replace the part without scheduling downtime. RAID systems have the concept of a "hot spare" disk that sits in the system, unused, ready to replace a failed disk. Assuming the system can isolate the failed disk so that it doesn't prevent the entire system from working, the system can automatically activate the hot spare disk, making it part of whichever RAID set needs it. This makes the system $n + 2$. This is also important because RAID systems often run slower until a failed component has been replaced and the RAID set has been rebuilt.

Hot-swappable components increase the cost of a system. When is this additional cost justified? When eliminated downtimes are worth the extra expense. If a system has scheduled downtime once a week and letting the system run at the risk of a double-failure is acceptable for a week, then hot-swap components may not be worth the extra expense. If the system has a maintenance period scheduled once a year, the expense is more likely to be justified.

When a vendor makes a claim of hot-swappability, always ask two questions: Which parts aren't hot-swappable? How and for how long is service interrupted when the parts are being hot-swapped? Some network devices have hot-swappable interface cards, but the CPU is not hot-swappable. Some network devices claim hot-swap capability, but do a full system reset after any device is added. This reset can take seconds or minutes. Some disk subsystems must pause the I/O system for as much as 20 seconds when a drive is replaced. Others run with seriously degraded performance for many hours while the data is rebuilt onto the replacement disk. Be sure that you understand the ramifications of component failure. Don't assume that hot-swap parts makes outages disappear. It just reduces the outage.

2.2.5   Separate Networks for Administrative Functions

Additional network interfaces in servers permit you to build separate administrative networks. For example, it is common to have a separate network just for backups and monitoring. Backups use significant amounts of bandwidth when they run, and separating that traffic from the main network means that it won't adversely affect customers' use of the network. This separate network can be engineered using simpler equipment and thus be more reliable or, more importantly, unaffected by outages in the main network, which means that the monitoring system is less likely to produce false errors for servers when there is a network problem. It also provides a way for SAs to get to the machine during such an outage. This is a form of redundancy that solves a very specific problem.

2.3 Opposing View: Many Inexpensive Workstations

There is an opposing view to the "buy server hardware when you build a server" rhetoric. The economics of hardware are changing. High-powered PCs have become a commodity, and prices are dropping. It is difficult to argue against using a desktop system as a server. If the performance is there, can't we forego the benefits of rack-mountable, redundant, reliable systems? If the commodity hardware is less than half the cost of a server, can't we save money by purchasing two systems and make up for the reliability through full redundancy?

We predict that this economic situation will be short lived, but it is reasonable to take advantage of it while it lasts. The economic situation will be short lived because server vendors are adapting their designs to utilize commodity components for key functions in their servers, reducing their purchase price. This achieves the best of both worlds. Take the right precautions and manage the risk.

Take advantage of this trend for as long as possible, whenever possible. As stated in Section 2.1.3, some computers are engineered to get the best price per unit of performance, whereas others focus on reducing the purchase price or total cost of ownership. Therefore comparing the initial purchase price of home computers to the initial purchase price of servers is an apples-to-oranges comparison.[7] The key is to not let yourself be blinded by the initial purchase price, but consider the other features listed in this chapter, such as remote console access, rack space utilization, additional SA overhead, and load-sharing issues.

Be careful about making up for reliability through full redundancy. Sometimes two cheap systems fail more often than one expensive one.

Case Study: Disposable Servers

Many e-commerce sites build mammoth clusters of low-cost 1U PC servers. Racks are packed with as many servers as possible, with dozens or hundreds configured to provide each service required. One site found that when a unit died, it was more economical to power it off and leave it in the rack rather than repair the unit. Removing dead units might accidentally cause an outage if other cables were loosened in the process. The site would not need to reap the dead machines for quite a while. We presume that when it starts to run out of space, it would adopt a monthly "day of reaping," with certain people carefully watching the service monitoring systems while others reap.

---

[7]For a full comparison of apples to oranges, look at the *Annals of Improbable Research (AIR)* (Abrahams 1997).

2.4   Conclusion

Servers are different from clients because more depends upon them. Therefore we make different decisions when purchasing servers. Different economics drive the server hardware market versus the desktop market, and understanding those economics helps one make better purchasing decisions. Servers, like all hardware, sometimes fail, and therefore one must have some kind of maintenance contract or repair plan, as well as data backup/restore capability. Servers should be in proper machine rooms, as described in Chapter 3, to provide a reliable environment for operation. Space in the machine room should be allocated at purchase time, not when a server arrives.

Server appliances are hardware/software systems that contain all the software that is required for a particular task preconfigured on hardware that is tuned to the particular application. Server appliances provide high-quality solutions engineered with years of experience in a "canned" package and are likely to be much more reliable and easier to maintain than homegrown solutions.

Servers need to be remotely administered. Hardware/software systems allow one to simulate console access remotely. This frees up machine room space and enables SAs to work from their offices and homes.

To increase reliability, servers often have redundant systems, preferably in $n + 1$ configurations. Having a mirrored system disk, redundant power supplies, and other redundant features enhances up-time. Being able to swap dead components while the system is running provides better MTTR and less service interruption. While this redundancy may have been a luxury in the past, it is often a requirement in today's environment.

This chapter illustrates our theme of completing the basics first so that later everything else falls into place. Proper handling of the issues discussed in this chapter go a long way toward making the system reliable, maintainable, and repairable. These issues must be considered at the beginning, not as an afterthought.

Exercises

1. What servers are used in your environment? How many different vendors are used? Do you consider this to be a lot of vendors? What would be the benefits and problems with increasing the number of vendors? decreasing?

2. Describe your site's strategy in purchasing maintenance and repair contracts. How could it be improved to be cheaper? How could it be improved to provide better service?

3. What are the major (and minor) differences between the hosts you install for servers versus clients?

4. Why would one want hot-swap parts on a system without $n + 1$ redundancy?

5. Why would one want $n + 1$ redundancy if the system does not have hot-swap parts?

6. Which critical hosts in your environment do not have $n + 1$ redundancy or cannot hot-swap parts?

7. An SA needed to add a disk to a server that was low on disk space. He chose to wait until the next maintenance period to install the disk, rather than do it while the system was running. Why might this be?

8. What services in your environment would be good candidates for replacing with an appliance (whether or not such an appliance is available)? Why are they good candidates?

9. What server appliances are in your environment? What engineering would you have to do if you had instead purchased a general-purpose machine to do the same function?

Chapter 3

Services

Services are what distinguish a structured computing environment that is managed by SAs from an environment where there are one or more standalone computers. Homes and very small nontechnical offices typically have a few standalone machines. Larger groups of computers and those used by technical people are typically linked together through shared services that ease communication and optimize resources. When a home computer connects to the Internet through an Internet Service Provider (ISP), it uses services provided by the ISP and the other people that the person connects to across the Internet. An office environment provides those same services and more.

A typical environment has many services. Fundamental services include domain name service (DNS), email, authentication services, network connectivity, and printing.[1] These services are the most critical, and they are the most visible if they fail. Other typical services are the various remote access methods, network license service, software repositories, backup services,

---

[1] DNS, networking, and authentication are services on which many other services rely. Email and printing may seem less obviously critical, but if you ever do have a failure of either, you will discover that they are the lifeblood of everyone's workflow. Communications and hardcopy are at the core of every company.

Internet access, DHCP, and file service. This is by no means an exhaustive list, but it demonstrates the diversity of services that SA teams create and maintain. Everything that you do while supporting your customers involves services that the SA team provides.

The previous chapter looked at selecting and building an individual server from a hardware perspective. A service may be built on several servers that work in conjunction with each other. This chapter looks at how to build a service that meets customer requirements, is reliable, and is maintainable.

Providing a service involves more than just putting together the hardware and software. It involves making the service reliable, scaling the service, and monitoring, maintaining, and supporting it. A service is not truly a service until it meets these basic requirements.

One of the fundamental duties of an SA is to provide the customers with the services they need. This work is on-going. As technologies evolve and customers' jobs evolve, the customers' needs will evolve. As a result, an SA spends a considerable amount of time designing and building new services. How well the SA builds those services determines how much time and effort will have to be spent supporting them in the future and how happy the customers will be.

3.1   The Basics

Building a solid, reliable service is a key role of an SA. There are many basics that the SA needs to consider when performing that task. The most important thing to consider at all stages of design and deployment is the customers' requirements. Talk to the customers and find out what their needs and expectations are for the service.[2] Then build a list of other requirements, such as administrative requirements, that are visible only to the SA team. Focus on the "what" rather than the "how." It's easy to get bogged down in implementation details and lose sight of the purpose and goals.

We have found great success through the use of open protocols and open architectures. You may not always be able to achieve this, but it should be considered in the design.

Services should be built on server-class machines that are kept in a suitable environment. They should reach reasonable levels of reliability and performance. The service and the machines that it relies upon should be monitored, and failures should generate alarms or trouble tickets, as appropriate.

---

[2]Some services, such as name service and authentication service, do not have customer requirements other than that they should always work and they should be fast and unintrusive.

Most services rely on other services. Understanding in detail how a service works will give you insight into the services on which it relies. For example, almost every service relies on name service (DNS). If there are machine names or domain names configured into the service, it relies on DNS; if its log files contain the names of hosts that used the service or were accessed by the service, it uses DNS; if the people accessing it are trying to contact other machines through the service, it uses DNS. Likewise, almost every service relies on the network, which is also a service. DNS relies on the network, and therefore anything that relies on DNS also relies on the network. Some services rely on email (which relies on DNS and the network); others rely on being able to access shared files on other computers. Many services also rely on the authentication and authorization service to be able to distinguish one person from another, particularly where different levels of access are given based on identity. The failure of some services, such as DNS, causes cascading failures of all the other services that rely on them. When building a service, it is important to know the other services on which it relies.

Machines and software that are part of a service should only rely on hosts and software that are built to the same standards or higher. A service can only be as reliable as the weakest link in the chain of services on which it relies. A service should not gratuitously rely on hosts that are not part of the service.

Access to server machines should be restricted to SAs for reasons of reliability and security. The more people who are using a machine and the more things that are running on it, the greater is the chance that memory leaks and other bugs will crop up, disrupting service. Machines that customers use also need to have more things installed on them so that the customers can access the data they need and use other network services. A server should be as simple as possible. Simplicity makes machines more reliable and easier to debug when they do have problems. Servers should have the minimum that is required for the service they run, only SAs should have access to them, and the SAs should log into them only to do maintenance. Servers are also more sensitive from a security point of view than desktops. If an intruder can gain administrative access to a server, he can typically do more damage than he can with administrative access to a desktop machine. The fewer people who have access and the less that runs on the machine, the lower is the chance an intruder has of gaining access, and greater is the chance that an intruder will be spotted.

An SA has several decisions to make when building a service, such as from what vendor to buy the equipment, whether to use one or many servers for a complex service, and what level of redundancy to build into the service. A service should be as simple as possible, with as few dependencies as possible, to increase reliability and make it easier to support and maintain.

Another method of easing support and maintenance for a service is to use standard hardware, standard software, and standard configurations and have documentation in a standard location. Centralizing services so that there are one or two large primary print servers, for example, rather than hundreds of small ones scattered throughout the company, also makes the service more supportable. Finally, a key part of implementing any new service is to make it independent of the particular machine that it is on by using service-oriented names in client configurations, rather than, for example, the actual hostname. If your OS does not support this feature, tell your OS vendor that it is important to you and consider using another OS in the meantime.

Case Study: Tying Services to a Machine

In a small company, all services run on one or two central machines. As the company grows, those machines will become overloaded and some services will need to be moved to other machines, so that there are more servers, each of which runs fewer services. For example, assume there is a central machine that is the mail delivery server, the mail relay, the print server, and the calendar server. If all these services are tied to the machine's real name, then every client machine in the company will have that name configured into the email client, the printer configuration, and the calendar server. When that server gets overloaded, and both email functions are moved to another machine with a different name, every other machine in the company will need to have its email configuration changed, which requires a lot of work and causes disruption. If the server gets overloaded again and printing is moved to another machine, all the other machines in the company will have to be changed again. On the other hand, if each service was tied to an appropriate global alias, such as "smtp" for the mail relay, "mail" for the mail delivery host, "calendar" for the calendar server and "print" for the print server, then only the global alias would have to be changed, with no disruption to the customers and little time and effort beyond building the service.

Once the service has been built and tested, it needs to be rolled out slowly to the customer base, with further testing and debugging along the way.

3.1.1   Customer Requirements

When building a new service, you should always start with the customer requirements. The customers are the reasons that the service is being built. If it does not meet their needs, then building the service was a wasted effort.

There are very few services that do not have customer requirements. DNS is one of those. Others, such as email and the network, are more visible to customers. Customers may want certain features from their email clients, and different customers put different loads on the network, depending on the work they do and how the systems they use are set up. Other services are very customer-oriented, such as an electronic purchase order system. SAs need to understand how the service affects customers and how customer requirements affect the service design.

Gathering the customer requirements should include finding out how they intend to use the new service, the features that they need, the features that they would like, how critical the service will be to them, and what levels of availability and support they will need for the service. Involve the customers in usability trials on demo versions of the service, if possible. Do not choose a system that they will find cumbersome to use, or the project will not be a success. Try to gauge how large the customer base for this service will be and what sort of performance they will need and expect from it, so that you can size it appropriately.

This is a good time to define a service level agreement (SLA) for the new service. An SLA enumerates the services that will be provided and the level of support they receive. It typically categorizes problems by severity and commits to response times for each category, perhaps based on the time of day and day of week if the site does not provide 24×7 support. The SLA usually defines an escalation process that increases the severity of a problem if it has not been resolved after a specified time and calls for managers to get involved if problems are getting out of hand. In a relationship in which the customer is paying for a certain service, the SLA usually specifies penalties for the service provider if the service provider fails to meet a given standard of service. The SLA is always discussed in detail and agreed on by both parties to the agreement.

The SLA process is a forum for the SAs to understand the customers' expectations and to set them appropriately, so that the customers understand what is and isn't possible and why. It is also a tool to plan what resources will be required for the project. The SLA should document the customers' needs and set realistic goals for the SA team in terms of features, availability, performance, and support. It should document future needs and capacity so that all parties will understand the growth plans. It is a document that the SA team can refer to during the design process to make sure that they meet their customers' and their own expectations and to help keep them on track.

3.1.2 Operational Requirements

The SA team may have other requirements for the new service that are not immediately visible to the customers. SAs need to consider the administrative interface of the new service, whether it interoperates with other existing services and can be integrated with central services such as authentication or directory services.

SAs also need to consider how the service scales. Demand for the service may grow beyond what was initially anticipated and will almost certainly grow with the growth of the company. They need to think of ways that the service can be scaled up without interrupting the existing service.

A related consideration is the upgrade path for this service. As new versions become available, what is the upgrade process? Does it involve an interruption of service? Does it involve touching every desktop? Is it possible to rollout the upgrade slowly, to test it on a few willing people before inflicting it on the whole company? Try to design the service so that upgrades are easy, can be performed without service interruption, don't involve touching the desktops, and can be rolled out slowly.

From the level of reliability that the customers expect and what the SAs predict as future reliability requirements for the system, the SAs should be able to build a list of desired features, such as clustering, slave or backup servers, or running on high-availability hardware and OSs.

SAs need to consider network performance issues related to the network between where the service is hosted and where the users are located. If some customers will be in remote locations across low-bandwidth, high-latency links, how will this service perform? Are there ways to make it perform equally well, or close to that, in all locations, or does the SLA need to set different expectations for remote customers? Vendors rarely do testing of their products over high-latency links—links with a large roundtrip time (RTT)—and typically everyone from the programmers to the salespeople are equally ignorant about the issues involved. In-house testing is often the only way to be sure.

❖ **Bandwidth Versus Latency**   *Bandwidth* is how much data can be transmitted in a second. *Latency* is the delay before the data is received by the other end. A high-latency link, no matter what the bandwidth, will have a long turnaround time (the time for a packet to go and the reply to return). Some applications, such as noninteractive (streaming) video, are unaffected by high latency. Others are affected greatly.

Suppose the client software accesses a server with many small requests, each of which must be completed before the next one is sent (lock-step or synchronous requests). In a low-latency network, performance may be fine. In a high-latency network, such as a transoceanic link, performance will degrade because each request must wait for the previous one to complete. The transit time will dominate performance. The link utilization will be minimal because most of the time is spent waiting for the reply, not sending data.

Mathematically speaking, the problem is as follows. The total time to completion (T) is the sum of the time each request takes to complete. The time it takes to complete each request is made up of three components: sending the request (S), computing the result (C), and receiving the reply (R). This is depicted mathematically as

$$T = (S_1 + C_1 + R_1) + (S_2 + C_2 + R_2) + (S_3 + C_3 + R_3)$$
$$+ \cdots + (S_n + C_n + R_n)$$

In a low-latency environment, $S_n + R_n$ is nearly zero, thus leading programmers to forget it exists, or worse, thinking that the formula is

$$T = C_1 + C_2 + C_3 + C_n$$

when it most certainly is not.

Programs written under this assumption will benchmark very well on a local Ethernet, but terribly once put into production on a global high-latency wide area network (WAN). This can make the product too slow to be usable. In this situation, many customers purchase additional bandwidth to solve a performance problem and then are very surprised when the improvement is minimal.[3] In these situations, bandwidth isn't important—latency is. Most network providers do not sell latency, just bandwidth. Therefore their salesperson's only solution is to sell the customer more bandwidth. One must either reduce the latency (possibly changing network technology) or improve the software.

Improving the software usually is a matter of rethinking algorithms. In high-latency networks, one must change the algorithms so that requests and replies do not need to be in lock-step. One solution (batched requests) sends all requests at once, preferably combined into a small number of packets, and waits for the replies to arrive. Another solution (windowed replies) involves sending many requests in a way that is disconnected from waiting for replies. A program may be able to track a "window" of n outstanding replies at any given moment.

---

[3]Sometimes, bandwidth is also a problem and queuing on the router is increasing latency. Monitoring your network devices will tell you if you have this problem. If you do, look into queuing options and quality of service (QoS) options on your network equipment, too.

**Case Study: *Minimize the Number of Packets in High-Latency
            Networks***

Even if an algorithm must process requests in lock-step, how the requests are sent
can greatly affect performance. RTT is per packet, so sending fewer large packets is
often better than sending many short packets. A global pharmaceutical company
based in New Jersey had a terrible performance problem with a database application. Analysis found that 4,000-byte Structured Query Language (SQL) requests
sent over a transatlantic link were being sent in fifty 80-byte packets one at a time. It
took five minutes just to log in. When the database connector was reconfigured to
send a few large packets, the performance problem went away. The users had been
demanding additional transatlantic bandwidth. This would have taken months to
order, been very expensive, and disappointed the users when it didn't solve the
problem.

Every SA and developer should be aware of how latency affects the
services they are creating. SAs should also look at how they can monitor
the service in terms of availability and performance. Being able to integrate a
new service into existing monitoring systems is a key requirement for meeting
the SLA. They should also look at whether the system can generate trouble
tickets in the existing trouble ticket system for problems that it detects, if
that is appropriate.

The SA team also needs to consider the budget that has been allocated
to this project. If the SAs do not believe that they can meet the service levels
that the customers want on the current budget, that constraint should be
presented as part of the SLA discussions. Once the SLA has been ratified by
both groups, the SAs should take care to work within the budget allocation
constraints.

3.1.3   Open Architecture

Wherever possible, a new service should be built around an architecture
that uses open protocols and file formats. In particular, we're referring to
protocols and file formats that are documented in a public forum so that
many vendors can write to those standards and make interoperable products.
Any service with an open architecture can be more easily integrated with
other services that follow the same standards.

The opposite of "open" is "proprietary." A service that uses proprietary
protocols and file formats will interoperate with fewer products because the
protocols and file formats are subject to change without notice and may
require licensing from the creator of the protocol. Vendors use proprietary

protocols when they are covering new territory or are attempting to maintain market share by preventing the creation of a level playing field.

Sometimes, vendors that use proprietary protocols do make explicit licensing agreements with other vendors, but typically a lag exists between the release of a new version from one vendor and the release of the compatible new version from the second vendor. Also, relations between the two vendors may break down, and they may stop providing the interface between the two products. That situation is a nightmare for people who are using both products and rely on the interface between them.

❖ **The Protocol Versus the Product** It is important that SAs understand the difference between the protocol and the product. One might standardize on Simple Mail Transfer Protocol (SMTP) (Crocker 1982) for email transmission. There is no product named SMTP. It is a document written in English that explains how bits are to be transmitted over the wire. This is different from a product that uses SMTP to transmit email from one server to another. Part of the confusion comes from the fact that companies often have internal standards that list specific products that will be deployed and supported. That's a different use of the word "standard."

The source of this confusion is understandable. Before the late 1990s, when the Internet became a household word, many people had experience only with protocols that were tied to a particular product and didn't need to communicate with other companies, because companies were not connected to each other as freely as they are now. This developed a mentality that a protocol is something that software implements and does not stand on its own as an independent concept. Although the Internet has made more people aware of the difference between protocols and products, many vendors still take advantage of customers who lack awareness of open protocols. They fear the potential for competition and would rather eliminate competition by locking people into systems that make migration to other vendors difficult. These vendors make a concerted effort to blur the difference between the protocol and the product.

Also, beware of vendors who "embrace and extend" a standard in an attempt to prevent interoperability with competitors. Such vendors do this so they can claim to support a standard without giving their customers the benefits of interoperability. That's not very "customer oriented." A famous case of this is when Microsoft adopted the Kerberos authentication system, which was a very good decision, but extended it in a way that prevented it from interoperating with non-Microsoft Kerberos systems. All the servers had to be Microsoft-based. The addition that they made was gratuitous, but it successfully forced sites to uproot their security infrastructure and replace it with Microsoft products if they were to use Kerberos clients of either flavor. Without this "enhancement," customers would be able to choose their server vendor, and those vendors would be forced to compete for their business.

The business case for using open protocols is simple: it lets you build better services because you can select the best server and client, rather than being forced to pick, for example, the best client and then getting stuck with a less than optimal server. Customers want an application that has the features and ease of use that they need. SAs want an application whose server is easy to manage. These are often conflicting requirements. Traditionally, either the customers or SAs have more "power" and make the decision in private, surprising the other with the decision. If the SAs make the decision, the customers consider them fascists. If the customers make the decision, it may well be a package that is difficult to administer, which will make it difficult to give excellent service to the customers.

A better way is to select protocols based on open standards and permit each "side" to select their own software. This "decouples" the client application selection process from the server platform selection process. Customers are free to choose the software that best fits their own needs, biases, and even platform. SAs can independently choose a server solution based on their needs for reliability, scalability, and manageability. The SAs can now choose between competing server products, rather than being locked into the (potentially difficult to manage) server software and platform required for a particular client application. In many cases, the SAs can even choose the server hardware and software independently if the software vendor supports multiple hardware platforms.

We call this the ability to decouple the client and server selections. Open protocols provide a level playing field that inspires competition between vendors. The competition benefits you.

For comparison, the next anecdote illustrates what can happen when the customers select a proprietary email system that does not use open protocols, but fits their client-side needs.

Hazards of Proprietary Email Software

A New Jersey pharmaceutical company selected a particular proprietary email package for their PC userbase after a long evaluation. Their selection was based on user interface and features, with no concern for ease of server management, reliability, or scalability. The system turned out to be very unreliable when scaled to a large user base. The system stored all messages from all users in a single large file that everyone had to have write access to, which was a security nightmare. Frequent data corruption problems resulted in having to send the email database to the vendor across the Internet for demangling. This meant that potentially sensitive information was being exposed to people outside the company and that the people within the company could have no expectation of privacy for email. It also caused long outages of the email system, because it was unusable while the database was being repaired.

Because the package was not based on open protocols, the system support staff could not seek out a competing vendor that would offer a better, more secure, and reliable server. Because of the lack of competition, the vendor considered server management low priority and ignored the requests for server-related fixes and improvements. If the company had selected an open protocol and then let customers and SAs independently select their solutions, they would have realized the best of both worlds.

Open protocols and file formats are typically quite static (or only change in upwardly compatible ways) and widely supported, giving you the maximum product choice and maximum chance of reliable, interoperable products.

The other benefit to using open systems is that you won't require gateways to the rest of the world. Gateways are the "glue" that connect different systems. Although a gateway can save your day, systems based on a common, open protocol avoid gateways altogether. Gateways are additional services that require capacity planning, engineering, monitoring, and, well, everything else in this chapter. Reducing the number of services is a good thing.

Protocol Gateways Reduce Reliability

In college, Tom's email system was a proprietary system that was not based around Internet standard protocols, such as SMTP. Instead, it was sold with a software package to gateway email to and from the Internet. The gateway used their proprietary protocol to communicate with the mail server and SMTP to communicate with the rest of the world. This gateway was slow, unreliable, and expensive. It seemed like the vendor engineered the gateway with the assumption that only a tiny fraction of the email traffic would actually go through the gateway. The gateway was yet another thing to manage, debug, do capacity planning for, and so on. The vendor had little incentive to improve the gateway because it let customers communicate with systems that were considered to be "the competition." The mail system had many outages, nearly all of which were gateway outages, rather than problems with the main mail system. None of these problems would have arisen if the system had used open protocols rather than requiring a gateway.

History repeated itself nearly a decade later when Microsoft's Exchange mail server was introduced. It used a nonstandard protocol and offered gateways for communicating with other sites on the Internet. These gateways added to the list of services that SAs needed to engineer, configure, plan capacity for, scale, and so on. Most of the highly publicized Exchange bugs were related to the gateway.

Remember these lessons the next time a salesperson tries to sell you a calendar management system, directory service, or other product that ignores Internet Engineering Task Force (IETF) standards and other industry standards, but promises excellent gateways at an extra (or even zero) cost. Using standard protocols means using IETF standards, not vendor-proprietary standards.[4] Vendor-proprietary protocols lead to big headaches in the future.

3.1.4   Simplicity

When architecting a new service, simplicity should be your foremost consideration. The simplest solution that satisfies all the requirements will be the most reliable, easiest to maintain, easiest to expand, and easiest to integrate with other systems. Undue complexity leads to confusion, mistakes, and potential difficulty of use and may well make everything slower. It will be more expensive in setup cost and in maintenance costs.

As a system grows, it will become more complex. That is a fact of life. Therefore starting out as simple as possible delays the day when a system becomes "too complex." Consider two salespeople proposing to provide systems. One has a list of 20 basic features, and the other has an additional 20 features. One can expect that the more feature-rich software will have more bugs, and the vendor will have a more difficult time maintaining the code for the system.

Sometimes one or two requirements from the customers or SAs may add considerably to the complexity of the system. During the architecture phase, if you come across such requirements, it is worth going back to their source and evaluating the importance of the requirement. Explain to the customers or SAs that these requirements can be met, but at a cost to reliability, support levels, and on-going maintenance. Then ask them to reevaluate those requirements in that light and decide whether they should be met or dropped.

---

[4]If the vendor offers gateways, that's a good sign that it's not using IETF standards. You can also ask for the Requests for Comments (RFCs) that the product follows, and check that way, if you are unsure.

Let's return to our example of the proposals from two salespeople. Sometimes the offer with the 20 basic features does not include certain required features, and you might be tempted to reject the bid. On the other hand, if the customers understand the value of simplicity, they may be willing to forego those features and gain the higher reliability.

3.1.5 Vendor Relations

When choosing the hardware and software for a service, you should be able to talk to sales engineers from your vendors to get advice on the best configuration for your application. Hardware vendors sometimes have product configurations that are tuned for particular applications, such as databases or web servers. If the service you are building is a common one, your vendor may have a canned configuration that will be suitable.

If there is more than one server vendor in your environment, and it seems that more than one of your server vendors has an appropriate product, you should use this situation to your advantage. You should be able to get those vendors bidding against each other for the business. Because you probably have a fixed budget, this means that you may be able to get more for the same price, which you can use to improve performance, reliability, or scalability. Or, you may get a better price and be able to invest the surplus in improving the service in some other way. Even if you know which vendor you will choose, don't let them know that you have decided until you are convinced that you have the best deal possible.

When choosing a vendor, particularly for a software product, it is important to understand the direction in which the vendor is taking the product. If you have a large installation, it should be possible to get involved in beta trials and to influence the product direction by telling the product manager what features will be important to you in the future. For key, central services, such as authentication or directory services, it is essential to stay in touch with the product direction, or you may suddenly discover that the vendor no longer supports your platform. The impact of having to change a central piece of infrastructure can be huge. If possible, try to stick to vendors who develop the product primarily on the platform that you use, rather than port it to that platform. It will typically have fewer bugs, receive new features first, and be better supported on its primary development platform. Vendors are much less likely to discontinue support for that platform.

3.1.6 Machine Independence

Clients should always access a service using a generic name that is based on the function of the service. For example, they should point their shared calendar clients to the server called `calendar`, their email clients to a Post

Office Protocol (POP) (Myers and Rose 1996) server called `pop`, an Internet
Message Access Protocol (IMAP) (Crispin 1996) server named `imap`, and an
SMTP server named `mail`. Even if some of these services initially reside on
the same machine, they should be accessed through function-based names to
enable you to scale by splitting the service across multiple machines without
reconfiguring each client.

The machine should never have a primary name that is function-based.
For example, the calendar server could have a primary name of `dopey`, and
also be referred to as `calendar`, but should never have a primary name
of `calendar` because ultimately the function may need to move to another
machine. Moving the name with the function is more difficult because other
things that are tied to the primary name (`calendar`) on the original machine are not meant to move to the new machine. Naming and namespace
management issues are discussed in more detail in Chapter 6.

For services that are tied to an IP address, rather than a name, it is
also generally possible to give the machine that the service runs on multiple
"virtual" IP addresses in addition to its primary real IP address and to use
a virtual address for each service. Then the virtual address and the service
can be moved to another machine relatively easily.

When building a service on a machine, think about how you will move
it to another machine in the future. Someone is going to have to move it
at some point. Make that person's life as simple as possible by designing it
well from the beginning.

3.1.7   Environment

A service is something that your customers rely on, either directly or indirectly through other machines and services that rely on it. They have an
expectation that the service will be available when they want to use it. A
fundamental piece of building a service is providing a reasonably high level
of availability, which means placing all the equipment associated with that
service into a data center environment.

A data center provides protected power, plenty of cooling, controlled humidity (vital in dry or damp climates), fire suppression, and a secure location
where the machine should be free from accidental damage or disconnection.
Data centers are described in more detail in Chapter 17.

Another reason to locate servers in the data center is that a server often needs much higher-speed network connections than its clients because
it needs to be able to communicate at reasonable speeds with many clients
simultaneously. A server also is often connected to multiple networks, including some administrative ones, to reduce traffic across the network backbone.
High-speed network cabling and hardware typically are expensive to deploy
when they first come out and so will be installed in the limited area of the

data center first, where it is relatively cheap to deploy to many hosts, and is the most critical. All the servers that make up your service should be in the data center, to take advantage of the higher-speed networking there.

None of the components of the service should rely on anything that runs on a machine that is not located in the data center. The service is only as reliable as the weakest link in the chain of components that need to be working for the service to be available. If one of those components is on a machine that is not in a protected environment, it is more likely to fail and bring your service down with it. If you discover that you are relying on something that is running on a machine that is not in the data center, find a way to change the situation: Move the machine into the data center, replicate that service onto a data center machine, or remove the dependence on the less reliable server.

Hazards of Servers Relying on Nonservers

A customer once exported a partition on his desktop UNIX host so that it could be mounted via a Network Filesystem (NFS). Several critical servers mounted this partition because of a promiscuous automount configuration. He shut off his machine and left for the day, and all those servers in the machine room started hanging. The SAs had to decide whether to get corporate security to open his office door to boot his machine or to reboot the servers, because this incident occurred before "forced" unmounting of filesystems was possible.

3.1.8 Restricted Access

Restrict access to the servers that are part of the service that you are building. Customers should not need login access to machines that offer a service across the network. The fewer people who log in to a machine, the more stable it is. The more people who log in to a machine on a regular basis, the more likely it is to crash. Even OSs that crash frequently on desktops can stay up for months at a time offering a network service when no one is logging in and doing other work. Stability is important for servers. A server crashing affects a lot more people than a single desktop crashing. There should be no reason for anyone to log in to a server other than an SA performing administrative work on the server.

If a customer becomes accustomed to logging in to a particular server, he probably will start running other jobs on it that take CPU and Input/Output (I/O) cycles away from the service, without realizing that he is adversely affecting the service. Restricting server access to the SA team from the outset is the best approach to ensure reliability and expected performance levels.

For example, suppose a server is providing file-service through NFS, and customers start experiencing NFS performance problems. The best thing to do is to open a ticket with the SA group and get them to fix the performance problems. However, the quick and easy thing for the customer to do is just log in to the server and run the jobs on the server. If the customer is able to log in, that is probably what he will do without considering the impact on the system. As more customers start running their jobs on the NFS server, the performance of the NFS service will deteriorate and the server will become more unstable and less reliable, resulting in more people running their jobs on the server. Clearly this does not benefit anyone. It is far better to know about the situation and start fixing the root problem as soon as the first customer notices it.

3.1.9   Reliability

Along with environmental and access concerns, there are several things to consider when architecting a service for reliability. In Chapter 2, we discussed how to build an individual server to make it more reliable. Having reliable servers as components in your service is another part of making the service reliable as a whole.

If you have redundant hardware available, use it as effectively as you can. For example, if a system has two power supplies, plug them into different power strips and different power sources. If you have redundant machines, get the power and also the network connectivity from different places (for example, different switches), if possible. Ultimately, if this service is meant to be available to people at several different sites, think about placing redundant systems at another site that will act as a backup if the main site has a catastrophic failure.

All of the components of each service, other than the redundant pieces, should be tightly coupled, sharing the same power source and network infrastructure, so that the service as a whole depends on as few components as possible. Spreading nonredundant parts across multiple pieces of infrastructure just means that there are more single points of failure in the service. Each of those single points of failure can bring the whole service down. For example, suppose that a remote access service is deployed, and part of that service is a new, more secure, authentication and authorization system. The system is designed with three components: the box that handles the remote connections, the server that makes sure people are who they say they are (authentication), and the server that determines what areas people are allowed to access (authorization). If the three components are on different power sources, a failure of any one of those three power sources will cause the whole service to fail. Each one is a single point of failure. If they are on the same power source, the service will be unaffected by failures of the other power sources. Likewise, if they are on the same network switch, only a failure of that switch will take the service down. On the other hand, if they are spread across three different networks, with many different switches and routers involved in communications between the components, many more components could fail and bring the service down.

The single most effective way to make a service as reliable as possible is to make it as simple as possible. Find the simplest solution that meets all the requirements. When considering the reliability of a service you are building, you need to break it down into its constituent parts and look at what each of them relies on and the degree of reliability, until you reach servers and services that do not rely on anything else. For example, many services rely on name service, such as DNS. How reliable is your name service? Do your name servers rely on other servers and services? Other common central services are authentication services and directory services.

The network is almost certainly one of the components of your system. When you are building a service at a central location that will be accessed from remote locations, it is particularly important to take network topology into account. If connectivity to the main site is down, can the service still be made available to the remote site? Does it make sense to have that service still available to the remote site? What are the implications? Are there resynchronization issues? For example, name service should remain available on both sides when a link is severed, because there will be many things that people at the remote site do that rely only on machines at that site. But they won't be able to do those things if they can't resolve names. Even if their name server database isn't getting updates, the stale database can still be useful. If you have a centralized remote access authentication service with remote access systems at other offices, those remote access systems probably still should be able to authenticate people who connect to them, even if the link to the central server is down. In both of these cases, the software should be able to provide backup servers at remote offices and cope with resynchronizing databases when connectivity is restored. However, if you are building a large database or file service, ensuring that the service is still available in remote offices when their connectivity has been lost is probably not realistic.

Soft outages are outages that still provide some functionality. For example, a DNS server can be down and customers can still function, though sometimes a little slower or simply unable to do certain functions.

Hard outages, on the other hand, are problems that disrupt all other services, making it impossible for people to get any work done. It's better to group customers and servers/services such that hard outages disrupt only particular customer groups, rather than all customers. The funny thing about computers is that if one critical function isn't working, such as NFS, then often no work can be done. Thus being 90 percent functional can be the same as being 0 percent functional. Isolate the 10 percent outage to well-partitioned subsets.

For example, a down NFS server hangs all clients that are actively using the data. Suppose there are three customer groups and three NFS file servers. If the customers' data are spread over the file servers randomly, an outage on one file server may affect all customers. On the other hand, if each customer group is isolated to a particular file server, then during an outage one third of the customers at most will be unable to work.

When two people from different groups need to share data, they can do so by sharing the existing file servers or deploying a new one. Using a new file server for all possible combinations of collaborating groups does not scale well. Sharing one group's file server with another group will increase the load on the server and potentially on the network traffic. It also means that people outside of the primary group using that file server may be affected by outages. However, if properly configured, outages will only affect those people who are actively using the data rather than the whole group.

Grouping Power Cords

This same technique relates to how hardware is connected. A new SA was very proud of how neatly he wired a new set of servers. Each server had three components: a CPU, an external disk chassis, and a monitor. There was one power strip for all the CPUs, one for all the disk chassis, and one for all the monitors. Every wire was neatly run and secured with wire ties—a very pretty sight. His mentor complimented him on a job well done, but, realizing that the servers weren't in use yet, took the opportunity to shut off the power strip with all the disks. All the servers crashed. The SA learned his lesson: It would be better to have each power strip supply power to all the components of a particular machine. Any single power strip failure would result in an outage of one third of the hosts. In both cases, one third of the components were down, but in the latter case, only one third of the service became unusable.

❖ **Windows Login Scripts**   Another example of reliability grouping relates to how one architects MS Windows login scripts. Everything the script needs should come from the same server as the script. That way the script can be fairly sure that the server is alive. If users receive their login scripts from different servers, the various things that each login script needs to access should be replicated to all the servers rather than having multiple dependencies.

3.1.10 Single or Multiple Servers

Independent services or daemons should always be on separate machines, cost and staffing-levels permitting. However, if the service that you are building is actually composed of more than one new application or daemon and the communication between those components is over a network connection, you need to consider whether to put all of the components on one machine or to split them across many machines.

This choice may be determined by security, performance, or scaling concerns. For example, if you are setting up a web site with a database, you will want to put the database on a separate machine, so that you can tune it for database access, protect it from general Internet access, and scale up the front end of your service by adding more web servers in parallel without having to touch the database machine.

In other cases, one of the components will initially only be used for this one application, but may later be used by other applications. For example, you could introduce a calendar service that uses a Lightweight Directory Access Protocol (LDAP) (Yeong, Howes, and Kille 1995) directory server, and is the first LDAP-enabled service. Should the calendar server and directory server reside on the same machine or different ones? If a service, such as LDAP, may be used by other applications in the future, it should be placed on a dedicated machine, rather than a shared one, so that the calendar service can be upgraded and patched independently of the (ultimately more critical) LDAP service.

Sometimes, two applications or daemons may be completely tied together and will never be used apart from each other. In this situation, all other things being equal, it makes sense to put them both on the same machine, so that the service is only dependent on one machine, rather than two.

3.1.11 Centralization and Standards

An element of building a service is centralizing the tools, applications, and services that your customers need. Centralization means that the tools, applications, and services are primarily managed by one central group of SAs on a single central set of servers, rather than by multiple groups across the company who duplicate each other's work and buy their own servers. Support for these services is provided by a central helpdesk. Centralizing services and building them in standard ways make them easier to support and lower training costs.

To provide good support for any service that a customer relies on, the SA team as a whole needs to understand it well. That means that service should be properly integrated into the helpdesk process and that it should use your standard vendor's hardware, where possible. It should be designed and documented in some consistent way, so that the SA answering the support call knows where to find everything and thus can respond more quickly. Furthermore, avoid too many little services that require the person on the helpdesk to look up in a table or a database what print server John Smith of Performance Engineering uses when he prints to printer `lp1`. Instead, it is better to have a single print server or small number of large print servers.

Centralization does not preclude centralizing on regional or organizational boundaries, particularly if each region or organization has its own support staff. Some services, such as email, authentication services, and networks, are part of the infrastructure and need to be centralized. For large sites, these services can be built with a central core that feeds information to and from distributed regional and organizational systems. Other services, such as file services and CPU farms, are more naturally centralized around departmental boundaries.

3.1.12   Performance

From a customer's perspective, two things are important in any service: does it "work"[5] and is it fast? When designing a service, you need to pay attention to its performance characteristics, even though there may be many other difficult technical challenges to overcome. If you solve all of those difficult problems, but the service is slow to use, it will not be considered a success by the people using it.

Performance expectations increase constantly as networks, graphics, and processors get faster. Performance that is acceptable now may not be six months or a year from now. Bear that in mind when designing the system. You do not want to have to upgrade it for years if possible. You have other work to do. You want the machine to out-last the depreciation being paid on it.

To build a service that performs well, you need to understand how it works and perhaps look at ways of splitting it effectively across multiple machines. From the outset, you also need to consider how to scale the performance of the system as usage and expectations rise above what the initial system can do.

If your testing shows that the system runs fine with a few simultaneous users, how many resources—random access memory (RAM), I/O, and so on—will be consumed when the service goes into production and is in use by hundreds or thousands of simultaneous users? The vendor's experience can be very helpful with these projects.

---

[5] "Work" covers such areas as reliability, functionality, and user interface.

Bad Capacity Planning Makes a Bad First Impression

Always purchase servers with enough extra capacity to handle peak utilization, as well as a growing number of customers. A new electronic voucher system was deployed at one site and immediately was overwhelmed by the number of simultaneous users accessing it. The customers who tried to use it found that the system was impossibly slow and unreliable, and so they switched back to the old paper method. This gave a bad first impression of the service. A memo was sent out stating that a root cause analysis was performed and the system needed more RAM, which would arrive shortly. Even when the new RAM arrived, the customers did not adopt the new system because everyone "knew" that it was too slow and unreliable. They preferred to stick with what they knew worked.

This new system was projected to save millions of dollars per year, yet the management had skimped on purchasing enough RAM for the system. The finance group hoped that the new system would be wildly popular and the basis for numerous future applications, yet the performance was specified for an initially small capacity rather than leaving some room for growth. There was a lot of internal publicity about this new service, so they shouldn't have been surprised that so many people would be trying the service on the very first day, rather than having a slowly increasing number of customers. Finally, the finance group had decided to flash-cut the new service, rather than gradually introduce it to more divisions of the company over time. This is something we will discuss more (and advocate against) in Section 13.1.5. The finance group learned a lot about introducing new electronic services from this experience. Most importantly, they learned that with customers, the saying "once burned, twice shy" holds true. It is very hard to get customers to accept a service that has failed once already.

When choosing the servers that run the service, consider how the service works. Does it have processes that do a lot of disk accesses? If so, choose servers with fast disk I/O and fast disks to run those processes. Optimize that further by determining whether the disk access is more reads than writes or vice versa. If the service keeps large tables of data in memory, then look at servers with lots of fast memory and large memory caches. If it is a network-based service that sends large amounts of data to clients or between servers in the service, get lots of high-speed network interfaces and look at ways of balancing the traffic across those interfaces. Ways to do that include having a separate network for server-to-server communications, having dedicated network interfaces on key client networks, and using technology that enables the client to transparently communicate with the closest available interface. Also look at clustering options and devices that allow loosely tied clusters or machines running the same service to appear as a single entity.

Performance of the service for remote sites may also be an issue. You may need to become very creative for providing reasonable remote performance if the service has a lot of network traffic, particularly if it has not been designed for placing a server or two at each remote site. In some cases, quality of service or intelligent queuing mechanisms can be sufficient to make the performance acceptable. In others, you may need to look at ways of reducing the network traffic.

Performance at Remote Sites

A large company was out-sourcing some of its customer support functions, hardware support in particular. The company needed to provide people at several locations around the world with interactive access to the customer support systems and the service that was used for ordering replacement parts for customers. These both had graphical interfaces that ran on the client PCs and talked to the servers. Previously, the clients and servers were all on the same campus network, but now long-distance links were being introduced.

One of the applications transferred huge bitmaps to the client display, rather than more concise pieces of data that the client could then put into a graphical window. This feature of the server software made the usual client-server configuration completely unusable over slow links. The people architecting the service discovered that they could run the client application on a machine on the same network as the server and remotely display the results across the wide area link to the end-user's desktop, resulting in much better interactive performance for the end-user. So they bought some new server-class machines to act as the "client" machines at the central site. The real clients connected to these new machines, which displayed the results back to the real clients over the WAN, yielding acceptable performance.

The performance issue over wide area links and the solution that yielded acceptable performances were found through systematic testing of a prototype early in the project. If this problem had been discovered at the last minute, it would have delayed the project considerably, because it would have required a complete redesign of the whole system, including the security systems. If it had been discovered when it was rolled out to an end-user of the service, the project would have visibly failed.

3.1.13   Monitoring

A service is not complete and cannot properly be called a service unless it is being monitored for availability, problems, and performance and there are capacity planning mechanisms in place. (Monitoring systems is the topic of Chapter 24.)

The helpdesk, or front-line support group, must be automatically alerted to problems with the service so that they can start working on fixing them before too many people are affected by the problems. If a customer always has to notice a major problem with a service and call up to report it before anyone starts looking into the problem, the customer is getting a very low standard of service. Customers do not like to feel that they are the only ones paying attention to problems in the system.

Likewise, the SA group should monitor the service on an ongoing basis from a capacity planning standpoint. Depending on the service, capacity planning can include network bandwidth, server performance, transaction rates, licenses and physical device availability. As part of any service, SAs can reasonably be expected to anticipate and plan for growth. To do so effectively, usage monitoring needs to be built in as a part of the service.

3.1.14   Service Rollout

The way that a new service is rolled out to the customers is every bit as important as the way that it is designed. The rollout and the customers' first experiences with the service will color the way that they view the service in the future. So make sure their first impressions are positive.

One of the key pieces of making a good impression is having all of the documentation available, the helpdesk familiar with and trained on the new service, and all the support procedures in place. There is nothing worse than having a problem with a new application and finding out that no one seems to know anything about it when you look for help.

The rollout also includes building and testing a mechanism to install any new software and configuration settings that are needed on each desktop. Methods for rolling out new software to the desktops were discussed in Section 1.1.2, including using a slow rollout technique that we named "one, some, many," which uses well-chosen test groups that gradually increase in number. Ideally, no new desktop software or configuration should be required for the service, because that is less disruptive for your customers and reduces maintenance, but installing new client software on the desktops is frequently necessary.

The web's biggest benefit to corporate applications is that a single client (web browser) supports all new web-enabled applications. Entire new services can be rolled out without requiring client software rollouts.

3.2   The Icing

Besides building a service that is reliable, monitored, easy to maintain and support, and meets all of our basic requirements and the customers' requirements for a service, some extra things should be considered. If possible, you should use dedicated machines for each service. Doing so makes them easier to maintain and support. It also reduces the chances that someone working on a server will forget about one of the smaller services on that machine. In large companies, using dedicated machines is one of the basics. In smaller companies, the cost is prohibitive.

The other ideal that you should aim for in building services is to have them fully redundant. Some services are so critical that they need full redundancy in any size company. You should aim to make the others fully redundant as the company grows.

3.2.1   Dedicated Machines

Ideally, services should be built on dedicated machines. Large sites should be able to justify this structure based on demands on the services, but small sites will have a much harder time justifying it. Having dedicated machines for each service makes services more reliable, debugging easier when there are reliability problems, outages more limited in scope, and upgrades and capacity planning much easier.

Sites that grow from a small company to a larger one generally end up with one central administrative machine that is the core of all the critical services. It provides name service, authentication service, print service, email services, and so on. Eventually, this machine will have to be split up and the services spread across many servers because of the increased load. Often, by the time that the SAs get funding for more administrative machines, there are so many services and dependencies on this machine that it is very hard to split it apart. IP address dependencies are the most difficult to deal with when splitting services from one machine to many. Some services, such as name service, have IP addresses hardcoded into all the clients; others may result in the IP address being used in security systems, such as router or firewall rules.

Splitting the Central Machine

As a small company, Synopsys started with the typical configuration of one central administrative machine. It was the Network Information Service (NIS) master, DNS master, time server, print server, console server, email server, SOCKS relay, token-card authentication server, boot server, NetApp admin host, file server, Columbia Appletalk Protocol (CAP) server, and more. It was also the only "head" in the machine room, so it was the machine that SAs worked on when they had to work in there. As the group grew and new SAs were working at its console, using the console server software to access other hosts' consoles, occasionally a new SA would accidentally type a `halt` key sequence on the central server rather than using the appropriate sequence to send a `halt` message through the console server software. Because everything relied on this machine, this effectively brought down the whole company at once.

The time had come to split the functionality of the machine across multiple servers, not only because of those occasional slips but also because the machine was becoming increasingly unreliable and overloaded. At this point, the central machine had so many services running on it that just figuring out what they all were was a large task in itself.

The primary services of NIS and DNS were moved to three machines with lots of network interfaces, so that each network had two of these machines connected to it. Other services were moved onto still more machines, with each new machine being the primary machine for one service and a secondary for another. Some services moved relatively easily because they were associated with a service-based name. Others were more difficult because they were tied to IP addresses. In some cases, machines in other parts of the company had been built to rely on the real hostname rather than the service-based name.

Years later, the original central machine was still in existence, though not nearly so critical or overloaded, as the SAs continued to find a myriad of dependencies that remote offices had built into their local infrastructure servers and desktops in nonstandard ways.

Splitting a center-of-the-universe host into lots of different hosts is very difficult and becomes harder the longer it exists and the more services that are built onto it. Using service-based names helps, but they need to be standardized and used universally and consistently throughout the company.

3.2.2 Full Redundancy

Full redundancy means having a duplicate server or set of servers that will be ready to take over from the primary set in the case of failure. The redundant systems may continuously run as backup servers, automatically come on line when the primary servers fail, or require a small amount of human intervention to take over providing the failed service.

The type of redundancy that you choose depends on the service. Some services, such as web servers and compute farms, lend themselves well to running on large farms of cloned machines. Other services, such as huge databases, do not and require a more tightly coupled fail-over system. The software you are using to provide a service may dictate that your redundancy is in the form of a live passive slave server that only responds to requests when the master server fails. In all cases, the redundancy mechanism must ensure that data synchronization occurs and data integrity is maintained.

In the case of large farms of cloned servers and other scenarios in which redundant servers run continuously alongside the primary servers, the redundant machines can be used to share the load and increase performance when everything is operating normally. If you use this approach, be careful not to allow the load to reach the point at which performance would be unacceptable if one of the servers were to fail. Add more servers in parallel with the existing ones before you reach that point.

Some services are so integral to the minute-to-minute functioning of a site that they are made fully redundant very early on in the life of the site. Others remain largely ignored until the site becomes very large or has some huge, visible failure of the service.

Name service and authentication services are typically the first services to have full redundancy. This is partly because the software is designed for secondary servers and partly because they are so critical. Other critical services, such as email, printing, and networks, tend to be considered much later because they are more complicated or more expensive to make completely redundant.

As with everything that you do, consider which services will benefit your customers most to have completely redundant, and start there.

Case Study: Design Email Service for Reliability

Bob Flandrena engineered an interesting redundant way for email to flow into and out of Bell Labs. Mail coming in from the Internet is spooled to a group of machines inside the firewall, which then forward the messages to the appropriate internal mail server. An external machine will queue mail in the event of the firewall being down. This external machine has a large spool area and could hold a couple of days' worth of mail. Logging, spam control, and various security-related issues are focused on the small set of internal hosts that are guaranteed to see all incoming email.

Internal mail servers route email between each other. However, their configurations are simplified by the fact that more difficult routing decisions can be deferred to two routing hosts, both inside the firewall. These routing hosts have more complicated configurations and can determine if email should be routed to the Internet.

Mail destined for the Internet is sent by the routing hosts to two redundant hosts outside the firewall dedicated to repeatedly retrying message delivery to external Internet domains. There is sufficient spool space on the routing hosts in case these two external relays are inaccessible and sufficient spool space on the external machines in case they have to retry some messages for a long time.

The firewall rules permit only outbound email (SMTP) traffic from the routing hosts to the external relays. The inbound rules permit only the appropriate paths for incoming email. All of these hosts use the same hardware and software, with slightly different configurations. A spare set of hardware is kept on hand so that broken hosts can be replaced quickly.

The system is slower when a single host is down, but as long as the firewall is operating, email gets through. If the firewall is down, it takes a simultaneous failure of a complete set of redundant systems before incoming or outgoing mail is not spooled.

The system scales very well. Each potential bottleneck is independently monitored. If it becomes overloaded, the simple addition of more hosts and appropriate DNS Mail eXchanger (MX) records adds capacity. It's a simple, clear design that is reliable and easy to support.

The only remaining points of failure are the mail delivery hosts within the company. Failure of any one of those affects only part of the company, however. This is the trickiest part to address.

Another benefit of such redundancy is that it makes upgrades easier. A "rolling upgrade" can be performed. One at a time, each host is disconnected, upgraded, tested, and brought back into service. The outage of the single host does not stop the entire service, though it may affect performance. Heck, if you really screw up an upgrade you can power off the machine and fix it when you have calmed down.

3.3 Conclusion

Designing and building a service is a key part of every SA's job. How well the SA performs this part of the job determines how easy each service is to support and maintain, how reliable it is, how well it performs, how well it meets customer requirements, and ultimately how happy the customers will be with the performance of the SA team.

You build services to provide better service to your customers, either directly by providing a service they need or indirectly by making the SA team more effective. Always keep the customers' requirements in mind. They are ultimately the reason that you are building the service.

An SA can do a lot of things to build a better service, such as building it on dedicated servers, making it as simple as possible, monitoring the servers and the service, following company standards, and centralizing the service onto a few machines. Some ways to build a better service involve looking beyond the initial requirements into the future to upgrade and maintenance projects. Making the service as independent as possible of the actual machines it runs on is one key way of keeping it easier to maintain and upgrade.

Services should be as reliable as the customer requirements specify. Over time, in larger companies, you should be able to make more services fully redundant so that any one component can fail and be replaced without bringing the service down. Prioritize the order in which you make services fully redundant based on the return on investment for your customers. You will have a better idea of which systems are the most critical only after gaining experience with them.

Rolling out the service smoothly with minimal disruption to the customers is the final, but possibly most visible, part of building a new service. Customers are likely to form their opinion of the new service based on the rollout process, so it is important to do that well.

Exercises

1. List all the services that you can think of in your environment. What hardware and software make up each one? List their dependencies.

2. Select a service that you are currently designing or can predict needing to design in the future. What will you need to do to make it meet the recommendations in this chapter? How will you roll it out to customers?

3. What services currently rely on machines that do not live in the machine room? How can you remove those dependencies?

4. What services do you currently monitor? How would you expand your monitoring to be more service-based rather than simply machine-based? Does your monitoring system open trouble tickets or page people as appropriate? If not, how hard would it be to add that functionality?

5. Do you have a machine that has multiple services running on it? If so, how would you go about splitting it up so that each service runs on dedicated machines? What would the impact on your customers be during that process? Would this help or hurt service?

6. How do you currently do capacity planning? Is it satisfactory, or can you think of ways to improve it?

7. What services do you have that have full redundancy? How is that redundancy provided? Are there other services that you should add redundancy to?

8. Reread the discussion of bandwidth versus latency in Section 3.1.2. What would the mathematical formula look like for the two proposed solutions (batched requests and windowed requests).

Chapter 4

Debugging

In this chapter, we dig deeply into what is involved in debugging problems. In Chapter 16, we will put this into the larger context of receiving problem reports, processing them, and so on, but that is an organizational issue called *customer care.* This chapter, on the other hand, is about you and what you do when faced with a technical problem.

Debugging is not simply making a change that fixes a problem. That's the easy part. Debugging begins by understanding the problem, finding its cause, and then making the change that makes the problem disappear for good. Temporary or superficial fixes (such as rebooting) that do not fix the cause of the problem only guarantee more work for you in the future. We'll continue that theme in Chapter 5.

Anyone reading this book has a certain amount of smarts and a level of experience[1] that means we do not need to be pedantic about this topic. You've debugged problems; you know what it's like. We're going to make you conscious of the finer points of the process, then discuss some ways of making it even smoother. We encourage you to be systematic. It's better than randomly poking about.

---

[1] And while we're at it, you're good looking and a sharp dresser.

4.1 The Basics

The basics of debugging can be narrowed down to these points:

- Learn the customer's failed goal (problem).
- Find the problem's cause and fix it.
- Have the right tools.

4.1.1 Learn the Customer's Problem

The first step in fixing a problem is to understand, at a high level, what the customer is trying to do and what part of it is failing. In other words, the customer is doing something and expecting a particular result, but something else is happening instead.

For example, customers may be trying to read their email and aren't able to. They may report this in many ways: "My mail program is broken," or "I can't reach the mail server," or "My mailbox disappeared!" Any of those statements may be true, but the problem also could be a network problem, a power failure in the server room, or a DNS problem. Therefore it is important to gain a high-level understanding of what the customer is trying to do.

Sometimes customers aren't good at expressing themselves, so care and understanding must prevail. "Can you help me understand what the document should look like?"

Some customers provide a valuable service by digging into the problem before reporting it. A senior SA partners with these customers but understands that there are limits. It can be nice to get a report such as, "I can't print, I think there is a DNS problem." However, we do not believe in taking such reports at face value. You understand the system architecture better than they do, so you still need to verify the DNS portion of the report, as well as the printing problem. Maybe it is best to interpret the report as two possibly related reports: printing isn't working for a particular customer and a certain DNS test failed. For example, a printer's name may not be in DNS, depending on the print system architecture. Often customers will ping a host's name to demonstrate a routing problem, but overlook the error message and the fact that the DNS lookup of the host's name failed.

Can't Ping a Server
One of Tom's customers was reporting that he couldn't ping a particular server located about 1,000 miles away in a different division. He provided traceroutes, ping information, and a lot of detailed evidence. Rather than

investigating potential DNS, routing, and networking issues, Tom stopped to ask, "Why do you require the ability to ping that host?" It turned out that pinging that host wasn't part of the person's job, but instead the customer was trying to use that host as an authentication server. The problem to be debugged should have been "Why can't I authenticate off this host?" or even better, "Why can't I use service A, which relies on the authentication server on host B?"

By contacting the owner of the server, Tom found the very simple answer: Host B had been decommissioned, and properly configured clients should have automatically started authenticating off a new server. This wasn't a networking issue at all, but a matter of client configuration. The customer had hard-coded the IP address into his configuration when he shouldn't have. A lot of time would have been wasted if the problem had been pursued as originally reported.

Now you understand that a reported problem is about an expected outcome not happening. Now let's look at the cause.

4.1.2 Find the Problem's Cause and Fix It

To build sustainable reliability, you must find and fix the cause of the problem, not just work around the problem or find a way to recover from it quickly. Although workarounds and quick recovery times are good things, fixing the root cause of a problem is better.

How many times has this happened to you: A coworker reports that there was a problem and he fixed it. "What was the problem?" you inquire.

"The host needed to be rebooted."

"What was the problem?"

"I told you! The host needed to be rebooted."

And a day later, the host needs to be rebooted again. If he really had determined what the problem was, it wouldn't have returned.

The same goes for: "The daemon or service needed to be restarted" and other mysteries. Many times we've seen someone fix a full-disk situation by deleting old log files. However, the problem returns as the log files grow again. Deleting the log files fixes the symptoms, but activating a script that would rotate and automatically delete the logs would actually fix the problem.

A vendor known for producing an unreliable OS got a lot of bad press when it reported that a major goal of its next release was to make reboots happen faster. Users would prefer it didn't need to be rebooted.

It is important to be methodical or systematic about finding the cause and fixing it. To be systematic, you must form hypotheses, test them, note the results, and make changes based on those results. Anything else is just making random changes until the problem goes away.

Two common processes used in debugging are the process of elimination and successive refinement. The *process of elimination* is the removing of different parts of the system until the problem disappears. The problem must have existed in the last portion removed. *Successive refinement* is the adding of new components to the system and verifying at each step that the desired change happens. The process of elimination is often used when debugging a hardware problem, for example, replacing memory chips until a memory error is eliminated, or pulling out cards until a machine is able to boot. Elimination is used with software applications, such as eliminating potentially conflicting drivers or applications until a failure disappears. Some OSs have tools that search for possible conflicts and provide test modes to help narrow the search. One such tool is ConflictCatcher in MacOS.

Successive refinement is an additive process. To diagnose an IP routing problem, `traceroute` tests connectivity one network "hop" away. It then tests connectivity two hops away, then three, four, and so on. When the probes no longer return a result, we know that the router at that hop wasn't able to return packets. The problem is at that last router. When connectivity exists but there is packet loss, a similar methodology can be used. You can send many packets to the next router and verify that there is no packet loss. You can successively refine the test by including more distant routers until the packet loss is detected.

Sometimes, successive refinement can be thought of as *follow-the-path* debugging. To do this, you must follow the path of the data or the problem, reviewing the output of each process to make sure it is the proper input to the next stage. It is common on UNIX systems to have an assembly-line approach to processing. One task generates data, the others modify or process the data in sequence, and the final task stores it. Some of these processes may happen on different machines, but the data can be checked at each step.

Short-cuts and optimizations can be used with these techniques. Based on past experience you might skip a step or two. However, this is often a mistake because you may be jumping to a conclusion.

We should point out, however, that we often find that the final problem is related to the most recent change made to the host, network, or whatever is having a problem. This usually indicates a lack of testing. Therefore, before you begin debugging a problem, ponder for a moment what changes were made recently: Was a new device plugged into the network? What was the last configuration change to a host? Was anything changed on a router or firewall? Often this directs your search for the cause.

4.1.3 Have the Right Tools

Debugging requires the right diagnostic tools. Some tools are physical devices, others are software tools that are either purchased or downloaded, and still others are home grown. However, knowledge is the most important tool.

Diagnostic tools let you *see* into a devices or systems to see its inner workings. However, if you don't know how to interpret what you see, all the data in the world won't help you solve the problem. Training usually involves learning how the system works, where to look to see its inner workings, and how to interpret what you see.

For example, when training someone how to use an Ethernet monitor (sniffer), teaching the person to capture packets is easy. Most of the training is spent explaining how various protocols work so that you understand what you see. That's not really a function of the tool, but a function of a deeper understanding of what the tool lets you see.

UNIX systems have a reputation for being very easy to debug. This is most likely because of the fact that so many experienced UNIX SAs have in-depth knowledge of the inner workings of the system. Such knowledge is easily gained. UNIX systems come with documentation about their internals; early users had access to the source code itself. Many books dissect the source code of UNIX kernels (McKusick, Bostic, and Karels 1996; Lions 1996; Mauro and McDougall 2000) for educational purposes. Much of the system is driven by scripts that can be read easily to gain an understanding of what is going on behind the scenes.

Windows NT developed an early reputation for being a difficult system to debug when problems arose. Rhetoric from the UNIX community claimed that it was a black box with no way to get the information you needed to debug problems on NT systems. In reality, there were mechanisms, but the only way to learn about them was through vendor-supplied training. From the perspective of a culture that is very open about information, this was difficult to adjust to. It took many years to disseminate the information about how to access NT's internals and how to interpret what was found.

Know Why a Tool Draws a Conclusion
It is important to understand not only the system being debugged but also the tools being used to debug it. Once Tom was helping a network technician with a problem: A PC couldn't talk to any servers, even though the "link" light was illuminated. The technician disconnected the PC from its network jack and plugged in a new handheld device that could test and diagnose a large list of local area network (LAN) problems. However, the output of

the device was a list of conclusions without information about how it was arriving at them. The technician was basing his decisions on the output of this device without question. Tom kept asking, "The device claims it is on network B, but how did it determine that?" The technician didn't know or care. Tom stated, "I don't think it is really on network B! Network B and C are bridged right now, so if the network jack was working, it should claim to be on network B and C at the same time." The technician disagreed, because the very expensive tool couldn't possibly be wrong, and the problem must be with the PC.

It turned out that the tool was guessing the network after finding a single host that was also on that LAN segment. This jack was connected to a hub, which had another workstation connected to it in a different office. The uplink from the hub had become disconnected from the rest of the network. Without knowing how the tool performed its tests, there was no way to determine why a tool would report such a claim and further debugging would have been a wild goose chase. Luckily, there was a hint that something was suspicious—it didn't mention network C. The process of questioning the conclusion drew them to the problem's real cause.

What makes a good tool? We prefer minimal tools over large, complicated tools. The best tool is one that provides the simplest solution to the problem at hand. The more sophisticated a tool is, the more likely it will get in its own way or simply be too big to carry to the problem! The smaller the tool, the better.

NFS mounting problems can be debugged with three simple tools: `ping`, `traceroute`, and `rpcinfo`. Each does one thing and does that one thing well. If the client can't mount from a particular server, one should make sure they can ping each other. If they can't, it's a network problem and `traceroute` can isolate the problem. If `ping` succeeded, then connectivity is good and there must be a protocol problem. From the client, the elements of the NFS protocol can be tested with `rpcinfo`.[2] One can test the `portmap traceroute` function, then `mountd`, `nfs`, `nlockmgr`, and `status`. If any of them fail, one can deduce that the appropriate service isn't working. If all of them succeed, one can deduce it is an export permission problem, which usually means the name of the host listed in the export list is not exactly what the server sees when it performs a reverse DNS lookup. These are extremely powerful diagnostics that are done with extremely simple tools. A similar process works for other RPC-based protocols (Stern 1991).

---

[2]For example, `rpcinfo -T udp servername portmap` in Solaris or `rpcinfo -u servername portmap` in Linux.

Transmission Control Protocol (TCP)-based protocols often can be debugged with a similar triad of tools: ping, `traceroute/tracert`, and `telnet`. These tools are available on every platform that supports TCP/IP (Windows, UNIX, and others). Again, `ping` and `traceroute` can diagnose connectivity problems. Then `telnet` can be used to manually "simulate" many TCP-based protocols. For example, email administrators know enough of the SMTP protocol (Crocker 1982) to telnet to port 25 of a host and type the SMTP commands as if they were the client. One can diagnose many problems by watching the results. Similar techniques work for NNTP (Kantor and Lapsley 1986) and FTP (Postel and Reynolds 1985) and other TCP-based protocols. *TCP/IP Illustrated, Volume 1* by W. Richard Stevens (Stevens 1994) provides an excellent view into how the protocols work.

Sometimes the best tools are simple home-grown tools or the combination of other small tools and applications as the following anecdote shows.

Finding the Latency Problem

Once Tom was tracking reports of high latency on an Integrated Service Digital Network (ISDN) link. The problem happened only occasionally. He set up a continuous (once per second) ping between two machines that should demonstrate the problem and recorded this output for several hours. He observed consistently good (low) latency, except that occasionally there seemed to be trouble. A small `perl` program was written that would extract pings with high latency (latency more than three times the average of the first 20 pings) and would reveal missed pings. He noticed that no pings were being missed, but every so often a series of pings took much longer to arrive. He used a spreadsheet to graph the latency over time. Visualizing the results helped him notice that the problem occurred every five minutes, within a second or two. It also happened at other times, but every five minutes he was assured of seeing the problem. He realized that there are protocols that do certain operations every five minutes. Could a route table refresh be overloading the CPU of a router? Maybe there was a protocol that overloaded a link?

By process of elimination he isolated the problem to a particular router. Its CPU was being overloaded by routing table calculations, which happened every time there was a real change to the network plus every five minutes during the usual route table refresh. This agreed with the previously collected data. The fact that it was an overloaded CPU and not an overloaded network link explained why latency increased but no packets were lost. The router had enough buffering to ensure that no packets were dropped. Once he fixed the problem with the router, the ping test and filter were used again to demonstrate that the problem had been fixed.

The customer who had reported the problem was a scientist with a particularly condescending attitude toward SAs. After confirming with him that the problem had been resolved, the scientist was shown the methodology including the graphs of timing data. He was no longer condescending to SAs after he saw that a scientific approach was in use.

4.2   The Icing

Now that we have covered the basics, the icing really improves those basics: better tools, better knowledge about how to use the tools, and better understanding about the system being debugged.

4.2.1   Better Tools

Better tools are, well, better! There is always room for new tools that improve on the old ones. Keeping up-to-date on the latest tools can be difficult, preventing you from being an early adopter of new technology. Several forums, such as USENIX and SAGE conferences, as well as web sites and mailing lists, can help you learn of these new tools as they are announced.

We are advocates for simple tools. Improved tools need not be more complex. In fact, sometimes a new tool brings innovation through its simplicity.

When evaluating new tools, assess them based on what problems they can solve. Try to ignore the aspects that are flashy, buzzword-compliant, and full of hype. *Buzzword-compliant* is a humorous term meaning that the product applies to all the current industry buzzwords one might see in the headlines of trade magazines, whether or not such compliance has any benefit.

Ask "what real-life problem will this solve?" It is easy for salespeople to focus you on flashy, colorful output, but does the flash add anything to the utility of the product? Is the color used intelligently to direct the eye at important details, or is it just to make the product pretty? Are any of the buzzwords relevant? Sure, it supports SNMP, but will I actually integrate it into my SNMP monitoring system? Or is SNMP simply used for configuring the device?

Ask for an evaluation copy of the tool and make sure you have time to actually use the tool during the evaluation. Don't be afraid to send it back if you didn't find it useful. Salespeople have thick skins, and the feedback you give will help them make the product better in future releases.

4.2.2 Formal Training on the Tools

Although manuals are great, formal training can be the icing that sets you apart from others. Formal training has a number of benefits, including the following.

- Training is usually provided off-site, which takes you away from the interruptions of your job and lets you focus on learning new skills.
- Formal training usually covers all the features, not just the ones with which you've had time to experiment.
- Often, you have access to a lab of machines where you can try things you couldn't try "at home" because of production requirements.
- Instructors often will reveal bugs or features that the vendor may not want revealed in print.
- You can list the training on your resume; this can be more impressive to prospective employers than actual experience, especially if you receive certification.

4.2.3 End-to-End Understanding of the System

Finally, the ultimate debugging "icing" is to have at least one person who understands, end-to-end, how the system works. On a small system, that's easy. As systems grow larger and more complex, however, people specialize and end up only knowing their part of the system. Having someone who knows the entire system end-to-end is invaluable when there is a major outage.

Case Study: Architects

How do you retain employees that have this kind of end-to-end knowledge? One way is to promote them.

Synopsys had "architect" positions in each technology area who were this kind of "end-to-end" person. They knew more than just their technology area in depth, and they were good cross-over people, too. Their official role was to track the industry direction; predict needs and technologies two to five years out and start preparing for them (prototyping, getting involved with vendors as alpha/beta customers, and helping to steer the direction of the vendors' products); architecting new services; watching what was happening in the group; steering people toward smarter, more scalable solutions; and so on. This ensured that such people were around when end-to-end knowledge was required for debugging major issues.

Mystery File Deletes

Here's an example of a situation in which end-to-end knowledge was required to fix a problem. A customer revealed that some of his files were disappearing. To be more specific, he had about 100MB of data in his home directory, and all but 2MB had disappeared. He had restored his files. The environment had a system that let users restore files from backups without SA intervention. However, a couple of days later the same thing happened; this time a different set of files remained. Again, the files remaining totaled 2MB. He then sheepishly revealed that this had been going on for a couple of weeks, but he found it convenient to restore his own files and he felt embarrassed to bother the SAs with such an odd problem.

The SA's first theory was that there was a virus, but virus scans revealed nothing. The next theory was that someone was playing pranks on him, or there was a cron job that was badly written. He was given pager numbers to call the moment his files disappeared again. Meanwhile, network sniffers were put into place to monitor who was deleting files on that server. The next day, the customer alerted the SAs that his files were disappearing. "What was the last thing you did?" Well, he had simply logged in to a machine in a lab to surf the web. The SAs were baffled. The network monitoring tools showed that the deletions were not coming from the customer's PC nor from a rogue machine or misprogrammed server. The SAs each had done their best to debug the problem using their knowledge of their part of the system, yet the problem remained unsolved.

Suddenly, one of the senior SAs with end-to-end knowledge of the system, including both Windows and UNIX and all the various protocols involved, realized that web browsers keep a cache that gets pruned to stay lower than a certain limit, often 2MB. Could the browser on this machine be deleting the files? After some investigation, it was discovered that the lab machine was running a web browser configured with an odd location for its cache. The location was fine for some users, but when this user logged in, the location was equivalent to his home directory because of a bug (or feature?) related to how Windows parsed directory paths that involved subdirectories that didn't exist. The browser was finding a "cache" with 100MB of data and deleting files until the space used was less than 2MB. That explained why every time the problem appeared a different set of files remained. After the browser's configuration was fixed, the problem disappeared.

The initial attempts at solving the problem (virus scans, checking for cron jobs, watching protocols) had proved fruitless because they were testing the parts. Only by someone having end-to-end understanding of the system was the problem solved.

4.3 Conclusion

Every SA debugs problems and typically develops a mental catalog of standard solutions to common problems. However, debugging should be a systematic or methodical process that involves understanding what the customer is trying to do, rather than just the symptoms that they are reporting, and fixing the root cause of the problem, rather than smoothing over the symptoms. There are many techniques for debugging; some are subtractive (process of elimination) and others are additive (successive refinement). Fixing the root cause is important, because if the root problem isn't repaired, the problem will recur, thus generating more work for the SA.

Although this chapter strongly stresses fixing the root problem as soon as possible, there are times when one must provide a workaround quickly and return later to fix the root problem. For example, one might prefer quick fixes during "production hours" and have a maintenance window (Chapter 12) reserved for more permanent and disruptive fixes. Such situations are more fully discussed in Chapter 16.

Better tools let one solve problems more efficiently without adding undue complexity. Formal training on a tool provides knowledge and experience that one cannot get from a manual. Finally, in a major outage or when a problem seems peculiar, nothing beats a person or a team of people that together have end-to-end knowledge of the system.

Simple tools can solve big problems. Complicated tools sometimes obscure how they draw conclusions.

Debugging is often a communication process between you and your customers. You must gain an understanding of the problem in terms of what the customer is trying to accomplish, as well as the symptoms discovered so far. Debugging is one of the basics that must be mastered before one can study the larger issue of handling customer requests (Chapter 16).

Exercises

1. Pick a technology that you deal with as part of your job function. Name the debugging tools you use for that technology. For each tool, is it home-grown, commercial, or free? Is it simple? Can it be combined with other tools? What training (formal or informal) have you received on this tool?

2. Describe a recent technical problem that you debugged and how you resolved it.

3. In Section 4.1.3 the customer was impressed by the methodology used to fix his problem. How would the situation be different if the customer was a nontechnical manager rather than a scientist?

4. What tools do you not have that you wish you did?

Chapter 5

Fixing Things Once

The point we make in this chapter is that fixing something once is better than fixing it over and over again. Although this sounds obvious, sometimes it just isn't possible given other constraints, or we find ourselves fixing something over and over without realizing it, or the quick fix is just emotionally easier. By being conscious of these things, we can achieve several goals. First, we can manage our time better. Second, we can become better SAs. Third, if necessary, we can explain better to the customer why we are taking longer to fix something than they expected.

The previous chapter described a systematic process for debugging a problem. This chapter is different in that it is about a general day-to-day philosophy.

- *The Basics*
  - Fixing something once rather than over and over.
  - Corollary A: "Fix the problem permanently."
  - Corollary B: "Don't reinvent the wheel."
  - Corollary C: "Fix the problem for all hosts at the same time."
  - Avoid the temporary fix trap.
  - Measure twice, cut once and other advice from carpenters.

- *The Icing*
  - Automation can fix the symptoms.
  - Automation should fix the problem.

5.1   The Basics

One of Tom's favorite mantras is "fix things once." If something is broken, it should be fixed once and fixed permanently. The fix should leverage the work of others to avoid reinventing the wheel. If a problem is likely to appear on other machines, it should be tested for and repaired on all other machines.

5.1.1   Fix Things Once, Rather Than Over and Over

Sometimes, particularly for something that seems trivial or that affects you only for the time being, it can seem easier to do a quick fix that doesn't fix the problem permanently. It may not even cross your mind that you are fixing a problem multiple times that you could have fixed once with a little more effort.

Fix It Once

Once Tom was helping an SA reconfigure two large Sun Solaris servers. The configuration required many reboots to test each step of the process. After each reboot, the SA would log in again. The root account on this host didn't have TERM, PATH, and other environment variables set properly. This usually wouldn't burn him. For example, it didn't matter that his TERM variable was unset, for he wasn't using any curses-based tools. However, this meant his shell wouldn't support command-line editing. Without that, he was doing much more typing and retyping than would normally be required. He was on a console, so he didn't even have a mouse with which to cut and paste. Eventually he would need to edit a file using a screen-based editor (vi or emacs), and he would set his TERM variable so that the program would be usable.

It pained Tom to see this guy manually setting these variables time and time again. In the SA's mind, however, he was being very efficient, because he only spent time setting a variable right before it was required, the first time it was required. Occasionally, he would log in, type one command, and reboot; a big win considering that none of the variables needed to be set that time. However, for longer sessions Tom felt the SA was distracted by having to keep track of which variables hadn't been set yet, in addition to focusing on the problem at hand. Often, the SA would do something that would fail because of unset variables; then he would set the required variables and retype the failed command.

Finally, Tom politely suggested that if the SA had a /.profile that set those variables, he could be more focused on the problem rather than his environment. *Fix the problem once, Corollary A: "Fix the problem permanently."*

The SA agreed and started creating the host's /.profile from scratch. Tom stopped him and reminded him that rather than inventing a /.profile from scratch he should copy one from another Solaris host. *Fix the problem once, Corollary B: "Leverage what others have done, don't reinvent the wheel."* By copying the generic /.profile that was on most other hosts in that lab, he was leveraging the effort put into the previous hosts. He was also reversing the entropy of the system, taking one machine that was dissimilar from the others and making it the same again.

As the SA copied the /.profile from another machine, Tom questioned why we were doing this at all. Shouldn't Solaris JumpStart have already installed the fine /.profile that all the other machines have? In Chapter 1, we saw the benefits of automating the big three deployment issues: loading the OS, patching the OS, and network configuration. This environment had a JumpStart server; why hadn't it been used?

It turned out that this machine came from another site, and the owner simply configured its IP address rather than JumpStart the machine. (The security risk of doing this is an entirely different issue.) This was "to save time," because it was unlikely that the host would stay there for more than a couple of days. A year later, it was still there. We were paying the price for customers who want to skip one of "the big three" to save their own time. They saved time, and cost us time.

Then Tom realized a couple more things. If the machine hadn't been JumpStarted, then it was very unlikely that it got added to the list of hosts that were automatically patched. This host had not been patched since it arrived. It was insecurely configured, had none of the recent security patches installed, and was missed by the Y2K scans: It was sure to have problems on January 1,2000.

Fix the problem once, Corollary C: "Fix a problem for all hosts at the same time." The original problem was that Solaris includes a painfully minimalist /.profile file. The site's solution was to install a better one at install time via JumpStart. The problem was fixed for all hosts at the same time by making the fix part of the install procedure. If the file needed to be changed, we could use the patch system to distribute a new version to all machines.

All-in-all, the procedure that Tom and his coworker were there to do took twice as long because the host hadn't been JumpStarted. Some of the delays were caused because this system lacked the standard configuration, which is mature and SA-friendly. Other delays came from the fact that the OS was a minefield of half-configured or misconfigured features.

This was another reminder about how getting the basics right makes things so good that you forget how bad things were when you didn't have the basics done right. Tom was accustomed to the luxury of an environment where hosts are configured properly for us. He had been taking it for granted.

5.1.2   Avoid the Temporary Fix Trap

The previous section is fairly optimistic about being able to make the best fix possible in every situation. However, that is not realistic. Sometimes, constraints on time or resources require a "quick fix" to hold one over until a complete fix can be scheduled. In Section 16.2.4, we discuss the fact that sometimes a complete fix can require an unacceptable interruption of service in certain situations, and a temporary fix will have to suffice until a maintenance window can be scheduled.

Sometimes, temporary fixes are required because of resource issues. Maybe software will have to be written or hardware installed to fix the problem. Those things will take time. If a disk is being filled by logs, a permanent fix might be to add software that would rotate logs. It may take time to install such software, but in the meanwhile old logs can be manually deleted.

It is important that temporary fixes be followed by permanent fixes. To do this, some mechanism is needed so that problems don't fall between the cracks. Returning to our full log disk example, on a busy day it can be tempting to manually delete the older logs and move on to the next task without recording the fact that one needs to return to the issue to implement a permanent fix. Recording such action items can be difficult. Scribbled notes on paper get lost. One might not always have one's Day-Runner to-do book on hand. It is much easier to email a reminder to oneself. Even better is to have a "helpdesk" application that permits new tickets to be created via email.

It is extremely convenient to be able to send email from the command line, as can be done on all UNIX systems. Even if a UNIX host isn't configured to receive email, they are almost always configured to be able to send email. Being able to generate email from the command line is much better than having to have a properly configured email client, with profile and configuration and other settings properly configured. UNIX SAs often take this ability for granted until they start doing more work with PCs. At Bell Labs, Tom had a reputation for having nearly as many self-created tickets as tickets from customers.

Temporary fixes are emotionally easier than permanent fixes. We feel like we've accomplished something in a small amount of time. That's a lot easier on our ego than beginning a large project to permanently fix a problem or adding something to our never-ending to-do list.

Fixing the same small things time after time is habit-forming. With Pavlovian accuracy, we execute the same small fix every time our monitoring systems warn us of the problem. When we are done, we admonish ourselves, thinking, "Next time I'll have the time to do the permanent fix!" Soon we are so efficient at the quick fix that we forget that there is a permanent fix. We get the feeling that we are busy all day but don't feel like we are accomplishing anything. We ask our boss or coworker to look at our day with "new eyes," and they see what we can no longer see, that we are spending our days mopping the floor rather than turning off the faucet.

We have grown so accustomed to the quick fix that we are now the expert at it. In shame, we discover that we have grown so efficient at it that we take pride in our efficiency, pointing out the keyboard macros we have written and other time-saving techniques we have discovered.

Such a situation is common. To prevent it we must break the cycle.

Case Study: Bounced Email

Tom used to run many mailing lists using Majordomo, a very simple mailing list manager that is driven by email messages to a command processor to request that subscriptions be started and discontinued. At first, there was an occasional bounce message, which he would diligently research to find that an email address on a particular list was no longer valid. If it remained invalid for a week, he would remove the person from the mailing list. He became more efficient by using an email filtering program to send the bounces to a particular folder, which he would analyze in batches every couple of days. Soon, he had shell scripts that helped hunt down the problem, track who was bouncing and if the problem had persisted for an entire week, and macros that efficiently removed people from mailing lists.

Eventually, he found himself spending more than an hour every day with this work. It was affecting his other project deadlines. He knew there was other software (Viega, Warsaw, and Manheimer 1998) that would manage the bounces better or would delegate the work to the owners of the individual mailing lists, but he never had time to install such software. He was mopping the floor instead of turning off the faucet.

The only way for Tom to break this cycle was to ignore bounces for a week and stay late a couple of nights to install the new software without interruption and without affecting his other project deadlines. Even then some project would have to slip at least a little. Once he finally made this decision, the software was installed and tested in about 5 hours total. The new software reduced his manual intervention to about 1 hour a week, for a 4 hour/week saving, the equivalent of gaining a half day every week. Tom would still be losing nearly a month of workdays every year if he hadn't stopped his quick fixes to make the permanent fix.

Let's dig deeper into Corollary A, "Fix the problem permanently." It certainly sounds simple; however, often we see someone fix a problem only to find it reappears after the next reboot. Sometimes, knowing which fixes are permanent and which need to be repeated on reboot is the difference between a new SA and a wizard.

Many OSs run scripts or programs to bring the machine "up." The scripts that are involved in booting a machine must be edited from time to time. Sometimes a new daemon must be started, for example, an Apache http server that must be started. Sometimes, a configuration change must be made, such as setting a flag on a funny network interface. Rather than running these commands manually every time a machine reboots, they should be added to the startup scripts. The danger with adding things to the startup scripts is that the next time the machine reboots it may not succeed in booting because of an error in the startup script. It is always wise to test such changes immediately with a quick reboot.

Case Study: Permanent Configuration Settings

The Registry on Microsoft Windows solves many of these problems. The contents of the Registry are, or at least supposed to be, permanent and survive reboots. They are also live and running as soon as they are made in newer versions of Windows. Every well-written program has its settings and configuration stored in the registry. No need for every program to reinvent the wheel. Each service (what UNIX calls "daemons") can fail to start without interrupting the entire boot process.

In a way, Microsoft has attempted to "fix it once" by providing software developers with the registry and the Services Control Panel and the Devices Control Panel rather than requiring each to reinvent something similar for each product.

5.1.3   Learning from Carpenters

SAs have a lot to learn from carpenters. They've been building and fixing things for a lot longer than we have.

Carpenters have an expression, "Measure twice, cut once." Measuring a second time prevents a lot of errors. Wood is expensive. A little extra care is a small cost compared with wasted wood.

Carpenters also understand how to copy things. When a carpenter needs to cut many pieces of wood all the same size, he cuts the first one to the proper length, and uses that first piece over and over to measure the others. This is much more accurate than using the second piece to measure the third piece, the third piece to measure the fourth piece, and so on. The latter technique easily accumulates errors.

SAs can learn a lot from these techniques. Copying something is an opportunity to get something right once and then replicate it many times. Measuring things twice is a good habit to develop. Double-check your work before you make any changes. Reread that configuration file, have someone else view the command before you execute it, load-test the capacity of the system before you recommend growing, and so on. Test, test, and test again.

❖ **Be Careful Deleting Files** UNIX shells make it easy to accidentally delete files. This is illustrated by the classic UNIX example of trying to delete all files that end with `.o`, but accidentally typing `rm * .o` (notice the space accidentally inserted after the `*`) and deleting all the files in the directory. Luckily, UNIX shells also make it easy to "measure twice." One can change `rm` to `echo` to simply list which files will be deleted. If the right files are listed, one can use command-line editing to change the `echo` to `rm` to really delete the files.

This technique is an excellent way to "measure twice," by performing a quick check to prevent mistakes. The use of command-line editing is like using the first block of wood to measure the next one. We've seen SAs who use this technique but manually retype the command after seeing the `echo` came out right, which defeats the purpose of the technique. Retyping a command opens one up to an accumulation of errors. Invest time in learning command-line editing for the shell you use.

Case Study: Copy Exact

Intel has a philosophy called *Copy Exact.* Once something is done right, it is copied exactly at other sites. For example, if a factory is built, additional capacity is created by copying it exactly at other locations. No need to reinvent the wheel. The SAs adopt the policy also. Useful scripts that are distributed to other sites are used without change, rather than ending up with every site having a mess of slightly different systems. This forces all SAs to maintain similar environments, develop code that works at all sites without customization, and feed back improvements to the original author for release to the world (thus not leaving any site behind).

You'll never hear a carpenter say, "I've cut this board three times and it's still too short!" Cutting the same board won't make it any longer. SAs often find themselves trying the same thing over and over, frustrated that they keep getting the same failed results. Instead, they should try something different. SAs complain about security problems and bugs, yet they put their trust into software from companies without sufficient quality assurance systems. They run critical systems on the Internet without firewalls. They fix problems by rebooting systems rather than fixing the root cause.

> ❖ **Excellent Advice**   In the famous "UNIX Room" at Bell Labs, there is a small sign on the wall that simply states, "Stop Doing Things That Don't Work."

5.2   The Icing

The icing for this chapter is having someone, preferably a nonhuman, that performs the fix for you. This falls into two categories: automation that fixes symptoms and alerts an SA so she can fix it permanently and automation that fixes things permanently on its own.

Automation that fixes problems can be worrisome. We've seen too much bad science fiction where the robot "fixes" a problem by killing innocent people or blowing up Earth. None of us want that to happen. Therefore automation should be extremely careful in what it does and should keep logs so that its work can be audited.

Automation often fixes symptoms without fixing the root cause. It is critical, in that situation, that the automation alert a human that it has done something, so that a permanent fix can be implemented. We have seen automation that reacts to a full-disk situation by deleting old log files. This works fine, until the consumers of disk space outpace the log files and suddenly there are very few logs to delete. Then the automation requests immediate human intervention, and the human finds an extremely difficult problem. If the automation had alerted the human that it was making temporary fixes, it would have given the human time to make a more permanent fix.

However, now we risk the "boy who cried wolf" situation. It is very easy to ignore warnings that a robot has implemented a temporary fix and that a longer-term fix is needed. If the temporary fix worked this time, it should work the next time too. It's usually safe to ignore such an alert the first time. It's only "the time after that" that the permanent fix is done. Because an SA's workload is virtually always more than the person has time for, it is just too easy to hope that "the time after that" won't be soon. In a large environment, it is likely that different SAs will see the alerts each time. If all of them assume they are the first to ignore the alert, the situation will degenerate into a big problem.

Fixing the real problem is rarely something that can be automated. Automation can dig you out of a small hole, but it can't fix buggy software. For example, it can kill a runaway process, but it can't fix the bug in the software that makes it run away.

Sometimes automation can fix the root problem. Large systems with virtual machines can allocate additional CPUs to overloaded computations, grow a full disk partition, or automatically move data to some other disk. Some types of file systems let you grow a virtual filesystem in an automated fashion, usually by allocating a spare disk and merging it into the volume. That doesn't help much if the disk was running out of space as a result of a runaway process generating an infinite amount of data, because the new disk will also fill. However, it does fix the daily operational issue of disks filling. You can add spares to a system, and automation can take care of attaching them to the next virtual volume that is nearly full. This is no substitute for good capacity planning, but it would be a good tool as part of your capacity management system.

The solution is policy and discipline, possibly enforced by software. It takes discipline to fix things rather than ignore them.

Sometimes the automation can take a long time to create. However, sometimes it can be done a little bit at a time. The essentials of a five-minute task can be integrated into a Makefile. Later, more of the task can be added or more recipes can be added to the Makefile. It may seem like five-minute tasks are taking an hour to complete, but you are saving time in the long run.

5.3   Conclusion

Fixing something once is better than fixing something many times over. Ultimately, fixes should be permanent, not temporary. You should not reinvent the wheel and should, when possible, copy solutions that are known to work. It is best to be proactive, and if a problem is found in one place, fix it on all similar hosts or places. An anecdote illustrated how easy it is to get into a situation in which an SA doesn't realize that things should be fixed the right way. However, sometimes limited resources leave an SA no choice other than to implement a quick fix and schedule the permanent fix for later. On the other hand, SAs must avoid developing a habit of delaying such fixes and the emotionally easier path of repeating small fixes rather than investing time in producing a complete solution. In the end, it is best to fix things the right way at the right time.

This chapter was a bit more philosophical than the others. In the first anecdote, we saw how critical it is to get the basics right early on. If automating the initial OS load and configuration had been done, many of the other problems would not have happened. Many times the permanent fix is to introduce automation. However, automation has its own problems. It can take a long time to automate a solution; and while waiting for the automation to be completed, we can develop bad habits or an emotional immunity to repeatedly fixing a problem. Nevertheless, good automation can dramatically lessen your workload and improve the reliability of your systems.

Exercises

1. What are some of the things you fix often rather than implementing a permanent fix? Why hasn't a permanent fix been implemented?

2. In what ways do you use carpenters' techniques described in Section 5.1.3?

3. Describe a situation in which you had to delay a permanent fix because of limited resources.

4. Does your monitoring system emulate "the boy who cried wolf?"

Chapter 6

Namespaces

In this chapter, we discuss how to organize and manage namespaces. *Namespaces* are all the lists and directories in your environment. Examples of namespaces include the account names in use, the printers available, the names of hosts, Ethernet addresses, service-name/port-number lists, and home directory location maps. Every namespace has attributes for each element. Account names have UIDs (UNIX) or SIDs (Windows), home directories, owners, and so on. Hostnames have IP addresses, customer/owner, serial number, Ethernet media access control (MAC) address, and so on.

The term *namespace* can be confusing because it can refer to either an abstract concept or a concrete thing. For example, usernames are a namespace. Every multiuser operating system (OS) has a namespace that is the list of identifiers for users. Therefore every company has the abstract concept of a username namespace. However, the namespace used by the multiuser OSs at my company is a different namespace than the one at your company (unless you've just hired all of my coworkers!). In that sense, they have different username namespaces (your set of users and my set of users). Most of this chapter uses the term *namespace* to refer to a particular (concrete) namespace database. We'll be specific when we feel it's worthwhile to differentiate the two.

Namespaces come in many shapes. Some namespaces are flat; that is, there are no duplicates. For example, in Windows, a **WINS** directory is a flat namespace. In UNIX, the set of UIDs is a flat namespace. Other namespaces are hierarchical, like a directory tree. No two files in a particular directory can have the same name, but there can be two different files called `example.txt` if they are in different subdirectories.

The larger and more sophisticated an environment becomes, the more important it is that namespaces be managed formally. Smaller environments tend to need very little formality with their namespaces. They all might be controlled by one person who keeps certain information in her head (if there are only five computers, why record where they are located?). On the other hand, mega-corporations must divide and delegate the responsibility among many divisions and people.

It is very powerful to simply acknowledge that your environment has namespaces in the first place. Until that happens, you just have piles of data. Each namespace is thought of independently, and we do not gain the potential benefits that can be seen by linking them. We develop wildly different processes and find ourselves reinventing the wheel over and over. It's like seeing the trees instead of the entire forest. New SAs see each namespace as a separate item (a tree), but over time they see a more global picture (the forest). When you can see a particular namespace in the context of a larger vision, you see more clearly.

In this chapter, we will examine the basics of namespace management and then explore more advanced topics on the management and use of namespaces. This chapter should help you see the forest, not just the trees.

6.1   The Basics

The basics of namespaces are very simple.

- Namespaces need policies: naming, longevity, locality, and exposure.
- Namespaces need procedures: adding, changing, and deleting.
- Namespace management should be centralized.

6.1.1   Namespaces Need Policies

Namespaces should be controlled by policies more than they are controlled by any technological system. The larger your SA team is, the more important it is for these to be written policies. As a team grows, these written policies become tools for communicating to SAs or training new SAs. One can't reprimand an SA for permitting a customer to name his new PC outside the permitted name rules if such rules are not in written form. Written policies should be the basis for the requirements specified when one creates automation for the maintenance of namespaces. Written policies also set expectations with customers.

Naming Policy

The namespace's naming policy should answer these questions: What names are permitted in this namespace? What names are not permitted in this namespace? How are names selected? How are collisions resolved?

One needs rules for what names can go into a namespace. Some may relate to the technology (UNIX login IDs can be only alphanumeric characters plus a limited number of symbols) or to corporate rules (login IDs shouldn't be offensive, however that may be defined). External standards bodies set rules too: before RFC1123 (Braden 1989; Section 2.1), DNS names couldn't begin with a digit, making it difficult for 3 Com, Inc., to register their domain.

When selecting names there are four methods:

- *Formulaic:* Names fit a strict formula. For example, some sites name all desktops "pc" followed by a four-digit number. Login names might be strictly the first initial followed by the first six letters of the last name, followed by a random series of digits to make a unique name.
- *Theme:* All names fit a theme, such as naming all servers after planets (and using planet names from science fiction when you run out of real planet names).
- *Functional:* Names have functions. Accounts for a specific purpose (`admin`, `secretary`, `guest`), hostnames that reflect the duties of the machine (`dns1`, `cpuserver22`, `web01`), or disk partitions that reflect the project for which they store data (`/finance`, `/devel`, `/housekeeping`).
- *No method:* Sometimes the formula is no formula. Everyone picks what they want. Conflicts and collisions are resolved by first-come, first-serve policies.

There is tension among these different methods. Once you use one scheme, it is difficult to change.

Functional names can make software configuration easier: Helpdesks can support software more easily if the mail server is called "mail" and the calendar server is called "calendar." However, if such services ever move to different hosts, a confusing situation can come about. It is better to have functional aliases that point to such hosts. Aliases (DNS CNAMEs) are great for noninteractive service machines, such as mail, web, DNS, and so on. They don't work nearly as well for interactive compute servers, because users will notice the hostname and start to use it. It can be confusing when logs are generated with the real hostname, rather than the functional alias, but it would be more confusing if they referred to the alias with no way to determine which specific machine was intended.

Sequential Names

Formulaic names give a false sense of completeness. A customer submitted a panicked trouble ticket when she noticed that hosts `software-build-1`, `-4`, `-5`, and `-7` weren't pinging. Of course, only `-2`, `-3`, `-6`, and `-8` exist anymore; the rest have been recycled for other uses. This is only a problem when a clear sequence is being used.

Theme names can be cute—sometimes too cute. One part of Bell Labs where Tom worked used coffee-related names (decaf, latte, java, froth) for their printers. Although cute, it was much less frustrating to locate a printer in the other divisions that named their printers after the printer's room number (plus the letter "c" if it was a color printer). Some naming conventions just make a lot more sense than others. The coffee names were more frustrating to new people. The formulaic names meant less need for lists of where to find printers.

The method that is used reflects the corporate culture. If one is trying to establish a progressive, fun, enlightened work atmosphere, then "froth" is a great name for a printer. If one is trying to reflect a culture where work is boring, not fun, and painfully dull, then require hosts to be named "pc" followed by a four-digit number. (Of course, in that case one should start numbering them with pc0011 so that nobody gets jealous of the special people with single-digit numbers. While you are at it, skip numbers ending with 00, primes, numbers with sexual connotations, and any of the "interesting" numbers discovered by the mathematician Ramanujan.)

Names have security implications. Intruders might find "sourcecodedb" a more interesting target than "server05." Alternatively, intruders have long known that SAs usually break the naming rules for their own systems. The goal of an intruder is to work for as long as possible without being detected. Therefore they avoid any host that might be closely watched, such as the desktop machines of the SA team. If they discover a network where all hostnames are strictly formulaic, except for a few random machines named after Star Trek characters, they will assume that the Star Trek hosts are the SAs' machines. They will avoid those hosts to decrease their chances of being detected. It's even reasonable to assume that the lead SA's host is the one named "picard," and the person in charge of security sits in front of "worf." Although we don't encourage anyone to rely on security through obscurity, there are benefits in camouflaging the SAs' machines with unremarkable names.

RFC1178 (Libes 1990) has excellent advice about selecting names for hosts. However, we'd like to interject that for desktop computers that have a single, primary user, it can make an SA's life a lot easier if the host's name reflects the name of that primary user. If one receives email from "ajay" reporting that "my machine is having a problem," it is very convenient to be able to rely on the fact that his host's name is "ajay." Of course, some directory services don't permit hostnames to be the same as names in the user directory, in which case names such as "ajaypc" can be sufficient.

Difficult-to-Type Names

A site had an architecture in which every cluster had a file server and a number of compute servers. Users were to do their work on the compute servers and not `telnet` directly into the file server. To discourage people from logging in to the file servers, those servers were given names that were long or difficult to spell and the compute servers were given easy-to-type names. One such cluster named its machines after famous mathematicians, naming the file server `ramanujan` and the compute server `boole`. Everyone preferred to log into `boole`.

Protection Policy

A namespace's protection policy should answer the following questions.

- What kind of protection or security does this namespace require?
- What are you trying to protect the names from and why?
- Do the names in the space need to be protected, or just their attributes?
- Who can add, change, or delete entire records?
- Can the owner of a record change certain fields within the record?

Whom should the contents of a namespace be protected from? It depends on the namespace. Everyone should be prevented from reading a namespace such as a list of passwords. Some namespaces are a secret held by a few people (users in the cluster, all employees, anyone except the competition) or by nobody (who cares how many people know that Tom's UID is 27830?).

The answer can be different for each namespace. For example, the login IDs of a UNIX system can be safely exposed in the outbound email message, on business cards, in advertisements, and so on. However, the complete list of IDs shouldn't be exposed externally, because spammers will use the list for their mail bombing. The password associated with that ID shouldn't be exposed, obviously. Thus on UNIX systems the `/etc/shadow` file that stores the password has stricter protection than the `/etc/passwd` file that stores the UID, person's full name, home directory, and preferred shell. On the other hand, although we don't mind the exposure of the UID internally, we generally don't want to expose all the UIDs to the outside world.

Printing /etc/passwd

An SA was setting up a printer and kept printing `/etc/passwd` to generate test pages. In an environment that didn't have a namespace protection policy, he didn't realize that exposing the contents of `/etc/passwd` was a bad thing. (He didn't realize that intruders were sometimes found looking through corporate dumpsters for just that kind of thing.[1]) It was recommended that it would be safer for him to print `/etc/motd` or create his own test file. A more experienced SA would have had a greater appreciation for namespace protection issues and wouldn't have done this.

Changes are a different matter. Customers should be able to change their own shell or password, but only specific people should be able to create or delete accounts. On the other hand, ISPs often have a policy that the user can create an account, based on the person's ability to provide a credit card number, and deleting an account is also customer-initiated. Universities often have systems on which professors can create dozens of accounts at a time for the students in their classes. However, non-SAs couldn't create a privileged account or delete other people's accounts. One major web-based email provider doesn't have a procedure to delete accounts. If the account is not used for a certain period, it is automatically deleted.

Another facet of protection includes change control and backup policies. Change control is discussed in Chapter 10, but suffice it to say that it is important to be able to roll back a change. Namespaces that are stored in plain text format can be checked into a revision control system such as Revision Control System (RCS) or Source Code Control System (SCCS) (Bolinger 1995) for simple change management or Concurrent Versions System (CVS) (Berliner 1990) for network-based management. Backup policies should pay particular attention to namespaces. Backups are the ultimate insurance policy.

How a namespace is protected from modification is another issue. Sometimes, a namespace is maintained in a flat text file, and modifications are

---

[1] This practice is called "dumpster diving."

prevented by using the appropriate file permission controls. In other instances, modifications are done through a database that has its own access controls. It is important to remember that a namespace is as secure as the methods that can be used to modify the namespace. The method used to update a namespace should be more secure than the systems that depend on that namespace for security.

Longevity Policy

A namespace's longevity policy should answer the question: When are entries in this namespace removed?

Some entries in a namespace need to expire on a certain date or after a certain amount of inactivity. You might prescribe that accounts for contractors must be sponsored by a regular employee who must renew the request once a year and are removed if no renewal is performed. IP addresses are scarce, and in a loosely controlled environment, you might expire the IP address that has been granted to a customer if a network monitoring system shows that the IP address hasn't been used in a certain number of months.

Names, once exposed to customers, last longer than you would ever expect. Once a name is established in the minds of your customers, it is very difficult to change. You should plan for this. If an email address is printed on a business card, it is difficult to recall all those cards if you require a person to change an email address. Once a document repository is announced to be on fileserver `fred`, don't even think of moving it to `barney`. Good technology lets you obscure names that shouldn't be interrelated. The UNIX automounter can be used so that customers refer to the repository as `/home/docs`, and the name of the fileserver is obscured. The location of the documents should not be tied to the name of the server. The fact that they are interrelated shouldn't matter to your customers. Aliases can be a good solution here, though some technologies (for example, NFS) require clients to be rebooted for such changes to take effect. Never name a web server "www." Give it a generic name, and make "www" an alias to it. Only announce the "www" name, and you can move the functionality to a different host without worry. If you consistently use aliases and other technologies that obscure names as appropriate, you can move functionality from one host to another without worry.

A Machine Named "Calendar"

For many years, the calendar server that Tom used was on a host named `calendar`. It seemed like a good idea at the time, because the host was purchased expressly for the job of being the calendar server. Eventually, it also became the main print server, and customers were confused that their print jobs were being spooled to a host named `calendar`. The hostname can't be changed because the software license is locked to that hostname. This problem could have been avoided if the host had been called something else and `calendar` was an alias for the machine. Surely someday the calendar service will evolve to a new machine and customers will question why they print to a machine named `calendar` and have their calendar server set to `fred`. Maybe that new machine should be called `printer` just to keep things consistently inconsistent.

Scope Policy

A namespace's scope policy should answer the question: Where is this namespace to be used? How global or local a particular namespace is can be measured on two axes: diameter (geographically, how widely it is used) and thickness (how many services use it).

The *diameter* is how many systems use a particular namespace database: single host, cluster, division, enterprise-wide, and so on. While your entire enterprise might use the Active Directory Protocol, a given namespace database (say, username/passwords) might only be usable for your department's machines. Other departments have different lists of users and passwords for their machines.

RADIUS (Rigney et al. 1997) an authentication protocol for modem pools, virtual private network (VPN) servers, and other network devices, can be implemented so that devices all around a global enterprise access the same database (both username and password). People can log in with the same username/password no matter which modem pool they use when traveling around the world.

Sites that use the Network Information Service (NIS, often UNIX systems) tend to implement namespaces that have a diameter of a single cluster of UNIX hosts. Each cluster has its own namespace databases.

The *thickness* of a namespace is based on how many services use it. For example, a company might allocate a unique ID (for example, `tal` or `chogan`) for each employee and use that for the person's email name, login ID, ID for logging into intranet services, name on modem pools, VPN services, and so on. Even though these are different databases and use different protocols (ActiveDirectory, NIS, RADIUS, and so on), the ID is used for all of them. In fact, even though each of those uses of the ID might involve a different password, it is still a measurement of the thickness.

The diameter of a namespace has a lot of implications. If each division has a different namespace for login IDs, what happens if a person has accounts in two namespace databases? For example, what if `tal` is Tom Limoncelli in one division and Terry Levine in another? This can be fine until Tom needs a login in Terry's division. Should Tom be `tal2` exclusively in Terry's division, or should Tom be required to change his account name everywhere? That would be very disruptive, especially if Tom needs an account on Terry's network for only a short time.

Case Study: Lucent's "Handles"

It can be useful to have a single, global namespace and encourage all other namespaces to align themselves with it. Lucent gives each employee a "handle" that is a unique identifier. Employees can select their own handles, but the default is a person's first initial followed by his or her last name. This namespace is globally unique, a challenge considering there were more than 160,000 employees at Lucent in 2000. The database of handles can be accessed as a field in the online corporate directory. Each division is encouraged to create account names that are the same as the person's handle. All services run by the central chief information officer (CIO) group (email, human resources, remote access, and so on) use the handle exclusively to model proper behavior. This system results in the best of both worlds. Locally run services can adopt login IDs that match the associate's "Lucent handle"; they may deviate if they wish, but they would have to accept the risk that collisions (current and future) will cause confusion. The benefits of using the Lucent handle, rather than letting customers select unique ones, are obvious, and thus little enforcement is required. During corporate acquisitions, the company being acquired has to deal with namespace collisions that may occur.

Sometimes, one does not want a globally "flat" namespace. In some cases, the technology in use provides for a hierarchical namespace instead. For example, it is not required that hostnames be unique within an entire corporation because DNS provides for zones and subzones. With departmental DNS zones, each department can have a host named "www." They could even name their desktop PCs "pc" followed by a number, and sites would have to coordinate between each other to ensure that no overlapping numbers are used.

Case Study: E-commerce Namespaces Can Be Wide and Thick

E-commerce sites usually are able to have a username namespace that is extremely wide and thick. The customer establishes one username and password and uses it for all the services at the site, whether these services are on one machine or hundreds. Yahoo is well known for this. Once a customer establishes a profile, it applies to all the services offered. The customer might have to activate those additional services, but they are all tied to one username and password for the person to remember.

Consistency Policy

A namespace's consistency policy should answer the question: Where the same name is used in multiple namespaces, which attributes will be kept consistent also?

High consistency means that a name used in one place will have the same attributes in all the places it exists. For example, you might establish a policy that if someone has a UNIX account, the numeric UID must be the same everywhere the person has UNIX accounts. You might establish a policy that although the same ID is used to access email and to connect to the company's modem pool, the passwords are not kept in sync. In fact, it would be wise to require different passwords for both systems.

Case Study: A Simple Way to Set Naming Standards

Bell Labs Research has many different UNIX environments, or clusters, but there are amazingly few conflicting UIDs. This was discovered, much to our surprise, when some of these environments were merged. How this happened is an interesting story.

Many years ago, someone invited all the SAs from all the different computing centers to lunch. At that lunch, they divided up the UID space, allocating large ranges to each research center. Everyone agreed to stay within their allocated space, except when creating accounts for people from other computing centers, in which case their UID from that center would be carried forward. No policy was created, no bureaucratic allocation czar was appointed, and no penalty scheme was implemented. Everyone agreed to follow the decisions because they knew it was the right thing to do. Shortly after the meeting, someone sent out email describing the ranges.

Years later, those UID ranges are still followed. When new SAs are hired, someone forwards them a copy of that email explaining what was agreed on many years ago. Each center has some kind of "create an account" script that embodies the guidelines in that email. It's worked very well all these years because it is truly the simplest solution for the problem.

Use the Same UID for an Account Everywhere

At Bell Labs, most people can log into all the general-purpose machines with the same username and password and using the same UID. However, there are special-purpose machines that not everyone can access. Tom inherited ownership of a DNS server that was one such machine. Only people that needed to make updates to DNS had accounts, and their UIDs were allocated starting at 1,000 and incrementing upward. The previous SA justified the situation by stating that the DNS server was considered relatively secure and would never speak NFS to other hosts, the UIDs didn't have to be the same as everywhere else, and it would have taken an entire 10 seconds per account to identify their regular UIDs. That might have been a minute per year that he saved in the three years he ran the machine. As a result, when backups of this machine were restored to other hosts, the UIDs mismatched. To forestall future problems, all new accounts were created using UIDs from their home system, and during an upgrade where downtime was permitted, the legacy UIDs were realigned.

Reuse Policy

The namespace's reuse policy should answer this question: How soon after a name has been deleted or expired can it be reused?

Usually, the name can be reused immediately. For example, not only might a printer name be reused immediately, but you might want to reuse it so that print jobs to the old name go to the new printer. You might be more concerned with email addresses. You might have a policy that once an email address is deleted, nobody else can reuse that address for six months, so that the new person is less likely to receive email intended for someone else. This prevents the following mischievous trick: some companies have an automated procedure to allocate "vanity email addresses" to be forwarded to your mailbox. For example, you might allocate `foosupport@companyname.com` to be forwarded to yourself—the person that supports product `foo`. If your job function changes, the address can be forwarded to your replacement. However, if John Doe (`jdoe@companyname.com`) leaves the company, you could use this process to have `jdoe`'s email forwarded to you and pick up his mail until all his correspondents learn his new email address. This would be particularly bad if it was the CEO that left the company. By requiring deleted email addresses to be invalid for six months, you can be fairly sure that allocating that address is safe again.

A reuse policy can be implemented in software. However, in small, infrequently changing namespaces, the SAs just should be sensitive to the ramifications of reuse. For example, if you are asked to give a customer's PC a name that was recently used for a popular server, you might suggest a different name to prevent confusion. The confusion will be particularly high if a lot of hardcopy documentation mentioning the server's name is still in the field.

Summary

Policies on naming, protection, longevity, scope, consistency, and reuse must be written, approved by management and technical staff, and available for reference to customers and SAs. This clearly establishes the rules of your namespaces. Much grief can be avoided by doing this. Small sites that run without such documentation and survive do so because the few SAs have to work closely together to have such policies as part of their culture. However, this doesn't scale. Such sites become large sites that suddenly find themselves with a larger group of SAs who have not been indoctrinated into the "standard" way of doing things. Many disagreements can be prevented by having these policies documented. If these policies are documented, a new SA who disagrees with them can discuss her proposed changes. Without documentation, each SA is free to assume that her way is the right way.

6.1.2   Namespaces Need Change Procedures

All namespaces need procedures for additions, changes, and deletions. These should be documented just as the policies are, but these procedures may not be available to the customers. Again, a small group may be able to operate without these procedures being explicitly written down. Often, the procedures are performed only by the people who invented the system and thus do not require documentation. However, as the system grows and new SAs are involved, confusion sets in because the new people didn't invent the undocumented procedures that are in use. Documentation can serve the dual purposes of providing a basis for training and providing step-by-step instruction when the task is being performed.

Case Study: Two Sets of Documentation

At Bell Labs, Cliff Miller created a system for maintaining a software depot for homogeneous UNIX environments. An important part of the depot's design was the namespace used for the various packages, some of which would be visible only on certain platforms or certain individual hosts. The process for adding new software packages into the namespace is a little tricky, but it is well documented. The documentation that explains how to add a new package contains a lot of hand-holding verbiage. Therefore the second time you go to add a new package, that documentation is cumbersome. His solution to this was to create a brief "quick guide" that includes just the commands to be entered, with brief reminders of what you are doing and hypertext links to the appropriate section of the full documentation. Now, both new and experienced SAs can easily execute the process and receive the right amount of documentation.

If something can be documented in a clear, concise manner, it can be automated. Not all automation needs to be complicated, as we will see in the next section.

6.1.3 Namespace Management Should Be Centralized

Namespace management should be centralized as much as possible for the given environment. With centralization, comes consistency. Otherwise, namespaces become scattered around various servers or even different directories on the same server. It is better to have a single host maintain your namespaces and have them "pushed" to all other hosts.

Case Study: A Namespace Clean-up

At one site, Tom found that some namespaces had their master copy on a particular host and were distributed to all hosts by the UNIX `make` command. A couple of other hosts stored the master copy of other namespaces. For those namespaces, the file would be edited and then a script would be run to push the data to other hosts. In fact, it wasn't just one script, but a set of scripts with names such as `update_printcap`, `aliases_push`, and `push_stuff`. The scripts were named inconsistently because the environment was the merger of a few smaller environments. The directory that stored the files and scripts often were different on the various hosts.

Part of Tom's indoctrination at this site was to be taught, for every namespace, what directory it was stored in, on which machine, and which script to run to "push" any changes to the other machines. All of this information was taught from memory by a senior SA, because none of it was documented. By the end of the week, Tom had assembled all of this information into a large chart. Tom doesn't have a very good memory, so this complicated system concerned him greatly.

None of the files were stored under RCS or SCCS, so SAs had to rely on tape backups for any kind of change control. They couldn't "roll back" any change without a lot of effort. Tom has his error-prone days, so this concerned him too.

After a month of effort, the master file for every namespace had been moved to a single directory on a single host. These files were maintained under RCS control so that changes could be rolled back. There was a new `Makefile` in that directory that fired off the appropriate legacy script, depending on which file had been changed. After this transition was made, not only was the system easier to administer, but it was more consistent. This made it easier to train new SAs.

Once the new system was stable, it could be optimized. Some of the legacy scripts were brittle or slow. With the system consolidated, there was a focus on replacing the scripts one at a time with better ways of doing things.

This consolidation also made it easier to introduce new automated processes, such as creating new accounts. Rather than requiring SAs to remember the names of scripts to create an account, for example, `make menu` would list a set of reminders. The scripts themselves were integrated into the `Makefile`. So, rather than remembering which script created an account, one simply issued the `make account` command and the script would ask the appropriate questions and complete the task.

Mark Burgess' GNU/Cfengine (Burgess 1995) is an excellent UNIX tool for maintaining master copies of namespaces and configuration files and distributing them to hosts. It has the benefit of being able to automatically maintain any kind of configuration on a UNIX host and can be programmed to know that certain hosts should have different configurations.

6.2   The Icing

Now that the basics are done, we can take things to the next level by centralizing further and automating further. Using namespaces can become a ubiquitous way of doing business.

6.2.1   One Huge Database That Drives Everything

Centralization is a good trend, and centralizing all namespaces into a large SQL database such as Sybase or Oracle is even better. You can develop web-based or forms-based frontends that let operators make most changes. Programs can then feed the data into systems such as LDAP and NIS, printer configurations, and so on. Jon Finke of Rensselaer Polytechnic Institute has written several papers on this topic (Finke, 1994a, 1994b, 1995, 1996, 1997).

6.2.2   Further Automation

Once the fundamentals are completed, further automation is easier. If the primary automation is done properly, higher levels of automation can be interfaces to the primary automation and provide, for example, additional data validation or the ability to iterate over the process many times.

If you can iterate over the elements of a namespace, automation can be driven by namespaces. For example, a simple iteration over the `passwd` namespace can be the basis of a system that audits various security parameters, such as the contents of `.rhosts` files. Many sites have one mailing list per department, and these mailing lists can be automatically generated from a corporate directory.

An inventory of all systems can be one of your most powerful namespaces if it is kept up-to-date. (Keeping it up-to-date can be partially automated itself!)

Automated Inventory
Tom once worked at a site that had an inventory database that could be easily queried from shell scripts. They also had a program that would run the same command on a list of hosts. Putting them together made it easy

to write a program that would make changes globally or on hosts with specific characteristics (for example, OS, OS revision, amount of memory, and so on). For example, a program that would change the root password on every Solaris box was fewer than ten lines long. When a new application was deployed, a query could quickly determine which hosts would need additional memory to support it. Driving maintenance processes off a database of hosts was very powerful.

6.2.3 Customers Do Many of the Updates

Automation can also lean in another direction: making customers self-sufficient. Every environment has many opportunities for automating services. You should not only review your request logs and workload but also talk to customers about what they would like to have automated. Section 1.1.3 describes a DHCP system that makes allocating IP addresses self-service.

> **Case Study: Account Creation at Rutgers**
>
> At Rutgers University, many of the computer science classes required that accounts be created for every student on machines in the computer science cluster. Automation was provided for mass-producing accounts. Teaching assistants had access to a command that would create a large number of accounts for a class by querying the enrollment database. A similar command would delete all the accounts for a particular class when the course was over. As a result of this automation, the SAs didn't have to be involved in maintaining this aspect of the namespace anymore—a major win at an academic institution!

6.2.4 "Next-level" Namespace Ubiquity

Although pervasive namespaces are useful in your computing infrastructure, they also can be useful in other infrastructures. There is a trend to reduce the administrative burden of noncomputer infrastructure by tying it to the namespaces from the computing infrastructure. For example, PBXs, voicemail systems, card-key access, and cafeteria credit card systems are increasingly speaking LDAP. Imagine making an addition to your corporate LDAP database when new employees are hired and having their email account created, their external home page template copied into place, their phone and voicemail box configured, and their card-key access configured to let them into appropriate parts of the building.

6.3   Conclusion

In this chapter, we have established some rules for namespaces. First we must acknowledge that namespaces exist. Once we do, it becomes obvious that there are certain qualities that all namespaces share. Namespaces need policies for naming, protection, longevity, scope, consistency, and reuse. Once policy is established, procedures can be established. The policies must be established before the procedures because the policies should drive the procedures. Namespaces can greatly benefit from central management and automation.

Once the basics are completed, new opportunities arise. Benefits can come from generating all namespaces from a single database system. Better automation can be created, including automation that permits customers to accomplish what they need without SA intervention. Finally, we like the trend of tying noncomputer infrastructure such as human resources, PBXs, and card-key systems to centralized databases.

Namespaces are part of the fundamental infrastructure of a computing environment. Well-managed namespaces are one of the key systems that will make all other systems run smoothly. You could, for example, maintain an email system without a well-managed namespace, but it would be difficult and cumbersome.

Automation is required to do a good job of maintaining namespaces, and yet good namespaces can aid further automation if the namespaces have good APIs. Moving all namespaces into a single large database system enables us to take this to an extreme.

Establishing written policies and procedures about namespaces improves communication within the SA team and communicates expectations to customers.

Exercises

1. What are the namespaces in your environment? How are they maintained?

2. One aspect of an environment's maturity can be measured by determining whether or not the basics listed in Section 6.1 are being observed for the namespaces in the environment. Evaluate your environment.

3. In your environment, what automation is in place for maintaining the namespaces? What automation should be created?

4. What namespace maintenance should be pushed down to your customers through automation?

5. Suppose you moved to a new organization and your login ID was already in use. What would you do?

6. Who was Ramanujan and which numbers did he find interesting?

Security Policy

In this chapter, we describe the basic building blocks that a company needs for a successful security program, some guiding principles, and some common security needs. There is much more to security than firewalls, intrusion detection, and authentication schemes. Although all of these are key components of a security program, security administrators also have to take on many different roles and the skills for those roles are quite diverse. This chapter looks at all aspects of security. At the end of the chapter, we briefly discuss how the approaches that we describe here apply in various-size companies and mention some ways in which the approach you take to security may differ in an academic environment.

Security is a huge area, with many fine books on the topic. Zwicky, Chapman, and Cooper (2000) and Cheswick and Bellovin (1994) are excellent books dedicated to the topic of firewalls. Garfinkel and Spafford (1996, 1997) have books on UNIX and Internet security and web security and commerce. Norberg and Russell (2000) and Sheldon and Cox (2000) provide details on Windows security. Miller and Davis (2000) cover the area of intellectual property. Wood (1999) is well known for his sample security policies. Kovacich (1998) deals with the topic of establishing an information protection program. Neumann (1997) and Denning (1999) cover the topics of risks and information warfare.

It is important to hire security specialists to take on the organization's security needs. Security is a huge, rapidly changing field, and to keep current, SAs working in security must focus all their attention on the security arena. Senior SAs with the right mind-set for security are good candidates for being trained by security specialists to join the security team.

Data security is the area of system administration that requires more negotiating skills and better contacts throughout the company than any other area. People in many companies perceive computer security as being an obstacle to getting work done. To succeed, you must dispel that notion and be involved as early as possible in any projects that affect the electronic security of the company.

Historical Perspective

Computer security needs have changed radically over time. Initially, only trained operators had access to the computer, and their job required physical access. Later, they would feed the computers programs that were written by a limited number of programmers. Mainframes accommodated access by more people but had very strict access controls in the OS and strict access policies enforced by the operators. Electronic access was obtained through clearly defined physical connections to the machine. The computer was as secure as the lock on the door to the terminal room.

With timesharing systems came the need for users to have protection from each other. With networks came the need for security from outsiders, and, as networks grew and connected to larger networks, the definition of outsiders grew too. With the advent of minicomputers, UNIX, networking, and the ARPAnet (the predecessor of the Internet), remote access to computers over shared networks became possible and computer security entered a new era. Initially, the ARPAnet was a small, friendly, trusting community. Over time, with more abuses of resources, more attacks, and more businesses connecting, organizations began to protect themselves from the Internet. They used firewalls, creating a clear boundary between their network and everyone else. Over time, close collaboration with business partners across a network became common, and as companies cross-connected to each other, the network boundary blurred again, necessitating another change in how the organization viewed security. Simultaneously, wireless communications became more popular, requiring technological controls to prevent the entire community from sharing one's network or eavesdropping on one's communications. Also, many companies started to depend on the Internet for conducting their daily business. Internet security became more critical and visible to the CEO and shareholders. All of these developments have affected the job of the security professional.

How will the computer and network access model change in the future, and what impact will it have on security? The trend so far has been a decreasing ability to rely on physical security and an increasing need to rely on technological solutions. We see this trend continuing.

7.1 The Basics

As with the design of other infrastructure components, the design of a security system should be based on simplicity and minimalism. Complexity obscures errors or chinks in your armor. An overly complex system will prove to be inflexible, difficult to use and maintain, and will ultimately be weakened or circumvented for people to be able to work effectively. In addition, a successful security architecture has security built into the system, not just bolted on at the end. Good security involves an in-depth approach with security hooks at all levels of the system. If those hooks are not there from the beginning, they can be very hard to add and integrate later.

Some consider security and convenience to be inversely proportional. That is, to make something more secure makes it more difficult to use. The reality is that this can be true, but when security is done correctly, it takes into account the customer's ease of use.[1] The problem is that often it takes several years for technology to advance to this point. For example, passwords are a good start, but putting a password on every application becomes a pain for people who use a lot of applications in a day's work. When security is inconvenient, your customers find ways around the system that are less secure than working within the system, which means that the level of security will deteriorate over time. When security technology advances sufficiently, however, the system becomes more secure and easier to use. For example, a secure single-sign-on system maximizes security and convenience by being much more secure yet nearly eliminating the users' need to type passwords.

Reliability and security go hand in hand because security is generally defined in a way that includes reliability. An unreliable system fails in unexpected ways, which means that the behavior is not fully known or carefully controlled. When a system is not working the way it is intended to, its security and integrity are unknown. If something is not reliable, it is not secure. Someone who wants to break your system will have nothing to do but wait. If something is not secure, it can't be reliable. If intruders can break in, any amount of reliability engineering is a waste.

---

[1] However, having no security is generally more convenient than having any security, no matter how good, unless you take into account the inconvenience of having to continually deal with break-ins and associated problems. Dealing with break-ins often adversely affects the customers in addition to the security team.

With all of these points in mind, we present the basic components of a security program. Security will develop cracks and fall down when not built on solid foundations. This section discusses the basic building blocks of security.

7.1.1   Build Security Using a Solid Infrastructure

Building an effective security program requires a solid computer and network infrastructure that is built with security in mind. Deploying security effectively requires that you have known, standard configurations, that you can build and rebuild secured systems quickly and cheaply, that you can deploy new software and patches quickly, and that you can track patch levels and versions well.

Another piece of infrastructure that is required for a good security program is a policy for someone leaving the company. The exit process typically involves notifying the human resources department, which notifies other appropriate departments, such as payroll, facilities, and information technology (IT). The most useful tool in the exit process is a checklist for the manager of the person who is leaving. It should remind the manager to ask for keys, access badge(s), identity badge(s), authentication token(s), home equipment, company phone card, company credit card, mobile phone, pager, radio, and any other equipment that the person might have. It should also remind the manager to contact the IT department at the appropriate time. The IT department must have an efficient process, which should be automated as much as possible, for disabling a person's access. Efficiently disabling access is particularly important for adverse terminations. This process is described in more detail in Chapter 31.

Case Study: Deploying Security Without Infrastructure

This story is the one we tell the most often when trying to explain how the techniques presented in the earlier chapters can be leveraged time and time again and how skipping those basics make things like security either very expensive or impossible.

A small team of security consultants was brought into a successful Internet commerce site that had experienced a break-in. After the initial clean-up operation, they were chartered to help this company build a security infrastructure that would enable them to increase security and maintain it efficiently on an ongoing basis.

The company needed to rebuild all of the machines that were part of their Internet commerce site so that the machines would be as secure as possible. They were also deploying new machines into their commerce site at a very rapid pace. Unfortunately, they had no system for automating OS loading, upgrading, or patching. Naturally, nothing was being done consistently across all the machines. Everything was done by hand, one host at a time, without even a written procedure because no one had time to stop their day-to-day work and build an automated system. As a result, the security consultants ended up building the automated systems, because they knew that a manual procedure would be error-prone and would take too long when the SAs were in a rush (which was all the time!). Although it would not normally be part of the security team's job description to build such a system, they required it in order to meet their charter.

They were lacking other pieces of infrastructure, which hampered the quick deployment of a security infrastructure. These included a centralized logging system, time synchronization, and console servers. In many ways, the security consultants became the infrastructure team because they could not deploy security systems without the infrastructure. This made the cost of "securing the site" seem very expensive, although it did have lots of efficiency and many reliability benefits for the company. Implementing the new security policies would not have been so expensive if the company would have had the basic site infrastructure in place.

It is important to build the basic system and network infrastructure and to get it right because other things, such as security, depend on it.

The earlier chapters of this book detail the basic infrastructure that makes it easier to maintain higher-level things such as security. They give you leverage. Without them, you will find yourself wasting time and effort repeatedly solving the same problems.

7.1.2 Ask the Right Questions

Before you can implement a successful security program, you must find out what you are trying to protect, from whom it must be protected, what the risks are, and what it is worth to the company. These are business decisions that should be made through informed discussion with the executive management of the company. Document the decisions that are made during this process and review the final document with management. The document will need to evolve with the company but should not change too dramatically or frequently.

Information Protection

Corporate security is about protecting assets. Most often, "information" is the asset that a company is most concerned about. The information that it wants to protect can fall into several different categories. A mature security program defines a set of categories and classifies information within those categories. The classification of the information determines what level of security is applied to it. For example, information could be categorized as public, company confidential, and strictly confidential. Public information might include marketing literature, user manuals, and publications in journals or conferences. Company confidential information might include organization charts, phone lists, an internal newsletter with financial results, business direction, articles on a product under development, or security policies. Strictly confidential information would be very closely tracked and available on a need-to-know basis only. It could include contract negotiations, employee information, top-secret product development details, or a customer's intellectual property (IP). Information protection includes protecting against malicious alteration, deliberate and accidental release of information, and theft or destruction.

Case Study: Malicious Alteration

Staff from a major New York newspaper revealed to one security consultant that although they were concerned with information being stolen, their primary concern was with someone modifying information without detection. What if a report about a company was changed to say something false? What if the headline was replaced with foul language? The phrase, "Today the [insert your favorite major newspaper] reported . . ." has a lot of value, which would be diminished if intruders were able to change their content.

Service Availability

In some cases, the company will want to protect service availability. If a company relies on the availability of certain electronic resources to conduct its business, part of the mission of the security team will be to prevent malicious denial of service attacks against those resources. Often, companies do not start thinking about this until they have Internet access because employees generally tend not to launch such attacks against their own company.

Theft of Resources

Sometimes, the company will want to protect against theft of resources. For example, if a production line is operated by computer equipment at less than full capacity because the computer has cycles being used for other purposes, the company will want to reduce the chance that compute cycles are used by intruders on that machine. The same applies to computer-controlled hospital equipment, where lives may depend on computing resources being available as needed. E-commerce sites are also concerned with theft of resources. Their systems can be slowed down by bandwidth pirates that hide FTP or IRC servers in the infrastructure, resulting in lost business for the e-commerce company.

Summary

In cooperation with your management team, decide what you need to protect and from whom, how much that is worth to the company, and what the risks are. Define information categories and the levels of protection afforded to them. Document those decisions and use this document as a basis for your security program. As the company evolves, remember to periodically reevaluate the decisions in that document with the management team.

Case Study: Decide What Is Important, Then Protect It

As a consultant, one gets to hear various answers to the question "What are you trying to protect?" The answer often, but not always, is predictable.

At a mid-size Electronic Design Automation (EDA) company, which had a cross-functional information protection committee, they considered that the most important thing for them to protect was their customers' and business partners' IP, followed by their own IP. Customers would send this company their chip designs if they were having problems with the tools or if they had a collaborative agreement for optimizing the software for the customers' designs. They also worked with business partners on collaborative projects that involved a two-way exchange of information. This third-party information always came with contractual agreements regarding security measures and restrictive access. They recognized that if they lost their customers' or business partners' trust in their security, particularly by inadvertently giving others access to that information, they would no longer have access to the information that made them the leader in their field and ultimately would lose customers. If someone gained access to the company's own IP, it would not be as damaging as the loss of customer confidence.

At a company whose entire business was e-commerce based, availability of their e-commerce site was most important, with protecting access to customers' credit cards coming in second. They were not nearly as worried about access to their own IP.

At a hardware manufacturing division of a large multinational electronics company, availability of and access to the manufacturing control systems was of the utmost importance.

At a large networking hardware and software company, the crown jewels were identified as the financial and order-processing systems. Surprisingly, neither their IP nor that of their customers was mentioned.

7.1.3   Document the Company's Security Policies

Policies are the foundations for everything that a security team does, and formal policies must be created in cooperation with people from many other departments. The human resources department needs to be involved in certain policies, especially acceptable use policies, monitoring and privacy policies, as well as creating and implementing the remedies for any policy breach. The legal department should be involved in policies, such as whether to track and prosecute intruders, and how and when to involve law enforcement when break-ins occur. Clearly, all policies need the support of upper management.

The decisions the security team makes must be backed by policy to ensure that the direction set by the management team is being followed in this very sensitive area. These policies must be documented and formally approved by the appropriate people. The security team will be asked to justify the decisions that it makes in many areas and must be able to make decisions with the confidence it is doing so in the best interests of the company, as determined by the management of the company, not by the security group, engineering, or any other group.

Different places need different sets of policies, and, to some degree, that set of policies will continually evolve and be added to as new situations arise. However, the following common policies are a good place to start in building your repertoire of policies.

Acceptable Use Policy   An acceptable use policy (AUP) describes who the legitimate users of the computer and network resources are and what they are permitted to use those resources for. It may also include some explicit examples of unacceptable use. The legitimate users of the computer and network resources are required to sign a copy of this policy, acknowledging that they have read and agreed to it before being given access to those resources. Multiple AUPs may be in place when a company has multiple security zones.

Monitoring and Privacy Policy   The monitoring and privacy policy describes the company's monitoring of their computer and network resources, including activity on individual computers, network traffic, email, web browsing, audit trails, and log monitoring. Monitoring may be considered an invasion of privacy; thus this policy should explicitly state what, if any, expectations of privacy an individual has while using these resources. Again, each individual should read and sign a copy of this policy before getting access to the resources.

Remote Access Policy   The remote access policy should explain the risks associated with unauthorized people gaining access to the network, describe proper precautions for the individual's "secret" information (pass-phrase, personal identification number [PIN], and so on), and provide a way to report lost or stolen remote access tokens so that they can be disabled quickly. It should also ask for some personal information (for example, shoe size and favorite color), through which people can be identified over the telephone. Everyone should complete and sign a copy of this policy before being granted remote access.

Network Connectivity Policy   The network connectivity policy describes how the company sets up network connections to another entity or some shared resources for access by a third party. In the current environment, every company will at some point want to establish a business relationship with another company that requires closer network access and perhaps some shared resources. You should prepare in advance for this eventuality. The policy should be distributed to all levels of management and stipulate that the security team be involved as early as possible. It should list different forms of connectivity and shared resources that are supported, which offices can support third-party connections, and what types of connections they can support.

Log Retention Policy   The log retention policy describes what is logged and for how long. Logs are useful for tracking security incidents after the event but take up large amounts of space if retained indefinitely. It is also important to know whether logs for a certain date still exist if subpoenaed for a criminal case. The policy may also address log reduction.

Case Study: Better Technology Means Less Policy

The easiest policy to follow is one that has been radically simplified. For example, password policies often include guidelines on what passwords are or are not acceptable and how often they need to be changed on different classes of machines. These details can be reduced or removed with better technology. Bell Labs' infrastructure includes a secure handheld authenticator (HHA) system, which eliminates passwords altogether. What could be simpler?

❖ **Handheld Authenticators**   An HHA is a device the size of a small calculator or a fat credit card that is used to prove that people are who they say they are. They generate a one-time password (OTP) to identify the user. For example, a host might ask the user to enter his predefined PIN and the number 1234 into his HHA and enter the output on the keyboard. The HHA will output a number that is a function of the private key stored in the HHA. No other HHA will output the same number if given the same input. Therefore the computer can know that the user is who he says he is or at least is holding the right HHA and knows the PIN for that person.

HHAs can be used to log into hosts, gain secure access (UNIX `su` command), and even gain access to web sites. With this infrastructure in place, password policies become much simpler. Hosts outside the firewall no longer require special password policies because they don't use plain passwords. Gaining root access securely on UNIX systems, previously difficult because of paranoia over password sniffing, was made more feasible by virtue of HHAs combined with encryption.[2] This is an example of how increased security, done correctly, made the system more convenient.

Lack of Policy Hampers the Security Team

Christine was once brought into a large multinational computer manufacturer as a consultant. They had no formal, approved written security policy. In particular, they had no Network Connectivity Policy. As a result, many offices had connections to third parties that were not secure, and, in many cases, the corporate IT department and the security group did not even know the connections existed because the remote offices were not under any obligation to report those connections.

One of the projects that Christine was asked to work on involved centralizing third-party access to the corporate network into three U.S. sites, two European sites, one Australian site, and one Asian site. While trying to discover where all the existing connections were, the estimate of the number of third-party connections increased from 50+ to 80+.

The security team spoke to the people who were responsible for the connections and described the new architecture and its benefits to the company. They then discussed with the customers what services they would need in this new architecture. Having assured themselves and the customer that all the services would be available, they then discussed the transition to the new architecture. In most cases, this is where the process began to fail.

---

[2]SSH provides an encrypted rsh/telnet-like system. (Yben 1996. See also Farrow 1997 and Thorpe 1998b.)

Because the new architecture centered around multiple hub sites, connections that were to a small sales office closest to the third party would need to be moved further away and so the costs would increase. Because there was no policy that stated the permissible ways to connect third parties to the network and no money had been allocated to pay the extra connectivity costs, the security group had no recourse when customers refused to pay the extra cost of moving the connection or adding security to the existing connection.

Although the initial third-party connection infrastructure was built at the main office, it saw very little adoption, and, as a result, the other connection centers were not deployed. If there had been a Network Connectivity Policy that was reasonable and supported by upper management, the result would have been very different. Management needed to support the project both financially and by instituting a formal policy with which the groups had to comply.

In contrast, Christine worked at another site that was very security-conscious and had policies and an information protection team. At that site, she set up a similar centralized area for third-party connectivity, which included access for people from other companies who were working on-site. That area was used by the majority of third-party connections. The other third-party connections had their own security infrastructure, as was permitted by the Network Connectivity Policy. There were no issues surrounding costs because this arrangement was required by company policy and everyone understood and accepted the reasons.

Get High-Level Management Support

For a security program to succeed, it must have high-level management support. The management of the company must be involved in setting the policies and ground rules for the security program, so that the right decisions are made for the business and so they understand what decisions were made and why. You will need to be able to clearly explain the possibilities, risks, and benefits if you are to successfully represent the security group, and you will need to do so in business language, not technical jargon.

In some cases, the security staff may disagree with the decisions that are made by the management of the company. If you find that you disagree with those decisions, try to understand why they were made. Remember that you may not have access to the same information or business expertise as the management team. Business decisions take into account both technical and nontechnical needs. If you represent the security group well, you must believe that the management team is making the decisions that it believes are best for the company and accept them.[3] Security people generally want to build the most secure environment possible. The cost of that security model may be more than the company can afford, however.

Once the corporate direction on security has been agreed upon, it must be documented and approved by the management team. It must then be made available and publicized within the company.

Ideally, there should be a security officer at a high level of the management hierarchy who is not a part of the IT division of the company. This person should have both business skills and experience in the area of information protection. The security officer should head up a cross-functional information protection team with representatives from the legal, human resources, IT, engineering, support and sales divisions, or whatever the appropriate divisions may be in the company. The security officer would be responsible for ensuring that appropriate polices are developed, approved, and enforced in a timely manner, and that the security and information protection team are taking the appropriate actions for the company.

No Management Support

When Christine arrived at the computer company described in the last anecdote, she asked about their security policy. A policy had been written by a cross-functional group, in the spirit of the company's informal policy, and submitted to management for formal approval two years earlier. The policy got stalled at various different levels within the IT management hierarchy for months at a time. No one in the senior management team was interested in pushing for it. The manager of the security team was periodically trying to push it from below, but with limited success.

This lack of success was indicative of the overall lack of interest in security within the company. The company had a very high turnover in security staff because they got no support for any of their projects, which is why they outsourced security to a consulting company.

If the security team cannot rely on high-level management support, the security program inevitably will fail. There will be large turnover in the security group, and money spent on security will be wasted. High-level management support is vital.

---

[3]If you think you didn't represent the security group well, figure out what you failed to communicate and how best to express it, and then see if you can get one more chance to discuss it. But it is best to get it right the first time!

Centralize Authority

At all levels there must be a central authority for decisions that relate to security. This includes business decisions, policymaking, architecture, implementation, incident response, and auditing. If the company feels that certain autonomous business units should have control over their own policymaking, architecture, and so on, then each unit should have its own central authority. The computer and network resources of each unit should be clearly divided from those of the rest of the company, and the interconnects should be treated as connections to a third party with each side applying its own policies and architectural standards to those connections.

If two parts of a company have different monitoring policies, for example, with no clear division between the two business units' resources, one security team could inadvertently end up monitoring traffic from an employee of the other business unit in contravention of that employee's expectation of privacy. This could lead to a court case and lots of bad publicity, as well as alienation of staff. On a technical level, your security is only as good as the weakest link. If you have open access to your network from another network whose security you have no control over, you don't know what your weakest link is and you have no control over it. You may also have trouble tracing an intruder who comes across such an open link.

Case Study: No Central Authority

At the company described in the previous two anecdotes, each site effectively decided on its own (unwritten) policies, but the network was undivided. As described earlier, many sites connected third parties to the network without any security. As a result, every few weeks there would be a security scare from one of the offices, and the security team would have to spend a few days tracking down the people responsible for the site to determine what, if anything, had happened.

On a few occasions, the security team was called in the middle of the night to deal with a security incident but had no access to the site that was believed to be compromised and was unable to get a response from the people responsible for that site until the next day.

By contrast, at the site that did have central authority and policies, there were no such scares or incidents.

It is impossible to implement security standards and effective incident response without a central authority that implements or audits security as dictated by companywide policies and a central incident response group that can trace all security incidents to their sources and handle them without depending on unrelated personnel.

7.1.4   Basics for the Technical Staff

As a technical member of the security team, you need to bear in mind a few other basics. The most important of these is to meet the business needs of the people who will be using the systems you design so they can work effectively. You must also stay up-to-date with what is happening in the area of vulnerabilities and attacks. If you do not, new vulnerabilities and attack methods will appear and your site will not be adequately protected. A critical part of the infrastructure that you will need, and that you should be responsible for selecting, is an authentication and authorization system. We will provide some guidelines on how to select the right products for security-sensitive applications.

Meet the Business Needs

When designing a security system, you must always find out what the business' needs are and meet those needs. Remember that there is no point in securing a company to the point that it cannot conduct its business. Also remember that the other people in the company are smart. If they cannot work effectively while using your security system, they will find a way to defeat it or find a way around it. This cannot be understated: *The way around it that they find will be less secure than the system you've put in place.*

To effectively meet the business' needs, you need to understand what people are trying to do, how they are trying to do it, and what their workflow looks like. You will also have to find out what all the reasonable technological solutions are and understand in great detail how they work before you can pick the right solution. The right solution:

- Enables people to work effectively
- Provides a reasonable level of security
- Is as simple and clean as possible
- Can be implemented within a reasonable time scale

Remember, if you make it easy to do the right thing, people will do it. People want to do what is right, but they will do what is easy. Making the secure thing the easy thing to do avoids the adversarial relationships that can develop over security policies.

Case Study: Enable People to Work Effectively

At one e-commerce site, the security group decided they needed to reduce the number of people who had super-user access to machines and that the SA groups would no longer be permitted to have super-user access on each other's machines. Although defining clean boundaries between the groups' areas of responsibility sounded fine in principle, it did not take into account shared responsibilities for machines that needed to run, for example, databases and complex email configurations. The database SAs and the mail SAs were in different groups and couldn't both have super-user access to the same machine under the new policy. The outcome was that about 10 to 15 percent of their trouble tickets now took two to three times as long because multiple groups had to be paged and one group had to direct the other verbally over the phone on how to fix the problem.

Both the SAs and the security team had a common desire for a policy that removed super-user access from approximately 100 developers who didn't need that access to get their work done and who were inadvertently causing problems when they did things as the super-user. However, the policy that was implemented prevented the SAs from working effectively and promoted an adversarial relationship between the SAs and the security team.

Preventing people from working effectively is not in the best interests of the company. Any policy that does so is not a good policy. The security team should have consulted the SAs and the engineers to understand how they worked and what they needed the super-user access for and implemented the policy accordingly.

Case Study: Designing a Shared Development Environment

Christine was once part of a team that needed to design a software development environment where a division of one company would be collaborating with a division of another company to develop a software product. The two companies competed with each other in other areas, so they needed to isolate the codevelopment effort from other development work.

The first question the team asked was, "What will the engineers need to do?" The answer was they would need to check code and designs into and out of a shared source code control system, build and run the code, and access the web, send and receive email, and access internal resources at their own company. Some of the engineers would also have to be able to work on software that was not shared with the other company. Engineers from one company would be spending time at the other company, working there for weeks or months at a time. There also needed to be a way for the release engineering group to retrieve a completed version of the software when it was ready for release. The support engineers also would need access to the shared code for customer support.

The next question that the team asked was, "Would two desktops, one on the shared network and one on the company's private network, provide an acceptable working model for the software developers?" After a reasonable amount of discussion with various engineers, it became apparent that this simple solution would not work from a workflow point of view. Most likely, if the security team had continued down this path, some of the engineers would have ended up connecting their computers to both networks in order to work effectively, thus circumventing any security the security team thought they had. The engineers needed to be able to do everything from a single desktop.

Based on what they had learned, they came up with a few possible technological solutions. Each had a different impact in terms of implementation speed, performance for the users, and differences in workflow for each group. In the end, they implemented a short-term solution that came as close as possible to the date the companies wanted to start working together, but didn't have the performance that the team wanted. They set the expectations correctly for the environment and started working on another solution that would have acceptable performance, but could not be ready for a few months because of some outside dependencies.

It was extra work and the first solution was not ideal, but it met the business need for enabling people to get started with the project on time and incorporated a plan for improving the performance and working environment so that the engineers would be able to work more effectively in the future.

Stay Up-to-Date: Attacks

A security professional must keep up-to-date with the current types of attacks and the ways to protect the company's systems from those attacks. This means tracking several mailing lists and web sites daily. The sorts of things that you need to track are security bulletins from vendors, advisories from organizations that track security issues, such as Bugtraq `http://www.securityfocus.com` (Levy 2001), Computer Incident Advisory Capability (CIAC) `http://www.ciac.org`, CERT/CC[4] `http://www.cert.org`, and Australian Computer Emergency Response Team (AUSCERT) `http://www.auscert.org.au`, and web sites and mailing lists that are more "full-disclosure" oriented. Full-disclosure lists generally provide exploits that you can test on your own systems to see if they are vulnerable. They often publicize a new vulnerability faster than the other lists because they do not need to develop and test a patch before releasing the news. A security professional should try to find out about new vulnerabilities as soon as possible to evaluate how best to protect the company's systems and how to check for attacks that take advantage of this vulnerability.

---

[4]The organization formerly known as the Computer Emergency Response Team/Coordination Center, now known as "CERT/CC: A registered service mark of Carnegie Mellon University."

Vulnerability Scanning
In the late 1990s, tools for scanning hosts or entire networks for known and possible vulnerabilities were in widespread use. A publishing company that produced both a paper and an online edition of its weekly magazine was working on a new web site. One of the people on the implementation team decided not to wait for the security consultant, who was to come out the next day to secure the machines, and connected the machines to the Internet. Within a few hours, she noticed something strange happening on one of the machines and realized that it had been broken into. She couldn't understand how anyone had found the machine because it didn't have a name in their external DNS yet. They had been scanned, and vulnerabilities in that machine's OS and configuration had been identified and exploited within hours of connecting. The vulnerabilities that were exploited were all well known and avoidable. Because she wasn't a security person and didn't receive or pay attention to security bulletins, she had no idea what vulnerabilities existed, how dangerous they were, or that so much automated scanning took place with break-in kits being used once vulnerabilities were identified.

In 1998, a friend of Christine's got a new DSL connection to his house, and he watched to see how long it would take before his small network was scanned. It took less than two hours. Fortunately, he had secured his machines before he brought up the connection and, because he read lots of security lists, he had up-to-date patches in place.

If you work in the area of security, it is vital that you keep up-to-date on what is happening in the areas of attacks and vulnerabilities.

Authentication and Authorization
One of the fundamental building blocks of a security system is a strong authentication system with a unique identity for each person and no accounts used by multiple people. Along with the authentication system goes an authorization system that specifies the level of access that each person is authorized to have. *Authentication* gives the person's identity, and *authorization* determines what that person can do.

A *role account* is one that gives people privileges to perform one or more functions they cannot perform with their normal account privileges. Typical examples include the SA role, the database administrator role, and the website administrator role. Shared accounts, even shared role accounts, should be avoided. Shared accounts make it difficult, if not impossible, to have accountability. If something goes wrong, there may be no way to tell who did what. It also makes it a lot harder to disable someone's access completely when he leaves the company. The SAs have to know what role accounts the person had access to and cause inconvenience to others by changing the passwords on those accounts. They need to make sure the person who has left no longer knows any valid username and password combinations. Most OSs have other mechanisms for providing the same level of access to multiple people who authenticate as separate entities. Check into the possibilities on your system before deciding to use a shared account. Fortunately, strong authentication systems, which we recommend you use, generally make it difficult to have shared accounts.

A strong authentication system gives you a high degree of confidence that the person the computer believes it has authenticated is actually that person and not someone else using that person's credentials. For example, a strong authentication system may be a biometric mechanism or it may simply be a token-based system, in which the person needs to have a physical device, as well as a secret that he remembers. If he gives the physical device to someone else, he no longer has access, which is often a sufficient deterrent against sharing. If the device is stolen, the thief should not automatically know the secret.

It can be useful to tie the strong authentication mechanism to something that has real value to the individual. For example, if it is tied to a credit card, phone card, money, house key, driver's license, or is biometric, the person is less likely to give it to someone else to use, especially for more than a few minutes. The more valuable it is, the less likely the person is to loan it out, especially to someone he does not know very well.

Case Study: Not Everyone Is Security-Aware

When one company switched from fixed passwords to HHAs, they received complaints from the sales team. Many on the sales team were unhappy that they could no longer give their username and password information to customers and potential customers to try out the company's products on the corporate network before deciding to buy them. If they loaned their HHA to someone, they couldn't send and receive email when they were on the road. The security team had to educate them about the problems with giving other people access to the corporate network and help them to establish more standard ways for customer trials, such as loaning equipment to the customer.

At times, something will go wrong with the strong authentication mechanism, and you will need a way to authenticate people over the telephone, particularly if they are traveling. For example, they could lose or break the

Group	Machines							
	Dev	RE	Fin	Res	HR	Ops	Inf	Sec
Developers	W	R		R				
Release Engineers	R	W		R				
Finance			W	R				
Human Resources				R	W			
Operations		R		R		W		
System Administration	A	A	A	A	A	A	A	
Security	A	A	A	A	A	A	A	A

Dev: Developer machines; **RE:** Release engineering machines; **Fin:** Finance machines; **Res:** Corporate resource machines (intranet, etc.); **HR:** Human resources machines; **Ops:** Operations/manufacturing machines; **Inf:** Infrastructure (mail servers, auth servers, etc.); **Sec:** Security machines (firewalls, intrusion detection, strong auth, etc.); **A:** Administrative rights; **R:** Read access; **W:** Write access

Table 7.1: Authorization Matrix

physical device, credit card, or whatever, or if there is a portable device for reading the card or fingerprint, it could break. You have to prepare for this eventuality when you initially set up people in the strong authentication system. Have them fill out a form, providing questions and answers that can be used to authenticate them over the phone. For example, they could supply their shoe size, their favorite fruit, the shop where they bought their dining room table, where they were for the Y2K New Year, their favorite subject in high school, or something that can be checked within the company, such as who sits in the office/cubicle beside them. If a person can successfully authenticate himself over the phone in this way, then another mechanism should be able to grant him temporary access to the systems until the problem can be fixed.

Earlier, we alluded to authorization. It is very useful to develop an authorization matrix based on roles within the company, categories of system, and classes of access, such as the one shown in Table 7.1. The authorization matrix describes the level of access that a given group of people has on a certain class of machines. It is a policy that should be developed in cooperation with management and representatives from all parts of the company. Then an authorization system should be linked to the authentication system that implements the policy. The set of identities and information stored in the authentication and authorization systems is one of the namespaces at a site. Managing this and other namespaces is discussed further in Chapter 6.

Shared Voicemail

At one fast-growing customer site, a group of people shared one telephone and voicemail box. One day, a new person started sharing that telephone and voicemail box. She asked what the password for the voicemail was. In answer, one of the other people in that group lifted up the handset and pointed to the number taped to the underside of the handset. Anyone could find the password and listen to potentially confidential information left in the voicemail box. Many sites consider voicemail a secure way to deliver sensitive information, such as news of a potential new customer, initial passwords, staff announcements, product direction, and other information potentially damaging to the company if the wrong people hear it.

The same site used shared accounts for administrative access, rather than associating authorization levels with authenticated individuals. The end result was a book with administrative account name and password pairs associated with each host. Someone who had authority to access the password for one host could easily obtain the password for others at the same time and then anonymously access the other machines using the administrative accounts. Lack of accountability because of shared accounts is a bad thing, as is having a book of passwords from which people can easily obtain a greater level of access than they are entitled to.

This site suffered several break-ins, and the use of shared role accounts made it harder to identify and track the intruder. This system was also not as easy to use as one that granted increased access based on each person's unique personal authentication token because everyone had to make periodic trips to check the book of passwords. Authorization based on individuals' authentication would have been easier to use and more secure.

Shared Role Accounts Make Identification Difficult

A site suffered several break-ins while the primary SA was away for an extended period and an inexperienced SA was standing in for her. The primary SA was able to provide some help through remote access, and they also enlisted the help of an experienced security administrator who was working at the site in a different role. The site used a shared super-user role account. At one point, the primary SA became afraid that the super-user account had been compromised because she saw logs of SSH access to that account from an unknown machine. Fortunately, the junior SA checked with the security administrator who was helping with the incidents and found out that she was the one accessing the super-user account from the unknown machine. If the group was much larger, it would have been difficult if not impossible to notice suspicious accesses and trace them to their sources. Failing to notice suspicious accesses could lead to machines remaining compromised when the problem was thought to be solved. Failing to trace those accesses to their (innocent) sources could lead to a huge amount of wasted effort and unnecessary outages rebuilding key machines that were not compromised. It is best to avoid this scenario by not using shared role accounts.

Select the Right Products and Vendors

When selecting a product for any security-sensitive purpose, it is important to select the right one. Evaluating a product from a security point of view is different from evaluating a product where security is not a priority.

A security-sensitive product is one that

- Is used by any third party who has a restricted level of access to that system or the network(s) that it is connected to
- Is part of the authentication, authorization, or access control system
- Is accessible from the Internet (or any untrusted network)
- Has access to the Internet (or any untrusted network)
- Provides authenticated access to sensitive data or systems (e.g., payroll data)

When evaluating a security-sensitive product, there are additional things that you need to consider. For example, you need some degree of confidence in the security of the product. You should consider several usability criteria that affect security. You also need to think about ongoing maintenance issues and the vendor's direction, along with some of the more usual concerns such as functionality and integration issues. We will discuss each of these in some detail.

Simplicity. Simple systems are more reliable and more secure than complex ones. A simple system performs a couple of basic functions. A complex system performs many different functions. For example, an email system that just sends and receives email is not as complex as one that also stores address books and notes and perhaps has a calendar service built in. The more basic email system can be augmented by other pieces of software that provide the extra functionality, if required. Several small, simple components that interact are likely to have fewer security problems than a single large complex system. The more complex a system, the harder it is to test in detail and the more likely it is to have unforeseen problems that can be exploited by an attacker.

Security.   Why do you believe that the product is reasonably secure? Research the product and find out who the principal designers and programmers are. Do you know (of) them; are they well respected in the industry? What else have they done? How well have their previous products worked, and how secure are those products? How does the product address some known problem areas? For example, for a firewall, you might ask how it addresses mail delivery, which is an area that has traditionally had many security problems. FTP is another service traditionally fraught with security problems (not only FTP server implementations, but handling the protocol at firewalls too). Look through a couple of years of security advisories and pick a recurring problem area to investigate.

Open Source.   Is this an open source product? The Open Source debate in a nutshell is as follows: If the source is available, intruders can find problems and exploit them; but on the other hand, it also gets reviewed by many people, problems are found more quickly, patches are available more quickly, and you can always fix it yourself if necessary. Closed source leads to suspicions of "security through obscurity": the mentality that keeping a method secret makes it secure even when it's fundamentally not secure. Security through obscurity does not work: the attackers find the problems anyway.

Usability.   How do the different components interact? How does a configuration change in one area affect other areas? For example, in a firewall that has both proxies and packet filters, if some separate configuration rules try to control something at both the network (packet filter) layer and the application (proxy) layer, which layer's rules are applied first and what happens? Does the application notice configuration conflicts? How long does it take to train new people on the product? Is it easy to understand and verify the configuration? How easy is it to configure the application in a way that is not secure?

Functionality.   It should provide the features that you need, but preferably no more. Superfluous functionality may be a source of problems, especially if it can't be disabled.

Vendor Issues.   Maintenance patches and updates are very important for a security-sensitive product. In most cases, you will also want to be able to report problems to a vendor and have a reasonable expectation of getting a quick fix or workaround for the problem. How security-conscious is the vendor? Do they release security patches for their products? What is their mechanism for notifying customers of security problems?

Integration. How well will this product integrate with the rest of your network infrastructure?

- Will it use your existing authentication system?
- What kind of load does it put on the network?
- What kind of load does it put on other key systems?
- If it has to talk to other systems or people through a firewall, are the protocols it uses supported adequately by the firewall? Open protocols usually are; proprietary ones are often not. The product should not embed communications into another protocol, such as HyperText Transfer Protocol (HTTP), that is widely supported by firewalls, because it can be difficult or impossible to control access to the new application independently from real use of that protocol (for example, web access in the case of HTTP).[5]
- Can its logs be sent to a central log host?
- What network services does it expect, and do you provide them already?
- Does it run on an OS that is already supported and understood at the site?

Cost of Ownership. How long does it take to configure this software? Are there "autoload" options that can help to standardize configurations and speed the setup time? How much day-to-day maintenance is there on this system—does it need lots of tuning? Are people in your organization already familiar with it? Are people that you hire likely to be familiar with it, or are you going to have to train them? How hard will it be to make a new person comfortable with your configuration?

Futures. How well does this product scale, and what are the scaling options when it reaches capacity? What direction is the vendor taking the product, and does it match your company's direction? For example, if you are in a UNIX-based company that does little with Windows and is not likely to move in that direction, then a product from a company that is primarily focused on Windows for the future is not a good choice. Is the product likely to die soon or stop being developed? How long are versions supported? How often do new releases come out? What is the market acceptance of this product? Is it likely to survive market pressures?

---

[5]If the product is web-based or has a web interface, it should obviously use HTTP for the web-based communication. However, if it is sending information back and forth between a client that is not a web browser and a server that is not a web server, it should not use HTTP, nor should it use port 80. The same rule applies to other protocols that are well supported by firewalls.

Internal Auditing

By *internal auditing,* we mean auditing that is performed by a group internal to the company. We believe that internal and external auditing groups should both be used, and we discuss the external audit function further in Section 7.1.5.

So, what do we mean when we say *auditing?* Different people may mean different things by this term. We mean it in a very broad sense. We intend it to cover all of the following:

- Checking whether security environments are in compliance with policies and design criteria
- Checking employee and contractor lists against authentication and authorization databases
- Physical checking on machine rooms, wiring, and telecom closets for foreign devices
- Checking that relevant machines are up-to-date with security patches
- Scanning relevant networks to verify what services are offered
- Launching sophisticated, in-depth attacks against particular areas of the infrastructure, with clearly specified success criteria and limitations

The role we recommend for the internal auditing team is performing those tasks that can be more thoroughly and easily performed using inside knowledge of the site.

Logging and Log Processing.   Logs, especially logs from security-sensitive machines and applications, are an important source of security information. Logs can help the security team trace what has happened in an attack. Logs can be analyzed to help detect attacks and gauge the seriousness of an attack. From a security standpoint, you can never have too many logs. From a practical standpoint, infinite logs consume an infinite amount of space and are impossible to search for important information. Logs should be processed by a computer to extract useful information and archived for a predefined period to be available for re-examination if an incident is discovered. All security-sensitive logs should go to one central place so that they can be processed together and the information from different machines can be correlated. Security-sensitive logs should not remain on security-sensitive machines, because the logs can be erased or modified by an attacker who compromises those machines. The central log host must be very well secured to protect the integrity of the logs.

Internal Verification.   Consider ways that you can check for anomalies on your network and important systems. Do you see any strange routes on the network, routes going in strange directions, or traffic from unexpected sources, for example? Try war-dialing all of the phone numbers assigned to your company to see if any modems answer on unexpected numbers.[6] Check what machines and services are visible on public networks to make sure that nothing new or unexpected has appeared. Does someone who is in the office also appear to be actively accessing the network using a remote access system? Intrusion Detection Systems (IDS) should make some of this type of anomaly detection easier, as well as other kinds of attack detection.

Per-project Verification. Periodically check on each security project that has been implemented to make sure that the configuration has not been materially changed. Make sure that it still matches the design specifications and conforms to all appropriate policies. Use this occasion to also check with the people who are using this security system to see whether it serves their needs adequately and whether they anticipate any new requirements arising.

Physical Checks. Check on areas that are key points in the computing, networking, or communications infrastructure. Look for additional devices, perhaps concealed, that may be monitoring and recording or transmitting data. Such areas include data centers, networking closets, telecommunications closets, video-conferencing rooms, wiring between such rooms, and wiring between buildings.

Physical Security Breach

The security team in a large multinational corporation did not perform regular physical checks of their data centers and communications closets. One day, someone from the company that supplied and maintained their telephone switch came to do some maintenance on the switch and discovered a device attached to it. Further investigation revealed that the device was monitoring all telephone communications within the building and across the outside lines and transmitting them off-site. It turned out that someone had come to the building dressed in the uniform of the telephone company, saying that he needed to bring in some new lines to the telephone closet. He had been let in without anyone checking with the telecom and networking groups to see if the phone company was expected. After this incident, they re-emphasized their policy that no one should be allowed into those rooms

---

[6] *War-dialing* means having a program dial all the numbers in a given list, which may include entire exchanges, and having it log which numbers respond with a modem sound. It can also include logging what greeting the machine at the other end gives, or trying certain combinations of usernames and passwords and logging the results.

without the consent and supervision of the telecom or networking group, and they instituted regular physical checks of all computer and communications rooms and the wiring between them.

7.1.5   Management and Organizational Issues

There are several areas in which the security team particularly needs management support. Maintaining reasonable staffing levels for the size of the company, with the appropriate roles within the group, is one such area. The manager of the security team can also help with coordinating with the rest of the system administration managers to establish an incident response team that is prepared for emergencies. Setting up a relationship with an outside auditing company and scheduling their work to fit in with the needs of the rest of the company is another task that will typically fall to the security team manager. We will also discuss some approaches for successfully selling security to other groups in the company.

Resources

The security team needs access to various resources. One key to success in the area of security is to have lots of contacts in the industry. They then get to know what other companies are doing and what others consider to be state of the art. Through their contacts security professionals also hear what attacks are happening before they become generally known, which enables them to be one step ahead and as prepared as possible. It also enables them to benchmark how the company is doing compared with other companies. Are they spending too much on security or too little? Are they lacking some important policies? They can also find out what experiences others have had in trying to implement some new technology and what the return on investment has been. Has anyone had any particularly positive or negative experiences with a new product that the security team is considering? Contacts are made through attending conferences regularly and becoming a part of some select intercompany security focus groups. They need to become known and trusted by other security professionals so that they can stay in touch with the industry.

The security team needs people with a variety of skills. In a small company, one person may need to take on all the roles, perhaps with some management assistance. In a larger company, however, the manager of the security team should look at hiring people for a number of different roles within the security team. Some of these roles require particular skill sets and personalities. The various roles include policy writers, architects, implementers, operations staff, auditors, and incident response team members.

Security Architect. The security architect represents the security group to the rest of the company. She should be on cross-functional teams within the company. She is responsible for staying in touch with what is happening within the company and finding out for which projects the group needs to prepare. She is the one who finds out what the requirements and business needs for each project are and identifies the key people. She also designs the security environment and takes an overview of what is happening with security within the company, including what infrastructure would help the group and the company. She should be involved with vendor relations, tracking technologies, products, and futures. She should decide when (or whether) the company should move toward a new technology.

Implementer. The implementer implements the architect's designs and works with the architect on product evaluations. The implementer becomes part of the cross-functional project teams when he is identified as the person who will be building that particular environment. He should also understand what the business requirements are, bring up issues that he sees, and suggest alternative solutions. He documents the setup and operational aspects of the systems that he implements and trains the operations staff on how to run these systems. He acts as a level of escalation for the security operations staff. He should also discuss future directions, technologies, and products with the architect and bring up any requirements that he sees arising in the future.

Operations. The security operations staff run the security infrastructure on a day-to-day basis. They are trained by the implementer and consult him when they run into problems that they can't resolve. In large companies if the operations staff provides 24×7 coverage, they can serve double-duty by also being the security operations staff. The security operations staff can respond to alerts or reports from the log monitoring system or other intrusion detection systems. They deal with the day-to-day issues that arise from the authentication and authorization system, such as lost or broken tokens, new employees or contractors, and departures from the company. They are also the people who the rest of the SA staff talk to when they suspect that there may be a problem with a piece of the security infrastructure. Where possible, they should help the implementer to build the infrastructure that they support.

Policywriter. The policywriter is responsible for writing corporate policies. That means that she needs to have contacts in key areas of the company and to be a part of some cross-functional teams where she can discuss policy with managers, the legal department, and the human resources department.

She needs to be able to identify what policies the company needs and to get support for those policies within the company, particularly at upper management levels. She should be aware of what other companies have in the way of policies, in particular other companies in the same industry, if possible. She should know what is "standard" and what is considered "state of the art" with respect to policies. She should be able to judge the business environment and spirit of the company to know what is appropriate to that company.

Auditor.   An auditor may be internal to the company or from an external consulting group. One company may use both kinds of auditors in different roles. The auditor builds a program for verifying that the security of the company matches expectations. He should work closely with the security team and management to determine if there are particular areas that should be tested in depth. Such testing may include "social engineering,"[7] which is typically the weakest part of any company's defenses. The role of auditors, in particular external auditors, is discussed later in this section. Internal audits were discussed in Section 7.1.4.

Incident Response Team.   The incident response team springs into action when there is an intrusion or suspected intrusion. The incident response team also meets on a regular basis to go over incident response procedures. Depending on the size of the company and the security team, the incident response team probably will be composed of people from across the SA organization, as well as the security team. The rest of the time, they have another role within the system administration organization, sometimes within and sometimes outside the security group.

Incident Response

In this section, we discuss establishing a process for security incident handling, the advance preparation needed for effective incident response, and how various company policies relating to incident response affect how the team works.

---

[7] *Social engineering* is the art of persuading people to give you access to that which you are not entitled to, normally by using a small piece of information you have ferreted out. An example would be finding out the name of a new sales engineer at a company, calling up the helpdesk pretending to be that engineer and saying that you need to dial in, and asking for the phone number. Then later you call the helpdesk pretending to be the same or a different person and say that you have lost your HHA, but you need access, and get them to give you some other way of authenticating, such as a password. Most people do their best to be helpful; social engineering exploits their helpfulness.

To handle an incident well, one must be prepared. One shouldn't be forming the team during a crisis. Ironically, the best time to form the team and the processes is when you feel you don't need them.

❖ **"Above the Fold"** The larger a company grows, the more likely it is that they are more concerned with the embarrassment of having an incident than the data or productivity that would be lost as a result of an incident. Embarrassment comes from not handling an incident well. Handle something properly and it becomes a minor article in the newspaper. Handle something badly and you become one of the headlines that is "above the fold" on the front page. That can affect the company's share price and the confidence of customers.

When setting up an incident response team, the first thing you need to establish is how reports of possible incidents are going to get to the team. To do so, you need to look at your problem reporting mechanisms, which we will discuss in detail in Section 16.2.2. If a person reports a potential incident, who do they report it to and how is it handled? Are there any electronic devices that may report a potential incident, and, if so, where do those reports go and how are they handled? During what hours are you willing to respond to potential security incidents, and how does this affect the reporting mechanisms? For example, if you provide internal customer support only during business hours, but you want to be able to respond to security incidents around the clock, how can someone report a potential security incident outside of business hours?

This first stage of the process must be integrated into your standard problem-reporting procedures because customers cannot be expected to know in the heat of the moment that network or system failures should be handled one way, but potential security incidents should be handled another way. Customers are not usually qualified to determine whether something is a security incident.

Whoever receives the report needs to have a process for handling a call relating to a potential security incident and for determining if this is a call that should be escalated to an incident response team member. There should be one or more points of contact for the team to whom calls are initially escalated and who are capable of deciding whether it is a full-blown incident that needs the team to respond. The points of contact should be members of the security team. The person who initially receives the report should be able to determine whether a call is a true potential security incident, but he should err on the side of caution and escalate any calls he is unsure about to the appropriate contact on the incident response team. Failing to escalate a security incident to the appropriate people is a bad thing.

No Incident Reporting Mechanism

At a computer manufacturer, there was no formal incident response team, but there was a security group that also responded to incidents and had a reasonably well-established set of procedures for doing so. The company also had 24×7 internal computer support coverage. An engineer in the web group was working late and noticed something strange on one of the machines in the web cluster. He looked closer and discovered that the machine had been broken into and that the attacker was actively defacing web pages at that moment. He did his best to get the attacker off the machine and keep him off, but realized that he was not up to the challenge because he did not know exactly how the attacker was getting on to the machine. He called the 24×7 internal support group at about 2 AM and told them what was happening.

Because they had no procedures for dealing with this and did not have outside hours contact information for the security group, they just opened a trouble ticket and assigned it to someone in the security group. When that security administrator came in at 8 AM, he found the trouble ticket in his email and set the incident response processes into motion. At this stage, both the engineer and the attacker had grown tired and gone to bed, making it harder to get complete details to track down the attacker.[8] The engineer felt let down by the SA organization because he had rightly expected that someone would come to his aid to deal with an attack in progress.

The SA organization and the security organization both failed, but in different ways. The security organization failed because it didn't give clear instructions to the internal support group on how to escalate a security incident. The SA organization failed because no attempts at escalation were made for something that merited at least escalation within the organization if an outside escalation path was unknown. After this incident, the security team made sure that the SA organization knew the escalation path for security incidents.

Once you have figured out how reports of potential security incidents will reach the incident response team contacts, you need to determine what course of action the team should take. That depends on preparation and corporate decisions made well in advance of an incident.

---

[8]He eventually was tracked down and successfully prosecuted for a number of incidents of breaking into and defacing web sites, including government sites.

Response Policy. The response policy determines what incidents you respond to and at what level. For example, if there is a large-scale attack on many machines, the entire incident response team is activated. However, if there is a small-scale attack on just one machine, a smaller group of people may be activated.

How do you respond if your network is being scanned? You may choose to log that and ignore it, or to try to track down the attacker. Based on the various ways that incidents are reported and the level of filtering that happens before an incident is passed on to the incident response team contact, you should build a list of general scenarios and determine how to respond to each of them. Regardless of whether you plan on pursuing attackers, detailed and timestamped logs of events, actions, and findings should be kept by the security team. You should also document how your response will be different if the incident appears to be of internal origin. How you respond will be partly determined by the company's prosecution policy, disconnection policy, and communication policies, as described next.

Prosecution Policy. The prosecution policy should be created by upper management and the legal department. The question that needs to be answered is "When does the company prosecute attackers?" This can range from "never," to "only when significant damage has been done," to "only in successful break-ins," to "always, even for scanning." The company may choose "never" because of the associated bad press cost and risks of gathering evidence. Once you have determined the criteria for prosecution, you also need to determine at what point law enforcement will be contacted. Training for all the incident response team members on how and when to gather evidence that is admissible in court will be necessary for any prosecution to be successful.

Disconnection Policy. The disconnection policy determines when, if ever, you sever connectivity between the machines that are being attacked (and possibly other company networks) and the attacker. In some cases, this may mean severing network connections, possibly Internet connectivity, possibly some form of remote access; perhaps powering down one or more machines; perhaps terminating some TCP sessions; perhaps stopping a particular service; or adding some IP filtering rules to a perimeter security device. You need to consider in advance what forms of connectivity you may wish to sever, how you would do it, and what the impact would be on the operations of the company. You also need to define the risks of not severing that connection in various scenarios. Remember to include the possibility that your site may then be used to launch an attack against another site.

When this data is clear and well organized, the management of the company needs to decide in what cases connectivity must be severed and how, when it should not be severed, when it may or may not be severed, and who gets to make that call. It also needs to state when the connection can be restored and who can make that decision.

> ❖ **Your Site Used to Launch New Attacks**   If your site is used as a launch pad for attacks against other sites, the company may well become involved in a court case against the attacker, even if the company decides not to prosecute in order to avoid adverse publicity. The next company to be attacked may have a different policy. To protect your site from being used as a launch pad for attacks against others, it is important to use egress filtering to restrict what traffic can leave your network.

Communication Policy.   Senior management needs to decide what communication should happen within and outside the company for the various sorts of security incidents. Depending on what is decided here, this may involve having contacts in marketing or press relations departments who need to be kept informed from the outset about what is happening. A company may choose to keep as many incidents as possible as quiet as possible in order to avoid bad press. This policy may include no internal communications about the incident for fear that it will accidentally reach the ears of the press. The communication policy affects the structure of the team if it needs someone to act as the communication contact, as well as how the team works, perhaps trying not to draw attention to itself, and how many people are involved in responding to the incident.

The communication policy may affect the disconnection policy, because a disconnection may draw attention to the incident. The prosecution policy also affects the disconnection policy, because disconnecting may make it more difficult to trace the attacker or may trigger an automated clean-up of a compromised system, thus destroying evidence. On the other hand, leaving the attacker connected may give him the opportunity to erase his tracks.

Responding to a security incident is a very detail-oriented process that is well described in the SANS *Computer Security Incident Handling: Step-by-Step* booklet (Northcutt 1999). The process is divided into six phases: preparation, identification, containment, eradication, recovery, and follow-up. These phases are composed of a total of 90 actions in 31 steps, with most of the actions being part of the preparation phase. Being prepared is the most critical part of responding to an incident effectively.

External Audits

We recommend employing outside security consultants in an auditing role. The security consultants should be people the technical team can recommend and work with or the company will not get the most out of the arrangement. Using external auditors has several benefits. It gives the security team independent feedback on how they are doing and provides extra pairs of eyes examining the company's security. The consultants have the advantage of distance from the work that is going on, and their approach will be unaffected by expectations and inside knowledge. Ideally, the auditing group should not be involved in the design or maintenance of the company's security systems. Senior management will usually value getting an outside view of the company's security, and if the security consultants are experienced in this area, they may well have more data to present to senior management on the existing state of the art in the industry, the resources that other similar companies assign to security, and the risks associated with any shortcomings they have found or have been told about by the security team. The external group may be able to help the internal security team to get more resources, if that is appropriate. They may also have good ideas on approaches to take or advice on software or hardware to use.

This external auditing role does not replace the internal auditing function. We recommend different roles and tasks for the internal and external auditing groups. The role of the external group is discussed here, and the role of the internal group is discussed in Section 7.1.4. Briefly, we recommend splitting the auditing function with the internal auditing team tracking things on an ongoing basis and the external group being brought in periodically for larger-scale audits and for the benefits associated with their external viewpoint.

The role we believe the external auditing team should take on is examining the security of the company from the outside, which would cover in-depth attacks against particular areas and scanning of exposed networks and remote access points.

What do we mean by "in-depth attacks against a particular area?" We mean giving the external auditing team a task such as getting access to the company's financials or customer database rather than a task such as "breaking through the firewall," which focuses on a particular security mechanism. The in-depth attack takes a more holistic approach to checking site security. The external auditing team may think of ways to get in that the security team did not consider. Specifying the security infrastructure to attack limits the consultants' scope in ways that a real attacker will not be limited. An in-depth attack is a more realistic test of how site security will hold up against a determined attacker.

For some of these tests, the security team may wish to deliberately exclude social engineering. Social engineering involves an attacker convincing people to give him certain information or access, usually by pretending to be someone else, such as a new employee or contractor. Social engineering is typically the weakest link. It is important to have an awareness program that addresses it. The success of the program can be periodically checked by permitting social engineering attacks. When social engineering is no longer a problem, it should no longer be restricted as a method.

Scanning exposed networks and remote access points is another area that lends itself to being delegated to an external auditing group. It may be a good source of statistics to use when talking to upper management about what the security team is doing. It is also a tedious task, and the consultants will often have better tools for it. In addition, they will be performing their work from a network or a location that will not be assigned an extra level of privilege because it belongs to the company or an employee.

External auditing should include penetration testing, if that is appropriate for your company. If consultants are doing penetration testing for you, there should be a written schedule of areas to be tested and bounds placed on the extent of the testing. Make sure that you are very clear on the goals, restrictions, and limitations for the group. For example, you may specify that they should stop as soon as they get inside your security perimeter, obtain access to a certain database, get super-user privileges on any of the target machines, or have shown that a denial-of-service (DoS) attack works on one or two machines. The consultants should coordinate carefully during testing with one or two points of contact at the company who may tell them to stop at any point during testing if they are causing unexpected damage. Be sure that you have approval from the highest level of management to conduct such audits.

Penetration Testing Must Be Coordinated

A consultant was employed to perform penetration testing on a large multinational networking company. There was a very clear contract and statement of work that described the dates, extent, and limits of testing. Part of the penetration testing was checking for DoS vulnerabilities. The consultant came across a cascading DoS vulnerability that disabled all of the European connections before he could stop it. Such a large network failure naturally caused a great deal of high-level management interest. Fortunately, the consultant had carefully followed the contract and statement of work, so the incident cost a lot less than it would have if a malicious attacker had come across the vulnerability first, or if the company had not been able to quickly figure out what was happening. Once the high-level managers found out what had happened and why, they were understanding and happy to accept the cost of finding that vulnerability before it could be used against them.

Cross-Functional Teams

The security group cannot work in isolation. They need to learn as quickly as possible any new business developments that may affect security. They need to be in touch with the company ethos and the key players when developing security policies. They need to have a strong relationship with the rest of the SA team to make sure that what they implement is understood and maintainable, and they must know that other SAs will not on their own do anything that will affect security. They need to be aware of the working models of other people in the company and how security changes will affect those people, especially in the field offices.

Legal. A strong alliance with the legal department of the company provides many benefits. The right person, or people, within that department typically will be glad to have a strong relationship with the security group because they will have questions and concerns that the security group can address. The right person in that group is usually the person who is responsible for IP, often known as the Intellectual Property Manager or simply IP Manager.

The IP manager is a good person to lead an information protection team that regularly brings together representatives from all over the company to discuss how best to protect IP within the company and how the proposed changes will affect each group. An information protection team needs representatives from the following departments: legal, risk management and disaster planning, facilities, (data) security, system administration, human resources, marketing and communications, engineering, and sales.

The IP manager within the legal department is interested in electronic security because how the company protects its information relates to how well they can defend the company's right to that information in court. She will also typically be involved in, or at least aware of, any partnership negotiations with other companies, mergers, and acquisitions because there will be IP issues to be discussed. If you have a good relationship with this person, she can make you aware of upcoming projects that you will need to plan for and get you involved with the project team from the outset. She will also be able to give you the basis for your security model based on the contractual agreement between the two companies. She will be able to help with the policies that need to surround the agreement and with providing training to the people who will be working with the other party to the agreement.

Case Study: *Importance of a Relationship with the Legal Department*

One division of a multinational EDA company, formed an alliance with a group within the EDA division of IBM. The alliance involved codevelopment of a software product, which meant that both groups were to have complete access to the source for that product and that they needed a workable development environment. However, other groups within the EDA division of IBM competed directly with other groups within the EDA company, and other parts of IBM competed with customers of the EDA company. The EDA company often received confidential information from its customers that typically related to the next generation of chips that the customer was designing. It was very sensitive and very valuable information. Therefore the EDA company needed to carefully limit the information that it shared with IBM.

The security group's contact in the legal department at the EDA company ensured that a design team for the shared development environment was formed long before the contract was signed and that the security group was a part of that team. Other members included the people responsible for the development tools, the release management team, the development manager for the product, technical support, and the equivalent people from IBM. Several other groups were formed to deal with other aspects of the agreement, and progress was tracked and coordinated by the people responsible for the deal. The IP manager also directed the group that developed training materials for the engineers who would be working on the codeveloped product. The training included a guide to the contractual obligations and limitations, the policies that were being implemented with respect to this project, and a technical overview on how to use the codevelopment area. The same training materials were to be presented to both sides.

With a project of this magnitude, involving so many different departments of the company, the security group would have failed if it had not been involved from the outset. It would also have failed without clear direction from the legal department on what was to be shared and what was to be protected. The other vital component for the success of the security group in this project was a spirit of cooperation within the cross-functional team that was designing the environment.

System Administrators.   Security needs to be a cooperative effort within the company in general and within the system administration team in particular. The SAs often will know what is happening or going to happen within their business units before the business unit thinks to get the security team involved. The SAs can help to get the security team involved at the outset, which will give the projects much better success rates. The SA team can also help by keeping an eye open for unusual activity that might indicate an attack, knowing what to do when they see such activity, and possibly by being involved in the incident response team described earlier in this section.

In some companies, the business applications support team (sometimes referred to as *MIS*) is considered a part of the SA team and in others it is not. These are the people who are responsible for a specific set of business applications such as human resource systems, payroll, order tracking, and financials. It is very important that the security team also has support from this group and knowledge of what is happening within this group. If the applications support team does not understand the security model and policies, they may select and deploy a software system that comes with dial-in support from the vendor or connectivity to the vendor and not arrange for an appropriate security model for this setup. Or they may deploy a security-sensitive application (see Section 7.1.4) without realizing it or using the appropriate security guidelines for selecting it. If the security team works well with this group, these pitfalls can be avoided.

Product Development. The product development group is the main profit center for the company. In a consulting company, this is the consultants; in a university, it is the academics and the students; in a nonprofit organization, it is the people who perform the primary functions of that organization. If they cannot perform their jobs efficiently, that will adversely affect the whole company, so it is very important to work closely with them so that you understand their requirements. The product development group is also the group most likely to need connectivity to business partners and to have complex security requirements. Getting to know them well and learning of the new projects before they become official allows the security team to be better prepared. The product development group are also the people who are most likely to be using the security environments on a regular basis. Therefore their feedback on how usable the environment is, what their work model looks like, and what they see as future requirements is very important.

Field Offices. The security function is normally based in one or more major offices of a company. The smaller field offices often feel that their needs are ignored or neglected because they often have different sets of requirements from people in the larger offices and they do not have much, if any, direct contact with the security group. Field offices typically house sales and support staff who frequently travel to customers and may need to access corporate information while on the road or at customer sites. At a customer site, there will be restrictions on the types of access available to connect to the company because of the customer's policies and facilities. If they cannot use one of the officially sanctioned methods, they may set up something for themselves at their own office so that they can get their work done. It may prove very difficult to discover that such access has been opened up at a remote office because of the lack of SA and security team

contact with that office. It is vital that the people in these offices know that
their voice is heard and that their needs are met by the security team. It is
also important that they understand what the security team is doing and
why going around the security team is a bad thing for the company.

Sell Security Effectively

Selling security is like selling insurance. There is no immediately obvious
benefit in spending the money, except peace of mind. But with insurance, at
least customers can see from year to year, or decade to decade, how they are
doing, and they can see the potential costs if they do not have the insurance,
even if the risks are hard for the average person to visualize. For security,
it is less easy to see the benefits unless the security team can provide more
data on failed attacks, trends in attacks on a global scale, and potential
losses to the company.

You need to sell security to senior management, to the people who will
be using the systems, and to the SAs who will have to install, maintain, and
support users on those systems. Each of these groups cares about different
things, and all of their concerns must be taken into account when designing
and implementing a security system.

To sell security to senior management, you need to show how your security helps the company meet its obligation to its shareholders and its customers and ways in which security could be considered a competitive advantage.[9] When trying to sell something to others, it is important to show them
how buying it is in their best interest, not your own. The legal team should
be able to help with information on legal obligations. If the company receives
confidential information from customers, good security is an asset that may
increase business. Universities may be able to get more lucrative industrial
sponsorship if they can show that they can keep confidential information
safe. Companies selling services or support can also gain customer confidence
from demonstrating their security consciousness. Think about what you
(a security-conscious person) would want from your company if you were
a customer. If you can provide it and market it, that is a competitive advantage.

Also gather data on what the company's competitors are doing in terms
of investing in security or at least data on other similar-size companies in
reasonably similar industries. Senior management will want to be able to
gauge whether they are spending too much, too little, or about the right
amount on security. If possible, produce metrics on the work that the security
team is doing. Metrics are discussed further in Section 7.2.3. Also consider
getting a formal risk analysis performed for your company by an outside

---

[9]In a university, the customers are the students and the funding bodies; in a nonprofit or
government organization, the customers are the constituents that they serve. All organizations
have an equivalent of customers and shareholders.

group. Senior management likes to have solid data on which to base its decisions.

> ### Case Study: Security Can Be a Competitive Advantage
>
> An EDA company received chip designs from its customers on a regular basis for a variety of reasons. The company had to be very careful with this extremely valuable third-party IP. The company was very security aware, with good security measures in place and an information protection team. The information protection team considered its security program to be a competitive advantage and marketed it as such to its customers and to the management team. This helped to maintain the high level of support for security within the company.

To sell security to the people who will be using the systems, you need to ensure that they will be able to work effectively in an environment that is comfortable for them. You also need to show them that it is in their best interests or the best interest of the company. If you can provide them with a system that does not interfere with their work, but provides extra security, they will be happy to use it. However, you do need to be particularly careful not to lose the trust of these customers. If you provide slow, cumbersome, or invasive systems, they will lose faith in your ability to provide a security system that does not adversely affect them and will be unwilling to try future security systems. Credibility is very important for a successful sale.

To sell security to the SAs who will be maintaining the systems, looking after the people who use those systems, and potentially installing the systems, you need to make sure that the systems you design are easy to use and implement; have simple, straight-forward setups; and are reliable and do not cause problems for their customers. You also will need to provide them with tools or access for debugging problems. Supporting a security system ideally should not put any more overhead on them than supporting any other system.

7.2 The Icing

This section discusses ideals for your security program. To be able to achieve these, you will need to have a solid infrastructure and security program already in place. One of the ideals of the security team and the information protection team should be to make security awareness pervasive throughout the company. The security team should also ideally stay up-to-date with the industry, which means maintaining contacts within the industry and tracking new technologies and directions. Another ideal for the security team is to be able to produce metrics to describe how the team is performing and the benefits of the security program.

7.2.1   Make Security Pervasive

A good information protection program will make everyone aware of security and IP issues. For example, the information protection team at a company where Christine worked ran an awareness campaign with the help of the marketing group that included a series of cartoon posters of some common ways that information was stolen and raising awareness of laptop theft at airports.

If you can make security a part of the way that people work and think, the job of the security team will become much easier. People will automatically get the security team involved early in projects, they will notice strange behavior on systems that may indicate a break-in, and they will be careful with sensitive information.

Case Study: Making Security Pervasive

At IBM, there was a "Clean Desk Policy," which said that all paperwork, confidential or not, was to be locked inside your desk every night and confidential documents had to be locked away at all times. In general, infractions caused a note to be left on your desk by either security, IT, or facilities, depending on who was responsible for checking that particular office. Multiple infractions were dealt with differently, depending on the site, but there was a specific set of punishment criteria. At least one person was fired for leaving highly confidential information out on her desk.

IBM had entire office blocks of offices or conference rooms without windows because of the possibility of people spying through the windows with telescopes. Security is pervasive and very much a part of the corporate culture.

Case Study: Raising Security Awareness

Motorola instituted a program for Protection of Proprietary Information (POPI). It was a security awareness program that included informational posters reminding people to be careful of proprietary information, even within the company's buildings. They had reminders at the printers that all printouts would be cleared away at a certain time in the evening, so that people didn't print something and leave it there for anyone to see or pick up. They had little table-tents reminding people: "Please don't leave proprietary information on my desk while I am out." They also had what they called "POPI cops" within each group who would periodically go around and check everyone's desks and whiteboards for sensitive information. They left either a green "Well done!" note or a red "You did the following things wrong...." note on each desk after it had been checked.

People generally want to do the right thing. If you keep reminding them what it is and they keep trying, it becomes second nature.

7.2.2 Stay Up-to-Date: Contacts and Technologies

Contacts within the security industry can be a good source of information on current attacks and vulnerabilities, varying product experiences, and emerging technologies. Going to security conferences is a good way to build these contacts and keeps you several months ahead of the rest of the industry. Security professionals are typically more paranoid about disclosing their experiences to people that they do not know well, so it is important to attend lots of conferences, get involved and recognized, and build a good rapport with others at the conferences.

You should also aim to keep up with all the new technologies that are being developed, their supposed benefits, how they work, and their deployment and operational needs. In doing this, you will need to develop a skill for distinguishing snake oil from a useful product. Advice can be found in Matt Curtin's *Snake Oil Warning Signs: Encryption Software to Avoid* (Curtin 1999a, b).

For any new product idea, there typically are several fundamentally different approaches taken by the vendors, and it is often difficult to tell how successful any of them will be. However, watching the development of the different approaches, understanding the operational implications, and knowing the people behind various products helps us to predict which products and technologies might succeed.

7.2.3 Produce Metrics

Metrics for security are very difficult. As mentioned in Section 7.1.5, selling security is like selling insurance. If you can produce some form of metrics that makes sense, describing at some level how the security team is performing and what value they are giving the company for its money, then it will be easier to convince management to fund security infrastructure projects.

Having an external auditing team, as discussed in Section 7.1.5, may be a useful source of metrics. For example, you could describe the area that was audited or attacked, the level of success, and the possible cost of a breach in security of that area. If problems were found with an area, you can provide information on what it would cost to fix it and then track your improvements over time.

If you have a clear security perimeter, you may be able (for example, using an intrusion detection system) to gather data on the number of attacks or possible attacks seen outside and inside the security perimeter, thus enabling you to graph the level of protection provided by your security perimeter.

You may be able to start with simple graphs of the number of machines that are visible to people outside the company, statistics on the number of services that each of those is making available, and the number of vulnerabilities. You could also graph the number of security patches that the team needed to make overall by OS and by application.

Good metrics should help management and other nonsecurity people within the company understand at some level what you are doing and how well you are doing it. Good metrics help build confidence in the security team for the rest of the company.

7.3   Organization Profiles

In this section, we present a brief overview of the stages of development of a reasonable company security program, depending on the size and function of the company. This section is meant as a guideline only to give you a sense of whether you are behind the curve or ahead of it and how your security program should develop as your company grows.

We describe as examples a sample security program at a small, medium, and large company, an e-commerce site, and a university. For these examples, a small company typically has between 20 and 100 employees. A medium-size company has around 1,000 to 3,000 employees, and a large company has more than 20,000 employees.

7.3.1   Small Company

In a small company with one or two SAs, security will be a fairly small component of one SA's job. They should have an acceptable use policy and should be thinking about a monitoring and privacy policy. The SAs will probably know just about everything that is going on and so will probably not need to form or participate in any formal cross-functional teams. The company will be primarily concerned with perimeter security, particularly if it is a young company. The SAs should be considering a strong authentication mechanism, making management aware of it, and deciding when it is appropriate for the company to invest in one.

If the small company is a start-up, particularly in the computer industry, there may well be a requirement for engineering to have very open access to the Internet for immediate access to new technologies as they become available. In this case, the company should look at whether a lab environment will work for that, and, if not, at how to protect engineering as best possible without interfering with their work and how to protect the rest of the company from engineering.

7.3.2 Medium-size Company

A medium-size company should have a small staff of full-time SAs. These people should have primary roles of an architect and some implementers and also take on secondary responsibilities from the other security roles described. The responsibilities of the security function should be centralized, even if SAs in remote locations take on some security work as all or part of their job. Remote SAs who have security responsibilities should report to the security group for that aspect of their work.

The security architect will do quite a lot of implementation, and the implementers will also take on the operations responsibilities. Policies will be the responsibility of the architect and possibly the manager of the group. Auditing may be taken on by an implementer or the architect, or they may work with some external consultants to build an auditing program. The company should have all of the basic policies mentioned in Section 7.1.3 and at least a rudimentary auditing program. There should be an information protection group with representatives from the legal, facilities, human resources, IT, and sales departments, and core business groups. The company should have a security awareness program driven by the information protection group.

The company should have significant security infrastructure. It should have a strong authentication system that is centralized, robust, and thoroughly deployed. It will probably have many remote access mechanisms that should all be linked to the authentication system. The company will almost certainly have connections to third parties for a variety of business reasons. These connections should make use of standard security mechanisms and share infrastructure where possible and appropriate. The company may have areas that require a higher level of security and have additional protection from the rest of the company. It may also have lab environments that are more exposed, but from which the rest of the company is protected.

7.3.3 Large Company

The biggest problems that large companies face are related to size. Incident response, policy conformance, and tracking changes all become more difficult.

A large company should have several dedicated staff for each of the different security roles. They will probably be split across administrative business units, each with their own policies and security perimeter, with clear methods of exchanging information between the business units. Each business unit should have all the policies described in Section 7.1.3 and more, as appropriate.

The company should have a large security infrastructure with a comprehensive auditing program. There should be many interdepartmental groups that focus on security and security awareness programs in each of the business units.

Many areas will have much higher physical and electronic security requirements than others. In large companies, typically there is less de facto trust of all employees. There is simply more opportunity for accidental or malicious disclosure of sensitive information.

There will certainly be many third-party connections, with many restrictions and contracts relating to their use. There may also be lab environments where research networks are more exposed to external networks.

Mergers and aquisitions bring new challenges. Resolving differences in security policies, culture and attitudes, and integrating network inventories (network discovery) become major endevours for large companies.

7.3.4   E-commerce Site

A company that conducts a significant amount of business over the Internet has special requirements, in addition to those already mentioned. In particular, it must have a clear division between "corporate" machines and "online service" machines. Online service machines are the machines that are used for conducting business over the Internet. Corporate machines are those that are used for anything other than providing the online services to customers.

No matter what the size of the e-commerce company, it must have at least one full-time security professional on staff. It will also need to scale its security staff a lot more quickly than other companies of similar size because of the nature of the business. The company will also need to develop policies, for example, regarding protecting customer information, more quickly than other companies of similar size.

E-commerce companies need separate policies governing access to corporate machines and online service machines. No matter what the size of the company, it is critical to have an authorization matrix that defines the level of access to each type of online service machine. The company must also pay special attention to customer billing information, including credit card information, addresses, and telephone numbers. An e-commerce company must also focus on trying to prevent DoS attacks against its online service infrastructure, which is clearly business-critical.

7.3.5   University

The university environment is typically very different from that of a business. In a business, the people who have legitimate access to the network are typically quite trusted by definition.[10] The company is normally willing to make the assumption that the employees are working toward the best interests of the company.[11] In a university, however, the people who have access to the network are typically not trusted by default, in part because physical access is quite open.

A university typically will have administrative networks and computers that have restricted access and tight security controls. It will also have academic networks that are quite open. Frequently, it will have open access to and from the Internet because it is a research environment where openness and learning are considered to go hand-in-hand.

Universities usually have less money to spend on their computing environment in general and security in particular and so are in some ways similar to a small company. A university must have an acceptable use policy and a monitoring and privacy policy that every computer user signs before getting access to the computing systems.

Recall that the first questions you need to ask involve what you are trying to protect, from whom it must be protected, and what it is worth. Universities typically share and publish their research, and thus the value of that research is not as high as the design of the next computer microprocessor or the details about a new drug. For academic networks, the management at the university may determine that they are interested in preventing large-scale loss of service or data. They may also determine that some people who have legitimate access to the systems should be considered a threat.

In a university environment, you will need to have in-depth security on key servers and additional security around the administrative networks. For the open access machines in labs, you need to have a good autoinstall and autopatch system, as described in Chapter 1, and you need to find the balance among security, research, and teaching needs.

7.4 Conclusion

Security is a large and complex area that requires even more communication skills than other areas of system administration and must be a cooperative effort that crosses administrative divisions. It should be built on solid foundations in policies that are approved and supported by senior management. Building security systems relies on the other systems infrastructure.

---

[10]There often are different levels of access and protection even within a company, but usually everybody in a company has access to all but the most sensitive information, unless it is a very large company that is effectively divided into smaller subcompanies.

[11]This may not be wise from a security point of view, but it is a pragmatic business compromise that most executives make.

There are some areas that the technical staff should concentrate on and others with which management can help. The technical staff must consider business needs, convenience for their customers, staying up-to-date with attacks and vulnerabilities, building a solid authentication and authorization system, and selecting good security software. Ideally, the technical staff should also do their best to keep up-to-date with what is happening in the security world by building good contacts within the industry and keeping an eye on new technologies.

The security group's management can help with resources and staffing, establishing an incident response team, engaging external auditors, and selling security to other groups within the company.

Ideally, security should be a pervasive part of the company culture. This sort of company culture takes a lot of time and effort to build and will only really succeed if it comes from senior management. One of the best ways to gain management support is to produce meaningful metrics on the work that the security team is doing.

Exercises

1. What security polices do you have? Which of them need to be updated? Which policies listed in this chapter are missing? What problems is this causing?

2. Why do you think we recommend that the Network Connectivity Policy stipulate the different forms of third-party connectivity that are supported?

3. What third party connections does your institution have? Do you know beyond all doubt that those are the only ones? What about small remote offices? Can you categorize those connections into types of access?

4. Do you have infrastructure to support bringing up a new third-party connection easily? If not, try designing such an infrastructure and afterward, see if you can fit your existing third-party connections into that infrastructure.

5. What three changes in security would you recommend right now to your management?

Chapter 8

Disaster Recovery and Data Integrity

A disaster recovery plan looks at what disasters could hit the company and sets out a plan for responding to those disasters. Disaster recovery planning also involves implementing ways to mitigate potential disasters and making preparations to enable quick restoration of key services. It also identifies what those key services are and how quickly they need to be restored.

All sites need to do some level of disaster recovery planning. Disaster recovery planners must consider what happens if something catastrophic occurs at any one of their organization's sites and how they can recover from it. We will concentrate on the electronic data aspects of disaster recovery. However, this part of the plan should be built as part of a larger program in order to meet the company's legal and financial obligations. Several books are dedicated to disaster recovery planning, and we recommend them for further reading (Fulmer 2000, Levitt 1997, and Schreider 1998).

Building a disaster recovery plan involves understanding the risks that your site faces and your company's legal and fiduciary responsibilities. From this basis, you can begin your preparations. This chapter will give you a feel for what is involved in building a disaster recovery plan for your site.

8.1   The Basics

Like any project, building a disaster recovery plan starts with understanding the requirements. To understand the requirements, you need to understand what disasters could afflict your site, what the chances are of those disasters striking, the cost to your company if they do strike, and how quickly the various parts of your business need to be revived. Once you and your management understand the requirements, you can get a budget allocated for the project and start looking at how to meet, and preferably beat, those requirements.

8.1.1   What Is a Disaster?

A disaster is a catastrophic event that causes a massive outage affecting an entire building or site. It can be a natural disaster such as an earthquake, hurricane, tornado, plague, lightning strike, fire, or flood. Or it can be a man-made disaster such as a bomb, a massive loss of power, or the ever-increasing problem of idiots with backhoes (Anonymous 1997) It is anything that has a significant impact on your company's ability to do business.

Lack of Planning Can Cause Risk-Taking

A computer equipment manufacturer had a facility in the west of Ireland. A fire started in the building, and the staff knew that the fire protection system was inadequate and the building would be very badly damaged. Several staff members went to the data center and started throwing equipment out of the window because it had a better chance of surviving the fall than the fire. Other staff members then carried the equipment up the hill to their neighboring building. The staff members in the burning building left when they judged the fire hazard was too great. All the equipment that they threw out the window actually survived, and the facility was operational again in record time. However, the lack of a disaster recovery plan and adequate protection systems resulted in staff members risking their lives. Fortunately, no one was badly injured in this incident. Their actions were in breach of fire safety codes and extremely risky because no one there was qualified to judge when the fire had become too hazardous.

8.1.2   Risk Analysis

The first step that is necessary in building a disaster recovery plan is to perform a risk analysis.

Risk management is a good candidate for outsourcing because it is a specialized skill that is required periodically, not daily. A large company may get external risk analysts to perform the risk analysis while having an in-house person responsible for risk management.

A risk analysis involves determining what disasters the company is at risk of experiencing and what the chances are of those disasters occurring. The risk analyst then looks at the likely cost to the company if a disaster of each type occurred. The company then uses this information to determine approximately how much money is reasonable to spend on trying to mitigate the effects of each type of disaster.

The approximate budget for risk mitigation is:

(probable cost of disaster – probable cost after mitigation) × *risk of disaster*

For example, if a company's premises has one chance in a million of being affected by flooding and a flood would cost the company $10 million, then the budget for mitigating the effects of the flood would be in the range of $10. In other words, it's not even worth stocking up on sand bags in preparation for a flood.

On the other hand, if a company has 1 chance in 3,000 of being within ten miles of the epicenter of an earthquake measuring 5.0 on the Richter scale, which would cause a $60-million loss, the budget for reducing or preventing that damage will be in the $20,000 range.

A simpler, smaller-scale example is a large site that has a single point of failure where all LANs are tied together by one large router. If it died, it would take one day to repair, and there is a 70 percent chance that failure will occur once every 24 months. The outage would cause 1,000 people to be unable to work for a day. The company estimates the loss of productivity to be $68,000. When the SAs go looking for redundancy for the router, the budget is approximately $23,800. They also need to investigate the cost of reducing the outage time to four hours, for example, by increasing support contract payments. If that costs a reasonable amount, then it further reduces the amount the company would lose and therefore the amount it should spend on full redundancy.

This is a somewhat simplified view of the process. Each disaster can occur to different degrees with different likelihoods and a wide range of cost implications. Damage prevention for one level of a particular disaster will probably have mitigating effects on the amount of damage sustained at a higher level of the same disaster. All of this complexity is taken into account by a professional risk analyst when he recommends a budget for the different types of disaster preparedness.

8.1.3   Legal Obligations

Beyond the basic cost to the company, additional considerations need to taken into account as part of the disaster recovery planning process. Commercial companies have legal obligations to their vendors, customers, and shareholders in terms of meeting contract obligations. Public companies have to abide by the laws of the stock markets on which they are traded. Universities have contractual obligations to their students. Building codes and work-safety regulations also must be followed.

The legal department should be able to elaborate on these obligations. Typically they are of the form "the company must be able to resume shipping product within one week" or "the company can delay reporting quarterly results by at most three days under these circumstances." Those obligations translate into requirements for the disaster recovery plan. They define how quickly various pieces of the physical and electronic infrastructure must be restored to working order. Restoring individual parts of the company to working order before the entire infrastructure is operational requires an in-depth understanding of what pieces of infrastructure those parts rely on and a detailed plan of how to get them working. Meeting the time commitments also requires an understanding of how long restoring those components will take. We will look at that further in Section 8.1.5.

8.1.4   Damage Limitation

Damage limitation is about reducing the cost of the disasters. Some damage limitation can come at little or no cost to the company through advance planning and good processes. Most damage limitation does involve additional cost to the company and is subject to the cost/benefit analysis that is performed by the risk analysts.

For little or no cost, there are ways to reduce the risk of a disaster causing significant damage to the company or limit the amount of damage that the disaster can inflict. For example, in an area prone to flooding, placing critical services above ground level may not significantly increase construction and move-in costs but avoids problems in the future. Choosing equipment that can be properly rack-mounted and reasonably sturdy racks to bolt it into rather than putting equipment on shelves can significantly reduce the impact of a minor earthquake for little or no extra cost. Using lightning rods in the construction of buildings in an area that is prone to lightning storms is also a cheap way of limiting damage. These are particularly economical steps because they fix the problem once, rather than requiring a recurring cost.

Limiting the damage caused by a major disaster is more costly and always should be subject to a cost/benefit analysis. For example, a data center could be built in an underground military-style bunker to protect against tornados and bombs. In an earthquake zone, there are very expensive mechanisms for allowing racks to move independently in a constrained manner to reduce the risk of computer backplanes shearing, the major issue with rigidly fixed racks during a strong earthquake. These mechanisms for limiting damage are so costly that only the largest companies are likely to be able to justify implementing them.

Other damage limitation mechanisms fall somewhere between "almost free" and "outlandishly expensive." Fire prevention systems typically fall into that category. It is wise to consider implementing a fire protection system that is designed to limit damage to equipment in the data center when activated. Local laws and human safety concerns limit what is possible in this area, but popular systems at the time of writing include inert gas systems and selective, limited-area, water-based systems with early warning mechanisms that permit an operator to detect and resolve a problem, such as a disk or power supply catching fire, before the fire protection system is activated. Systems for detecting moisture under raised data center floors or in rarely visited uninterruptible power supply (UPS) or generator rooms are also moderately priced damage limitation mechanisms.

Another area that often merits attention is loss of power to a building or campus. Short power outages, power spikes, and brown-outs are not unheard of and can cause lost productivity and equipment damage. UPS systems condition the power so that the equipment gets a consistent smooth power supply. They also protect against short outages on the order of a few minutes. Protection against longer power outages requires a generator in addition to the UPS and some gear to switch between utility and generator power. Some sites may need to provide protected power to other locations in addition to the data center. For example, a biotechnology company may require protected power to freezers that contain samples. Other companies may need to keep their call centers running. The more things that are on protected power and the longer the company needs to be able to keep them running, the more expensive the protected power solution will be.

These issues are also covered in Chapter 17, particularly Section 17.1.11.

8.1.5 Preparation

Even with a reasonable amount of damage limitation controls in place, your organization may still experience a disaster situation. Part of your disaster planning must be preparation for this eventuality. Being prepared for a disaster means being able to restore the essential systems to working order in a timely manner, as defined by your legal obligations, which were discussed in Section 8.1.3.

Restoring services after a disaster involves rebuilding the necessary data and services on new equipment if the old equipment is not operational. That means that you need to arrange a source of replacement hardware in advance from companies that provide this service. You also need to have another site to which this equipment can be sent if the primary site cannot be used because of safety reasons, lack of power, or lack of connectivity. Make sure that the company providing the standby equipment knows where to send it in an emergency. Make sure that you get turnaround time commitments from them and that you know what hardware they will be able to provide on short notice. Don't forget to take the turnaround time on this equipment into account when calculating how long the entire process will take. If a disaster is large enough to require their services, chances are they will have other customers that are also affected. Find out how they plan to handle the situation in which both you and your neighbor have the right to the only large Sun server that was stockpiled.

Once you have the machines, you need to rebuild the data and services on them. Typically, this process involves first building the system to the point at which it is capable of restoring data and then restoring it. This involves having backups of the data with an off-site storage and retrieval service. It also means being able to easily identify which tapes are required for restoring the essential services. This part of the basic preparation is built on infrastructure that your site should have already put in place. An ongoing part of the disaster preparation is to try retrieving tapes from the off-site storage company on a regular basis to see how long it takes. This time is subtracted from the total amount of time available to completely restore the relevant systems to working order. If it takes too long to get the tapes, it may be impossible to complete the rebuild on time.

These issues are also covered in Chapter 21, particularly Section 21.2.2.

A site usually will need to have important documents archived at a document repository for safekeeping. These sites specialize in disaster recovery scenarios. If your company has such a site, you may want to consider also using that site to house the data tapes.

Remember that you may need power, telephone, and network connectivity as part of restoring the services. Work with the facilities group on these aspects. It may be advisable to arrange an emergency office location for the critical functions as part of the disaster plan.

Good Preparation for an Emergency Facility

A company had a call center in California that was used by its customers, who were predominantly large financial institutions. The company had a well-rehearsed procedure to execute in case of a disaster that affected the call center building. They had external outlets for providing power and the call center phone services and appropriate cables and equipment standing by, including tents and folding tables and chairs. When a strong earthquake struck in 1991, the call center was rapidly relocated outside and was operational again within minutes. Not long after they were set up, they received lots of calls from their customers in New York, who just wanted to make sure that their services were still available if they required them. The call center staff calmly reassured their customers that all services were operating normally. Their customers had no idea that they were talking to someone who was sitting on a chair in the grass outside the building. The call center had to remain outside for several days until the building was certified safe. But from the customers' perspectives, it remained operational the entire time.

The plan to relocate the call center outside in the case of emergency worked well because the most likely emergency was an earthquake and the weather was likely to be dry, at least for long enough for the tents to be put up. The company prepared well for its most likely disaster scenario.

8.1.6 Data Integrity

Data integrity means ensuring that data is not altered by external sources. Data can be corrupted maliciously by viruses or individuals. It can also be corrupted inadvertently by individuals, bugs in programs, and undetected hardware malfunctions. For important data, consider ways to ensure integrity as part of day-to-day operations or the backup or archival process. For example, data that should not change can be checked against a read-only checksum of the data. Virus-checking programs should be ubiquitous and constantly upgraded to stay current. Databases that should experience small changes or should only have data added, such as source code control systems or databases of gene sequences, should be checked for unexpectedly large changes or deletions. Exploit your knowledge of the data on your systems to automate integrity checking.

Disaster planning also involves ensuring that a complete and correct copy of the corporate data can be produced and restored to the systems. For disaster recovery, it must be a recent, coherent copy of the data with all databases in sync. Data integrity meshes well with disaster recovery.

Industrial espionage and intellectual property (IP) theft are not uncommon, and a company may find itself needing to fight for its IP rights in a court of law. The ability to accurately restore data as it existed on a certain date can also be used to prove ownership of IP. To be used as evidence, the date of the information retrieved must be accurately known and the data must be in a consistent state. For both disaster recovery purposes and use of the data as evidence in a court, the SAs need to know that the data has not been tampered with.

It is important to make sure the implementers put in place the data integrity mechanisms that the system designers recommend. It is inadvisable to wait for corruption to occur before recognizing the value of these systems.

8.2   The Icing

The ultimate preparation for a disaster is to have fully redundant versions of everything that can take over when the primary fails. In other words, have a redundant site with redundant systems. In this section, we look at having a redundant site and some ways a company might be able to make it more cost-effective.

8.2.1   Redundant Site

For companies where high availability is critical, the next level of disaster planning is to have a fully redundant second site in a different location that will not be affected by the same disaster. For most companies, this is an expensive dream that they can only aspire to be able to afford. However, if a company has two locations with data centers, it may be possible to duplicate some of the critical services across both data centers so that the only problem that remains to be solved is how the people who use those services get access to the redundant site.

Rather than permanently having live redundant equipment at the second site, it can instead be used as an alternative location for rebuilding the services. If the company has a contract for an emergency supply of equipment, that equipment could be sent to the alternative data center site. If the site that was affected by the disaster is badly damaged, this may be the fastest way to have the services up and running.

Another option is to designate some services at each site as less critical and to use the equipment from those services to rebuild the critical services from the damaged site.

Sometimes, you are lucky enough to have a design that compartmentalizes various pieces, making it easy to design a redundant site.

Case Study: Security Boundaries Can Ease Implementing Redundancy

Lumeta's service delivery architecture included well-defined security zones with trust relationships between those zones. The zones were well segmented, which enabled reliability requirements to be attached to each one. The barriers were well defined, which enabled connectivity arrangements to be designed for each. The most secure zone was isolated and therefore could physically be anywhere in the world or cloned for redundancy. Having a well-defined set of zones made it possible to plan appropriate disaster recovery plans for each zone.

8.2.2 Security Disasters

A growing concern is security disasters. Someone breaks into the corporate web site and changes the logo to be obscene. Someone steals the database of credit card numbers from your e-commerce site. A virus deletes all the files it can access. These are different from natural disasters because no physical harm may be done and the attack may not be from a physically local phenomenon.

A similar risk analysis can be performed to determine the kind of measures required to protect data. Architecture decisions have a risk component. One can manage the risk many ways—by building barriers around the system or by monitoring the system so that it can be shut down quickly in the event of an attack.

We constantly see sites that purchase large, canned systems without asking for an explanation of the security risks of such systems. Although there is no such thing as a perfectly secure system, a vendor should be able to explain the product's security structure, the risk factors, and how recovery would occur in the event of data loss.

Constructing security policies and procedures that take into account disaster recovery plans is covered in Chapter 7, Security Policy.

8.2.3 Media Relations

When a disaster occurs, there is a good chance that the media will want to know what happened, what effect it is having on the company, and when services will be restored. Sadly, the answer to all three questions is usually, "We aren't sure." This can be the worst answer you can give a reporter. Handling the media badly during a disaster can cause bigger problems than the original disaster.

There are two simple recommendations on this topic: First, have a public relations (PR) firm on retainer before a disaster so that you aren't trying to hire one as the disaster is happening. Some PR firms specialize in disaster management and some are proficient at handling security-related disasters. Second, plan ahead. Have a plan ahead of time that details how you will deal with the media. This plan should include who will talk to the media, what kind of things will and will not be said, and what the chain of command is if the designated decision-makers aren't available. Anyone who talks to the media should receive training from your PR firm.

Notice that these recommendations have one thing in common: They both require planning ahead of time. Never be in a disaster without a media plan.

8.3   Conclusion

The most important aspect of disaster planning is understanding what services are the most critical to the business and what the time constraints are for restoring those services. The disaster planner also needs to know what disasters are likely to happen and how costly they would be before he can complete a risk analysis and determine the company's budget for limiting the damage.

A disaster plan should be built with consideration of those criteria. It should account for the time to get new equipment, retrieve the off-site backups, and rebuild the critical systems from scratch. Doing so requires advance planning for getting the correct equipment and being able to quickly determine which backup tapes are needed for rebuilding the critical systems.

The disaster planner must look for simple ways to limit damage, as well as more complex and expensive ways. Preparations that are automatic and become part of the infrastructure are most effective. Fire containment, water detection, earthquake bracing, and proper rack-mount equipment fall into this category. The disaster planner also must prepare a plan for a team of people to execute in case of emergency. Simple plans are often the most effective. The team members must be familiar with their individual roles and should practice a few times a year.

Full redundancy, including a redundant site, is an ideal that is beyond the budget of most companies. If a company has a second data center site, however, there are ways to incorporate it into the disaster plan at reasonable expense.

Exercises

1. Which business units in your company would need to be up and running first after a disaster, and how quickly would they need to be operational?

2. What commitments does your company have to its customers, and how do those influence your disaster planning?

3. What disasters are most likely to hit each of your sites? How big an area might that disaster affect, and how many of your company's buildings could be affected?

4. What would the cost be to your company if a moderate disaster hit one of its locations?

5. What forms of disaster limitation do you have in place now?

6. What forms of disaster limitation would you like to implement? How much would each of them cost?

7. If you lost use of a data center facility because of a disaster, how would you restore service?

8. What are your plans for dealing with the media in the event of a disaster? What is the name of the PR firm you retain to help you?

Ethics

What are the policies that a site should have related to ethics? What is considered ethical behavior for system administrators? This chapter discusses both of these issues.

Ethics are the principles of conduct that govern a group of people. Ethics are different from morals. *Morals* are a proclamation of what is right and good; such a discussion is beyond the scope of this book.

If your organization involves you in drafting the ethical guidelines for all network users or just the SAs, bring this chapter along. We hope to provide you with the tools you need to get the job done.

9.1 The Basics

Organizations usually have various ethics-related policies for their employees and other affiliates. Ethics policies concerning computer use fall into two categories: those that apply to all users and those that apply only to privileged users, such as SAs and database administrators. In general, as an SA, you need to be especially careful about following company policies. You have access to confidential information that most other employees cannot see; as a result, you have special responsibilities.

9.1.1   Informed Consent

SAs can draw on medical ethics for comparison because doctors and SAs both operate on live subjects. There is a principle in medical ethics known as *informed consent*. It has two parts: Before something is done to a person, she should be fully educated as to all the treatment options, all the possible benefits and detriments of those options, and the various probabilities of success—this is the "informed" part. It should be explained in whatever way the person is competent to understand, and she must be given the opportunity to permit the treatment or refuse it, without coercion of any sort—this is the "consent" part. This is not possible in some situations such as someone being legally incompetent (unable to understand the ramifications) or unable to give consent (for example, the person is in a coma and has no next of kin). In these cases, the generally accepted standard is to fully satisfy all three of the following conditions: The procedure must have a high likelihood of success; it must be in the patient's best interest (rather than the doctor's or someone else's), such that if the procedure is successful, it is felt that the person would be thankful in retrospect; and, finally, all other avenues must have been attempted first. In other words, violating informed consent must be a last resort.

These principles can be applied in many SA tasks. People should understand the rules under which they are living. For example, a service level agreement (SLA) should specify that maintenance will be done only in certain hours, and your customers should be aware of those hours. Sometimes, a compute server is designated for long-term jobs such as simulations. If the simulation software doesn't have a checkpointing feature, a reboot might lose days or weeks of work. If a reboot is absolutely unavoidable, the SLA might specify that the current users of the machine will be notified (informed consent). On the other hand, compute servers for shorter jobs might have a blanket SLA that just specifies a 15-minute warning. The SLA informs your customers how you will be operating in various situations.

9.1.2   Professional Code of Conduct

SAGE, the System Administrators' Guild, has granted us permission to print their Code of Ethics.[1] We are doing so because we feel that it does an excellent job of putting into words our feelings regarding the need for SAs to maintain an extremely high level of professionalism. It's a useful

---

[1]SAGE http://www.sage.org is a Special Technical Group of The USENIX Association, 2560 Ninth Street, Suite 215, Berkeley, CA 94710; http://www.usenix.org. Hal Miller is the original author of the Code of Ethics.

starting point for writing your own corporate Code of Conduct policy. It is intentionally *not* a set of enforceable laws, an enumeration of procedures, proposed responses to situations, all-encompassing, or an enumeration of sanctions and punishments.

The SAGE Code of Ethics

Canon 1: *The integrity of a system administrator must be beyond reproach.*

A system administrator may come into contact with privileged information on a regular basis and thus has a duty to the owners of such information to both keep confidential and to protect the confidentiality of all such information.

Protecting the integrity of information includes ensuring that neither system administrators nor unauthorized users unnecessarily access, make any changes to, or divulge data not belonging to them. It includes all appropriate effort, in accordance with industry-accepted practices, by the system administrator to enforce security measures to protect the computers and the data contained on them.

System administrators must uphold the law and policies as established for the systems and networks they manage, and make all efforts to require the same adherence from their users. Where the law is not clear, or appears to be in conflict with their ethical standards, system administrators must exercise sound judgment, and are also obliged to take steps to have the law upgraded or corrected as is possible within their jurisdiction.

Canon 2: *A system administrator shall not unnecessarily infringe upon the rights of users.*

System administrators shall not act with, nor tolerate from others, discrimination between authorized users based on any commonly recognized grounds (e.g., age, gender, religion, etc.), except where such discrimination (e.g., with respect to unauthorized users as a class) is a necessary part of their job, and then only to the extent that such treatment is required in dealing with the issue at hand.

System administrators will not exercise their special powers to access any private information other than when necessary to their role as system managers, and then only to the degree necessary to perform that role, while remaining within established site policies. Regardless of how it was obtained, system administrators will maintain the confidentiality of all private information.

Canon 3: *Communications of system administrators with all whom they may come in contact shall be kept to the highest standards of professional behavior.*

System administrators must keep users informed about computing matters that might affect them, such as conditions of acceptable use, sharing and availability of common resources, maintenance of security, occurrence of system monitoring, and any applicable legal obligations. It is incumbent upon the system administrator to ensure that such information is presented in a manner calculated to ensure user awareness and understanding.

Honesty and timeliness are keys to ensuring accurate communication to users. A system administrator shall, when advice is sought, give it impartially, accompanied by any necessary statement of the limitations of personal knowledge or bias. Any potential conflicts of interest must be fully and immediately declared.

Canon 4: *The continuance of professional education is critical to maintaining currency as a system administrator.*

Since technology in computing continues to make significant strides, a system administrator must take an appropriate level of action to update and enhance personal technical knowledge. Reading, study, acquiring training, and sharing knowledge and experience are requirements to maintaining currency and ensuring the customer base of the advantages and security of advances in the field.

Canon 5: *A system administrator must maintain an exemplary work ethic.*

System administrators must be tireless in their effort to maintain high levels of quality in their work. Day to day operation in the field of system administration requires significant energy and resiliency. The system administrator is placed in a position of such significant impact upon the business of the organization that the required level of trust can only be maintained by exemplary behavior.

Canon 6: *At all times system administrators must display professionalism in the performance of their duties.*

All manner of behavior must reflect highly upon the profession as a whole. Dealing with recalcitrant users, upper management, vendors, or other system administrators calls for the utmost in patience and care to ensure that mutual respect is never at risk.

Actions that enhance the image of the profession are encouraged. Actions that enlarge the understanding of the social and legal issues in computing are part of the role. System administrators are obligated to assist the community at large in areas that are fundamental to the advancement and integrity of local, national, and international computing resources.

9.1.3   Network/Computer User Code of Conduct

A User Code of Conduct offers guidelines for acceptable uses of an organization's computers. Every organization needs one. A code of conduct might address some of the following points: Under what circumstances is personal use of employer equipment permitted? What types of personal use are forbidden? For example, can you run a fledgling "dot com" out of your cubicle? How about using your computer for surfing "adult" web sites? How do the rules change if you're using company equipment at home? A code of conduct should define and forbid threatening or harassing communications, explain how to report them, and explain how reports are processed.

Sometimes, these guidelines are part of the acceptable use policy mentioned in Chapter 7.

Codes of conduct at academic institutions are usually very different from codes of conduct in industry. The differences are due to requirements for academic freedom and the fact that, for many students, the campus *is* home.

You can find sample policies through various industry and academic consortia. They often have a web site with a collection of actual policies from various organizations. Dijker (1999) is one such archive. The best way to write a policy is to use an archive to find a policy whose philosophy is close to your own and use it as a base document.

9.1.4 Privileged Access Code of Conduct

Some users need privileged access to do their jobs. The ability to write and debug device drivers, install software for more than just yourself, and perform many other tasks all require root or administrator access. Organizations need special codes of conduct for these people; as we all know, privileges can be abused.

This code of conduct should include the following points:

- The individual acknowledges that privileged access comes with a responsibility to use it properly.
- The individual will use elevated access privileges solely for necessary work-related uses. Management should explicitly describe these uses.
- The company acknowledges that mistakes happen, and encourages procedures for minimizing the damage a mistake may cause. For example, SAs should make backups before they make any changes to something.
- Procedures for what to do if privileged access gives someone information about something that wouldn't have otherwise been made public.

  For example, say an SA is fixing a problem with a mail server, and she accidentally sees a message implying that someone is running a gambling operation from his cubicle. What should the SA do? The policy should describe what the organization expects from her.

  In another scenario, say a privileged user learns about something that is less nefarious, but just as important. Say she sees a message about a pending merger. What should she do? Again the code of conduct should be explicit, and should explain what an employee should do if she comes across privileged company information.

- A warning about the possible penalties for violating the policy. The list should include termination.

People with privileged access should sign a statement saying that they have read the code of conduct for privileged users, and they should be given a copy of it for their files. As a good security measure, the SA team should track who has privileged access to which systems. This practice is especially useful for alerting the SAs to remove access privileges when a privileged user leaves the organization. Some organizations have a policy that privileged access expires every 12 months unless the form is re-signed. This practice encourages regular policy reviews. Automatic reminders are another good tool.

❖ **The Right Reminder at the Right Time**   sudo (Snyder et al. 1986) is a popular program that controls privileged access to UNIX systems. Certain versions of sudo print this message:

```
We trust you have received the usual lecture from the local
System Administrator. It usually boils down to these two
things:
#1) Respect the privacy of others.
#2) Think before you type.
```

sudo does an excellent job of reminding people about a policy at the right time.

Case Study: Have a Witness

A company's buggy email server was mangling people's mailboxes. While the SAs waited for a software patch, they discovered that the mailboxes could be fixed with a text editor. However, an SA could see someone's messages while fixing the mailbox. When the CEO's mailbox was mangled, the SAs faced a challenge. There was a high level of merger activity in the industry, and the SAs didn't want the responsibility that would come with accidentally seeing a critical email message in the CEO's mailbox. They decided that the CEO's assistant would watch the SA while he fixed the CEO's mailbox. That way, she would see that the SA wasn't nosing around for confidential information, and she would also understand how much exposure the CEO's confidential email had received. This protected the CEO and the SA alike.

Sometimes these policies are governed by federal law. For example, the Securities and Exchange Commission (SEC) has rules against monitoring networks used to trade stock, which can make debugging a network problem on Wall Street very difficult. Also, the Federal Communications Commission (FCC) has rules about how telephone operators and technicians can use information accidentally obtained while doing their jobs. They can only discuss the information with its source, and they can't use it for personal gain.

Finally, network users have to understand that monitoring may happen as part of running the network. A monitoring and privacy policy should be in place, as discussed in Section 7.1.3.

9.1.5 Copyright Adherence

Organizations should have policies stating that their members abide by copyright laws.

For example, software piracy is pervasive and many people don't realize that "borrowing" non–freely redistributable software is actually *stealing* it.[2]

Companies are very concerned about being caught using pirated software. The financial liabilities and bad public relations that result are not what company executives want to deal with in weekly meetings. Add this fact to the highly publicized raids conducted by anti–software piracy organizations, and you get a recipe for disaster. The bottom line: Don't use pirated software on company equipment, and don't let users sneak it past you.

Telling people not to pirate software isn't all that useful; they're always convinced that what they're doing is not software piracy. Many people don't understand what constitutes software piracy. Even if they do, they will try to plead ignorance when they are caught. "I thought we had a site license." "I didn't know it was also installed on another machine." "Someone told me it was OK."

To solve this problem, a copyright adherence policy should give three or four examples of the most common violations. It might, for example, state that individually licensed PC software packages should be purchased for individual PCs and that a single-use installation disc should not be used on multiple machines. The policy could also require that manuals and media for software be stored in the room with the PC using the software.

Some companies bar employees from installing *any* software without explicit management approval. Alternatively, and for the sake of simplicity, a policy statement might specify software that employees may download at will, such as new versions of Adobe Acrobat Reader or new versions of web browsers. Installing software not on the list would require management approval.

Finally, a statement along the following lines might be useful: "We are always striving to reduce overhead costs, and we appreciate your efforts in

---

[2]Pirated software is also a vector for spreading computer viruses and therefore is a security concern. Nowadays, because Internet email is a much larger vector, viruses introduced via pirated software are barely noticed. However, we would be remiss if we didn't point out that there have been a couple of famous cases where commercial, shrink-wrapped software was a vector!

this area. That said, software piracy is a recipe for trouble, and we do not consider it to be a valid cost-saving measure. No one at this company is authorized to pirate software; if anyone pirates software or asks you to do so, please follow this procedure."

The easiest way to ensure policy compliance is to mold your policy into the path of least resistance. One major benefit of Open Source software is that the licenses permit, if not actively encourage, copying. For non–Open Source software, you can ensure proper licensing by buying bulk or site licenses for software that is preinstalled with every PC. One useful trick is to have someone in the purchasing chain look for purchasing trends, and then use them to select new packages for bulk licensing. Users will use the prepurchased licenses because delivery time should be faster than ordering it themselves.

Look for Simple Solutions

Administrating bulk licenses need not be complicated. Tom once ordered 50 *right to use* licenses of a software package and one copy of the documentation and media. He then numbered 50 lines on a piece of paper, and, when someone requested the software, he wrote the person's name on a line. He taped the paper inside the installation manual. This solution worked extremely well and required very little effort—there was no database to maintain and no overhead. It short, it was the simplest solution that met all the requirements. A larger operation might have kept such lists in a binder.

Another important point that employees must know is that companies, when faced with a copyright violation lawsuit, rarely will accept the blame. Instead, they'll implicate whoever let the violation happen and relay the damages to that person. Therefore, and not surprisingly, clearly communicating an organization's copyright adherence policy is important.

9.1.6   Working with Law Enforcement

Organizations should have a policy on working with law enforcement agencies so that SAs know what to do if one contacts them. Law enforcement officials sometimes contact SAs to help with investigations in areas of computer-related crime, as well as with harassment issues or other instances in which evidence is needed. Panicking can be a natural response in these situations; for this reason, and to avoid violating the law or company policy, SAs need a procedure to guide them. Generally speaking, working with these agencies through a manager is a good idea. One company had this procedure:

1. Relax. Be calm.
2. Be polite. *(SAs often have problems with authority and need to be reminded that being rude to an investigator is A Bad Thing.)*
3. Refer the issue to your manager. Suggested words are, "As a policy, we gladly cooperate with law enforcement. I need to refer this matter to my boss. Can I take your phone number and have her call you?" *(Law enforcement will always give a phone number. Pranksters and scam artists will not.)*
4. If you are a manager, contact the legal department for advice.
5. Keep a log of all requests, all related phone calls, and any commands typed.
6. The SA that collects evidence should give it to the legal department, who will give it to law enforcement unless the manager directs otherwise. *(This policy protects the SA.)*
7. If the law enforcement agency is the internal corporate security department, the evidence should be given to the SA's manager, who will give it to corporate security. Again, use polite verbiage when explaining this policy to corporate security: "We always comply with requests from your group. However, it is department policy for me to collect these logs and give them to my boss, who will then give them to you. This protects all of us."

An organization *must* verify the identity of a person claiming to be from a law enforcement agency before telling him *anything*. Perform this verification even before you admit that you are an SA. The best way to do this is to tell him you want to verify his identity. Ask for his phone number and his agency's switchboard number, and then call the switchboard and ask for him. If you question whether the switchboard number is real, look up the number in the phone book. (Yes, the FBI, CIA, and even the NSA are all listed!)

Failing to verify the identity of someone claiming to be a law enforcement official can turn out to be A Bad Thing. Why? Because, unfortunately, some of society's seamier characters pretend to be officials when they steal company information by using a tactic termed *social engineering*. How do they get away with it? Basically, it works like this:

1. Start with a small piece of information.
2. Make telephone calls while pretending to be an official or a new employee.

3. Leverage the piece of information into more useful information. Repeat with the new piece of information.

4. Repeat the previous steps until there is sufficient information to wreak havoc.

A Failed Experiment in Social Engineering

A naive young SA once received a phone call from someone claiming to be from the local police. The guy claimed that he was trying to understand how local companies secured their computer networks. He asked several pointed questions, which the SA happily answered.

Over the next few days, other people at the company received phone calls from the same guy, this time claiming he was a new member of their computer security group. He certainly sounded knowledgeable about the system. Luckily, one woman tried to verify his identity, and, when she couldn't, she alerted the SA team's manager. As a result, an executive warned everyone in the company that a scam was afoot, that no one should reveal sensitive information over the phone, and that any unusual requests for sensitive information should be reported to a manager. These actions stopped the guy in his tracks.

If the guy had continued, he might have used his techniques to gain access to the corporate network. For example, when he claimed to be from the security group, he sounded authentic, because he had learned so much about the company's security system from the naive SA. If he had continued, he could have collected enough small bits of information to leverage them into full system access.

Real cops and real employees provide information that will verify their identities, and they will not be offended when you ask them for this information. Cops don't mind a direct question. Employees, however, might be upset if you do not ask in a tactful manner.

Sometimes, would-be social engineers hatch their plans by starting with the information they find by rooting through dumpsters and rubbish bags. This is referred to as "dumpster diving." They look for anything that might help them harm your company: names, phone numbers, or project information.

Say a dumpster diver finds a memo on company letterhead about a mysterious Project Zed in the R&D department. Attached to it is a list of people involved in the project and their phone numbers. The diver will use this starting material and the telephone tactics we described to get whatever he can out of unsuspecting employees. These people can sound *very* smooth on the phone, and they can succeed if employees aren't on their toes. They may start by claiming to be new on Project Zed, working with [insert the name of someone listed on the memo], and are trying to find out how to have an account created, find out the phone number to the modem pool, and so on. Once the account is created, they can walk right into your systems.

The moral of this story is to tell people to be careful about what they say on the phone and to shred documents that may contain sensitive information—even if they feel silly doing it!

If you run your organization's Internet gateway, you are much more likely to be contacted by law enforcement. If law enforcement agencies contact you regularly, it's time to consider streamlining your procedures for dealing with them to avoid making mistakes or becoming a target. You might get training from the legal department and establish a procedure that lets you handle a standard police inquiry yourself and simply notify the legal department about the existence of the inquiry. This way, the legal department won't need to hold your hand every step of the way. Of course, exceptional cases should still be referred to the legal department. In the best case, a problem is quickly fixed and no future reports are generated. However Internet Service Providers (ISPs) and web-hosting companies may have a constant stream of problems.

Being Too Accommodating Is Not Necessarily a Good Thing

Once upon a time, a company offered a web-based service that let people surf the web anonymously. Crackers used this service occasionally to harass other sites; this activity, unfortunately, was traced back to the anonymizer service. This was *not* good. Whenever the problem would happen, law enforcement would contact the company's SA instead of the people that ran the anonymizer service because the SA was responsible for the gateway. Initially, he tried to handle the complaints himself. When it got to be too much work, he worked with the manager of the anonymizer service to establish a single point of contact for all law enforcement calls. However, the number and frequency of the calls increased, which worried the SA. He advised the group how they could change their service to make it less susceptible to abuse, but they ignored him. Finally, the FBI started contacting the SA many times a week. He found himself being listed on subpoenas and his work was affected. Not surprisingly, he became extremely frustrated and burned out.

The problem here is that the SA was being too nice. By continually accommodating his customers, who were the root of the problem, he allowed the crackers to continue, which made his company look bad, created work for the FBI, and made his own life very difficult. Instead, he should have adopted the "fix things once" philosophy in Chapter 5, which would require one of two things:

1. Force the customer to improve its security
2. Cut the customer off altogether

In the end, the SA realized that he had to stop accommodating people who were doing things that were bad for the business, bad for him, and bad for the Internet community. He got management approval to cut off their service in 30 days if they didn't fix their software. Complaints would be referred directly to the legal department, and the SA was not to spend time on any such issues, except to give the complainer the phone number of the legal department.

The corporate legal department shut down the service within minutes of receiving the first complaint. They didn't wait the entire 30 days. They were shocked that the problem had been permitted to persist at all. In hindsight, the SA should have been tougher with the customer from square one. If he didn't have the backbone or the authority to shut them down, he should have turned the problem over to the legal department, who would have been much firmer. The moral of this story is to be firm with people who are harming your company, even if they're customers. If they turn into bullies, sometimes it's better to find a bigger bully to fight for you.

Printer Log Panic
A young SA who ran the print system for a large company was contacted by corporate security. As part of a sexual harassment investigation, security wanted logs related to what had been printed on a particular color printer. This printer was in the SA's building, which meant that he might know the suspect. He panicked. He collected all the logs from that printer and copied them to his own computer at home. Next, he deleted the logs at work. Finally, he sought advice from two friends. "Someone could be fired! What should I do?" They both gave him the same advice: To avoid getting fired himself, he should restore the logs and give corporate security what they wanted. By hiding evidence, he had endangered his own position and made himself look like an accomplice to the accused.

No matter how you feel about a policy, your duty is to follow the requests from corporate security. If you feel uncomfortable with their requests, take the issue to your manager, don't take the situation into your own hands.

9.2   The Icing

Now that policies are set, this section discusses setting expectations and some example situations one might encounter.

9.2.1   Setting Expectations on Privacy and Monitoring

We've already covered the need for a policy on privacy and monitoring in Section 7.1.3. Establishing such a policy is a fundamental ethical issue. This section, however, emphasizes the need to remind the customers time and time again about this policy and its implications.

Setting employee expectations on privacy is important because putting people in situations in which they don't know the laws governing them is unfair. Punishing someone for violating a rule they've never been told about is abusive. There are many ways to set expectations. When hired, employees should be required to sign a statement that they have read the privacy and monitoring guidelines. Companies can also require employees to sign these statements annually. Companies should occasionally reprint privacy statements in newsletters or bulletins.

Allowing employees to remain uninformed about privacy policies can be dangerous for business reasons. For example, if system users do not realize what risks their actions involve, they might not be able to manage those risks. For example, suppose customers discuss proprietary business details via email, which they think is secure. If it is not, security could be compromised. Because they were misinformed, they exposed the company to unnecessary risk.

In the financial community, email is regularly monitored for SEC violations such as insider trading. The threat of monitoring may be enough to prevent illegal exchanges of insider information via email. Of course, it also could simply push insider trading back to channels that are more difficult to monitor, such as the telephone. However, that decision is for the SEC to make, not you.

E-commerce sites, and any site doing international business, must be concerned with privacy laws as they vary from country to country. For example, if you do business with European Union citizens, there are strict regulations on how you must protect private information.

Setting expectations also protects the reputations of SAs because a lack of information will result in customers assuming the worst. Tom once had a customer that had previously been at a site that fired their SA for reading other people's email. The customer now assumed that all SAs read other people's email (once burned, twice shy). However, some customers believe that email is somehow magically private in all situations and will take unreasonable risks, for example emailing salary data. Companies that understand the realities of networked computing environments keep their most critical data on removable media (for example, floppies, Zip, Jazz) rather than putting it on network file and email servers.

Case Study: Email Forwarding

A company had a liberal policy permitting email to ex-employees to be forwarded to their new email addresses for a year. The policy created problems because proprietary business information was often bulk emailed to lists that hadn't been updated. It was assumed that email within the company was private, even if it was sent to an entire department. Until everyone in the company was told about the problem, current employees weren't aware that they were risking security breaches by sending bulk emails. A better email forwarding policy is to set up autoreply systems that reply with a message that includes the person's new email address and an explicit statement that the sender's message had not been forwarded. That solution was not workable at this location for other reasons.

9.2.2   Being Told to Do Something Illegal/Unethical

No chapter on ethics would be complete without a discussion of what to do if your manager tells you to do something illegal, unethical, or against company rules. We hope that you won't ever need the information in this section, but it is better to be prepared with an understanding of the issues rather than facing them cold.

The most important thing to remember in this situation is to keep logs. Keep logs of when such requests are made, when related phone calls happen, what commands you type to execute such requests, and so on. Logs are your friends.

We recommend a basic process: Verify the request (maybe you didn't hear it right), verify that it's illegal or against company policy (check the written policy or ask someone for advice), and, if the request is against policy, assert yourself and reject the request explicitly.

If the manager persists, you have the choice of going along with it, going to a higher authority, or both. Many companies have an ombudsperson that you can confidentially talk to about these situations. In highly regulated industries such as financial institutions, there are clearly established guidelines for what to do next.

Asked to Read Someone Else's Email

Let's follow this through in a fictional example: Bob, a department head, asks you to read another department head's email (Alice) to see if her department is planning on canceling a project on which Bob's department relies. A good response would be to ask, in person, if you heard the request right. "What did you want me to do?"

If the request is confirmed, verify that it's against company policy by finding the appropriate paragraph in your organization's privacy and monitoring guidlines. Use it to provide a gentle reminder to Bob. Bob might rationalize his request, explaining that Alice has cancelled other commitments and that he's only trying to help you because he knows you rely on this project, too.

At this point, you have a decision to make. You can stall and use the time to talk with an ombudsperson, corporate security, or Bob's manager. You can also go along with the request. However, doing so will make you an accessory to the crime. Also, Bob might make more requests of you, possibly pointing out that if you don't comply, he'll reveal the previous incident, claiming that you did it on your own initiative. He might also claim that if you do not comply, he'll simply find someone else who will do it. This tactic is a very threatening way for someone to convince a person to do something.

Obviously, we cannot make this decision for you. However, we can give you this advice: When you aren't sure if you should do something, get the request in writing and keep a log of exactly what you do. Never act on verbal instructions that you find questionable. Even if you think it might be OK, get it in writing. This is critical not only to cover yourself, but also to assist the person making the request to be sure he really wants it done. If someone is not willing to put a request in writing, the person is not willing to take responsibility for the action. Your log should note the time, the request, who made it, why it was done, and what was done. Also note anything unusual about the request. Not creating a log is something that people regret when it is too late. When in doubt, log it.

9.3   Conclusion

Our ethics are the principles of conduct that govern what we do. The word *ethics* is scary and vague to many people. We hope to have laid some guiding principles for you to consider, but also to have left things open-ended enough that you can make your own choices.

The SAGE Code of Ethics seeks to enhance the professionalism and image of SAs through a standard for conduct. The policies an organization should create include a network/computer user code of conduct, privileged access code of conduct, copyright adherence policy, and a policy on working with law enforcement. Informed consent decrees that we have a monitoring and privacy policy that is clearly communicated to all customers. All of these policies must include a penalty for violations that is enforced consistently, or they have no "teeth."

Having thought about potential situations greatly prepares you for the situations when they arise. Try to think about potential ethical dilemmas you might encounter and what you would do in those instances. This might be a good thing to discuss occasionally at staff meetings or at lunch. This should be done with your manager present so that you can develop an understanding of the official policy.

If you learned one thing in this chapter, we hope it was that when you are in a gray area, the best way to protect yourself is to keep logs. Log when you receive phone calls, log what you are asked to do, and log what you do. Log everything!

Exercises

1. Describe an experience in which the SAGE Code of Ethics or the informed consent rule would (or did) affect your actions.

2. Do you follow Canon 3 of the SAGE Code of Ethics? In particular, consider the areas of conditions of acceptable use, sharing and availability of common resources, and system monitoring. How would you improve your performance in this area?

3. Think of an incident in which you or another SA were not following Canon 6 of the SAGE Code of Ethics. How would you have handled the incident with Canon 6 in mind?

4. Of the policies discussed in this chapter, which does your site have? If you are at a large site with corporate policies, do you have policies specific to your division?

5. Describe the policies detailed in the previous question as being easygoing or strict. Give examples. How would you change things and why?

6. Ask three users if they know where to find any of the policy documents mentioned in this chapter.

7. Suppose you were debugging a problem and as a result accidentally heard (in the case of voice over IP) or read (in the case of email) that a coworker was dealing drugs from the office. What would you do? What if the person was instead planning on sabotaging the company? Stealing office supplies? Stealing pieces of equipment for resale on an Internet auction site? Having an affair with the boss? What if the person was not your coworker, but was a high-level executive?

8. How long do you keep various logs on your system (printer, log in/log out, and so on)? If you had been involved in the printing log anecdote in Section 9.1.6, how long would you now retain such logs? Why?

9. You work at a web-based e-commerce site. An engineer who doesn't have the skill or patience to properly test his code in the development environment asks you to let him look at his logs on a production machine, then let him quickly change a logging parameter so he gets more information. Before you know it, you have an engineer doing development on the live production hosts. How would you have handled this situation? Realistically, how could you have prevented it?

10. An executive asks you to allocate additional disk space for someone. You respond that you don't have the space, but are told "Make space, this person is important." Soon the same request is made for another person. You are told, "You did it for the last person. This guy is just as important." How would you have handled this situation? Realistically, how could you have prevented it?

11. A person who is not an SA has privileged access to her workstation because the software she uses requires it. Friends ask for accounts on her system. It's against policy, but she does it anyway. One of her friends starts engaging in illegal activity on the workstation. How would you have handled this situation? What if the employee that violated policy was above you in management? A peer? Realistically, how could you have prevented the problem?

PART II

The Processes

Chapter 10

Change Management
and Revision Control

Change management is the process that ensures effective planning, implementation, and postevent analysis of changes made to a system. It means that changes are well documented, have a back-out plan, and are reproducible. Change management yields an audit trail that can be used to determine what was done when and why. Part of change management is communicating with customers and other system administration (SA) teams about the project before implementation. A small component of change management is revision control, which is a low-level process for controlling the changes to a single configuration file. Revision control should not be confused with change management—it is only a fraction of the picture.

Change management is one of the core processes of a mature system administration team. It is a mechanism through which a group of people can make sure that changes that may have an impact on each other do not occur simultaneously. It is a mechanism for reducing outages or problems by making SAs think through various aspects of a change before they implement it. It is a communication tool that makes sure everyone is "on the same page" when changes are made. In other words, it means having a lower "oops-quotient" and being able to deal more quickly with an "oops" when it happens. Change management is crucial in e-commerce companies whose revenue stream relies on 24×7 availability.

10.1   The Basics

Change management involves communication and scheduling: Communicate with the customers and other SAs so that they know what is happening, and schedule changes to cause the least impact. It also involves lots of preparation and documentation. Changes must be well planned with all eventualities covered. They must be documented and approved before they are implemented. Change management also involves using tools for revision control and automation.

The change management process should take into account different categories of systems that are changed, types of changes that are made, and the specific procedures for each combination. For example, the machine categories may include desktops, departmental servers, corporate infrastructure systems, business critical systems, Internet presence, and production e-commerce systems. Categories of changes may include adding an account or changing the privilege level of an account, updating a directory such as DNS, installing a new service or software package, upgrading an existing service or software package, hardware changes, security policy changes, or a configuration change.

Significant changes to anything other than a single desktop should be coordinated with a group of people and should go through a change review or change management process. What counts as "significant" should be defined locally. This process means that SAs can't make a change without following the correct procedure, which involves communicating with the right people and scheduling the change for an appropriate time. For important or large changes on critical systems, it may involve writing up a small project plan, with test procedures and a back-out plan, which is reviewed by peers or more senior SAs, and it may also involve appointing a "buddy" to observe and help out with the change. Sections 10.1.2 and 10.1.3 discuss the communications structure and scheduling of changes in more detail.

Each company must decide what level of change management process to have for each point in the machine category/type of change matrix. Having too cumbersome a process for relatively minor changes will prevent the SAs from working efficiently, but not having enough process and review for changes on more critical systems will result in more, potentially costly, mistakes.

10.1.1   Technical Issues

You need to have a documented procedure that everyone in the SA team follows for updating system configuration files. It should be consistently used everywhere that configuration files are updated. It should be documented clearly in a step-by-step manner, including the procedure to follow if any of the steps fail, and given to all SAs as they join the team. The procedure should include creating revision histories, locking the configuration files so that only one person can edit them at once, running automated checks on the format of, or information in, the files, and, if appropriate, notifying other systems or applications that an update has occurred. It is a fundamentally good practice that should be followed at all times by everyone because it is simple and can save the day surprisingly often.

Revision History and Locking

A revision history lets anyone with appropriate access review the changes that have been made to a file, step-by-step. It also gives you the ability to return quickly to a previous version of the file, which is very useful if the current version becomes corrupt. Typically, it also will record who made the change and when, and it can add an optional comment along with the change. Revision control software usually also provides a locking mechanism, which should be used to prevent two people from trying to modify the same configuration file at once.

Having each person's identity attached to his changes is useful. If a junior SA makes a mistake, the more senior person who discovers it can take him aside and use the opportunity to do some mentoring on that area of the system.

Source code control systems that are used by software developers are the sorts of tools that you should look at for this functionality. Under UNIX, there are Revision Control System (RCS) (Bolinger 1995), Source Code Control System (SCCS) (Bolinger 1995), and Concurrent Versions System (CVS) (Berliner 1990), which store the differences from version to version, along with identity and a comment, and also provide locking. Many commercial systems also are available and may already be in use by developers at a given site.

❖ **Maintaining Revision History in UNIX** It's easy to get started maintaining revision history of a file in UNIX with RCS. Start doing this the next time you edit any file and, before you know it, you'll have simple but efficient revision history on all your important configuration files.

Suppose the file is `/etc/named.conf`. Create a directory named `/etc/RCS`. Start the revision history with the command `ci -l named.conf`. The revision history of the file will now be stored in `/etc/RCS/named.conf,v` (note the `,v` at the end of the file). To edit the file, check it out with `co -l named.conf`, and then edit it with your favorite editor. When you are satisfied with your changes, check in the revision with `ci -u named.conf`. This three-step process is traditionally put into a

shell script named `xed` or `vir`. It is always advisable to run `rcsdiff`
`named.conf` before running `co`. That way, if someone has made changes
but forgotten to use RCS, you will see the changes and can commit
them to RCS before you proceed. To commit someone else's changes, use
`rcs -l named.conf` followed by the usual command to check in changes:
`ci -u named.conf`. Taking the extra time to ensure that you don't clob-
ber someone else's changes can save much heartache and debugging later.
RCS has other useful commands. `rlog named.conf` will show you the
history of the file's changes, and `rcsdiff -r1.1 -r1.2 named.conf` will
show you the changes between revision 1.1 and 1.2. You can see what
version 1.2 looked like explicitly with a command such as `co -p -r1.2`
`named.conf`.

A good reference, for example Bolinger (1995), will explain more complicated issues such as backing out of changes. Create a simple text file to
experiment with while reviewing the manual pages. You'll be an expert in
no time.

Revision History Saves the Day

A mid-size software company had a script that automated the process of
account creation. One day, the disk that contained the account database
filled up while the program was rewriting the database. Because the script
did almost no error checking, it failed to notice. It proceeded to push out
the new account database to all the authentication servers, even though
it was missing most of the accounts. The SAs quickly realized what had
happened and were able to immediately clear some space and go back to
the old account database as it existed immediately before the script was
run. If they had not had a revision history, they would have had to restore
the file from backup tape, which would have taken much longer and meant
that any password changes customers had made since the backup would
have been lost. The automated program had identified itself in the optional
comment field, and thus it was easy to track down the entity responsible for
the truncation. The script was subsequently changed to do a lot more error
checking.

Automated Checks

The final steps in updating a file or a set of files are to verify that each
file is syntactically correct and then ensure that the applications that
use these files start to use the new information. These steps should be

performed by an automated program, which also should tell various servers that their configuration files have changed or push files to other locations, as necessary.

Sometimes, you may need to separate these two steps. If getting the applications to use the new configuration information will cause a small service outage, and the update can wait until a time that will cause less, or no, disruption the syntax should be checked immediately, but the update process should be scheduled for a later time.

Some system configurations are difficult to check with an automated program and ideally should be generated by a program so that they are at least syntactically correct. Establish a practice of testing these components in some other way that gives you a high level of confidence that they are working correctly. For example, under UNIX, the system boot scripts are often modified by hand to change the set of services that are started at boot time or perhaps to configure the behavior of the network interfaces. It is important that these scripts be tested carefully because an error may prevent the system from completing the reboot cycle. In most commercial UNIX systems, the start scripts are split into many small pieces, one for each service, that can be individually tested so that you can be reasonably confident that changes and additions are correct.

If the start scripts are not tested in advance, problems with them will not be found until the next reboot. Therefore it is critical to make boot scripts completely reliable. Machines seem to reboot at the most inconvenient times. Systems crash late at night, when you are on vacation, and so on. If you only find out that a script you wrote has a typo at the next reboot, you are making this discovery at a very bad time. To make matters even worse, good systems stay up for months on end. It is extremely difficult to remember what changes have been made since the last reboot, particularly when it happened months ago. Even if the site has a policy of logging changes in a log book or a trouble ticket system, it can be difficult to find the relevant change if months have gone by.

The Reboot Test

Before distributed computing, most sites (or sometimes entire colleges) had only "one big computer" that everyone would access through terminals or modems. Tom's "one big computer" was a VAX 11/750 running Digital's VMS operating system. Now, before you young whippersnappers yawn at the antique 1980s technology and skip to the next section, there is a lesson here that is still valuable today, so keep reading. The script that executed on boot-up was rarely changed. The SAs had a simple rule: If you changed the startup script at all, you had to reboot the VAX soon after.

They usually rebooted the machine once a month, as part of their "stand-alone backup" procedure. First, they would reboot the VAX to make sure it could come up on its own. In theory, that step should be unnecessary. Then they would make changes to the system files that were needed. Another reboot would test their changes (and potentially other reboots after bugs were fixed). After that, they would do the reboot that was required for the tape backup procedure. The benefit of this technique is that it meant mistakes were discovered soon after they were made, when the change was still fresh in the SA's mind. With distributed computing, it is more likely that a reboot is not such a terrible thing. Machines also reboot faster now. However, it is even more important today to reboot a machine or perform some kind of rigorous testing of changes to such critical code. In the old days, a typo would have meant the VAX would be down until the morning, when the SAs arrived to fix it. In today's world, business comes to a halt when a computer is down, and such an outage would result in you, the SA, being awakened in the middle of the night or pulled out of vacation to fix the problem *right now*. An extra reboot is a strategic investment in your sleep!

If your customers have been notified that a certain host will not be available at a certain time, take the opportunity to give it an extra reboot after you think you are done.

10.1.2   Communications Structure

You need to develop a communications structure for informing your customers about the changes you are making. If the changes involve a hard cut-over, after which the old service, system, or software will not be available, you must make sure that all of your customers who use the old version will be able to continue to work with the new version. If a soft cut-over is involved, with the old version available for a time, then you should ensure that everyone knows in advance when it is happening, how they use the older version if they need to, and when or whether the old version will no longer be available. If you are adding a service, you need to ensure that the people who requested it, and those who might find it useful, know how to use it when it is available. In all three cases, let your customers know when the work has been successfully completed and how to report any problems that occur.

Although it is necessary and good practice to inform customers whose work may be affected about changes and the schedule for implementation, you must take care not to flood your customers with too many messages, or they will ignore them, thinking them irrelevant. Targeting the correct groups for each service requires understanding your customer base and your services, so that you can make appropriate mappings. For example, if you know that group A uses services A to K and group B uses services B, D, and L to P, then you only need to let group A know about changes to service A, but you should let both groups A and B know about modifications to service B. This task may seem tedious, but when it is done well, it makes a huge difference to your customers.

The most effective communication method will vary from company to company and depends on the company culture. For example, in some companies, a newsgroup that people choose to subscribe to, where they can quickly scan the subjects of the messages for relevance, may be the most effective tool. However, other companies may use newsgroups very little or not at all, and so email may work more effectively. For significant changes, we recommend that you use a "push" mechanism, meaning that you send a message out to people, rather than a "pull" mechanism, meaning your customers have to check a certain web page every couple of days. A significant change is one that is either sensitive or major, as defined in Section 10.1.3.

Case Study: Bell Lab's Demo Schedule

At Bell Labs, the research area has a very relaxed computing environment that does not require too much in the way of change management. However, there is a need for an extremely stable environment during demos. Therefore they maintain a simple calendar of when all the demos are using the UNIX "calendar" command. Researchers notify the SAs of demos via the usual "helpdesk" procedure, and the SAs pay attention to this calendar when scheduling downtime. They also avoid risky changes on those days and avoid any kind of "group lunch" that might take too many SAs away from the building. If the demo includes CEOs or heads of state, an SA stands ready outside the door.

10.1.3   Scheduling

A key component of change management is timing. When you make the change can be a significant factor in how much it affects your customers. We will briefly discuss the scheduling of three different types of changes: routine updates, sensitive updates, and major updates.

A *routine update* is one that can happen at any time and is basically invisible to most of the customer base. These are changes that happen all the time. Examples of routine changes are updating the contents of a directory server or an authentication database, helping an individual customer to customize his environment, debugging a problem with a desktop or a printer, or altering a script that processes log files to produce statistics. You do not need to schedule a routine update; the scope of the problem that an error would cause is very limited because of the nature of the task.

Major updates are those that affect many systems or require a significant system, network, or service outage or that touch a large number of systems.[1] Major updates include upgrading the authentication system, changing the email or printer infrastructure, or upgrading the core network infrastructure. These updates must be carefully scheduled with the customer base, using a "push" mechanism such as email. Major updates should not be happening all the time. If they are, consider whether you should change the way you are classifying some updates. Some companies may want them performed at off-peak times, and others may want all the major updates to happen in one concentrated maintenance window. Maintenance windows are discussed in detail in Chapter 12.

A *sensitive update* is one that may not seem to be a large update, or even one that will be particularly visible to your customers, but that could cause a significant outage if there is a problem with it. Sensitive updates include altering router configurations, global access policies, firewall configurations, or making alterations to a critical server. You should have some form of communication with your customers about a sensitive update before it takes place, in case there are problems. These updates will happen reasonably often and you do not want to over-communicate them, so a "pull" mechanism, such as a web page or a newsgroup, is appropriate. The helpdesk should be told of the change, the problems that it might cause, when work starts and finishes, and who to contact in the event of a problem.

Sensitive updates should happen outside of peak usage times, to minimize the potential impact and to give you time to discover and rectify any problems before they affect your customers. Peak usage times may vary, depending on who your customers are. If you work at an e-commerce site that is primarily used by the public in the evenings and on the weekends, the best time for making changes may be at 9 AM. Sensitive updates also should not be immediately followed by the person who made the change going home for the evening or the weekend. If you make a sensitive change, stay around for a couple of hours to make sure you are there to fix any problems that you may have caused.

---

[1]What is considered "large" varies from site to site. For most sites, anything that affects 30 percent or more of the systems is a large update.

Case Study: No Changes on Friday

One of Tom's customers did a lot of system administration tasks, and Tom was affected by his customer's changes and schedule, rather than the other way around. When his customer made a mistake, Tom was blamed because some of the group's systems depended on the customer's systems. The customer and Tom had the following debate.

Within his own area, Tom instituted the rule that no changes should be made on Friday, because if they made mistakes that were discovered over the weekend, response times would be slower, increasing the risk of adversely affecting his customers' work. Tom also didn't want his weekend ruined, and he thought the customer should abide by this guideline also.

The customer believed that no matter what day Tom's group made changes, they should check their work more thoroughly and then wouldn't have to be concerned about making changes the day before a weekend or vacation. Even though the customer's own changes often caused problems, he refused to acknowledge that even when changes are carefully checked before they are made, the unexpected may happen or an error may occur. He also refused to acknowledge the increased risk to other customers and that lowering that risk was in everyone's best interest.

The customer also felt that the SAs should make their changes during the day, because there's no better test of a change than having live users try to work on the system. He felt that if changes were made during off-hours, the SAs wouldn't find the problem until people who used the system returned in the morning or after the weekend. He preferred to make changes during lunch, so that there was a half day of testing before he went home. There was no "lunch hour" at that company. The cafeteria was open from 11:15 to 13:30, and at least a third of their customers were active on the network at any time.

Both Tom and this customer had valid points, and no one rule will do for all situations. However, ignoring the risks to other customers is not appropriate, and saying that more careful checking is sufficient is not a valid point. More careful checking is always good, but it is not a sufficient reason to ignore a higher risk to the customers.

Many sites like to make some changes during the working day for the same reason that they don't like to make them on a Friday: because they want people to be around when the change happens to notice and fix any problems. However, many sites like to wait until no one, or almost no one, is around to make changes that require an outage.

You need to figure out what is right for your situation. However, you should try to avoid situations in which people outside the SA organization can make changes that may have an adverse impact on important systems.

Different people have different philosophies on performing sensitive updates. More senior SAs typically are more cautious than junior SAs, because they understand the potential impact better and they have been burned by lack of caution in the past. In a mature system administration organization, everyone will have been made aware of a documented, consistent set of guidelines to follow. These guidelines will include acceptable times to make certain kinds of changes.

When trying to classify updates as routine, sensitive, or major, take into account that some changes may be considered to be routine updates at some sites and sensitive updates at other sites or even in different areas at the same site. For example, at an e-commerce company, attaching a new host to the corporate network may be considered a routine update, but attaching a new host to the customer-visible service network may be considered a sensitive update. Consider how various sorts of updates should be categorized in the different areas of your site, and institute a scheduling practice that reflects your decision.

10.1.4   Process and Documentation

An important part of change management is processes and documentation. Following the processes and producing the documentation force SAs to prepare thoroughly for significant changes. They have to fill out *change control* forms, also referred to as *change proposal* forms. These forms detail the changes they will make, the systems and services affected, the reasons for the change, the risks, the test procedure, the back-out plan, how long the change will take to implement, and how long the back-out plan takes to implement. Sometimes, SAs are required to list all the commands they will type. The level of detail required varies from site to site and usually is dependent on how critical the affected machine or service is. For very critical machines, the SA cannot type anything that is not listed on the change control form that was approved. However, the process and documentation requirements for less critical machines should be less stringent, or SAs will find that their hands are tied by change management red tape and they are unable to work effectively.

If a site can readily identify one or two machines that are absolutely critical to the running of the business, those machines should be covered by stringent change management processes. For example, the main database machines and credit card processing machines at an e-commerce site could fall into this category. At a drug development company, machines involved in that process often are required by law to comply to very strict change management controls. Machines that fall into this category usually are not servers that provide important services such as email, printing, DNS, or authentication. Machines that provide those services should be covered by less stringent change-management policies to strike a balance between the benefits of change management and the benefits of SAs being able to quickly respond to customers' needs. However, significant changes to these servers or services do need to follow good change management process so that they happen smoothly with few surprises.

Later chapters cover in detail the processes associated with various types of changes. In particular, Chapter 11 covers server upgrades, Chapter 12 covers maintenance windows, and Chapter 13 covers service conversions.

10.1.5 Quiet Times

It is useful to institute quiet times when only minor updates can be performed. Quiet times typically occur at the end of a quarter and the end of the fiscal year. Figure 10.1 on the next page is an example of a quiet time announcement that is sent out to all system administration staff and department heads. It includes a change control form that is part of the change management process.

10.2 The Icing

Once you have basic change management in place that describes a process for configuration updates, the communication methods that are used, and how to schedule a change, there are some other change management techniques that you can employ to improve stability at your site. In particular, you can create automated front-ends for common configuration updates that perform all the locking, revision history, checking, and updating for the SAs. You should also institute formal change management meetings with cross-functional change councils to review change proposals.

10.2.1 Automated Front-Ends

In Section 10.1.1, we saw how automatically checking system files for format and syntax errors before bringing an update live brings greater stability to your systems. The next step along that path is to provide a front-end interface to those system files that asks the appropriate questions, checks the answers for errors, looks for omissions, and then updates the file correctly using the information supplied. If everyone uses this front-end, there is only one place to check for errors and test for correctness, rather than a changing staff of people who all need to be trained.

```
Subject:  FYI - QUIET TIME IS COMING   09/25 - 10/06

Team
Just a reminder for you all that QUIET TIME will be here in three weeks.
It is scheduled to begin on 9/25 and go to 10/06.
Change control 96739 is below:

              CHANGE SUMMARY DISPLAY          CHANGE: 00096739
   Assignee Class/Queue... GNSC              Change Status/Type OR/INF
   Assignee Name........  _____ IPL/Service Disrpt N/N
   Requester Name........ FRED/ADDAMS         Risk/Chg Reason... 1/QT
   Enterer's Name........ FRED/ADDAMS         Proc Ctr/Cntl Ctr. NET/GNS
   Enterer's Phone....... (555)555-8765       Problem Fixed..... _____
   Enterer's Class/Queue.. GNSC               Business Unit..... ALL
   Plan Start Date/Time... 09/25/2000  00:01  Location Code..... GLOBAL
   Plan End Date/Time..... 10/06/2000  24:00  COI.............. ALL
   Date/Time Entered...... 04/10/2000  14:26  Approval Status... PENDING
   Date/Time Last Altered 06/22/2000  16:02  User Last Altered. NCCOFHA
   Date Closed.......... _____           Associated Doc.... N/A
   System.............. _____
   Component/Application.. FISCAL-PROCESS&NTWK-QUIET-TIME
   Description.......... 4Q00/1Q01 FISCAL EXTENDED AVAILABILITY
   System edited........ _____ Loc added.... _____

Fiscal processing, email, and network quiet time to support
quarterly book close/open activities.
Changes that may impact access to or data movement
between server/mainframe applications or email should be
rescheduled.  Only emergency changes to prevent or
fix outages will be  reviewed for possible implementation.
All changes will require a change exception form be
submitted to the CMRB.
See URL for Quiet Time Guidelines and contact information:
   http://wwwin.foo.com/gnsc/quiet-time.html

   Customer Impact: None
   Test plan: None
   Contact and Phone/Pager Numbers:
       JOHN SMITH.........(555)555-1234
       JANE JONES.........(555)555-4321
       ALICE WALTER.......(555)555-7890   800-555-5555 pin 123456

   Backout Plan: None
   *** BOTTOM OF DATA ***
```

Figure 10.1: Sample quiet time announcement.

10.2.2 Change Management Meetings

Change management meetings, where proposed changes are reviewed, discussed, and scheduled (if approved) are a valuable tool for increasing the stability of the systems. This formal process asks the SAs what they plan to do and when, how long it will take, what can go wrong, how they will test it, how to back out the change, and how long that will take. It forces the SAs to think about the implications of what they are doing, as well as to prepare for problems that might arise.

It also makes other people aware of changes that are being made so that they can recognize the potential source of problems. The people who approve, refuse, or reschedule proposed changes should be drawn from across the company, so that representatives from each area that might be affected can alert everyone as to how it will affect their groups and prepare their groups for the changes that will be made.

It also gives the people who attend the meetings an overall view of what is happening at the site. It provides an opportunity for senior SAs or managers to spot a change that will cause problems before it happens and prevent it from happening. It reduces entropy and leads to a more stable environment. Typically, a change management meeting will occur once a week or once a month, as appropriate for the rate of change at the site.

Case Study: Daily Change Management Meetings

At a popular e-commerce site that handles a large and ever-increasing volume of traffic, the service network is constantly being updated to handle the increased demand. It has an unusual change-management process, which involves daily change management meetings. Change proposals are submitted before the cutoff time each day. The SAs who have proposed changes, all the SA managers, and some representatives from the engineering and operations attend the meetings, where the change proposals are discussed, approved, postponed, or refused with an alternative approach suggested. Each change proposal includes a proposed date and time for making the change. If it is approved, the change should be made at the approved time; otherwise, it needs to be discussed in another change management meeting.

This company's service is primarily used by the consumer market in the United States. Because the company is on the West coast of the United States, its peak usage times are after 2 PM on Monday to Friday (that is, after 5 PM on the East coast of the United States) and all day during the weekend. The time specified in a change proposal is typically the following morning, before peak time. Another thing that is decided at the change management meeting is whether the change should go ahead regardless of "the weather" or wait until there is "good weather." The *weather* refers to the operating status of the service. In other words, some changes are approved on condition that the service is operating normally at the time the SA or engineer wants to make the change. Other changes are considered so critical that they are made regardless of how well or badly the service is functioning.

This approach is unusual for a couple of reasons. It is certainly a step better than having no change management, because there is at least a minimal review process, a defined off-peak time in which changes are performed, and a process for postponing some tasks to avoid possibly introducing extra problems when the system is unstable. However, the frequency of the meetings and the changes to the service network mean that it is difficult to look at the big picture of what is going on with the service network, that entropy and lots of small instabilities that may interact with each other are constantly introduced, and that the SAs and the engineers are not encouraged to plan ahead. Changes may be made quickly, without being properly thought out. It is also unusual that changes are permitted to happen while the service network that is the company's revenue stream is unstable. Changes at such a time can make debugging existing problems much more difficult, particularly if the instabilities take a few days to debug. The formal process of checking with the operations group before making a change and giving them the ability to prevent at least some changes from happening is valuable, however.

Although the site was often successful in handling a large number of transactions, for a while it was known for having stability problems and large, costly outages, the source of which was hard to trace because of the rapidly changing nature of the network. It was not possible to draw a line in time and say "the problems started after this set of changes, which were approved in that change management meeting." That would have enabled them to narrow their search and perhaps find the problem more quickly.

A mature change management process can also take on overtones of project management, with a proposed change being carefully considered not only for its impact on other systems, but also on other deadlines the group must meet. If making the change will cause other, more important deadlines to slip, it will be refused.

Case Study: IBM's Nagano Olympics

IBM built and operated the computer infrastructure to support the 1996 Summer Olympics in Atlanta and the 1998 Winter Olympics in Nagano. In the 1996 Atlanta Games, they did not have a change management review process, and many "small" changes were made by programmers who were unaware of the impact their "small" changes would have on the rest of the system. Some systems were completed "just in time," with no time for testing. Some were still being developed after the Games had started. There were many problems, all heavily reported by the press, much to IBM's embarrassment. The outages prevented the press from getting information about the athletic events and left them little to write about except the fact that IBM's computer system wasn't working.

A root cause analysis was performed to make sure these problems were not repeated at the 1998 Winter Olympics. It was determined that better change management was required. They implemented "change management boards" that had up to ten representatives from different areas of the project to review change proposals. Through this mechanism, they successfully managed to prevent several similar "small" changes from occurring, and all the hardware and software was completed and fully tested before the events, with many problems discovered and fixed in advance. The final result was that the information system for the 1998 Winter Olympics ran smoothly when the events started (Guth and Radosevich 1998).

Case Study: Change Management Makes Large-Scale Events Succeed

When Cisco ran the NetAid event, they had roughly four weeks to build and run a distributed network that had to handle 125,000 simultaneous video streams across 50 ISPs. They had to develop mechanisms that scaled across the planet. In the end, they had nearly 1,000 pieces of hardware to manage and occasionally change. They did this with a full-time staff of about five people and many volunteers.

Nobody had ever scaled to the size they were engineering toward. Thus they knew they would face operational challenges that would require them to change the router and server configurations. With lots of people and a volatile environment, it was important for them to maintain configuration control, particularly because the reasoning behind certain routing configurations was not intuitively obvious (for example, why did Paul put in that particular route filter?). In addition, they used an intrusion detection system to guard their e-commerce site. Any time such a system is configured, it must be tailored to the environment in which it will run. This process usually takes about four weeks. It was important to keep track of the changes made so that they knew the reasons for those filters. The change management process provided a documentation trail that enabled everyone working on the system to understand what had been done before, why it had been done, and how their changes fit in with the others' work. Without this documentation, it would have been impossible to get the system working correctly in time. Such processes all contributed to the project's success.

10.2.3 Streamline the Process

Ultimately, when you think you have everything in place, you should look at your process to see if there are ways to streamline it. Are there questions on your change proposal form that are not used? Are there paper-based parts of the process that could be done more efficiently? If the forms are online, is there a way that each person can save defaults for some of the fields (such as name and contact information)? What problems do the people who use the system have with the current setup?

10.3 Conclusion

Change management is a valuable tool that is used at mature sites to increase the reliability of the site, both through restricting when certain changes can happen and by having a process for reviewing changes in advance to catch any adverse effects the SA may have missed or interactions that the SA might not have known about. Change management also helps with debugging problems because changes are tracked and can be reviewed when a problem arises.

The frequency with which you have change management meetings depends on their scope and how rapidly the environment that they cover changes. Instituting a mechanism through which SAs check that the site is operating normally before they make their changes reduces the risk that a change made during debugging of an existing problem complicates the debugging process or makes the site even less stable.

Exercises

1. Describe the change management process in your organization.

2. How would you define the off-peak times for your site?

3. Look at the sort of tasks you perform in your job and categorize them as routine, sensitive, or major updates.

4. What kind of communication process would work best for your company? Would you have both a "push" and a "pull" mechanism? Why? What would you use each of them for?

5. How would you organize change management meetings in your company? Who do you think should attend? How often would you have them?

6. To what extent would change management affect the way that you do your job?

7. Consider how different sorts of updates should be categorized in the various areas of your site, and institute a scheduling practice that reflects your decision.

8. What problems do the people who use the system have with the current setup?

9. In reference to the case study in Section 10.1.3, about making big changes on Friday or before a vacation, pick a side and defend your decision.

Chapter 11

Server Upgrades

This chapter has a very specific focus: How do you upgrade the operating system (OS) of a single host? This is a deceptively simple task. There is a lot of preparation to do beforehand and a lot of testing afterward. There are also many different ways to perform the upgrade itself. The more critical the host is, the more important it is to do it right. This technique is a building block. Once mastered, one can move on to larger upgrade projects, such as those described in Chapter 12.

A single tool is required to do this task successfully no matter what OS is involved. This tool is a piece of paper that will be used to maintain a checklist. There is no excuse for not using this tool. Our publisher, Addison-Wesley, has graciously agreed to include a blank piece of paper in the back of this book for your convenience.[1]

Some choose to simulate a piece of paper by using a web page or a spreadsheet. These high-tech solutions have many benefits, which are described later. However, the fundamental issue is the same: There is no excuse for upgrading a server without using a checklist to guide you. Grab a pencil. Let's begin.

---

[1] If you desire additional blank paper, we highly recommend purchasing additional copies of this book.

11.1   The Basics

The hope of any OS upgrade is that all the services provided before the upgrade will be working after the upgrade. With this in mind, the process looks like this:

1. Develop a service checklist:
   (a) What services are provided by the server?
   (b) Who are the customers of each service?
   (c) What software package provides which service?
2. Verify that each software package will work with the new OS or plan an upgrade path.
3. For each service, develop a test to verify that it is working.
4. Write a back-out plan.
5. Select a maintenance window.
6. Announce the upgrade as appropriate.
7. Execute the tests developed earlier to make sure they are correct.
8. Do the upgrade with someone watching/helping (mentoring).
9. Repeat all the tests developed earlier. Follow the usual debugging process.
10. If all else fails, rely on the back-out plan.
11. Communicate completion/back-out to the customers.

11.1.1   The Steps in Detail

Let's look a little closer at each step.

Step 1: Develop a Service Checklist

The *service checklist* is a tool that you use to drive the entire process. The list should record *what* services are provided by the host, *who* are the customers of each service, and *which* software package provides each service.

Spreadsheets are an excellent way to maintain such information. The biggest benefit of maintaining this information in electronic form is that it can be easily shared both within the team and with customers. Making the file accessible via the web is better than mailing it to individuals because the web version can be rapidly updated. People will always see the latest updates. However the web is a pull mechanism. People won't seek it out on their own. You can include the URL in every email about the project, but that will not guarantee that it actually gets read.

If you really need your plans double-checked, hold a meeting with key representatives of the affected community and then walk them through the plan, step by step, asking specific questions. It is most effective to begin the process with a meeting and then use email for updates, possibly having another face-to-face meeting only at key points in the process.

Customer Dependency Check

An SA once had a meeting of 10 experienced SAs, all of whom looked at a plan and agreed right away that it looked fine to them. When the SA started stepping through it asking, "What's going to happen when we turn this off?" they started saying things like "Oops, no, if you do that, the billing system won't work any more. I guess we need to add a step where we move the billing information." In the end, they had a completely different plan with three times as many steps. If they hadn't done an in-person meeting, the original plan would have created a major disaster.

Including the customers as part of the decision and planning processes gives them a feeling of participation and control. They are invested in the outcome. They become part of the team. This generally leads to a more positive experience for them and a better relationship between the SA and business units. Sharing dependency and status information with customers on the web and in email helps ensure this process.

A machine may be dedicated to providing a single service or it may provide many services. Either way, many software packages may be involved in providing the complete service.

❖ **What's on a Machine?**   Sometimes, you know what a machine is being used for, and it is easy to create the initial document. However, over time, additional services, features, and software are added to a machine (Evard 1997). We can cross-check ourselves by analyzing the host itself. You can review the software that is installed on UNIX by looking in `/opt`, `/usr/local`, and various places that are common on such systems. Microsoft OSs usually put programs in a directory named `Program Files,` though some sites adopt local conventions such as installing them in `C:\apps`. You can look at which processes are running on the system. UNIX and NT systems will list all the TCP/IP and UDP/IP ports being listened to with the command `netstat -an`. UNIX has various boot-time scripts that can be analyzed. NT has the Services console. UNIX has `crontab` files to browse through. Every OS has some way to list all the software packages that have been installed. Some have more than one. A couple of examples include `pkginfo` (Solaris and SVR4) and `swlist` (HP-UX 10 and higher).

Usually, each service is directly related to a single software package. Sometimes a service is related to multiple packages, such as a calendar server that relies on an LDAP server. Document all of these interdependencies in the checklist.

It is also important to determine who is dependent on the various services. If they are people, they should be included in the process or at least notified that the process is happening. If other machines are dependent on the services, then users of those machines should be included.

Often, you will find some services with no dependents, and the services can be eliminated. These are always happy moments, but be careful: You might find the dependency after the service no longer exists. Consider having the service in a ready-to-run but not actually active state so that it is easy to bring up if necessary. Make sure that you document why the service is there but not running, so that it gets cleaned up next time through, if it has not been reenabled by then. The best place for this documentation is in one of the configuration files that will be edited to reenable the service.

Step 2: Verify Software Compatibility

The next step is to verify that each software package will work with the new OS and plan an upgrade path for those that don't. Using the list developed earlier, contact the vendor and find out if the software release in use will work after the upgrade. Vendors often list such information on their web sites.

You may wish to test this yourself or find another customer that has already performed the upgrade. Vendors' ideas about what it means for a version to work often don't include the features your site needs or the exact configuration you're going to use. Doing the tests yourself can be expensive but reduces the risk of failure. The point of this is risk management. If only one system is being upgraded, and the application is not critical, then personally testing it might be a waste of time. If the upgrade is going to be repeated thousands of times, in an automated fashion and in a way that failure would be highly visible, then testing is a requirement.

If the software release being used will work on the new OS release, document where you found this information for future reference. If the software isn't supported on the new OS, you have many options as follows:

Upgrade to a release that supports both OSs: If you are lucky, the software can be upgraded to a release that works on both the current release and the future release. If this is so, schedule an upgrade to that release. The tests developed in Step 3 can be useful here.

An upgrade is available, but it only works on the new OS: In this case, you must schedule the software upgrade after the OS upgrade is complete.

Depending on the customer requirements, this upgrade may be required as part of the OS upgrade or a service gap may be negotiated if the customers do not require constant access. For example, if a host is a busy web server, the customers may request that the new web server software be installed immediately because it is a major function of the host. However, if a little-used compiler requires an upgrade, they may simply request that it be upgraded in the next week or before a certain development cycle is complete. This is especially true if some other host can be used (for compilation) in the meantime.

The product is no longer supported: Sometimes, it is only when we are upgrading an OS that we find out that a product is no longer being supported by the vendor. This may block the upgrade, or customers may be willing to change vendors or go without this product.

Step 3: Verification Tests

As each service is identified, a test should be developed that will be used to verify that the service is working properly after the upgrade. The best scenario is to have all the tests recorded as scripts that can be run unattended. A master script can be written that outputs an "OK" or a "FAIL" message for each test. Tests can then be run individually as specific problems are debugged. For more complicated services, customers may write the tests or at least review them or offer to be on call to execute their own set of manual tests. Some software packages have an installation verification suite that can be run.[2]

The software world uses the term *regression testing* to describe such tests. You capture the output of the old system, make a change, and then captures the output of the new system. The output should match exactly. If the new output is expected to be slightly different, you might edit the captured output by hand or use a "fuzzy match" algorithm. Simple tools such as UNIX `diff` are very useful here. `diff` is an extremely useful program that compares two text files and points out the differences between the two. (Although `diff` first appeared in UNIX, there are ports to nearly every OS in existence.) `diff` has a limited fuzzy match capability; the `-w` option makes all whitespace the same. More sophisticated regression testing software can be programmed to ignore certain specific changes, usually based on a system of regular expressions. However, such complexity is not required. You can manually change the old output (Make a backup first!) to reflect the differences that are expected in the new output. For

---

[2] All software packages should have such a verification procedure, but they rarely do. Sometimes, the verification procedure is broken. One supercomputer vendor was notorious for having bad verify databases, especially in the beta OS releases.

example, you might change the version numbers in the output to match the new software. Excellent examples of regression testing are included in Kernighan and Pike's *The Practice of Programming* (1999), as well as the installation procedure for `perl` (look how `make tests` is implemented).

Sometimes, the tests can be as simple as a "Hello, world!!" program that is compiled and run to verify that a compiler works. It may be a particular sequence of commands or mouse clicks. However, be careful to make sure the tests are not superficial.

Hello, World!!

Tom was once responsible for maintaining a large range of compilers for many different operating systems. He maintained a library of simple programs; most only printed "Hello, world!!" then exited. He could always verify that a new compiler installation was at least fundamentally correct if the appropriate program(s) compiled and ran. When new languages were added to the mix, he would often recruit the programmers to write the test program. The programmers enjoyed being asked to help out!

You must test the tests with the same level of scrutiny as any other service. When the tests are put into use, you don't want to be debugging the tests.

It is tempting to perform these tests manually. However, remember that each test will be done a minimum of three times and more if there are problems. There will be benefits to automating the tasks. If they are general enough, they can be reused during future upgrades. Ultimately, they can be reused on a regular basis just to debug problems or notice outages before your customers do.

Scripted tests work fine for programs that produce predictable text output, but they're much more difficult for graphical programs, protocols like NFS, or physical issues such as printing. For something such as NFS, you can try to access a file rather than test the protocol itself. For other systems, you can find specialized test systems, but those are extremely expensive. In these cases, you will simply end up testing these features by hand, documenting a couple specific features to test or a sequence of operations to perform. Everyone is in this situation at one time or another, and we should all complain to vendors until they instrument their products so that such testing can be automated.

Step 4: Write a Back-Out Plan

If something goes wrong during the upgrade, how will you revert back to the old state? How long will that take? Obviously, if something small goes wrong, the usual debugging process will try to fix it. However, you can use up the entire maintenance window trying "just one more thing" to make an upgrade work. It is therefore important to have a particular time at which the back-out plan will be activated. Take the agreed upon end time and subtract the back-out time, as well as the time it would take to test that the back-out is complete. When you reach that time, you must either declare success or begin your back-out plan. It is useful to have the clock watcher be someone outside of the group directly performing the upgrade, such as a manager.

Small to medium-size systems can be backed up completely before the upgrade begins. It can be even easier to clone the disks and perform the upgrade on the clones. If there are serious problems, the original disks can be reinstalled.[3] Larger systems are more difficult to replicate. Replicating the system disks and doing incremental backups of the data disks may be sufficient in this case.

Step 5: Select a Maintenance Window

The next step is a test of your technical and nontechnical skills. You must come to agreement with your customers on a maintenance window, that is, when the upgrade will happen. However, to do that, you must know how long the process will take and have a plan if the upgrade fails. That is more of a technical issue.

When? Customers usually have a good idea of when they can withstand an outage. Most business systems are not needed at night or on the weekend. However, SAs might not want to work those hours, and vendor support might not be available at certain times. A balance must be found. Sites that are required to be up 24×7 have a maintenance plan (that might include fall-back systems) engineered into the entire operation.

How long? The length of the maintenance window equals the time the upgrade should take, plus the time testing should take, plus the time it will take to fix problems, plus the time it takes to execute the back-out plan, plus the time it takes to ensure the back-out worked. Initially, it is best to double or triple your estimates to adjust for hubris. As time goes on, your estimates will become more accurate.

Whatever length of time you have calculated, announce the window to be much longer. Sometimes, you may get started late. Sometimes things just take longer than you expect for technical reasons (hardware, software, or unrelated or unexpected events) or nontechnical reasons (weather or car problems).

---

[3]It is better to perform the upgrade on the clone rather than the original. If it turns out that the original wasn't cloned properly, you don't want to have destroyed the original.

What time is the back-out plan initiated?   It is a good idea to clearly document the exact time that the back-out plan will be initiated for reasons described in Step 4.

> ❖ **Scotty Always Exaggerated**   In the *Star Trek: The Next Generation* episode "Relics," James Doohan made a cameo appearance as Scotty from the original series. Among Scotty's interesting revelations was that he always exaggerated when giving estimates to Captain James T. Kirk. Thus he always looked like a miracle worker when problems were solved faster than expected. Now we know why the warp drive was always working sooner than predicted and the environmental systems lasted longer than were indicated. Follow Scotty's advice! Exaggerate your estimates!

Case Study: The Monday Night Carte Blanche

When Tom worked at a division of Mentor Graphics, the SA staff had the luxury of a weekly maintenance window. Monday night was "SA Carte Blanche Night." Users were expected to be logged out at 6 PM on Monday night, and the SA staff could use this evening to perform any kind of major upgrades that would require bringing down service. Every Monday by 4 PM, the customers were informed what changes would be happening and when the systems should be usable again. Users eventually developed a habit of planning non-work-related activities on Monday nights. Rumor has it that some spent the time with their family.

Although it required a big political investment to get this approved through management, it was a factor in creating high reliability in their network. There was rarely a reason to put off timely system upgrades. Problems during the week could be taken care of with quick fixes, but long-term fixes were done efficiently on Monday night. Unlike some environments where the long-term fix never gets implemented, those were always put in relatively soon.

When there wasn't much to be done, one supervisor believed it was important to reboot some critical servers at 6 PM to "encourage" users to go home for the night. He believed this helped the users maintain their habit of not planning anything critical for Monday night. Of course, the SAs were flexible. When the customers were up against a critical deadline and would be working around the clock, the SAs would cancel the Monday night maintenance or collaborate with the customers to determine which outages could happen without interfering with their work.

Step 6: Announce the Upgrade as Appropriate

Now announce the upgrade to the customers. Use the same format for all announcements so that customers get used to them. Depending on the culture of your environment, the message may best be distributed by email,

```
To: all-users
Subject: SERVER REBOOT: 6 PM TODAY
From: System Administration Group <help@example.com>
Reply-To: tom@example.com
Date: Thu, 16 Jun 2001 10:32:13 -0500


WHO IS AFFECTED:

        All hosts on DEVELOPER-NET, TOWNVILLE-NET, and BROCCOLI-NET.


WHAT WILL HAPPEN:

        All servers will be rebooted.


WHEN?

        Today between 6-8 PM (should take 1 hour)


WHY?

        We are in the process of rolling out new kernel tuning
        parameters to all servers. This requires a reboot. The
        risk is minimal. For more information please visit:
                http://portal.example.com/sa/news0005


I OBJECT!

        Send mail to "help" and we will try to reschedule. Please
        name the server you want us to keep up today.
```

Figure 11.1: Sample upgrade message.

voicemail, desk-to-desk paper memo, newsgroup posting, web page, note on door, or smoke signals. No matter what format, the message should be brief and to the point. Many people read only the first sentence, so make it a good one, as shown in Figure 11.1.

It is better to have a blank template that is filled out each time than to edit previous announcements to include new information. This prevents the form from mutating over time. It also prevents the common problem of forgetting to change some parts. For example, when creating the above example we initially used a real announcement that referred to a router reboot. We changed it to be about servers instead but forgot to change the Subject: line. The example went four rounds of proofreading before anyone noticed this. This wouldn't have happened if we had started with a blank template instead.

Step 7: Execute the Tests

Right before the upgrade begins, perform the tests. This last-minute check assures you that you won't be chasing problems after the upgrade that existed before the upgrade. Imagine the horror of executing the back-out plan only to discover that the failing test is still failing.

Step 8: Do the Upgrade (with Someone Watching)

This is where most system administration books begin. Aren't you glad you bought this book instead?

Now, the moment you've all been waiting for: Perform the upgrade as your local procedures dictate.

System upgrades are too critical to do alone. First of all, we all make mistakes, and a second set of eyes is always useful. Upgrades aren't done every day, so everyone is always a little out of practice. Second, a unique kind of mentoring goes on when two people do a system upgrade together. System upgrades often involve extremes of our technical knowledge. We use commands, knowledge, and possibly parts of our brains that aren't used at other times. You can learn a lot by watching and understanding the techniques that someone else uses at these times.

If the upgrade isn't going well, it is rarely too early to escalate to a colleague or senior member of your team. A second set of eyes often does wonders, and no one should feel ashamed about asking for help.

Step 9: Test Your Work

Now repeat all the tests developed earlier. Follow the usual debugging process if they fail. The tests can be repeated time and time again as the problem is debugged.

Customers should be involved here. As with the helpdesk model in Chapter 16, the job isn't done until customers have verified that everything is complete. This may mean having the customer called at a prearranged time, or they may agree to report back the next day, after the maintenance window has elapsed. In that case, getting the automated tests right is even more critical.

Step 10: If All Else Fails, Rely on the Back-Out Plan

If the clock watcher announces that it is time to begin the back-out plan, you have to begin the back-out plan. This may happen if the upgrade is taking longer than expected or if the upgrade is complete but the testing persists in failing.

Reverting the system back to its previous state should not be the only component of the back-out plan. Customers might agree that if only certain tests fail, they may be able to survive without that service for a day or two while it is repaired. You should decide in advance the action plan for each potential failure.

After the back-out plan is executed, the services should be tested again.

Step 11: Communicate Completion/Back-Out

At this point, the customers are notified that the upgrade is complete (or if the back-out plan was initiated), what was accomplished, what didn't get accomplished, and the fact that the systems are usable again. This has three goals. First, it tells people that the services they have been denied access to are now usable. Second, it reminds the customers what has changed. Finally, if they find problems that were not discovered during your own testing, it lets them know how to report problems they have found. If the back-out plan was initiated, customers should be informed that the system should be operating as it had before.

Just as there are many ways to announce the maintenance window, there are many ways to communicate the completion. There is a catch-22 here. Customers cannot read an email announcement if the email service is affected by the outage. However, if you keep to your maintenance window, then email, for example, will be working and customers can read the email announcement. If customers hear nothing, they will assume that at the end of the announced maintenance window, everything is complete.

Such announcements should be short. Simply list which service should be functioning again and provide a URL that people can refer to for more information and a phone number to call if a failed return to service might prevent people from being able to send email. One or two sentences should be fine.

Big Red Signs

Customers tend to ignore messages from SAs. Josh Simon reports that at one client site he tried leaving notes—black text on bright red paper taped to the monitors—saying "DO NOT LOG IN—CONTACT YOUR SYSTEM ADMINISTRATOR AT [phone number] FIRST!" in 36-point font. Over 75 percent of the customers ripped the paper off and proceeded to log in rather than calling the phone number. The lesson to be learned here is that it is often better to actually disable a service than to ask customers not to use it.

11.2   The Icing

Once the basics of upgrading a server have been mastered, what can we do to expand on the process?

11.2.1   Add and Remove Services at the Same Time

During an upgrade, sometimes you must add or remove services at the same time. This complicates matters because more than one change is being made at a time. Debugging a system with two changes is much more difficult because it affects the tests that are being executed. Adding services has all the same problems as bringing up a new service on a new host, but you are now in a new and possibly unstable environment and you cannot prepare by creating appropriate tests. However, if the new service is also available on a different host, tests can be developed and run against that host.

Removing a service can be both easy and hard at the same time. It can be easy for the same reason that it is easier to tear down a building than to build one. However, you must make sure all the residents are out of the building first. Sometimes, we set up a network sniffer to watch for packets that indicate someone is trying to receive that service from the host. That can be useful to find stragglers. We prefer to disable a service in a way that makes it easy to re-enable quickly if forgotten dependencies are discovered later. For example, the service can be halted without removing the software. It is usually safe to assume that if no forgotten dependencies are discovered in the next week or month, it is safe to remove the software. However, don't forget to come back to clean up! Create a ticket in your helpdesk system, send yourself email, or create an `at` job that emails you a reminder sometime in the future.

11.2.2   Fresh Installs

Sometimes, it is much better to do a fresh install than an upgrade. Doing upgrade after upgrade can lead to a system with a lot of damage. It can result in files left over from old patches, fragmented file systems, and a lot of "history" from years of entropy as described in Chapter 1.

Earlier we mentioned the luxury of cloning the appropriate disks and doing the upgrade on the clone. An even more luxurious method is to perform the upgrade as a fresh install on a different system because it doesn't require an outage of the old system. You can do the fresh install on a temporary machine at a leisurely pace, make sure all services are working, then move the disks into the actual machine and adjust network configuration settings as appropriate. Note that the machine on which the rebuild takes place must be almost identical to the machine that is to be upgraded, to ensure that the new OS disks have all the appropriate hardware support and configurations.

11.2.3 Reusing the Tests

If the tests are properly scripted, they can be integrated into a real-time monitoring system. In fact, if your monitoring system is already doing all the right tests, you shouldn't need anything else during your upgrade. See Chapter 24 for more discussion about service monitoring.

11.2.4 System Changelog

Building the service checklist is much easier if you've kept a log of what's been added to the machine as it was added. Why not start maintaining a log of all the changes that have been made right now? If not, why not begin at the next upgrade? At Bell Labs, we put this file in `/var/adm/admin/CHANGELOG` and maintain it under RCS (Bolinger 1995). A script called `xed` edits a file and does the boring RCS manipulations for you. We put a reminder as follows in `/etc/motd`:

```
If you make any changes to this system,
as root, you must document them with:

    cd /var/adm/admin; /opt/default/bin/xed CHANGELOG
```

11.2.5 A Dress Rehearsal

Take a lesson from the theater world: Practice makes perfect. Why not perform a dress rehearsal on a different machine before you perform the upgrade? This might reveal unexpected roadblocks, as well as give you an indication of how long the process will take. A dress rehearsal requires a lot of resources and may be unrealistic. However, if you are about to perform the first upgrade of many, this can be a valuable tool to estimate the time the upgrades will require. An absolutely complete dress rehearsal results in a new machine that can simply replace the old machine. If you have those resources, why not do just that?

The theater also has what's referred to as the *Tech Rehearsal*. This is a rehearsal for the lighting and sound people more than the actors. The actors run through their lines with the right blocking as the lighting and sound directions are put through their paces. The SA equivalent is to have all the involved parties walk through the tasks.

Also from theater we borrow the fine art of pantomime. Sometimes, a major system change involves a lot of physical cables to be changed. Why not walk though all the steps looking for problem areas such as cable lengths, crossover/straight-through mismatches, male/female connector mismatches, incorrect connectors, and conflicting plans? Pantomime the change exactly how it will be done. It can be helpful to have someone else with you and explain the tasks as you act them out. Verify to them that each connector is correct, and so on. It may seem silly and embarrassing at first, but the problems you prevent will be worth it.

11.2.6   Install Old and New Versions on the Same Machine

Sometimes, one is simply upgrading a single service on a machine, rather than the entire OS. In that situation, it is helpful if the vendor permits the old versions of the software to remain on the machine in a dormant state while the new software is installed and certified.

The web server Apache on UNIX is one such product. We usually install it in `/opt/apache-x.y.z` (where `x.y.z` is the version number), but place a symbolic link from `/opt/apache` to the release we want to be using. All configurations and scripts refer to `/opt/apache` exclusively. When the new version is loaded, the `/opt/apache` link is changed to point to the new version. If we find problems with the new release, we revert the symbolic link and restart the daemon. It is a very simple back-out plan.

In some situations, the old and new software can actually run simultaneously. If a lot of debugging is required, we can run the new version of Apache on a different port while retaining the old version.

11.2.7   Minimal Changes from the Base

Upgrades become easier when there is little work to do. With a little planning, all add-on packages for UNIX can be loaded in a separate partition, thus leaving the system partitions as "generic" as possible. Such additions to the system can be documented in a CHANGELOG file, as mentioned before. Most changes will be in `/etc`, which is small enough to be copied before any upgrades begin and used as a reference. That is preferable to the laborious process of restoring files from tape.

In a dataless UNIX environment, usually only `/var` needs to be preserved between upgrades, and then only the crontabs and at jobs, the mail spool, and, for systems such as Solaris, the calendar manager files. A version control system such as RCS is good for tracking changes to configuration files.

Case Study: Upgrading a Critical DNS Server

This case study combines many of the techniques discussed in this chapter. During the rush to fix Y2K bugs before January 1, 2000, Tom found a critical DNS server that was running on hardware that was not Y2K compliant and that the vendor had announced would not be fixed. Also, the OS was not Y2K compliant. This was an excellent opportunity to perform a fresh load of the OS on entirely new hardware.

He developed a service checklist. Although he thought that the host provided only two services, he found many other services running on the machine, using `netstat -a` and listing all the running processes. He discovered that some of those extra services were no longer in use and found one service that nobody could identify!

They knew that all the software packages involved would work on the new OS because they were in use on other machines with the newer OS. However, many of the services were homegrown, and there was a panic when it was thought that the author of a home-grown package was no longer at the company and the source code couldn't be found immediately. Luckily, it was found.

Tom built the new machine and replicated all the services onto it. The original host had many configuration files that were edited on a regular basis. He needed to copy these data files to the new system to verify that the scripts that processed them worked properly on the new machine. However, because the upgrade was going to take a couple of weeks, those files would be modified many times before the new host would be ready. The tests would be done on aging data, and when the new system was cut in, he stopped all changes on the old host, recopied the files to the new system, and verified that the new system accepted the new files.

The tests that were developed were not run just once before the cut-over, but were run over and over as various services on the new system became usable. However, Tom did leave most services somewhat disabled when they weren't being tested because of concern that the old and new machines might conflict with each other.

The cut-over worked as follows: The old machine was disconnected from the network but left running. The new machine's IP address was changed to that of the old one and the machine rebooted. After five minutes, the ARP caches on the local network timed out, and the new host was recognized. If problems appeared, he could unplug the new machine from the network and reconnect the network cable of the legacy machine. The legacy machine was left running so that not even a reboot would be required to bring it back into service.

The actual maintenance window could have been quite short—a minimum of five minutes if everything went right and the machine could be rebooted instantly. However, a 30-minute window was announced.

Tom decided to have two people looking over his shoulder during the upgrade because he wasn't as familiar with this version of UNIX as he is with others and didn't get much sleep the night before. It turned out that having an extra pair of hands helped with unplugging and plugging wires.

The group pantomimed the upgrade hours before the maintenance window. Without actually changing anything, they walked through exactly what was planned. They made sure that every cable would be long enough and that all the connectors were the right type. This process cleared up any confusion that anyone on the team might have had.

The upgrade went well. Some tests failed, but they were soon able to fix the problems. One unexpected problem resulted in certain database updates not happening until a script could be fixed. The customers that depended on that data being updated were willing to live with slightly stale data until the script could be rewritten the next day.

11.3   Conclusion

We have described a fairly complete process for upgrading the OS of a computer, yet we have not mentioned a particular vendor's OS, particular commands to type, or buttons to click. The important parts of the process are not the technology, which is a matter of reading manuals, but rather communication, attention to detail, and testing.

The basic tool we used is a checklist. We began by developing the checklist then used it to determine which services required upgrading, how long the upgrade would take, and when we could do it. The checklist drives what tests we develop, and those tests are used over and over again. We use the tests before and after the upgrade to ensure quality. If the upgrade fails, we activate the back-out plans included in the checklist. When the process is complete, we announce this to the list of concerned customers on the checklist.

A checklist is a simple tool. It is a single place where all the information is maintained. Whether you use paper, a spreadsheet, or a web page, the checklist is the focal point. It keeps the team "on the same page," keeps the individuals focused, lets the customers understand the process, helps management understand the status, and brings new team members up to speed quickly.

Like many SA processes, this requires communication skills. Negotiation is a communication process, and we use it to determine when the upgrade will happen, what needs to happen, and what the priorities are if things go wrong. We give the customers a feeling of closure by communicating to them when we are finished. This helps the customer–SA relationship. We cannot stress enough the importance of putting the checklist on a web page. The more eyes that can review the information, the better.

When the tests are automated, we can repeat them with accuracy and ensure completeness. These tests should be general enough that they can be reused not just for future upgrades on the same host, but on other similar hosts. In fact, the tests should be integrated into your real-time monitoring system. Why only perform these tests after upgrades?

This is a simple, 11-step process that can be easily understood and practiced. This is one of the basic processes that an SA must master before moving on to more complicated upgrades. The real-world examples we used all required some kind of deviation from the basic process, yet still encompassed the essential 11 points.

Exercises

1. Select a server in your environment and figure out what services it provides. If you maintain a documented list of services, what system commands would you use to cross check the list? If you do not have the services documented, what are all the resources you might use to build a complete list?

2. In your environment, how do you know who depends on which services?

3. Select a location that should be easy to walk to from your machine room or office, such as a nearby store, bank, or someplace at the other end of your building if it is very large. Have 3 or 4 fellow students, coworkers, or friends estimate how long it will take to walk there and back. Now, all of you should walk there and back as a group, recording how long it takes. (Do this right now, before you read the rest of the question. Really!) How long did it take? Did you start walking right away or were you delayed? How many unexpected events along the way (ran into customers, people that wanted to know what you were doing, and so on) extended your trip's time? Calculate how close each of you were to being accurate, the average of these, and the standard deviation. What did you learn from this exercise? If you repeat it, how much better do you think your estimate will be if you select the same location? A different location? Would bringing more people have affected the actual time? Relate what you learned to the process of planning a maintenance window.

4. In Section 11.1.1, the claim is made that the tests that are developed will be executed "a minimum of three times, and more if there are problems." What are the three minimum times? What are some additional times the tests may be run?

5. Section 11.2.7 includes a case study in which the source code to a home-grown service almost couldn't be found. What would you do in that situation if the source code couldn't be found?

6. How do you announce planned outages and maintenance windows in your environment? What are the benefits and problems with this method? What percentage of your customers ignore these announcements?

7. Customers often ignore announcements from SAs. What can be done to improve this situation?

8. Select a host in your environment and upgrade it. (Ask permission first!)

9. What steps would you take if you had to replace the only restroom in your building?

Chapter 12

Maintenance Windows

In the previous chapter, we focused on doing a single system change well. What about the other extreme, when you must perform many changes or bring down all systems? What if your machine room is almost out of space and needs to be split across two machine rooms in different buildings, or you need to completely redesign your authentication architecture so that it can scale? Or you may be at a site that wants all maintenance that requires interruption of service (such as hardware upgrades, replacing broken parts, or network changes) to be performed at a prescheduled time, once a month, or once a quarter. As a result, a lot of work that is delayed until then needs to be coordinated. Larger projects require more planning, more orderly execution, and considerably more testing. We call this the "flight director" technique, named after the role of the flight director in NASA space launches.[1]

Although most people clean their house or apartment on a weekly or monthly basis, an annual "spring cleaning" is certainly useful. Similarly, networks sometimes need massive, disruptive cleaning. Cooling systems must be powered off, drained, cleaned, and refilled. Messy nests of wires become

---

[1]The origin of this terminology was with Paul Evans. Paul is an avid observer of the space program. The first flight directors wore the "flight director vest," like the vest worn by the flight director in *Apollo 13*.

Stage	Activity
Preparation	Schedule the window
	Pick a flight director
	Prepare change proposals
	Build a master plan
Execution	Disable access
	Shutdown sequence
	Execute plan
	Perform testing
Resolution	Announce completion
	Enable access
	Have a visible presence
	Be prepared for problems

Table 12.1: The Three Stages of a Maintenance Window

impediments to working effectively and sometimes must be tidied. Large volumes of data must be moved between file servers to optimize performance for users or simply provide room for growth. Network improvements that involve many changes can be done much more efficiently if all users agree to a large window of downtime. The flight director technique guides the activities before the window, during execution, and after execution. It is summarized in Table 12.1.

Some companies are willing to schedule regular maintenance windows for major systems and networking work in return for better availability during normal operations. Depending on the size of the site, this could be one evening and night per month or perhaps an entire weekend, from Friday evening to Monday morning, once a quarter. These maintenance windows are necessarily very intense, so consider the capacity and well-being of the system administration staff, as well as the impact on the company, when deciding to schedule them.

SAs often like to have a maintenance window during which they can take down any and all systems and stop all services, because it reduces complexity and makes testing easier. It's difficult to change the tires while the car is driving down the highway. For example, in cutting email services over to a new system, you need to transfer existing mailboxes, as well as switch the incoming mail feed to the new system. Trying to transfer the existing mailboxes without cutting the feed and the read access for those mailboxes, and yet ensure consistency, is a very tricky problem. However, if you can bring email services down while you do the transfer, it becomes a lot easier. In addition, it is a lot easier to check that the system is working correctly before you turn the mail feed and the read access on again than it is to deal with having dropped or bounced mail if something didn't work quite right with the live cut-over.

However, you will have to sell the concept to the company in terms of a benefit to them, not in terms of it making the SA's life easier. That means that you need to be able to promise better service availability the rest of the time. In other words, you need to plan in advance: If you have one maintenance window per quarter, you need to make sure that the work you do this quarter will hold you through the end of the next quarter, so that you won't need to bring the system down again. Every member of the team must commit to high availability for their systems for this to work. You should also be prepared to provide metrics to back up your claims of higher availability[2] from before and after you have succeeded in getting scheduled maintenance windows.

Many companies will not agree to a large scheduled outage for maintenance. In that case, an alternative plan must be presented, explaining what would be entailed if the outage was granted, demonstrating that customers, not the SAs, are the real beneficiaries. A single large outage can be much less annoying to customers than many little outages (Limoncelli et al. 1997).

Other companies are unable to have a large outage for business reasons. E-commerce sites and ISPs fall into this category. Those sites need to provide high availability to their customers, who typically are off-site and not easily contacted. They do, however, still need maintenance windows. The end of this chapter looks at how the principles learned in this chapter apply in a high availability site.

12.1 The Basics

A *maintenance window* is by definition a short period in which a lot of systems work must be performed. It is disruptive to the rest of the company, and so the scheduling must be done in cooperation with the customers. A group of SAs must perform various tasks, and that work must be coordinated by the flight director.

Scheduling the maintenance window, the role of the flight director, developing a coordinated plan, preparatory work, communicating with the customers, the mechanics of running a maintenance window, and complete

---

[2]The most effective way of doing this is to use an existing monitoring system that can produce historical graphs. The most popular ones at the time of writing are MRTG (Oetiker 1998a) and Cricket (Allen 1999). It should be able to monitor any form of availability, such as responding to pings, daemons listening on a certain port, or a response to an SNMP query. You can then decide how you want to define the "availability" levels that you report. A detailed discussion on such metrics is beyond the scope of this book.

system testing are some of the basics that you need for success. We discuss each of those further below.

12.1.1   Scheduling

In scheduling periodic maintenance windows, you must work with the rest of the company to coordinate dates. In particular, you will almost certainly need to avoid the end-of-month, end-of-quarter, and end-of-fiscal-year dates so that the sales team can enter rush orders and the accounting group can produce financial reports for that period. You also will need to avoid product release dates, if that is relevant to your business. Universities have different constraints around the academic year. Some businesses, such as toy and greeting card manufacturers, may have seasonal constraints. You must set and publicize the schedule far in advance, preferably more than one year ahead, so that the rest of the company can plan around those times.

Case Study: Maintenance Window Scheduling

In a mid-size software development company, we had quarterly maintenance windows. We had to avoid dates immediately before and after scheduled release dates, when the engineering and operations divisions would rely on the systems being operational to make the release. Releases typically occurred three times a year. We had to avoid dates leading up to and during the major trade show for the company's products, because engineering typically produced new alpha versions for the show, and demos at the trade show might rely on equipment at the office. We also had to avoid end-of-month, end-of-quarter, and end-of-year dates when the sales support and finance departments rely on full availability to enter figures.

In addition, events likely to cause a spike in customer-support calls, such as a special product promotion, needed to be coordinated with outages, although they were typically scheduled after the maintenance windows were set. As you can see, finding windows that did not conflict with other people in the company being able to meet important deadlines was a tricky business. However, maintenance schedules were set at least a year in advance and well advertised so that the rest of the company could plan around them.

Once the dates were set, reminders were posted six, four, two, and one weeks in advance of each window, with additional notices the final week. At the end of each notice, the schedule for all the following maintenance windows was attached, as far ahead as they had been scheduled.

The maintenance notice would highlight a major item from those that were scheduled, to advertise as the benefit to the company of the outage period, such as bringing a new data center online or upgrading the mail infrastructure. This helped the customers understand the benefit they received in return for the interruption of service.

> Unfortunately for the SA group, the rest of the company saw the maintenance weekends as the perfect times to schedule company picnics and other events, because no one would feel compelled to work (except for the SAs, of course).

12.1.2 Planning

As with all planned maintenance on important systems, the tasks need to be planned by the individuals performing them, so that no original thought, or problem solving, should be involved in performing the task on the day. There should be no unforeseen events, only planned contingencies.

Planning for a maintenance window also has another dimension, however. Because maintenance windows occur only occasionally, the SAs need to plan far enough in advance to allow time to get quotes, submit purchase orders and get them approved, and have any new equipment arrive a week or so before the maintenance window. The lead-time on some equipment can be six weeks or more, so this means starting to plan for the next maintenance window almost immediately after the preceding one has ended.

12.1.3 Flight Director

The flight director is responsible for crafting the announcement notices and making sure that they go out on time. She is also responsible for scheduling the submitted work proposals based on the interactions between them and the staff required, deciding which ones (if any) don't make the cut for that maintenance window, monitoring the progress of the tasks during the maintenance window, ensuring that the testing occurs correctly, and communicating status to the rest of the company at the end of the maintenance window.

The person who fills the role of flight director must be a senior SA who is capable of assessing work proposals from other members of the SA team and spotting dependencies and effects that may have been overlooked. The flight director also must be capable of making judgment calls on the level of risk versus need for some of the more critical tasks that affect the infrastructure. She must have a good overview of the site, understand the implications of all the work, and look good in a vest.

In addition, the flight director cannot perform any technical work during that maintenance window. Typically, the flight director is a member of a multiperson team, and the other members of the team take on the work that would normally have been the responsibility of that individual. The flight director is not normally a manager, unless the manager was recently promoted from a senior SA position, because of the skill requirements described above.

Case Study: *Selecting a Flight Director*

Depending on the structure of the SA group, there may be an obvious group of people from which the flight director is selected each time. In the mid-size software company we discussed earlier, there were about 60 SAs, most of whom took care of a division of the company. About 10 SAs formed the "core services" unit and were responsible for central services and infrastructure that were shared by the whole company, such as security, networking, email, printing, and naming services. The SAs in the core services unit provided services to each of the other business units, and thus had a good overview of the corporate infrastructure and how the business units relied on it. The flight director was typically a member of core services who had been with the company for a while.

Other factors also had to be taken into account, such as how the person interacted with the rest of the SAs, whether she would be reasonably strict about the deadlines but show good judgment where an exception should be made, and how the person would react under pressure and when tired. There were some excellent senior SAs in that group, who performed flight director duties once and never wanted to do it again, so we also had to make sure that the flight director we selected was a willing victim.

12.1.4   Change Proposals

One week before the maintenance window, all change proposals should have been submitted. A good way of managing the change proposal process is to have all the change proposals online in a revision-controlled area. Each SA edits documents in a directory with his name on it. The documents supply all the required information. One week before the change, this revision-controlled area is frozen, and all subsequent requests to make changes to the documents have to be made through the flight director. A change proposal form should answer at least the following questions:

- What changes are going to be made?
- What machines will you be working on?
- What are the premaintenance window dependencies, and due dates?
- What needs to be up for the change to happen?
- What will be affected by the change?
- Who is performing the work?
- How long will the change take in active time and elapsed time, including testing, and how many additional helpers will be needed?
- What are the test procedures? What equipment do they require?
- What is the back-out procedure and how long will it take?

Change Proposal: Sample 1

What change are you going to make?
Upgrade the SecurID authentication server software from v1.4 to v2.1.

What machines are you working on?
`tsunayoshi` and `shingen`

Prewindow dependencies and due dates?
The v2.1 software and license keys are to be delivered by the vendor and should arrive on September 14. Perform backups the night before the window.

Dependencies on other systems?
The network, console service, and internal authentication services (NIS).

What will be affected by the change?
All remote access and access to secured areas that require token authentication.

How long will the change take?
Time: 3 hours active; 3 hours elapsed.

Who is performing the work?
Jane Smith.

Additional helpers?
None.

Test procedure?
Try to: dial in, establish a VPN in, connect over ISDN, and access each secured area. Test creating a new user, deleting a user, and modifying a user's attributes; check that each change has taken effect.

Equipment required:
Laptop with modem and VPN software, analog line, external ISP account, ISDN modem, and BRI.

Back-out procedure?
Installing new software in a parallel directory, and copying the database into a new location. Don't delete old software and database until after a week of successful running. To back out (takes 5 minutes, plus testing), change links to point back to the old software.

Change Proposal: Sample 2

What change are you going to make?
Move `/home/de105` and `/db/gene237` from `anaconda` to `anachronism`.

What machines are you working on?
`anaconda, anachronism,` and `shingen`.

Prewindow dependencies and due dates?
> Extra disk shelves for `anachronism` need to be delivered and installed; due to arrive September 17 and installed by September 21. Perform backups the night before the window.

Dependencies on other systems?
> The network, console service, and internal authentication services (NIS).

What will be affected by the change?
> Network traffic on 172.29.100.x network, all accounts with home directories on `/home/de105`, and database access to `/db/gene237`.

How long will the change take?
> Time: 1 hour active; 12 hours elapsed.

Who is performing the work?
> Greg Jones.

Additional helpers?
> None.

Test procedure?
> Try to mount those directories from some appropriate hosts; log in to a desktop account with a home directory on `/home/de105`, check that it is working; start the gene database, check for errors, run test database access script in `/usr/local/tests/gene/access-test`.

Equipment required:
> Access to a non-SA desktop.

Back-out procedure?
> Old data gets deleted *after* successful testing; change advertised locations of directories back to the old ones and rebuild tables. Takes 10 minutes to back out.

12.1.5   The Master Plan

One week before the maintenance window, the flight director freezes the change proposals and starts working on a master plan. The master plan takes into account all the dependencies and elapsed and active times for the change proposals. The result is a series of tables, one for each person, showing what task each person will perform during which time interval and identifying the coordinator for that task. A master chart shows all the tasks that are being performed over the entire time, who is performing them, the team lead, and what the dependencies are. The master plan also takes into account complete system-wide testing after all work has been completed.

If there are too many change proposals, the flight director will find that scheduling all of them produces too many conflicts, in terms of either machine availability or the people required. You need to have slack in the schedule to allow for things to go wrong. The difficult decisions about which projects should go ahead and which ones must wait should be made beforehand, rather than in the heat of the moment when something is taking too long and blowing the schedule, and everyone is tired and stressed. The flight director makes the call on when some change proposals must cut and assists the parties involved to choose the best course for the company.

Case Study: *Building a Master Plan Template*

Once we had run a few maintenance windows, we discovered that a formula that worked well for us. The systems on which most people were dependent for their work were operated on during Friday evening. The first thing to be upgraded or changed was the network. Next on the list was console service, then the authentication servers. While these were in progress, all the other SAs helped out with hardware tasks such as memory, disk, or CPU upgrades, replacing broken hardware, or moving equipment within or between data centers. Last thing on Friday night, large data moves were started so that they could run overnight.

The remaining tasks were then scheduled into Saturday, with some people being scheduled to help others in between their own tasks. Sunday was reserved for comprehensive systemwide testing and debugging, because of the high importance placed on testing.

12.1.6 Disabling Access

The very first task in the maintenance window is to disable or discourage system access and provide reminders that it is a maintenance window. Depending on what the site looks like and what facilities are available, this process may involve

- Placing notices on all doors into the campus buildings with the maintenance window times clearly visible.
- Disabling all remote access to the site, whether by dial-in, dedicated lines, or wireless or over a public network.
- Making an announcement over the public address system in the campus buildings to remind everyone that systems are about to go down.
- Changing the helpdesk voicemail message to announce that this is a maintenance window, and stating when normal service should be restored.

These steps reduce the chance that people will try to use the systems during the maintenance window, which could cause inconsistencies, or accidental loss or damage of their work. It also reduces the chance that the person carrying the on-call pager will have to respond to urgent helpdesk voicemails saying that the network is down.

12.1.7   Mechanics and Coordination

Some key pieces of technology enable the maintenance window process described here to proceed smoothly. These are not solely useful for maintenance windows, but they are critical to their success.

Shutdown/Boot Sequence

In most sites, there are some systems or sets of systems that must be available for other systems to shutdown or boot cleanly. If a machine tries to boot when machines and services that it relies on are not available, it will fail to boot properly. Typically, the machine will boot, but it will fail to run some of the programs that it usually runs on start-up. These programs might be services that others rely on or programs that run locally on someone's desktop. In either case, the machine will not work properly, and it may not be apparent why. When shutting down a machine, it may need to contact file servers, license servers, or database servers that are in use in order to properly terminate the link. If it cannot contact those servers, it may hang for a long time, or indefinitely, trying to contact those servers before completing the shutdown process. It is important to understand and track the dependencies that machines have on each other during boot up and shutdown. You do not want to have to figure it out for the first time when a machine room unexpectedly loses power.

The most critical systems, such as console servers, authentication servers, name-service machines, license servers, application servers, and data servers, typically need to be booted before other machines such as compute servers and desktops. There also will be dependencies between the critical servers. It is vital to maintain a boot sequence list for all data center machines, with one or more machines at each stage, as appropriate. Typically, the first couple of stages will have few machines, maybe only one machine in them, but later stages will have many machines. All data center machines should be booted before any non-data-center machines, because no machine in a data center should rely on any machine outside a data center (see Section 3.1.7).

One site created the shutdown/boot list as shown in Table 12.2. The shutdown sequence is typically very close to, if not exactly the same as, the reverse of the boot sequence. There may be one or two minor differences.

The shutdown sequence is a vital component to starting work at the beginning of the maintenance window. The machines that are operated on at the start of the maintenance window are typically those with the most dependencies on them, so any machine that needs to be shut down for hardware

Stage	Function	Reason
1	Console server	So that SAs could monitor other servers during boot.
2	Master authentication server	Secondary authentication servers contact the master on boot.
	Master name server	Secondary name servers contact the master on boot.
3	Secondary authentication servers	So that SAs could log in to other servers as they booted. UNIX hosts contact NIS servers when they boot. Rely on nothing but the master authentication server.
	Secondary name servers	Almost all services rely on name service. Rely on nothing but the master name server.
4	Data servers	Applications and home directories reside on data servers. Most other machines rely on data servers. Rely on name service.
	Network config servers	Rely on name service.
	Log servers	Rely on name service.
	Directory servers	Rely on name service.
5	Print servers	Rely on name service and log servers.
	License servers	Rely on name service, data servers and log servers.
	Firewalls	Rely on log servers.
	Remote access	Relies on authentication service, name service, log service.
	Email service	Relies on name, log, and directory services and data servers.
6	All other servers	Rely on servers previously booted and not on each other.
7	Desktops	Rely on servers.

Table 12.2: Template for a Boot Sequence

maintenance/upgrades or moving has to be shut down before the work on the critical machines starts. It is important to shut down the machines in the right order, to avoid wasting time bringing machines back up so that other machines can be shut down cleanly. The boot sequence is also critical to the comprehensive system testing that is performed at the end of the maintenance window, as we shall see later.

Emergency Use of the Shutdown Sequence

At a company that had quarterly maintenance windows and maintained a shutdown and reboot list, that list got some unexpected exercise one day. The data center had a raised floor, with the usual mess of air-conditioning conduits, power distribution points, and network cables hiding out of sight. One Friday, one of the SAs was installing a new machine and needed to run cable under the floor. He got the tile puller, lifted a few tiles, and discovered water under the floor, surrounding some of the power distribution points. As usual in these situations, the air-conditioning unit was the source of the water, and unfortunately that site didn't have an under-floor water detection system. The SA who discovered the water notified his management (by finding them over the radio), and after a quick decision, radio notification to the SA staff and a quick company-wide broadcast, out came the shutdown list, and the flight director for the upcoming maintenance window did a live rehearsal of shutting everything in the machine room down. It went flawlessly because of the shutdown list.

In fact, management chose an orderly shutdown over tripping the emergency power cut-off to the room because they knew that there was an up-to-date shutdown list, and they had an assessment of how long they had before water and electricity would actually meet. If they hadn't had the list, they would have just had to cut power to the room, with potentially disastrous consequences.

Console Service

All of the equipment in the computer room that is capable of supporting a serial console should have its serial console connected to some kind of console concentrator such as a networked terminal server. The console servers should be running console server software that securely allows authenticated access to machine consoles from authorized hosts across the network. This enables people to work from their own desks, rather than having to try to coordinate access for many people to the very limited number of monitors in the computer room, or having to waste computer room space, power, and cooling with more monitors. If possible, the console software should log all output to disk for future reference. It is also more convenient for the individual SAs to work in their own workspace with their preparatory notes and reference materials around them.

Radios

Because the maintenance window is tightly scheduled, there are many dependencies, and system administration work can be unpredictable at times, everyone has to check with the flight director to let her know when they are finished with a task, and before they start a new task, to make sure that the prerequisite tasks have all been completed.

We recommend using handheld radios to communicate within the group. Rather than seeking out the flight director, an SA can just call her over the radio. Likewise, the flight director can contact the SAs to find out status, and team members and team leaders can find each other and coordinate over the radio. If SAs need extra help, they can also ask for it over the radio. There are multiple radio channels, and long conversations can move to another channel to keep the primary one free. The radios are also essential for systemwide testing at the end of the maintenance window, which will be described later, in Section 12.1.9.

Selecting Radios It is useful to use radios, cell phones, or some other effective form of two-way communication for campuswide instant communication between SAs. We recommend radios because they are not billed by the minute like cell phones and typically work better in data center environments than do cell phones. Remember that anything that is transmitted on the airwaves can be overheard by others, so sensitive information such as passwords should not be communicated over radios, cell phones, or pagers.

Several options exist for selecting the radios, and what you choose depends on the coverage area that you need, the type of terrain in that area, availability, and your skill level. It is useful to have multiple channels, or frequencies, available on the handheld radios, so that long conversations can switch to another channel and leave the primary hailing channel open for others (see Table 12.3).

Line-of-sight radio communications are the most common and typically have a range of around 15 miles, depending on the surrounding terrain and buildings. Your retailer should be able to set you up with one or more frequencies and a set of radios that use those frequencies. Make sure that the retailer knows that you need the radios to work through buildings and the coverage that you need.

Repeaters can be used to extend the range of a radio signal, and are particularly useful if there is a mountain between campus buildings that would block line-of-sight communication. It can be useful to have a repeater and an antenna on top of one of the campus buildings in any case for additional

Type	Requirements	Advantages	Disadvantages
Line of sight	Frequency license Transmits through walls	Simple	Limited range Doesn't transmit through mountains
Repeater	Frequency license Radio operator license	Better range Repeater on mountain enables communication over mountain	More complex to run Skill qualifications
Cellular	Service availability	Simple Wide range Unaffected by terrain Less to carry	Higher cost Only available in cell phone providers' coverage area Company contracts may limit options Multiple channels may not be available

Table 12.3: Comparison of Radio Technologies

range, with at least the primary hailing channel using the repeater. This configuration usually requires that someone with a ham radio license sets up and operates the equipment. Check your local laws.

Some cellular phone companies offer a radio service in addition to the telephone service. It will work wherever the telephones operate. The provider should be able to provide maps of the coverage areas. The company should supply all SAs with a cell phone with this service. This has the advantage that the SAs only have to carry the phone and not a phone and radio. This can be a quick and convenient way to get a new group established with radios, but may not be feasible if it requires everyone to change to the same cell phone provider.

If radios won't work, or work badly, in your data center because of radio frequency (RF) shielding, put an internal phone extension with a long cord at the end of every row, as shown in Figure 17.13. That way, SAs in the data center can still communicate with other SAs while working in the data center. At worst, they can go outside the data center, contact someone on the radio, and arrange to talk to her on a specific telephone inside the data center.

12.1.8   Deadlines for Change Completion

A critical role of the flight director is tracking how the various tasks are progressing and deciding when a particular change should be aborted and the back-out plan for that change executed. For a general task that had no other dependencies, and where those involved had no other remaining tasks, that time would be 11 PM on Saturday evening, minus the time required to implement the back-out plan, in the case of a weekend maintenance window. The flight director should also consider the performance level of the SA team. If they are exhausted and frustrated, the flight director may decide to tell them to take a break or to start the back-out process early if they won't be able to implement it as efficiently as they would when they were fresh.

If other tasks depend on that system or service being operational, it is particularly critical to predefine a cut-off point for task completion. For example, if a console server upgrade is going badly, there might not be time to start the large data moves on Friday night, which would prevent them from happening at all, which could cause a cascade of catastrophic effects for people within the company, until the next downtime.

12.1.9   Comprehensive System Testing

A maintenance window is like taking a very complicated piece of machinery completely to pieces and then putting it back together again under a time constraint. Sometimes there are bits left over when you think you should be finished.

The final stage of a maintenance window must involve comprehensive system testing. Depending on the length of the window, you may be able to test only the few components that you worked on. However, if you have a weekend maintenance window and have a lot of people performing work on may different components, you should plan on spending all day Sunday doing system testing.

Sunday system testing starts with a complete shutdown of all machines in the data center, and then stepping through the boot sequence in order. An individual is assigned to each machine on the reboot list. The flight director calls out the stages during the shutdown sequence over the radio, and each individual calls in each machine he is responsible for when it has completely shut down. When all the machines at the current stage have shut down, the flight director calls the next stage. When everything is down, the flight director calls out the stages on the boot list and tracks the progress. If problems occur with a machine at any stage, those must be debugged and fixed before moving on to the next stage. The person assigned to each machine is responsible for ensuring that all services started correctly before calling it in as being operational.

Finally, when all the machines in the data center have been successfully booted in the correct order, the SA team is split into groups. Each group has a team leader and is assigned an area in one of the campus buildings. The teams are given instructions on what to do and which tests to perform. The instructions always include rebooting every desktop machine to make sure it comes up cleanly. They could also include logging in, checking for a particular service, or trying to run a particular application, for example. Each person in the group has a stack of colored sticky tabs used for marking offices and cubicles that have been completed and verified as working. They also have a stack of sticky tabs of a different color that they use to mark cubicles that have a problem. When SAs run across a problem, they spend a short time trying to fix it before calling it in to the central core of people who are assigned to stay in the main building to help debug problems. As a team finishes its area, it is assigned to a new area or to help another team to complete an area, until the whole campus has been covered.

The central command center, with the flight director and the senior SA troubleshooters, keeps track of problems on a whiteboard. The SAs and flight director decide who should tackle each problem, based on the likely cause and who is available. By the end of testing, all offices and cubicles should have tags, preferably all indicating success. If any offices or cubicles still have tags indicating a problem, a note should be left for that customer explaining the problem, and someone should be assigned to meet with that person to try to resolve it first thing in the morning. This method has caught many potentially serious problems before people came into work the following day, for example, disconnected or incorrectly connected network segments after wiring closet clean-up, a failed push to a software depot server, inoperable NIS slaves, AppleTalk problems, and license server problems. Be warned, however, that there may be machines that weren't working in the first place. The reboot teams should always make sure to note when a machine did not look operational before they rebooted it. They can still take time to try to fix it, but it is lower on the priority list and does not have to happen before the end of the maintenance window.

Ideally, the system testing, and site-wide rebooting should be completed sometime on Sunday afternoon, giving the SA team time to rest after a stressful weekend, before coming into work the next day.

12.1.10   Postmaintenance Communication

Once the maintenance work and system testing is completed, the flight director sends out a message to the company informing everyone that service should now be fully restored. The message briefly outlines the main successes of the maintenance window. It also briefly lists any services that are known not to be functioning and when they will be fixed.

This message should be in a fixed format and largely written in advance, because the flight director will be too tired to be very coherent or upbeat if she writes the message at the end of a long weekend. There is also little chance that anyone who proofreads the message at that point is going to be able to help, either.

12.1.11 Re-enable Remote Access

The final act before leaving the building should be to re-enable remote access, and restore the voicemail on the helpdesk phone to normal. Make sure that this appears on the master plan and the individual plans of those responsible. It can be very easily forgotten after an exhausting weekend, but it is a very visible, inconvenient, and embarrassing thing to forget, especially because it can't be fixed remotely if all remote access was turned off successfully.

12.1.12 Visible Presence the Next Morning

It is very important for the entire SA group to be in early and to be visible to the company the morning after a maintenance window, no matter how hard they have worked during the outage. If there are company or group shirts that everyone has, coordinate in advance of the maintenance window so that all the SAs wear the same shirt on the day after the outage. Have the people who look after particular departments roam the corridors of those departments, keeping eye and ear open for problems.

Have the flight director and some of the senior SAs (from the central core-services group, if there is one) sit in the helpdesk area to monitor incoming calls and listen for problems that may be related to the maintenance window. They should be able to detect and fix them sooner than the regular helpdesk staff, who won't have such an extensive overview of what has happened.

A large visible presence when the company returns to work sends the message "we care, and we are here to make sure that nothing we did disrupts your working hours." It also means that any undetected problems can be handled quickly and efficiently, with all the relevant staff on-site and not having to be paged out of their beds. Both of these are important factors in the overall satisfaction of the company with the maintenance window. If the company is not satisfied with how the maintenance windows are handled, the windows will be discontinued, which will make preventive maintenance more difficult.

12.1.13 Postmortem

By about lunchtime of the day after the maintenance window, most of the remaining problems should have been found. At that point, if it is sufficiently quiet, the flight director and some of the senior SAs should sit down and talk about what went wrong, why, and what can be done differently. That should all be noted and discussed with the whole group later in the week. Over time, with the postmortem process, the maintenance windows will become smoother and easier. Common mistakes early on are taking on too much, not doing as much preparatory work as you could, and underestimating how long something will take.

12.2 The Icing

Although a lot of basics must be implemented for a successful large-scale maintenance window, there are still a few more things that are nice to have. After completion of some successful maintenance windows, you should start thinking about the icing that will make your maintenance windows more successful.

12.2.1 Mentoring a New Flight Director

It can be useful to mentor new flight directors for future maintenance windows. This requires selecting your flight directors far enough in advance so that the flight director for the next maintenance window can work with the current flight director.

The trainee flight director can produce the first draft of the master plan using the change requests that were submitted, adding in any dependencies that he notices are missing, and tagging those additions. The flight director then goes over the plan with the trainee, adds or subtracts dependencies as she goes, and reorganizes the tasks and personnel assignments as appropriate, explaining why she makes the changes. Alternatively, the flight director can create the first draft along with the trainee, explaining the process as she goes along. The trainee flight director can also help out during the maintenance window, if he has time, by coordinating with the flight director to track status of certain projects, and suggesting reallocation of resources where appropriate. He can also help out before the downtime by discussing projects with some of the SAs if the flight director has questions about the project and by ensuring that the prerequisites listed in the change proposal are met in advance of the maintenance window.

12.2.2 Trending of Historical Data

It is useful to track how long particular tasks take, so that you can analyze the data later and improve on the estimates in the task submission and planning process. For example, if you find that moving a certain amount of data between two machines took eight hours and you have a large data move between two similar machines on similar networks another time, you can more accurately predict how long it will take. If a particular software package is always difficult to upgrade and takes far longer than anticipated, that will be tracked, anticipated, allowed for in the schedule, and watched closely during the maintenance interval.

Places where trending proves particularly useful is in passing along historical knowledge. When the person who used to perform a particular function has left the group, the person who takes over that function can look back at data from previous maintenance windows to see what sort of tasks are typically performed in this area and how long they take. This can give those who are new to the group and to planning a maintenance window a valuable head-start so that they don't waste a maintenance opportunity and fall behind.

12.2.3 Providing Limited Availability

It is highly likely that at some point you will be asked to keep service available for a particular group during a maintenance window. It may be something unforeseen, such as some serious bug has been found that engineering needs to work on all weekend, or it may be a new mode of operation for a division, such as customer support switching to 24×7 service and needing continuous access to their systems to meet their contracts.

Planning for this requirement could involve rearchitecting some services or introducing added layers of redundancy to the system. It may involve making groups more autonomous or separating them from each other. These can be significant tasks and probably require implementing during a maintenance window, so it is best to be prepared for these requests before they arrive, or you may be left without time to prepare.

To approach this, find out what the customers will need to be able to do during the maintenance window. Ask a lot of questions and use your knowledge of the systems to translate these needs into a set of service availability requirements. For example, they will almost certainly need name service and authentication service. They may need to be able to print to specific printers. They may need to be able to exchange email within the company or with customers. They may require access to services across wide area connections or across the Internet. They may need to use particular databases; find out what those machines depend on. Look at ways to make the database machines redundant so that they can also be properly maintained without loss of service. Make sure that the services they depend on are redundant. Identify what pieces of the network must be available for the services to work. Look at ways to reduce the number of networks that must be available by reducing the number of networks that the group uses and locating redundant name servers, authentication servers, and print servers on the group's networks. Find out if small outages are acceptable, such as a couple of ten-minute outages for reloading network equipment. If not, the company needs to invest in redundant network equipment.

Devise a detailed availability plan that describes exactly what services and components must be available to that group. Try to simplify it by consolidating the network topology and introducing redundant systems for those networks. Incorporate availability planning into the master plan by ensuring that redundant servers are not down simultaneously.

12.3   High-Availability Sites

By the very nature of their business, high-availability sites cannot afford to have large planned outages.[3] This also means that they cannot afford *not* to make the large investment necessary to provide high availability. Sites that have high availability requirements need to have lots of hot redundant systems that continue providing service when any one component fails. The higher the availability requirement, the more redundant systems that are required to achieve it.[4]

These sites still need to perform maintenance on the systems in service. Although the availability guarantees that these sites make to their customers typically exclude maintenance windows, they will lose customers if they have large planned outages.

12.3.1   The Similarities

Most of the principles described here for maintenance windows at a corporate site apply at high-availability sites.

- They need to schedule the maintenance window so that it has the least impact on their customers. For example, ISPs often choose 2 AM (local time) midweek; e-commerce sites need to choose a time when they do the least business. These windows will typically be quite frequent, such as once a week, and shorter, perhaps four to six hours in duration.
- They need to let their customers know when maintenance windows are scheduled. For ISPs, this means sending an email to the customer contacts. For an e-commerce site, this means having a banner on the site. In both cases, it should only be sent to those customers who may be affected and should contain a warning that small outages or degraded service may occur during the maintenance window and give

---

[3]High availability is anything above 99.9% availability. Typically, sites will be aiming for three nines (99.9%) (9 hours downtime per year), four nines (99.99%) (1 hour per year) or five nines (99.999%) (5 minutes per year). Six nines (99.9999%) (less than 1 minute a year) is more expensive than most sites can afford.

[4]The term $n + 1$ *redundancy* is used for services where any one component can fail without bringing the service down, $n + 2$ means any two components can fail, and so on.

the times of that window. There should be only a single message about the window.

- Planning and doing as much as possible beforehand is critical because the maintenance windows should be as short as possible.
- There must be a flight director who coordinates the scheduling and tracks the progress of the tasks. If the windows are weekly, this may be a quarter-time or half-time job.
- Each item should have a change proposal, as described in Section 12.1.4. The change proposal should list the redundant systems and include a test to verify that the redundant systems have kicked in and service is still available.
- They need to tightly plan the maintenance window. Maintenance windows are typically smaller in scope and shorter in time. Items scheduled by different people for a given window should not have dependencies on each other. There must be a small master plan that shows who has what tasks and their completion times.
- The flight director must be very strict about the deadlines for change completion.
- Everything must be fully tested before it is declared complete.
- Console servers benefit all sites.
- The SAs need to have a strong presence when the site approaches and enters its busy time. They need to be prepared to quickly deal with any problems that may arise as a result of the maintenance.
- A brief postmortem the next day to discuss any remaining problems or issues that arose is useful.

12.3.2 The Differences

There also are several differences in maintenance windows for high-availability sites.

- There is a prerequisite that there is redundancy at the site if it is to have high availability.
- It is not necessary to disable access. Services should remain available.
- It is not necessary to have a full shutdown/boot list, because a full shutdown and reboot does not happen. However, there should be a dependency list if there are any dependencies between machines.[5]
- Because the customers of ISPs and e-commerce sites are not on-site, being physically visible the morning after is irrelevant. However, being available and responsive is still important. Find ways to increase your

---

[5]Usually high-availability sites avoid dependencies between machines as much as possible.

visibility and ensure excellent responsiveness. Advertise what the
change was, how to report problems, and so on.

- A postmaintenance communication is usually not required, unless
  there are remaining problems about which the customers must be
  informed. Customers don't want to be bombarded with email from
  their service providers.
- The most important difference is that the redundant architecture of
  the site must be taken into account during the maintenance window
  planning. The flight director needs to make sure that none of the
  scheduled work can take the service down. The SAs need to make sure
  that they know how long failover takes to happen.[6] If redundancy is
  implemented within a single machine, the SA needs to know how to
  work on one part of the machine while keeping the system operating
  normally.
- Availability of the service as a whole must be closely monitored during
  the maintenance window. There should be a plan for how to deal with
  any failure that causes an outage as a result of temporary lack of
  redundancy.

12.4   Conclusion

The basics for successfully executing a planned maintenance window fall into
three categories: preparation, execution and postmaintenance customer care.
The advance preparation for a maintenance window has the most effect on
whether or not it will run smoothly. Planning and doing as much as possible
in advance is key. The group needs to appoint an appropriate flight director
for each maintenance window. Change proposals should be submitted to the
flight director. The flight director uses this to build a master plan and set
completion deadlines for each task.

During the maintenance window, remote access should be disabled and
infrastructure, such as console servers and radios, should be in place. The
plan needs to be executed with as few hiccups as possible. The timetable
must be adhered to rigidly; it must finish with complete system testing.

Good customer care after the maintenance window is important to its
success. Communication about the window and a visible presence the morning after are key.

Integrating a mentoring process, saving historical data and doing trend
analysis for better estimates, providing continuity, and providing limited
availability to groups that request it can be incorporated at a later date.
Proper planning, good back-out plans, strict adherence to deadlines for

---

[6]For example, how long does the routing system take to reach convergence when one of the
routers goes down or comes back up?

change completion, and comprehensive testing should avert all but some minor disasters. Some tasks may not be completed, and those changes will need to be backed out. In our experience, a well planned, properly executed maintenance window never leads to a complete disaster. A badly planned or poorly executed one could, however.

These kinds of massive outages are not easy and are risky. Hopefully, you will find the planning techniques in this chapter useful.

Exercises

1. Read the paper on how the AT&T/Lucent network was split (Limoncelli et al. 1997), and consider how having a weekend maintenance window would have changed the process. What parts of that project would have been performed in advance as preparatory work, what parts would have been easier, and what parts would have been more difficult? Evaluate the risks in your approach.

2. A case study in Section 12.1.1 describes the scheduling process for a particular software company. What are the dates and events that you would need to avoid for a maintenance window in your company? Try to derive a list of dates that would work for your company, approximately three months apart from each other.

3. A case study in Section 12.1.3 describes how potential flight directors were identified at a particular software company. Consider the SAs in your company. Who do you think would make good flight directors and why?

4. What tasks or projects can you think of at your site that would be appropriate for a maintenance window? Create and fill in a change request form. What preparation could you do for this change in advance of the maintenance window?

5. Section 12.1.6 discusses disabling access to the site. What specific tasks would need to be performed at your site, and how would you re-enable that access?

6. Section 12.1.7 discusses the shutdown and reboot sequence. Build an appropriate list for your site. If you have permission, test it.

7. Section 12.2.3 discusses providing limited availability for some people to be able to continue working. What groups are likely to require 24×7 availability? What changes would you need to make to your network and services infrastructure to keep services available to each of those groups?

8. Research the flight operations methodologies used at NASA. Relate what you learned to the practice of system administration.

Service Conversions

Sometimes, you need to convert your customer base from an existing service to a new replacement service. The existing system may not be able to scale or may have been declared "end of life" by the vendor, requiring you to evaluate new systems. Or, your company may have merged with another company that uses different products, and both parts of the new company need to integrate their services with each other. Or, perhaps your company is spinning off a division into a new, separate company, and you need to replicate and split the services and networks so that each part is fully self-sufficient. Whatever the reason, converting customers from one service to another is a task that SAs often face.

Like many things in system and network administration, your goal should be for the conversion to go smoothly and be completely invisible to your customers. To achieve, or even approach that goal, you need to plan the project very carefully. This chapter describes some of the areas to consider in that planning process.

An Invisible Change

When AT&T split off Lucent Technologies, the Bell Labs research division was split in two. The SAs who looked after that division had to split the

Bell Labs network so that the people who were to be part of Lucent would not be able to access any AT&T services and vice versa. Some time after the split had been completed, one of the researchers asked when it was going to happen. He was very surprised when he was told that it had been completed already because he had not noticed that anything had changed. The project was successful in causing minimal disruption to the customers.

13.1   The Basics

As with many high-level system administration tasks, a successful conversion depends on having a solid infrastructure in place.

Rolling out a change to the whole company can be a very visible project, particularly if there are problems. You can decrease the risk and visibility of problems by rolling out the change slowly, starting with the SAs and then the most suitable customers. With any change you make, be sure that you have a back-out plan and can revert quickly and easily to the preconversion state if necessary.

We saw in Chapter 1 how an automated patching system can be used to rollout software updates. This system may be a key component of your rollout plan. Chapter 3 describes how to build a service, including some of the ways to make it easier to upgrade and maintain. Some of those techniques will also help in the conversion process.

Communication plays a key role in performing a successful conversion. It is never wise to change something under your customers' feet without making sure they know what is happening and have told you of their concerns and timing constraints.

In this section, we touch on each of those areas, along with ways to minimize the intrusiveness of the conversion for the customer, and discuss two approaches to conversions. You need to plan every step of a conversion well in advance to pull it off with minimum impact on your customers. This section should shape your thinking in that planning process.

13.1.1   Small Groups First, Then Expand

When performing a rollout, whether it is a conversion, a new service, or an update to an existing service, you should do so gradually to minimize the potential impact of any failures. Start by converting your own system to the new service. Test and perfect the conversion process, and test and perfect the new service before converting any other systems. When you cannot find any more problems, convert a few of your coworkers' desktops and debug and fix any problems that arise from that process and their testing of the new system. Expand the test group to cover all the SAs before starting on your customers. When you have successfully converted the SAs, start with customers who are better able to cope with problems that might arise and who have agreed to be on the cutting edge, and gradually move toward more conservative customers.

We referred to this approach as the "one, some, many" technique for rolling out new revisions and patches in Section 1.1.2. That technique actually applies more globally across rollouts of any kind, including conversions.

13.1.2 Communication

Although the guiding principle for a conversion is that it be invisible to the customer, that does not mean that you do not communicate the conversion plan to your customers. On the contrary, communicating a conversion far in advance is critical.

Customers need to know what is taking place and how the change is going to affect them. They need to be able to ask questions about how they will perform their tasks in the new system and need to have all their concerns addressed. Customers who use the system extensively should be involved early in the project to make sure that their needs will be met.

If the conversion will require service outages, changes to customers' machines, or visits to their offices, they need to know that in advance. By communicating with the customers about the conversion, you will find people who use the service in ways you did not know about that you will need to support on the new system. You should also find out about dates when the system needs to be absolutely stable or customers' important deadline dates.

Even if the conversion should go seamlessly, with no interruption or visible change for the customers, they still need to know that it is happening. You can schedule it to have the minimum impact just in case something goes wrong.

13.1.3 Minimize Intrusiveness

Aim for the conversion to have as little impact on the customer as possible. Try to make it seamless. When planning the conversion rollout, pay close attention to the impact on the customer.

Does the conversion require a service interruption? If so, how can you minimize the time that the service is unavailable? When is the best time to schedule the interruption in service so that is has the least impact?

Does the conversion require changes on each customer's machine or in their office? If so, how many, how long will they take, and can you organize the conversion so that the customer is only disturbed once?

Does the conversion require that the customers change their work methods in any way, for example, by using new client software? Can you avoid changing the client software? If not, do they need training? Sometimes training is a larger project than the conversion itself. Are they comfortable with the new software? Are their SAs and the helpdesk familiar enough with the new and the old software that they can help with any questions the customers might have? Have the helpdesk scripts (Section 15.1.5) been updated?

Look for ways to perform the change without service interruption, without visiting each customer, and without changing their workflow or user interface. Make sure that the support organization is ready to provide full support for the new product before you roll it out. Remember, your goal is for your customers to not even realize that the conversion has happened because it was so smooth. If you can't minimize intrusiveness, at least you can make the intrusion fast and well-organized.

The Rioting Mob Technique

When AT&T was splitting into AT&T, Lucent, and NCR, Tom's SA team was responsible for splitting the Bell Labs networks in Holmdel, New Jersey (Limoncelli et al. 1997). At one point, every host needed to be visited to perform several changes, including its IP address. A schedule was announced that listed which hallways would be converted on which day. Mondays and Wednesdays were used for conversions. Tuesdays and Thursdays were for fixing problems that arose. Fridays were unscheduled in the hope that we wouldn't cause any problems that would make us lose sleep on the weekends.

On conversion days we used what we called the "The Rioting Mob Technique." At 9 AM, we would stand at one end of the hallway. We'd psych ourselves up, often by chanting, and move down the hallways in pairs. Two pairs were PC technicians, two pairs were UNIX technicians, one set for the left side of the hallway and another for the right side. As the technicians went office to office, they kicked out the inhabitants and went machine to machine making the needed changes. Sometimes, machines were particularly difficult or had problems. Rather than trying to fix it themselves, the technicians would call on a senior team member to solve the problem as the technicians moved on to the next machine. Meanwhile, a final pair of people stayed at our "command central," where people could phone in requests for IP addresses and provide updates to the host, inventory, and other databases.

The next day was spent cleaning up anything that had broken. We also met to refine the process. A brainstorming session revealed what went well and what needed improvement. It was decided that it would be better to make one pass through the hallway calling in requests for IP addresses, giving customers a chance to log out, and identifying nonstandard machines for the senior SAs to focus on. On the second pass through the hallway, everyone had the IP addresses they needed and things went more smoothly. Soon we could do two hallways in the morning and our cleanup in the afternoon.

The brainstorming session between the first and second conversion day was critical. What we learned in the first session inspired us to completely change the process. When the brainstorming sessions were not gathering any new information, the breather days became planning sessions for the next day. Many times a conversion day went smoothly enough that we were done by lunch, had the problems resolved by the afternoon, and had nothing to do on our breather day except normal work.

Consolidating all the customer disruption to a single day (for any given customer) was a big success because customers were expecting some kind of outage, but would have found it unacceptable if it was prolonged or split up over many instances.

13.1.4 Layers Versus Pillars

A conversion project, as with any project, will be divided into discrete tasks. Some of these tasks will have to be performed for every customer of the service. For example, with a conversion to new calendar software, the new client software must be rolled out to all the desktops, accounts will need to be created on the server, and existing schedules must to be converted into the new system. As part of the project planning for the conversion, you need to decide whether to perform these tasks in "layers" or "pillars."

The *layers* approach means that you perform one task for all of the customers before moving on to the next task and doing that for all of the customers. The *pillars* approach means performing all the required tasks for each customer at once, before moving on to the next customer. In general, pillars is the best approach because it minimizes intrusiveness.

Tasks that are not intrusive to the customer, such as creating the accounts in the calendar server, can be safely performed in layers. However, tasks that are intrusive for a customer, such as installing the new client software, freezing his schedule and converting it to the new system, and getting him to connect for the first time and initialize his password, should be performed in pillars.

With the pillars approach, you need to schedule only one period with each customer, rather than many small ones. By performing all the tasks at once, you need to disturb each customer only once. Even if it is for a slightly longer time, a single intrusion is typically less disruptive to your customer's work than many small intrusions.

Case Study: Bell Labs Pillars Versus Layers

When AT&T split off Lucent Technologies, and Bell Labs was divided in two, many changes needed to be made to each desktop to convert it from a "Bell Labs" machine to either a "Lucent Bell Labs" machine or an "AT&T Labs" machine. Very early on, the SA team responsible for implementing the split realized that a pillars approach would be used for most changes, but sometimes the layers approach would be best. For example, the layers approach was used when building a new web proxy. The new web proxies were constructed and tested, and then customers were switched to their new proxies. However, more than 30 changes had to be made to every UNIX desktop, and it was determined that they should all be made in one visit, with one reboot, to minimize the disruption to the customer. There was great risk in doing this. What if the last desktop was converted and then it was realized that one of those changes was made incorrectly on every machine? To reduce this risk, client machines with the new configuration were placed in public areas, and customers were invited to try them out. This way, they were able to find and fix many problems before the 30 big changes were implemented on each of the customers' machines. This approach also helped the customers become comfortable with the change. Some customers were particularly fearful of the change because they lacked confidence in the SA team. They were physically walked to the public machines and asked to log in, and problems were debugged in real time. This calmed their fears and increased their confidence. The network split project is described in detail in a USENIX LISA paper (Limoncelli et al. 1997).

E-commerce sites, while looking monolithic from the outside, can think about their conversions in terms of layers and pillars, too. A small change or even a new software release can be rolled out in pillars (one host at a time) if the change interoperates with the older systems.

13.1.5   Avoid Flash-Cuts

Wherever possible, avoid converting everyone simultaneously from one system to another. The conversion will go more smoothly if you can convert a few willing test subjects to the new system first, as discussed in Section 13.1.1. Avoiding a flash-cut may mean budgeting in advance for duplication of hardware, so remember to think about how you will perform the conversion rollout when you prepare your budget request.

In other cases, you may be able to use features of your existing technology to slowly rollout the conversion. For example, if you are renumbering a network or splitting a network, you might use IP multinetting network ("secondary IP addresses") in conjunction with DHCP (see Section 1.1.3) to initially convert a few hosts without using additional hardware.

Alternatively, you may be able to make both old and new services available simultaneously and encourage people to switch during the overlap period. That way, they can try out the new service, get used to it, report problems with it, and switch back to the old service if they prefer. It gives your customers an "adoption" period. This approach is commonly used in the telephone industry when a phone number or area code change is introduced. For a period of a few months, both the old and new numbers work. For the following few months, the old number gives an error message that tells the caller what the new number is. Then the old number stops working, and some time later it becomes available for reallocation.

Physical Network Conversion

When a mid-size company converted their network wiring from "thin" Ethernet to 10Base-T, they divided the problem into two main preparatory components and had a different group attack each preparatory part of the project. The first group had to get the new physical wiring layer installed in the wiring closets and cubicles. The second group had to make sure that every machine in the building was capable of supporting 10Base-T, by adding a card or upgrading the machine if necessary.

The first group ran all the wires through the ceiling and terminated them in the wiring closets. Next they went through the building and pulled the wires down from the ceiling and terminated them in the cubicles and offices and tested them, visiting each cubicle or office only once.

When both groups had finished their preparatory work, they gradually went through the building, moving people to the new wiring but leaving the old cabling in place, so that they could switch back if there were problems.

This conversion was done well from the point of view of avoiding a flash-cut and converting people over gradually. However, the customers found it too intrusive because they were interrupted three times, once for wiring to their work areas, once for the new network hardware in their machines, and finally for the actual conversion. Although it would have been very difficult to coordinate and would have required extensive planning, the teams could have visited each cubicle together and performed all the work at once. Realistically, though, this would have complicated and delayed the project too much. It would be simpler to have better communication initially, letting the customers know that they would be disturbed three times, one of which would require a reboot, scheduling the disturbances, and letting them know all the benefits of the new wiring. Customers find interruptions less of an annoyance if they really understand what is going on, have some control over the scheduling, and know what they are going to get out of it ultimately.

13.1.6   Successful Flash-Cuts

Sometimes a conversion, or a part of a conversion, must be performed simultaneously for everyone. For example, if you are converting from one corporate-wide calendar server to another, where the two systems cannot communicate and exchange information, you may need to convert everyone at once or people on the old system will not be able to schedule meetings with people on the new system, and vice versa.

Performing a successful flash-cut requires a lot of careful planning and some comprehensive testing, including load testing. Persuade a few key users of that system to test the new system with their daily tasks in advance of making the switch. If you get the people who use the system the most heavily to test the new one, you are more likely to find any problems with it before it goes live, and the people who rely on it the most will have become comfortable with it before they have to start using it in earnest. People use the same tools different ways, so more testers will gain you better feature test coverage.

For a flash-cut, two-way communication is particularly critical. Make sure that all of your customers know what is happening when and that you know and address their concerns in advance of the cut-over. Also, be prepared with a back-out plan, as discussed in the next section.

Phone Number Conversion

In 2000, British Telecom converted the city of London from two area codes to one, and lengthened the phone numbers from seven digits to eight, in one large number change. Numbers that were of the form (171) xxx-xxxx became (20) 7xxx-xxxx, and numbers that were of the form (181) xxx-xxxx became (20) 8xxx-xxxx. More than six months before the designated cut-over date they started advertising the change, and the new area code in combination with the new phone number started working. For a few months after the designated cut-over date, the old area codes in combination with the old phone numbers continued to work, as is usual with telephone number changes.

However, for London customers dialing a local number, without an area code, that began with a 7 or an 8, the designated cut-over date meant a flash-cut from seven digits to eight. One day, seven-digit phone numbers would work and eight-digit numbers would not, and the next day it would be the reverse. Because this sudden change was certain to cause confusion, British Telecom telephoned every single customer who would be affected by the change to explain person-to-person what the change meant and to answer any questions that their customers might have. Now that's customer service!

13.1.7 Back-Out Plan

When rolling out a conversion, it is critical to have a back-out plan. A *conversion,* by definition, means removing one service and replacing it with another. If the new service does not work correctly, the customer has been deprived of one of the tools that she uses to do her job, which may seriously affect her productivity. If a conversion fails, you need to be able to restore the customer's service quickly to the state it was in before you made any changes and then go away, figure out why it failed, and fix it.

In practical terms, this means that you should leave both services running simultaneously if possible and have a simple, automated way of switching someone between the two services.

Bear in mind that the failure may not be instantaneous or may not be discovered for a while. It could be as a result of reliability problems in the software, it could be caused by capacity limitations, or it may be a feature that the customer uses infrequently or only at certain times of the month. So you should leave your back-out mechanism in place for a while, perhaps a couple of months, until you are certain that the conversion has been completed successfully.

A major difficulty with back-out plans is deciding when to execute them. When a conversion goes wrong, the technicians tend to promise that things will work with "one more change," but management tends to push toward starting the back-out plan. It is a good idea to have decided in advance the point at which the back-out plan will be put into use. For example, one might decide ahead of time that if the conversion isn't completed within two hours of the start of the next business day, then the back-out plan must be executed. Obviously, if in the first minutes of the conversion one meets insurmountable problems, it can be better to back out of what's been done so far and reschedule the conversion. However, getting a second opinion can be useful. What is insurmountable to you may be an easy task for someone else on your team.

13.2 The Icing

When you have become adept at rolling out conversions with minimal impact for your customers, there are a couple of things that you should consider to further reduce the impact of conversions on your customers. The first of these is to have a back-out plan that allows for instant roll-back, so that no time is lost in converting your customers back to the old system the moment that a problem with the new one is discovered. The other is to try to avoid doing conversions altogether. We discuss some ways of reducing the number of conversion projects that might arise.

13.2.1   Instant Roll-Back

When performing a conversion, it is nice to be able to instantly roll every-thing back to a known working state if a problem is discovered. That way, any disruption to customers resulting from a problem with the new system can be minimized.

How you provide instant roll-back depends on the conversion that you are performing and how you do the conversion. However, one component of providing instant roll-back will be to leave the old systems in place. If you are doing a conversion that just involves pointing your customers' clients to a different machine, you should be able to perform the conversion by making a DNS change and roll-back by changing the DNS record back to the original value. DNS can be configured so that clients frequently look up the name of the server, even if they have accessed it recently. The field that controls how often the clients look up the name of the server to get its address is called the *time to live* (TTL). It tells the client how long it should cache the answer that it receives. Another field tells the DNS secondary servers how often they should check to see if the master DNS server has been updated. If both of these fields are left set low, DNS updates should reach the clients quickly, and therefore roll-back can happen quickly and simply. Another approach would be to perform the conversion by stopping one service and starting another, which would also provide instant roll-back. In some cases, you may have two client applications on the customers' machines, one of which uses the old system and another that uses the new one.

Sometimes a flash-cut involves upgrading to new server software. If the old software can exist dormant on the server while the new software is in use, you can instantly perform a roll-back by switching to the old soft-ware. Vendors can do a lot to prevent this from happening, and they can also be very careful in their installation procedure to make sure that it is possible. For example, if version 1.2 and 1.3 of a server get installed in /opt/example-1.2 and /opt/example-1.3, respectively, but a symbolic link /opt/example points to the version that is in use, you can roll-back by simply replacing a single symbolic link.

These simple methods either violate the principle of doing a slow roll-out or make the change more visible to the customer. Providing instant roll-back with minimal customer impact and using a gradual roll-out method is more complex and requires careful planning and configuration. One way of accomplishing this would be to set up extra DNS servers that provide the information for the new servers and all the common information to clients that use them, and then use your automated client network configuration tool, described in Chapter 1, to selectively convert a few hosts at a time to the alternative DNS servers. At any stage, you can roll those hosts back to the original configuration by changing their network configuration back to its original state.

13.2.2 Avoid Explicit Conversions

In an ideal world, you should avoid explicit conversions wherever possible. Where some sort of conversion is unavoidable, you ideally should avoid having to convert something on every desktop, but rather just change the infrastructure transparently to the customers.

Some conversions can be avoided with good planning and good vendor relations. Select a product that scales well, integrates with other systems that you use,[1] provides the features that you need, seems to be developing in the right direction, and is a leader in its market. Talk to the vendor about future directions for the product, large installations, and how it scales. By selecting the right product initially, you minimize the chances that you will need to switch to another one in the future because of new feature requirements, scaling problems, or the end of the product's life cycle.

Advance planning, careful product selection, and well-designed infrastructure can also help avoid having to convert the customers to new software or new configuration settings. Where possible, select products that use standard protocols to communicate between the client on the desktop and the server that is providing the service. If the client and server use a proprietary protocol, and you want to change the server, you will also have to change the client software. This is disruptive to the customers. However, if they use standard protocols, you should be able to select another server that uses the same protocol and avoid converting your customers to new client software.

You should be able to avoid explicitly converting customers' configurations by using methods that are part of building a good infrastructure. For example, using automatic network configuration (as described in Chapter 1) with good documentation as to which service is located on which host (as described in Chapter 6) provides a solid basis on which to start splitting a network transparently to the customer base. Using names that are service-based aliases for your machines (as described in Chapter 3) enables you to move a service to a new machine or set of machines without having to change client configurations.

---

[1]Such as your authentication system, even if you don't see the need for such integration when you select the product.

13.2.3   Vendor Support

When doing large conversions, make sure you have vendor support. Contact them to find out if there are any pitfalls. This can prevent major problems. If you have a good relationship with a vendor, they should be willing to be involved in the planning process, sometimes even lending personnel. If not, they may be willing to make sure their technical support hotline is properly staffed on your conversion day (for example, it isn't the day of their annual picnic) or that someone particularly knowledgeable about your environment is available.

13.3   Conclusion

A successful conversion project is based on lots of advance planning and a solid infrastructure. The success of a conversion project is measured on how little adverse impact it had on the customers. The conversion should intrude as little as possible into their work routines.

The principles for rollouts of any kind, updates, new services, or conversions are the same. Start with lots of planning, deploy slowly with lots of testing, and be ready to back the changes out if you need to.

Exercises

1. What conversions can you foresee in your network's future? Choose one and build a plan for performing it with minimum customer impact.

2. Now try to add an instant roll-back option to that plan.

3. If you had to split your network, as described in the "The Rioting Mob" anecdote, what services would you need to replicate and how would you convert people from one network and set of services to the other? Consider each service in detail.

4. Can you think of any conversions that you could have avoided? How could you have avoided them?

Chapter 14

Centralization and Decentralization

This chapter seeks to help an SA decide how much centralization is appropriate, how to centralize a service that was previously decentralized, and how to decentralize a service that was previously centralized.

Centralization means one focus of control. One might have two DNS servers in every department of a company, but they all might be controlled by a single entity. Alternatively, decentralized systems distribute control to many parts. In our DNS example, each of those departments might maintain and control their own DNS server. Each would be responsible for maintaining the skill-set to stay on top of the technology as it changes, to architect the systems as they see fit, and to monitor the service. Centralization refers to nontechnical aspects also. Organization charts can structure a company to be centralized or decentralized.

Centralization is an attempt to improve efficiency by reorganizing to take advantage of potential economies of scale. Decentralization is an attempt to improve speed and flexibility by reorganizing to increase local control and execution of a service. Neither is always better, and neither is always possible in the purest sense. When each is done well, it can realize the benefits of the other (odd paradox, isn't it?).

Decentralization means breaking away from the prevailing hegemony. It is a revolt against the frustrating bureaucratic ways of old. It means someone has become so frustrated with a centralized service that "do it yourself" has the potential of being better.

Centralization means pulling groups together to create order and enforce process. It is cooperation for the greater good. It is a leveling process. It seeks to remove the frustrating waste of money on duplicate systems, extra work, and manual processes. New technology paradigms often bring opportunities for centralization. For example, although it may make sense for each department to have slightly different processes for handling paper forms, no one department could fund building a pervasive web-based forms system. Therefore a disruptive technology such as the web creates an opportunity to replace many old systems with a single, more efficient, centralized system.

14.1   The Basics

It seems as if every couple of years management decides to centralize everything that is decentralized and vice versa. In this section, we discuss guiding principles you should consider before making such broad changes. We then discuss some sample "good candidates" for centralization and decentralization.

14.1.1   Guiding Principles

There are a several guiding principles related to centralizing and decentralizing. They are similar to what anyone making large, structural changes should consider.

Understand Your Motivation for Making the Change.   Maybe you are seeking to save money, increase speed, become more flexible. Maybe your reasons are political: You are protecting your empire or your boss, making your group look good, or putting someone's personal business philosophy into action. Maybe you are doing it just to make your own life easier; that's valid too. Write down your motivation and remind yourself of it from time to time to verify that you haven't strayed.

Know What Specific Problem You Are Solving.   Clearly define what problem you are trying to fix. Some examples include: "Reliability is inconsistent because each division has different brands of hardware." "Services break when network connections to sales offices are down." Again, write down the specific problem or problems and communicate these to your team. Use this list as a reality check later in the project to make sure you haven't lost sight of the goal.

Centralize as Much as Makes Sense for Today, with an Eye to the Future. You must find the balance between centralization and decentralization. There are time considerations: Building the perfect system will take forever. You must set realistic goals, yet keep an eye to future needs. For example, in six months the new system will be complete and at that time it will be expected to process a million widgets per day. However, a different architecture will be required to process two million widgets per day, the rate that will be needed a year later, and will require considerably more development time. You must balance the advantage of having a new system in six months (with the problem of needing to start building the next-generation system immediately) versus the advantage of waiting longer for a system that will not need to be replaced so soon.

The More Centralized Something Is, the More Likely It Is that Some Customers Will Need a Special Feature or Some Kind of Customization. An old business proverb is, "All of our customers are the same: They each have unique requirements." One size never fits all. You can't do a reasonable job of centralizing without being flexible. You'll doom the project if you try. Instead, you should always look for a small number of models. Some customers require autonomy. Some may require performing their own updates, which means creating a system of access control so that customers can modify their own segments without affecting others.

If It Has Become a Commodity, Consider Centralization. A good time to consider centralizing something is when the technology path it has taken has made it a commodity. Network printing, file service, email servers, and even workstation maintenance used to be highly specialized technologies or services. However, now these things are commodities and excellent candidates for centralization.

Be Circumspect About Unrealistic Promises. You should thoroughly investigate any claims that you will save money by decentralizing, add flexibility by centralization, or have an entirely new system without pain—the opposite is usually the case. If a vendor promises a new product will perform miracles but requires you to centralize (or decentralize) how something is currently organized, maybe the benefits come from the organizational change, not the product!

Use Your Best Judgment. Sometimes, you must use experience and "a hunch" rather than specific scientific measurements. For example, we've found that when centralizing email servers, our experience has developed these "rules of thumb": Small companies (five departments with 100 people) tend to need one email server. Larger companies can survive with an email server per thousands of people, especially if there is one large headquarters and many smaller sales offices. When the company grows to the point of having more than one site, each site tends to require its own email server (as discussed in Section 14.1.3), but is unlikely to require its own Internet gateway. Extremely large or geographically diverse companies start to require multiple Internet gateways at different locations.

It's Like Rolling Out Any New Service.   Although more emotional impact may be involved than with other changes, both centralization and decentralization projects have issues similar to building a new service. Chapter 13 offers detailed advice.

Listen to the Customers' Concerns.   Consult with customers to understand their expectations: Retain the good qualities and fix the bad. Focus on the qualities that they mention, not the implementation. People might say that they like the fact that "Karen was always right there when we needed new terminals installed." That is an implementation. The new system might not include on-site personnel. What should be retained is that the new service has to be responsive—as responsive as having Karen standing right there. That may mean the use of overnight delivery services or pre-configured and "ready to eat" systems[1] stashed in the building, or whatever it takes to meet that expectation. Alternatively, you must do expectation-setting if the new system is not going to deliver on old expectations. Maybe people will have to plan ahead and ask for terminals a day in advance.

You Only Have One Chance to Make a Good First Impression.   A new system is never trusted until proven a success, and the first experience with the new system will set the mood for all future customer interactions. Get it right the first time, even if it means spending more money up front or taking extra time for testing.

Listen to the Customers, but Remember that Management Has the Control.   The organizational structure can influence the level of centralization that is appropriate or possible. The largest impediment to centralization often is management decisions or politics. Lack of trust makes it difficult to centralize. If the SA team has not proven itself, management may be unwilling to support the large change. Management may not be willing to fund the changes, which usually indicates the change is not important to

---

[1]Do not attempt to eat a computer. "Ready to eat" systems are hot spares that will be fully functional when powered up. Absolutely no configuration files to modify and so on.

them. For example, if the company hasn't funded a central infrastructure group, SAs will end up decentralized. It may be better to have a central infrastructure group, but lacking management support, the fall-back is to have each group make the best subinfrastructure they can. Either way, the end goal is to meet the customer's needs.

14.1.2 Candidates for Centralization

Centralization does not innately improve efficiency. It brings about the opportunity to introduce new economies of scale to a process. SAs constantly find new opportunities to centralize processes and services.

The cost savings of centralization comes from the presumption that there will be less overhead than the sum of the individual overheads of each decentralized item. Centralization can create a simpler architecture. Reliability through simplicity is a time-tested tradition.

To the customers of the service being centralized, centralization is about giving up control. Divisions that previously provided their own service now have to rely on a centralized group for service. SAs who previously did tasks themselves, their own way, now have to make requests of someone else who has his own way to do things. They will want to know if the new service provider can do things better than they were previously done.

When taking control away from the previous SA or customer, you must consider many issues. What will the customer's psychological response be? Will there be attempts to sabotage the effort? How can you convince people that the new system will be better than the old system? How will damage control and rumor control be accomplished? What's the best way to make a good first impression?

The best way to succeed in a centralization program is to pick the right services for centralization. Here are some good candidates for centralization.

Centralize the Management of Distributed Systems. Historically, each department of an organization configured and ran their own DNS servers. As the technology got more sophisticated, less customization of each DNS server was required. Eventually, there was no reason not to have each DNS server configured exactly the same way, and the need for rapid updates of new binaries was becoming a security issue. The motivation was to save money by not requiring each department to have a high level of DNS server expertise. The problem being fixed was the lack of similar configurations on each server. A system was designed to maintain a central configuration repository that would update each of the servers in a controlled and secure manner. The "customers" that were affected were the SAs of each department, who were eager to give up a task that they didn't always understand.

Consolidate Services onto Fewer Hosts.   In the past, for reliability's sake, you would put one service on each physical host. However, as technology progresses, we find it can be beneficial to have many services on one machine. The motivation is to decrease cost. The problem being fixed is that every host has overhead costs such as power, cooling, administration, machine room space, and maintenance contracts. Usually, you can find a larger machine that costs less to operate than many smaller hosts. The customers that are affected may be different depending on the service.

Centralize System Administration.   In Chapter 25 we discuss different organizational structures. When redesigning your organization, your motivation may be to reduce cost, improve speed, or to provide services consistently throughout the entire enterprise. The problem may be the extra cost of having technical management for each team or that the distributed model resulted in some divisions having worse service than others. Centralizing the SA team can fix these problems.

To provide customization and the "warm fuzzies" of personal attention, subteams might focus on particular customer segments. However, one common mistake is to take this to an extreme. We've seen at least one amazingly huge company that centralized to the point that "customer liaisons" were hired to maintain a relationship with the customer groups, and the customers hired liaisons to the centralized SA staff. Soon these liaisons numbered more than 100. At that point, the savings in reduced overhead were surely diminished. A regular reminder and dedication to the original motivation may have prevented that problem.

Consolidate Expertise.   In decentralized organizations, there is a good chance that a few of the groups have more expertise in particular areas than the others. This is fine if they maintain casual relationships and help each other. However, certain expertise can become critical to business, and therefore an informal arrangement becomes an unacceptable business risk. In that case, it may make sense to consolidate that expertise into one group. The motivation is to ensure that all divisions have access to a minimum level of expertise in one specific area or areas. The problem is that the lack of this expertise causes uneven service levels, for example, if one division had unreliable DNS while others didn't, or one division had superior Internet email service, whereas others were still using UUCP-style addresses. (If you are too young to remember UUCP-style addresses, just count your blessings.) That would be intolerable! Establishing a centralized group for one particular service can bring uniformity and improve the average across the entire company. Some examples of this include highly specialized skills such as maintaining an Internet gateway, a software depot, various security issues

(VPN service, intrusion detection, security hole scanning, and so on), DNS, and email service.

Centralize Infrastructure Decisions. The creation of infrastructure and platform standards can be done centrally. This is a subcase of centralizing expertise. The motivation at one company was that that infrastructure costs were high and interoperability between divisions was low. There were many specific problems to be solved. Every division had a team of people researching new technologies and making decisions independently. Each team's research duplicated the effort of the others. Volume purchasing contracts could not be signed because each individual division was too small to qualify. Repair costs were high because so many different spare parts had to be purchased. When divisions did make compatible purchasing decisions, multiple spare parts were still being purchased because there was no coordination or cooperation. The solution was to reduce the duplication in effort by having one standards committee for infrastructure and platform standards. Previously, new technology was often adopted in pockets around the company because some divisions were less averse to risk; these became the divisions that performed product trials or became early adopters of new technology.

This last example brings up another benefit of centralization. The increased purchasing power should mean that better equipment can be purchased for the same cost. Sometimes, money can be saved through centralization. Other times, it is better to use the savings to invest in better equipment.

Case Study: Big, Honkin' File Servers

Tom's customers and even fellow SAs fought the concept of large, centralized file servers long and hard. They complained about the loss of control and produced (in his opinion) ill-conceived pricing models that demonstrated that the old UNIX-based file servers were the better way to go. What they were really fighting was the notion that network file service was no longer very special; it had become a commodity and therefore an excellent candidate for centralization. Eventually, an apples-to-apples comparison was done. This included a total cost of ownership model that included the SA time and energy to maintain the old-style systems. The value of some unique features of the dedicated file servers (such as filesystem snapshots) was difficult to quantify. However, even when the cost model showed the systems to cost about the same per gigabyte of usable storage, the dedicated file servers had an advantage over the old systems: consistency and support. The old systems were a mish-mash of various manufacturers for the host, for the RAID controllers, for the disk drives, cables, network interfaces, and in some cases even the racks they sat in! Each of these items usually required a level of expertise and training to maintain efficiently, and no single vendor would support these Franken-stein monsters. Usually, when the SA who purchased a particular RAID device left the group, the expertise left with him. Standardizing on a particular product resulted in a higher level of service because the savings were used to purchase top-of-the line systems that had fewer problems than "inexpensive" competitors. Also, having a single phone number to call for support was a blessing.

Printing is another commodity service that has many opportunities for centralization, both in the design of the service itself and when purchasing supplies. In Section 20.1.1 we will see more examples.

14.1.3   Candidates for Decentralization

Decentralization does not automatically improve speed. When done correctly, it creates an opportunity to do so. Even when the new process is less efficient or inefficient in different ways, people can be satisfied to be in control of their own destiny. We've found that people are more tolerant of a mediocre process if they feel they control it. (In the United States, Senator Jesse Helms was re-elected year after year in North Carolina by people who said, "He's a jerk, but he's *our* jerk.")

Decentralization often trades efficiency for something even more valu-able. In these examples, we decentralize to democratize control, gain fault tolerance, acquire the ability to have a customized solution, or remove our-selves from clue-lacking central authorities. ("They're idiots, but they're *our* division's idiots.") One must seek to retain what was good about the old system while fixing what was bad.

Decentralization democratizes control. The new people gaining control may require training; this includes both the customers and the SAs. Your goal may be autonomy, the ability to control your own destiny, or the ability to be functional when disconnected from the network. This latter feature is also referred to as *compartmentalization,* the ability to achieve different reliability levels for different segments of the community. Here are some good candidates for decentralization.

Fault Tolerance.   The duplication of effort that happens with decentral-ization can remove single points of failure. A company with growing field of-fices required all employees to read email off servers located in the headquar-ters. There were numerous complaints that during network outages people couldn't read or even compose email because composition required access to directory servers that were also at the headquarters. Divisions in other time zones were particularly upset that maintenance times at the headquarters were their prime working hours. The motivation was to increase reliability, in particular access during outages. The problem was that people couldn't use email when wide area network (WAN) links were down. The solution was to install local LDAP caches and email servers in each of the major locations. (It was convenient and effective to also use this host for DNS, authentication, and other services.) Although mail would not be transmitted site to site during an outage, customers could access their email store, local email could be delivered, and messages that needed to be relayed to other sites would transparently queue until the WAN link recovered. This could have been a management disaster if each site was expected to have the expertise required to configure and maintain such systems or if different sites created different standards. Instead, it was a big success because management was centralized. Each site received preconfigured hardware and software that simply needed to be plugged in. Updates were done via a centralized system. Even backups could be performed remotely if required.

Customization.   Sometimes, certain customer groups have a business requirement to be on the bleeding edge of technology, whereas others require stability. A research group required early access to technology, usually before it was approved by corporate infrastructure standards committees. The motivation was political because the group maintained a certain status by being ahead of others within the company, as well as in the industry. There was also business motivation: The group's projects were far-reaching and futuristic, and they needed to "live in the future" if they were going to build systems that would work well in the networks of the future. The problem was that the group was being prevented from deviating from corporate standards. The solution was to establish themselves as their own system administration group. They participated in the committees that created the corporate standards and were able to provide valuable feedback because they had experience with technologies that the remainder of the committee was just considering. Their participation also guaranteed that they would be able to establish interoperability guidelines between their rogue systems and the corporate standards. This local system administration group was able to meet the local requirements that were different from those of the rest of the company. They could provide special features and select a different balance of stability versus cutting-edge features.

Meeting Your Customers' Needs.   Sometimes, the centralized services group may be unable to meet the demands placed on them by some of the groups in the company. Before abandoning the centralized service, try to understand the reason for the failures of the central group to meet your customers' needs. Try to work with them to find a solution to those problems that works for both groups, such as the one described above. Your ultimate responsibility is to meet your customers' needs and to make them successful. If you cannot make the relationship with the central group work, your company may have to decentralize the necessary services so that you can meet your group's needs. Make sure that you have management support to make this move; be aware of the pitfalls of decentralization and try to avoid them. Remember why you moved to a centralized model and periodically re-evaluate whether it still makes sense.

Advocates of decentralization sometimes argue that centralized services are single points of failure. However, when centralization is done right, the savings can be reinvested into technology that increases fault tolerance. Often, the result of decentralization is many single points of failure spread all over the company. When decentralizing, don't fall into this trap.

Another point in support of decentralization is that there are benefits to having diversity in your systems. For example, different OSs have different security problems. It can be beneficial to have only a fraction of your systems taken out by a virus. A major software company had a highly publicized DNS outage because all of their DNS servers were running the same OS and the same release of DNS software. If they had used a variety of OSs and DNS software, one of them might not have been susceptible to the security hole that was being leveraged. If you are the centralized provider, accept that this may sometimes be necessary.

14.2   The Icing

Centralization and decentralization can be major overhauls. If you are asking people to accept the pain of converting to a new system, you should be proposing a system that is not just cheaper, but better too.

There is an old adage that often appears on buttons and bumper stickers: "Cheap, fast, good. Pick two." This pointed statement reveals a time-tested truism. In general, you must sacrifice one of those three items to achieve the other two. In fact, if someone tries to claim that they provide all three simultaneously, look under the tablecloth of their slick demo and check for hidden wires. This section describes some examples that achieved or promised to achieve all three.

14.2.1   Consolidate Purchasing

In this example, centralization resulted in better products being delivered faster for less money. A system administration group was able to position themselves to approve all computer-related purchasing for their division. In fact, they were able to have the purchasing agent who handled such purchases moved into their group so they could work closely on contracts, maintenance agreements, and so on. As a result, they were able to monitor what was being purchased. Particular purchases, such as servers, would alert them to contact customers to find out what special requirements the server would create: Did it need machine room space, special networking, or configuration? This solved a problem whereby customers would blindside the SAs with requests for major projects. Now the SAs could contact them and schedule these large projects.

Centralized purchasing's biggest benefit was the fact that the SAs now had knowledge of what was being purchased. They noticed certain products being purchased often and would arrange volume purchasing deals for them. Certain software packages would be preordered in bulk. Imagine the customers' surprise when they would try to purchase a particular package and instead receive a note saying that their department would be billed for one fiftieth of a 50-license package that was purchased earlier that year and were given a password they could use to download the software package and manuals. That certainly beat waiting for it to be delivered!

The most pervasive savings came from centralizing the PC purchasing process. Previously, customers would order their own PCs. They would spend days looking through catalogs, selecting each individual component to their particular needs. The result was that the PC repair center had to handle many types of motherboards, cards, and software drivers. Although a customer might take pride in saving ten dollars by selecting a nonstandard video card, he would not appreciate the cost of a technician at the PC repair department spending half a day to get it working. With the repair group unable to stock such a wide variety of spare parts, the customers were extremely unhappy with having to wait weeks for replacement parts to arrive.

To make matters worse, the average time for a PC to be delivered was six weeks. It would take a week to determine what was to be ordered and push it through the purchasing process. The vendor would spend a couple of weeks building the PC to the specifications and delivering it. Finally, another week would pass before the SAs had time to load the OS, with possibly an additional week if there were difficulties. A company cannot be "fast paced" if every PC requires more than a month to be delivered. To make matters worse, new employees would have to wait weeks before their PC would arrive. This was a morale killer and reflected badly on the company. The temporary solution was that management would beg the SAs to cobble together a PC out of spare parts to be used until the person's real PC was delivered. This means that twice as much work was being done because two complete PC deliveries were required.

The centralized purchasing group was able to solve these problems. They found that by standardizing the PC configuration, they could achieve a volume discount that would reduce cost. In fact, they were actually able to negotiate a good price even though they had negotiated four configurations: server, desktop, ultralight laptop, and ultrapowerful laptop. Because they feared people would still opt for a custom configuration, they used some of the savings to ensure the standard configuration would be more powerful, with better audio and video than any previously purchased custom PC. Even if they matched the old price, the savings to the PC repair department would be considerable. The ability to stock spare parts would be a reduction in lost productivity by customers waiting for repairs.

The purchasing group realized that they wouldn't be able to "push" a standard on the customers because the customers could simply opt for a fully custom solution if the standard configuration wasn't to their liking. Therefore they made sure to "pull" people to their standard by making it amazingly good. With the volume discounts, the price was so low and quality so high that most of the customization options remaining would result in a less powerful machine for more money! How could anyone not choose the standard? Using "push" instead of "pull" is also termed "using the carrot, not the stick." It refers to two common ways to get a mule to move forward.

One more benefit was achieved. Because the flow of new machines being purchased was relatively constant, the purchasing group was able to preorder batches of machines that would be preloaded with their OS by the SAs. New employees would have a top-notch PC installed on their desk the day before they arrived.

Ordering time for PCs was reduced from six weeks to six minutes. When faced with the choice between ordering the exact PC they wanted and waiting six weeks or waiting six minutes and getting a PC that was often more powerful than they required, for less money, it was difficult to reject the offer.

Any company that is rapidly growing, purchasing a lot of computer-related items, or deploying PCs should consider these techniques. Other advice on rapid PC deployment can be found in Chapter 1. More information about how PC vendors price their product lines is in Section 2.1.3.

14.2.2   Outsourcing

Outsourcing is often a form of centralization. Outsourcing is a process by which an external company is paid to provide certain technical functions for a company. Some commonly outsourced tasks include running the corporate PC helpdesk, remote access, WAN and LAN services, computer deployment, operations, and so on. Sometimes specific tasks, such as building the infrastructure to support a particular application (web site, e-commerce site,

Enterprise Resource Planning system) are outsourced, though often vendors will refer to that as "professional services" instead.

The process of outsourcing usually involves centralization to reduce redundant services. That is one way outsourcing saves money. It eliminates any political battles that were preventing such efficiencies.

Advocates for outsourcing emphasize that outsourcing lets a company focus on their core competency rather than all the technological infrastructure required to support the core. Some companies become bogged down in supporting their infrastructure to the detriment of their business goals. In that situation, outsourcing can be an appealing solution.

The key in outsourcing is to know what you want and make sure it is specified in the contract. The outsourcing company isn't required to do anything that isn't in the contract. Although the salespeople may paint an exciting picture, once the contract is signed, you should only expect what is specified in ink.

We've seen three related problems with signing an outsourcing contract. Together they create an interesting paradox. Outsourcing to gain new technical competence means the people you are negotiating with have more technical competence than you. This gives the outsourcing firm the power seat in the negotiations. Second, to accurately state your requirements in the contract you must have a good understanding of your technical needs; however if your executive management had a good handle on what was needed and was skilled at communicating this, you wouldn't need outsourcing. Finally, sometimes companies don't decide to outsource until their computing infrastructure has deteriorated to the point that outsourcing is being done as an emergency measure. Being desperate eliminates any ability to gain the upper hand in the negotiations. Therefore typically a company negotiating to outsource their computing needs doesn't know what to ask for, doesn't know what they want, and is in a rush to get the deal done. Be careful!

You should research the outsourcing process, discuss the process with peers at other companies, and talk with customer references. Make sure the contract specifies the entire life cycle of services (design, installation, maintenance and support, decommissioning, data integrity, and disaster recovery), service level agreements, penalties for not meeting performance metrics, and a process for adding and removing services from the contracts. Negotiating an outsourcing contract is extremely difficult, requiring skills far more sophisticated than our introduction to negotiating in Section 27.2.1.

Outsource Negotiations

When one Fortune 500 company outsourced its computing support infrastructure, the executive management feared a large backlash by both the computing professionals within the company and the office workers being supported. Therefore the deal was done quickly and without consulting the people who were providing the support. As a result, it was missing key elements such as data backups, quality metrics, and a clear service level specification. The company had no way to renegotiate the contract without incurring severe penalties. Don't negotiate an outsource contract in secret, get buy-in from technical people.

Critically Examine Metrics
Executives at one company were very proud of their decision to outsource when, after a year of service, the metrics indicated that calls to the helpdesk were completed, on average, in five minutes. This sounds good; but why were employees still complaining about the service they received? Someone thought to ask how this statistic could be true when so many calls included sending a technician to the person's desk. Certainly a moderate percentage of calls like that would destroy such an excellent average. It turned out that the "desk-side support technicians" had their own queue of requests, which had their own time-to-completion metrics. A call to the helpdesk was considered "closed" when a ticket was passed on to the desk-side technician's queue. Always question any metrics you receive from a vendor.

Make sure your contract specifies an exit strategy. When transitioning, the outsourcing company usually retains a right to hire your current computing staff. However, the contract never says you get them back if you decide outsourcing isn't for you. Even switching to a different outsourcing company is difficult, because the old company certainly isn't going to hand over their employees to the competition. Make sure the contract specifies what will happen in these situations so you do not get trapped. Switching back to in-house service is extremely difficult.

Our coverage of outsourcing is admittedly centric to our experiences as SAs. Many books give other points of view. Some are general books about outsourcing (Gay and Essinger 2000; Rothery and Robertson 1995), whereas Williams (1998) gives a CIO's view of the process. Mylott (1995) discusses the outsourcing process with a focus on managing the transfer of MIS duties. Group Staff Outsource (1996) has a general overview of outsourcing. Kuong (2000) discusses the specific issue of provisioning outsourced web application service provider services. Jennings and Passaro

(1999) is an interesting read if you want to go into the outsourcing business yourself. Finally, Chapman and Andrade (1997) discuss how to get out of an outsourcing contract and offer an excellent sample of outsourcing horror stories. We'll pick up the topic of outsourcing again in Section 25.1.8.

14.3 Conclusion

Centralization and decentralization are complicated topics. Neither is always the right solution. Technical issues, such as server administration, as well as nontechnical issues, such as organizational structure, can be centralized or decentralized.

Both topics are about making changes. They are active words, not just descriptive. When making such pervasive changes, we recommend you consider these guiding principles: Understand your motivation for making the change; know what specific problem you are solving; centralize as much as makes sense for today; recognize that as in rolling out any new service, it requires careful planning; and, most importantly, listen to the customers.

It is useful to learn from other people's experiences. The USENIX LISA conference has published many case studies (Van Epp and Baines 1992; Ondishko 1989; Schafer 1992b; and Schwartz, Cottrell, and Dart 1994). Harlander (1994) and Miller and Morris (1996) describe useful tools and the lessons learned from using them.

Centralizing purchasing can be an excellent way to control costs, and our example showed that it can be done not by preventing people from getting what they want to purchase, but by helping them make purchases in a more cost-effective manner.

We ended with a discussion of outsourcing. Outsourcing can be a major force for centralization and will be a large part of system administration for a very long time.

Exercises

1. How centralized or decentralized is your current environment? Give examples.

2. Give an example of a service or an aspect of your organization that should be centralized. Relate guiding principles in Section 14.1.1 to such a project.

3. Give an example of a service or an aspect of your organization that should be decentralized. Relate guiding principles in Section 14.1.1 to such a project.

4. In Section 14.1.3, we describe decentralizing email servers to achieve better reliability. How would you construct a similar architecture for print servers?

5. Describe a small centralization project that would improve your current system.

6. Share your favorite outsourcing horror story.

PART III

The Practices

Chapter 15

Helpdesks

This chapter is a macro view of helpdesks: what they are, how to organize them, how to manage them, and so on. Handling an actual call is covered in the next chapter.

A helpdesk is a place, real or virtual, where people can get answers to their computing questions, report problems, and request new services. It may be a physical desk that people walk to, or it may be a virtual helpdesk that people access electronically.

Nothing is more important than your helpdesk. The helpdesk is the face of your organization. These are the people who make the first impression on your customers and maintain your relationship, good or bad, with them. The helpdesk staff fix the daily problems that are part of living with modern computers, and they are the heroes who are called when customers have an emergency. A good helpdesk reflects well on your organization. The typical customer sees only the helpdesk portion of your organization. They often assume this is your entire organization. They have no idea what "back office" operations and infrastructure are also performed. In short, a helpdesk is for helping the customers. Don't forget the "help" in "helpdesk."

15.1   The Basics

The basics of running a helpdesk are first to simply have one and that
it should have a friendly face. It should have enough staff to support the
traffic, a defined scope of coverage, processes for staff, an escalation process
for when things go badly, and call tracking software.

15.1.1   Have a Helpdesk

All organizations have a helpdesk. Some are physical (a walk-up counter),
and others are virtual (phone-in, or email-in virtual helpdesk). Others are
unofficial (the portion of each day spent directly helping customers).

SA teams of 1 or 2 people often only have an unofficial helpdesk. This
usually doesn't last forever. As the organization grows, small SA teams
become big SA teams and big SA teams become enterprise organizations.
Organizations don't realize they need to institute a formal helpdesk until it
is too late.

The best time to institute a formal helpdesk is nine months before you
realize that you should have done this six months ago. Organizations without access to time-travel devices need other techniques. Organizations grow
through planning, and adopting a formal helpdesk should be part of that
planning. If growth is slow, you can simply look for warning signs. One
warning sign is when SAs start to notice that their group has grown to the
point that communication problems are occurring. Alternatively, SAs might
notice that they aren't able to get "project work" done because they are
constantly being interrupted by customer requests. Typically, the SAs might
decide that it would be better if, for example, one SA could be interrupt-
driven in the morning and focus on project work in the afternoon and the
other SA could do the opposite. If you are considering such a structure, you
are in the formative stage of adopting a formal helpdesk. We believe "earlier
is better."

The transition from ad hoc to helpdesk can be uncomfortable to customers. SAs should expect this and do their best to ease the transition.
Clearly communicating the new helpdesk procedures is important.

People Assume Nothing Changes If They Aren't Told Otherwise
When establishing a formal helpdesk, whether physical or virtual, people
must be told that this is being done. When Lumeta was small (fewer than
ten people), most people did their own computer support, and Tom would intervene for more difficult problems. Eventually, the company grew, and there
were three SAs, including one who was dedicated to PC-related problems and
any "customer-facing issues" (where "customers" refers to other employees,

not clients of Lumeta). For all intents and purposes, this person was "the helpdesk." The customers didn't understand that the various SAs had specializations. This frustrated both the SAs, who felt pestered with inappropriate questions, and the customers, who were confused why every SA wasn't able to help in every situation. The problem was fixed when email went out explaining which SAs to contact for what kind of problems, and the message was repeated at weekly staff meetings two meetings in a row. You can prevent this confusion by making such announcements as the change happens.

Where's Karen?

A department (75 people) had a self-administered network. People who were more knowledgeable about the systems did more of the SA duties, and others did less. They had one semitechnical clerk on staff, named Karen (not her real name), who took care of backups and was trained to do most installations and other semiautomated tasks. Nearly every bit of user documentation included the instruction, "Email Karen to get started." As a result of business changes, they eventually were required to use the centralized support that other departments in that building used. Customers were frustrated that instead of sending email to Karen, they had to send email to "help." The personal touch had been lost. Rather than deal with the emotional issue head-on, management just kept pushing people to use the new process. Karen held a lot of political weight in the department because everyone knew her, and she could spread pessimism effectively if she chose to do so. Because she was not made part of the process, but was shoe-horned into it, she felt she was being pushed out. She eventually quit, and it took a couple of years of effort for the new helpdesk system to be fully accepted by the customers. This could have been prevented if the transition had been handled better, first by understanding what the customers were used to and then by integrating that culture into the new process.

Helpdesks do not need to be purely physical objects. Virtual helpdesks are very popular. Problems can be reported and replies can return via email. Other solutions include text-based and audio chat that let people interact with a human without using a phone.

Self-help systems are also popular, but should not be considered replacement for systems that involved human interaction. With the pervasiveness of the web, there is no excuse not to have at least a simple repository of documentation for customers on topics that include how to get help, how to request service activation, and solutions to common problems. Web-based systems let customers help themselves by offering documentation, lists of frequently asked questions (FAQs) and their answers, and "just in time help." These systems can reduce the workload of helpdesk attendants, but cannot provide the interactive debugging and "workflow" issues that require real-time interaction. At least, there should be a phone number to call to report that the self-help system is down.

15.1.2   A Friendly Face

A helpdesk should have a friendly face. If it is a physical helpdesk, the interior design should be pleasant and welcoming. A virtual helpdesk should be equally welcoming, which often means a design that uses soothing colors and readable fonts with the most commonly selected items at the top left of the first page.

The faces of the staff also should be welcoming and friendly, as should their personalities. Some people have personalities that are suited for customer service and others don't. That should be a consideration when hiring people for your staff. The tone set by the staff will reflect that which is set by the supervisor. A supervisor who yells at the staff will find staff yelling at customers. A supervisor who is good natured, can laugh, and is always friendly will attract similar staff, who will reflect such an attitude with customers. It is easier to build a reputation for being friendly initially than to restore a bad reputation. In short, if you are the supervisor, be the friendly person you want your staff to be. Be a role model.

15.1.3   Staff Sizing

A helpdesk can be helpful only if there are enough people to serve customers in a timely manner. Otherwise people will look elsewhere for their support.

Sizing a helpdesk staff is very difficult because it changes from situation to situation. Universities often have thousands of students per helpdesk attendant. Corporate helpdesks sometimes have a higher ratio or sometimes a lower ratio. In a commercial research environment, the ratio is often 50:1 and the first-tier SAs are of a similar skill level as second-tier SAs at other helpdesks. E-commerce sites usually have a seperate helpdesk for internal questions and a "customer-facing" helpdesk to help resolve issues reported by paying customers. Depending on the services being offered, the ratio can be 10,000:1, or a million to one.

Ratios are a "can't win" situation. Management will always push to have a higher ratio; customers will always demand a lower ratio. You can always "increase" the ratio by providing less service to the customers, which usually costs the organization more because the customers spend time doing their own SA work inefficiently.

Rather than focus on customer-to-attendant ratios, it is better to focus on call volume ratios and time-to-call completion. For example, you can monitor the rate at which customers receive busy signals or how long they wait to receive a response to their email or the number of minutes issues take to be resolved (minus, of course, time spent in "customer wait," as described in Section 16.2.6).

These metrics focus on issues that are more important to the customer. Customer-to-attendant ratios are an indirect measurement of benefit to the customers. In metric-based management, the direct metrics are better.

Managing resources based on call volume also presents a more diverse set of potential solutions. Instead of one solution—headcount management—companies can invest in processes that let customers help themselves without need for human intervention. For example, new system commands can be created that empower customers to do tasks that previously required privileged access, online documentation can be provided, new services can be provisioned automatically via web interfaces, and so on.

Case Study: Human Web Browsers

Making the customers more self-sufficient can backfire if not done correctly. One company established a web site to give easy access to all the documentation and FAQs that previously had been the domain of the helpdesk staff. By monitoring the logs of the web site, the management saw an interesting trend. At first, the web site was wildly successful. The hits to the site were coming from the customers. The volume of phone calls was reduced, and everything was happening as planned. However, by the third month, the logs indicated a new trend: The web site was seeing an increasing number of hits from the helpdesk itself. Investigation showed that people had returned to calling the helpdesk, and the helpdesk staff was reading answers off the web site. The helpdesk was acting as a human web browser! The situation was rectified when the helpdesk attendants were instructed to try to refer people to the appropriate web page rather than give answers directly. Customers were reminded to visit the web site before calling the helpdesk.

You need to have appropriate metrics to make decisions about improving processes. Metrics can reveal good candidates for new automation and documentation. Metrics can reveal which processes are more effective, which are used heavily or which are not used at all.

15.1.4 Defined Scope of Coverage

A helpdesk should have a well-defined scope of coverage. Scope has "what," "who," "where," "when," and "how long" components.

What: What is being supported? Just the PCs or the network itself? All
PCs no matter what OS is being used, or just certain OSs and certain

revisions? Which applications are being supported? How are unsupported platforms handled?

Who: Who will be supported? A particular department, building, division, enterprise, university? What if a person has offices in multiple buildings, each with its own helpdesk? Only people that pay? Only people of a certain management level and higher (or lower)?

Where: Where are the customers? This is similar to "who" if one is supporting, for example, all the people in a particular building or location. However, "where" also includes support of traveling customers, customers visiting external customer sites, customers performing demos at trade shows, and whether people are supported when they are working from home.

When: The hours of operations must be defined. Is the support provided 8 AM to 6 PM five days a week or 24×7? How are things handled outside of these hours? Do people have to wait until the helpdesk reopens, or is there a mechanism to reach people at home? If there is no support in the off-hours, what should facilities management do if environmental alarms (HVAC, power) sound or if there is a fire?

How long: "How long" should the average request take to complete? Certain categories of requests should be instant, and other categories of requests should take longer. Establishing these goals sets expectations for the staff and customers. Customers expect everything to be immediate if they aren't told that certain tasks should be expected to take longer (see Section 26.1.3).

Case Study: Wide Scope, Narrow Responsibility

Scope of support also means scope of responsibility. The New Jersey engineering division of a computer-aided design (CAD) company was entirely in one building. The helpdesk's policy was that no question was inappropriate, but the SAs had a sharply defined scope of responsibility. This worked because they understood where their responsibility ended. They had complete responsibility for certain issues: If someone reported a problem with their workstation, they would fix it. Other issues they would advocate on behalf of the customer: If the problem was with a WAN link that they didn't control, they would take responsibility for contacting the corporate Network Operations Center (NOC) and seeing that it got fixed. With other issues, they acted as a referral service: If someone reported that the light in their office had burned out, they referred the person to facilities management and would not take responsibility for seeing the issue to completion. They became a clearing house for information.

> To save money, the regional sales office was in the same building. The helpdesk was funded by the engineering division, not the sales office, and therefore the scope of responsibility for the sales staff was different. They could refer the sales engineers to the proper documentation or suggest where they could get more training, but they could not be involved in helping to set up machines for demos or presentations. The sales staff used the central email server that was run by the engineering group, so email support was complete, but only if the salesperson was using the email client supported by the engineering group. However, because the support of the sales staff was "free," there usually was a limit to how far the helpdesk staff would go to support their requests.
>
> Having a clearly defined scope of responsibility prevented the helpdesk from taking on more work than they could handle, yet let them provide an extremely friendly referral service. It also prevented the sales group from abusing their service by giving the helpdesk the ability to say "no" in a way that had management support.

A helpdesk must have a good process for dealing with requests about technologies that are out of scope. The helpdesk can simply state that the request is out of scope and refuse to help, but that is an unfriendly response. It is much better to clearly state the scope of what the helpdesk can and can't do for the person and then offer a little help, but give a time limit before you begin. For example, you might say, "We don't support systems with that video card, but I'll try my best for 30 minutes. If I can't fix it, you are on your own." You might spend 45 minutes on the problem, and then politely tell the customer that you've reached your limit. The customer will appreciate the effort.

Set Expectations When Working Outside of Job Scope

One of Jay Stiles' favorite stories is about a time he worked in a place that had one set of technicians who installed network jacks in offices. The customers were supposed to configure their own PCs or call a different set of technicians, who did that kind of work. The customers often asked the first group of technicians to configure their PC. The technicians soon learned that if they made a mistake, their boss would be called and put in a difficult position: How do you answer a complaint about an employee that didn't do a task right, when she wasn't supposed to do that task? Later, the technicians learned that if they were asked to configure a PC, they should stop what they were doing, back away from the machine, and explain, "Well that really isn't my job, but I happen to know a little about these PC computers and I can give it a try. However, if I can't figure it out, I'm going to ask you to call the people that are supposed to do that kind of thing." If they said those magic words, the entire process was different. If they were successful, the customer was very happy, especially because they now knew they had received special service that was above the call of duty for that person. If they weren't successful, the customer would be ecstatic that the technician tried. The boss started receiving calls that were compliments: "The technician tried to configure my PC and couldn't, but I want to thank him for trying so hard!" It's all in how you sell it.

15.1.5   Defined Processes for Staff

Helpdesk staff should have well-defined processes to follow. In a smaller environment, this is not as important, because the processes are more ad hoc or are undocumented because they are being used by the people that built them. However, for a large organization, the processes must be well documented.

Very large helpdesks use "scripts" as part of their training. Every service that is supported has an associated flow of dialogue to follow to support that service. For example, if someone is calling to request remote access service, the script captures the appropriate information and tells the operator what to do, be it enable remote access directly or forward the request to the appropriate service organization. Another example would be password resets: For security reasons, the script would require callers to prove who they are (possibly by knowing something that only they would know), then a new password would be set.

Chapter 16 discusses a formal process that helpdesk attendants can use to process individual trouble reports.

15.1.6   An Escalation Process

Escalation is the process by which the issue is moved from the current staff person to someone with more experience. The first line of operators should be able to handle 80 to 90 percent of all calls. The remaining calls are escalated to a second tier of support. This second tier may have more experience, more training, and possibly other responsibilities. Depending on the size of the organization; the third or fourth tier may be the people that created the service themselves or the manager of the service.

It is common to have a policy that the first tier of support should escalate all calls that get to the 15-minute mark. This has a carry-over effect in that the second tier, who may be responsible for project-oriented work, now has less time for projects. This can be alleviated by designating one second-tier person to sit with the first-tier people each week. That is, make "helpdesk" his or her "project" for the week. Although upper-tier staff will usually dislike this policy, a sizable organization will require this of people only once every six weeks or so. A side benefit to this strategy is that the first-tier staff will learn from the second-tier person. The second-tier person will also get a better understanding of the kind of issues that are coming into the helpdesk, which will help them decide which new projects will be the most help to the first tier and the customers.

The escalation process is also what customers use when they are dissatisfied with the support they are receiving. One hopes this happens as little as possible, but inevitably someone will want to talk to a manager. The helpdesk should be prepared for this. If large numbers of calls are escalated to the second tier, it is a warning sign that there is a problem. Usually, this is an indication that the first-tier staff need more training or they do not have the tools to do their job properly. If large numbers of calls are escalated to management, there may be systemic problems with the support the helpdesk is providing.

Escalation Is Just an Arm's Reach Away

Escalation should not exist just to pacify angry customers. One small ISP's helpdesk often receives calls from angry individuals who demand to speak to a manager. Their process is to hand the phone to the person to their left, who then claims to be "the manager." Although this works in the short term or when business growth is at a staggering rate, we do not feel this is a sustainable way of maintaining a helpdesk. Escalation should actually get results.

15.1.7 Helpdesk Software

Every helpdesk needs some kind of software to help manage it. The alternative we have seen is a collection of notes written on scraps of paper. Although it is simple in the beginning and sufficient for environments with one or two SAs, this solution doesn't scale. Requests get lost, and management has no ability to oversee the process to better allocate resources. Those are the first qualities that you need in helpdesk software. As a helpdesk grows, software can help in other areas. The scripts mentioned in Section 15.1.5 can be displayed automatically, and they can be "smart" by being part of the information gathering process rather than just a static screen.

Helpdesk software should permit some kind of priority to be assigned to tickets. This not only helps meet customer expectations but also helps SAs manage their time. An SA should be able to easily list the top priority issues that have been assigned to her.

Another important aspect of helpdesk software is that it collects logs about what kind of requests are made and by whom. Statistical analysis of such logs can be useful in managing the helpdesk. However, if the software doesn't capture that information, one can't gain the benefits of such statistics. This often happens when there is a lot of walk-up and phone traffic. In such cases, it can be useful for the software to have a one-click way to log common questions or issues. Caller ID can be used to populate fields with the caller's information.

Helpdesk software can also automate the collection of customer satisfaction data. Every day it can select a random sample of yesterday's customers and survey them about the service they received.

Case Study: From Good to Bad

A software company of about 1,500 people was using an enhanced version of a freely available call tracking system. It was very simple to use, with a few different interfaces, the most popular of which was the email interface. The system tracked customer, department, category, status, who the call is assigned to, how much time has been spent on it and by whom, priority, due date, and so on. Custom scripts produced metrics that management could use to track how things were going. Customers could use a web interface to see the history of their call and all of the other fields associated with it. They could also look at the call queue for the person that it was assigned to and see where it was in their priority list. Although the system wasn't glitzy, everyone was comfortable with it and could get the information they needed out of it.

The MIS group, which provided support for databases and the applications that ran on top of them and was not a part of the SA group, was commissioned to build a new call tracking system for the Customer Support Center. The management chain of that group expanded the scope of the project to make this into one unified call tracking system to also be used by the operations group, MIS, and the SA group. Neither the operations group nor MIS had a call tracking system, and no one in the SA group was told of the project, so their needs and the needs of their customers were not taken into consideration in the design. The system that resulted was entirely windows-based,[1] with no email interface and no command-line interface. Creating a new call involved bringing up ten different windows. Updating a call required five or six different windows. It was impossible for many SAs (who dialed in using company-standard Apple Mac laptops) to use the system from home and impossibly slow for the others who had nonstandard UNIX or Windows machines at home. It frequently took longer to open a trouble ticket than it took to solve the

---

[1] Refers to Microsoft Windows and X Windows.

problem, so the numerous small calls were no longer tracked. What was once a quick email process had become a ten-minute endeavor. Several SAs went back to tracking projects on pieces of paper or in their heads.

Customers complained because they could no longer see the status of their calls or where those calls were in the priority queues. They also complained because they couldn't open a ticket via email any more and because the new system sent them far too much email whenever a small field in the call was changed. All of these complaints were predicted by the SA group when they were suddenly presented with the new system that they were going to have to start using, but it was too late to change anything.

The system was supposed to provide better tools for producing metrics. However, because a lot of the data was no longer entered into the system, it clearly didn't, even though the tools it provided for metrics may have been better.

It is critical that helpdesk software match the workflow of the people that use it. If one ticket is opened per week, it is reasonable for the creation of a ticket to take a long time. However if you expect hundreds of tickets per day, initiating the new ticket should be almost instantaneous, such as sending email. Do not use helpdesk software to introduce radical new workflow concepts.

Choosing helpdesk software is not an easy process. Most software will need a lot of customizing to your environment. When you decide to invest in helpdesk software, you need to be prepared to invest in the customizations also, so that the SAs can use it effectively. If it is a burden to use, they will not use it or will only use it for large projects.

15.2 The Icing

Now that we have a solid helpdesk, the icing helps us expand it on many different axes: quality, coverage, clarity of policy, and scaling.

15.2.1 Statistical Improvements

More sophisticated statistics can be gathered about a helpdesk. You can monitor the rate of escalations to determine where more training is needed. However, when dealing with upper management for budgeting and planning purposes, historical statistics become much more valuable. You can make a better case for your budget if you can show multiyear trends of customer growth, call volume, types of calls, technologies, services provided, and customer satisfaction. When being asked to support a new technology or service, one can use past data to predict what the support costs may be.

The value of statistics increases as the organization grows, because the management becomes less directly involved in the work being done. It is often difficult to collect statistics in small organizations because practices are often less automated and can't be instrumented to collect data. As an organization grows, statistics are easier to collect and it becomes more important that they be collected.

15.2.2   Out of Hours and 24 × 7 Coverage

As computers become critical to an ever-expanding list of business processes, customers are asking for 24 × 7 coverage more often. Although full "three-shift coverage" may be required in some organizations, there are some very simple ways to provide 24 × 7 coverage that are not as expensive.

You can set up a voicemail box that alerts a pager when new messages arrive. The pager can be passed to various staff members on a rotation basis. The responsibility of the staff person may not be to fix the problem, but to simply alert the appropriate person or keep calling various people until someone is found. This requires all staff to have a list of everyone's home phone number.

A variation on this technique is to have all managers of the customer groups know the home phone number of the helpdesk's supervisor, who then takes responsibility for calling SAs in turn until one is found. This has the benefit of spreading personal information around to fewer people. This can wear down a helpdesk supervisor and doesn't take into account the supervisor's vacations. However, local solutions can be found, such as rotating this duty among a couple of supervisors.

You can also treat the issue the same way other industries treat alarms, because the modern equivalent of a researcher's laboratory catching fire at night is a major file server being down. Security personnel at factories always have a "call list" in case of alarms, fires, and so on. They start at the top of the list and keep calling numbers until they find someone. Depending on the issue, that person may advise the security guard on who is the most appropriate person on the list to call. At IBM's T.J. Watson facility, they extended that process to the computer systems. If a major computer is down, customers can call the security desk and report the issue. The security guards have a separate list of people to call if the problem is computer related.

No matter how SAs are contacted out of hours, the person must be compensated or there is no incentive to fix the problem. Some organizations have a salary incentive for "on call" time equivalent to a fraction of the employee's salary and time and a half if they are called. Other organizations issue comp time[2] either officially or unofficially.

---

[2]Compensation time allows the employee to take off that much time (or 1.5 times that amount in some cases) without claiming it against vacation time.

15.2.3   Better Advertising for the Helpdesk

Having your policies defined and announcements available for all to see on a web site is nice and should be included in "The Basics" of this chapter. However, rarely will anyone seek them out to read them. In this section, we talk about getting your policies and announcements "out there" and understood.

With the introduction of the web, it is easy to make all policies accessible to all customers. There is no excuse for not doing this. However, you must get customers to that web site. Some SA organizations choose to have a "portal" web site that is the gateway to all their services, policies, and documentation. By making it the way customers receive information that is important to them, they also will know where to go for information that is important to you.

Pick the right message. Talk with customers to find out what is important to them. It's difficult to get people to read something that isn't important to them. They may not care that `server3` will be down during the weekend, but knowing that the database that is stored on `server3` won't be accessible all weekend will draw their attention.

New policies can be emailed to customers or sent via paper memo if they are particularly critical. Portals can highlight a "policy of the month." If the message will benefit from repetition, put posters in appropriate places. A physical helpdesk should have its hours posted at all entrances. Students spend a lot of time staring at the wall while waiting for their computer; fill those blank walls with the message you want them to remember. Posters that say "Change your password every 30 days!" or "`Server3` is being decommissioned on May 1." Give good advice and warn of upcoming changes.

Messages are most effective when received at the right time. If `server3` is being decommissioned in a month, it is best to tell people that every time they use `server3`.

15.2.4   Different "Desks" for Service Provision Versus Problem Resolution

When an organization grows, there may be times when it makes sense to have two separate helpdesks: one for requesting new services and the other for reporting problems that arise after the service has been successfully enabled. Often a third group of people deals with installing the new service, if it requires physical work, and possibly an internal helpdesk that installers can call to escalate installation problems (though this is usually the second tier of one of the other helpdesks).

The benefit of dividing the helpdesk this way is that the three (or four) groups can be under different supervisors. A supervisor can effectively manage only a certain number of people. This division of labor makes it clear where to place various supervisors. They should all report to the same manager to make sure that communication happens and finger-pointing doesn't (or is restricted to within a small organization).

Another benefit is that the different groups can be separately trained for the different skills required for their task. This tends to be less expensive than hiring people who are experienced enough to be able to do all the tasks.

Provisioning service is a process that should be "cookie cutter"—the same for all customers. The initial collection of data does not have to be done by a highly technical person, just someone who can be trained to ask the right questions. They may have more sales experience than the other staff. Solving installation problems is a highly technical issue but has a narrow focus, and training can be customized to those issues. The separate helpdesk for reporting problems requires a staff with wider technical experience and background. This division of labor is critical to scaling the organization to very large sizes.

15.3   Conclusion

To your customers, the helpdesk is how they see you, how they get service, and how they have their problems fixed. It is the number one component to your reputation. To you, a helpdesk is a tool to create once your organization has grown to a certain size and a tool for creating a division of labor as you grow. A helpdesk is not needed for small organizations, but there is a particular growth point at which it becomes useful and, later, critical.

The helpdesk is the "face" of your organization, so make it a happy, friendly one no matter if it is physical or virtual. Properly sizing the helpdesk is important and affects not only your budget but your customer satisfaction rating. In planning your helpdesk, you must define what is supported, who is supported, where they are, when you provide support, and how long customers should expect an average call to last. Constructing accurate budget and staffing plans is made easier by collecting the statistics mentioned in Section 15.1.7.

Processes should be defined for staff to follow regarding how they provide support for various services and how issues are escalated. Software must be used to collect statistics on all calls and to track issues that last longer than a single call.

Once those things are established, a helpdesk can grow in other areas. "Out of hours" coverage can be instituted; policies can be better advertised; and, with high growth, the helpdesk can be split into separate groups for new service provisioning and trouble reporting.

Much was discussed in this chapter, and every issue in some way touched on communication. The helpdesk is how customers communicate with our organization, and yet it is often the role of the helpdesk to communicate to customers how, when, and why things are done. How we communicate can determine if we are perceived as friendly or unfriendly. The statistics that are collected help communicate to management the needs of the organization during planning cycles. Escalation procedures keep the communication flowing when things stall. Having a written out-of-hours support policy sets expectations with customers and prevents the frustration of unexpected calls late at night.

Exercises

1. Describe your helpdesk staff structure.

2. How many attendants does your helpdesk have at any given moment? How is that number selected?

3. Which helpdesk attendant in your organization is perceived as the least friendly by the customers? How would you know? How would you help them improve?

4. How "hands on" are you with your helpdesk? What statistics do you use to manage it or what statistics are given to your management? If you were one step less "hands on," what new statistics would you need then?

5. Report a problem tonight at 10 PM. Describe how well it went.

Customer Care

SAs spend much of their time responding to requests from customers. In this chapter, we present a structured process defining how customer requests are gathered, evaluated, fixed, and verified.[1] This is a more specific task than the general issues that surround running a helpdesk (the topic of the previous chapter).

By "customer requests" we mean "trouble tickets," "calls," "problem reports," or whatever your site calls them. Examples include: "I can't print," "The network is slow," or "A program that compiled yesterday won't compile anymore."

SAs do many tasks, but often customers see only the parts that involve responding to their requests. They do not see all the "back office" work, and they shouldn't have to see it. Therefore how well you respond to customer requests is critical to maintaining customer satisfaction.

The method for processing these trouble reports has nine steps, which can be grouped into four phases.

- Phase A: The Greeting ("Hello")
  - Step 1: The Greeting

---

[1] This process is based on a paper by Tom titled "Deconstructing User Requests and the Nine Step Model" (Limoncelli 1999).

- Phase B: Problem Identification ("What's wrong?")
  - Step 2: Problem Classification
  - Step 3: Problem Statement
  - Step 4: Problem Verification
- Phase C: Planning and Execution ("Fix it")
  - Step 5: Solution Proposals
  - Step 6: Solution Selection
  - Step 7: Execution
- Phase D: Verification ("Verify it")
  - Step 8: Craft Verification
  - Step 9: Customer Verification/Closing

This gives structure to what is, for newer SAs, a more haphazard process. It helps you solve problems more efficiently by keeping you focused. It increases effectiveness because it is explicit about planning before you begin and verify afterward that work is truly complete. It introduces a common set of terminology that, when used by the entire SA team, increases the ability to communicate within the group.

This tool does not bestow any additional technical expertise on the people using it, but it may help the junior people gain insight into how the senior SAs approach problem solving. Creativity, experience, the right resources, tools, and personal and external management are other influences that contribute to productivity.

In addition to this model being useful to SAs, if customers understand it, they become more skilled in getting the help they desire. They will be prepared with the right information, and they can nudge the SA through the process if necessary.

Historical Comparison

At the close of World War II, the United States found itself with a huge excess of manufacturing capacity. As a result, companies started producing hundreds of new products that households and businesses never had access to previously. Thousands of returning G.I.s found jobs selling these new products. The new manufacturing capacity, the new products, and the large number of returning G.I.s looking for work combined to produce a new era for the United States economy.

As time went on, competition grew. Companies found that it was no longer sufficient just to have a large sales force; a *good* sales force was needed. They started to ask, "What makes the high-performing salespeople different from the others?"

Industry encouraged business schools to increase their study of the sales process. They discovered that the better salesmen, whether or not they realized it, had a specific, structured method they employed. It involved specific phases or steps. Mediocre salespeople deviated from these phases in varying ways or performed certain phases badly. The low performers had little or no consistency in their methods.

The method, once identified, could be taught. Thus sales skills went from an intuitive function to a formal function with well-defined parts. Previous sales training consisted mostly of explaining the product's features and qualities. Subsequently, training included exploration of the selling process itself.

This deconstruction of the process permitted further examination and therefore further improvement. Each step could be studied, measured, taught, practiced, and so on. Focus was improved because a single step could be studied in isolation. Also the entire flow of steps could be studied (a holistic approach).

We imagine that if anyone explained the structured process to the high-performing salespeople, it would sound strange. To them it comes naturally. It would be like explaining to Picasso how to paint. However, to the beginners, this framework gives structure to a process they are learning. After they master it, they may modify or customize it for their situation. Without first learning one structured system, it is difficult to get to the place where you need to be to invent your own.

In the 1990s, system administration began a similar journey. Previously it was a craft or an art practiced by few people. With the explosive growth of corporate computing and intranet/Internet applications, the demand for SAs was similarly explosive. A flood of new SAs arrived to meet the need. The quality of their work varied. Training often took the form of teaching particular product features, similar to when a salesperson's training consisted mostly of learning the product line. Other training methods included exploring manuals and documentation, trial by fire, training by social institutions (for example, IRC, mailing lists, and so on) and professional institutions (for example, SAGE, SANS, and others).

System administration needed to mature in ways similar to how the sales process matured. In the late 1990s there was an increase in the academic study of system administration (Burgess 2000). In fact, this book's inspiration comes from that same need to provide training founded on non-platform-specific themes, principles, and theoretical models rather than specific details about particular technologies, vendors, and products (Limoncelli and Hogan 2001).

16.1 The Basics

The basic process described in this chapter contains nine steps grouped into four phases. As seen in Figure 16.1, the phases deal with:

- How the customer reports the problem
- Identifying the problem
- Planning and executing a solution
- Verifying that the problem resolution is complete

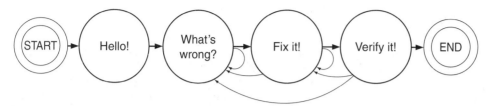

Figure 16.1: General flow of problem solving

Readers should be forewarned that sometimes certain steps are iterated as required. For example, during Step 4 (Problem Verification), the SA may realize the issue has been misclassified and he must return to Step 2 (Problem Classification). This can happen at any step and requires returning to any previous step.

16.1.1   Ticket Tracking Software

Although we already discussed it in Section 15.1.7, we cannot overemphasize the importance of using a software package to track problem reports. This is not as controversial a point as it used to be, but in the 1980s and early 1990s, it was rare that SAs would use software to track such requests. Installing such software is profoundly transformational. It affects your ability to manage your time and deliver consistent results to customers.

Although we could fill a chapter with what makes for good trouble-tracking software, we instead choose to focus elsewhere. Any software is better than no software. If you find a site that has no trouble-tracking software, simply install whatever you were comfortable with at a previous site or software that has an Internet mailing list of active supporters.

Now let's look at the process in detail.

16.1.2   Phase A: The Greeting

The first phase only has one deceptively simple step (Figure 16.2). Issues are solicited from the customers.

Figure 16.2: Greeting phase

Step 1: The Greeting—"The Greeter"

Step 1 includes everything related to how the customer's request is solicited. This step is where someone or something asks, "How may I help you?" either literally (on the phone) or figuratively (a web site that collects problem reports). It should welcome the customer to the system and start the process on a positive, friendly, helpful note.

The entities that respond to the requests are called *greeters*. There are many greeters: calling a customer care center, walking up to a physical "helpdesk," email, web form, and so on. Multiple ways to collect reports are needed for easy and reliable access. If the customer's problem is an inability to send email, requiring him or her to report this issue via email is silly.

Sometimes problems are reported by automated means rather than by humans. For example network monitoring tools such as "Big Brother," (Peacock and Giuffrida 1988) HP OpenView, and Tivoli can notify SAs that a problem is occurring. This is still the same process, although some of the steps may be expedited by the tool.

Every site and every customer is different. What is an appropriate way to report issues is different for every part of every organization. Is the customer local or remote? Is the customer experienced or new? Is the technology being supported complicated or simple? These questions can help when you select which greeters to use.

How do customers know how to find help? There are various ways to advertise the available greeters. Examples include signs in hallways, newsletters, stickers on computers or phones, and even banner advertisements on internal web pages.

Although this certainly isn't a complete list, the greeters we have seen include: email, phone, walk-up helpdesk, visiting the SA's office, submission via web, submission via custom application, and report by automated monitoring system.

16.1.3 Phase B: Problem Identification ("What's Wrong?")

The second phase is focused on classifying the problem and recording and verifying it (Figure 16.3).

Step 2: Problem Classification—"The Classifier"

In Step 2, the request is classified to determine who should handle it. This role is known as *the classifier*. The classifier may be a human or it may be automated. For example, at a walk-up helpdesk, staff might listen to the problem description to determine its classification. A phone response system may ask the user to press 1 for PC problems, 2 for network problems, and so on. If certain customer groups are helped by certain SAs, their requests

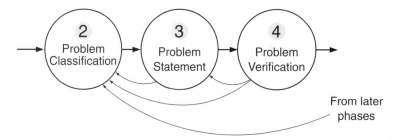

Figure 16.3: What's wrong?

may be automatically forwarded based on the requester's email address, manually entered employee ID number, or by the phone caller's caller ID information.

When the process is manual, a human must have the responsibility to classify the problem from the description or to ask the customer more questions. A formal decision tree may be used to determine the right classification.

You need to ask more questions when you aren't as familiar with the customer's environment. This is often the case at the helpdesk of e-commerce sites or extremely large corporate helpdesks.

No matter how the classification is performed, the customer should be told how the request is classified. This creates a feedback loop that can detect mistakes. For example, if a classifier tells a customer, "This sounds like a printing problem. I'm assigning this issue to someone from our printer support group," the customer stays involved in the process. The customer may point out that their problem is more pervasive than just printing, leading to a classification such as a network problem.

If a phone response system is used, the customer has classified the request already. However, a customer may not be the best person to make this decision. The next person who speaks with the customer should be prepared to validate the customer's choice in a way that is not insulting. If the customer had misclassified the request, it should be remedied in a polite manner. We feel the best way to do so is for the customer to be told what he should have done (that is, told the correct phone number to call or button to press), and then the SA should do it for him (that is, transfer the call to the right number). Some companies do one or the other, but doing both is better.

When asking a customer to classify the problem the choices presented must be carefully constructed and revised over time. You should gather statistics to detect mismatches between customers' perceptions of what the classifications mean versus what you intended them to mean or at least you should monitor for customer complaints.

Marketing-Driven Customer Support
A large network equipment manufacturer once had their phone menu based on the marketing terminology that segments their product lines rather than the technical terminology that most of their customers used. This caused no end of confusion because the marketing terminology had little basis in reality from the typical technician's point of view. It was particularly confusing for customers of any company that was acquired by this company because the acquired company's products were reclassified into marketing terms unfamiliar to the acquired company's customers. Phone menus should use terminology that the customers expect to hear.

Many requests may be transferred or eliminated at this stage. For example, if the customer is requesting a new feature, she should be transferred to the appropriate group that handles requests for features. If the request is outside the domain of work done by the support group, the customer might be referred to another department. If the request is against policy and therefore it must be denied, the issue may be escalated to management if the customer disagrees with the decision. For this reason, it is important to have a well-defined scope of service and a process for requesting new services.

At very large sites, you are more likely to find yourself acting on behalf of your customer, coordinating between different departments or even the helpdesks of different departments! Complicated problems that involve network, application, and server issues can require the helpdesk attendant to juggle conversations between three or more organizations. Navigating such a twisty maze of passages for the customer is a valuable service you can provide.

Step 3: Problem Statement—"The Recorder"
Step 3 is where the customer states the problem in full detail and this information is recorded. The person performing this role is referred to as *the recorder* and often is the same person as the classifier. The skill required by the recorder in this phase is the ability to listen and ask the right questions to draw out the necessary information from the customer. The recorder extracts the relevant details and records them.

A problem statement describes the problem being reported and records enough clues to reproduce and fix the problem. A bad problem statement is vague or incomplete. A good problem statement is complete and identifies all hardware and software involved, as well as their location, the last time it worked, and so on. Sometimes, not all of that information is appropriate or available.

An example of a good problem statement is "PC talpc.example.com (a PC running Windows NT 4 SP4) located in room 301 cannot print from MS-Word97 to printer 'rainbow,' the color PostScript printer located in room 314. It worked fine yesterday. It can print to other printers. The customer does not know if other computers are having this problem."

Certain classes of problems can be completely stated in simple ways. Internet routing problems can best be reported by listing two IP addresses that cannot ping each other, but that both can communicate to other hosts; including a traceroute from each host to the other (if possible) helps considerably. All other information is superfluous.

It is unreasonable to expect problem statements from customers to be complete. Customers require assistance. The above problem statement comes from a real example in which a customer sent email to an SA that simply stated, "Help! I can't print." That is about as ambiguous and incomplete as a request can be. A reply was sent asking, "To which printer? Which PC? What application?"

The customer's reply included a statement of frustration. "I need to print these slides by 3 PM. I'm flying to a conference!" At that point, email was abandoned and the telephone was used. This permitted a faster "back and forth" between the customer and classifier. No matter the medium, it is important that this dialog take place and that the final result be reported to the customer.

Sometimes, the recorder can perform a fast loop through the next steps to accelerate the process. The recorder might find out if the device is plugged in, if the person has checked the manual, and so on. However, questions such as "Is it plugged in?" and "Have you checked the manual?" are questions that put customers in defensive positions. They have only two possible answers and only one clearly "right" answer. Avoid putting customers in a defensive position where they feel compelled to lie. Instead, ask what outlet it's plugged into; ask them to confirm, while you're on the phone, that the cable is firmly seated at both ends. Tell them that you've checked the manual, and for future reference the answer is on page 9, if the problem comes up again.

You also should make sure to never make the customer feel like an idiot. We cringed when we heard that a helpdesk attendant informed a customer that "an eight year old would understand" what he was explaining. Instead, reassure the customers that they'll get better at using computers as they gain experience.

Flexibility is important. In the previous example the customer indicated that there was an urgent need to have the slides printed. Here it might be appropriate to suggest using a different printer that is known to be working, rather than fixing the problem right now. This accelerates the process, which is important for an urgent problem such as this one.

Large sites often have different people recording requests and executing the requests. This added "hand-off" introduces a challenge because the recorder may not have the direct experience required to know exactly what to record. In that case it is prudent to have preplanned sets of data to gather for various situations. For example, if the customer is reporting a network problem, the problem statement must include an IP address, the room number of the machine that is not working, and what particular thing the person is trying to do over the network that is not working. If the problem relates to printing, you should record the name of the printer, the computer being used, and the application generating the print job.

Most sites use some kind of "trouble ticket" software to record the customer's report. It can be useful if the software records different information depending on how the problem has been classified.

Step 4: Problem Verification—"The Reproducer"

Step 4 is where the SA tries to reproduce the problem. This role is known as *the reproducer*. If the problem cannot be reproduced, often the problem being reported is not being properly communicated and you must return to Step 3 (Problem Statement). If the problem is intermittent this process becomes more complicated but not impossible.

Nothing gets you a better understanding of the problem than seeing it in action. This is the single most important reason for doing problem verification. Yet, we see naive SAs skip it all the time. If you do not verify the problem, you may work on the problem for hours before you realize that you aren't even working on the right issue. Often, the customer's description is misleading. A customer who doesn't have the technical knowledge to accurately describe the problem can send you on a wild goose chase. Just think about all the times you've tried to help someone over the phone, failed, and then visited the person. One look at the person's screen and you say, "Oh! That's a totally different problem!"—and a few keystrokes later the problem is fixed. What happened was that you weren't able to reproduce the problem locally, so you couldn't see the whole problem and therefore couldn't figure out the real solution.

It is critical that the method used to reproduce the problem is recorded for later repetition in Step 8 (Craft Verification). Encapsulating the test in a script or batch file will make verification easier. One of the benefits of command-driven systems such as UNIX is the ease with which such a sequence of steps can be automated. Graphical user interfaces make this phase more difficult when there is no way to automate or encapsulate the test.

The scope of the verification procedure must not be too narrowly focused, nor too wide, nor misdirected. If the tests are too narrow the entire problem may not be fixed. If the tests are too wide the SA may waste time chasing non-issues.

It is possible that the focus may be misdirected. Another, unrelated problem in the environment may be discovered while trying to repeat the customer's reported problem. Some problems can exist in an environment without being reported or without affecting users. It can be frustrating for both the SA and the customer if many unrelated problems are discovered and fixed along the way to resolving an issue. If an unrelated problem is discovered that is not in the critical path, it should be recorded so that it can be fixed in the future. On the other hand, determining if it is in the critical path is difficult, so fixing it may be valuable. Alternatively, it may be a distraction or may change the system enough to make debugging difficult.

Sometimes, direct verification is not possible or even required. If a customer reports that a printer is broken, the verifier may not have to reproduce the problem by attempting to print something herself. It may be good enough to verify that new print jobs are queuing and not being printed. Such superficial verification is fine in that situation.

However, at other times exact duplication *is* required. The verifier might fail to reproduce the problem on her own desktop PC and may need to duplicate the problem on the customer's PC. Once the problem is duplicated in the customer's environment, it can be useful to try to duplicate it elsewhere to determine if the problem is local or global. When supporting a complicated product, you must have a lab of equipment ready to reproduce reported problems.

Verification at E-commerce Sites

E-commerce sites have a particularly difficult time duplicating the customer's environment. Though Java and other systems promise "write once, run anywhere," in reality you must be able to duplicate the customer's environment for a variety of web browsers, web browser versions, and even firewalls. One company needed to test access to their site with and without a firewall. Their quality assurrance (QA) effort had a PC that was "live on the Internet" for such testing. Because it was unprotected, it was isolated physically from other machines and the OS was reloaded regularly.

16.1.4 Phase C: Planning and Execution ("Fix It")

In the previous phase the problem was identified. In this phase it is fixed. This involves planning possible solutions, selecting one, and executing it (Figure 16.4).

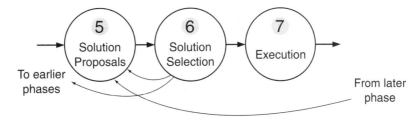

Figure 16.4: Flow of repair

Step 5: Solution Proposals—"Subject Matter Expert"

This is the point where the possible solutions are enumerated. This is performed by the Subject Matter Expert (SME). Depending on the problem, this list may be large or small. For some problems, the solution may be obvious and there is only a single proposed solution. Other times, there are many possible solutions. Often, verifying the problem in the previous step helps to identify possible solutions.

The "best" solution varies depending on context. At a bank, the help-desk's solution to a client-side NFS problem was to reboot. It was faster than trying to fix it, and it got the customer up and running quickly. However, in a research environment, it would make sense to try to find the source of the problem, perhaps unmounting and remounting the NFS mount that reported the problem.

Case Study: Radical Print Solutions

In our printing example, because the customer indicated that he needed to leave for the airport soon, it might be appropriate to suggest alternative solutions such as recommending a different printer that is known to be working. If the customer is an executive flying from New Jersey to Japan with a stop-over in San Jose, it might be reasonable to transfer the file to an office in San Jose where it can be printed while the customer is in flight. A clerk could hand the print-out to the executive while he waits for his connecting flight at the San Jose airport. Tom witnessed this solution actually being used. The printer, in this case, was a very expensive plotter. Only one such plotter was at each company location.

Some solutions are more expensive than others. Any solution that requires a deskside visit is generally going to be more expensive than one that can be handled without such a visit. This kind of feedback can be useful in making purchasing decisions. Lack of remote support capability affects the total cost of ownership of a product. There are tools (commercial and noncommercial) that add remote support to such products.

If the SA does not know any possible solutions, the issue is escalated to other, usually more experienced, SAs.

Step 6: Solution Selection

Once the possible solutions are enumerated, one of them is selected to be attempted first (or next, if we are looping through these steps). This role is also performed by the SME.

Selecting the best solution tends to be either extremely easy or extremely difficult. However, solutions often cannot and should not be done simultaneously, so possible solutions must be prioritized.

The customer should be included in this prioritization. Customers have a better understanding of their own time pressures. If the customer is a commodities trader, she or he will be much more sensitive to downtime during the trading day than, say, a technical writer or even a developer (provided he or she is not on deadline). If solution A fixes the problem forever but requires downtime, and solution B is a short-term fix, the customer should be consulted as to whether A or B is "right" for his or her situation. It is the responsibility of the SME to explain the possibilities, but the SA should know some of this based on her environment. There may be predetermined service goals for downtime during the day. SAs on Wall Street know that downtime during the day can cost millions, so short-term fixes may be selected and a long-term solution may be scheduled for the next maintenance window. In a research environment, the rules about downtime are more relaxed and the long-term solution may be selected immediately.[2]

When dealing with more experienced customers, it can be useful to let them participate in this phase. They may have useful feedback. In the case of inexperienced customers, it can be intimidating or confusing to hear all these details. It may even unnecessarily scare them. For example, listing every possibility from a simple configuration error to a dead hard disk may cause the customer to panic and is generally a bad idea (especially when the problem turns out to be a simple typo in `CONFIG.SYS`).

Even though customers may be inexperienced, they should be encouraged to participate in determining and choosing the solution. This can help educate them so future problem reports can flow more smoothly and even enable them to solve their own problems. It can also give the customer a sense of ownership—the warm fuzzy feeling of being part of the team/company, not a "user." This approach can help break down the "us versus them" mentality common in industry today.

---

[2]Some sites centralize their helpdesks to a bizarre extreme that results in SAs no longer knowing into which category their customers fall. This is rarely a good thing.

Step 7: Execution—"The Craft Worker"

Step 7 is where the solution is attempted. The skill, accuracy, and speed at which this step is completed depends on the skill and experience of the person executing the solution.

The term "craft worker" refers to the SA, operator, or laborer who performs the technical tasks involved. This term comes from other industries, for example, the foreman at a construction site plans what is done when, and the craft workers (for example, carpenters, plumbers, and so on) do the physical work. In the telecommunications industry, others receive the order and plan the provisioning of the service, and the craft workers run the cables, connect circuits, and so on. In a computer network environment, the network architect might be responsible for planning the products and procedures used to give service to customers, but when a new Ethernet interface needs to be added to a router, the craft worker installs the card and configures it.

Sometimes the customer becomes the craft worker. This is particularly common when the customer is remote and using a system with little or no remote control. In that case, the success or failure of this step is shared with the customer. A dialog is required between the SA and the customer to make the solution work. Has the customer executed the solution properly? If not, is the customer causing more harm than good?

The dialog has to be adjusted based on the skill of the customer. It can be insulting to spell out each command, space, and special character to an expert customer. It can be intimidating to a novice customer if the SA rattles off a complex sequence of commands. Asking, "What did it say when you typed that?" is better than "Did it work?" in these situations.

This kind of bidirectional communication is not how we grow up learning to talk. It is a special skill that we must learn. Training is available. Workshops that focus on this area often have titles that include the buzzwords "Active Listening," "Interpersonal Communication," "Interpersonal Effectiveness," or simply "Advanced Communication."

At this point, it is tempting to think that we have finished. However, we haven't finished until the work has been checked and the customer is satisfied. That brings us to the final phase.

16.1.5 Phase D: Verification ("Verify It")

At this point, the problem *should* have been remedied, but we need to verify that it really has been. This phase isn't over until the customer agrees the problem is fixed (Figure 16.5).

Step 8: Craft Verification

In Step 8, the craft worker who executed Step 7 (Execution) verifies that the actions taken to fix the problem were successful.

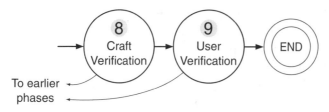

Figure 16.5: Verification flow

If the process used to reproduce the problem in Step 4 (Problem Verification) is not recorded properly or not repeated exactly, the verification will not happen correctly. If the problem still exists, return to Step 5 (Solution Proposals) or possibly an earlier step.

> ❖ **The UNIX diff program**   The UNIX command `diff` can be useful in this situation. `diff` is a program that displays the difference between two text files. Capture the output generated when the problem is reproduced. As attempts are made to fix the problem, run the program again, capturing the output to a new file. Run `diff` against the two captures to see if there is any difference. Alternatively, you might copy the output that demonstrates the problem to a new file and edit it the way it should be on a working system. (You might have a working system to generate sample "good" output.) `diff` can then be used to compare the current output with the corrected output. You'll know you've made the right changes when `diff` claims the files are the same. Some systems do not generate output that is well suited to `diff`, but Perl and other tools can pare down the output to make it more palatable to `diff`.

Case Study: T_EX Installation Problem

Once a customer was able to provide Tom with a sample T_EX file that processed fine in his previous department's T_EX installation but not on the local one. Because Tom had an account on the computers of the customer's previous department, he could establish a basis for comparison. This was extremely useful. Eventually, he was able to fix the T_EX installation through successive refinement of the problem and comparison on both systems.

Step 9: Customer Verification/Closing—"The Customer"

The final step is for the customer to verify that the issue has been resolved. If the customer isn't satisfied, the job isn't done. This role is performed by the customer.

Presumably, if the craft worker positively verified that the solution worked (Step 8, Craft Verification), this step should not be needed. However, often customers report at this point that the problem still exists. This is such a critical problem at some sites that we chose to emphasize it by making it a separate step.

Customer verification reveals mistakes made in previous phases. Communication problems include the customer not properly expressing the problem, the SA not understanding the customer, or the SA not properly recording the problem. Errors may have crept into the planning phase. The problem that was verified in Step 4 (Problem Verification) may have been a different problem that also exists, or the method that verified the problem may have been incomplete. The solution may not have fixed the entire problem or may have turned the problem into an intermittent one.

In either case, if the customer does not feel the problem is fixed, there are many possible actions. Obviously, Step 4 (Problem Verification) should be repeated to find a more accurate method to reproduce the problem. However, at this point, it may be appropriate to return to other steps. For example, the problem could be reclassified (Step 2, Problem Classification) or restated (Step 3, Problem Statement), or escalated to more experienced SAs (Step 5, Solution Proposals). If all else fails, you may have to resort to escalating the problem to management.

It is important to note that "verification" isn't to verify that the customer is happy, but that the customer's request is satisfied. Customer satisfaction is a metric to be measured elsewhere.

Once customer verification is complete, the issue is "closed."

16.1.6 Perils of Skipping a Step

Each step is important. If any step in this process is performed badly, the process can break down. Many SAs skip a step, either because of lack of training or an honest mistake. Many stereotypes about bad SAs are the result of SAs that skip a particular step. We assigned Seinfeldesque names to each of these stereotypes and list possible ways of improving the SAs process.

The Ogre: Grumpy, caustic SAs are trying to scare customers away from Step 1. They are preventing the greeting from happening. Suggestion: Management must set expectations for friendliness. Also, it is important to set expectations with customers.

The Mis-Delegator: If you've called a large company's technical support line and the person that answered the phone refused to direct your call to the proper department, you know what it's like to deal with a mis-delegator.

They skip Step 2. Suggestion: Design a formal decision tree of what issues are delegated where.

The Assumer: Step 3 usually isn't skipped; these SAs just assume that they understand what the problem is when they really don't. Suggestion: An "active listening" class usually helps this kind of SA.

The Non-Verifier: An SA who skips problem verification (Step 4) is usually busy fixing the wrong problem. One day Tom was panicked by the news that "the network was down." In reality, a nontechnical customer couldn't read his email and reported that "the network is down." This claim hadn't been verified by the newly hired SA, who hadn't yet learned that certain novice customers report all problems that way. The customer's email client was misconfigured. Suggestion: Teach SAs to replicate problems, especially before escalating them. Remind them that it isn't nice to panic Tom.

The Wrong Fixer: Inexperienced SAs sometimes are not creative or are too creative in proposing and selecting solutions (Steps 5 and 6). But skipping these steps entirely results in a different issue. After being taught how to use an Ethernet monitor (a network sniffer), an inexperienced but enthusiastic SA was found dragging out the sniffer no matter what problem was being reported. He was a Wrong Fixer. Suggestion: Provide mentoring or training. Increase the breadth of solutions with which the SA is familiar.

The De-Executioner: Incompetent SAs sometimes cause more harm than good when they execute incorrectly. It is quite embarrassing to apply a fix to the wrong machine; however, it happens. Suggestion: Train the SA to check what has been typed before pressing ENTER or clicking OK. It can be vital to include the hostname in your shell prompt.

The Hit-and-Run Sysadmin: This SA walks into a customer's office, types a couple of keystrokes, and waves as he walks out the door saying, "That should fix it." The customers are frustrated to discover that the problem was not fixed. In all fairness, what was typed really should have fixed the problem, but it didn't. Suggestion: Management needs to set expectations on verification.

The Closer: Some SAs are obsessed with "closing the ticket." Often, SAs are judged on how quickly they close tickets. In that case, they are pressured to skip the final step. We borrow this name from the term used to describe high-pressure salespeople who are focused on "closing the deal." Suggestion: Management should not measure performance based on how quickly issues are resolved but on a mixture of metrics that drive the preferred behavior. Metrics should not include time waiting for customers when calculating how long it took to complete the request. Tracking systems should permit a request to be put into a "customer wait" state while waiting for them to complete actions, and that time should be subtracted from the time-to-completion metrics.

16.1.7 Team of One

The solo SA can still benefit from using the model to make sure that customers have a well-defined way to report problems; that problems are recorded and verified; that solutions are proposed, selected, and executed; and that both the SA and the customer have verified the problem is resolved.

Solo SAs may feel they have nowhere to escalate problems, but that is not true. Problems can be escalated to vendor support lines. Often the solo SA's site is part of a larger company that has a larger IT organization.

16.2 The Icing

Once the basic process is understood, there are ways to improve it. On the micro level, you can look into improving each step; on the macro level, you can look at how the steps fit together.

16.2.1 Training Based on the Model

Internal training should be based on this model so that it is consistently used among the SA staff. After the initial training, more experienced staff should mentor newer staff to help them retain what they have learned. Certain steps can be helped by specific kinds of training, as was mentioned in section 16.1.6.

Improvements can be made by focusing on each step. Entire books could be written on each step. This has happened in other professions that have similar models, such as nursing, sales, and so on.

A lack of training hurts the process. For example, an ill-defined delineation of responsibilities makes it difficult for a "classifier" to delegate the issue to the right person. Inexperienced "recorders" don't gather the right information in Step 3 (Problem Statement), which makes further steps difficult and may require contacting the customer unnecessarily. A written chart of who is responsible for what, as well as a list of standard information to be collected for each classification will reduce these problems.

16.2.2 The Single Point of Contact

In addition to focusing on improving each step you may also focus on improving the entire process. Transitioning to each new step should be fluid.

If the customer sees an abrupt, staccato hand-off between each step, the process can appear amateurish or disjointed.

Every hand-off is an opportunity for mistakes and miscommunication. The fewer hand-offs, the fewer opportunities there are for mistakes. A site small enough to have a single SA has zero opportunities for this class of error. However, as systems and networks grow and become more complicated, it becomes impossible for a single person to understand, maintain, and run the entire network. As a system grows, hand-offs become a necessary evil. This explains a common perception that larger SA groups are not as effective as smaller ones. However, it shows an area for improvement: When growing an SA group, you should focus on maintaining high-quality hand-offs. Or, you might choose to develop a single point-of-contact or customer advocate for an issue. That results in the customers seeing a single face for the duration of a problem.

16.2.3   Increasing Customer Familiarity

If a customer talks to the same person every time she calls for support, there is a likelihood that the SA will become familiar with the customer's particular needs and be able to provide better service. There are ways to improve the chance of this happening. For example, subteams of the SA staff may be assigned to particular groups of customers, rather than to the technology they support. Or, if the staff answering the phone is extremely large, they may be using a telephone "call center" system, in which customers call a single number and the call center routes the call to an available operator. Modern call center systems can route calls based on caller ID. They can use this functionality, for example, to route the call to the same operator that the caller spoke to last time if that person is available. This means there will be a tendency for customers to be speaking to the same person each time. It can be very comforting speak to someone who recognizes your voice.

16.2.4   Special Announcements for Major Outages

During a major network outage, many customers may be trying to report problems. If customers report problems through an automatic phone response system ("Press 1 for ..., press 2 for ..."), usually such a system can be programmed to announce the network outage before listing the options. "Please note the network connection to Denver is currently experiencing trouble. Our service provider expects it to be fixed by 3 PM. Press 1 for ... press 2 for ...."

16.2.5　Trend Analysis

Spend some time each month looking for trends and take action based on them. This does not have to be a complicated analysis, as this case study describes.

Case Study: Who Generates the Most Tickets?

At one site we simply looked at which customers opened the most tickets in the last year. We found that 3 of the 600 people opened 10 percent of all tickets. That's a lot! It was easy to visit each person's manager to discuss how we could serve them better; if they were generating so many tickets, we obviously weren't matching their needs.

One person opened so many tickets because he was pestering the SAs for workarounds to the bugs in the old version of the LaTeX typesetting package that he was using and refused to upgrade to the latest version, which fixed most of the problems he was reporting. This person's manager agreed that the best solution would be for him to require his employee to adopt the latest LaTeX, and took responsibility for seeing to it that the change was made.

The next manager felt that his employee was asking "basic questions" and decided to send the customer for training to make him more self-sufficient.

The last manager felt that his employee was justified in making so many requests. However, the manager did appreciate knowing how much the employee relied on us to get his job done. The employee did become more self-sufficient in future months.

Here are some other trends to look for:

Does a customer report the same issue over and over? Why is it recurring? Does the customer need training, or is that system really that broken?

Are there many questions in a particular category? Is that system difficult to use? Could it be redesigned or replaced, or could the documentation be improved?

Are many customers reporting the same issue? Can they all be notified at once? Should such problems receive higher priority?

Are there categories of requests that can become self-service? Often, a customer request is that they need an SA to do something that requires privileged access (for example, superuser or administrator). Look for ways to empower customers to help themselves. Many of these requests can become self-service with a little bit of web programming. In the UNIX world, there is the concept of set user ID (SUID) programs, which, when properly administered, permit regular users to run a program that performs privileged tasks but then lose the privileged access once the program is finished executing. Individual SUID programs can give users the ability to perform a particular function, and SUID wrapper programs can be constructed that gain the enhanced privilege level, run a third-party program, and then reduce the privileges back to normal levels. Writing SUID programs is very tricky, and mistakes can turn into security holes. Systems such as `sudo` (Snyder et al. 1986) let you manage SUID privilege on a per-user and per-command basis and have been analyzed by enough security experts to be considered a relatively safe way to provide SUID access to regular users.

Who are your most frequent customers? Calculate which department generates the most tickets or who has the highest average tickets per member. Calculate which customers make up your top 20 percent of requests. Do these ratios match your funding model, or are certain customer groups more "expensive" than others?

Is a particular time-consuming request one of your frequent requests? If customers often accidentally delete files and you waste a lot of time each week restoring files from tape, you can invest time in helping the user learn about `rm -i`, or use other "safe delete" programs. Or, maybe it would be appropriate to advocate for the purchase of a system that supports snapshots or lets users do their own restores. If you can generate a report of the number and frequency of restore requests, management can make a more informed decision (or decide to talk to certain users about being more careful).

This chapter does not discuss metrics, but a system of metrics grounded in this model might be the best way to detect areas needing improvement. The nine-step process can be instrumented easily to collect metrics. Developing metrics that drive the right behaviors is difficult. For example, if SAs are rated by how quickly they close tickets, one might accidentally encourage "the closer" behavior described above. As SAs proactively prevent problems, reported problems will become more serious and time-consuming. If average time to completion grows, does that mean minor problems were eliminated or that SAs are slower at fixing all problems?

16.2.6   Customers That Know the Process

A better educated customer is a better customer. If customers understand the nine steps that will be followed they can be better prepared when reporting the problem. They can provide more complete information when they call because they understand the importance of complete information in solving the problem. In gathering this information, they will have narrowed the focus of the problem report. They might have specific suggestions on how to reproduce the problem. They may have narrowed the problem down to a specific machine or situation. Their additional preparation may even lead them to solve the problem on their own! Training for customers should include explaining the nine-step process to facilitate interaction between customers and SAs.

16.2.7 Architectural Decisions That Match the Process

Architectural decisions may impede or aid the classification process. The more complicated a system is, the more difficult it can be to identify and duplicate the problem. Sadly, some well-accepted software design concepts, such as delineating a system into layers, are at odds with the nine-step process. For example, a printing problem in a large UNIX network could be a problem with DNS, "lpd" on the servers, "lpr" on the client, the wrong version of lpr, misconfigured user environment, the network, DHCP, the printer's configuration, or occasionally even the printing hardware itself. Typically, many of those layers are maintained by separate groups of people. To diagnose the problem accurately requires the SAs to be experts in all of those technologies or that the layers cross-check each other.

You should keep in mind how a product will be supported when you are designing a system. The electronics industry has the concept of "design for manufacture"; we should think in terms of "design for support."

16.3 Conclusion

This chapter presents a formal, structured model for handling requests from customers. The process has four phases: The Greeting, Problem Identification, Planning and Execution, Fix and Verify. Each phase has distinct steps, summarized in Table 16.1.

By following this model the process becomes more structured and formalized. Once it is in place, it exposes areas for improvement within your organization. You can integrate the model into training plans for SAs, as well as educate customers about the model so they can be better advocates for themselves. The model can be applied for the gathering of metrics. Trend analysis, even in simple, ad hoc ways, can be performed.

We cannot stress enough the importance of using automation to reduce the tedium of managing incoming requests and collecting statistics. Let us use our "brain power" for the job of helping people, not the meta issues. Software that tracks tickets for you saves time in real ways. Tom once measured that a group of three SAs was spending an hour a day per person to track issues. That is a loss of two staff-days per week!

Phase	Step	Role
Phase A "Hello!"	1. The Greeting	Greeter
Phase B "What's wrong?"	2. Problem Classification	Classifier
	3. Problem Statement	Recorder
	4. Problem Verification	Reproducer
Phase C "Fix it"	5. Solution Proposals	Subject Matter Expert
	6. Solution Selection	
	7. Execution	Craft Worker
Phase D "Verify it"	8. Craft Verification	
	9. Customer Verification	Customer

Table 16.1: Overview of problem solution phases

The process described in this chapter brings clarity to the issue of customer support by defining what steps must be followed for a single successful call for help. We show why these steps are to be followed and how each step prepares you for future steps.

Although knowledge of the model can improve an SA's effectiveness by leveling the playing field, it is not a panacea; nor is it a replacement for creativity, experience, or having the right resources. The model does not replace the right training, the right tools, and the right support from management, but it must be part of a well-constructed helpdesk.

A lot of people react negatively to structured techniques like this one. We find that people who dislike structured techniques are really complaining that the structure being prescribed isn't their own structure, which they adhere to without realizing it. We're happy for those who have found their own structure and use it with consistently great results. We're sure it has many of the rudiments discussed here. Do what works for you. However, for the millions of SAs who have not found the perfect structure for themselves, consider this structure as a good starting point.

This chapter has been about communication. The process helps us think about how we communicate with customers, and it gives us a base of terminology to use when discussing our work. All professionals have a base of terminology to use to effectively communicate with each other.

Exercises

1. Are there times when you should not use the nine-step model?

2. What are the tools used in your environment for processing customer requests, and how do they fit into the nine-step model? Are there ways they could fit better?

3. What are all the ways to greet customers in your environment? What ways could you use but don't? Why?

4. In your environment, you greet customers by various methods. How do the methods compare by cost, by speed (faster completion), and by customers' preference? Is the most expensive method the one that customers prefer the most?

5. Some problem statements can be stated concisely, such as the routing problem example in Step 3. Dig into your trouble-tracking system to find five typically reported problems. What is the shortest problem statement that completely describes the issue?

6. Query your ticket tracking software and determine who were your top ten ticket creators overall in the last 12 months, then sort by customer group or department. Then determine what customer groups have the highest per-customer ticket count. Which customers make up your top 20 percent? Now that you have this knowledge, what will you do? Examine other queries from Section 16.2.5.

7. Which is the most important of the nine steps? Justify your answer.

Chapter 17

Data Centers

This chapter focuses on building a data center or machine room. A data center is anywhere that you keep machines that are shared resources and where your customers do not need physical access to in the normal course of events. A data center is more than just the room that your servers live in, however. A data center also typically has cooling, humidity control, power, and fire suppression systems. These systems are all a part of your data center. The theory is that you put all of your most important eggs in one basket and then make sure it is a really good basket.

Building a data center is expensive, and doing it right is even more expensive. You should expect your company's management to balk at the cost and to ask for justification. Be prepared to justify spending the extra money up front by showing how it will save time and money in the years to come. Some anecdotes in this chapter should help.

Small sites will find it difficult to justify many of the recommendations in this chapter. However, if your small site is intending to grow into a larger one, use this chapter as a roadmap to the data center that your company will need when it is larger. Plan for improving the data center as the company grows and can afford to spend more to get higher reliability. Do what you can now for relatively little cost, such as getting decent racks and cable management, and look for opportunities to improve.

Because the equipment in the data center is generally part of a shared infrastructure, it is difficult to upgrade or fundamentally alter a data center in any way without scheduling at least one maintenance window (see Chapter 12 for tips on doing that), so it is best to get it right the first time, when you initially build the data center. Obviously, as technologies change, the data center requirements will change, but you should aim to predict your needs eight to ten years into the future.

Historical Perspective

In the early days of computing, the computers were huge and could be operated only by a few trained people. Their size alone required that they be accommodated in a dedicated data center environment. Later, large mainframes had special cooling and power requirements and also had to live in a special data center environment, although they could be accessed over serial lines from more places. Mini-computers generated less heat and had lower power requirements. They were also housed in special computer rooms. Supercomputers generally needed water cooling, had special power requirements, and typically had to be housed in a data center with a specially strengthened and reinforced raised floor. Early PCs generally were not used as servers but rather resided on people's desks without special power or cooling. PCs were the radical anti-mainframe tool, and their users prided themselves in being far from the data center. Unix workstations were used as desktops and servers from the beginning, as are current PCs. Here the line between what should be in a data center versus what can be on, or under, a desk elsewhere in the building becomes less obvious and must be determined by function and customer access requirements, rather than by type of machine. We have come full circle: The PC world is now being required to build reliable, 24×7 systems, and they are learning to put their PCs in the data centers that they had previously rebelled against.

17.1 The Basics

At first glance, it may seem fairly easy to build a data center. You just need a big room with tables, racks, or wire shelves in there and voilà! In actual fact, the basics of building a good, reliable data center that enables SAs to work efficiently is a lot more complicated than that. To start with, you need to select good racks, you need good network wiring, you need to condition the power that you send to your equipment, you need lots of cooling, and you need to consider fire suppression. You also should plan for the room to survive natural disasters reasonably well. Organizing the room well means thinking ahead about wiring, console service, labeling, tools, supplies, workbenches, and designating parking places for mobile resources.

You also need to consider how you will move equipment in and out of the room and security mechanisms for the data center.

17.1.1 Picking a Location

The first thing that you need to do is decide on a location for the data center. If this data center is to be a hub for worldwide offices or for a geographic area, this will first involve picking a town and a building within that town. Once the building has been chosen, a suitable place within the building must be selected. For all of these stages, you should take into consideration the natural disasters that the area is subject to as part of the decision process.

Selecting a town and a building is typically out of the hands of the system administration staff. However, if the data center is to serve a worldwide or significant geographic area, and it will be located in an area that is prone to earthquakes, flooding, hurricanes, lightning storms, tornados, ice storms, or other natural disasters that may cause damage to the data center or loss of power or communications, you must prepare for these eventualities. You also must be prepared for someone with a backhoe to accidentally dig up and break your power and communication lines, no matter how immune your site is from natural disasters (Anonymous 1997). Preparing for power loss is discussed further in Section 17.1.4. For communications loss, you can deploy additional technologies as communication backups should your primary links fail, such as satellite backup for land lines. You can also raise the issue of having another site to take over the data center services completely if the primary site fails. This approach is expensive and can only be justified if loss of this data center for a time will have a considerable adverse impact on the company. Such risk analysis is covered in Chapter 8.

When it comes to selecting the location for the data center within the building, the system administration team should have some influence. Based on the requirements you build from the rest of this chapter, you should be able to discuss your space needs. You should also be able to provide the facilities department with requirements that will help them select an appropriate location. At a basic level, you should make sure that the floor will be strong enough to take the weight of the equipment. There are also other factors to consider. For example, if the area is prone to flooding, you will want to avoid having the data center in a basement or even at ground level, if possible. You should also consider how this affects the location of the support infrastructure for the data center, such as the UPS systems, automatic transfer switch (ATS), generators, and cooling systems. If these support systems have to be shut down, the data center will, too. Remember, the data center is more than just the room in which your servers live.

Having a data center in an earthquake zone affects several things in the data center. You must choose racks that can withstand a reasonable amount of shaking, and you must ensure that equipment is secured in the rack and will not fall out during an earthquake. You should install appropriate earthquake bracing that provides support but is not too rigid. If you have a raised floor, you should make sure that it is sufficiently strong and compliant. Consider how power and network cables are run through the data center. Are they able to cope with some stretching and compressing forces, or will they come apart? There are different levels of earthquake readiness for a data center. A good data center contractor should be able to discuss possibilities and costs with you, so that you can decide what is appropriate for your company.

Areas exposed to a lot of lightning require special lightning protection; architects can offer advice about that.

Lightning Protection Is Important

There is a hill in New Jersey that has a large amount of iron ore in it. On top of it is a very large building that has an all-copper roof. The hill and the roof attract many lightning strikes. The building has an extremely large amount of lightning protection. However, when unexplainable outages happen in that building, the SAs have a fun time blaming the iron ore and the copper roof even when it isn't raining. Hey, you never know!

> ### *Case Study: Bunkers Can Provide the Ultimate Secure Data Center*
>
> When you need a secure building, you can't go wrong following the United States military as an example. There is an agency that provides insurance for members and families of the United States military. Most of the people that work there are ex-military, and their data center is in the strongest kind of building they could think of: a real military bunker. People who have visited the site say that they have to stifle a chuckle or two, but they appreciate the effort. These buildings will survive all kinds of weather, natural disasters, and, most likely, terrorist attacks and mortar fire.

17.1.2   Access

Local laws will determine to some degree the access to your data center and, for example, may require at least two exits or a wheelchair ramp if you have a raised floor. Aside from those considerations, you also must examine how you will move racks and equipment into the room. Some pieces of equipment are wider than standard door widths, so you may want extra-wide doors. If you have double doors, make sure that they don't have a post in the middle. You also may want to look at the spacing between racks for getting the equipment into place. If you have a raised floor, you need either a ramp for wheeling the equipment up or elevator access. You may need to strengthen certain areas of the floor and the path to them for supporting extra-heavy equipment. You also need to consider access from the delivery dock all the way to the data center. Remember that equipment is usually delivered in a box that is larger than the equipment itself. We've seen equipment unboxed at the delivery dock so that it could be wheeled into the elevator and to its final destination.

Delivery Dock?

At one Silicon Valley start-up company, there was no delivery dock. One day a large shipment of servers arrived and was delivered onto the street outside the building, because there was no immediate way to get them inside the building from the truck. Some of the servers were on pallets that could be broken down, and individual pieces were carried up the entrance stairs into the building. Other pieces were small enough that they could be wheeled up the narrow wheelchair ramp into the building. But some were too large for either of these approaches. In the end, they were wheeled down the steep ramp into the parking garage, where they could be squeezed into the small elevator, and brought up to the entrance level where the computer room was. Fortunately, because it was summer in California, it didn't start to rain during this rather lengthy process.

17.1.3 Security

Your data center should have good physical security that does not impede the SAs' work, insofar as that is possible. Only SAs, their managers, and the appropriate people from the physical security and safety departments should have access. The fire safety wardens (or in some places, the emergency search teams) assigned to that area should be drawn from people who have access already.

Restricting data center access to SAs increases the reliability and availability of the equipment in there and increases the chance that wiring and rack-mounting standards will be followed. Machines that live in the data center should be servers on which the corporate infrastructure relies, servers that are shared by a group of people, or servers that are required for business-critical tasks. By definition, they have high availability requirements and therefore should be subject to all the change management processes and procedures that the SA group abides by to meet or exceed their service level commitments. People outside of the system administration group do not have those commitments and will not have been trained on the system administration group's key processes. People outside the system administration's group spend less time maintaining infrastructure equipment, and thus they are more likely to make mistakes that could cause a costly outage. If some of your customers need physical access to machines that are in the data center, those machines cannot be considered highly reliable or infrastructure machines. These machines should be moved to a lab environment, where your customers can have access to them. If the machines have special power, HVAC, or security requirements, those should be provided in the lab, rather than compromising the site's reliability by putting them in the data center.

Ideally, access to the data center should not use simple key access. Keys are easy to copy, and it is impossible to audit who has access or check who entered the room in a given period if there is a problem. They are also awkward to use while carrying equipment and relatively time-consuming if an SA needs to go in and out a lot, which is likely to result in the door being propped open.

Proximity badges[1] work well for data centers. If the card reader is at an appropriate height, the badge can be kept on a chain or in a back pocket and brought close to the card reader without requiring the use of your hands.[2] A badge system allows you to associate a badge with a person and keeps logs of what badges were used to open the door at what time. This information allows you to audit who has access, easily disable the access of people who should no longer have access, and bring up an access history when there is a problem.

Some data centers may have higher security requirements for legal or insurance reasons. For example, a data center that has machines that contain individuals' medical records might require biometric locks in addition to proximity badges. A data center that contains banking systems may require at least two people to badge in and out together, leaving no one in the room alone, and activating motion detectors when the room is believed to be empty, based on the badge-in, badge-out records.

Biometric locks have brought up a new ethical issue. Is it ethical to install a security system that can be bypassed by cutting off an authorized person's finger or removing their eyeball? If the data is sufficiently valuable, the biometric lock system may put the lives of authorized personnel in danger. Newer biometric security systems also check for life, by looking for a pulse or body heat from the finger or eye, as well as scanning the

---

[1] Badges that unlock the door when they are brought in close proximity to a badge reader.
[2] SAs with style do this with Elvis-like precision. Others look just plain silly.

pattern. Others also look for a PIN or do voice recognition, in addition to the fingerprint or retina scan. We recommend that you select a biometric system that checks to see that the person is still alive, if you do install a biometric system. Still, there are ethical issues related to the fact that employees cannot change their fingerprints, voices, or DNA, when they leave a company.

17.1.4 Power and Air

When deciding how much power and cooling a data center needs, you should aim to reach capacity on your power systems at the same time as you reach capacity on your cooling systems, which should be at the same time as you run out of space. Bear in mind that equipment tends to get smaller over time, so in a few years the same amount of space will be capable of consuming more power and needing more cooling. Even with that knowledge, we find that one ton of cooling for every 5,000 square feet of data center tends to be the correct rule of thumb. Humidity control is another component of air-conditioning. It is important to regulate the humidity in the data center because high humidity leads to condensation and equipment failure and low humidity causes static discharge that can damage equipment. A humidity level between 45 and 55 percent is ideal. Power systems and HVAC[3] systems are large, complicated to replace, and will almost certainly require outages, so you want to plan for these systems to last at least eight to ten years.

Data center power must be conditioned to protect equipment from the spikes, brownouts, and power cuts that are a fact of life with utility power. That means having at least one UPS that provides sufficient power at a constant voltage to the whole data center. A UPS normally supplies power from battery banks, which it is constantly recharging from its in-bound power feed, when that feed is clean enough to use (see Figure 17.1). Power from the UPS is then brought to distribution panels in the data center and any other locations that get protected power.

Normally, a data center also has a generator for backup power if utility power fails. The generator is connected through an ATS, which turns on the generator a configurable amount of time after utility power goes out of tolerance and then switches the power feed to the UPS over to generator power. When utility power returns to within tolerance, the ATS switches the power feed to the UPS back to utility power after a configurable amount of time and turns the generator off. An ATS usually has a manual switch (Figure 17.2) as well, so that you can force it to feed utility power (or generator power) to the UPS if necessary.

---

[3]We have yet to come across anyone who needed heating in their data center. Even the computers at Amundsen-Scott South Pole Station are reported to not need heating. The computers at the top of the ski slopes in Nagano at the 1998 Winter Olympics did have electric blankets because everything was turned off at night (Guth and Radosevich 1998).

Figure 17.1: A modular UPS at GNAC, Inc.

Always install a switch that allows you to bypass the UPS if it fails. All power for the data center runs through the UPS all the time, so you will need to bypass it if it fails or if you need to do maintenance on it. This switch must be external to the UPS and a reasonable distance away from it. A UPS is full of batteries, and if it catches fire you do not want to go into the UPS room to bypass it. The UPS will probably come with a bypass switch that is integral to the unit. That switch is insufficient, particularly in the case of a fire.

Studies show that power outages tend to be extremely short (seconds) or extremely long (half a day or longer). The majority of power outages last less than three seconds. Statistically speaking, if an outage lasts longer than ten minutes, there is a high likelihood that it will last the rest of the day, and you should consider sending staff home. Therefore there are two ways to make your purchasing decision. One is to purchase a UPS that could last for an hour. That will cover extremely short outages and give you enough time to power down all the systems if it looks like the outage is going to last the rest of the day. Alternatively, you can purchase a smaller UPS that lasts for about 15 minutes and combine it with a generator and an ATS so that you can survive multihour outages (see Figures 17.3 and 17.4). Trying to purchase a UPS that can last more than an hour without a generator is expensive, and, statistically, you are unlikely to have an outage of that length.

When purchasing the UPS, you should also consider its maintenance and environmental requirements. The UPS may need periodic maintenance,

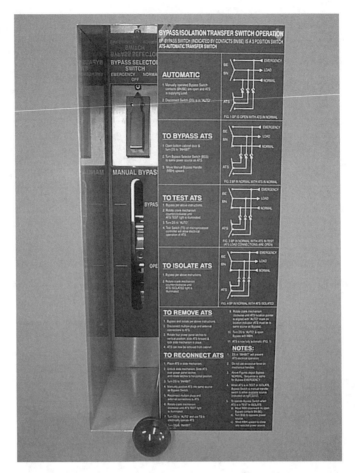

Figure 17.2: ATS bypass switch at GNAC, Inc.

and it will certainly need to have its batteries replaced about once every three years. It may also require cooling and humidity control, which may dictate its location within the building. Also consider whether the UPS can be forced to trickle-charge its batteries, rather than charging them as fast as it can. When a UPS fast-charges its batteries, it puts a huge load on the rest of the power system, which may bring the power down. When it trickle-charges, the additional load placed on the rest of the power system is much less.

Generators have to be carefully maintained, tested weekly, and periodically refueled, or they will not work on the few occasions when they are needed, and you will have wasted your money.

Figure 17.3: A 1,000-gallon tank to power the generators at GNAC, Inc.

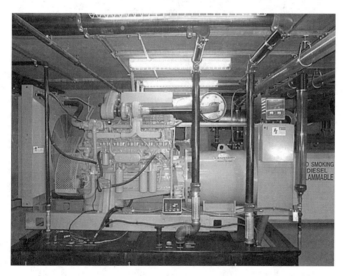

Figure 17.4: The redundant generators at GNAC, Inc. each have a 200-gallon
tank that is filled from the main 1,000-gallon tank.

The HVAC system must also be on protected power, or at least have a
feed directly from the ATS if it does not need very clean power. If utility
power is not available for an extended period, and the HVAC systems cannot
access the generator power, you will need to shut down everything in the
data center anyway, or the overheating will result in more hardware failures
than normal in the ensuing weeks.

Case Study: A Failing HVAC System Causes Problems

A biotechnology company was building its first data center. At the time, it was just a small start-up of about 50 people and had just moved into a large building that they were planning to stay in for at least ten years. They did not have a senior SA on staff at the time. The facilities manager didn't realize how much heat a data center can generate and decided to save some money on the HVAC system by getting a less powerful one than recommended by the data center contractors. Instead, they went with the unit recommended by the HVAC sales person. The HVAC sales person apparently was not familiar with data center planning. A few years later, the data center was full of equipment and the HVAC system was failing every few months. Each time this happened, the SAs would shut down the less essential machines, get huge buckets of ice (which the labs had lots of) and fans, and try to keep the most critical parts of the data center running for the rest of the day. They would then shut everything off overnight. Over the following two or three weeks, they would suffer a multitude of hardware failures, mostly disks. Then things would even out for a while, until the next HVAC failure. The HVAC engineers would always tell them that the problem was that the unit was unable to keep up with the amount of heat the room was generating.

Heat sensors distributed around the data center that are connected to the monitoring system are a useful tool for detecting hot spots. A quick, cheap alternative is to use digital thermometers that record the high and low temperatures and move them around the room. If you are good at judging temperatures, you can also check for hot spots with your hand. Hot spots with no airflow are particularly problematic because they will get hotter. When there are known hot spots, the equipment can be redistributed to address the problem or the HVAC can be altered to provide better airflow to those areas. If hot spots go unnoticed, they can be the source of equipment failure. Some hardware vendors provide a way to monitor the temperature at one or more points inside their equipment. If this feature is provided, it should be used because doing so can provide better coverage than deploying heat sensors. Research has been conducted into building boards that are mounted inside machines to provide this and other monitoring facilities (Drzyzgula 2000). HVAC systems often fail silently and sometimes return to service without anyone noticing. Because HVAC failures cause hardware to fail more quickly, it is important to notice when the HVAC system fails. Monitoring heat sensors is one way to do this, if the HVAC system itself does not provide a monitoring mechanism that can be plugged into the helpdesk systems.

In addition to having the HVAC systems on generator power, it can be useful to put other building circuits onto power circuits that have generator backup. These circuits should be tolerant of small outages and spikes. Lights are good candidates, particularly in the operations and helpdesk areas. For groups such as the helpdesk, operations (for example, shipping and receiving), or a customer service center that need to stay up during power outages, it can be useful to have the light and power circuits on generator backup with small deskside UPS systems. All areas should at least have emergency lighting that comes on automatically when the power fails, even if it is not part of the building code in that region. If you have the luxury of being able to switch off utility power to the building, it can be useful to try it and see what else you would like to have on emergency power. In the absence of a full trial, mime all the things that you would do in a power outage and note what you rely on that would not be available.

Lighting Is Important

One site did not have emergency power brought to the lights in the generator room. They discovered this omission when they had a power outage and needed to refuel the diesel generator in the dark.

All of the components of the electrical system, described above, and the wiring and trip switches between them must be sized to deal with your data center at maximum load and the HVAC system running at maximum capability, with the added load of the UPS charging its batteries. Maximum load is more than just what the equipment in the data center can draw.

Adding Extra Capacity

A small company moved into new premises and had the foresight to allocate a large area for data center space, because they knew that their data center needs were going to grow a lot during the coming years. At the time, they did not have enough money to build in all the power and air-conditioning capability that they eventually would need, so they put in a system that they knew would be only temporary and would be replaced in a year or two with the full-capacity system.

Adding the extra electrical capacity involved getting new service from the local power company to a new dedicated transformer, which meant cutting power to the building. It also involved new generators, a new ATS unit, new UPS systems, and new power distribution panels in the data center.

The local power utility company would switch the service to the new transformer only in the middle of the day on a midweek day. The power company claimed it would take half an hour, but the SAs at the company assumed that it would take at least two hours. They had a UPS, an ATS, and a generator for the data center already, so they planned on running on generator power during the outage. However, because the generator had sometimes proved unreliable in running under load for more than a few minutes in the past, they wisely decided to rent a second generator for the day in case their primary one stopped working.

When the second generator arrived, they ran the cables from it to the ATS ahead of time, so that they would be on hand if they needed to be connected. They also had their electrical contractors on-site that day to deal with that eventuality.

When the day arrived, they manually switched over to generator power a couple of minutes before the utility company cut power to the building. The generator ran fine for about ten minutes and then failed. The electrical contractors sprang into action, pulled out the failed generator's cables from the ATS, quickly connected the second generator's cables, powered up the new generator, waited for its power to stabilize, and finally switched on the electrical feed from the generator to the ATS. All the while, a person was standing by the UPS in the data center on a cell phone to another person on a cell phone, who was with the electrical contractors (they didn't have radios, as described in Chapter 12). The person in the data center was giving the UPS' countdown time (for power remaining) to the people downstairs, who in turn were letting him know their progress.

As in all the best movies, the power feed from the generator to the ATS was turned on with two seconds of remaining time showing on the UPS display. The feeling of having just averted a disaster was short-lived, however. The UPS did not like the power that it was getting from the new generator, so it ran down its batteries completely and then went into bypass mode, feeding the generator power directly through to the data center.

In the rush, the three-phase power cables from the generator were connected to the ATS the wrong way around because the ATS had been mounted upside-down on the wall. So, despite having prepared very well for the event, they still had to take a small power hit later in the day when they switched back to utility power because the UPS had no battery power available during the transition.

That was not the end of the problems, however. It also turned out that the temporary electrical system had a thermal circuit breaker that was undersized and could not deal with the load of charging the UPS batteries on top of the load of the data center. After the data center was switched back to utility power and everything remained stable, the SAs started charging the UPS batteries. A few minutes later, the thermal breaker overheated and tripped. The UPS ran its batteries down again, and a few seconds before the circuit breaker had cooled down enough to be reset, the data center lost power for a second time.

The rest of the electrical cut-over involved switching to a new UPS, ATS, generators, and power distribution panels. For those remaining components, everything was comprehensively tested with load banks for a couple of weeks before the switch was made. Lots of bugs were worked out, and the switch went flawlessly.

Even if you are installing a system that you know will be temporary, you must still examine every component with the same attention to detail as if it will be your permanent system. No component should be undersized. No component should be installed in a nonstandard way. Otherwise, no matter how much you try prepare for every eventuality, the unexpected quirks of the system will bite you when you least expect it.

Power Distribution

Once you have the appropriate amount of conditioned power in the data center, you need to distribute it to the racks. An overhead power bus is a good way to do that, giving you the option of bringing different voltages into each rack, in case you have equipment that requires nonstandard power, as some high-end equipment does (see Figures 17.5 and 17.6). Overhead power also mitigates the risks associated with anything that may cause water to be on the floor or under a raised floor, such as a leak from an air-conditioning unit or overhead pipes. Power outlets can be located away from anything that might drip on them and protected with something to deflect dripping

Figure 17.5: The GNAC, Inc. data center with prewired overhead network and power

Figure 17.6: Host racks at GNAC, Inc. with a patch panel at the top and consoles wired into the patch panels. (A different color is used to differentiate console cables from network cables.)

water. Sites with raised floors must install water sensors under the floor. A builder should be able to help you locate the low spots where water will accumulate first. Sensors also should be placed under the air-conditioning units.

Overhead power also provides some flexibility in how much power can be brought into a rack because some racks may need more than others, and you should avoid running power cords between racks. If equipment in one rack takes power from another rack, it may be inadvertently deprived of power by someone working in the next rack who is unaware of the interrack dependency. Good practice dictates keeping everything within the rack as far as possible. A power distribution unit (PDU) may look like a power strip but has internal wiring that connects different sockets onto different circuits. A PDU doesn't suffer from overload whereas a simple power strip can.

The power should be properly distributed using PDUs within the rack. If there are different power sources within the data center, such as protected and unprotected power, or power from two separate UPS and generator systems, they should be clearly identified using different color sockets or PDUs. Many different kinds of PDUs are available, including vertical and horizontal rack-mount options. If they work with your racks and equipment depths, the vertical ones can be nice, as discussed in Section 17.1.7. In all cases, look at where the power switch on the PDU is located and how easy it is to accidentally turn off. Some PDUs have switches that are protected inside a small box that must be lifted to trip the switch. You do not want someone to accidentally cut power to the whole rack.

Upside-Down PDUs Prevented Accidental Power-Downs

The technical lead at Synopsys always mounted the (horizontally rack-mounted) PDUs upside-down in the racks. The reason was that the PDUs had large trip switches on them that cut the power to that PDU when it was pushed down. He had realized that it was easy to accidentally lean on the PDU, perhaps trying to balance oneself, and knock the switch into the off position. However, if the unit was the other way up, it was much less likely that someone accidentally would knock the switch upward. One PDU did not get mounted upside-down by a new SA, who had not been told about this practice and had not read the documentation. A few months later, as fate would have it, another SA accidentally bumped this PDU and tripped the switch, shutting down several important servers. After that, everyone made it a point to indicate this feature to all new SAs.

HVAC and UPS systems should be able to notify staff in case of failure or other problem. It's a good idea to have a network-attached thermometer that can alert you in case of HVAC or high heat. The UPS should connect to your network so that servers can power themselves off when the batteries are getting low.

17.1.5   Fire Suppression

It's a good idea to have a fire suppression system in your data center, even if local laws do not require it. Power supplies burn out, disks catch fire, as do batteries in UPS systems, and electrical wiring can develop a fault that sparks a massive fire.

Typically, local laws will not only require a fire suppression system, but they will also be very explicit about what systems you can and can't use. This list changes constantly as dangers of new systems, particularly to those in the room when they are activated, are discovered.

If you do have a choice, consider the dangers to the people working in the room, environmental hazards of the system, the damage that it might do to the equipment that is not on fire, and how well that system deals with electrical fires.

Another thing to consider is whether to link activation of the fire suppression system with a switch for turning off power in the computer room. If you are going to dump water on all the equipment, for example, you need to cut the power to the equipment first. Such a harsh method of turning off the equipment may cause some hardware fatalities, but not as many as dumping water on live equipment.

Find out if your choice of fire suppression system will allow other equipment to continue operating. If not, is there a way of localizing the fire suppression to a small set of racks? Some systems have a preactivation facility that enables on-site staff to check on a small amount of localized smoke before the fire suppression system activates. This permits them to turn off the equipment that is smoking before a fire starts and the fire suppression system activates fully.

In addition to the technology of your fire suppression system, there are also some important procedural components to put in place. If your fire suppression system is linked to your operations center, you need to train the operations staff on what to do if there is an alert. If the people who are on-site 24 hours a day are not computer professionals, you need to train them on a process they should follow in response to a fire alert. If the fire suppression system activates, you are probably going to be without fire suppression until the system is recharged. If the fire reignites after the fire suppression system has activated, you may lose the whole building. You need a procedure to both minimize the chance of the fire reactivating and for monitoring it and dealing with it effectively if it does.

17.1.6 Racks

You need to consider rack selection and layout. These issues will influence the amount and type of space you need, so it is best to consider them before consulting with the facilities department on your space requirements.

A data center should have proper racks for equipment because otherwise all sorts of problems will ensue. Machines get stacked on top of each other, making it difficult to work on a lower machine without bringing down those on top of it. Cables from different machines will become tangled and often end up on the floor and being walked on because there are no facilities for cable management. This results in cable damage and accidental disconnection of cables. It will be difficult, if not impossible, to trace cables without the risk of pulling another cable and disconnecting or damaging it. Power provisioning will be haphazard and may increase the risk of fire caused by chaining power strips. The resulting mess will be unreliable and a nightmare to support.

Rack selection is not as simple as it may appear on the surface. There are many factors to consider. The most obvious are the number of posts (two or four) and height, width, and depth of the rack. You also will want to look at air circulation in the rack, strength of the rack, whether it has threaded mounting holes, and the options for the vertical rails and shelves. You need to consider whether you want fronts, backs, or sides for the racks, and what the cable management options are.

Two Posts or Four?

Two-post racks are cheaper than four-post racks, so many sites use them. However, four-post racks are nicer to work with. Two-post racks are often used for networking and telecommunication equipment, which is often designed to be center-mountable, as well as front- and/or rear-mountable. However, it is often easier and safer to mount some of the heavier networking and telecommunications equipment in a four-post rack. Four-post racks provide more protection for the equipment from accidental knocks that may loosen or damage cables. Four-post racks typically provide better horizontal cable-management options.

Most server equipment is only front-mountable, although some servers have options for center or rear mounting. If equipment is front-mounted in two-post racks, it sticks out at the back, and different-depth equipment sticks out different distances, which can be hazardous for people walking behind the racks (and for the equipment). Full-depth shelves for two-post racks are center-mounted (often as two half-depth shelves, one at the front of the rack and one at the back). Having front-mounted equipment with either shelves or center-mounted equipment in the same rack or row of racks means that the effective depth of the rack (with equipment) is more than the depth of a four-post rack, in which everything lines up at the front.

If your site decides to get two-post racks, make sure that you leave lots of space between the rows. The aisles must be wide enough to accommodate the depth of one and a half pieces of equipment plus the width of the aisle where people will walk. A minimum aisle width usually is specified in fire safety regulations. The machines can't protrude into that space. The reason for a depth of one and a half machines plus the regulation aisle width is that there must be sufficient aisle space left when a deep machine is front-mounted in one rack and a center-mounted piece of equipment or a shelf in the rack is immediately behind it.

Case Study: Insufficient Aisle Space

One company rented a cage and some racks in a data center. They selected the data center based on the cost of the rack space. The racks were two-post racks and didn't have much aisle space between them. Once the equipment was installed in both rows of racks, it was impossible to access the equipment in the back rack. In fact, the cables for the back row of machines were so close to the edge of the cage that they could be reached from outside of the cage, which defeated the point of having a secured cage. The SAs who had to work on machines in the cage hated it, but they were stuck with it. The contract specified the number of racks and the size of the cage. They should have measured carefully before they signed the contract.

Height

The height of the rack may have an impact on reliability if it is very tall and an SA has to stretch across other equipment to access a machine. Taller racks also may not fit beneath anything that might be attached to the ceiling, such as power buses, cooling systems, or fire suppression apparatus. They also may not give adequate clearance for overhead air circulation or fire suppression systems to work correctly. It may not be safe to pull roll-out shelves from the high part of the rack. On the other hand, they use data center floor space more efficiently.

Width

There are a couple of standard rack widths at the time of writing. Most equipment fits into 19-inch racks, but telecommunications equipment is usually in NEBS-compliant racks, which are 21 inches between poles. However, NEBS-compliant equipment tends to come in its own rack, so one need only allocate space for the rack and not worry about purchasing the rack itself. Based on the type of equipment that you will have, you need to allocate an appropriate mix of spaces on your floor plans, which may include only one width, if that is appropriate.

Depth

For four-post racks, several rack depths are available because there are several different machine depths. You want to have racks that are deep enough for your equipment to fit completely inside, so that the cables are more protected from accidental knocks and so that horizontal cable management can be used within the rack where necessary. Having machines protrude into the aisles is a safety hazard and may be in contravention of local safety laws if it causes the aisle to be less than the regulation width. It also looks neater and more professional to have the equipment fully contained within the rack.

However, if the racks are too deep, you may consume floor space too rapidly and not be able to accommodate enough equipment in the room. Having excess unused space may tempt people to mount extra equipment into the back of the rack, if they can squeeze it in. This makes it difficult to access the cables or rear panels of other machines or perform maintenance on other machines in the rack and may cause equipment in the rack to overheat as a result of insufficient air circulation.

Wasted Space Gets Used When Space Is Short

A company had a shortage of space in its data center. An additional data center was under construction, but in the meantime SAs still had to install machines. They realized that many of the older freestanding machines had unused space inside where extra boards or disks could have been installed. They started installing smaller machines inside the (still running) older machines. They diligently labeled the main machine with its own name and listed the machines that were inside. It was an unusual practice and made machines harder to find if SAs didn't remember to look at the larger machines as additional racks. However, the only real problem was that they were consuming more power per square foot than the UPS could manage, because they had outgrown that data center. Ideally, the new data center should have been commissioned before they reached this point.

Air Circulation

Some racks have fans built into them for air circulation. If you are looking at these, you need to consider how air will reach the racks. They may require raised perforated floors with air pushed into the rack from below. If it is a simpler rack that does not have its own air circulation system, you probably don't want to get doors for the front, back, or side panels because that will restrict airflow to equipment in the rack. Having doors and side panels can make the data center look neater, but it also can hide many cabling sins, and it makes neat interrack wiring more difficult unless it is all prewired (see Section 17.1.7). Neat wiring is possible, as shown in Figures 17.6 and 17.7. It just takes discipline.

❖ **Racks with Doors**   Tom prefers racks with doors so he can institute an "if the door doesn't close, you're not done" policy. This keeps SAs from leaving dangling wires after they make changes. Christine prefers no doors so that she can see at a glance what has not been done correctly and get it fixed before things get out of hand.

Figure 17.7: Network racks in GNAC, Inc. have patch panels in one rack and the network gear in the adjacent rack.

Cable Management

The cable management options are important to consider when selecting racks. Almost always it should be purchased separately from the rack. To decide what you need in this department, you should consider how you are wiring your data center, as discussed in Section 17.1.7. Consider both horizontal and vertical cable management options. Keeping cables neatly organized within and between racks is vital for being able to work efficiently without disturbing other equipment. Cleaning up a rat's nest of cables is painful and cannot be done without taking equipment down. If you don't provide reasonable cable management, people will wire equipment in all sorts of interesting ways, and you will later discover that you can't take a piece of equipment out of the rack to replace broken hardware without bringing down three other critical pieces of equipment that have nothing to do with the machine you are trying to work on.

Horizontal cable management usually screws into the mounting rails. It can be open or closed. Open cable management has a series of large split hoops that all the cables go behind. Cables are slotted through the gaps in the hoops as they are run from one place to the other. The hoops keep the cables within a confined channel or area. Closed cable management consists of a channel with a cover. The cover is removed, cables are placed in the channel, and then the cover is replaced. Open cable management can look messier if not maintained well, but closed cable management often is used to hide huge loops of cables that are too long. When closed cable management fills up, it becomes difficult or impossible to replace the covers so they are left off, and it becomes even messier than open cable management. Closed cable management is also more tedious to work with and becomes a nuisance for very little gain.

Some racks are designed to have vertical cable management as a recessed channel between the racks. Others can have it within the rack, going down the sides just inside the back posts. Others can have cable management only attached externally to the back posts. Cable management that is between the racks makes cables take up more valuable floor space. Cable management that attaches to the back of the racks protrudes into the aisles, which makes the cables more vulnerable and may be a safety concern. Cable management that goes within the rack requires racks that are deep enough to contain the cable management, in addition to the deepest piece of equipment. Wherever it is placed, the cable management can be either open or closed.

Cable management also comes in a variety of widths. A data center will typically require different widths for different rack functions. Racks that have lots of patch panels and network or console equipment will have lots of cables in them and require much wider and deeper cable management than racks that contain a few hosts with a few network and console connections. Racks with lots of wires also require lots of horizontal cable management well distributed between the pieces of equipment and the various patch panels. Having too little cable management space is bad. It makes it difficult to access the cables, and SAs may damage cables by trying to force them into the cable management. It is better to overestimate rather than underestimate your space requirements.

Strength

The racks must be strong enough to carry the weight of the equipment that will be mounted in them. In an earthquake zone, they also should be able to withstand moderately strong quakes.

Environment

If your racks are going to be deployed in remote locations, consider the atmosphere of the location. Rust can be an issue if there is high water vapor content, salt, or other pollutants. Racks with special coatings are available.

Mounting Rails and Shelves

The mounting rails are another important component to consider. Threaded holes in the mounting rails are simple to deal with. You just need to be sure the right size of rack screws are in stock. For rails without threaded holes, you need nuts at the back of the rail to screw into, so you require both nuts and screws. When mounting equipment, you need to work with nuts at the back of the rail. It is often impossible to get your hand around to the back of the rail to hold a nut in place, particularly if you have several side-by-side racks. For that reason, you can usually get clip-on nuts for rails with nonthreaded holes, so that you shouldn't have to get your hand around the back. The clip-on nuts can be a nuisance, though, because they tend to move when you're trying to line the equipment up and get the screw in and can be impossible to move when you need to switch them from one hole to another. The only advantage of rails without threaded holes is that it is possible to rack-mount equipment that is not Electronic Industry Association/Telecommunications Industry Association (EIA/TIA) compliant, instead of resorting to shelves. We much prefer threaded rails.[4]

Another thing to consider is how shelves and various pieces of rack-mount equipment will fit into the rack and how, or whether, you can combine different rack-mount units in the same rack, or if you can still mount shelves in the rack when a rack-mount unit requires the vertical rails to be moved forward or backward. Often, large rack-mount units need the vertical rails to be a particular distance apart so they can be attached at all four corners. In some cases, the positioning of these rails may prevent you from mounting other pieces of equipment that require a different spacing of the rails. Worse yet, the shelves may require an exact positioning of these vertical rails that is not compatible with your rack-mount equipment. Make sure that the racks that you choose allow mounting the shelves with the vertical rails in various positions. You also may want to get extra vertical rails so that you can mount a couple of units with different depths in the same rack.

Extra Floor Space

Consider how many large freestanding pieces of equipment you might have, with a footprint the size of a rack or larger, that cannot be rack-mounted.

---

[4]We also prefer to only get data center equipment that is EIA/TIA compliant.

Leaving space for these will affect the number of racks that you order and how you wire the data center.

17.1.7   Wiring

It is difficult to keep data center wiring tidy. However, there are several of ways you can make it easier for all the SAs to keep the wiring neat when you are designing the data center.

Hiding the mess does not mean that it is not there or that it will not affect SAs trying to work in the data center. A raised floor can hide sloppy cabling, with cables following all sorts of random paths to go between two points. When you go to pull cables out from under the floor, you will find them tangled up in many others and extracting them probably will be difficult. This may cause some people to just leave them there "until later, when I have time."

Wiring Under a Raised Floor Can Become a Mess
At one company, the original data center had a raised floor. Several cables were prerun from the front of the room to the back for network connections, but most wiring was done under the floor as needed. Not long after a new network administrator started, he set about pulling out all the unused cables from under the floor in his spare time, because some places had so many cables that it was difficult for them all to fit. He pulled out two miles of cable over the course of three months.

The biggest gain that you can make is by prewiring the racks as much as possible. Choose a section of your data center that will house only network equipment, for example, the back row. Then put a clearly labeled patch panel at the top of each rack, with more jacks than you think you will need, and clearly label the rack. Racks should be labeled based on their row and position within the row. Some companies put these labels high on the walls so that they can be seen from anywhere and racks are easy to locate. Figures 17.8 and 17.9 show this form of rack location labeling, and how it is used on patch panels.

Wire the rack's patch panel to a patch panel in your network row that has corresponding labels and is clearly labeled with the rack number. If you are using serial console servers, put one of those at the top of every rack too, if they are small. If they are large, put a patch panel in every rack for the serial consoles that is connected to a console server box mounted a couple of racks away, or increase the number of jacks you have wired to the back

Figure 17.8: Numbering high on the walls of the data center in Synopsys is used for rack naming and makes it easy to locate a given rack.

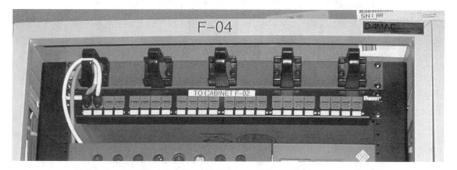

Figure 17.9: Racks at Synopsys are clearly labeled at the top and have a patch panel that indicates the rack to which it is wired.

of the room and put the console servers with the network equipment (see Figure 17.10).

Some sites choose to color code their network cables. At the very least, different-quality cables (Category-3, Category-5) and cables with different wiring (straight through, crossover) should be different colors. Some sites choose to have different subnets use different colors.

All network and console wiring for servers in a rack should stay within that rack, other than what has been prewired. Make sure there is adequate cable management within the rack for the intra-rack cabling. Get cables in a variety of lengths so that you will always be able to find a cable that is almost the right length. It always should be possible to find a cable that will run through the cable management with sufficient slack for sliding the machine forward a little and for seismic events. The cable should not have so much slack that it leaves a long trailing loop. If your hosts are on shelves that pull out, make sure there is enough slack in the cables so the machines

Figure 17.10: Synopsys stores serial console concentrators
in the network racks and uses special cables
to wire them directly into the patch panel.

can keep functioning even when the shelves are completely extended. Cables
should never run diagonally across the rack where they will get in the way
of someone working in the rack later. Make it easy for people to do the right
thing by having a full selection of cable lengths in stock. Otherwise, you
will have to deal with either a rat's nest of cables on the floor or a web of
criss-crossing cables at the back of the rack.

The cabling in the network row will require a lot of cable management
and discipline, but at least it is confined to one area (see Figure 17.11). You
also may be able to optimize this area if there are networks common to most
or all machines, such as a dedicated network for backups, an administrative
network, or serial console connections. If you know that a certain percentage

Figure 17.11: Network racks at GNAC, Inc. (Patch panels
are connected to overhead cabling to prewired
patch panels at the top of each host rack.)

of connections from a rack are going to be to particular destinations, you
can have all of those connections prewired, live, and ready to go, which
will reduce entropy in your cabling. Alternatively, if you can configure your
network equipment to map a particular port to a particular network, you
may be able to prewire everything.

A word of caution, however, about doing too much prewiring within
your network racks. You need to be able to deal gracefully with hardware
failures, which may require being able to rapidly move a lot of connections
to a different piece of hardware while you get replacement parts. You also
need to be able to deal with the exceptions that will inevitably crop up.
Don't paint yourself into a corner by making your wiring too inflexible.

Case Study: Good Wiring Pays for Itself

Prewiring a dozen network connections to every rack may sound expensive, but the payback is immeasurable. Once Tom oversaw two machine rooms in buildings that were 40 miles apart. One wasn't prewired and the other one was. In the data center that was not prewired, installing any new machine was an all-day event. Running the networking cable plus a cable for its console would take hours. Sometimes it would take an entire day because, as a two-person task, it took a while to find a second person to help. The constant wear and tear on the floor tiles over the decades resulted in them becoming wobbly and dangerous. The difficulty and danger of working in the room resulted in SAs procrastinating. It can be difficult to find a two- to three-hour block of free time to do an installation. New hosts would be delayed by a week as a result. The successful installation of a host was a cause for celebration. Conversely, the other data center was prewired with a dozen Category-5 cables to each rack drawn back to an orderly patch panel near all the network equipment. Installing a new host in this room was a breeze, usually taking less than 15 minutes. The installations were done without procrastination or fanfare. The cost of the prewiring is more than compensated for by the productivity it affords.

The major trade-offs for prewiring are rack space consumption and upfront cost. But the increases in reliability, productivity, and manageability through not having to deal with rat's nests and cables crossing all over the place at the backs of the racks are huge.

Some places may not be able to prewire their racks. For example, a colocation center that will have customer equipment in the racks cannot know when building the data center what kind of equipment will be in the racks and how many connections will be leaving a set of racks to be connected to other sets of racks or to the colocation center's own network equipment.

Another trick for optimizing your cabling is to have vertical power distribution units, with lots of outlets, mounted at the sides of the racks. Buy a lot of really short power cords in a couple of different lengths (for example, one foot and two feet long), and plug each piece of equipment into the power socket next to it. That avoids having long power cords trailing all over the rack next to the data cables and possibly causing interference problems in addition to the mess (see Figure 17.12).

Power and Data Cables Should Be Separated

At a site where Christine performed consultant work, an SA received a report of a network problem. The customer who reported the problem found that data transfer between two hosts was very slow. The SA verified the problem and did further tests. She found that the network interface of one

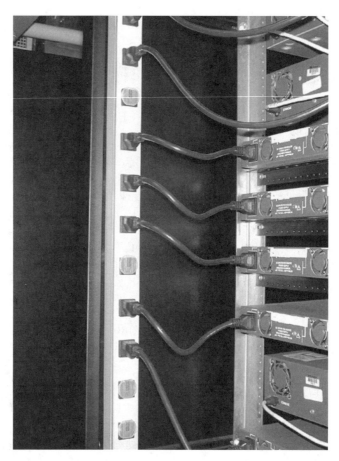

Figure 17.12: Vertical PDUs at GNAC, Inc. with short power cables
are convenient and help to keep the wiring neat.

of the machines was recording a lot of errors. She went down to the data
center to check the cabling. It all seemed solid, and replacing the cables
made no difference. While she was doing that, however, she noticed that
the power cord of the machine that she had installed in a rush earlier in
the day was crossing over the network cable that went into the interface
that was having problems. All the other power cords were carefully kept
away from network cables and neatly run through the cable management.
She remembered Christine telling her about keeping network and data cables apart because of electromagnetic interference, so she took the extra
minute or so to run the power cord through the cable management with the
rest of the power cords. When she tested again, the network problem had
vanished.

17.1.8   Labeling

Good labeling is essential to a smooth-running data center. All equipment should be labeled on both the front and the back with its full name as it appears in the corporate namespace (see Chapter 6) and in the console server system (see Section 17.1.10).

If a machine has multiple connections of the same kind and it is not obvious from looking at the machine which one is used for what function, such as multiple network interfaces that belong on different networks, both the interfaces and the cables should be labeled. Color coding the network cables can also help, perhaps using a different color for each security domain.[5] For example, on a firewall that has three network interfaces, one for the internal, protected network; one for the external, unprotected network; and one for a service network that is accessed from untrusted networks through the firewall. The interfaces should at least have "int," "ext," and "serv" next to them, and cables should have labels with corresponding tags attached. When you are debugging a problem, you will then be able to easily say "the external network card has no link light." When you have to pull it out of the rack to work on a hardware fault, you will be able to put it back in and reconnect all the cables without having to think about it or trace cables.

For high-port-density network equipment, labeling every port will be impractical. However, maintaining a label on the equipment that associates ports with networks or virtual LANs (VLANs) should be possible. For example, such a label might read "192.168.1/24: cards 1-3; 192.168.15/24: cards 4,5,8; 192.168.27/24: cards 6,7."

For network equipment that connects to WANs, both the name of the other end of the connection and the link vendor's identity number for the link should be on the label. This labeling should be on the piece of equipment that has the error lights for that link. For example, a CSU/DSU for a T1 would have a label that reads "T1 to San Diego office" or "512k link to WAN Frame Relay cloud," as appropriate, and the T1 provider's circuit ID and telephone number.

Network equipment typically also has facilities for labeling ports in software. The software labeling facility should be used to its full potential, providing at least as much information as is available from the physical labels. As network equipment becomes smaller and more integrated, and detailed physical labeling becomes more difficult, the software labels will become the most convenient way to store information that you need for debugging.

---

[5]Large sites find it difficult to have a different color for every network.

Using both physical labeling and software labeling leads to having multiple sources of the "truth." It is important to make sure they are synchronized so they give the same information. Make someone responsible for ensuring that physical and software labels match, finding out the correct information, and fixing the labels when they do not match. Nothing is worse than having multiple sources of information all disagreeing when you are trying to debug a problem. It takes diligence, time, and effort to keep labeling up to date, but it saves lots of time during an outage, when it is important to be able to respond quickly. It can also prevent accidental outages from happening when someone traces a cable to the wrong spot.

Labeling both ends of every cable becomes tedious, especially when cables get reused and old labels must be removed and new ones attached. Cables are also notoriously difficult to label because not many labels stick well to their PVC shells over the long term. A useful alternative is to get prelabeled cables that have their type and their length encoded into the label, along with a unique sequence number, and have the same label at each end. Your cable vendor should be able to do this for you, including tracking the sequence numbers. You then have an easier way of finding the other end of the cable (if you know approximately where it is already), rather than tracing it. Even if you have to trace it, you can confirm you have the right cable before disconnecting it by checking the numbers. Another alternative is to find cable ties with a flat tab at the end that normal labels will stick to. The cable ties can be permanently attached to either end of the cable, and labels on the tabs can be changed relatively easily.

Policy for Enforcing Labeling Standards

Eircom has a very strict labeling policy. Servers must be labeled front and back, and every power cord must be labeled at the far end with the name of the machine that it is attached to. Network cables are color coded rather than labeled. The policy is briefly and clearly described in a sign on the data center wall (see Figure 17.13). They make periodic sweeps to check labels; if any server or power cord is not labeled, it will be removed. Their policy makes it very clear that any resulting problems are the fault of the person who installed the machine without labeling it or the power cord, rather than the fault of the person who disconnected the machine. Because these sweeps happen frequently, however, machines that do not comply with labeling standards are typically only disconnected before they go into production.

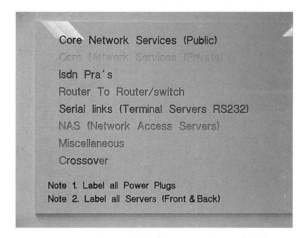

Figure 17.13: Sign in the Eircom data center showing
the cabling and labeling policy. (Each line is
in the color of the cable it describes.)

17.1.9   Communication

SAs working in the data center often need to communicate with customers or other SAs outside the data center. They may need someone else to test whether a problem has been fixed; someone to monitor service availability; or someone to find information, equipment, or another person. We recommend that SAs carry radios to facilitate communication because many SAs are rarely at their desks. However, radios often do not work well in data centers because of high levels of electromagnetic interference or, at some sites, because of RF shielding. Simple telephone extensions sometimes work better. We recommend putting a telephone at each end of a row of racks, with a long enough cord to the receiver to enable SAs to work on any part of the row and still be able to talk on the phone, if necessary (see Figure 17.14).

17.1.10   Console Servers

Console servers allow you to maintain console access to all of the equipment in the data center without the overhead of attaching a monitor and a keyboard to every system. Having lots of "heads" in the data center is an inefficient way to use the valuable resource of data center floor space and the special power, air-conditioning, and fire suppression systems that are a part of it. Keyboards and monitors in data centers also typically provide a

Figure 17.14: SAs at Synopsys all have radios, but
they find that phone extensions at the end of
each row work better in the data center.
(Note the extremely long cord.)

very unergonomic environment to work in if you spend a lot of time on the
console of a server attached to a "head" in a data center.

Console servers come in two primary flavors. There are switch boxes
that allow you to attach the monitor, keyboard, and mouse ports of many
machines through the switch box to a single "head." Try to have as few such
heads in the data center as you can, and try to make the environment they
are in an ergonomic one.

The other flavor is a console server for machines that support serial
consoles. The serial port of each of these machines is connected to a serial
device such as a terminal server. These terminal servers are on the network.
Typically some software on a central server controls them all (Fine and
Romig 1990) and makes the consoles of the machines available by name,
with authentication and some level of access control. The advantage of this
system is that if an SA is properly authenticated, he can access the console of a system from anywhere, including his desk, home, and when he is
on the road and connected by remote access. Installing a console server,

particularly one that uses serial consoles, dramatically improves productivity and convenience, as well as cleans up the data center and yields more space (Harris and Stansell 2000).

It can also be useful to have a few carts with dumb terminals or laptops that can be used as portable serial consoles. These carts can be conveniently wheeled up to any machine and used as a serial console if the main console server fails or an additional monitor and keyboard is needed. One such cart is shown in Figure 17.15.

Figure 17.15: Synopsys has several serial console carts that can be wheeled up to a machine if the main console server fails, or if the one machine with a "head" in the machine room is in use.

17.1.11   Workbench

Another key feature for a data center is easy access to a workbench with plenty of power sockets and an antistatic surface where SAs can work on a machine that has a hardware fault or on adding extra memory, disks, or CPUs to new equipment before it goes into service. Ideally, the workbench should be in a room that is attached to the data center so that the SAs do not have far to go, and yet it will not be used as "temporary rack space," or cause an overspill of messiness into the data center. These work spaces generate a lot of dust, especially if new hardware is unboxed there. Keeping this dust outside of the data center is important.

If there is nowhere for SAs to perform this sort of work, they will end up doing repairs on the data center floor, which is a fire hazard, and new installs in their desk area, leading to the unprofessional messy offices or cubicles with boxes and pieces of equipment lying around often associated with SAs. A professionally run SA group should look professional, which means having a properly equipped and sufficiently large work area that is designated for hardware work.

17.1.12   Tools and Supplies

Your data center also should be kept fully stocked with all the different cables, tools, and spares you need. This is actually easier to say than do. With a large group of SAs, it takes constant tracking of the spares and supplies and support from the SAs themselves to make sure that you don't run out, or at least run out only occasionally and not for too long. If an SA notices that the data center is running low on something or that she is about to use a significant quantity of anything, she should inform the person responsible for tracking the spares and supplies, so that he can order more.

Tools ideally should be kept in a cart with drawers, so that it can be wheeled to wherever it is needed. In a large machine room you should have multiple carts. The cart should have screwdrivers of different sizes, a couple of electric screwdrivers, Torx drivers, hex wrenches, chip pullers, needle-nose pliers, wire cutters, knives, static straps, a label maker or two, and anything else that you find yourself needing, even occasionally, to work on equipment in the data center.

Spares and supplies must be well organized so that they can be quickly picked up when needed and so that it is easy to do an inventory. Some people hang cables from wall hooks with labels above them, others use labeled bins of varying sizes that can be attached to the walls in rows. A couple of these arrangements are shown in Figures 17.16 and 17.17. The bins provide a more compact arrangement, but need to be planned for in advance of laying out the racks in the data center because they will protrude significantly into

Figure 17.16: Different sizes of labeled blue bins are used to store a variety of different data center supplies at GNAC, Inc.

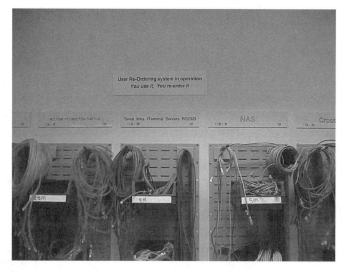

Figure 17.17: Eircom uses a mixture of blue bins and hanging cables.

the aisle. Small items such as rack screws and terminators should be in bins or small drawers. Many sites prefer to keep spares in a different room with easy access from the data center. A room with a workbench connected to the data center is ideal. Keeping spares in another room may also protect them from the event that killed the original. Large spares, such as spare machines, should always be kept in another room so that they don't use valuable data center floor space. Valuable spares, such as memory and CPUs, are usually kept in a locked cabinet.

If possible, you should keep spares for the components that you use or that fail most often. Your spares inventory might include standard disk drives of various sizes, power supplies, memory, CPUs, fans, or even entire machines if you have arrays of small dedicated machines for particular functions.

It is useful to have many different kinds of carts and trucks: two-wheel hand-trucks for moving crates, four-wheel flat carts for moving mixed equipment, carts with two or more shelves for tools, and so on. Mini-forklifts with a hand-cranked winch are excellent for putting heavy equipment into racks. They enable you to lift and position the piece of equipment at the preferred height in the rack. After locking the wheels, the lift is stable and the equipment can be mounted in the rack safely and easily.

17.1.13 Parking Spaces

A simple, cheap, but effective way to improve the life of people who work in the data center is to have designated parking spaces for mobile items. Tools live in carts. The carts should have parking spaces where they are returned to when no longer in use. Carts for wheeling equipment around should also have their own parking spaces. If you have a raised floor, pick a spot for your tile pullers to be stored when not in use. The chargers for battery-operated tools should have a secure area. In all cases, the mobile items should be labeled with the location where they should be returned.

Case Study: Parking Space for Tile Pullers

In the original Synopsys data center that had a raised floor, there were two tile pullers. However, because there was no designated place to leave them, the SAs would just put them somewhere out of the way so that no one tripped over them. Whenever SAs wanted a tile puller, they had to walk up and down the rows until they found one. One day, a couple of SAs got together and decided to designate a parking space for them. They picked a particular tile where no one would be in danger of tripping over them, labeled the tile to say, "The tile pullers live here. Return them after use," and labeled each of the tile pullers with, "Return to tile at E5" (using the existing row and column labeling on the walls of the data center). The new practice was not particularly communicated to the group, but as soon as the SAs saw the labels, they immediately started following the practice because it made sense and they were relieved that they wouldn't have to search the data center for tile pullers any more.

17.2   The Icing

You can improve your data center above and beyond the facilities that we described earlier. Equipping a data center properly is expensive, and the improvements that we outline here can add substantially to your costs. But if you are able to, or your business needs require it, you can improve your data center by having much wider aisles than necessary and by having greater redundancy in your power and HVAC systems.

17.2.1   Greater Redundancy

If your business needs require very high availability, you will need to plan for redundancy in your power and HVAC systems, among other things. For this sort of design, you need to understand circuit diagrams and building blueprints and consult with the people who are designing the system to make sure you catch every little detail, because it is the little detail that you miss that is going to get you.

For the HVAC system, you may want to have two independent parallel systems that run all the time. If one fails, the other will take over. Either one on its own should have the capacity to cool the room. There are other alternatives too, and your HVAC engineer should be able to advise you.

For the power system, there are many things that you need to consider. At a relatively simple level, consider what happens if a UPS, a generator, or the ATS fails. You can have additional UPSs and generators, but what if two fail? What if one of the UPSs catches fire? If all of them are in the same room, they will all need to be shut down. Likewise, the generators should be distributed. Think about bypass switches for removing pieces of equipment that have failed from the circuit, in addition to the one that you hopefully already have for the UPS. Those switches should not be right next to the piece of equipment that you want to bypass, so that you can still get to them if the equipment is on fire. Do all the electrical cables follow the same path, or meet at some point? Could that be a problem?

Within the data center, you may want to make power available from several different sources. You may want both AC and DC power, but you may also want two different sources of AC power for equipment that can have two power supplies, or to power each half of a redundant pair of machines.

Figure 17.18: GNAC, Inc., brings three different "legs" of UPS power into a single power strip. Redundant power supplies in a single piece of equipment are plugged into different legs to avoid simultaneous loss of power to both power supplies if one leg fails.

Equipment with multiple power supplies should take power from different power sources (see Figure 17.18).

❖ **High-Reliability Data Centers** The telecommunications industry has an excellent understanding about how to build a data center for reliability, because the phone system is used for emergency services and must be reliable. The standards were also set forth when telecommunication monopolies had the money to go the extra distance to ensure that things were done right. The United States standard for equipment that may be put in a phone company's central office is called

Network Equipment Building System (NEBS). In Europe, the equipment must follow the European Telecommunication Standards Institute (ETSI) standard. NEBS and ETSI set physical requirements and testing standards for equipment, as well as minimums for the physical room itself. These document in detail topics such as space planning, floor and heat loading, temperature and humidity, earthquake and vibration, fire resistance, transportation and installation, airborne contamination, acoustic noise, electrical safety, electromagnetic interference, electrostatic discharge (ESD) immunity, lightning protection, DC potential difference, and bonding and grounding. We only mention this to show how anal retentive the telecom industry is. On the other hand, when was the last time you picked up your telephone and didn't receive a dial tone in less than a second? The NEBS and ETSI standards are good starting places when creating your own set of requirements for a very-high-availability data center.

For a high-availability data center, you also need good process. The SAS-70 standard applies to service organizations and is particularly relevant to companies providing services over the Internet. SAS-70 stands for Statement of Auditing Standards No. 70, which is entitled "Reports on the Processing of Transactions by Service Organizations." It is an auditing standard established by the American Institute of Certified Public Accountants (AICPA).

17.2.2   More Space

If space is not at a premium, it is nice to have more aisle space in your computer room than you need to meet safety laws and to enable you to move equipment around. One data center that Christine visited had enough aisle space to pull a large piece of equipment out of a rack onto the floor and wheel another one behind it without knocking into anything. Cray's data center in Eagan, Minnesota had aisles that were three times the depth of the deepest machine. If you are able to allocate this much space, based on your long-term plans (so that you will not have to move the racks later), then treat yourself. It is a useful luxury, and it makes the data center a much more pleasant environment.

17.3   Ideal Data Centers

Different people like different features in a data center. To provide some food for thought, we both have described the features we would like in a machine room.

17.3.1   Tom's Dream Data Center

When you enter my dream data center, the first thing you notice is the voice-activated door. To make sure that someone didn't record your voice and play it back, you are prompted for a word from a dictionary, which you must then repeat back. The sliding door opens. It is wide enough to fit a very large server such as an SGI Challenge XL. Even though the room has a raised floor, the floor is the same height as the hallway, which means no ramp is required.

The room is on the fourth floor of a six-story building. The UPS units and HVAC systems are in the sixth floor attic, with plenty of room to grow and plenty of conduit space if additional power or ventilation needs to be brought to the room. Flooding is unlikely.

The racks are all the same color and from the same vendor, which makes them look very nice. In fact, they were bought at the same time, so the paint fades evenly. There is a pull-out drawer at the halfway point of every third rack. The drawer has a pad of paper and a couple of pens. (I never can have too many pens.) There are five shelves in each rack, two below the drawer, one just above the drawer, and two further up the rack. The shelves are at the same height on all racks so that it looks neat. They are strong enough to hold equipment and still roll out. Machines can be rolled out to do maintenance on them, and there is enough slack in all the cables to permit this. When equipment is to be mounted, the shelves are removed or installed on racks that are missing shelves. You only now notice that some of the racks (the ones at the far end of the room) are missing shelves in anticipation of equipment that will be mounted and not require shelves.

The racks are 19-inch racks with doors on the front and open in the back. The side panels are removed, which saves an inch per rack and, although it is discouraged, means you can pass cables between two adjacent racks. The racks are locked together so that each row is self-stable.

Each rack is as wide as a floor-tile, two feet. That means that there is one rack per floor-tile. Each rack is three feet deep, which makes it one and a half floor-tiles deep. A row of racks takes up one and a half tiles and the walkway between them takes an equal amount of space. That means that every three tiles is a complete rack and walkway combination that includes one tile that is completely uncovered and can therefore be removed when access is required. If we are really lucky, some or all rows have an extra tile between them. The extra two feet makes it much easier to rack-mount bulky equipment. (See Figure 17.19.)

The racks are in rows that are no more than 12 racks long. Between every row is a walkway large enough to bring the largest piece of equipment through. Some rows are missing, or simply missing a rack or two nearest the

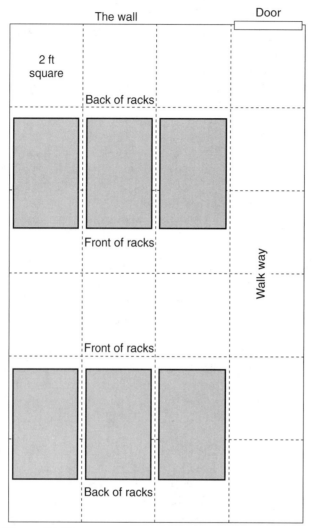

Figure 17.19: Simple floor plan that provides open space.

walkway. This space is reserved for machines that come with their own rack or are floor-standing servers.

If the room is large, there are multiple walkways. If the room is small, the walkway is in the middle of the room where the door is. There is another door, used less frequently, in the back for fire safety reasons. The main door gives an excellent view of the machine room when tours come through. There is a large glass window into the machine room. On the inside of the window is a desk with three monitors. The monitors display the status of the LAN, WAN, and services.

The back of each rack has 24 network jacks with cable certified for Category 6 or GigaSPEED wire. The first 12 go to a patch panel near the network equipment. The next 12 go to a different patch panel near the console consolidator. Although the consoles do not require Category 6 copper, using the same copper consistently means one can overflow network connections into the console space. If there is an indication that fiber may someday be needed, every rack (or just every other rack) has six pairs of fiber that run back to a fiber patch panel.

The last row of racks is dedicated for network equipment. The patch panels have so much wire coming into them that they can never be moved, so this row is in the far back corner. Also, in this part of the room is a table with three monitors and keyboards. One is for the KVM switch, the second connects to the serial console concentrator, and the third is a simple X Terminal for getting work done. One rack is dedicated to connections that go out of the room. Near it is a row of fiber-to-copper adaptors. Vendors now make a single unit that supplies power to many such adaptors that slide into it. This eliminates the rat's nest of power cables and power bricks.

The network equipment rack also has a couple of non-UPS outlets. There are times when the UPS will be down but the network must be up, and the redundant power supplies can be plugged into these non-UPS outlets.

Air-conditioning is fed under the floor. Every other floor tile in the walkways has pin holes to let air out. The tiles under each rack have large holes to let air in, so air can flow up the back of each piece of equipment. A fan at the top pulls air up and out.

Along the left and right sides of the back of each rack is a power strip with widely spaced outlets. Each pair of racks is on a different circuit that comes from the UPS. Each is marked with a circuit number so that redundant services can be placed on different circuits.

Every cable is labeled on each end with a unique number, and every host is labeled with name, IP address, and MAC address. There are two label printers in the room, each labeled with the room number of the data center and a warning that stealing the device will lead to certain death.

Also under the floor are cable trays, with separate ones for power and for networking. Because power and networking are prewired, there should be little need to ever open the floor.

Outside the machine room through the other door is a work area. It is separated from the main room to keep out the dust. In this room are wide wire shelves that hold new machines being installed. There are workbenches with power sockets and an antistatic surface where repairs can be done without doing more damage to the equipment. Also in this room is a set of drawers filled with tools, spare parts, and bins of cables of various lengths and types. There are 20 extra pairs of wire cutters, 40 extra Phillips screw drivers, and 30 extra flathead screw drivers (at the rate they are stolen, that should last a year).

This ends our tour of Tom's dream data center. As you leave, the tour guide hands you a complimentary Linux box.

❖ **The Floor Puller Game**   Here's a great game to play in a wide open space in a room with a raised floor, such as the open area behind the desk at a helpdesk. This game should be played when your boss isn't around. You will need two people and one floor puller.

Each person sits or stands at a different end of the room. One player throws the floor puller at a tile. If it sticks, the player removes the tile and accumulates it in a pile in her end of the room. The two players alternate taking turns until all the floor tiles are missing. You must walk on the grid and not touch the floor below the tiles. If you fall into the floor you must return a floor tile to one place. When all the tiles are removed, whoever has the largest pile of floor tiles wins.

If you play this enough, the edges of the tiles will be damaged in a year and you will need to purchase a new floor. We don't actually recommend that our readers play this game, but if you are in the business of installing and repairing raised floors, teaching it to your customers might increase your sales. (You didn't hear that from us!)

17.3.2   Christine's Dream Data Center

Christine's dream data center has double doors that are opened with a hands-free security system, such as proximity badges or voice activation, so that it is easy for people carrying equipment to get access. The double doors are wide enough to get even the largest piece of equipment through. It is on the same level as, and is convenient to, the receiving area, with wide corridors between the two.

The data center has backup power from a generator with enough capacity to hold the machines and lighting in the data center, the HVAC system, the UPS charging, the phone switches, the SA work area, and the customer service center. The security access system is also on the protected power system. The generator has large tanks that can be refueled while it is running. The generator is tested once a week.

There is an ATS that is tunable for what is considered to be acceptable power.[6] There is a UPS protecting the data center. It has enough power to run for 30 minutes, which should be enough to manually switch to a backup generator, providing the backup generator is there already.

The data center does not have a raised floor. The air is pumped in from overhead units. The room has a high ceiling with no tiles. It is painted matte black from a foot above the racks, with drop-down lights that are at the level where the black paint starts. This makes the overhead HVAC inconspicuous.

There is an overhead power bus. I would love to have two different power sources—different UPS, ATS, generator, and power distribution panels and power bus for each, with different physical locations for each set of equipment, but I couldn't justify it for the average site data center.

The data center is prewired with one 36-port, two rack-units-high patch panel at the top of each rack, brought back to racks in the network row. In the network row, patch panel racks are interspersed between racks that hold the network equipment. There is lots of wire management.

The data center has seven-foot tall, four-post racks (black), with 19-inch wide rack mount spaces that are 36 inches deep with no backs, fronts, or sides. They have threaded mounting holes, and the sides of the shelves mount onto vertical rails, which can be moved just about anywhere. The shelves are not as deep as the racks—just 30 inches—to leave room for cables that are plugged into the machines and PDUs and vertical wire management within the racks. Extra vertical rails can be moved for rack-mounting different depth equipment. The racks have vertical PDUs with lots of outlets down one side. If there are different power sources in the machine room, the racks have power available from both. Lots of one- and two-foot power cables are available so that there are no dangling power cords. There is vertical wire management down the other side and horizontally on an as-needed basis. There are several short step-ladders so that vertically challenged SAs can reach the top.

The data center has network patch cables from 3 feet to 10 feet at every 1-foot interval, plus a few that are 15, 20, 25, 30, 35, 40, 45 and 50 feet long. All network cables are prelabeled with unique serial numbers that also encode length and type. There are blue bins for storing all of the different kinds of cables and connectors in the data center where it is convenient.

The machines are labeled front and back with the DNS name. Network interfaces are labeled with the network name or number.

There are a couple of carts with drawers that have all the tools you could possibly need. There are battery-powered screwdrivers, as well as manual

---

[6]Christine once saw an ATS that found utility power acceptable when the UPS didn't, so the UPS ran off batteries, and the generator didn't get switched on—what a nightmare.

ones. Each cart has a label-maker. A work area is off the machine room with a nice wide bench, lots of power, and static protection. Sets of tools are kept to hand in there also.

17.4   Conclusion

A data center takes a lot of planning to get right, but whatever you build, you will be stuck with for a long time, so it is worth doing right. A badly designed, underpowered, or undercooled data center can be a source of reliability problems, whereas a well designed data center should see you safely through many problems.

Power, air-conditioning, and fire suppression systems are key components of the data center that are relatively immutable. They can also have the greatest effects if they go wrong. Bad wiring is something that everyone has experienced and would rather not have to deal with. With good advance planning, you can reduce your nightmares in that area.

Access to the room for getting equipment in and moving it around is another key area that you need to plan in advance. And along with access, comes security. The data center is a business-critical room that holds a lot of valuable equipment. The security access policies must reflect that, but the mechanism selected should be one that is convenient for people with armloads of equipment to use.

Building a good, reliable data center is costly but has significant payback. However, there also are simple, inexpensive things you can do to make the data center a nicer and more efficient environment to work in. Everyone appreciates having a convenient place to work on broken equipment with all the tools, spares, and supplies that you need on hand, and, relatively speaking, the cost for that is very low. Labeling all equipment well and having designated parking spaces for mobile resources will provide you with inexpensive, time-saving benefits. Seek ideas from the SAs; all of them will have features that they particularly like or dislike. Incorporate the good ones and learn from the negative experiences of others.

For companies with lots of space, it is nice to make the data center more spacious than it really needs to be. And for those with lots of money and very high reliability requirements, you can do much with the key systems of power and air-conditioning to add greater redundancy that will make the room even more reliable.

To get the most out of a data center, you need to design it well from the start. If you know that you are going to be building a new one, it is worth spending a lot of time up front to get it right.

Exercises

1. What natural disasters is your area prone to? What precautions have you taken for natural disasters, and what improvements could you make?

2. What problems have you found with your racks? What would you like to change?

3. Could you make use of prewiring in your current data center, if you had it? If not, what would you have to do to make it useful? How much do you think prewiring would help in cleaning up the wiring in your data center?

4. What is the power capacity of your data center? How close are you to reaching it?

5. If you have separate power circuits from different UPSs in your data center, how well are they balanced? What could you do to balance them better?

6. How much space is currently occupied with monitors in your data center? How many could you pull out with the use of serial console servers? How many could you pull out by deploying KVM switch boxes?

7. Where do you work on broken machines at the moment? Is there an area that could be turned into a workbench area?

8. What tools would you want in a cart in the data center?

9. What supplies do you think you would want in the data center, and how many of each? What should the high and low supply levels be for each item?

10. What spares would you want, and how many of each?

11. What equipment do you have that is always "walking off?" Can you think of good parking spaces for it?

Chapter 18

Networks

A site's network is the foundation of its infrastructure. A poorly built network affects everyone's perception of all other components of the system. It cannot be considered in isolation. Decisions made as part of the network design and implementation process influence how infrastructure services are implemented. Therefore the people who are responsible for designing those services should be consulted as part of the network design process.

We cannot explain every detail of network design and implementation in this short chapter. There are entire shelves of books on the topic. However, we can relate the key points we have found to be the most important. An excellent starting point is Perlman (1999). For TCP/IP, we recommend Stevens (1994) and Comer (2000). To understand how routers and switches work, see Berkowitz (1999). Berkowitz (1998) also has written a book on network addressing architectures. For more information on specific technologies, see Black (1999). For WANs, see Marcus (1999) and Feit (1999). For routing protocols, there is Black (2000). Other books concentrate on a single protocol or technology, such as OSPF (Moy 2000, Thomas 1998a), EIGRP (Pepelnjak 2000), BGP (Stewart 1999, Halabi and McPherson 2000), MPLS, VPNs, and QoS (Black 2001, Guichard and Pepelnjak 2000, Keagy 2000, Lee 1999, Della Maggiora et al. 2000, and Vegesna 2001), Multicast (Williamson 2000), ATM (Pildush 2000), and Ethernet (Spurgeon 2000).

Networking is an area of rapid technological development, and therefore the approaches and implementation possibilities change significantly over the years. In this chapter, we will identify areas that change over time, as well as some of the constants in the networking realm.

This chapter is primarily about an organization's internal LANs and WANs. Sections 18.1.4, 18.1.5, and 18.1.10 focus on a campus environment rather than an e-commerce site. However, the recommendations in the remaining sections are also applicable to e-commerce environments.

18.1   The Basics

When building a network, your basic goal is to provide a reliable, well-documented, easy to maintain network that has plenty of capacity and room for growth. Sounds simple, doesn't it?

Many pieces at different layers combine to help you reach (or fail to reach) that goal. This section discusses those building blocks. It covers everything from physical network issues to logical network topologies, documentation, host routing, routing protocols, monitoring, and administrative domains. It also discusses how components of the network design interact with each other and with the design of the services that run on top of the network.

There is also a big difference between WAN and LAN design. Over time, cyclic trends make them more similar, less similar, then more similar again. For example, at one time, it was popular for LAN topologies to be dual-connected rings of Fiber-Distributed Data Interface (FDDI) connections to provide fault tolerance. This lost popularity as Fast Ethernet (100Mb Ethernet) arose, which was a bus architecture. Meanwhile WANs were adopting ring architectures such as SONET (Synchronous Optical Network) and MONET (Multiwavelength Optical Network). As we write this, draft proposals for 10Gb Ethernet LAN technology return to ring architectures. We have come full circle.

18.1.1   The OSI Model

The Open Standards Interconnection (OSI) reference model for networks has gained widespread acceptance and is used throughout this chapter. It looks at the network as logical layers and is briefly described in Table 18.1.

Network devices decide the path that data travels along the physical network, which consists of cables, wireless links, and network devices. A network device that makes those decisions based on hardware or MAC address of the source or destination host, is referred to as a layer 2 device. A device that makes decisions based on the IP (or AppleTalk, or DECnet) address of the source or destination host is known as a layer 3 device. One that uses transport information such as TCP port numbers is a layer 4 device.

Layer	Name	Description
1	Physical	The physical copper or fiber connection between devices
2	Data Link	Interface (or MAC) addressing, flow control, low-level error notification
3	Network	Logical addressing (e.g., IP addresses) and routing
4	Transport	Data transport, error checking and recovery, virtual circuits (e.g., TCP sessions)
5	Session	Manages communication sessions (e.g., AppleTalk name binding, or SCP)*
6	Presentation	Data formats (e.g., MPEG), character encoding, compression, encryption
7	Application	Application protocols such as SMTP (email), HTTP (web), and FTP (file transfer)

*SCP is not commonly used in the TCP/IP world. SCP is the session control protocol.

Table 18.1: The OSI Model

18.1.2 Clean Architecture

A network architecture should be as clean and simple to understand as it can be. It should be possible to briefly describe the approach used in designing the network and to draw a few simple pictures to illustrate that design. A clean architecture makes debugging network problems much easier. You can quickly tell what path traffic should take from point A to point B. You can tell which links affect which networks. Having a clear understanding of the traffic flow on your network puts you in control of it. Not understanding the network puts you at the mercy of its vagaries.

A clean architecture encompasses both physical and logical network topologies and the network protocols that are used on both hosts and network equipment. It also has a clearly defined growth strategy, both for adding LAN segments and for connecting new remote offices. A clean network architecture is a core component behind everything that is discussed later in this chapter.

Case Study: Vendors Can't Support Too Much Complexity

If a network architecture can't be explained easily, it can be difficult to get support from vendors when you have a problem. A network administrator discovered that the hard way. There was an outage in an overly complicated network. Anyone he talked to, either locally or at a vendor, spent a lot of time just trying to understand the configuration, let alone coming up with suggestions to fix the problem. Calling vendor support lines wasn't very useful because the front-line support people could not understand the network being debugged; sometimes the vendor simply had difficulty believing that anyone would use such a complicated design! After being escalated to higher levels of customer support, he was told that the products weren't supported in such odd configurations and the suggestion was made to simplify the design rather than push so many different vendors' products to their limits.

Case Study: Network Administrators Can't Support Too Much Complexity

When debugging a complicated network, the network administrator at one site found herself spending more time figuring out what network paths existed rather than debugging the actual problem. Once the network architecture was simplified, problems were debugged in less time.

18.1.3   Network Topologies

Network topologies change as technologies and cost structures change. They also change as companies grow, set up large remote offices, or buy other companies. We introduce some of the common topologies here.

One topology that is often seen in wide area, campus area, and local area networks is a "star," where one site, building, or piece of network hardware is at the center of the star and all other sites, buildings, or networks are connected to the center. For example, within a single building or a campus there might be one layer 2 or layer 3 device to which all hosts or all networks are connected. That device is the center of a star. A LAN with a star topology is illustrated in Figure 18.1. For WAN, if all wide-area connectivity is brought into one building, that building is the center of the star, as illustrated in Figure 18.2. A star topology has an obvious single-point-of-failure problem: A failure at the center of the star disrupts all connectivity between the points of the star. In other words, if all hosts in a building are connected to a single switch, all connectivity is lost. If all wide area sites are connected through one building and that building loses power, the wide area sites cannot communicate with each other or with the site they connect through, but communication within each individual wide area site still works. However, a star topology is easy to understand, simple, and often cost-effective to implement. It may be the appropriate architecture to use, particularly for relatively small organizations. One simple improvement on this design is to have each link be redundant between the two end points and have a spare for the center point.

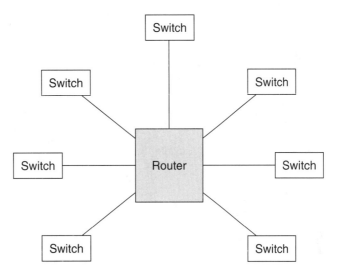

Figure 18.1: A local-area or campus-area network with a star topology

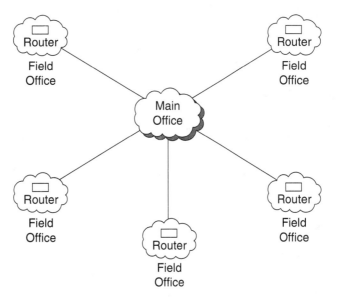

Figure 18.2: A wide-area network with a star topology

A common variant of the star topology is one that consists of multiple stars, the centers of which are connected to each other with redundant high-speed links (Figure 18.3). This approach limits the effects of a failure of a single star-center point. Companies with geographically disparate offices often will use this approach to concentrate all long-distance traffic from a

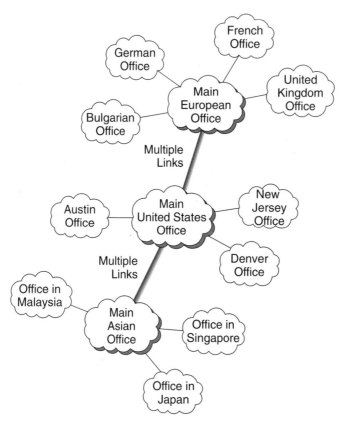

Figure 18.3: A multiple-star topology for a WAN, based on geographic hubs

single geographic area onto one or two expensive long-haul lines. Such a company would also typically provide lots of application-layer services at each of the star-center sites to reduce long-haul traffic and dependence on the long-distance links.

Ring topologies are also not uncommon. They are most often used for particular low-level topologies such as SONET rings. They are also found in local area and campus area networks and are sometimes useful for WANs. In a ring topology, each network entity[1] is connected to two others so that the network connectivity essentially forms a ring, as shown in Figure 18.4. Any one link or network entity can fail without affecting connectivity between functioning members of the ring. Adding new members to the ring, particularly in a WAN, can involve reconfiguring connectivity at multiple sites, however.

---

[1] Piece of network hardware, building, or site.

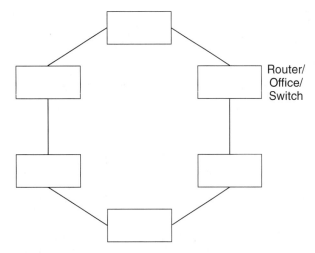

Figure 18.4: A ring topology in which each network device
is connected to two others

Another architecture that is used by sites that are concerned about redundancy and availability is one that looks like a multistar topology, but where each leaf node[2] has a backup connection to a second star center, as shown in Figure 18.5. If any star center node fails, its leaf nodes revert to using their backup connections until the primary service has been restored.

There are many other possible network topologies, including the "chaos" topology that largely describes the topology of the Internet in the year 2001. A chaotic topology ensues when each node can pick any one or more willing "upstream" nodes to use as a path to the rest of the networks. However, you cannot expect anyone to accurately describe or draw a connectivity map for a chaotic network without the aid of complicated mapping software.[3] If no one can draw or describe it without aids, it is not a clean architecture. The Internet survives, however, because it is highly adaptive and fault tolerant. But remember that no one cares about or tracks small failures that only affect a few sites on the Internet. That is not true in a corporate or university network. The chaos approach is not a reliable model to use in a network where availability of every component matters.

---

[2]A leaf node is a network entity that only handles traffic originating at or destined for local machines and does not act as a conduit for other traffic. In a simple star topology, every node except the center node is a leaf node.

[3]However, attempts to produce maps of the Internet have generated interesting and useful pictures. In particular, the February, 1998 issue of *Wired* magazine contains one of Bill Cheswick's Internet maps.

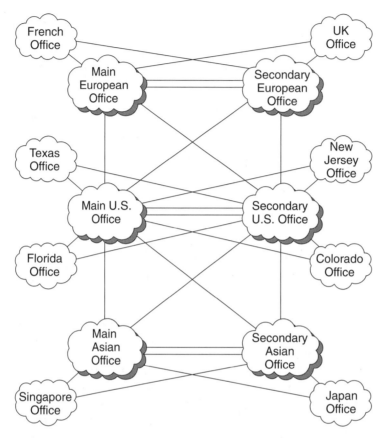

Figure 18.5: A redundant multiple-star topology for a WAN

Logical Network Topology

The logical network topology is what is normally drawn as the "network map." It generally shows only network devices that operate at layer 3 and above (for example, routers), and represents each subnetwork that is handled by one or more layer 2 devices (for example, switches) as a single entity. The logical network topology that makes the most sense for any given site varies with technologies and cost structures. Differing logical network maps of a single network may sometimes be drawn depending on what specific features need to be highlighted for the audience.

There is a simple rule of thumb about limiting network complexity: Network architects and senior network administrators at a site should all be able to sketch without aids the key features and basic structure of the network topology. If they need to resort to other sources of information, then the architecture is not clean and easy to understand.

The logical network topology cannot be designed in isolation. It influences, and is influenced by, other aspects of the computing infrastructure. In particular, the logical network design, its physical implementation, and the routing topologies that will be employed across that network are all interdependent. In addition, the architecture of network services such as email, Internet access, printing, and directory services must influence and be influenced by the network architecture.

Case Study: Inconsistent Network Architecture

A large multinational computer manufacturing company needed to redesign its WAN to bring it up to date with (then) current technologies. Both the implementation of the physical intersite connectivity and the routing architecture for the site were to be redesigned. The new routing protocol was chosen relatively quickly through evaluating the constraints and requirements. The physical architecture, in particular the bandwidth between certain key sites, was later chosen independently of the routing protocol choice. The metrics used by the routing protocol for path determination were not taken into consideration.[4] As a result, some high-bandwidth links were underused and some low-bandwidth connections suffered delays and packet loss as a result of overuse. Incorrectly sizing the connections is an expensive mistake to make.

The network must be considered as a unit. Choices made in one area affect other areas.

Case Study: Network Services Design

A large multinational software company had a "core services" team, a field office team, and a network team that worked closely together. The network team determined that they would connect small field offices to the corporate backbone through small, inexpensive, wide area links. Redundancy through Integrated Services Digital Network (ISDN) backup connections would be provided at a later date, so network hardware that would be able to accommodate a backup ISDN link was used from the outset. Based on this decision and discussions with the network team, the core services and field office teams decided to make the field offices as independent as possible so that they would be able to conduct the majority of their business while connectivity to the corporate backbone was unavailable.

Each field office, however small, had a server that handled local email, authentication, name service, file service, and printing. They also had a remote access box that was configured to fall back to a local authentication server if it could not

---

[4]The protocol chosen did not take bandwidth into consideration, only hop-counts.

contact the primary corporate authentication server. This architecture worked well because the field office sites were almost fully functional even when they were cut off from the rest of the company. For the few tasks where they needed to connect to another site, they had ordinary corporate remote access available to use if necessary.

If each field office had had high-speed redundant connectivity to the corporate backbone, they could have chosen an alternative service architecture that relied on that network connectivity more heavily, though this would have been much more expensive.

The star, multistar, and ring topologies that are described previously can appear at the physical level, the logical level, or both. Other topologies that are common at the logical network level include a flat network topology, a functional group-based topology, and a location-based topology.

In a flat topology, there are no layer 3 devices except at the egress point(s). In other words, all machines reside in the same address block with the same network number and network mask. For example, machines with IP addresses 10.1.1.1 and 10.1.1.2 and network masks of 255.255.255.0 are both in the 10.1.1.0/24 network block. Machines with addresses 10.1.1.1 and 10.1.2.1 and network masks 255.255.255.0 are not in the same network block. One is in the 10.1.1.0/24 block and the other is in the 10.1.2.0/24 block. However, if the machines with addresses 10.1.1.1 and 10.1.2.1 had network masks of 255.255.0.0, they would both be in the 10.1.0.0/16 network block. All machines in a network block must have the same network mask. Machines that are in the same network block are also in the same broadcast domain, which means that when one machine sends a broadcast to that network, all machines on that network receive the broadcast. A flat topology has only one network block with all the machines in it. All services, such as file, print, email, authentication, and name services are provided by servers on that network. Layer 3 devices connect that flat network to other networks. These might include a remote access server, a firewall, or a router connection to a remote office. The other networks connected to the layer 3 devices will be in different network address blocks.

In a location-based topology, layer 2 networks are assigned based on physical location. For example, a company might associate a layer 2 network with a floor of a building and use layer 3 devices to connect the floors together. For example, there would be a layer 2 switch on each floor of the building, and each switch would have a high-speed connection to a layer 3 device (router). All of the machines on the same floor of a building would be in the same network address block. Machines on different floors would be in different network address blocks and communicate through at least one layer 3 device.

In a functional group–based topology, each member of a group that works as a functional unit is connected to the same (flat) network regardless of location (within reason). For example, a building may have four LANs: sales, engineering, management, and marketing. Network ports at each group member's desk would be patched from wiring closet to wiring closet, potentially across interbuilding links, until reaching a place where there was a layer 2 switch for that network. The group network typically also includes services such as file, name, and authentication services to that group on that same network, which means that the network would also extend into the data center. One or more layer 3 devices connect the group network to the main company network. The main company network also provides services to the group network, such as email, intranet, and Internet access. Some of the services provided on the group network, such as authentication and name services, will exchange information with master servers on the main company network.

18.1.4 Intermediate Distribution Frame

An Intermediate Distribution Frame (IDF) is a fancy name for a wiring closet. This distribution system is the set of network closets and wiring that brings network connectivity out to the desktops. The need for IDFs, and how to design them and lay them out, is not something that has changed rapidly over time. The technologies and wiring specifics are what change with time.

New innovations in network hardware require higher-quality copper or fiber wiring to operate at increased speeds. If you use the newest, highest-specification wiring available when you build your cable plant, it is reasonable to expect it to last for five years before networking technology outpaces it. However, if you try to save money by using older, cheaper, lower-specification wiring, you will need to go through the expense and disruption of an upgrade sooner than if you had selected better cabling. Sites that "saved money" by installing Category-3 copper when Category-5 was available paid heavily to convert their cable plants when Fast Ethernet became commonplace.

The primary debate on wiring in an IDF is whether to use punch down blocks or standard network jacks to terminate the connections to the desktops. A punch down block separately terminates each of the individual wires that go to each network jack. For example, a Category-5 network jack uses eight wires, each of which would be terminated separately on the punch down block using a special tool. Making a connection to the desktop involves terminating another eight wires in the right place on the punch down block. Usually, those wires will go to the back of a standard network jack in a patch panel in the IDF. That jack is then connected to a switch using a patch cable. The other approach is to terminate all connections to the desktops directly onto patch panels, without going through a punch down block. Bringing a network port live simply involves running a patch cord between the appropriate jack and a switch.

The following sidebar lists arguments for and against punch down blocks and standard network jacks.

Arguments for Punch Down Blocks

- The punch down block approach does not take up as much space because not all ports will be used, and therefore not all ports need to be terminated on patch panels, which are larger.
- Only people who know what they are doing will touch a punch down block, so this approach produces more reliable network closets and effectively controls who can make network changes.

Arguments Against Punch Down Blocks

- Debugging flaky or failed connections on a punch down block is tedious and difficult.
- Tracing wires and installing new connections can cause wires to become loose.
- Patch panel jacks that are connected after the initial batch will not be in a logical order and may not be well labeled.
- The termination points can get damaged by misuse or overuse, which may put a jack out of use.
- Punch down connections may not reach the correct impedance standards for the speed of the connection.

Arguments for Standard Network Jacks

- Permanent connections to jacks in a patch panel are tested and certified when they are initially installed.
- The only things that are touched in normal use are the patch cables, which can be easily replaced if they are damaged.
- Standard network jacks can take much more use and abuse than punch down blocks.
- They will be laid out logically when they are installed and can be permanently labeled at that time.
- It is easier to train people to use a network closet that doesn't use punch down blocks.

Arguments Against Standard Network Jacks

- People outside the network group will connect additional switch ports to people's desks, and the network group will be unable to track switch port usage. This may result in closets running out of switch port capacity without the network team realizing it.
- The network will be less reliable if just anyone feels they know how to rewire network ports.
- Connecting all the desktop jacks that are not in use to jacks in patch panels is a waste of space and money.

We prefer to terminate connections to desktop jacks directly onto jacks in patch panels. It makes labeling and documentation easier and more consistent. In our experience, it makes for more reliable closets, assuming physical access is controlled.

There are two ways to make a connection between two IDFs. One way is to run bundles of cables between IDFs within a building. However, if there are large numbers of IDFs, the number of links can make this very expensive and complicated to maintain. The other way is to have a central location and only run bundles from IDFs to this central location. Then to connect any two IDFs, one simply creates a cross-connect in the central location. This central location is referred to as a *main distribution frame* (MDF) and is discussed later.

You generally only get a chance to lay out and allocate space for your IDFs before moving into a building. It is difficult and expensive to change at a later date if you decide that you did the wrong thing. Having to run from one floor to another to debug a network problem at someone's desk is frustrating and time-consuming. You should have at least one IDF per floor, more if the floors are large. You should align those IDFs vertically within the building (in other words, located in the same place on each floor so that they stack on each other throughout the building). Vertical alignment means that cabling between the IDFs and the MDF is simpler and cheaper to install and it is easier to add extra cabling between the IDFs at a later date, if necessary. It also means that the support staff need to learn only one floor layout, which eases the support burden. Likewise, if a campus consists of several similar buildings, the IDFs should be located at the same place in each of them. Figure 18.6 illustrates the connections between the IDFs and an MDF.

The IDFs should be numbered with the building number, floor number, and closet number. The closet numbers should be consistent across all the floors and all the buildings. Network jacks that are served by the IDFs should be labeled with the IDF number and a location number.[5] If there are multiple network jacks at a single location, a common convention is to use letters after the location number. The location numbers and letters must correspond with the location number and letters on the corresponding jacks in the IDF. When that numbering is inconsistent or nonexistent, debugging desktop network problems becomes very difficult. Color coding multiple jacks in a single location works well for people who are not color blind, but can cause problems for those who are. If you want to color code

---

[5]A location is a network drop point, where one or more cables are terminated. Typically, an individual office or cubicle will have a single location number corresponding to a single point in the room that has one or more network jacks. But a larger room, such as a conference room, may have multiple network drops and therefore multiple location numbers.

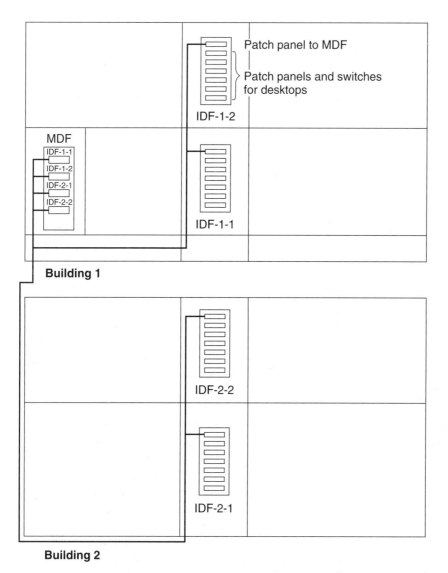

Figure 18.6: A patch panel in each IDF connects back to a patch panel in the MDF

the jacks, you should also use letters to avoid those problems. Each wiring closet should have, solidly mounted on the wall, a permanent, laminated floorplan for the area that it serves, showing the locations and location numbers of the network jacks. You will be surprised how often it gets used. It is also a good idea to install a small whiteboard in dynamic locations to track changes. For example, in an IDF that serves training rooms that are used for both in-house and customer training, a whiteboard could be used to track rooms for classes, dates, attendees, and network connections. The board should also have an area for freeform text for tracking current issues.

IDFs always should be locked and subject to restricted access. It is easy to wreak havoc in a wiring closet if you think you know what you are doing, but you have not been trained. If your environment has a high volume of changes made by a team with large turnover, it is advisable to have frequent, but brief, wiring closet training classes. If these are regularly scheduled for the same time and location each month, people who have access to the closets but rarely work in them can attend whenever they feel the need and keep up to date with what is happening.[6] Another reason for IDFs to be locked is security. IDFs are good places to hide network snooping devices because they typically have little human traffic and have lots of other equipment to obscure their existence. They are also easy targets for malicious changes.

Malicious Changes in the IDF

One large company found that the number of outages created by "unexplainable" and "unrequested" wiring changes increased soon before or during layoffs or contract negotiations with the local unions. They found it prudent during such events to perform daily checks to ensure the IDFs were securely locked.

The IDF closets themselves should be larger than you expect to need for your networking equipment, but not so large that people will be tempted to store servers or noncomputer equipment there. The IDF closet should only contain the network equipment for the area that it serves. If servers are stored in unexpected places such as wiring closets, they are more likely to suffer problems as a result of accidental knocks or cable disconnections, and they will be harder to locate when they do have problems. Sometimes, more people have access to the wiring closets than have access to the server room. Perhaps some trusted, trained people from your customer base may have access to the closet to bring ports live in a lab that has a high equipment turnover, for example. Very large labs may be configured similarly to an IDF and even be labeled as one in network diagrams. That should bring sufficient networking to the lab. In some situations, smaller labs can be configured as substations of the IDF by connecting the IDF to a network switch in the lab via a high-speed connection.

---

[6]We suggest monthly meetings in fast-growing environments so that new people get training shortly after joining. More static environments may want to have wiring closet training less frequently.

Wiring closets should also be on protected power, as described in Section 17.1.4, if possible. Desktops do not typically need protected power, other than surge protection, although a customer support center is often an exception to that rule. However, laptops that can run on battery power for significant lengths of time are increasingly common in the office, and occasional groups of people will have small UPS power supplies for their desks to keep working through an outage. These people should not experience a network outage because their workstation or laptop is better equipped to survive a power outage than is the network infrastructure.

IDF closets also should have special cooling beyond what the building air-conditioning can supply. Network equipment is compact, so you will have lots of heat-generating devices packed into a small area. Network devices are typically robust, but they do have operating limits. A small IDF closet can get very hot without extra cooling.

You should also provide remote console access to all the devices located in the IDFs that support that functionality. The console ports on all devices should be appropriately protected using strong authentication, if available, or passwords at a minimum.

Wiring to the Desktop

It is less expensive to install jacks at construction time rather than add them one at a time afterward as needed. Therefore it is reasonable to install one or two more jacks at every desk than you think any of your customers will ever need. Extra wiring to the closet is very expensive and disruptive to add later. Rather than trying to determine, for example, that engineering offices will have more jacks than marketing offices, install the same number of jacks at every desk and have the same amount in the ceiling. Initial location assignments are never permanent. Over time, engineers will end up in what used to be the marketing area, and you will need to bring the cable plant in that area up to the standard of the rest of the engineering locations. The same is true when running fiber to the desktop. Fiber cable is cheap compared with the cost of terminating the fiber itself. Some sites run fiber to the desk but only terminate what they actually plan on using (plus another 5 to 10 percent in case of failures). Later, if more desktops require fiber connections, the termination cost is less than the cost and disruption of new fiber runs to the IDFs. The cost of running extra fiber that may not be used is minimal in comparison.

When the desktop wiring is installed initially, ensure that the installers test every network jack and provide you with test data to prove it. All wiring contractors in our experience promise this book of test data, but only a few deliver it. Go to sites that they have previously wired, look at the work, and ask to see their test book before you decide which contractor you will choose. Often the contractor who is the most expensive will be the only one to pass this test. Building wiring is expensive, and it is not a place for cost savings because the expense of fixing it later, or trying to debug network problems that turn out to be caused by the building wiring, is even more expensive. It is not uncommon to find faults, particularly with the second or third jacks at a desk, years after the wiring contractor has left, and realize that the network jack could never have worked or passed a test.

Case Study: *The Value of Cable Test Printouts*

A CAD company in Oregon maintained a catalog of the cable tests performed on every jack in their campus. When inconsistent or difficult to reproduce problems were reported with a particular jack, they found that a quick review of the jack's test results would usually reveal that it had only marginally passed the quality tests. The debugging process would be short-circuited by trying a different jack and labeling the old jack as "do not use." The connections for the bad jack would be scheduled for retermination. The added cost of having the full notebook of test results delivered by the installers easily paid for itself.

Another thing to consider about installing network jacks is their orientation. Jacks are installed in some kind of termination box or face-plate, which determines which way the jacks face. If the face-plate is flush, a cable that plugs into it will stick out from the wall, requiring space to make sure that the cable is not bent or crimped. Make sure that space is available. Termination boxes tend to be mounted on the wall and therefore stick out. If the jacks are on the side of the box they can face up, down, left, or right. (We don't wish to ruffle feathers by taking sides in the contentious debate over which is best. Wars have been waged on this issue, and archeologists now believe that the Roman Empire fell because they weren't able to agree on this point.[7]) Jacks that face upward become buckets that catch dust and construction particles. That's bad. If they face down, it can be difficult for people to see how to insert cables into them and loose connections will fall out. That's not good either. Therefore we recommend having the jacks on the left or right of the termination box.

18.1.5 Main Distribution Frame

The main distribution frame, or MDF, is what connects the IDFs together and to the data center(s). There should always be plenty of cabling between the MDF and the IDFs. It is not uncommon for part of the data center to

---

[7]We're exaggerating here. In fact, Rome didn't use RJ48 jacks at all. They used a predecessor to 802.11 wireless networks and therefore didn't need to be concerned with many of these cabling issues.

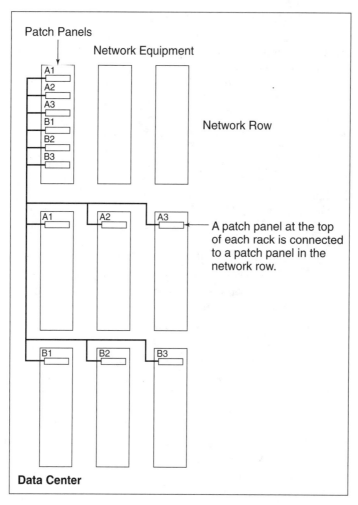

Figure 18.7: A patch panel in each data center rack connects back
to a patch panel in the MDF or network row

be the MDF. In a data center, the MDF is often referred to as the *network row* or *network racks*. Patch panels in these racks connect to a patch panel at the top of each rack in the data center, as shown in Figure 18.7. Data center layout is described in detail in Chapter 17.

The MDF must have protected power because it connects all the server networks that are on protected power to each other; it often connects the Internet, WANs, and remote access customers to the data centers; and it connects the IDFs to each other and everything else. It also needs adequate cooling.

Typically, there is a single MDF per campus. A large campus, or one that is particularly concerned about redundancy, may have more than one, with high bandwidth between them and redundant links to each of the IDFs and to wide-area, remote access, or Internet connections.

An MDF should have the same level of restricted access as the data center. It is the central core of the network. Only the network administration team should need access to it.

18.1.6 Demarcation Points

A demarcation point is the boundary between your organization and a utility company, such as a telephone company or network provider. It can be a fiber cabinet, a set of punch down blocks, a board in a rack, a piece of network hardware or a small plastic box[8] on the wall with a jack or socket for plugging in a cable. The telephone company is only responsible for the wiring up to its demarcation point (demarc). If you have a fault with a line, you need to be able to show the service engineer where the correct demarc is so that he doesn't end up trying to test and fix another operational line. You also need to be able to test your cabling from the demarc all the way back to the network equipment. The main thing to know about your demarcation points is where they are. Make sure they are properly labeled.

18.1.7 Documentation

Network documentation takes on many forms, the most fundamental of which is labeling. The need for documentation and the forms it should take are not likely to change with time.

Maps of both the physical and logical networks should be part of the network documentation. The physical network map should show where the wires go and the end points or ranges of wireless links. If redundancy was part of the physical network design, it should clearly indicate and document the physically diverse paths. The amount and type of connectivity available for each link should be indicated. For example, if there are 200 pairs of copper wires and 20 pairs of fiberoptic cables between a pair of buildings, the documentation should specify how both sets are rated and terminated and the distances between the termination points.

The logical network map should show the logical network topology, with network numbers, names, and speeds. It should also show routing protocols and administrative domains if those vary across the network. Both the physical and logical network maps should reach to the perimeter of the organization's network and identify its outer boundaries.

---

[8]Often termed a "brick" or a "biscuit."

Labeling is the single most important component of the network documentation. Clear, consistent labeling on patch panels and long-distance connections is particularly important. A patch panel should clearly indicate the physical location of the corresponding patch panel or jacks, and each of the connections on the patch panel should be clearly and consistently labeled at both ends. Long-distance connections should clearly indicate where the circuit goes, who to report problems to, and what information will be required when reporting a problem, such as the circuit ID and where it terminates. Placing this label immediately beside the unit's fault indicator light can be helpful. Doing so eliminates the need to trace cables to find the necessary information when a fault occurs. For example, one might otherwise have to trace cables from a channel service unit/data service unit (CSU/DSU) to the punch down block at the telephone company's demarcation point or to a jack on the wall.

Less-permanent connections, such as the network connection for each host on the network, also should be labeled. Labeling on each wire is easier to maintain in a relatively static environment and harder to maintain in a highly dynamic one. You should only attempt to do this level of labeling if you can maintain it. Incorrect labels are worse than none at all.

A compromise between no labels and full cable labeling is to purchase cables with a unique serial number shown at each end. With a serial number, you can quite quickly trace exactly where a cable goes if you have an approximate idea of the location of the other end. The serial number label can also indicate length and the way that the cable is wired. For example the first two digits can indicate straight-through, cross-over, twisted-pair, FDDI, or other wiring arrangements. That can be followed by a dash and three digits indicating the cable length and then another dash and the serial number. Colored covers on the connectors can also be used to indicate cable type.

Network cables are often difficult to label. One of the most effective ways we have seen is to use a cable tie with a protruding flat tab, to which standard sticky labels can be affixed. It is securely attached and can be easily altered.

The other key location for documentation is online, as part of the configuration of the network devices themselves. Wherever possible, comment fields and device names should be used to provide documentation for the network administrators. Naming standards for devices can go a long way toward making network administration easier and more intuitive.

Case Study: Naming Conventions

A midsize multinational software company used a multistar topology for its wide area connectivity. One of the star centers was in Mountain View, California. The router at each remote site that connected to Mountain View was called "*location*2mtview," for example "denver2mtview" or "atlanta2mtview." The router at the Mountain View end of the connection was called "*location*-router," for example "denver-router" or "atlanta-router," in addition to any other names that it might have. When a remote site suffered connectivity problems, everyone could immediately identify which routers served that site without resorting to network maps or tracing cables. This standardization vastly improved the level of support that remote sites could expect from the average SA. All those capable of performing basic network debugging were given read-only access to the network equipment and were able to perform basic diagnostics before handing the problem to the network team.

Routers usually permit a text comment to be recorded with each interface. For WAN connections, this comment should include all the information a technician would need in an emergency involving the link going down. This includes the name of the vendor providing the link, their phone number, the circuit identifier, and the maintenance contract number that the vendor needs to provide service. For LAN connections, include the name of the subnet and the contact information for the owner of the subnet, if it is not the main SA team.

18.1.8 Simple Host Routing

We highly recommend that routing within a site be simple, deterministic, predictable, and easy to understand and diagnose. Use simple routing techniques on hosts. Making routing or hosts simple makes it possible to have the same configuration on all host devices and know that they will all behave in the same deterministic way. Redundancy for such hosts should be taken care of by the network devices and should be transparent to the hosts.

If a host is single-homed,[9] it should have a single default route. It should not listen to any dynamic routing information. If a host is multi-homed, it should not route packets from other hosts. It should only accept traffic addressed to it. It should have a static routing table and not listen to dynamic routing information. It should be configured as simply as possible. If a multi-homed host is connected to networks A, B, and C, and it needs to communicate with another host on network B, it should use its network interface that is connected to network B to communicate with that host. This path is the simplest, most obvious, and most direct. In the absence of compelling reasons to do otherwise, all traffic to networks that are not directly connected to the multi-homed host (that is, to hosts that are not on

---

[9] A single-homed host is one with a single network interface that has an IP address on a single network or subnet.

networks A, B, or C) should be directed to a single static default router. This is the simplest routing configuration for a multi-homed host. Occasionally, it may be necessary to have some additional static routes on the multi-homed host to direct traffic along preferred paths. For example, the multi-homed host may be configured to send traffic for network D via a router on network C and to send traffic for networks other than A, B, C, or D via a router on network A. However, it is best to avoid even this much complexity if possible.

Simple host routing makes debugging network problems easier and more predictable. When every host on a network is configured the same way, they should all behave the same way. When hosts listen to dynamic routing, the unexpected can happen. Worse yet, when hosts actively participate in dynamic routing, an environment can become completely unpredictable. If possible, enforce the policy that hosts cannot participate in your dynamic routing infrastructure by using any security or authentication mechanisms that the protocol provides.

Case Study: Complex Host Routing Causes Problems

A large, multinational computer manufacturer ran routing software on all the desktops and servers in the company at a time when basic routing protocols were still under development. Whenever any device on the network sent out incorrect or rogue information, every machine was affected. They also had persistent problems with incompatibilities between their implementation and a network device vendor's implementation of some protocols. If the hosts on the network had used simple, static host routing, these problems would not have arisen.

There is also a performance problem with requiring hosts to perform routing. As the number of routes in a network grows, the routing protocol updates become more difficult to process. We have seen large networks where every host paused every 300 seconds as Routing Information Protocol (RIP) broadcasts are sent out and simultaneously processed by all hosts on a LAN. If a subnet contains exactly one router, there is no need for it to broadcast the routing protocol to that subnet (that is, it can use "passive mode"). In fact, if the routing protocol uses broadcasts, also known as *advertising*, there can be a noticeable performance issue even if the hosts are not configured to speak any routing protocols. Not only do the broadcasts consume network bandwidth, but every host on a subnet stops to process the broadcasts even if the "processing" is to simply throw the packet away.

18.1.9   Use Network Devices

The building blocks of any modern network should be dedicated network devices, such as routers and switches, rather than general-purpose hosts that have been configured to do routing. These network devices should be designed to perform only tasks directly related to pushing packets, managing the traffic and the device itself. They should not be "all-purpose" devices that are configured to handle just network traffic, and they should most definitely not be devices that are also trying to perform other tasks or to provide additional services. Network devices are optimized to move packets as quickly as possible, they integrate better into network management tools, they provide better monitoring facilities, and they are simpler devices, which means they are less prone to failure and have fewer moving parts. The one common exception to this rule is firewalls because they are often more involved in the application layer than a highly tuned network device can be. However, a firewall should still be treated as a single-purpose device, and under no circumstances should anything other than the firewall software be installed or run on it, nor should it be used for any purpose other than acting as a firewall.

Case Study: *Central Host*

One computer hardware manufacturer[10] had a network built around a single multi-homed host that primarily routed traffic. However, because it was a multipurpose machine and it was conveniently multi-homed on all key networks, other services were added to it over time. Sometimes these other services would have problems or become over-loaded, resulting in loss of network connectivity or serious network performance problems.

When the time came to replace that machine with a different dedicated machine, the work was considerably more difficult than it should have been. The new hardware only routed packets. It was not a multipurpose machine. All the other services that ran on the old central machine had to be tracked down and rearchitected for an environment where they would not be running on a single machine that touched every network.

Even as the UNIX workstation community seems to have finally moved away from using workstations and servers as routers, we see a disturbing trend in the Windows and Novell environments as they use general-purpose machines as routers, firewalls, or RAS devices. Although sometimes this is

---

[10]A manufacturer who, ironically, designed and built boxes dedicated to providing a single service well across the network.

done for economic reasons, we feel that this trend will reverse itself yet again in the future as they learn this lesson for themselves.

18.1.10   Overlay Networks

An overlay network is a logical topology that rides on top of a physical topology. Examples include VLAN (virtual LAN), Frame Relay, and ATM. This lets us design simple physical architectures that can support whatever complexity we require in the logical overlay, yet maintain simplicity on the physical layer.

You can build a very simple (and therefore stable), flat physical network and then construct overlay networks on top of the solid base to give the appearance of the more complicated connections that are needed.

On the WAN level, this could mean that all sites have a single connection to the ATM or Frame-Relay cloud. The Frame-Relay or ATM switches are then configured to provide virtual connections (circuits) between sites. For example, each remote office might have a virtual circuit to the main office. If any two remote sites exchange a lot of traffic, it is then a simple matter of changing the switch configurations so that a virtual circuit is added between those two sites. The shared connection to the main site is then not burdened with that traffic passing through it, and the company did not have to go to the delay and expense of having a new physical circuit installed. Another wide area example is the use of encrypted tunnels (virtual private networks, or VPNs) across the Internet. A company can just give each site a firewall, a VPN device, and an Internet connection and build its WAN over the Internet. An ISP can also use this approach to build and maintain one solid infrastructure that is literally sold time and time again to different customers.

On the LAN level, an overlay network usually means creating a simple, flat physical topology and using IEEE 802.1q VLAN protocols to overlay the subnetworks that are needed by the customers. For example, each IDF can connect to the MDF using high-speed redundant links all mediated at layer 2 (Ethernet link layer) using the spanning tree protocol.

Case Study: Large LAN Using VLANs

The largest single-building LAN that Tom ever experienced included nearly 100 IDFs and supported 4,000 people spread out all over the building. All IDFs were connected exclusively to a single MDF. This simplicity meant that to connect two IDFs the connection would pass through the MDF. Although this sounds wasteful when the IDFs were sometimes only one floor away, it is much better than the nightmare that would exist if they chose to create direct connections between all IDFs. One aspect was, however, painful to maintain. Some customers needed their subnetworks to appear in a single IDF or a couple of IDFs, whereas others needed theirs to appear in nearly every IDF. Every subnetwork was individually tied back to the MDF as needed. For example, if a jack was requested in a wing served by an IDF that didn't already include the necessary subnetwork, fiber would be allocated between that IDF and the MDF, a hub in that IDF would be allocated, and the new hub would be connected to that subnet's hub in the MDF. This made the first request for a subnet in any part of the building take a long time. As the network grew to include hundreds of subnetworks, it became a nightmare to maintain. It was difficult just to track which subnets appeared in which IDFs, and it required huge amounts of manual labor nearly every time a new jack was activated.

The replacement for this network maintained the same physical plant but replaced the individual fibers with overlays on a large flat network. A large Fast Ethernet switch was installed in each IDF. Each switch was connected to larger switches in the MDF. These connections were redundant Gigabit Ethernet connections. Although this was a huge flat network from a layer 1 perspective, VLANs were overlaid onto it at layer 2. Then, network change requests involved configuration changes on the switches, which were done without a walk to the closet. To bring a particular subnet to an IDF, an SA did not have to allocate and connect fiber pairs; instead he configured the appropriate VLAN to extend into that IDF and configured the switch in the IDF to provide that VLAN to the appropriate port. The result was a greatly reduced cost of maintenance and quicker response to requests for change.

This design is future-proofed. The links to the MDF can be replaced by faster technology (as long as future technologies work on the type of fiber that was installed and support VLANs). If new technology brings back ring topologies, the ring could follow the star-shaped pattern of the IDFs and the switches become nodes on the ring.

18.1.11 Number of Vendors

Using equipment from many vendors can add unnecessary complexity to managing the network. The more vendors whose equipment is on the network, the more interoperability problems you are likely to experience. In addition, there is extra overhead for the network administration staff in learning the configurations and quirks of the diverse equipment and in tracking software upgrades and bugs. Minimizing the number of vendors makes the network more reliable and easier to maintain. It also gets the company bigger discounts on the equipment thanks to larger volume purchasing.

However, exclusive use of a single vendor has its own problems. A single vendor cannot possibly make the best product in every area. Exclusive use of a single vendor also leaves your protocol interoperability untested, which can lead to a surprise the first time a new vendor is introduced.

Somewhere between the extremes is a reasonable balance. Some sites find choosing a single vendor for each protocol layer or each tier of the network works well. For example, one might consistently use a particular router vendor, a different vendor for the core LAN switches, and yet another vendor for offices that require hubs.

18.1.12   Standards-Based Protocols

An organization's network should be built using standards-based protocols. This is not a rule that changes over time. It is a constant. Vendor-proprietary protocols lock you into a single vendor by making it difficult to integrate equipment from competing vendors. Being locked into a single vendor makes it difficult to negotiate for better prices and prevents you from adopting another company's products to take advantage of their improvements. It also leaves you vulnerable to that vendor's business problems.

If you require features that are only provided by vendor-proprietary protocols, you should pressure the vendor to open the standard. Ideally, the standards should also be well established, rather than new, so that all hardware is likely to be fully compliant with the standard. Using established IETF standards means that any hardware or software that you choose should comply with that standard. Established IETF standards are stable and do not suffer from interoperability problems between different versions. When a vendor brags about a new feature, it can be useful to ask which IETF Request for Comments (RFC) number or IEEE document defines the standard. If the new feature is not standards-based, the vendor should be questioned on how this equipment will interoperate with your other devices.

18.1.13   Monitoring

To build a fast, reliable network you need network monitoring. It is also the best way to scale the network in advance of growing demand and to maintain its reliability. You don't know how your network is performing or how reliable it is until you monitor it. There are two primary types of network monitoring. One is real-time availability monitoring and alerting. The other is gathering data to do trend analysis to predict future demand or for usage-based billing purposes. For companies that are providing a service across the Internet, whether they be ISPs, application service providers, or e-commerce sites, both types of monitoring are an essential part of running the business. Within a corporate environment, they are good things to implement but usually are not business critical.

Real-time monitoring of the network should be incorporated into any existing trouble ticket and alerting system used at your site. At a minimum, it should be able to alert you to network interface state transitions. In other words, it should tell you when a network interface goes down and preferably when it comes back up again. Ideally, it should also inform you of routing problems, though exactly what form that monitoring takes is completely dependent on the routing protocol. You also can consider alerts based on unusual conditions, such as sudden, unexpected spikes or drops in traffic that may indicate a problem.

The most common and important use of historical data collection is to predict future needs. For most sites, it is sufficient to simply monitor all network interfaces that are of interest to see how much traffic is going over them and perform trend analysis to predict when more bandwidth will be required. Other sites, particularly those in the Internet services industry, will want to gather data on the traffic flow within their network to determine whom they should establish direct connections to, what size they should be, and where those connections should be made geographically to optimize the traffic on the network. Gathering historical data on faults, errors, and outages can also prove useful and informative. It can show when problems start or deteriorate. Analysis of the historical data can also be used to detect behavioral anomalies that can indicate problems (Brutlag 2000). Or it may be useful in building availability statistics for management or customers. Monitoring is discussed in detail in Chapter 24.

18.1.14 Single Administrative Domain

Properly designing networks, maintaining them, and debugging problems across multiple organizations are always difficult. A network should be a single organism that moves traffic around in a coherent, coordinated fashion. It should be governed by a single set of policies and practices that are implemented consistently across the entire network. The more independent groups there are directing the movement of the traffic, the more likely the network is to become incoherent and uncoordinated. Having a single administrative domain means having a single, closely tied network administration team with a single management structure. When parts of the network team are managed by management structures that meet only at the CEO level, different parts of the company inevitably go in different directions following their own sets of policies and practices.

Case Study: Lack of a Single Administrative Group Causes Problems

A large, multinational computer manufacturing company had different groups of people responsible for different parts of the network. The groups reported through different management structures. A closely tied group was responsible for the WANs and a loosely tied group was responsible for LANs at each site. The different groups could not agree on a single routing protocol to use across the company. In part, the disagreement was related to the different management chains. Some of the site-specific networking groups reported through the engineering organization, which wanted the desktops[11] to participate in the routing. That desire severely limited the available network protocols, none of which were suitable for the other requirements that the wide area group had to meet. Ultimately, both groups used different routing protocols and identified some redundant locations for exchanging routing information. However, because of the lack of cooperation between the groups, they could never quite get the configuration right and ended up with routing loops if both of the redundant hand-off points were connected at once. A single, coherent network administration group would not have had this problem.

There are security issues associated with not having a single administrative domain. When different groups have control over different parts of the network, they probably will also have different policies with respect to connecting other networks to their piece of network and the security that should surround those connections. This results in an unknown level of security for the network because it is a single entity and only as secure as the weakest link.

Having a single administrative domain does not exclude the possibility of having regional or divisional network teams that all report to the same management structure and are all governed by the same set of policies and practices. The network will still act as a single organism if multiple teams work closely together in a coordinated fashion.

However, sometimes it is not possible to have a single administrative domain for the network. We briefly discuss how to make multiple administrative domains work well in Section 18.2.2.

18.2   The Icing

There are a few additional things beyond the basic tasks that are involved in building a network you can do to further improve your network. You must strike a balance between the risk of using cutting-edge, "hot" technologies

---

[11] All of which used the company's hardware and software.

and staying with older but more reliable equipment and technologies. Finally, if you find yourself in a situation that requires multiple administrative domains, we discuss ways to mitigate the problems that occur.

18.2.1 Leading-Edge Versus Reliability

Typically, the most important quality people seek in their networks is reliability. Older products that have gone through many firmware and hardware revisions tend to be more reliable. The bugs have been shaken out. On the other hand, newer features and faster connectivity are often only available in new products, which may not have been field tested. You must find a balance.

There are different ways to manage this risk. You might perform your own certification of new products in a lab before they are put into production situations and then only slowly deploy them to establish confidence before beginning a major installation.

You might have separate customer groups that differ in the amount of risk they are willing to accept. Some may be willing to accept slightly lower reliability in exchange for having access to newer features. Even then, such equipment should be tested in the lab first. People who want cutting edge performance still want reliability.

Sometimes, the customer groups that are willing to take the risks are in a different SA team's domain of control. They may have customer groups with business requirements that mean they must use some of the new technologies when they become available. Let them suffer through the teething problems, if you can, and take advantage of your chance to let others work out the bugs for you.

If you use leading-edge gear, make sure that each person who is going to be affected by its early problems knows that he is likely to suffer outages because the technology is so new. If you don't do that in advance, your customers will be unhappy and the reputation of your network as a whole will be adversely affected. If a high-level manager approves the risk, make sure the end-users and their direct managers are aware of this decision so that outages are not blamed on you.

18.2.2 Multiple Administrative Domains

For political, practical, or security reasons, it is sometimes impossible to have a single administrative domain. If different organizations manage different parts of the network and are not governed by the same set of policies or managed by the same management chain, the network needs a different model. The various pieces of the network should have explicit borders between them, making use of border routing protocols (for example, BGP) and security mechanisms (such as firewalls) to provide routing stability and known levels of security in each of the administrative domains, independent of the others.

If you must have multiple administrative domains, you should do it the right way. The choices and actions of one network administration team should be completely independent of what the other teams are doing and unable to affect the operations or reliability of other networks.

18.3   Conclusion

In this chapter, we looked at the various aspects of designing and building a network. Because network technology changes rapidly, some of these areas change significantly over time. But there are other components of building a network that are constants. In this chapter, we discussed ways that technology has changed networks, as well as the areas that always need to be considered.

Constants in Networking

- Have a clean architecture
- Build for reliability
- Have good labeling and documentation
- Build IDFs and MDFs to the highest standards of wiring available
- Provide protected power and cooling to the IDFs and MDF
- Have a consistent IDF layout across floors and buildings
- Know your demarcation points
- Have a single administrative domain where possible, and a clean separation of responsibilities where it is not
- Use open Internet (IETF and IEEE) standard protocols
- Use simple host routing
- Only use dedicated network hardware to push packets
- Use a minimal number of vendors' hardware
- Avoid leading-edge gear whenever possible

Things That Change in Network Design

- The type of intrabuilding and interbuilding wiring required
- The physical and logical network topologies
- The network devices and protocols
- Wide-area connectivity options
- Internet connectivity architectures
- Strategies for redundancy
- Monitoring technologies

So, although many of the key pieces that determine exactly how you are going to build your network constantly change, there are some solid building blocks you can use as foundations for your network that will make it easier to achieve a reliable network and to move with the times.

Exercises

1. Draw a physical network map for your organization.

2. Draw a logical network map for your organization.

3. How do hosts route packets in your environment? Where is there redundancy in the network? If there isn't any, how would you implement it?

4. If your organization was just moving into the campus that you now occupy, and you had the opportunity to lay out the IDFs and MDF, how would you do it? How is this different from the current situation?

5. Where are your demarcation points? How are they documented and labeled?

6. What protocols do you use on your network and what are the corresponding RFC numbers for those protocols? Are any of them proprietary protocols? If so, how could you avoid using those protocols?

7. What vendors' equipment do you use in your network? How could you reduce the number of vendors that you use? What would be the advantages and disadvantages of doing so?

8. What policy, informal or otherwise, does your organization have for using leading-edge hardware? How do you limit the impact of reliability problems with that hardware?

9. If your organization had multiple administrative domains, as described in the anecdote in Section 18.1.14, how would you implement the approach suggested in Section 18.2.2?

10. What do you monitor on your network? What would you like to monitor and how would you go about it?

Chapter 19

Email Service

Email is a service that companies rely on to conduct business. Everyone expects email to just work, and outages are unacceptable. Nearly 45 percent of business-critical information is housed in email message storage (Osterman 2000). For many companies, it is one of the primary ways for existing and potential customers to contact the sales and support staff. Reliability should be the focal point of building an email service. It also needs to scale well.

The guiding principles of simplicity, clarity, generality, automation, communication, and basics first are all key to successfully building a reliable email service. The email system interacts with other parts of a company's infrastructure. It is dependent on namespaces, which are described in Chapter 6. It is a service that must be monitored by the monitoring system discussed in Chapter 24. And it has implications for both the security architecture (Chapter 7) and the backups service (Chapter 21).

19.1 The Basics

A reliable, scalable email service must be built on strong foundations. An SA who is designing and building an email service must put the basics first, before trying to add features or scale the service to deal with high traffic volumes.

A simple, clear, well-documented architecture for the email system is fundamental to building a reliable service. It also is important to use open protocols and standards throughout the email system to ensure maximum interoperability with other sites and other applications within the site. In particular, one key piece of infrastructure that the email system needs to interact with is the namespace management system that implements the organizational structure of the corporate namespaces that relate to email. Remember from Chapter 3 that nothing can be called a service until it is monitored.

Finally, because email is a method of communicating with the rest of the world, some parts of the service will always be a target for potential attackers. Security must therefore be considered during the design and implementation of the email system.

19.1.1　Privacy Policy

Every site must have an email privacy policy that is communicated to and acknowledged by every employee. The privacy policy must explain under what circumstances a person's email may be read and by whom. It must also explain that email may be inadvertently seen by administrative staff during the course of their work, usually when performing diagnostics. It should also state that email that crosses over other networks such as the Internet cannot be considered private and that company-confidential information should not be emailed to an address on or across another entity's network unless it is encrypted.

At many companies email that arrives on or crosses over corporate servers is not considered private. Others state that corporate machines should not be used for personal communication, which typically amounts to the same thing. Some automatically monitor incoming and outgoing mail for certain key words. Others state that people using the corporate email system have a reasonable expectation of privacy and outline the circumstances when an expectation of privacy may no longer hold.

Whatever the policy decided by the upper management of the company, the SAs must implement it. The SA management team should ensure that everybody who uses the company's email service is aware of the policy and has acknowledged it.

19.1.2　Namespaces

Namespaces are discussed in detail in Chapter 6. Email addresses at a site form the namespace that is the most visible to the company's customers and business partners. It is also one of the most visible to the people within the company, and it is critical to get it right.

The most fundamental part of getting the email namespace right is to use the same email addresses for internal and external email. If one address is used for internal mail and a different one for mail coming from outside the company, people will inevitably give the wrong email address to customers and business partners, which can lead to lost business. Don't expect people to remember that they have two email addresses and which one they should give to whom. It is far simpler for all concerned, including the SAs debugging problems, if everyone just has one email address for both internal and external email.

Standardizing email addresses by using a `first.last`-style email address such as `John.Smith@foo.com` is popular, particularly with management. However, we generally discourage `first.last`-style email addresses. There is just too much of a chance that your company will employ two people with the same name, or even same first, last, and middle initial. When your second John Smith is hired, "John.Smith" becomes "John.A.Smith" to avoid being confused with the new hire, "John.Z.Smith." At that point, the first person's business cards become invalid. Business cards, once distributed, are difficult to update. Some email systems deal with ambiguous `first.last`-style addresses by generating an automatic reply that tries to help the sender figure out which "John Smith" he was trying to reach, possibly listing the first ten matches in the corporate directory. Although this sounds nice, it is not a perfect solution. The replies are only useful if a human receives them. If the person was on any email mailing lists, those messages will now bounce.

Eric Allman, author of Sendmail (1985), explains why this kind of formatting is problematic in this quote from Sendmail's `cf/README` file (Shapiro and Allman 1999):

> As a general rule, I am adamantly opposed to using full names as email addresses, since they are not in any sense unique. For example, the UNIX software-development community has two Andy Tannenbaums, at least two well-known Peter Deutsches, and at one time Bell Labs had two Stephen R. Bournes with offices along the same hallway. Which one will be forced to suffer the indignity of being Stephen.R.Bourne.2? The less famous of the two, or the one that was hired later?

Instead, we prefer making a namespace that is unique corporation-wide using name tokens such as `chogan`, `tal`, `jsmith`, and so on. A directory service can be provided to help people look up the email address of the person they want to contact. Customers should be able to select their own token, though an initial default should be preselected based on an algorithm that combines initials and first or last names. It should be relatively difficult to change once it has been set to discourage people from making gratuitous changes. Tokens should not be reused for a couple of months to prevent someone from hijacking the token of a recently removed employee to see what residual email he receives.

19.1.3   Reliability

Email is a utility service. People expect to be able to send and receive email at all times, just like they expect to always have a dial tone when they lift the phone and power when they turn on a light. As with other utilities, they don't realize how much they rely on it until it is no longer working.

A failure of the email system is a very stressful event. It results in lots of support calls over a short period. It will inevitably occur when someone has to urgently send important documents, because that is happening all the time, unseen by the SAs. Because the email system is so critical, failures will be emotional times for both the SAs and the customers. The email service is not a service with which SAs should experiment. New systems and architectures should be deployed into the email service only after extensive testing.

More important, there are costs associated with a malfunctioning email system. Missed email can cause business panic. Contractual obligations are missed, customers turn to other vendors, and time is lost as people revert to older, slower forms of communication.

Case Study: Don't Use the Email Service for a Beta Test

A major technology company was promoting the concept of centrally located server farms for business applications such as email. As a proof of concept, they quickly moved 100,000 email users to a server farm. The network connections into the server farm were overloaded to the point of being unusable. As a result, the entire company was unable to communicate for nearly a month until more network capacity was added. Not one to learn from mistakes, the company then decided to use this server farm to demonstrate a new release of their email software. This may have been the single largest beta test ever attempted. It was also a disaster. Eventually the company learned to not take such risks with such a critical application. It was, however, too late. By this time, many organizations had created rogue email servers for their local members, making the situation worse. Your corporate email system is just too critical to use as a playground or experimenter's lab.

The national power grids and telephone networks of all developed countries are highly redundant systems. They are designed and built with reliability in mind. The design of an email system should have a similar focus on reliability, though on a smaller scale.

Start with a clear, simple design. Select hardware and software for their reliability and interoperability, rather than their full-featuredness. Complex software with lots of additional features is typically less reliable. See Chapter 2 for details on how to build a reliable server.

Having hot spares for all of the email machines is ideal. Many companies cannot justify that expense, however. If you do not have the luxury of hot spares, have a plan that you can execute rapidly to restore service if anything fails.

19.1.4 Simplicity

The email system should be simple. Complexity decreases reliability and makes the system harder to support. Limit the number of machines involved in the email service. That limits the number of machines that have to be reliable and the number of places SAs must look to debug a problem. Above all, do not involve desktop machines in the mail delivery process. Desktops should be limited to having an email client.[1] For more information about how and why desktops are different from servers, refer to Section 2.1.3, and for how they are networked differently, refer to Section 3.1.7.

There are three main aspects to an email service: mail transport, mail delivery, and list processing. Mail transport is how email gets from place to place; mail delivery occurs when email reaches its destination; mailing list processing is how one message gets delivered to a group of people on a list.

For small sites, a simple architecture typically means having all three functions provided by the same machine, possibly with an additional Internet-facing mail relay system being the interface between the company and the rest of the world. For larger sites, simplicity often involves separating the three functions out onto different systems or groups of systems. Several dedicated mail relays will deliver mail to either the list processing machines or the delivery machines. The list processing machines also use mail relays to deliver messages to the individual recipients on each list.

At a large site, there may be many types of mail machines. It is best to avoid having too many. Avoid delivering mail to people's desktops and make sure their mail clients are configured to send email by contacting a mail relay rather than routing mail themselves. Desktops should not even listen on the SMTP port. Servers that are not part of the email service should be configured the same way as the desktops. Doing so means that the SAs always know where all the mail for a particular account is being

---

[1] An email client is also referred to as a *mail user agent* (MUA). This is separate from the *mail transport agent* (MTA), which carries email from one server to another.

delivered. A configuration that can lead to email being delivered in several possible places for a single account inevitably leads to confusion and "lost" mail.[2]

Case Study: Bad Mail Delivery Scheme

A computer manufacturer had a mail scheme that permitted email delivery on any machine on which the recipient had an account. Their scheme also exposed the full hostname of the machine from which the person sent the email. Whenever someone replied to one of these emails, the reply would be addressed to the person at the machine from which the mail was sent, so it would be delivered there, rather than to the person's primary email box. This meant that when someone sent an email from a machine that he did not normally use, the reply went to that machine and was "lost." The helpdesk frequently received complaints about lost email, but because their email system was so unstructured, they had a hard time finding out what had happened.

They should have implemented an email system that passed all mail to a central relay that rewrote the senders email address so that it did not contain the name of the machine that it came from (known has "hostname masquerading"). That way, all replies would automatically go through the central mail relay, which would direct email to each person's primary email box.

Simplicity also means avoiding gateways and other email translation devices. Use the same standards throughout the network and for communication with other sites. Gateways translate email between two or more different formats, often between a proprietary (or nonstandard format or protocol) and a standard one. They add complexity and are typically the source of endless problems at sites that use them. They also typically strip off delivery history information because it is in a different format, and this makes it harder to trace problems. Anecdotes that should sway you against gateways are in Section 3.1.3.

Simplicity also means using a single mechanism for implementing and managing email lists. There are many different ways of doing it, and sites that have been around for a few years are typically using more than one. This makes it harder to maintain the lists and much harder to implement automated list maintenance and pruning mechanisms. Forcing customers to learn multiple different email procedures and expecting them to remember which to use for each mailing list is unacceptable.

---

[2]The mail is lost in the sense that the intended recipient is unaware of it and doesn't see it because it has arrived in an unexpected place, and it doesn't bounce back to the sender because it was successfully delivered, albeit to the wrong recipient.

19.1.5   Generality

One of the fundamental reasons for the existence of an email system is to open communication paths within and outside the company. To successfully communicate with the maximum number of people, the email system should be built around open protocols that are universally accepted and implemented.

For mail transport, this means using an SMTP-based protocol. Because mail transport involves communicating with many other sites, the well-established Internet-standard SMTP protocol will continue to be supported for a long time to come. It is extremely pervasive on the Internet. It is more likely that a new email protocol would be an extension of SMTP rather than a completely new and incompatible protocol. All sites must support SMTP as a transport protocol, and, for simplicity and generality, it should be the only transport protocol that a site uses.

Generality is also about communications within the company and mail user agents. It applies to the methods that are available for people to read their email. The number of protocols in this area is a little larger and changes more easily with time because it is usually easy to add support for an additional email client/server protocol without affecting the existing ones. Most sites support one or two of the most popular email client protocols, thereby supporting almost all mail readers. A site can trivially support lots of mail clients on lots of different OSs if the mail delivery and relay systems use Internet-standard protocols. Supporting the maximum number of clients by supporting a small number of standard protocols means that people who have a strong preference for one client over another are able to use that client. Typically, email clients will also support multiple protocols, and it is not hard to find a protocol in common between the client and the mail delivery server. On the other hand, when a site uses a proprietary protocol, the customers will be locked into one or two clients from a single vendor that may not have the features they need or want.

Nonstandard Protocols Are Expensive

A small, successful Internet start-up company in Silicon Valley was bought by a large, well-established company based in Washington. The Internet start-up used standard protocols for its email service. The clients were primarily UNIX machines but also included a significant number of Macintoshes and a handful of Windows PCs. Its email system worked well and was accessible to everyone in the company. When the company was bought and integrated into the parent company, the employees of the start-up had to switch to the parent company's email service. It was based on Microsoft proprietary standards, rather than Internet standards.[3] No clients were available for the UNIX machines or the Macintoshes. The company had to buy a PC running Windows for each of the UNIX and Macintosh users (which was almost everyone), just so that they could continue to send and receive email. It was an outrageously expensive solution!

More philosophy and anecdotes on this subject can be found in Section 3.1.3.

19.1.6   Automation

As with everything that SAs do, automation can simplify common tasks and ensure that they are performed reliably and accurately. Many areas of email administration should be automated as part of the process of building the service or should be incorporated into existing email services.

In particular, setting up an email account should be automated as part of the account creation process. The automation should include putting the person onto any relevant email lists, such as company-wide and group-specific lists. Equally, removing the email account should be an automated part of account deletion. We have found that it is best not to provide email forwarding for people who have left the company, because sensitive information may be inadvertently sent to that person by someone who does not realize he has left. Implementing a "redirect" message that automatically replies with the new email address and a message stating that the person has left the company is often beneficial, however. Automating the process of moving an email account from one server to another can also be useful if that is a task that needs to be performed even occasionally. It is often a complicated process.

A departing employee should be removed from all internal mailing lists when he leaves. Periodic automatic checks of active email accounts against the personnel database should also be implemented, along with checks to ensure that email to local accounts is not forwarded outside the company and checks to ensure that disabled accounts are not on any internal mailing lists. A site can also automate examining sensitive internal mailing lists for unauthorized members.

Another useful form of email service automation is automating mailing list administration so that the lists can be created, deleted, and administered by the people who need them, rather than by the SAs. This provides a

---

[3]Microsoft Exchange now supports a large number of open protocols, such as POP and IMAP, so this issue would not arise with this choice of platform today.

better, more responsive service for the list owners and relieves the SAs of an annoying, trivial duty.

19.1.7 Basic Monitoring

Chapter 3 introduced the notion that a service isn't properly implemented until it is monitored. Email is no exception to that rule. There is a basic level of monitoring that must be performed on an email service. In particular, every machine that is part of the service should be monitored to ensure that it is up and on the network, which can be as simple as using the `ping` command, which sends Internet Control Message Protocol (ICMP) echo messages (Postel 1981) and waits for the responses. All email servers should also be monitored for disk space usage because a series of huge messages could put them out of service.

Email servers also should be monitored to ensure that they are responding to requests on the relevant IP ports. For example, all email servers running an SMTP server listen on the SMTP port, Transmission Control Protocol (TCP) port 25. Mail delivery hosts should also be responding to requests on the ports that are used by the supported email clients so that customers can read their email. These ports vary from protocol to protocol. All of the protocols that are supported should be monitored.

Email to the `postmaster` also must be monitored. The `postmaster` address at every site receives email messages showing mail delivery errors or bounces. By monitoring the email sent to this address, the person in charge of the email service will notice when failures occur and be able to address them. The bounces sent to `postmaster` contain all the headers from the failed email and the error message indicating why it failed. This information is vital for debugging email problems and often is not supplied when endusers report problems.

Finally, the logs on the email machines should be monitored to track the message flow rate, which can help with historical predictions, noticing when mail delivery has stopped for some reason, and debugging problems that can arise when the message flow rate increases unexpectedly.

These are the basics of monitoring an email system. Advanced monitoring techniques are covered later in this chapter, in Section 19.2.3. Chapter 24 is entirely about monitoring.

19.1.8 Redundancy

Because email service is central to the operation of all modern companies, sites should introduce redundancy into the email system as soon as they can afford to. Section 3.1.9 describes some general ways of building reliability into a service. This chapter concentrates on email-specific issues.

When there is no redundant hardware for the email systems, there must be a recovery plan in case of failure that can be implemented quickly. It is easy to introduce redundancy for mail relay hosts and list processing hosts using DNS Mail eXchanger (MX) records and multiple servers with the same configuration.

Redundancy of mail delivery hosts is different because entire hosts cannot easily be redundant for each other. Instead, you can make the server internally redundant with RAID and other techniques. You can replicate the host that accesses a shared message storage facility using Network Attached Storage (NAS) or Storage Area Network (SAN) technology (Katcher 1999). However, in that case, you must be extremely careful to ensure that proper locking and access control is performed.

The client access must be made redundant with transparent failover. To do so, you must understand how the client works. Clients typically cache the result of the initial DNS query that occurs when they try to contact the mail delivery server to download email, therefore simple DNS tricks will not suffice. Redundancy for the client must happen at the IP level. Several technologies are available for permitting a host to take over answering requests directed to a specific IP address when the original machine at that address dies. Two common techniques are the use of load-balancing (layer 4 or layer 7) switches (Black 1999) and using Virtual Router Redundancy Protocol (VRRP) (Knight et al. 1998).

Consider all components of the system and how they function when deciding on a redundancy strategy. Consider how the various mechanisms work, what impact they will have on the rest of your environment, and how other machines will interact with them as part of the decision-making process.

19.1.9   Scaling

All three aspects of the mail system need to scale in advance of demand. Mail transport systems must be prepared to deal with higher volumes of traffic; mail delivery systems must deal with more people picking up their email; and list processing systems must handle spikes in traffic and more list members. All three need to scale in advance of new technologies that significantly increase message sizes.

Mail transport systems need to scale to meet increased traffic levels. Three independent variables govern email traffic levels: The size of the messages, the number of messages per person, and the number of people using the email system. The more people that use the email service, the more email messages it will need to handle. The number of messages per person typically increases gradually over time with spikes around holidays. The size of the messages tends to increase in jumps with new technologies.

The email service also needs to scale to cope with large bursts of traffic that might be triggered by promotional events or significant, unexpected problems. Sudden increases in traffic volume through mail transport systems are not unheard of. The mail transport system should be designed to deal with unexpectedly high traffic peaks. Mail transport systems should also be prepared to store the large quantities of email that might accumulate if there are problems passing the messages downstream.

Mail delivery systems need to scale predictably as the number of people who are served by the delivery system increases. The mail delivery server will have to scale with time even if there is no increase in the number of people that it serves because of increases in the number and size of messages that people receive. If customers store their email on the delivery server for a long time after they have read it, the delivery server will also have to scale to meet that demand. Mail delivery systems always should have plenty of extra mail spool capacity; the usual rule of thumb for peak use is twice the size of regular use. Sudden, unexpected bursts of large messages can occur. More importantly, new technologies are emerging all the time that result in dramatically increased message sizes.

The Wrong Way to Scale

A department in a university had its own email delivery server. When it became overloaded, it sometimes refused Post Office Protocol (POP) (Myers and Rose 1996) client connection requests. To fix the problem, the SA sent an email around the department publicly berating people who were using email clients that automatically checked for new email at a predefined interval, such as every 10 minutes. It was the default configuration for the email clients, not a deliberate, selfish choice as her message had implied. However, several of them did take the time to figure out how to turn the feature off in their email clients, and the problem was resolved, at least temporarily. However, the problem kept reoccurring as new people arrived and the traffic volume increased. As we saw in Chapter 5, it is better to fix things once than partially fix them many times. It provides better service to the customers and ultimately less work for the SAs.

Instead of trying to embarrass and blame her customers, the SA should have been monitoring the mail server to figure out what lack of resources was causing the refused connections. She could then have fixed the problem at its root and scaled the server to deal with the increased demand. Alternatively, some mail server products optimize a client checking for new email by quickly replying that there are no new messages if the client has queried in the last 10 minutes. This requires fewer resources than actually checking if new mail has arrived for that user.

As new technologies emerge, message sizes typically increase significantly. In the early days, email was simple text and was transmitted over slow modem connections. When people started sharing basic images and large programs, the larger files were turned into text and broken into small chunks that were sent in separate messages so that they could still be transmitted over modems. Early images were of low resolution and black and white. Higher-resolution monitors and color monitors resulted in significant increases in the size of images that were emailed. When email became common on PC and Macintosh systems, people started sharing documents and slide presentations, which were large files and had the potential to be huge. More document formats and documents including more higher-resolution images continue to increase message sizes. The introduction of standard video and audio file formats and the subsequent sharing of those files also increased the volume of data sent in email.

Always have plenty of spare mail spool space. Watch for emerging technologies and be prepared to scale rapidly when they emerge. Every new generation of technology tends to use more disk space than its ancestors. Most mail systems let the SAs set message size limits. These can help with size problems, if handled well. However, if they get in the way of people's work, people will find a way around the limitation, such as by splitting the email into several smaller chunks that will pass the size limit. We recommend using size limits only as a temporary stopgap measure to deal with an overload problem while you find a permanent solution, or with a really huge limit to prevent people accidentally sending something enormous.

List processing systems have the same volume concerns as delivery and relay systems. However, they also have to deal with an increased and more diverse list membership. When a list processing machine has to deliver messages to a large number of other machines, it is likely that a number of them will be unavailable for some reason. The list processing system needs to deal gracefully with this situation without delaying the delivery of the message to other systems that are available. Some parts of scaling a list processing system are related to software configuration (Chalup et al. 1998). However, disk space usage, network usage, and CPU and memory usage should all be monitored and scaled appropriately, too.

19.1.10 Security Issues

Mail relay hosts that communicate with places outside the company are traditionally targets for attackers because such communication inherently requires exposure to the Internet or other extranets. Mail delivery is a complex process and therefore prone to bugs that, historically, have been leveraged as security holes. When building an email system, consider security from the outset. Security is always difficult to add later, and your mail system will be a target.

The mail system is also a conduit through which undesirable content, such as viruses, can get into the company. Several vendors offer products that scan email content for viruses and other undesirable or destructive content before it is accepted and delivered to the recipient. Consider whether your site should implement such content scanning and whether it conflicts with the site's privacy policy. If content scanning is implemented, try to make sure that the maximum number of possible data formats are understood by the application so that it can examine all the files in, for example, a zip archive attachment. Be aware that some things will slip through the net, however, and that similar scanning should take place on your customers' desktop machines too. When processing thousands or millions of email messages a day, such virus scanning can be a big bottleneck. If you use such systems, plan for high disk I/O rates.

Also consider how the email system fits into the security architecture. For example, if the site has a perimeter security model, what protection does the firewall system provide for email? Does it have a facility to prevent transmission of messages with suspicious headers that might be trying to exploit security holes? If not, where can that function best be implemented? Can the external mail relay systems be used by unauthorized persons to relay email that is not destined for the company? How can unauthorized mail relaying be prevented? How do customers access their email when they are on the road or at home? Many of the easiest and most common ways of providing people access to their email when they are traveling involve transmitting passwords and potentially confidential email unencrypted across public, unsecured networks. The system's design should include a secure mechanism for remote email access, such as described in Chapter 22.

19.1.11 Communication

An important part of building any service is communication, particularly telling people what its features are and how to use it. Another important component of communication about a service is the documentation of the system for SAs.

For the customers of an email service, it is important to ensure that everybody who uses the system understands the policies associated with the system. Everyone should be aware of the privacy policy discussed previously and the policy relating to forwarding email off-site, mentioned in Section 19.1.6. They should also be aware of the email backup policy and schedule, if any. Email backup policies are discussed further in Section 19.2.2. They should also be aware of the content filtering, or lack thereof, mentioned in Section 19.1.10 and what the implications are. They should be made aware of the risks associated with email, such as the privacy issues on noncompany networks, and the risks of viruses and running programs of any description that they are sent. They should understand how to check incoming mail for viruses and why they should always do so. They should be made aware of chain letters so that they recognize them and do not propagate them. They should know the company's acceptable use policy, discussed in Section 7.1.3, and how it applies to the email system. They should also be aware of any features that may be available to them, such as encryption mechanisms and mailing list administration tools discussed in Section 19.1.6.

The email system should be well documented for SAs. Failover and emergency recovery procedures should be clear and well documented. The design of the system should be well documented, including diagrams that show the flow of mail and what processing happens on what systems. SAs who do not work directly with the email system should be able to perform some preliminary debugging before reporting a problem, and that process should also be well documented. It is particularly important that SAs at remote sites who may be in different time zones understand the mail system architecture and are able to perform basic debugging tasks on their own.

19.2   The Icing

A site can do several things to improve its email service after covering all the basics. In the interest of protecting people's privacy and company-confidential information, a site can look at making email encryption a simple, easy-to-use option, particularly for the senior management. Also, the legal departments at many sites may want the SAs to implement an email-specific backup policy that discards email backups more quickly than others. A site that has an email service that is very visible to customers will want to implement more advanced monitoring. Some sites, such as ISPs or e-commerce sites, may need to scale the list processing system to handle very-high-volume, high-membership lists. We look at all of these in more detail.

19.2.1   Encryption

One enhancement to the basic email system is the addition of an easy-to-use encryption mechanism. Encryption is especially useful for senior management who are constantly working with highly confidential information, but it must be quick and easy so it does not take extra time to encrypt the message before sending it. It needs to be fully integrated into the email client, so that they can just press the ENCRYPT WHEN SENDING button, configure automatic encryption for certain recipients, or turn encryption on by default for all messages.

Available commercial encryption packages are integrated with email clients to varying degrees of transparency. When looking at the various products, consider both the user-interface issues and key-management issues. An encryption system needs a repository for everyone's encryption keys and a way for those keys to be rescinded if they are compromised. Consider also the issue of what to do in a disaster scenario in which something catastrophic happens to a key staff member and important emails are encrypted so that only he can read them. Some systems have key-recovery mechanisms, but those mechanisms should have adequate controls to ensure that the keys cannot be compromised.

Encryption systems and key management are complex topics and should be researched in detail before being implemented at a site. A well-implemented encryption service is an asset to any company. However, there are many cryptography vendors that are selling snake oil and should be avoided. Advice on detecting them can be found in Matt Curtin's *Snake Oil Warning Signs: Encryption Software to Avoid* (Curtin 1999a,b). For more information on email encryption standards see Garfinkel (1994) and Oppliger (2000).

19.2.2   Backup Policy

Although SAs consider backups to be an essential part of good system administration practice, they also can be harmful to the company in a somewhat unexpected way. Therefore, many companies have a policy of not performing backups on email or of discarding those backups after a predefined short period.

The problem is that if the company becomes involved in a legal battle of any sort, such as defending its patent or intellectual property rights, there is a high probability that all documents relating to the case will be subpoenaed. That means searching through all backup tapes for relevant documents. Typically, formal documents relating to the topic will have been kept in well-known places. However, informal documents such as emails can be in any mailbox, and all email then has to be searched for potentially relevant documents. Whether on backup tapes or disk, emails that match the search criteria then have to be individually examined by someone who is able to determine whether the document is relevant and should be turned over to the court. This is a very expensive and time-consuming process that the legal department would rather avoid regardless of whether it turns up documents in the company's favor. The process of having to search through years' worth of old email on backup tapes is just too expensive.

Medium-size and large companies usually have a document retention policy that specifies how long certain types of documents should be kept. This policy is in place to limit the amount of document storage space that is needed and to make it easier to find relevant documents. The document retention policy is typically extended to cover email at some point. At that point, the legal department will request that the SAs implement the policy. If email is distributed across many machines and in some nonstandard places, implementing the policy becomes difficult. In particular, if the email is stored on the laptops and desktops of people who use POP servers, then the policy needs to cover the laptop and desktop backups, and somehow separate the email backup from the system backup, so that the former can be discarded sooner. When designing your email service, it is best to bear in mind that you may be asked to implement this policy, and consider how you will do so.

19.2.3   Advanced Monitoring

For companies where email is tied quite closely into the revenue stream, it is advisable to implement some more advanced monitoring methods for the email system. Because email transmission and delivery is a complex series of events, SAs can easily overlook some small aspect of the system if they try to perform just basic monitoring on each component. Although basic monitoring is very useful and necessary, a more complex end-to-end model must be implemented at sites where email is truly mission-critical.

End-to-end monitoring means building a test that emulates someone sending email to someone served by this email system. It should emulate a customer or revenue-generating transaction as closely as possible to detect all possible problems, including those that are only visible from outside the site network. Chapter 24 covers the topic of monitoring in detail. In particular, Section 24.2.4 discusses end-to-end monitoring in general and includes an example that directly applies to email.

19.2.4   High-Volume List Processing

Most sites have mailing lists, and many have mailing lists that serve paying customers. For example, a company might have a mailing list that announces product upgrades or new products to its customers. It might have a mailing list that keeps customers up-to-date with events at the company, or one that announces serious bugs with its products. Other companies have mailing lists for people who are beta-testing a product. A nonprofit organization may have one or more mailing lists for its members, to keep them up-to-date with what is happening and what events are being organized. A university may have mailing lists for the students in each class. A service provider will almost certainly have mailing lists for its customers to let them know of outages that might affect them.

Mailing lists are handled centrally on mail servers, rather than as an alias in one person's mail client. Everyone can send email to the same address to reach the same list of people. Mailing lists can be protected so that only a few authorized people can send to them, or so that messages have to be approved by an authorized person before they are sent, or so that only people who are members of the list can send messages to it. They can also be open so that anyone can send email to all the list recipients. Most list management software gives the SAs the ability to delegate control of list membership, posting restrictions and message approval to the person who manages the list from a business perspective. The list management software should also be able to permit end-users to create and delete their own mailing lists without SA involvement. For example, if a company starts a beta-test program for a particular product, the manager in charge of the beta test should be able to set up the mailing list for the beta users, add people to the list, remove people from the list, control who sends messages to the list, and delete the list when the beta test is over.

Relatively few companies will have high-volume, high-membership lists that require special scaling. Sites that fall into this category have special scaling and redundancy concerns. The requirements for the average site's list processing service can be met using basic, freely available software. However, high-volume lists often exceed the capabilities of those systems. For sites that have high-volume needs, we recommend investing in commercial software that is capable of handling those large volumes but still uses IETF standard protocols for mail delivery and processing. High-volume list services should also be built across several redundant systems to avoid cascading outages caused by the list server getting swamped with work as soon as it recovers from an outage. On a high-volume list server, it is important to monitor the total length of elapsed time from when it starts sending a message to the first person on the list to when it finishes sending it to the last person on the list, excluding sites that it has problems contacting. It is important to members of the lists not to suffer from a large time-lag. If people at the end of the list receive the message a day after people at the beginning of this list, it is difficult for them to participate in the conversation in a meaningful way because they are so far behind the other people on the list.

The USENIX LISA conference and the IETF have published many useful papers on the subject of list servers (Chapman 1992, Houle 1996) and list management (Bernstein 1997, Chalup et al. 1998). Email list server technology has changed dramatically over the years as the demands placed on it have increased. Like many areas of system administration, it is important to keep up with technology improvements in this area.

19.3   Conclusion

Email is an important service to get right. People rely on it even more than they realize. In many ways, it is like a utility such as power or water. Scaling the system to meet increasing demand, monitoring the service, and building redundancy should not be an afterthought. Security should be considered from the outset, too, because email servers are a common target for attackers and email is a common vector for viruses.

Before building an email system, you must consider several policies. Companies should carefully consider the email namespace policy and make sure that the same namespace is used internally and externally to the company. In addition, a privacy policy should be defined and communicated to people who use the service.

Some companies may want to consider integrating encryption into the email service to provide extra protection for sensitive information. Larger companies may want to implement a policy for reducing how long backups of email are retained, and to protect themselves from the expense of searching through old email to find messages of relevance to a court case. Sites where the email service is linked to the revenue stream should consider implementing end-to-end monitoring of the email service. Those that run high-volume list servers have special needs that must be addressed and should invest in a commercial package.

Exercises

1. What is the email privacy policy at your site? How many people know about it?

2. How many different email namespaces are at your site? Who controls them?

3. Identify your mail relay machines. Do they have other functions?

4. Identify your mail delivery machines. Do they have other functions?

5. Where does list processing happen at your site?

6. When do you anticipate having to scale up your existing email system? What aspect do you expect to scale and why? How do you predict when it will run out of capacity?

7. How do you monitor your email system at the moment? Is there anything you would like to change or add?

8. How reliable is email service at your site? How did you arrive at that figure?

9. If your site has multiple delivery machines, explain why each one exists. Could you reduce the number?

10. If your company has remote offices, can people in those offices access their mail when the connection to the main site is down?

11. How is email security handled at your site?

12. How does email flow from the Internet into your enterprise? How does it flow out to the Internet? What security risks and exposures are involved, and how does your design mitigate them? What improvements can be made?

13. How would you implement a six-month retention schedule for email backups? Would you need to include desktops in this policy? How would you implement that component?

Chapter 20

Print Service

Printing is about getting paper[1] copy of the information you want, when you want it. Printing is a critical business function. In our experience, customers tend to rank it as one of the most critical services that is provided, second only to email.

Oddly, many SAs have disdain for printing or even anyone who prints a lot. "What happened to the paperless office?" laments the anti-printer crowd. Many SAs pride themselves on how little they print, refusing to work with paper when an electronic version is available. However, SAs who do not appreciate how important printing is to their customers will not provide good printing support. The priorities of the SAs must align with those of the customers.[2]

Printing is important to customers because, like it or not, business still runs on paper. Contracts need to be signed in ink. Diagrams need to be posted on walls. Paper can go places that computers can't. When you are driving it is easier to read directions on paper than on a laptop. People find

---

[1] You can print on a lot of things besides paper, but for the sake of simplicity, we will refer to paper in this chapter. Transparencies are just paper that didn't come from trees.

[2] We, however, are still chagrined when we discover people who print every interesting web page they see.

different mistakes when proofreading from paper than on the screen, possibly as a result of our ability to take the document to new environments. Even technocrats use paper: Although it may shock you, dear reader, every chapter of this book was proofread on white, bond, laser printer–compatible . . . paper.

When a contract must absolutely, positively get there overnight, missing the overnight delivery truck because of a printer jam is an unacceptable excuse. Printing is a utility; it should always work. However, printing technology has radically changed many times during our careers. We therefore choose not to discuss the pros and cons of various print technologies—those choices may not even be available by the time the ink on these pages is dry. Instead, we will discuss the invariants of printing: making sure the ink gets to the page, creating policies about printing, and designing print servers. Finally we will discuss ways to encourage environmentally friendly printer use. All of these things are important regardless of the evolution of the technology used to actually print anything.

20.1   The Basics

A successful print system begins with an understanding of the requirements for a good policy, followed by solid design. Without proper policy, the design will be without direction. Without design, printing functions will be unstable and harder to use.

20.1.1   Select the Level of Centralization

What would the perfect print environment look like? Some people want their own printers attached to their own computers. In their perfect world, every machine would have its own high-speed, high-quality printer. This is extremely expensive, but very convenient for the customers. For others, the key issue is that no matter how many printers exist, they should be able to print from any host to any printer. This has the benefit of being able to "borrow" someone's high-quality (possibly color) printer as needed and is certainly a flexible configuration. Finance people look at the high cost of printers and printer maintenance and would prefer to centralize printing, possibly recommending each building have one high-speed printer, one high-quality printer, and one color printer.[3] To others, it doesn't matter how many printers there are or who can access them, as long as every penny of cost is recouped via a chargeback system. Somewhere is middle ground.

---

[3]We have nightmares of a CFO requesting one printer for an entire multinational company and arranging for printouts to be distributed by next-day delivery. However, Internet-based services that do specialty printing are very promising.

The primary requirement of a print system is that people can print to any printer they have permission to use, which might encompass all printers or just a well-defined set of printers. Costs are recouped either in per-page increments, as part of a "tax," or by having each group (center, department, division) fund its own. If your life is too simple, try using completely different cost recovery methods for the hardware, supplies, and maintenance.

A typical office arrangement is to have one printer per section of a building, be it hallway, wing, or floor. These can be accessed either by anyone in the company or in the same cost center. Some individuals may have private printers because of confidentiality issues (they need to print documents containing confidential information), ego (they're important and demonstrate this by having their own printers), or some other business reason. There also may be special printers (high-speed printers, photographic-quality printers, wide-format plotters, and so on) that have special access control because of their special cost or operating requirements.

There is a trade off between cost and convenience. More printers usually means more convenience. It may mean a shorter walk to the printer or may add to the variety of types of printers available. However, having more printers costs more in a variety of ways.

On the other hand, a shared, centralized printer can be so much less expensive that you can use some of the savings to purchase a significantly higher-quality printer. Suppose inexpensive desktop printers cost $500 each. If ten people share a network printer, the break-even point is $5,000. At the time of this writing, $5,000 can purchase an extremely nice network printer and still have room for a few years of maintenance. If 20 people share that same printer, they now have a better printer at half the price of individual desktop printers, plus they get a little exercise walking to get their printouts.

Case Study: No Standards for Printers

Where there is little or no control over spending, costs will get out of control. One company had few restrictions on spending for items less than $600. When the cost of desktop printers dropped below that limit, droves of employees started purchasing them. This introduced dozens of new models to the support load of the SA team, which often had to install the printer, maintain printer drivers, and debug problems. Without maintenance contracts, people were throwing away printers rather than repairing them. Management began to crack down on this problem, and in an "informal audit" found that many of the printers that were purchased were now attached to the employee's home computer. Cost controls were put into place, and soon the problem was halted. Most of the printers purchased were slow and had low-quality output compared with the centrally purchased printers located in each hallway. However, employees were more concerned with a printer being within inches of their desk rather than being of higher quality or more cost effective.

20.1.2   Print Architecture Policy

Every site should have certain written architecture policies related to printing.

The first policy is a *general printer architecture policy* about how centralized printing will be. The goal of this document is to indicate how many people will share a printer for general printing (that is, one printer per desktop, one per hallway, one per building, one per floor), who qualifies for personal printers, and how the printers will be networked.

For reasonable reliability, networking printers requires a central print-spool. This is the device that receives jobs for a printer and holds them until the printer is ready to receive them. The spooler is often part of the access control system because it decides who can print to which printer. Spoolers also can reroute print jobs around broken printers and permit such intelligent decisions as "print this on letterhead to any printer on the fourth floor."[4] Modern printers have a built-in spooler, but their memory may be limited, so a separate spooling host may still be required. The policy should indicate the level of redundancy required. One spooler often can handle dozens or hundreds of printers, but that creates a single point of failure. Some print spoolers can have hot standbys, or redundant spool hosts can be configured. Some OSs cannot spool to a machine that runs a different OS without losing features. You may choose to have such machines spool to a central host that uses the same OS but has gateway software that can spool to the main print system, which talks directly to the printer (Limoncelli et al. 1998).

This policy also should detail how maintenance is handled: in-house, time and materials, or service contract. It should indicate the point at which maintenance costs, including labor, time, and downtime or other impact, become high enough that replacing the printer is more cost effective.

A site should also have an *accounting policy*. This policy should determine whether printers are purchased by the department that uses the printer, from a central budget, or via an ad hoc source. Similar decisions must be made regarding paying for maintenance and repairs. Paying for supplies (media, toner) can be a contentious issue if printers are not obviously dedicated to particular financial units of the organization. Photocopiers and laser printers use the same paper, and thus it can be confusing if they are covered by different budgets. The simplest method is to have everything paid for out of a central budget. On the other hand, billing on a finer granularity may discourage wasting resources. Universities often bill per page with different cost schedules for different kinds of printers. Students may receive a certain number of "free" pages every semester. There is no perfect solution,

---

[4]Of course, they must be able to notify the customer which printer was eventually selected!

but the money has to come from somewhere. The objective is to create the least objectionable solution.

The issue of who orders supplies and who resupplies the printers should also be part of the written policy. Some offices simply have the department secretary order the supplies, but sometimes the ordering is centralized. At some sites, the users of a particular printer are expected to refill the paper and change toner; at others, operators monitor printers and perform these tasks. We recommend against permitting customers to handle toner cartridges themselves. Sometimes, this procedure is complicated and error prone, not something that should be left to the typical customer. Moreover, it is our experience that customers will change toner at the slightest sign of quality problems, whereas a trained operator can take other steps. Changing toner cartridges needlessly is a waste of money and has environmental implications.

There should be a documented *printer equipment standard*. This policy should have two parts. The first part should change rarely and should specify long-term standards such as whether PostScript or PCL will be used, whether duplexing units (when available) should be purchased, what protocol printers must speak (Line Printer Daemon Protocol [LPD] over TCP/IP [McLaughlin 1990], NT's Server Message Block [SMB] print protocol [Epps et al. 1999], AppleTalk, or parallel/USB cable connection), how they are connected to the network, and so on. The second part should be a list of currently recommended printers and configurations. For example, you might list an approved configuration or two for someone purchasing a color printer, a color printer for transparencies, and a couple of black and white printers of two or three different price ranges. This part should be updated on a regular basis. These standards can also save money because they may qualify your company for volume discounts. Problems can also be avoided by having all equipment orders filtered through the SA team (or other knowledgeable people), as described in Section 14.2.1. They can verify the completeness of orders and schedule installations so SAs are not caught unprepared when the devices arrive. Limiting the number of models in use also reduces the number and types of supplies you have to inventory, which saves money and confusion.

Case Study: Recommended Configurations Save SA Time

Recommended configurations should include all the items that customers might forget but that SAs will need to complete the installation. A site had a centralized printer for each group, which was always the same model. New groups made a valiant effort to purchase the same model they saw the other groups use. However, they didn't know to purchase the optional duplexing unit, cable, and network connectivity package. When the SAs were asked to install such printers they would have to give the customer the sad news that there would be a delay while the proper add-ons were purchased so that the device would be usable. This problem continued until a printer standards document was written.

A *printer access policy* should determine who can access which printers and how that will be enforced. For example, people may be permitted to print to all printers, only to printers that their department paid for, or somewhere in between. This policy should also specify who can cancel print jobs on printers: For example, people other than administrators only should be able to cancel their own print jobs, with administrators being able to cancel any print job on the spoolers they control. Universities may have to meticulously control this because students may be prone to having "cancel wars." We take an overly optimistic, utopian stance for the office environment. In business, inside a firewall, it is reasonable to permit everyone within the company to print to every printer and cancel any job on any printer. Being able to print to any printer in the company makes it possible for people to replace faxing with printing. A designer in San Jose can print to the printer in Japan over the corporate WAN, saving the cost of the international phone call. Can this be abused? Absolutely. However, this is extremely rare and will be even rarer if the cover page names the perpetrator. If employees have a private printer that they don't want others to print to, they can lock their doors. If someone has to ask for a printout, this can be an opportunity to tell the person not to print to the private printer. If people can print to any printer, it needs to be clear to them where the printers are located. You don't want people to print to the wrong country by mistake.

Case Study: An "Open" Cancellation Policy

Permitting anyone to cancel other people's printouts seems like asking for trouble. However, this policy was used successfully when Tom was at Bell Labs. Peer pressure prevented canceling any job but your own. However, during the common event of a print job going out of control (most commonly PostScript code, rather than PostScript output, being printed by mistake), paper waste was prevented because the first person to notice the problem could cancel the print job. This won't be as successful in less cooperative environments or where camaraderie between employees is not as good.

A *printer naming policy* should be established. Often printers have a two-part name. The first part indicates the printer's common name, such as the room number. The second part may be a code for what kind of printout will be produced. For example, printer "2t408-d" may send the job to the printer in room 2t408 in duplex (double-sided) mode, and "2t408-s" may be an alias that prints to the same printer but in single-sided mode. We prefer printers to be named geographically, that is, the name indicates where the printer is located. Nothing is more frustrating than having printers named with a theme that is not helpful in locating the printer. Although it may be creative and "cool" to have printers named `decaf`, `latte`, `mocha`, and `froth`, it makes it difficult for people to find their printouts.

There is one major pitfall to naming a printer after its location. If the location changes, everyone must update their printer configuration. This is less likely to happen if floorplans have designated printer areas that are unlikely to move or are the wrong shape to be used for anything else. If the printer is likely to move, a more general name might be more appropriate, such as a name that indicates what floor it is on, possibly concatenated with the word "north," "east," "south," or "west."

20.1.3   Designing the System

Once the policies have been defined, you can design and implement the print system architecture. Some print systems give very little flexibility, others too much.

Peer-to-peer: A peer-to-peer print architecture is very decentralized. This is where all hosts spool jobs directly to the destination printer over a network. This is the simplest to set up because often you only need to know the IP address or name of the printer in order to send print jobs to it. However, this configuration can be the most difficult to administer. Any printer change that requires host-side (client) changes must be propagated to all clients. For example, if the printer is replaced by a newer model, all hosts may require a new printer driver.

The central funnel: A more centralized architecture gives a higher level of control. In the simplest version of this architecture, all hosts send their print jobs to a central server, which then distributes the jobs to the various printers under its control. This server acts as a funnel that collects the print jobs. It can then make intelligent decisions. For example, it can convert various print formats (PostScript to PCL or vice versa), collect per-page billing information, and so on. It can also do intelligent printer selection. For example, customers could submit jobs to "the first available printer on the fourth floor" or "any color printer" or "the highest-quality color transparency printer." Only this one host needs the particular printer drivers and utilities that require maintenance so there is only one place for upgrades to be done. On the other hand, this introduces a single point of failure.

There are several variations on these two architectures. One problem with peer-to-peer architectures is that they become more complex and chaotic as they grow larger. This can be mitigated by either adopting a more centralized approach or using some kind of automated client update mechanism. For example, you might use whatever automated software deployment mechanism is used to distribute a patch that updates a printer driver or changes a printer setting. UNIX systems can distribute "printcap" information via various mechanisms (NIS, `cfengine`, and so on). Although most UNIX print clients cannot read their configuration directly from NIS, replacements such as Line Printer Remote, next generation (LPRng) (Powell and Mason 1995) can. Alternatively, a simple script can turn information stored in an NIS database into the local configuration file.

The problem with the centralized funnel is that it creates a single point of failure. However, because you can save money through centralization, some of those savings can be used to build in redundancy. The funnel can be two redundant print spoolers that can either manually or automatically fail over. This also makes server upgrades cleaner because one server can be taken out of service for upgrading without a reduction in service. Sometimes, automatic failover can be difficult to achieve. Considering how rare a hardware failure is, you can choose manual failover if the process is well documented and something that all SAs can be trained to do.

Other variations on these architectures include per-group spoolers, multiply-redundant spoolers, one spooler per building, and so on. Some sites have two spoolers, each serving half of their customers (possibly divided between two buildings), but the spoolers have the ability to fail over to each other. Every spooler in the print system increases the work the administrators must do to maintain the service. Much of this work can be mitigated through automation, but be aware that not everything can be automated.

20.1.4   Documentation

It goes without saying that the architecture, operations procedures, and software used in your print system should be documented. Documentation is a critical part of any well-run system. SAs must provide three kinds of printing documentation to their customers.

How to print: This document should explain how to print. It may include which menus and buttons to click on to connect to the printer of the customer's choosing, or it may explain which commands must be executed. For example, a UNIX environment might explain the environment variables that must be set, whether `lpr` or `lp` is used, and what options to use to get simplex, duplex, letterhead, or other specialty output. This document shouldn't need to change very often. It should be made available as part of the "getting started" manual or web site that new customers are given.

List of printers: This document should be a catalog of all the printers available, where they are located, and what special features they have such as color, quality, and so on. It should tell customers where they can find the "How to Print" document just mentioned. This catalog needs to be updated every time a new printer is added or removed from the system. This document should be posted on the wall near every printer it lists, in addition to being part of the "getting started" manual or web site that new customers are given.

Printer labels: The final piece of documentation is that every printer should be well labeled with its name (or names). Trays should be labeled if they are intended for transparencies, letterhead, and so on.[5] Labeling printers is such a simple thing, yet we have seen many environments where SAs forget to do it. The users of the printer will feel that this is the most important documentation you can provide. The rest can usually be figured out!

20.1.5 Monitoring

As we said in Chapter 3, it doesn't deserve the name "service" until it is monitored. Two aspects need this attention. The first is the spooling and printing service itself. The SAs need to monitor each spooler to make sure the queue hasn't stalled, the spool disk hasn't filled, logs are being recycled, the CPU is not overloaded, the spool disk hasn't died, and so on. This should be a part of your normal monitoring system.

The second aspect that needs to be monitored is the status of each printer. Toner and paper trays need to be refilled. Shelves of paper need to be restocked. Most network printers speak SNMP and can alert your monitoring system that they are jammed, low on toner, or out of paper. Hopefully, some day printers will be able to monitor exactly how much paper they have remaining so that SAs can be alerted when they are nearly out of paper. Meanwhile, a simple trick can be used. Some printers have

---

[5]We recommend a consistent tray scheme. For example, transparencies are always "tray 2." This will help prevent the situation in which documents are accidentally printed on transparencies or slides are printed on paper.

two paper trays and alternate between them. If the trays are individually monitored, you can pretty much ensure that some paper is always available to the printer if the trays are refilled in a staggered manner, that is, don't refill both trays at the exact same time.

Although there are automated means to tell if a printer is out of paper, there is no automated way to tell if a good supply of paper is sitting near the printer. SAs can either visit the printers on a regular basis, or deputize customers to alert them when paper supplies are running low.

Case Study: Print Tests

Newer printers will indicate when they are low on toner, but older printers require a test print. One site used a program to generate a test print on every printer each Monday morning. The page included a time, date, a warning to customers not to throw it out, and a large test pattern. An operator was assigned to retrieve these printouts and add toner if the test pattern was unreadable. The operator pulled a cart of paper along and restocked the supply cabinets under each printer. This very simple system maintained a high level of service.

20.1.6   Environmental Issues

There is an environmental aspect to printing. Printing kills trees and the disposal of printouts fills up landfills. A page that is not printed has a lower impact than a page that is printed and then recycled; however, there also is a cost and environmental impact to recycling. We must design our print systems to minimize waste. Toner cartridges should be recycled. We should be sensitive to the environmental impact of the chemicals used in the printing process. We should discourage wasteful printing and encourage paperless solutions when possible.[6] We must also comply with environmental laws that require recycling.

Some of these issues are directly the SA's responsibility. For example, a recycling program is not something that customers can be expected to create on their own. If such a program does not exist, customers will not recycle paper. It is up to the SAs to coordinate with the facilities department to create such a system or, if one is in place, to make sure that proper "paper only" wastebaskets are located near each printer, instructions are posted, and so on. The same can be said for recycling used toner cartridges. This is an opportunity to collaborate with the people in charge of the

---

[6]Considerable cost savings are also gained by the reduction in paper and toner to be purchased. Waste disposal charges usually are lowered if recyclable paper is separated.

photocopying equipment in your organization because many of the issues overlap.

Some issues are the responsibility of the customers, but SAs can facilitate them by giving customers the right tools. SAs must also avoid becoming road-blocks that encourage their customers to adopt bad habits. For example, making sure preview tools for common formats such as PostScript are available to all customers helps them print less. Printers and printing utilities should default to duplex (double-sided) printing. Don't print a "burst page" before each printout. Replacing paper forms with web-based, paperless processes also saves paper, though making them as easy to use is a challenge.

Case Study: Creating a Recycling Program

A large company didn't recycle toner cartridges, even though new ones came with shipping tags and instructions on how to return old ones. The vendor even included a financial incentive to those that returned old cartridges. Their excuse for not taking advantage of this system was simply that nobody had created a procedure within the company to do it! Years of missed cost savings went by until someone finally decided to take the initiative to create a process. Once the new system was in place, the company saved thousands of dollars per year.

20.2 The Icing

SAs can build some interesting add-ons into their print service to make it more of a Rolls-Royce quality of service.

20.2.1 Automatic Fail-Over and Load Balancing

We discussed redundant print servers; often the failover for such systems is manual. SAs can build automatic fail-over systems to reduce the downtime associated with printer problems.

If the printing service deals with high volumes, the SAs might consider using the redundant systems to provide load balancing. For example, there may be two print spoolers, with each handling half of the printers (to balance the load) and substituting for each other if one dies (to mitigate downtime).

There are two components to automated fail-over. First is the detection of a problem. Next is the actual cut-over to the other spooler.

Detecting that a service is down is difficult to do properly. A spooler may be unable to print even if it responds to pings, accepts new connections, answers requests for status, and permits new jobs to be submitted. It is best if the server can give a more detailed diagnostic without actually generating printout. If there are no jobs in the queue, you can make sure that the server is accepting new jobs. If there are jobs in the queue, you can make sure that the current job has not been in the process of being printed for an inordinate amount of time, which may indicate that there is a problem. You must be careful because small PostScript jobs can generate many pages or can run for a long time without generating any pages. It is important to devise a way to avoid false positives. You must also differentiate between the server being out of service and the printer being out of service.

This solves the problem of an outage at the print server. Outside of server problems, we find most printing problems to be on the PC side, particularly the drivers and the application software. At least having reliable print servers to print documents to can reduce the chance of multiple simultaneous failures.

20.2.2   Dedicated Clerical Support

Printers are mechanical devices, and often their reliability can be increased by keeping untrained people away from their maintenance tasks.[7] Therefore it can be advantageous to have a dedicated clerk or operator service them. Many sites have enough printers that it can be a part-time job for someone to simply visit every printer every few days to verify that it is printing properly, has enough paper, and so on. This person can also be responsible for getting printers repaired. Although a company may have a service contract "to take care of that kind of thing," someone still has to contact, schedule, and baby-sit the repair person. Arranging service and describing the problem can be very time-consuming, and it's less expensive to have a clerk do this task than an SA. This kind of position has a lot of room for career growth. It can be an excellent way for people to get their foot in the door of the company or the SA team.

20.2.3   Shredding

People print the darnedest things: private email, confidential corporate information, credit card numbers, and so on. We've even met someone that tested printers by printing UNIX's /etc/passwd file, not knowing that the encrypted second field could be cracked. Some sites shred very little, some have specific shredding policies, and others shred just about everything.

---

[7]We don't mean to disparage our customers' technical abilities, but we've seen brilliant people break printers by trying to change the toner cartridge without following the instructions.

We don't have much to say about shredding except to note that it is good to shred anything that you wouldn't want on the front page of the *New York Times*, and that you should err on the side of caution about what you wouldn't want to see there. Something that isn't printed is even more secure than something shredded.

The other thing to note is that there are on-site shredding services that bring a huge shredder on a truck to your site to perform the shredding services, and off-site shredding services that take your papers back to their shredding station for treatment. Now and then we hear stories that an off-site shredding service was found to not actually shred the paper as they had promised. We aren't sure whether these are true or just urban legends, but we highly recommend regular spot-checks of your off-site shredding service if you choose one. Shredding services are typically quite expensive, so you should make sure you are getting what you pay for.

20.2.4   Dealing with Printer Abuse

An old Usenet saying goes, "You can't solve social problems using technology," and this applies to printing as well. You can't write a program to detect nonbusiness use of printers and you can't write a program to detect wasteful printing. However, the right peer-pressure and policy enforcement can go a long way. Your acceptable use policy (Section 7.1.3) should include what constitutes printer abuse.

Billing on a per-page basis can create a business reason for conserving paper. If the goal is to control printing costs rather than to recover funds spent by the SA team on supplies, you might give each person a certain amount of "free" printing per month or let departments pool their "free" allotment. A lot of psychology is involved in a scheme like that. You wouldn't want to create a situation in which people waste time doing other things because they fear that the boss will punish them for going over their allotment.

One site simply announced the "top 10 page generators" each month as a way to shame people into printing less. The theory was that people would print less if they learned they were one of the largest consumers of printing services. However, a certain set of employees took this as a challenge and competed to appear in the listing for the most consecutive months. This technique might have been more effective if the list had been shown just to management, or if an SA personally visited the people and politely let them know of their status. Shame can work in certain situations.

The 500-Page Printout

SAs were perturbed to find a 500-page printout of "game cheats" (tricks for winning various computer games) at the printer one day. When this was brought to the attention of the director, he dealt with it in a very smart way. Rather than scolding anyone, he sent email to all employees saying that he found this printout by the printer without a cover page to indicate who made the printout. He reminded people that a small amount of nonbusiness printing was reasonable and that he didn't want this obviously valuable document to accidentally go to the wrong person. Therefore he asked the owner of the document to stop by his office to pick it up. After a week, the printout was recycled, unclaimed. Nothing more needed to be said.

20.3 Conclusion

Printing is a utility. Customers expect it to always work. The basis of a solid print system is well-defined policies on where printers will be deployed (desktop, centralized, or both), what kind of printers will be used, how they will be named, and what protocols and standards will be used to communicate with them. Print system architectures can run from very decentralized (peer-to-peer) to very centralized. It is important to include redundancy and fail-over provisions in the architecture. The system must be monitored to ensure quality of service.

Users of the print system require a certain amount of documentation. How to print, and the location of the printers they have access to, should be documented. The printers themselves must be labeled.

There is an environmental impact to printing; therefore SAs have a responsibility to work with other departments to create and sustain a recycling program, but they also must provide the right tools so that customers can avoid printing whenever possible.

The best print systems also have automated fail-over and load balancing, rather than manual failover. They have clerks that do maintenance and refill supplies rather than SAs spending time with these tasks or inflicting untrained users on the printers' delicate components. The best print systems provide shredding services for sensitive documents. They also recognize that many printing issues are social problems and therefore can't be solved purely with technology.

Exercises

1. Describe the nontechnical print policies in your environment.

2. Describe the print architecture in your environment. Is it centralized, decentralized, or a mixture?

3. How reliable is your print system? How do you quantify that?

4. When there is an outage in your print system, what happens and who is notified?

5. When new users arrive, how do they know how to print? How do they know your policies regarding acceptable use?

6. How do you deal with the environmental issues associated with printing at your location? List both policies and processes you have, in addition to the social controls and incentives.

7. What methods to avoid printing are provided to your customers?

Chapter 21

Backup and Restore

Everyone hates backups. They are inconvenient. They are costly. Services run slower (or not at all) when servers are being backed up. On the other hand, customers *love* restores. Restores are why we perform backups.

Being able to restore lost data is a critical part of any environment. Data gets lost. Equipment fails. Humans delete it by mistake and on purpose. Judges impound all documents related to a lawsuit that were stored on your computers on a certain date. Shareholders require the peace of mind that comes with the knowledge that a natural (or other) disaster will not make their investment worthless. Data also gets corrupted, either by mistake, on purpose, or by gamma rays from space. Backups are like insurance: you pay for it even though you hope to never need it. In reality, you need it.

Although the goal is to be able to restore lost data in a timely manner, it is easy to get caught up in the daily operational work of doing backups, and forget that restoration is the goal. As evidence, the collective name typically used for all the equipment and software related to this process is our "backup system." It should really be called our "backup and restore systems" or, possibly more fittingly, simply our "data restoration system."

This book is different in the way it addresses backups and restores. Readers of this book should already know what commands their OSs use to backup and restore data. We will not cover that information. Instead, we will discuss the theory of how to plan your backups and restores in a way that should be useful no matter what backup products are available.

After we discuss the theory of planning the backups and restores, we will discuss the three key components of modern backup systems: automation, centralization, and inventory management. These should help guide your purchasing decision. Once the fundamentals are established, we will discuss how to maintain the system you've designed well into the future.

The topic of backups and restores is so broad that we cannot cover the entire topic in detail. We have chosen to cover the key components. Books such as Preston's *Unix Backup and Recovery* (Preston 1999) and Leber's *Windows NT Backup and Restore* (Leber 1998) cover the details for Unix and Microsoft environments in great detail.

Backup and restore service is a part of any data storage system. One study found that the purchase price of the disk is merely 20 percent of the total cost of ownership, with backups being nearly the entire remaining cost. Buying a raw disk and slapping it into a system is easy. Providing data storage as a complete service is hard. The price of disks has been decreasing at a constant rate, but total cost of ownership has risen mostly because of the increasing cost of backups. Therefore an efficient backup and restore system is your key to cost-effective data storage.

With regard to terminology, we will use "full backup" to mean a complete backup of all files on a partition (Unix users call this a "level 0 backup"). The term "incremental backup" refers to copying all files since the previous full backup (Unix users call this a "level 1 backup"). Incremental backups grow over time. That is, if we perform a full backup on Sunday and an incremental backup each day of the week that follows, the amount of data being backed up should grow each day because Tuesday's incremental backup includes all the files from Monday's backup, as well as what changed since then. Friday's incremental backup should include all the files that were part of Monday's, Tuesday's, Wednesday's, and Thursday's backups, in addition to what changed since Thursday's backup. Some systems perform an incremental backup that collects all files changed since a particular incremental backup, rather than the last full backup. We will borrow the Unix terminology and call those "level 2 incremental backups" if they contain files changed since the last level 1, or "level 3" if they contain files changed since the last level 2, and so on.

21.1   The Basics

Engineering your backup and restore system should begin by determining the desired end result and working backwards from there. The end result is the desired restore capability of the system. There are different reasons that restores are requested, and the reasons that apply to your environment affect further decisions such as creating a policy and a schedule.

We start by defining Corporate Guidelines, which drive your Service Level Agreement (SLA) for restores based on your site's needs, which becomes your backup policy, which dictates your backup schedule.

Corporate Guidelines: The corporate guidelines define terminology and dictate minimums and requirements for data recovery systems

Service Level Agreement: The SLA defines the requirements for a particular site or application and is guided by the corporate guidelines

Policy: The policy documents the implementation of the SLA in general terms, written in English

Schedule: The detailed schedule shows which disk will be backed up when. This may be static or dynamic. This usually is the policy translated from English into the backup software's configuration.

Beyond policies and schedules are operational issues. Consumables can be expensive and should be included in the budget. Time and capacity planning are required to ensure that we meet our SLA during both restores and backups. The backup and restore policies and procedures should be documented from both the customer and the SA perspective.

Only after all that is defined, can we actually build the system. There are three key components of modern backup systems: automation, centralization, and inventory management. Each of these will be discussed in turn.

21.1.1 Three Reasons for Restores

There are three reasons why restores are requested. If we do not understand these, we will create a backup and restore system that may miss the target. Each reason has its own requirements. The reasons are as follows:

Accidental file deletion: A customer has accidentally erased one or more files and needs to have them restored.

Disk failure: A hard drive has failed and all data needs to be restored.

Archival: For business reasons, a snapshot of the entire "world" needs to be made on a regular basis for disaster recovery, legal, or fiduciary reasons.

Accidental File Deletion

In the first case, customers would prefer to quickly restore any file as it existed any instant. However, that usually isn't possible. Typically, in an office environment, you can expect to be able to restore a file to what it looked like at any one-day granularity and that it will take three to five hours to have the restore completed. Obviously, special cases such as those found in the financial and e-commerce world are much more demanding. Making the restores convenient is easier now that modern software (Moran and Lyon 1993) permits customers to do their own restores either instantly (if the tape[1] is still in the jukebox) or after waiting for some operator intervention (if they must wait for a tape to be loaded).

Self-service restores are not a new feature. Systems dating back to the 1980s provided this feature.

- In the early 1980s, the VAX/VMS operating system from Digital (then DEC, now Compaq) actually retained previous versions of files, which could be accessed by specifying the version number as part of the file name.
- In 1988 (Hume 1988), Bell Labs invented the File Motel, a system that stored incremental backups on optical platters permanently. AT&T's CommVault[2] offered this "infinite backup" system as one of its products.
- In the 1990s, NetApp introduced the world to their "Filer" line of file server appliances that have a built-in snapshot feature. Hourly, daily, and weekly snapshots of a filesystem are stored on disk in an efficient manner. Data blocks that haven't changed are only stored once. Filers serve their filesystems to UNIX hosts via the NFS protocol, as well as to systems running OSs using Microsoft's CIFS file protocol, making them the darling of SAs in multi-OS shops. Customers like the way snapshots permit them to "cd back in time." Other vendors have added snapshot and snapshot-like features with varying levels of storage efficiency.

Systems such as these are becoming more commonplace as technology becomes cheaper and as information's value increases. To an SA, the value of snapshots is that it reduces their workload because the most common type of request becomes self-service.

The value of snapshots to customers is that it gives them new options for managing their work better. Customers' work habits change as they learn they can rely on snapshots. If the snapshots are there forever, as is possible with CommVault, customers manage their disk utilization differently, knowing that they can always get back what they delete. Even if snapshots are only available going back a fixed amount of time, customers develop creative, new, and more efficient workflows.

---

[1]We refer to the backup media as *tape* in this chapter, even though we recognize that there are many alternatives.

[2]CommVault is now a separate company.

Another way that snapshots increase customer productivity is that they reduce the amount of manually reconstructed lost data. When customers accidentally delete data, they may reconstruct it rather than wait for the restore, which may take hours or even days. Everyone has made a change to a file and later regretted making the change. Reconstructing the file manually is an error-prone process, but it would be silly to wait hours for a restore request to be completed. With snapshots, customers are less likely to attempt to manually reconstruct lost data.

The most common reason for requesting a restore is to recover from accidental file deletion. We have seen that modern software coupled with jukeboxes can make this kind of restore a self-service function. Even better, fancy systems that provide snapshots not only take care of this without requiring the SA to be involved for each restore, but can positively affect the customer's work environment.

Disk Failure

The second kind of restore is related to disk failure (or any hardware or software failure resulting in total filesystem loss). When a disk fails, there are two problems: loss of service and loss of data. On critical systems (such as e-commerce and financial systems), RAID should be deployed so that disk failures do not affect service, with the possible exception of a loss in performance. However, in noncritical systems, customers can typically[3] expect the restore to be completed in a day, and although they do not like losing data, they usually find a single day of lost work to be an acceptable risk. Sometimes, the outage is between these two extremes: a critical system is still able to run, but data on a particular disk is unavailable. In that case, there may be less urgency.

This kind of restore often takes a long time to complete. Restore speed is critical because gigabytes of data are being restored, and the entire volume of data is unavailable until the last byte is written. To make matters worse, a two-step process is involved: First, the most recent full backup must be read, and then the most recent incremental(s) are read.

Archival

The third kind of restore request is archival. Corporate policies may require you to be able to reproduce the entire environment with a granularity of a quarter, half, or full year in case of disasters or lawsuits. The work that needs to be done to create an archive is similar to the full backups required

---

[3] Again, *typical* refers to a common office environment.

for other purposes with four differences:

1. Archives are full backups. In environments that usually mix full and incremental backups on the same tapes, archive tapes should not be so mixed.
2. Some sites require archive tapes to be separate from the other backups. This may mean that archive tapes are created by generating a second, redundant set of full backups. Alternatively, archival copies may be generated by copying the full backups off previously made backup tapes. Although this alternative is more complicated, if it is automated, it can be performed unattended when the jukebox is otherwise unused.
3. Archives are usually stored off-site.
4. Archive tapes age more than other tapes. They may be written on media that will become unavailable. You might consider storing a compatible tape drive or two with your archives, as well as appropriate software for reading the tapes.

When making archival backups, do not forget to include the tools that go with the data. Tools get upgraded frequently, and if the archival backup is used to snapshot the environment, the tools (and their specific set of bugs and features) should be included. Make sure that the tools required to restore the archive and the required documentation are stored with the archive.

There are other types of restores that are required. Certainly there are more specialized types of restores, such as those for databases and specialized applications, but they all tend to fit into one of these three categories.

Different Restores, Different Customers

It is interesting to note that the three types of restore requests typically serve three different customers. Individual file restores serve the customer who accidentally deleted the data; the direct users of the data. Archival backups serve the needs of the legal and financial departments that require them, people that are usually far detached from the data itself.[4] Complete restores after a disk failure serve the SAs who committed to providing a particular SLA. Backups for complete restores are therefore part of the corporate infrastructure.

In an environment that bills for services with a fine granularity, these different kinds of backups can be billed for differently. If possible, these customer groups should be individually billed for these special requirements just as they would be billed for any service. Different software may be required, and there may be different physical storage requirements and different requirements for who "owns" the tapes.

---

[4]Increasingly, the legal requirement is to *not* backup data or to recycle tapes in increasingly short cycles. Judges can't subpoena documents that aren't backed up.

Passing the Cost to the Right Customer

During a corporate merger, the United States Department of Justice required the companies involved to preserve any backup tapes until the deal was approved. This meant old tapes could not be recycled. The cost of purchasing new tapes was billed to the company's legal department. They required the special service, so they had to pay for it.

Corporate Guidelines

Organizations need a corporate-wide document that defines terminology and dictates requirements for data-recovery systems. Global corporate policy-makers should strive to establish minimums based on legal requirements rather than list every specific implementation detail of the items that are discussed later in this chapter.

The guideline should begin by defining why backups are required, what constitutes a backup, and what kind of data should be backed up. A set of retention guidelines should be clearly spelled out.

The guidelines should list a series of issues that each site needs to consider, so that they are not overlooked. For example, it should require sites to carefully plan when backups are done, not just do them at the default "midnight until they complete" timeframe. It wouldn't be appropriate to dictate the same window for all systems. Backups usually have a performance impact and thus should be done during off-peak times. E-commerce sites with a global customer base will have a very different backup window than offices with nine-to-five schedules.

Backups Slow Down Services

The time that backups run must be carefully planned, or you will face embarrassing results. A large telecommunication equipment company received a lot of bad publicity in 1999 when a technology columnist reported that their web site was excruciatingly slow. His major complaint was that a company in the bandwidth business seemed to be miserly in the amount of bandwidth given to its own web site. He claimed this showed how telecom company's don't "get it" when it comes to the importance of the Internet. The company's investigation determined that the real problem was not bandwidth but that the system was slow because backups being performed at peak times. The operational aspects of the host (backups, tape changes, and so on) had been outsourced to a company that had ignored a request to move the backup window to nonpeak hours. If you fail to plan your backup windows well, you might not find your problems in the national media, but the results could be embarrassing nonetheless.

If you are the person writing the global corporate requirements document, you should begin by surveying various groups for requirements: consult your legal department, your executive management, the SAs, and your customers. It becomes your job to reach consensus among them all. You can use the three major types of restores listed above as a way of framing the subject.

For example, the legal department might need archival backups to prove copyright ownership or intellectual property rights. Insurance might require general backups that are retained for at least six months. The accounting department might need to have tax-related data kept for seven years, but only record it on a quarterly basis. Increasingly, legal departments are requiring a short retention policy for email, especially in light of the fact that key evidence in the Microsoft lawsuit was gained by reviewing Microsoft's email archives. Most companies insist that email archives be destroyed after six months.

It is important to balance all of these concerns. You might have to go through several rounds revising the requirements until they are acceptable to all involved.

Some companies, especially start-ups, may be too small to have guidelines beyond "there will be backups." As the company grows, consider adopting corporate guidelines based on the requirements of your investors and legal counsel.

A Data-Recovery SLA and Policy

The next step is to determine the service level that's right for your particular site. An SLA is a written document that specifies what kind of performance and service customers expect. This should be written in dialog with your customers. Once the SLA is determined, it can be turned into a policy. The policy specifies how the SLA will be achieved. For example, how often backups will be performed.

To establish an SLA, list the three types of restores from Section 21.1.1, along with the desired time to restoration, the granularity and retention period for such backups (how often the backups should be performed and how long the tapes should be retained), and the window of time during which the backups may be performed (for example, midnight to 8 AM).

Most SAs are in a position where there is already a corporate standard with vague, high-level parameters that they must follow. Make sure your customers are aware of these guidelines. From there, building the policy is usually very straightforward.

The example SLA we will use in the remainder of this chapter is as follows: Customers should be able to get back any file with a granularity of one business day for the last six months and with a granularity of one month for the last three years. Disk failures should be restored in four hours, with no more than two business days of lost data. Archives should be full backups on separate tapes generated quarterly and kept forever. Critical data will be stored on a system that retains user-accessible snapshots made every hour from 7 AM until 7 PM, with midnight snapshots held for one week. Databases and financial systems should have higher requirements that should be determined by the application's requirements and therefore are not within the scope of this example policy.

The policy based on this SLA would indicate that there will be daily backups and that the tapes will be retained as specified above. The policy can determine how often full versus incremental backups will be performed.

21.1.2 The Backup Schedule

Now that we have an SLA and policy, we can set the schedule. The schedule is specific and lists details down to which partitions of which hosts are backed up when. Although an SLA should change rarely, the schedule changes often, tracking changes in the environment. Often the schedule is not written out, but simply specified in the backup software's configuration.

Following our example from above, except for the snapshots handled by the server itself, the smallest granularity of backups in our example is a single business day. Thus a single day's backups can fail and we will still meet our disk failure scenario of two days. That means that Sunday through Friday night some kind of backup will be performed. Full backups take significantly longer than incrementals, so we schedule them for Friday night and let them run all weekend. Otherwise, incremental backups will be performed.

Backup software has become increasingly automated over the years. It is common to simply list all partitions that need to be backed up, and to have the software generate a schedule based on the requirements. The backups are performed automatically, and email notification is generated when tapes must be changed.

You usually have to manually decide how often full backups run. In our example, the smallest granularity for full backups is one month. We could, in theory, perform one quarter of our full backups each weekend. This leisurely rate would meet the requirements of our policy, but it would be unwise. As we noted earlier, incremental backups grow over time until the next full backup is completed. The incrementals would be huge if each partition received a full backup only once a month. It would save tape to perform a full backup more often.

Let's look at an example. Suppose that a partition with 4GB of data is scheduled to have a full backup every four weeks (28 days) and an incremental all other days. Let's also assume that the size of our incremental backup grows by five percent every day. On the first day of the month, 4GB of tape capacity is used to complete the full backup. On the second day, 200MB, third day, 400MB, the fourth day, 600MB, and so on. The tape capacity

Day Number	Cycle					
	Daily	7-day	14-day	21-day	28-day	35-day
1	4.0	4.0	4.0	4.0	4.0	4.0
2	4.0	0.2	0.2	0.2	0.2	0.2
3	4.0	0.4	0.4	0.4	0.4	0.4
4	4.0	0.6	0.6	0.6	0.6	0.6
5	4.0	0.8	0.8	0.8	0.8	0.8
6	4.0	1.0	1.0	1.0	1.0	1.0
7	4.0	1.2	1.2	1.2	1.2	1.2
8	4.0	4.0	1.4	1.4	1.4	1.4
9	4.0	0.2	1.6	1.6	1.6	1.6
10	4.0	0.4	1.8	1.8	1.8	1.8
11	4.0	0.6	2.0	2.0	2.0	2.0
12	4.0	0.8	2.2	2.2	2.2	2.2
13	4.0	1.0	2.4	2.4	2.4	2.4
14	4.0	1.2	2.6	2.6	2.6	2.6
15	4.0	4.0	4.0	2.8	2.8	2.8
16	4.0	0.2	0.2	3.0	3.0	3.0
17	4.0	0.4	0.4	3.2	3.2	3.2
18	4.0	0.6	0.6	3.4	3.4	3.4
19	4.0	0.8	0.8	3.6	3.6	3.6
20	4.0	1.0	1.0	3.8	3.8	3.8
21	4.0	1.2	1.2	3.8	3.8	3.8
	...	...	...	...	...	...
42-day total	**168**	**49.2**	66.6	91.6	94.6	107.2
Worst case	100%	29%	40%	55%	56%	64%
Best case	341%	100%	135%	186%	192%	218%

Table 21.1: 4GB data, 5 percent change. Tape capacity used when full backups done daily, versus on 7-, 14-, 21-, 28- and 35-day cycles.

used on the eleventh and twelfth day is 2GB and 2.2GB, respectively, which total more than a full backup. This means that on the eleventh day, it would have been wiser to have done a full backup.

Table 21.1 shows this hypothetical situation in detail with daily, 7-day, 14-day, 21-day, 28-day, and 35-day cycles. We assume zero growth after day 20 (80 percent) in the longer cycles because the growth of incrementals is not infinite.

The worst case would be doing daily full backup (168 GB of data written to tape). This would waste tape and time. Most environments have more data than could be backed up in full every day. Compared with the best case, daily full backups use 341 percent tape. This chart shows that the longer the cycle the closer we get to that worst case.

The best case in this example is the seven-day cycle (49.2 GB of data written to tape). The jump to a 14-day cycle is about a one-third increase in tape usage, with the same amount to the 21-day cycle. Longer cycles have insignificant increases because of our assumption that incrementals never grow beyond 80 percent of the size of a full backup. If this example was our actual environment, it would be relatively efficient to have a 7-day or 14-day cycle or anything in between.

Figure 21.1 graphs the accumulated tape used with those cycles over 41 days, a running total for each strategy. The "daily" line shows a linear growth of tape use. The other cycles start out the same but branch off each at its own cycle.

This first example demonstrates the fundamentals of tape utilization for a very simple situation. However, the situation is not very realistic. A more realistic situation involves the 80/20 rule. The 80/20 rule simply states that 80 percent of the data accesses in a system are repeatedly accessing the same 20 percent over and over. Therefore it is more typical that customers touch 20% of their data and modify half of what they touch (10%). Which 10 percent is modified varies each day. Thus a more "real world" study would

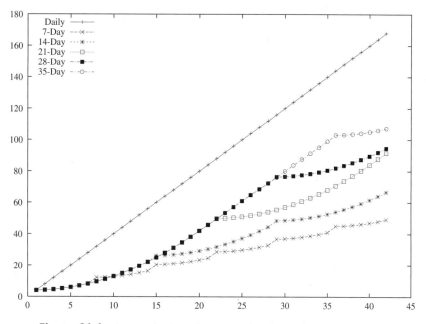

Figure 21.1: Accumulation of tape use by the cycles in Table 21.1

find that the first incremental backup after a full backup is 10 percent of the total data size, and it grows slightly each day.

Therefore we build a new model in which the first incremental is 10 percent of the full, and the incrementals that follow grow by 1 percent (10 percent of 10 percent) until the next full backup resets the cycle (Table 21.2).

In this case, the 14-day cycle is the best case, with the 21-day cycle a close second. The 7-day cycle, which had been the most efficient cycle in our previous example, comes in third place because it does too many costly full

Day Number	Cycle					
	Daily	7-day	14-day	21-day	28-day	35-day
1	4.00	4.00	4.00	4.00	4.00	4.00
2	4.00	0.40	0.40	0.40	0.40	0.40
3	4.00	0.44	0.44	0.44	0.44	0.44
4	4.00	0.48	0.48	0.48	0.48	0.48
5	4.00	0.52	0.52	0.52	0.52	0.52
6	4.00	0.56	0.56	0.56	0.56	0.56
7	4.00	0.60	0.60	0.60	0.60	0.60
8	4.00	4.00	0.64	0.64	0.64	0.64
9	4.00	0.40	0.68	0.68	0.68	0.68
10	4.00	0.44	0.72	0.72	0.72	0.72
11	4.00	0.48	0.76	0.76	0.76	0.76
12	4.00	0.52	0.80	0.80	0.80	0.80
13	4.00	0.56	0.84	0.84	0.84	0.84
14	4.00	0.60	0.88	0.88	0.88	0.88
15	4.00	4.00	4.00	0.92	0.92	0.92
16	4.00	0.40	0.40	0.96	0.96	0.96
17	4.00	0.44	0.44	1.00	1.00	1.00
18	4.00	0.48	0.48	1.04	1.04	1.04
19	4.00	0.52	0.52	1.08	1.08	1.08
20	4.00	0.56	0.56	1.12	1.12	1.12
21	4.00	0.60	0.60	1.16	1.16	1.16
	. . .	. . .	. . .	. . .	. . .	. . .
42-day total	**168**	42	**36.96**	39.2	41.16	47.04
Worst case	100%	25%	22%	23%	25%	28%
Best case	455%	114%	100%	106%	111%	127%

Table 21.2: 4GB of data, 10 percent change for the first day, then 1 percent additional change after that. Tape capacity used when full backups done daily versus on 7-, 14-, 21-, 28- and 35-day cycles.

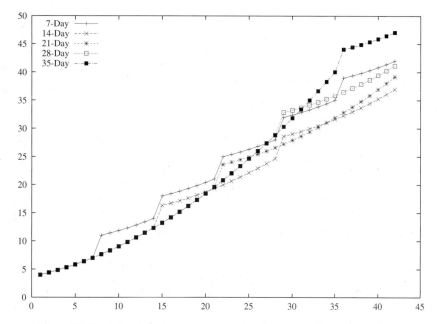

Figure 21.2: Accumulation of tape use by the cycles listed in Table 21.2

backups. Again, the worst case would be doing daily full backups. Compared with the best case, daily full backups use 455 percent of tape.

We also observe that the 7- thru 28-day cycles are all more similar to each other (between 6 percent and 15 percent of the best case), whereas in our previous example they varied wildly.

When we graph accumulations as before, we see visually how similar the cycles are. In this graph (Figure 21.2), we do not graph the daily full backups, so as to expose greater detail for the other cycles.

The best length of a cycle is different for every environment. So far, we have seen an example in which a 7-day cycle was the obvious best choice and another in which it was obviously not the best. Careful tuning is required to determine what is best for your environment. If you are starting from scratch and have no past data on which to base your decision, it is reasonable to start with a 14-day cycle and tune it from there. By reviewing utilization reports and doing a little math, you can determine if a longer or shorter cycle would use less tape. Obviously, these decisions should be in compliance with the SLA and policy.

Modern software has a dynamic schedule that tunes itself. Although it is difficult to keep track of the growing needs of hundreds of disk volumes, it is simple bookkeeping to a computer. We feel that eventually all commercial backup software will provide some kind of dynamic schedule.

Case Study: *The Bubble-Up Dynamic Backup Schedule*

Dynamic schedules do not need to be complicated. Tom once created a simple dynamic schedule as follows. The SLA was that every partition on every server was to have a backup done each night, whether it was incremental or full, and full backups should be done every seven to ten days.

The list of partitions would be sorted by backup date, so the least recently backed up partitions would be at the front of the list. The first partitions were designated for full backups that night, which would be handled on a separate set of tape drives. The remainder of the partitions would receive incremental backups.

As a result, any failed backups would tend to bubble up toward the top of the list and be the first priority the next night. Backups would typically fail because of a down host or, more likely, because the tape would run out of space. The software wasn't capable of continuing a backup onto a second tape. (This was in the days before affordable jukeboxes.)

The system could be tuned two ways. If the partitions weren't receiving full backups often enough, additional tape units would be allocated to that function. If the incremental tapes were filling, more tape drives could be allocated for that function. In this case, they had to watch to see if the incrementals were not just getting dangerously full, but also to see if they were taking longer than their backup window permitted.

Another way to reduce tape utilization is to perform two levels of incrementals. For example, a full backup is run on the first day of the month, followed by nightly incremental backups that capture any files that have been modified since the original full backup. We'll call these "level-1 incrementals." The size of these incrementals grows to an excessive size by the middle of the month. On the fifteenth of the month, we begin "level-2 incrementals." These record any file that has changed since the last level 1 backup. The incremental on the fifteenth should return to being fairly small. This saves tape in the same way that doing incrementals instead of full backups saves tape. However, there are two downsides. First, it is much more complicated to keep track of, although this is not a problem if the system is fully automated and maintains a good inventory. Second, it makes restores more difficult and error prone: You must now read the level 0, the level 1, and the level 2 tapes to make sure that all the files have been restored. This takes more time and, if the process is manual, the extra complication means it is more prone to error. There is also a reliability factor: If there is a 1:1,000 chance that a tape is bad, then having to rely on three tapes instead of two is an increased risk.

Some systems only have a single level of incremental backup. Some systems have incremental backups that record all the changed files since the last backup of the same level (sometimes called "true incrementals"). It is important to understand what your vendor means by "incremental." Be safe rather than sorry, and take the time to test the system yourself to make sure you understand how your vendor's backup system operates.

21.1.3   Time and Capacity Planning

Restores and backups are constrained by time. Restores need to happen within the time permitted by the SLA of the service, which may be disabled until the restore is complete. Backups can be done only during certain time windows. Most systems slow down considerably when backups are being performed.

The speed of a backup is affected by the following factors: read performance of the disk, write performance of the backup medium, bandwidth, and latency of the network between the disk and the backup medium. Restore time is affected by the reverse of those. Tape units often have wildly different read speeds versus write speeds.

Restores are slow for many reasons. Finding a single file on a tape can take longer than the restore itself. If the system is not able to fast-forward to the right place on the tape, reading through a long tape to find a single file can take nearly as long as restoring the entire disk itself. Restoring an entire disk is painfully slow, too. The time it takes to restore a disk is not the same length of time it takes to back up a disk. It can take 5 to 15 times longer. This is a very nasty surprise for most people. Many new administrators believe that vendors' statements about tape drive speeds and capacities bear some relationship to actual performance, which is not the case. The main issue on restore speed is not drive read speed but filesystem write speed. Writes are much less efficient than reads on almost every filesystem, and reconstructing a filesystem is often worst-case performance. People almost always underestimate the difference, figuring it will be 150 percent of the time; it's often closer to 1,500 percent. Vendors constantly tune and refine their backup algorithms for speed but often ignore restore speed time; most of their customers aren't demanding fast restores, and the ones who need it are willing to pay extra for it.

The slowest link in the chain will determine the speed at which the backup or restore will happen. The process is also affected by mechanical issues. Most tape drives write at a high speed if they are being fed data as fast as they can write ("streaming mode"), but down-shift to a considerably slower speed if they are being fed data at a slower rate. If, for example, there is network congestion slowing the data from getting to the tape host, backups may be significantly slower than if the congestion was not an issue. A similar situation can be found during restores.

When building a backup and restore system, you must take into account the speed of the various interconnections and plan to make sure the slowest link does not prevent you from meeting your time goals. It is common to use a dedicated network that is used exclusively by file servers to talk to their backup host. One of the first benefits that popularized SANs was the ability to move backup traffic off the primary network.

The only way to know for sure if your time goals have been met is to actually try it. Timing both a test backup and a test restore can validate your design. Over time, experience will help you determine what will work and what won't. However, it can be difficult to gain usable experience when backup and restore systems tend to be reengineered every couple years. You can instead rely on the experience of others, either a friendly sales engineer or a consultant who specializes in backup and restore systems.

21.1.4   Consumables Planning

Your policy and schedule affect how quickly you will use consumables: tapes, tape cleaners, and so on. Again we find ourselves doing math.

Using our example policy again, incrementals can be recycled after being stored six months, and full backups (except what we'll set aside as archives) can be recycled after three years.

Initially, there are no tapes to recycle. For the first six months, we will need to purchase new tapes for everything we do. Mathematically, we can project how many tapes will be needed by examining our schedule. Suppose six days a week there will be 8 tapes used per day. That is 48 tapes a week, or 1,248 tapes for the first six months. DLT tapes cost about $80 each, or about $99,840 for the first six months.[5]

Because the cost of tapes is constantly shrinking, we recommend purchasing them in monthly or quarterly batches. A rule of thumb is to make the first batch a "double batch" to establish a cache of blank tapes in case future orders are delayed. Otherwise, the cost of tapes often decreases faster than the volume discounts you might receive by purchasing large batches up front.

In the second six months, you can recycle all the incrementals, needing to purchase new tapes only for full backups. Let's assume that nine tapes per week are full backups, and our incrementals are growing at a rate that requires us to purchase an additional one tape per week. That means we will need only 260 tapes in the second half of the year, costing us $18,200 if we assume the cost per tape has dropped to $70 by then. If these estimates are correct, recycling tapes will make our budget for tapes in the second

---

[5] And you thought that jukebox was expensive!

six months only about 18 percent as much as what we paid in the first six months.

Tape cost (first year): $118,040

The second and third year should also require about 260 new tapes per six months, or $36,400 per year.

Tape cost (second and third year): $36,400/year

Tape cost (first 3 years): $190,840 total, or $5,301/month average

After three years, you can recycle all tapes from the first year (1,508 tapes), except those marked as "archival." If we do full backups every 14 days, this means that the archival tapes should be all the full-backup tapes created in the first two weeks of any quarter or 72 tapes per year ($9 \times 2 \times 4$). The remaining tapes total 1,436. This means we only need to purchase about 70 to 80 tapes per year. Assuming $70 per tape, that means our budget for new tapes is reduced to $5,000 to $6,000 per year.

Tape cost (fourth and future years): $6,000/year

Tape cost (first 4 years): $196,840 total, or $4,100/month average

Although year four is our least expensive, sadly it is likely that it is the last year before we must upgrade to new technology with an incompatible medium. If the old system is still around serving legacy systems, the tapes available for recycling should be sufficient for your diminished needs.

Let's look at how things would be different if the policy kept full backups (except for archival copies) for only one year instead of three. The four-year tape cost will be significantly lower. During the second and future years, we'd be able to recycle all tapes except the 72 tagged as archives. The second, third, and fourth years would cost less than $6,000 each.

Modified policy—3-year cost: $129,240 total, or $3,590/month average

Modified policy—4-year cost: $134,840 total, or $2,809/month average

This single policy change didn't affect the first year cost at all, but reduced both the three-year and four-year average cost by approximately 32%.

When setting the backup and restore policy, it is common for technical people to want backups that are retained forever and financial people to want a policy that saves as much money as possible. To strike a balance requires calculations based on your best predictions on the cost of consumables. It can be helpful to show people the cost models of what they have requested.

21.1.5   The Restore Process

Important issues involving the restoration process require a lot of thought and planning. First, it is important to set expectations with customers. They should know what the backup policy is, and they should know how to request a file restore. Even a simple explanation such as this is sufficient:

> Backups are performed only on data stored on servers (your PC's "Z:" drive, or UNIX "/home" directory) every night between midnight and 8 AM. **We never do backups of your PC's local C: drive.** If you need a file recovered, go to this URL [*insert URL*] for more information or send email to "help" with the name of the server, the file's complete path, and which date you need the restore from. Barring problems, simple restores are done in 24 hours.

It is a good idea to include this information in any kind of "new user orientation" documents or presentations and have it as a banner ad on your internal web portal. If your policy excludes certain machines from being backed up, it is particularly critical that people are aware of this.

You must think about the security implications of any restore request. Does this person have the right to receive these files? Will the file permissions and ownership change as a result of the restore? Will the data be restored to the same place with the same permissions or to a new place with possibly different security implications? Will it overwrite existing data?

There is a critical security issue here: restore requests must be validated. Millions of dollars of security infrastructure can be defeated by a careless restore. Obviously, a restore of someone's files to his own directory on the server they originated from has few security implications. However, restoring a directory that is part of a project to someone's home directory may have security implications, especially if the person is not on the project!

Although this kind of security attack may sound rare, it is a bigger risk as larger domains of control are outsourced. In a small company, it may be normal for a manager to request a restore of files from the directory of one of his staff, and the SA can verify that the staff-manager relationship is valid because everyone knows everyone. However, in a 50,000-person company, how do you verify who is in which organization? Therefore as a company grows larger, it becomes more critical that a well-defined procedure exists for validating restore requests.

It is key that multiple people be able to perform restores, not just the person who designed the system. Commonly, the engineer who designed the system invests time in automating the daily ritual of changing tapes so the process is as simple as possible. This allows a lower-paid clerk to do the task. However, designers often forget that it isn't wise to be the only person who knows how to do a restore. The restoration process should be well documented. This documentation should be kept online, and a printed version should be stashed on or near the backup hardware. The amount of effort taken to document and train people on a type of restore should be proportional to how often the restore is requested. Many people should be trained on the most common request: simple file restoration. The procedure for this should be well documented and easy to follow. A couple of people should be trained on how to restore an entire disk volume. This may require additional technical knowledge because it may involve replacing failed disks or knowing who has hardware training. Finally, a few senior SAs should be trained on how to restore a failed boot disk. This may be difficult to document because every server is a little different, but the key issue to document is how to do a restore on a system that is in some "half up" state, or how to do a restore when the machine with the tape inventory is down. All of these documents should list the customer support contact information for all vendors involved, as well as the maintenance contract numbers and passwords required to receive service.

21.1.6 Backup Automation

Not automating backups is dangerous and stupid. It is dangerous because the more you automate, the more you eliminate the chance of human error. Backups are boring, and if they aren't automated, they will not be reliably done. If they aren't done properly, it will be very embarrassing to have to face your CEO when he asks, "But why weren't there backups?"

Three aspects of the backup procedure can be automated: the actual backup commands, the schedule, and tape management and inventory. In the early days, there was no automation. Individual commands were typed by hand every time backups were done. Often, they would be started by the last shift before they left for the night. The schedule was simple. There was little or no inventory except the labels on the tapes. The first step in automation was scripts that simply replicated those commands that were previously typed manually. However, deciding what was to be backed up when was still a human task, and very little inventory management was done. Soon, software implemented the scheduling algorithms that humans had done manually. Eventually, they improved upon the algorithms by offering dynamic schedules that went beyond the scope of what humans could reasonably do. Finally, the task of physically manipulating tapes was automated through the use of jukeboxes. Automated systems would alert a clerk to remove a certain set of tapes from a jukebox and to replace them with new tapes. With a well-maintained inventory, a fully automated system can even automate the process of tracking which tapes are to be recycled and print reports of tapes that are due for recycling.

Not all sites need such sophisticated automation, but all sites need to have at least the first two levels of automation in place. All of this may seem obvious, but every site has one or two machines that have manual backups. Often, they are outside a firewall and unreachable from the central backup system. It is critical to introduce at least simple, rudimentary automation for these systems. If it is not automated, it will not happen.

Not automating backups is stupid because it is a waste of skills and time. With automation, the daily task of performing backups can be done by someone who has a lower skill level and therefore will be less expensive. Having a highly paid SA spend an hour a day changing tapes is a waste of money. Even if it takes a clerk twice as long to perform the function, it will be less expensive because during those hours highly skilled SAs will be able to work on tasks that only they can accomplish. This is why corporate executives do not send their own faxes.[6] It is better business practice to have executives do things that only they can do and move all other tasks to lower-paid employees.

The only thing worse than no automation is bad automation. Bad automation automates many aspects of a task, but does not alleviate the "think work" that must be done. Good automation doesn't just "do stuff for you," it reduces the brainwork you must do.

Backup System That Required Brainwork

Once upon a time, there was an SA who had to reckon with a backup system that automated the major aspects of the task at hand and even printed pretty labels for the tape covers. However, it failed to reduce the thinking aspect of the job. The software did a grand job of issuing the right backup commands at the right time and used a highly dynamic schedule to optimize tape use. It dealt with the security and political issues that were in place, which had the side-effect of requiring about ten small tape drives in the main data center and an additional ten scattered in various labs around the building. (This was before tape jukeboxes were inexpensive). However, every morning the SA responsible for backups had to review 20 email messages, one for each tape unit, and decide if that tape had enough space remaining to fit the next day's backups. To change a tape, a program was run, and much later the tape would be ejected. As a result, it took an hour or two to complete the daily tape changes. He, being lazy, did not want to think through 20 tapes per day and make a decision for each one. He knew that if he could eliminate this daily task, it would be like gaining five to ten hours of additional time for other projects.

---

[6]The gentleman in the back row who is trying to point out that many executives can't figure out how to operate a fax machine should please sit down.

His solution was based on his realization that he could buy more tapes but not more time. He noticed that the tape drives connected to large servers needed to be changed often, whereas the tape drives scattered in labs required infrequent changes. Rather than spending each morning with an hour of fretting over which tapes should be changed to optimize tape use, stop world hunger, and find a cure for cancer, he simply stopped changing tapes on Tuesdays and Thursdays. That gained him nearly four hours. If a new tape was started on Monday, Wednesday, and Friday, the risk of filling a tape by the next day was quite rare. He had not noticed this pattern previously because he hadn't spent the time to study the logs in that much detail. The time gained would be more valuable than the occasional full tape/missed backup situation. Next, he determined that the tape drives in the labs filled up very rarely, and he eliminated the grand tour of the facilities to change all the lab tape drives, except for once a week. That gained about three hours. By restructuring how the tape changes were performed, he gained an additional day[7] of project time each week.

The software being used was homegrown, and it would have been politically difficult to replace it before the author left the group (which he eventually did). Until that happened, this new process was a real time saver. In fact, the new procedure was so simple to explain to others that the SA was able to shift the daily process to a clerk, thus eliminating the task from his daily workload altogether. Victory!

Manual backups and homegrown backup software used to be very commonplace. Tracking new technologies, hardware, and OSs is costly. The more complicated backup requirements become, the more reason you have to purchase commercial software rather than trying to build your own system. With commercial products, the cost of development and support of the software is divided over their entire customer base.

21.1.7 Centralization

Another fundamental design goal of modern backup systems is centralization. Backups should be centralized because they are expensive and important. If we make the right investments, the cost of our backup and restore system is spread over many systems.

Two major costs can be reduced through centralization. Tape changes are costly because they are labor intensive. The equipment itself is costly because it involves precision mechanical parts spinning at high speeds. The tolerance for error is low.

---

[7] $4 + 3$ is an eight-hour day for large values of three.

Without centralization, we must have a tape unit attached to every machine that needs to be backed up and pay someone to walk to every machine to change tapes. We are now paying for many expensive pieces of hardware and a large amount of physical labor.

Network-based backup systems let us attach large backup machinery to one (or a few) hosts that contact other others to initiate backups. Network-based backups were adopted once networks were plentiful and reliable.

Jukeboxes are large devices that hold dozens, hundreds, or even thousands of tapes and contain robotic arms that shuttle tapes from their storage locations into one of multiple tape units. Jukeboxes are expensive, but their cost is amortized over all the systems for which they perform backups and vastly reduce labor costs. Tape drives, being mechanical, often break. The right software can detect a broken tape unit and simply use the remaining units in a jukebox to complete its tasks. Without network-based backup systems, we must either forego backups on a system if its tape unit has died or install an extra tape unit on each system to ensure there will always be one working tape unit. Certainly a jukebox is less expensive than that! Jukeboxes also are an enabling technology that permit much of the sophisticated automation described elsewhere in this chapter.

21.1.8   Tape Inventory

A pile of backup tapes with no index or inventory is only slightly more useful than no backups at all. The inventory is critical to being able to do restores in a timely manner. In large, automated backup systems that inventory is maintained on-line by the backup system. Often, special precautions must be taken in backing up the inventory because the system that does the backups will want to update the inventory as it is being copied. You might consider printing a minimal tape index at the end of your nightly backups and keeping those printouts in a notebook. The inventory is a good candidate for storage on a RAID system.

Being able to restore files is dependent on the quality of your inventory. The better the inventory is, the faster that the restore can be done. If there was no inventory, you would have to read tapes in reverse chronological order until the needed data was found. If the inventory only lists which partitions are on which tape, you would have to read each tape with data from that partition until the requested file was found. If the customer can remember the last time the file was modified, this can help the search, but it will still take a long time. Full restores would not be so impaired.

If the system stores a file-by-file inventory of each tape, the entire search process can be performed quickly in database queries; the exact tapes required would then be loaded. For example, if a couple of files on various directories plus a couple of entire directories need restoration, the software can deduce exactly which full and incremental backup tapes have the data that needs to be restored. All the required tapes would be loaded in the jukebox, and the software would perform all the restores using all the available tape drives in the jukebox.

Keeping a file-by-file inventory requires a lot of disk space. Some commercial products can strike a balance by maintaining the file-by-file listing for recent tapes and a simple partition listing for all others. The file-by-file listing can be reconstructed on demand if older files must be restored.

Software should be able to rebuild the inventory if it is lost or destroyed. In theory, you should be able to load the jukebox with the most recent tapes, click on a button, and in hours (or days) have rebuilt the inventory. A site could do backups by night and inventory-reconstruction by day.

A good inventory should also track how often a particular tape is reused. Most tape technologies become unreliable after being reused a certain number of times. You should expect backup software to be able to tell you when to destroy a tape.

In extreme situations, you may need to do a restore without access to the inventory, without access to a license server, and without the complete backup system working. Although a good inventory is critical to normal operations, make sure that the system you use doesn't prevent you from reading the data off a tape when you have nothing but the tape and a manual. Look for all of these features when selecting your backup and restore solution.

21.2 The Icing

Now that we've described the fundamentals of a solid, mature backup and restore system, certain things need to be established to maintain this system well into the future. First we must ensure that the system is working by performing fire drills. Off-site storage of tapes protects the backup media that we've worked so hard to generate. Finally, we end with a technical yet somewhat philosophical explanation of why a backup system is always one step away from needing an upgrade.

21.2.1 Firedrills

The only time you know the quality of your backup media is when you are doing a restore. This is generally the worst time to learn that you have problems. You can better assess your backup system if you do an occasional "fire drill." Pick a random file and restore it from tape to verify that your process is working.

Automated Fire Drill Requests

The first time Tom saw a backup fire drill was when he was working with Tommy Reingold at Bell Labs. Tommy wrote a small program that would randomly select a server, then randomly select a file on that server, then email the SAs asking for a copy of that file as it was a week ago. He was able to sleep better at night knowing that these weekly requests were satisfied successfully.

It can be useful to do an occasional fire drill that involves restoring an entire disk volume. The speed at which an entire disk volume can be restored is often unknown because it is so rarely requested. Restoring a file (or even a directory of files) as regularly requested by customers will not help you determine how long a full disk restore will take because of the huge difference in the quantity of data being restored. Bottlenecks go unnoticed until an emergency happens. It is better to restore an entire disk volume occasionally than to discover a bottleneck when you are under the gun to bring a system back into service. When doing these fire drills, it is important to time them and monitor things such as disk, tape, and network utilization. If you are not seeing the performance you expect, you can review the statistics you have collected to help determine what needs to be improved.

If you think you don't have enough free disk space to do a full disk fire drill, you might want to do this anytime you have installed a new server, but before it goes into production. You should have at least one spare partition available, and the drill will be a good "burn in" for the new hardware.

If some tapes are stored off-site, the fire drills should include both off-site and on-site tapes to completely exercise the system.

The person who verifies that the data recovered in the fire drill is valid should not be the same person who is responsible for performing the backups. This creates a system of checks and balances.

21.2.2 Backup Media and Off-Site Storage

Backup tapes must be stored somewhere safe. It doesn't make sense to spend large amounts of money and time on security systems to protect your data, yet store backup tapes in an unlocked room or cabinet. Your backups are the company's crown jewels. Finding storage space for them that is secure and convenient can be difficult in today's cramped office buildings. However, a set of well-locked cabinets or a large safe in an otherwise unsecure room may be sufficient.

If your backups are to hedge against the risk of a natural disaster that would destroy your entire machine room, they should not be stored in the machine room itself, nor in a room that would be flooded if your data center was also the victim of a broken pipe.

Off-site storage of backup media is an even better idea. This is where a set of backup tapes or archival copies are kept at a safe distance from the computers that generated them. This need not be complicated nor expensive.

The off-site storage facility can hold the actual backup tapes or copies of them. It is a trade-off in convenience versus risk. Storing copies hedges against the risk that the tapes may be damaged or lost in transit. However, making the additional copies may be laborious. Instead, the actual tapes usually are stored off-site. This affects your ability to do restores in a timely manner. You may choose to keep "last month's full backups" off-site, seeing that most restore requests are from the current month's backups, and customers should understand that restore requests from tapes that are more than 30 days old but newer than 60 days may incur a delay.

When selecting an off-site storage facility, consider all the same things that should be considered for the on-site storage facilities: Is the space secure? Who has access to the facilities? What policies, guarantees, or confidentiality contracts are in place? There are many ways to go about this, ranging from informal systems to using large commercial "digital warehouse" services.

Informal Off-Site Storage

In some situations, an informal policy is sufficient. A fledgling start-up had a policy that every Wednesday the head of their data processing department would take home the backup tapes that were one week old. On Wednesday morning of the following week, she would bring in the tapes she had brought home the week before. One concern was that if she was in an auto accident, the tapes could be destroyed. The risk could be reduced by increasing the cycle to once a month. The risk could be completely eliminated by having her only bring copies of the tapes home. The other concern was the security of her house. The company provided a fireproof safe for her house to store the tapes in. The safe was secured so that it could not be stolen.

Many companies use an off-site records storage service. This used to be a luxury service that only big financial companies used, but it has grown into a large market that serves all. These services provide pick-up and drop-off service, a four- or eight-hour turnaround time on requests to have particular tapes returned, and so on. Although their cost may sound prohibitive initially, they save a lot of hassle in the long run. They can also provide suggestions about typical policies that companies use for off-site storage. They even provide cute little locked boxes for you to put your tapes in when they are ready to be picked up.

There are security issues with storing tapes off-site. If a third-party company is paid to store the tapes, they must be bonded and insured. Read the contract carefully to understand the limits of their liability. You'll find it disappointingly small compared with the value of the data on the tapes. The horror stories are true. We've gotten back other people's tapes from storage facilities. In one case, we were not able to retrieve a tape that was sent to them for storage and had to request the tape that contained the previous backup of that file. The author of the file was not happy.

It is important to keep good track of what tapes are sent out and record every tape that is received back. Audit this tape movement and watch for mistakes; mistakes are an indicator of overall quality. This can be your best defense. Imagine not being able to retrieve a critical tape and later finding out from your operators that "occasionally the wrong tapes come back." Look for tapes that should have come back but didn't, tapes that shouldn't have come back but did, and tapes from the wrong company coming to you. If you are going to bring a complaint to the vendor, it is critical to have a written log of every mistake made in the past. Obviously, if these mistakes aren't "one in a million," you need to change vendors.

Homegrown Off-Site Storage

Companies with multiple buildings can provide their own off-site storage systems. One division of a company had its people spread out across two different buildings that were 40 miles apart. They exchanged tapes on a regular basis. Because they were all one division, they could even perform quick restores across their corporate network if waiting an hour or two for delivery was unreasonable.

Networked Off-Site Backups

A research center in New York had a lot of bandwidth between its two facilities and discovered that it was nearly unused at night. For several years, they performed backups for each other's site over this WAN link. This had the benefit of making all tapes "off-site." The bandwidth between the two facilities was large enough that restores could still be done in a reasonable amount of time. The management figured that it was an acceptable risk to assume that both buildings would not be simultaneously destroyed.

As network bandwidth becomes cheaper, the economics of performing backups to other sites via a network becomes more reasonable. Commercial backup services have sprung up within Internet colocation facilities to service the needs of ".com's." This is easy because extremely high-speed networks can be installed within a colocation facility. As bandwidth becomes cheaper and over-the-network backup technology becomes more reliable, secure, and accepted, we foresee this kind of service becoming even more common.

> ❖ **Internet-Based Backup Systems** When Tom was 13 years old he thought that an over-the-network backup service would be a fine idea, but was discouraged when he realized that it would take hours to backup his 160KB floppy disks over his 300-baud modem. When cable modems and xDSL service brought high-speed Internet access to homes, companies sprang up offering over-the-net backup services. Even without high-speed access, these services are fine for backing up small things, such as a student's doctoral dissertation. Tom started backing up his personal computer to one of these services the moment he got cable modem access at his house to vindicate his age 13 inventiveness.

21.2.3 High DB Availability

Some applications, such as databases, have specific requirements for ensuring a backup is successful. A database manages its own storage space and optimizes it for particular kinds of access to its complex set of data tables. Because the layout and data access methods are usually opaque to the backup software, the database usually is written to tape as a single unit, or file. If the data in that file changes as it is being written, information may be lost or corrupted because the records for locating the data may be missing or incorrect on the backup tape. Databases often need to be shut down so that no transactions can occur during the backup to ensure consistency.

If the database has high-availability requirements, it is not acceptable to shut it down each night for backups. However, the risks associated with not doing a backup or performing the backup while the database is live are also unacceptable. Some vendors of backup software offer modules for performing backups of particular databases. Some of these substantially reduce the risks associated with a live database backup. However, it is generally safest to backup the data when the database is not running. This is usually achieved through having the database mirrored, using RAID 1+0, for example. The database can be stopped long enough to disconnect a mirror and then restarted. The disconnected mirror disks are in a consistent state and unaffected by database transactions and can be safely written to tape. When the backup is finished, the mirror disks can be reconnected to the live database. Ideally, a high-availability database should be triple mirrored: one set of disks actively mirroring the database and one set detached and being backed up.

21.2.4   Technology Changes

Free your mind of the notion that there is one good piece of software or hardware that you will use for backups during your career as an SA. Instead, start thinking in general terms and move with the changes in technology.

There is one constant in backup and restore systems: Disk technology and tape technology keep leapfrogging each other, never at the same pace. Embrace this rather than fight it. Some years, tape technology will zoom ahead, and you'll feel like you can backup anything. Other years, you'll see disk technology be ahead and wonder if you will ever be able to backup all that you have. To understand why this happens, let's look at the historical growth patterns of each technology.

Disk size grows in small increments. Every couple of months, slightly larger drives are available. Overall disk capacity doubles every 15 to 18 months, and, historically, applications have been quick to use what is available. This means that about every other year you will be backing up disks that contain twice as much data.

Tape capacity over the years has grown in larger leaps but spread out over years rather than months. Consumers are less willing to upgrade tape backup hardware, and therefore the industry tends to provide "forklift upgrades" every two to three years. Resist the urge to upgrade your tape technology very often because it simplifies life to not have to deal with many, many different tape formats. Most sites tend to primarily use what was the latest technology when their system was installed and may also have a couple of legacy systems on the old platform. These legacy systems either haven't been upgraded yet or are to be decommissioned soon, and upgrading the tape technology would be a waste of money. They then retain one or two tape drives for all previous tape technologies that they still have in their archives.

Keep One Nine-Track Tape Drive

Here's a way to amass "favors" owed to you. An SA at a large company discovered that he was the only person in the main complex with the ability to read those old reel-to-reel nine-track tapes. Although it was rare that anyone would need to read such a tape, anyone who did need such a tape read would be desperate to do so. Outside companies will do tape conversions at a very high price, and he knew that people within the company would not want to pay such fees. He made sure the tape drive was in a place that he wouldn't mind visitors using and attached it to a machine on which he could create guest accounts. Every year he gained a couple valuable favors, which he would redeem later. It also helped him gain a reputation as a "nice guy," which can be more valuable in a large company than you would expect. You might want to remember this story the next time you think about decommissioning an old tape unit.

The unbalanced growth of disk and tape technologies affects how you can do backups. In the old days, it was extremely difficult to split a backup of a single partition across two tapes.[8] Most backup software was homegrown and tapes were small. Therefore when QIC tapes could store 150MB, SAs would split disks into partitions of 150MB. Then 8-mm tapes with 2.5GB capacity became popular because disks were commonly holding half to a full gigabyte. SAs thought their problems with mismatched tape and disk sizes were over; data disks could be one huge partition. The upgrade to 5GB-capacity 8-mm tapes came around the same time as disk capacity grew to 4GB. However when disks grew to their next leap (9GB), the tape industry had not caught up. This stalled the sale of these larger disks and was a boon to the commercial backup software industry, which could invest in making software to drive jukeboxes and handle the complicated task of splitting backups over multiple tapes. Next came DLT technology, which could hold 70GB, again leapfrogging disk size. And history repeated itself when disks grew beyond 70GB.

What can we learn from this? Change is constant. Trust your vendors to provide leaps in both areas, but don't be surprised when they become out of sync.

21.3 Conclusion

This chapter is about restores, for which backups are a necessary evil. This is a policy-driven issue. We are constantly surprised to find sites that do not predicate their backup system on a sound policy. There are three kinds of restore requests: accidental file deletion, recovery from disk failure, and archival. Each of these have different SLAs, expectations, and engineering requirements. More importantly, they each serve distinctively different customer groups, which you may want to bill separately. We set the policy based on these parameters.

Once we have a policy, all decisions flow easily. From the policy, we can then develop a backup schedule that is a specific list of which systems

---

[8]It still can be a risky thing to do; most systems only put the index on the first tape.

are backed up and when. One of the most difficult parts of determining the schedule is deciding how many days of incremental backups should be done before the next full backup. Modern software does these calculations for us and can create a highly dynamic schedule. The policy helps us plan time, capacity, consumables, and other issues. Communicating the policy to the customers helps them understand the safety of their data, which systems are not backed up, and the procedure they should use if they need data restored. Making customers aware of which systems are not backed up is important.

A modern backup system must be automated to minimize human labor, human thought, human decisions, and human mistakes. In the old days, backups were a significant part of an SA's job, and therefore it was reasonable that they consumed a significant amount of an SA's time. Now, however, an SA is burdened with many new responsibilities. Backups are a well-defined task that can be, and should be, delegated to others. We delegate the creation of the software to commercial vendors. We delegate the daily operational aspects to clerks. We can even delegate simple restores to the customers who request them. We focus our time, instead, on designing the architecture, installing the system, and handling the periodic scaling issues that come up. All this delegation leaves us more time for other tasks.

Modern backup systems are centralized. Doing backups over the network to a central, large backup device saves labor. The cost of large jukeboxes is amortized over the number of machines it serves.

Modern backup systems have excellent inventory systems. The system must have an excellent file inventory so that restores are done quickly and an excellent tape inventory so that tapes are recycled according to schedule.

We've also learned that backups cost a lot of money, both in equipment cost and consumables. Section 8.1.2 discusses the economics you can use to justify systems that reduce risk.

Backup technology is changing all the time. As disk capacity grows, we must upgrade our ability to maintain backups. We must free our minds of the notion that any backup and restore system we install is our final solution. Instead, we must be prepared to scale it constantly and replace it every three to five years.

Once the Basics are in place, there are two issues that are the Icing. First, we must test the validity of our backups with fire drills. We select a random piece of information and verify that we are able to successfully restore it. Second, we must establish safe, off-site storage for our backup media. We don't want our backups to be kept in the same place as the computers they are backing up.

Restores are one of the most important services you provide to your customers. The inability to restore critical data can bankrupt your company. The flawless execution of a restore can make you a hero to all.

Exercises

1. What is your restore policy? Do you have to work within corporate guidelines (what are they?), or is your policy created locally?

2. Tables 21.1 and 21.2 do not take into consideration the fact that tapes are usually changed every day, whether they are full or not. Why are the examples still statistically valid? Why might it be a bad idea to put multiple days' backups on the same tape?

3. Section 21.1.2 mentions that some vendors' incremental backups only record files changed since the last incremental. How does this affect how restores are done? What are the pros and cons of this technique?

4. Section 21.1.2 highlights that vendor terminology for "incrementals" varies. How would you construct a test to find out what variation is actually implemented by a vendor? Perform this test on two different OSs.

5. What are the benefits and risks of using a backup system that can continue a dump onto a second tape if the first tape gets full?

6. The example in Section 21.1.4 assumed that tapes could be recycled with no limit. Assume a tape can be used 15 times before it must be discarded. Calculate how many tapes would have to be discarded each year for the first four years of the example.

7. Section 21.1.4 didn't calculate how much would be spent on cleaning tapes. Assume that drives need to be cleaned every 30 days and a cleaning tape can be used 15 times. Calculate how many cleaning tapes are required for the two examples in Section 21.1.4.

8. Section 21.1.4 assumed that the amount of data being backed up didn't change over the four years. This is not realistic. Reproduce the calculations in that section based on the assumption that the amount of data stored doubles every 18 months.

9. What aspects of your current backup and restore system should be automated better?

10. Consider the summary, "A modern backup system must be automated to minimize human labor, human thought, human decisions, and human mistakes." What point is being made here?

Chapter 22

Remote Access Service

A remote access service is one that gives authorized individuals a way to access the company network from home; customer sites; or other locations around the country, the continent, or the world. In the early days, it was something that weird technical people wanted to use so that they could do extra work from home out of normal working hours. More recently it has become a core service that everyone in a company uses.

Many different problems get lumped together in the "remote access" category. One aspect of remote access is that people want to be able to check their email and access data when they are on the road. Almost as common is people wanting to work from home in the evenings, weekends, a few days a week, or full-time. Another aspect is that some people are semipermanently stationed at a customer's site, but still need to be able to access the corporate network on a regular basis. This chapter shows how all these different aspects have slightly different requirements, but also have much in common.

Remote access is one of the areas in which technology is constantly changing. This chapter will look at how that affects the design and administration of a remote access service. It will not examine what technologies to use because that will have changed even between the time of writing and publication. The information in this chapter should give you a basis for evaluating current technologies and solutions and making architectural decisions.

22.1   The Basics

To provide a remote access service you should start by understanding your customers' requirements, which will be many and varied. You should also decide with your customers what service levels the SAs will provide for the different aspects of the system and document those decisions for future reference.

Once you have defined the requirements and the service levels, you are ready to build the service, or to not build it. One of the basics of building a remote access system is to outsource as much of it as possible. However, there still are several components that must be built or managed internally to the company. In particular, the security aspects of authentication, authorization, and maintaining perimeter security should be managed internally.

22.1.1   Remote Access Requirements

The first requirement of a remote access service typically will be assumed and not explicitly stated by your customers. That requirement is that everyone must have access to a low-cost, convenient remote access solution. If the SA team does not provide one, then customers will build something for themselves that will not be as secure or well-managed as the service that the SAs would provide. It is quite likely that the SAs will ultimately be expected to support the service that their customers have built when it develops problems. It typically also will be more difficult to support than an SA-built service.

The other requirements are based on how the customers intend to use the remote access system. The most common customers of remote access are people who are traveling and want to check or send email. Other common customers are people who want to log in for an hour or two in the evening to catch up on a few things. These different groups of people have something in common, which is that they only use the remote access service for fairly short periods of time. They differ in that one group expects to be able to use the service from anywhere and the other just needs to use it from home. The requirement that they both introduce is that they need a way to connect to the office network that is reliable and economical for short-duration connections. They do not need very high bandwidth, but they want as much as they can get. Where they differ is that the people who are traveling need to be able to connect from anywhere they may travel. Depending on the company, that area may be anything from a small region to the entire world. To provide global remote access, the technology used must be ubiquitous. When setting up a remote access system for these customers, it is important to know what the coverage area needs to be for the service and what the cost model is for the different areas.

If people want to work from home on a regular basis, there are three primary things to take into account. First, outages will have a significant impact on the day-to-day work of those people, so the service they use must be reliable. Second, they will need high-speed access because the speed of the connection will affect their day-to-day productivity, and they will typically be doing tasks that require higher bandwidth and/or faster response time. Finally, the economics are different from the occasional or short-time user. A person who is working from home is typically using the remote access service for 8 to 10 hours a day. Per-minute charges add up rapidly under this usage profile, so always-on connections may be cheaper.

Often, people within the company may want to use a high-bandwidth connection to the Internet that they have access to at a conference or at home. This is particularly common in technical companies. This situation often requires a very different technology from what is used to meet the requirements described above. It requires encryption between the person's computer and the corporate network because company-confidential information is being transmitted over the public Internet and can be intercepted. Transmission of information unencrypted over the Internet may also be considered publication of the information in legal terms, which causes the company to lose intellectual property rights. In addition, transmitting passwords unencrypted over the Internet is a sure way to get broken into. Typically, the server-side of this encrypted connection is part of the corporate firewall. The encryption mechanism needs to provide access to everything that the person needs on the corporate network, be reliable, and have reasonably high throughput.

Another group of people that the service needs to cater to are those who need to access the network from another company's site, such as support engineers or consultants who are at a customer site. They introduce the added complexity of combining the policies, security, and practical issues of two, possibly unrelated, sites. These people usually are not in a position to be demanding of the customer, so they need to be able to work with whatever restrictions are in place, rather than try to change the security policies or the firewall rules. Typically bringing an "always-on" line of some description to the person's desk at the customer site is not an acceptable solution for either company's security team, because the person needs access to both networks and may inadvertently bridge them together. Sometimes, adding an analog line to the person's desk is acceptable, but often it is not, for the same reason. So the usual method involves building an encrypted channel between the person's machine and the company firewall, crossing the customer's firewall and the Internet. This means that you need to provide a remote access mechanism that is likely to be permitted to pass through most firewalls, as they typically are configured, and that is not too difficult to add to firewalls that don't already permit it.[1] It also needs to be flexible enough that the person can access everything needed on the corporate network. That often is not as easy as it may sound because some applications use protocols that are difficult to tunnel across some of the encryption mechanisms that meet the other requirements. Some compromises may have to be made between the different requirements to find products that will work. Ideally, this situation should be able to use the same software as was selected for the high-bandwidth, no-firewall situation described above, but that may not be the case. Supporting these people with remote access is often the most difficult challenge, especially because each customer site will have different security policies.

Because of all the different requirements that remote access services may be expected to meet, they normally are composed of several different components, each of which supports one or more of the groups of people described above.

22.1.2   Define a Remote Access Policy

Before starting to provide a remote access service, the company must define a policy for remote access. The policy should define what acceptable use of the service is, the security policies surrounding the service, and the responsibilities attached to having access to the service. It should also state who gets what kind of remote access and who pays for it. Section 7.1.3 discusses the remote access policy and other security policies in more detail.

22.1.3   Define Service Levels

It is important to clearly define the service levels for the various remote access services in consultation with the customers of those services. Remote access can be a sensitive area because failures are discovered by people who want to do some work and are unable to do anything until service is restored. This is frustrating for them and can cause the problems to have a high visibility. If the service levels are clearly defined, communicated, and understood before problems arise, the customers should know what to expect

---

[1]A new protocol is not too difficult to add if it only uses one TCP port and doesn't have security issues for the client side, such as permitting tunneling back to the client network across established connections.

for an estimated time to repair (ETR), which should reduce tension and frustration levels.

A lone SA at a small site should negotiate service levels that permit her to get some sleep so she can function properly during the day. Large organizations with a 24 × 7 helpdesk should have more customer-oriented service levels. The helpdesk staff should be trained on the remote access service and when to escalate problems. New services that are in a trial phase should have lower service levels because the helpdesk will not be fully trained and only a few senior SAs will be familiar with the trial service. However, customers of the trial service should have a backup access method. Services that are being phased out and used by only a few people are also candidates for lower service levels, because new staff may not be trained on old technologies.

Choose Customers for Trial Services Carefully

Several years ago, a software company was introducing a higher-speed remote access service based on ISDN. The first stage of this project was to determine what equipment to use for the corporate side and the home side of the connection, testing reliability, compatibility, feature sets, and scalability. A couple of possibilities for each end of the connection had been identified and needed to be tested. The network team planned to use only a few SAs for the initial tests, so the SAs could help with the debugging. However, several people in engineering demanded the service, saying they would build it themselves if the SA team did not deliver it quickly. The director of the SA team explained to engineering that the service would be available shortly because initial trials were beginning. The engineering directors identified some engineers who were working from home and desperately needed higher-speed access and asked that they be included in the trial. The SA team had to agree to ensure that the engineers did not build their own service. The network team made it clear to the engineers who participated in the trial that this was not yet a service and that outages could potentially last for several days, so they were not to rely on it and must have a backup access method. However, it was not long before one of the engineers on the trial program had a problem with his ISDN connection and quickly escalated it through his management chain so that it became a priority-one trouble ticket, requiring SAs to pay attention to it rather than many tickets relating to supported services. He was not an appropriate trial customer because he became reliant on the higher speed instantly, and he was not tolerant of outages or willing to revert to the old dial-in access method.

The root of the problem was that the ISDN investigation project was not funded until the engineers were already clamoring for it, which was more than a year after the budget request had been made by the network architect who had foreseen the need. At that stage it was impossible to restrict the trial team to appropriate people, which led to lots of stress and frustration for both the SAs and the engineers.

Major bandwidth increases are addictive. Reverting to the old system is not an option after using a faster one, no matter how clear the SAs try to be about the service levels that can be expected of the prototype service. A new service must have passed the initial prototyping phase, and at least the customer-side equipment must be determined, before early adopters are given access to the system; otherwise it is a recipe for disaster. Try to squeeze important projects like this into the budget before they become political disaster areas, even if they are not officially funded.

22.1.4   Centralization

Remote access is an area that benefits from centralization. From a security standpoint, the authentication component of the remote access service must be centralized to ensure proper auditing and access control. From a cost standpoint, new technologies are emerging all the time, and the research costs for how best to implement and support a new technology are high and so should not be duplicated across the company. Also, significant economies of scale can be achieved in concentrating all the usage onto centralized equipment and lines. The ultimate form of centralization is to outsource the remote access service.

22.1.5   Outsourcing

The best way to deal with the constantly changing technologies in the remote access area is to get someone else to do it. It is a losing battle to try to keep evaluating new technologies and figuring out how to scale and support them, only to replace everything within a year or two with newer technology.

Several remote access outsourcing companies, usually ISPs, can take on at least some aspects of a company's remote access service. One way they can do it is by installing VPN software on the customers' machines, with the customers dialing into the ISP's normal modem pools or other connection options, and using a VPN to connect to the corporate network. Another is through the use of "virtual circuits" that set up security filters and route customers' traffic based on the customers' authenticated identities. The customers usually use modem pools dedicated to this service offering from the ISP and dedicated connections from the ISP back to the company.

A more immediate benefit of outsourcing remote access is that the time spent supporting remote access is dramatically reduced. The cost becomes a visible, predictable number that can be in the budget, rather than a hidden, unquantifiable, variable number. A predictable charge is good for cost management and budgeting. From the SA's point of view, outsourcing remote access means fewer support calls out of business hours and not having to track down the errant broken modem that is preventing customers from dialing in. Some outsourcing services may deal with all remote access issues, others may deal with everything except the VPN software, for example. Anyone who has had to support a modem pool will appreciate that getting someone else to do it is desirable.

The economies of scale mean that it is easier and more cost-effective for the outsourcing company to evaluate new technologies and how to support them. It is part of their core business, so evaluation projects will be funded.

Some aspects of remote access should not be outsourced. In particular, the authentication database should be maintained within the company so that it can be incorporated into the exit process for departing employees and contractors, it can be audited, and sensitive terminations can be handled discreetly at short notice.

When a company decides to outsource any part of the computing environment, the SAs must choose the outsourcing vendor carefully. The vendors should be evaluated on the following criteria:

Coverage area: The outsourcing company should cover at least the areas that are needed by the customer base, which includes both employees' homes and the areas to which people are likely to travel. It is best to find an outsourcing company with global coverage and an option to select and pay for smaller coverage areas. You can expand to larger coverage areas when necessary. An area can be considered to be fully covered if any connection to the remote access service within that area is charged at local rates or is free of charge to the caller, other than the remote access provider's charges. It may be less cost-effective to outsource if you require only a small coverage area.

Supported technologies: Evaluating the outsourcing companies also involves looking at what technologies they support and their rate of technology adoption. If they don't keep up with new technologies, the problem of customers building their own faster remote access system will raise its head.

First-level support: Does the outsourcing company provide first-level support, or does it only provide support through escalation from the SA staff? Although problems that may be related to misconfiguration of the customers' machines could be solved by internal SA staff, they will not be as familiar with a service that was not built in-house, and will not have access to all the relevant parts of the system for debugging problems. The extra level of indirection also costs time in resolving the customer's problem.

Service level agreement: It is important to get and evaluate a written SLA before selecting an outsourcing vendor. What do the response times look like? What nonperformance clauses are there? How can you track their performance? What speed and latency is typical, what is guaranteed?

Billing structure: What is the cost model and the billing structure for the service? Ideally, all costs should be incorporated into the outsourcing company's charges so that the company and the employees do not have to deal with filing and processing expense reports for remote access. Understand what all the costs are and how they differ across service areas. Check whether it is possible to maintain a database for the outsourcing vendor that maps users to departments that the outsourcing company will then use to bill each department separately, or at least provide a cost breakdown for the company.

Authentication interface: Check what mechanisms the vendor supports for authentication. The vendor should support a few standard authentication and authorization protocols so that the SAs can choose an appropriate protocol for use with their authentication scheme. The vendor must have a facility for the authentication and authorization database to be managed by the customer company.

Security: The security team at the company still has responsibility for the site's overall security, which includes the outsourced remote access system. The security staff must liaise with the outsourcing company to ensure that appropriate security is maintained within the remote access architecture, perhaps by implementing something at the corporate site that works in conjunction with authentication information passed along by the outsourcing vendor. Find out what their security architecture is and the options available before selecting the outsourcing company.

Take the time to do the vendor evaluation thoroughly and to make the decision carefully. It is difficult to change remote access vendors if it doesn't work out, because it involves changing configurations, and perhaps software, on everyone's machines, as well as ordering new lines to all the places that had permanent connections to this vendor and giving everyone the new information that they need to carry with them when traveling.

22.1.6 Authentication

The authentication and authorization system is one component that always should be built and maintained in-house, even if everything else is outsourced. All remote access methods should use the same authentication database to reduce administrative overhead and the chances that one of the databases might be overlooked when disabling employees' access after they leave. There can be many interfaces into that database through different protocols, if necessary.

The authentication mechanism should use one of the many one-time password, or token-based, systems that are available. It should not be based on reusable passwords. Small companies may have to start with a simple password-based system for cost reasons, but they should budget for switching to a more secure system as soon as they can.

22.1.7 Perimeter Security

The remote access service is part of the company's perimeter, even if it is outsourced to another company. If the company bases some of its security around having a secure perimeter, then that perimeter must be maintained. Remote access services can breach the perimeter security through misconfiguration of some of the components. In particular, hosts or networking equipment can be configured for dynamic routing with no restrictions on what traffic they route or what routes they propagate. This can result in the remote access service providing a back door into the network.

Restrict Traffic and Routing Across Remote Access Links

A married couple worked in the computer industry. At one point, they worked for companies that were direct competitors. Both companies used perimeter security models. Both companies installed a high-bandwidth remote access service to their employee's home. The couple had a home network in the house with some shared resources, such as a printer. The networking equipment from each of the companies was not restricted in what traffic it would route or what routes it would propagate. Each company ended up with a full routing table for the other company. Company A used the same DNS table inside and outside the company, which resulted in company B's mail servers sending all mail for company A across the couple's home network directly to the internal mail server. The problem was only spotted and traced when one company noticed that the mail headers were not quite right.

The companies should have restricted what routes could get into their network tables, and they should have installed at least minimal security on these connections that restricted traffic to only go to and from the one authorized host on that connection. These measures would prevent the accidental connection of two networks, but not deliberate break-in attempts. More complex security measures and policies are needed to fully secure these remote access connections.

22.2   The Icing

There are a few ways to improve on a remote access service once it is up and running. For people who work from home on a regular basis, consider their other business needs beyond simple network access. Look at ways to reduce costs and automate some of the cost analysis component. For SAs who are providing remote access services, there are some ways to keep up with new technologies without making remote access support a complete nightmare.

22.2.1   Home Office

Working from home inevitably involves more than simply establishing network connectivity. Frequently, the SA team is called on for solutions to other problems.

One problem that directly affects the SA team is the issue of who provides the home office equipment, who supports it, and to what level. Support that requires a visit to someone's home to install new equipment or fix broken equipment is very expensive to provide. The SLA must be very specific on these issues, and if that level of support is provided, there must be a model for recovering those support costs from the home employee's department.

The other issues that inevitably arise are that the employee working from home needs to make business calls, send and receive faxes, print, photocopy, and initiate and participate in conference calls. Depending on their jobs they may want to be able to be connected to the network, on the telephone, and still able to receive a fax. They also don't want to have to go through their phone bill and expense back all the business calls every month. The company may want to consider remote access services that include telephony, or to simply install additional phone lines that are billed back to the company. If the lines can't be billed directly to the company, the cost of employees vouchering their individual bills can be a large, hidden cost. The SA team should bear these requirements in mind when deciding on the home office remote access solution and be ready to provide a solution for the customers.

The other issue that arises for people who work from home is that they feel they are losing touch with what is happening at the company because they are not involved in corridor conversations or group meetings or lunches. Look for ways to break down the distance barrier and make casual communication easier. Some common solutions include one-on-one video conference systems and equipping all conference rooms with the ability to broadcast presentations over the network.

22.2.2 Cost Analysis and Reduction

Remote access costs can accumulate quickly, and they are typically hidden from those who incur them. Once the remote access system is operational, look at ways to reduce the costs without adversely affecting the service. Most remote access services provide toll-free numbers for people to call, which have high charges for the company. Providing local dial-up numbers in a high-volume area and converting people to that number can reduce costs.[2] Also, look at the people who use the service the most (from a fixed location) and see if an always-on connection to that location is possible and would prove more cost-effective. Automate as much of this process as possible, including a notification mechanism for people who are using the toll-free number when they could use a local number.

Case Study: Reducing Costs by Billing Analysis

Lucent was able to significantly reduce the cost of its dial-in service using some interesting techniques. The system provided modem pools in areas that were highly populated by employees, so that the calls would be local and therefore toll-free. People that were not local to a modem pool expensed portions of their phone bills, which was time consuming for employees, expensive to process for Lucent, and wasteful because the individual's per-minute charges were often higher than Lucent could negotiate with phone companies. The use of a toll-free (1-800) phone number greatly reduced the vouchering process and saved costs. The 800 number was sophisticated enough to direct the call to the nearest modem pool, and route around modem pools that were low on capacity. The toll-free number was so convenient that sometimes people would use it even though there was a local number that was less costly to the company.

A system was created that detected the phone number of the incoming call and dynamically generated a sign-on banner that would alert the caller to the phone

---

[2]This is particularly applicable in countries that have free local calling, or even flat-rate local calls, but not so useful in countries that charge per-minute for local calls. Avoid this approach if it will lead to people expensing their dial-up costs.

number they should call instead. If the user had dialed in via the most cost-effective phone number, the normal banner would be displayed. Billing records were examined, and employees not dialing the most cost-effective dial-in numbers would receive email once a month explaining how much money they would have saved the company if they had dialed the right number.

When VPNs were first being introduced, billing records were used to identify which users could be supported for less money if they used a VPN service over an always-on Internet technology such as cable modems and xDSL. People whose conversions would save the company the most money (the top ten percent) were actively sought out to be some of the first customers for this new service. From time to time, billing records were again examined to identify new candidates.

22.2.3   New Technologies

SAs who have to build and support remote access services are faced with the problem of trying to keep up with new technologies and deciding which ones to implement. They then need to support all of the new and old technologies simultaneously, which leads to ever-increasing support costs. Traditional modems have a benefit in this area, in that they are backward-compatible. It is possible to upgrade the company modem pool to the latest, fastest technology and still support all the people who have older modems. Other remote access technologies do not have this benefit.

Introducing a new technology increases the support costs significantly until that technology has been widely adopted and is well understood. Supporting old technologies also has a high cost because the equipment becomes less reliable, and when only a few people use it, SAs are less familiar with the system.

The key to keeping support costs under control is to avoid the high support costs at the end of the curve where an old technology is still in use by only a few people. Do this by supporting at most two technologies, in addition to traditional modem dial-in access. When a new technology is going to be deployed, aggressively phase out the older of the two existing technologies by converting those people to a newer technology and having a hard cut-over date when the old service will be discontinued.

22.3   Conclusion

Supporting a remote access service can be a very time-consuming and thankless task. Technology moves rapidly and your customers want to move with it, but you may not be funded for it at the right time. Understand the requirements before attempting to build a remote access service; they may be many and varied. Define a remote access policy that customers must agree to before they have access to the service. Agree on and communicate service levels for the various components of the service.

The remote access service benefits from centralization because of the rate of technological change. It is a good area to outsource to benefit from the economies of scale and large coverage areas that an outsourcing vendor can achieve. The major benefit of outsourcing is that it relieves the SA team from the burden of maintaining a modem pool and debugging remote access problems. Keep control of the authentication and authorization components of the remote access service, however, and pay attention to the security of the service, particularly if your site relies on perimeter security.

Improve the remote access service by solving some of the other home office issues before they even arise. Find ways to reduce costs, and automate as much of that as possible. When faced with the challenge of supporting a remote access service, control the support costs by limiting the number of technologies in use.

Exercises

1. What technologies does your remote access service currently support? Which of these is the most expensive to support and why?

2. What is the next access technology you will adopt? Describe what will be involved in adopting it.

3. What is your site's remote access policy? How is it advertised to the customers?

4. What requirements does your remote access system have to meet?

5. Follow a new hire through the process of procuring remote access services from your organization. Watch, but don't help, them find out what is available, sign up for the service, complete the installation, and become functional. What should be improved about the process to make it a more pleasant experience for the customer?

6. How would you provide remote access for employees who are at a customer's site? What compromises would you need to make?

7. What are your site's service levels for the different areas of your remote access system?

8. If you do not outsource any of your remote access, what would the cost of outsourcing it be? How does that compare with the cost of supporting it in-house? What would the benefits be? What would the disadvantages be?

9. If you are outsourcing some of your remote access, how did you decide what parts to outsource, and how did you determine the vendor?

10. What authentication mechanism do you use for your remote access service?

11. How many authentication databases are there in your system?

12. What security controls are on your remote access service?

13. How many people in your company work from home on a regular basis? What is the support model for the equipment in their homes? What services does the company provide beyond simple network connectivity?

14. If you were to design a remote access service to support people who work from home within a reasonable distance of the main office, what support model would you choose? What technology would you use and why? How would you support your customers' additional needs, such as phones and faxes? How would your answer change if the people were 2,000 miles away from the nearest office?

15. How could you reduce the costs of your remote access service?

Chapter 23

Software Depot Service

A software depot is a way of making a large number of software packages available to many hosts. UNIX has a tradition of a globally accessible `/usr/local/bin` that is shared among all hosts in a cluster. Windows sites have a different tradition involving a repository of installable packages.

UNIX is known for providing a large number of tools to do various tasks. However, this number seems small compared with the tools that are available for free via the Internet. Selecting and installing these tools is a huge responsibility. Replicating these tools to dozens, hundreds, or thousands of machines is impossible without automation. If a software depot is not provided, nontechnical customers will simply lack these tools and will not reach their full productivity, whereas technical customers will install these tools themselves, most likely duplicating the work of others doing the same. Either way, customers will lose productivity if the SAs do not provide this service.

A good software depot makes the most anemic operating system (OS) rich and useful. It can become easy for customers to take the benefits for granted.

We Forget How Bare Vendor Installations Can Be

On a mailing list, a Solaris user asked how she could download a web page to disk in a shell script. One reply stated that it was a shame that she wasn't using Linux because she would then have access to a great program called `wget` (Niksic 1998). Tom was surprised because he had `wget` on every machine of every UNIX and UNIX-like OS to which he had access. He had forgotten that not everyone's UNIX environment included a rich software depot that tracked all the latest software. If your software depot is rich and widely distributed to all machines, customers will forget that it isn't part of the vendor's OS. This incident made Tom realize that much of the attractiveness of Linux distributions is that they include such a rich collection of tools without requiring a full-time software depot maintainer, unlike Solaris. It was a luxury he'd always had and therefore had taken for granted.

Conversely, while this reduces the barrier to entry, it makes future upgrades more difficult. Upgrading to a new release of any of those packages requires work on each and every machine because they are not accessing a repository shared over a network. Sites that have adopted Linux have had to refine (or rewrite) their software depot systems in response.

UNIX software often is delivered in source form with an installation process that is much more complicated than the average customer could follow. Even commercial UNIX software can be equally difficult to install. The installation of UNIX software often requires "root" access, something that UNIX users don't tend to have. In UNIX environments, it therefore is wise to have one person (or a team of people) build packages and distribute them to all hosts, often keeping hundreds or thousands of hosts in sync. This centralization leverages expertise.

Windows systems usually handle software depots differently for historical, technical, and cultural reasons. Windows systems tend to be self-administered. Windows systems also tend to access software from the local hard drive rather than from a file server because, historically, Windows-based file servers were slow, Windows-based networks were unreliable, and Windows software typically required some files or registry settings to be installed on the local machine, even if the software was run from a network disk. Windows software also tends to come as binary distributions, often with extremely user-friendly installation. Although those things aren't always true for modern Windows environments, this history resulted in the Windows culture evolving differently.

As a result, Windows software depots usually take one of three forms. One form is a *network disk* that includes certain software packages that are specifically written to run off a network disk. The first execution of such software installs the necessary local files and registry settings. Another form is some kind of *network-based software "push" system* such as Microsoft's System Management Service (MS-SMS), which lets centralized administrators push packages to all machines. The last form that this takes is the *distribution-server model*: a repository of software packages (usually .ZIP files) is made available to the local community for manual installation.

For the purpose of this chapter, Windows software depots will mean the distribution-server model whether the installation files are accessed via FTP, the web, or a network disk. Running software off a network disk is similar to UNIX software depots and systems such as MS-SMS have already been discussed in Chapter 1.

Software depots often are thought of as something found in corporate or university "general-purpose computing platform" environments rather than, for example, e-commerce sites that need to tightly control which software is on which hosts. Although the number of software packages may not be as large in e-commerce environments, important principles such as consistency and leverage still apply.

23.1 The Basics

We will begin by understanding the business justifications and technical requirements of software depots. Then we will discuss the policies and documentation you should create. With those foundations, we will follow the process of selecting from the many preexisting software depot management packages, then design simple software depot systems for both UNIX and Windows systems. The system we design fulfills our requirements yet requires very little programming.

23.1.1 Understand the Justification

A software depot is a service for customers that finds, installs, and maintains a library of software. Considerable cost savings can be achieved by reducing duplication of effort through using a software depot.

A depot saves people from searching for the software on the Internet, provides a simple cache that saves network bandwidth, and consolidates software purchases. (Section 14.2.1 describes the economic benefits and ramifications of volume software purchasing.)

Without a depot, customers and fellow SAs will waste a lot of time searching for software on the Internet, in catalogs, and other places. The depot provides a single place for customers to look for software. Without a depot, software will be installed in many places around the network. The people who maintain software depots are librarians. They cull through new software and select what they feel their customers will need. Like a DJ, they take requests. If one person has requested a package then there is a good chance that other people will find such software useful, too. Self-supporting subcommunities may spring up around certain packages.

Depots leverage software installation expertise. Compiling and installing software is difficult. We take it for granted after years of editing `Makefiles`, installing patches, and porting code.

SAs who maintain packages should always be watching for and installing new versions of a package as they are released. Bug fixes, especially security-related bug fixes, are particularly important to look for. By maintaining a centralized depot, we can be assured that all customers have access to the updated release if a push model is used.

The consistency that comes from having the same software on all hosts benefits SAs and customers alike. SAs benefit because their effort is leveraged to all hosts. Customers benefit because all machines that access the depot become somewhat interchangeable. They can select hosts based on their hardware differences (speed, memory, and so on), rather than which software packages are available.

Small sites often believe they don't need a software depot. We assert that all machines need a consistent layout for storage of software; otherwise, the inconsistencies will create a rat's nest of confusion. They may not need a complicated depot system, but a consistent layout and process is important. Small sites tend to grow into larger sites. Small sites should be on the lookout for signs that they are growing and would soon benefit from a more complicated software depot. Some warning signs are that you find yourself micro-managing your software library, duplicating the build process unnecessarily, and having an inconsistent set of software packages on your machines has become a hindrance.

23.1.2   Understand the Technical Expectations

A software depot must be based on the requirements of the people who use it. Get an understanding of what customers want from a depot. They might require a fixed set of tools or a broad range of tools. Maybe management only wants tools installed that are approved as part of the development chain, or they might want a veritable salad of interesting tools.

Customers also may have a requirement to have multiple versions of a key tool, such as a compiler, available simultaneously while they cut over from one tool to the newer version.

Consider the reliability requirements. If the files are stored locally, there is less concern because local files tend to be available if the machine is available. If the files are on a remote file server, network and server reliability and scaling are factors. If the depot is more like an FTP server that is accessed occasionally, customers will be more tolerant of outages.

Replication is often used to gain higher levels of reliability. You can replicate the depot on various servers, one or two per customer group (or collections of customer groups), or you can use RAID to increase the chance that the depot will be available.

23.1.3   Set the Policy

There needs to be a policy that describes who can contribute software packages to the depot. It can be dangerous to permit anyone to provide software that everyone will run. Someone could install a Trojan Horse, a malicious program with the same name as some other program. Or someone who is not aware of all the customer requirements might upgrade a tool and inadvertently create compatibility problems. The policy should address the following questions:

- Who may build and install packages? There might be one or more people who do this as their full-time job. Maybe all SAs can create packages, but one person does a quality-control check and actually installs the package. Maybe certain customers are able to update certain packages, but the initial installation must be gated by an SA.
- What happens if the maintainer leaves the organization? If particular packages are maintained by a particular person, the policy should specify what to do if that person leaves.
- Which OSs are supported? Is there a depot for each OS in use, or just a few? In UNIX it is possible to have one depot for all OSs and use *wrapper scripts* to work around system differences. A wrapper script is a batch file that discovers what platform it is running on and calls the appropriate binary. Usually, the binaries have been renamed so that the wrapper script can have the name that customers expect to type. Wrappers can set environment variables, verify that configuration files exist, and so on. Alternatively, if there is a depot for each OS, are packages expected to run on all releases of that OS or are wrappers used when different binaries are required even for different versions within that OS?
- If you do use wrappers, is there a standard wrapper that everyone should adopt?
- How are upgrades handled? When there is a new release of a package, who is responsible for installing it?
- How are bugs handled? Is the maintainer expected to try to debug open source packages, or are customers simply told to report the bug to the maintainers and wait for the next release?

- How are packages deleted from the depot? Many sites have a strict deletion policy. Packages may be deleted as the official development environment progresses to newer tools, or packages may stay around forever, simply depending on the fact that only popular packages are carried forward to the new depot created for the next release of the OS.
- What is the scope of distribution? Is this depot for a cluster, a department, or an entire enterprise?
- How do customers request that packages be added to the depot? Is there a depot committee that decides these things?

The policy must be advertised and published, preferably where customers will see it.

23.1.4   Selecting Depot Software

For UNIX systems, we recommend selecting an existing depot management package rather than writing one from scratch. Even if you feel your environment is particularly special, customizing an existing package is easier than inventing a new one. Many free software depot packages are available. Depot (Colyer and Wong 1992) is one of the seminal publications on this topic. GNU Stow (Glickstein 1996) is simple and powerful. Many other packages are available, such as "LUDE" (Dagenais et al. 1993), "Modules" (Furlani and Osel 1996), and "SEPP" (Oetiker 1998b).

For our definition of a Windows software depot, there are also choices. You can make a network directory "share," an FTP server, or a web site that provides the software. Section 23.1.7 describes how the questions of organization and documentation of the Windows depot can be addressed in the architecture of the depot system.

23.1.5   Create the Process Manual

No matter what software you choose, it is important to document the local procedure for injecting new software packages into the system. Although the documentation that comes with the package manager is useful, this document should include local specifics such as the names of the hosts that control the system and so on.

After people have used this documentation to inject a couple of packages, it can be useful to create a shorter "quick guide" document that summarizes the steps without much explanation as to why they are doing each step. This guide helps the experienced SA simply not forget any steps. The SA should be able to cut and paste command lines from this document into a shell so that the process goes quickly. An example of this is in the sidebar, "Two Sets of Documentation," in Chapter 6.

23.1.6 A UNIX Example

We will now describe a simple yet powerful software depot for UNIX. It is usable on a single system, as well as a medium-size distributed network. It can be extrapolated for large networks with a little automation.[1] In our example, the packages we are installing will be various versions of the programming language `perl` and the mail reader `mutt`.

Packages are built on a particular server for each OS being supported. It is important to document which build machines are used so that the process can be repeated exactly. This makes it easier to track down problems, especially strange library issues that pop up now and then.

The source code for each package is stored in `/home/src`, with a subdirectory for each package. Inside the subdirectory are the `tar` files for all the versions of the package that are currently supported, plus the untarred source code where the builds are performed. For example, `/home/src/perl` might contain `perl-6.0.tar.gz` and `perl-6.1.tar.gz`, as well as appropriate subdirectories. In multi-OS environments, there may be another subdirectory level to separate the copies of source code compiled for each OS, though some packages use the VPATH facility in `make` to permit one copy of the source to be used when building for multiple OSs.

Also in `/home/src` is a script named `SOURCEME` which is sourced to set up the build environment properly. If a special environment is required for a particular package, a `SOURCEME` file specific to those requirements is stored within the package subdirectory (for example, `/home/src/perl/SOURCEME` or `/home/src/perl/SOURCEME-6.1`). Creating such a file is a small investment of your time that promotes institutional learning, results in less reinventing of wheels, and leaves a "paper trail" for future SAs who must repeat the process. The large effort to build the first release of a package is leveraged when the newer releases arrive.

Packages are installed in directories that encode the name of the package, as well as the release number of the package. For example, `/sw/perl-6.0` would contain a `bin`, `man`, and `lib` directory of Perl 6.0. Other packages might be stored in `/sw/perl-6.1`, `/sw/mutt-1.2.6`, and `/sw/mutt-2.0.1`. This enables the SAs to satisfy a requirement to maintain multiple versions simultaneously.

The name of the package without a version number is a link to the latest supported release of that package. For example, `/sw/perl` would be a symbolic link pointing to `/sw/perl-6.1`. This means that to specifically use the older, 6.0, release of `perl`, you would include `/sw/perl-6.0/bin` in your

---

[1] We would like to specifically recommend against installing third-party software directly in `/bin` or `/usr/bin` as other books and articles have recommended. It is too difficult to track changes when you are modifying the vendor-provided namespace.

PATH.[2] However, to "go with the flow" and use the latest stable release of Perl, you would include `/sw/perl/bin` in your PATH.

New packages can be installed and tested before they are released to the general public by simply not updating the generic (`/sw/perl`) symbolic link until that release is ready for public use. For example, if Perl 6.1 is in common use and Perl 7.0 has just been released, this new release would be installed in `/sw/perl-7.0`. Testers could include `/sw/perl-7.0/bin` in the front of their PATH. After they certify the new release, the `/sw/perl` symbolic link is adjusted to point to the 7.0 directory. Because of the way symbolic links work, processes currently accessing the older version will usually continue to operate without trouble because the old version isn't removed. Instead, only new invocations of the software will see the new package.

If you used the system as described so far, each user's PATH would be very long and difficult to manage if there were many packages. To solve this, create a directory called `/sw/default/bin` that includes symbolic links to all the most popular programs. Now, typical depot users only need to add this one directory to their PATH to access the typical software. For example, `/sw/default/bin/perl` would be a link to `/sw/perl/bin/perl`. Similar links would be included for other parts of the Perl package, such as `a2p`, `s2p`, and `perldoc`. Notice that these links would be relative to `/sw/perl` rather than `/sw/perl-6.1` because `/sw/default/bin` should refer to what most people commonly need, not specific versions. Also, if a new version of Perl was installed, it would be a bother to have to update all the links in `/sw/default/bin`. If a person wants access to the entire package, he can add the package's `bin` directory to his PATH.

Guessing at the "popular" programs in a package can be hit or miss, but without automation it is easier to guess than create links for every item in a package. A little automation can help here by making it just as easy to link to all the files in the package rather than just what the SAs think the typical customer will want. A program such as GNU Stow (Glickstein 1996) can be used to manage the symbolic links. Stow is easy to use and always generates the minimal number of symbolic links such that it becomes just as easy to generate symbolic links for all the binaries in `bin`, as well as man pages, libraries, and other files.

So far, what we've described works for a single host. For a network of hosts, we want to give clients access to the same software. We can do this by copying the packages to the appropriate machines or we can provide access over the network, possibly via NFS. We can use the automounter to make the `/sw` of other servers appear on the clients.

---

[2]You should also include `/sw/perl-6.0/man` in your MANPATH. In the future, any time we suggest adding something to your PATH we will assume that the appropriate "man" directory is added to your MANPATH.

Assuming that `bester` is the file server that supports the Solaris 8.0 hosts, the automounter map of `/sw` for Solaris 8.0 might look like this:

```
default       bester:/sw/default
perl-6.0      bester:/sw/perl-6.0
perl-6.1      bester:/sw/perl-6.1
perl          bester:/sw/perl-6.1
mutt-1.2.5    bester:/sw/mutt-1.2.5
mutt-1.2.6    bester:/sw/mutt-1.2.6
mutt-2.0.1    bester:/sw/mutt-2.0.1
mutt          bester:/sw/mutt-2.0.1
```

When Solaris 9.0 is introduced into the environment, the automounter map for Solaris 9.0 systems is created by copying the map from 8.0. However, not all packages compiled for Solaris 8.0 are binary compatible for Solaris 9.0. Specific packages that require recompilation can point to those new binaries. In our example above, `mutt` is binary compatible across Solaris 8.0 and 9.0, but Perl requires recompilation. Supposing that our Solaris 9.0 server is named `lyta`, our 9.0 map would look like this:

```
default       lyta:/sw/default
perl-6.1      lyta:/sw/perl-6.1
perl          lyta:/sw/perl-6.1
mutt-1.2.5    bester:/sw/mutt-1.2.5
mutt-1.2.6    bester:/sw/mutt-1.2.6
mutt-2.0.1    bester:/sw/mutt-2.0.1
mutt          bester:/sw/mutt-2.0.1
```

Notice that `perl-6.0` is missing. This is to demonstrate that obsolete packages are not brought forward to new operating systems unless specifically requested.

You can adapt a couple of policies to support older OSs. Obviously, a new package should be built for the latest OS. However, if it requires special recompilation for older OSs, you can end up spending a lot of time and effort to support only a few legacy hosts. You might decide that the current and one previous release of an OS will have actively maintained depots. The depots for older OS releases are "frozen in time," except possibly for security-related fixes. This means that host `bester` can't be decommissioned until it is the last Solaris 8.0 host. Alternatively, the data can be copied to any NFS server, and, after a simple adjustment to the automounter map, `bester` can be decommissioned.

Additional OSs can be handled the same way—one tree per OS and an additional automounter map configured on the clients. These new depots usually will start out nearly empty because it is rare that any package can be reused for a completely different OS.

The reliability requirements gathered for your depot often can be implemented using automounter features. Replication can be handled by using the more sophisticated automounter syntax options that let you specify multiple servers. In fact, some automounter implementations permit maps to make decisions based on which OS the client uses. In that case, one super map can be created that "does the right thing" depending on what OS is in use and which servers are up.

Managing symbolic links and the many automounter maps can be a hassle. Even if a new package is binary compatible across many OS releases, many automounter maps must be updated. Odd problems can appear if the maps get out of sync. Humans aren't very good at keeping such things in sync, but computers are. Therefore it can be useful to automate this process to reduce mistakes and hassle. Create a master file that describes the various packages, versions, OSs, and servers. Use this master file to generate the automounter maps. Use this master file to generate the GNU Stow commands that need to be run. Of course, use a program such as `make` to automate all of the above so that you only have to edit the master file and type `make`.

Following our example, we introduce `talia`, which is a server that is redundant for `lyta` in that it provides the same software on a different host. The master file might look like

```
default      sol80         bester       /sw/default
default      sol90         lyta,talia   /sw/default
perl-6.0     sol80         bester       /sw/perl-6.0
perl-6.1     sol80         bester       /sw/perl-6.1
perl         sol80         bester       /sw/perl-6.1
perl-6.1     sol90         lyta,talia   /sw/perl-6.1
perl         sol90         lyta,talia   /sw/perl-6.1
mutt-1.2.5   sol80,sol90   bester       /sw/mutt-1.2.5
mutt-1.2.6   sol80,sol90   bester       /sw/mutt-1.2.6
mutt-2.0.1   sol80,sol90   bester       /sw/mutt-2.0.1
mutt         sol80,sol90   bester       /sw/mutt-2.0.1
```

Using such a master file requires defining a standard way of specifying OSs. In the above example, we defined `sol80` and `sol90` to mean Solaris 8.0 and Solaris 9.0 respectively. Some companies have created complicated codes to specify an exact vendor, processor, OS, and OS release 4-tuple, but we recommend that you keep it simple and use codes that you understand.

Deleting packages is as easy as removing the directory from the server and deleting the appropriate lines from the master file. A more conservative approach might be to rename the directory on the server so that it cannot be accessed. It is prudent to not actually delete the files for a week or so. If someone complains that the package is missing during that time, the package can be added back easily. (Of course, the removal should be announced to your customers using whatever method is appropriate for your site.)

The system as described has the potential to infinitely increase in disk utilization until it exhausts all available disk space. However, we find that the system manages disk space on its own. Now and then, new OSs are adopted that are incompatible enough that none of the previous packages can be carried over into the new automounter map. Rather than rebuilding every single package for the new OS, usually only the critical and popular packages get rebuilt. Eventually, the legacy OSs are eliminated from the environment, eliminating older, unused packages. As long as this happens, the system is relatively self-limiting in its disk consumption.

Control over who can add packages in this system is based on the UNIX permissions of the files and directories involved. Obviously, all these packages should be read-only for all nonprivileged users. In fact, you should NFS export the packages as read-only when possible.

If customers would like to be able to maintain software in this tree, it is best to have them hand the software to an SA who installs it. This ensures that the installation media has been archived in a central place. If the software is distributed in source code form, this prevents the situation in which the only person with the source code leaves the company.

It can be useful to provide an area where customers can install software on their own to share with others. This delegates work away from the SAs, which is always a good thing. The additional control given to the package owner means that he can provide rapid updates. Without this ability, sharing of such software often will involve customers including other customers' `bin` directories in their PATHs. That generally isn't safe practice. Given the system as described so far, we can extend it to permit this kind of "customer-initiated" software. You can create a `/sw/contrib` directory that is writeable by any user ID, possibly only from a particular host. Customers can create subdirectories in this area for packages that they wish to install. A couple of rules should be put into place to ensure some reasonable security. Obviously, if anyone installs virulent software, it can be traced to the source because that person owns the files that were installed in `/sw/contrib`. That is usually enough incentive to be careful selecting what is installed. The person who owns the files should be responsible for supporting the package. It would be unreasonable to expect the SAs to support a homegrown package in `/sw/contrib`. Another precaution that can be taken is to forbid people from including `/sw/contrib` directories in their PATH. Sadly, this can only be enforced through education and peer pressure. Rather than directly adding such packages to their PATHs, people should create symbolic links from

$HOME/bin to the specific program in /sw/contrib that they need to access. Although this isn't perfect, it balances convenience with safety. You should document the policies related to the /sw/contrib directory in a file named /sw/contrib/POLICY, or at least use that file to direct people to a web page that explains the policy.

One advantage of the system we've described is that it doesn't require the use of wrappers. We've seen well-written wrappers and poorly written wrappers, and, in our experience, we'd prefer to see no wrappers at all. Wrappers sometimes have strange effects on programs that react badly to being renamed, take options in a strange format, and so on. Of course, there surely will be an extreme case where a wrapper is still needed. You might put all wrappers in a special area, such as /sw/wrappers/bin, or they can be directly installed in /sw/default/bin. Some feel it is more "pure" to have only symbolic links in /sw/default/bin, whereas others feel that symbolic links and wrappers can share that space.

These wrappers might set environment variables, then call the program in the package's bin directory, or they may do a lot more. If you have a highly technical customer base, a sufficient wrapper might simply print out instructions on how to set the environment so that the program they are trying to run is accessible.

Wrappers can be a slippery slope. If you use a wrapper to avoid creating an automounter map for a new OS release, suddenly there may be many more wrappers to maintain. It's better to invest a little time to make it easy to create new automounter maps than start creating wrappers.

This system can grow quite large by adding additional packages, replicating the various packages onto additional servers, and creating new automounter maps for new OSs. As it grows, it makes sense to automate these processes, especially replication.

In this section, we have described a simple yet powerful software depot for UNIX. It leverages off preexisting elements such as the UNIX permission system, automounter, and NFS. It is self-documenting—the master file and filesystem layout describe the system itself. It is simple enough to be sufficient for a single host or a small cluster, and it has a clear path to growing to larger, even global, systems.

23.1.7 A Windows Example

Windows environments historically have more self-administered hosts than UNIX environments. The traditional Windows software depot is more akin to an FTP server or file server directory that contains installable packages (.ZIP files or self-installing .EXEs) of software that can be installed by the PCs' users.

Environments differ in their policies regarding self-installed software. Some completely forbid it, others permit only approved software to be installed, and others give users the freedom to install whatever they want on their PCs. A software depot should reflect this policy.

Here is an example of a simple software depot that would be suitable for an environment where certain products are approved for all systems, but others have special installation prohibitions and controls. In this depot, a "share" is created on a Windows (CIFS) file server named `software`. The users would access it as `\\server1\software`. Within it they would find a document named `POLICY`, which explains the general policy toward user-installed software on PCs and specific policies related to particular software packages. For example, it might explain how to acquire licensed software. There would also be a series of directories, as follows:

Standard: This directory contains software that has been approved for all machines but not installed by default on newly delivered PCs. This is the first place people would check when they want to see if a piece of software is available in the depot. Site-licensed software might be appropriate here.

Preinstalled: This contains software that should already be installed when PCs are delivered and/or is updated automatically via MS-SMS. Although redundant, it is useful to have the preinstalled software available for reinstallation, or installation on machines that escaped the regular PC deployment process. Example software found here would include site-licensed software such as WinZip, virus scanners, and office suites.

Disc Images: This directory contains images of CD-ROMs and DVDs that have been licensed, or whose license permits free distribution. For example, images of BSD and Linux distributions belong here. The benefit of providing these images here is that it saves bandwidth at your Internet gateway.

Experimental: This is for software packages that are not yet approved, but are being considered for approval. This directory might be password protected or may have a restrictive ACL, so that only evaluators are able to access the contents.

Admin: In here are tools that only SAs should access, or more importantly, software that is specially licensed. This should be a password- or ACL-restricted directory that only the SAs can access. The directory structure inside this area may include Standard, Preinstalled, Disc Images, and Experimental directories. One way of handling licensing issues is to require that software without site licenses be installed by an SA or someone trusted to follow all the license procedures. For example, they might verify that the software license was acquired for this particular host before it is installed. If software is prepurchased in bulk (as described in Section 14.2.1), the SA might simply record this installation as consuming one of the prepurchased licenses.

Within each directory there may be subdirectories for various flavors of Windows where version-specific packages are stored. There may be a directory named "Obsolete" where old packages that are no longer supported are moved. Although such old packages shouldn't be needed any more, emergencies do occasionally arise in which having the old packages around is beneficial. It's a balance of risk management versus disk space.

It is useful to create a directory for each package, rather than having a single directory full of packages. Package names are not always understandable to the casual observer, whereas directory names can be very specific: `FooSoft Accounting Client 4.0` is more clear than `FSAC40.ZIP`. Most packages include a separate README file, which should be in that directory. If packages are all stored in one directory, there is a good chance that the names of the READMEs will conflict.

For every directory, it is useful to create a document by the same name (with the addition of `.txt` of course) that includes notes about the software, what the license restrictions are, and if there are any special installation tricks or tips. You should adopt a standard format for the first part of the file with freeform text following.

If the software depot is extremely successful, you might choose to replicate it in various parts of the company. This can save network bandwidth, improve installation speed, and offer more reliability. The point at which such replication becomes useful is much different than with the UNIX depot. Windows software depots are relatively light on networks compared with the network activity required for a UNIX depot that accesses the network for every execution of a program. A Windows software depot is also less "real time" than UNIX depots because installation happens once and the server is not accessed again. An occasional slow install is painful, but not a show-stopper. However, slow NFS access to a UNIX depot can destroy productivity. For these reasons, you may choose not to replicate a Windows software depot, but instead simply locate it somewhere with excellent network connectivity.

In this section, we have described a simple yet powerful software depot for a Windows environment. It takes into account the unique culture of Windows systems with respect to software installation. It requires no software, unless replication is required, at which time one of many fine directory replication systems can be used. It leverages the access controls of Windows' CIFS file access protocol to restrict access as needed. It is self-documenting, because the directory hierarchy describes what software is available and local installation notes and policy documents can be colocated with the packages for easy access.

23.2 The Icing

Although the purpose of a software depot is to provide the same software to all hosts, the Icing is to be able to provide customizations for various hosts. Here we include suggestions for handling a couple of different customizations that are frequently requested: slightly different configurations, locally replicated packages, commercially licensed software, and smaller depots for OSs that do not receive full support.

23.2.1 Different Configurations for Different Hosts

A commonly requested feature of UNIX software depots is the ability to have slightly different configurations for certain hosts or clusters of hosts.

If a package's configuration must vary wildly from host to host, it may be useful to have the configuration file in the depot simply be a symbolic link to a local file. For example, `/sw/megasoft/lib/megasoft.conf` might be a symbolic link to `/etc/megasoft.conf`, which could contain specific contents for that particular host.

If there are a couple of different "standard" configurations that you might want to choose from, they could be included in the packages. For example, `/etc/megasoft.conf` might itself be a symbolic link to one of many configuration files in `/sw/megasoft/lib`. You might have standard server and client configurations (`megasoft.conf-server` and `megasoft.conf-client`) or configurations for particular customer groups (`megasoft.conf-mktg`, `megasoft.conf-eng`, `megasoft.conf-dev` and `megasoft.conf-default`). Because the series of symbolic links "bounce" from the depot, to the local disk, and back to the depot, they are often referred to as "bounce links."

23.2.2 Local Replication

If your UNIX depot is accessed over the network, it can be good to have commonly used packages replicated on the local disk. For example, a developer's workstation that has disk capacity to spare could store the most recent edition of the development tools locally. Local replication reduces network utilization and improves performance. You should make sure that access to a local disk is faster than access to a network file server, which is not always the case. The problem becomes managing which machines have which packages stored locally, so that updates can be managed.

Depot management software should make all this easy. It should provide statistics to help select which packages should be cached or at least permit SAs and customers to indicate which packages should be replicated locally. In our UNIX example above (Section 23.1.6), if a sophisticated automounter is used, it can specify that for a particular machine, a package can be found on a local disk.

New releases of packages require special handling when local replication is being performed manually. In some systems, a new, uncached release overrides the local copy. If the intention was that customers always see the most recent release of a package, the right thing would happen, though performance would suffer if nobody remembered to copy the new release to this machine's local disk. It's better to have the right thing happen slowly than the wrong thing happen with excellent performance. On the other hand, if someone directly changed the master copy of a package without changing the release number, then the SA must remember to also update any copies of the package that may be on other clients. This can become a management nightmare if tracking all these local copies is done manually.

The general solution to this is to use an NFS cache. This is where files accessed via NFS are cached to the local disk. NFS caches such as Solaris' `cachefs` work best on read-only data such as a software depot. There is a huge potential for performance improvement with such a system. Most importantly it is adaptive, automatically caching what is used rather than requiring SAs to manually try to determine what should be cached and when. It is a "set it and forget it" system.

23.2.3   Including Commercial Software in the Depot

Including commercial software in the depot is as difficult as the software's license is complex. If there is a site-license, the software packages can be included in the depot like anything else. If the software automatically contacts a particular license server, which in turn makes a "licensed/not-licensed" decision, then the software can be made available to everyone because it will be useless to anyone not authorized.

If, however, software may only be accessed by particular customers, and the software doesn't include a mechanism for verifying that customer is authorized, it is the SA's responsibility to make sure the license is enforced.

In our Windows depot example, we discussed gating licensed software installation by requiring SAs to perform the installation. In a UNIX environment there are additional options. If the software is licensed for all users of a particular host, the software can be installed on that host only. You should install it in the usual depot nomenclature if possible (in other words, depot management software shouldn't panic when it detects locally installed software in its namespace). Alternatively, a UNIX group can be created for people who are authorized to use the software, and key files in the package can be made executable only by members of that group.

UNIX environments often face a situation in which various small groups all use the same software package, but for each group a different license server must be accessed.[3] This is another problem that can be solved using the "bounce link" technique (described in Section 23.2.1) to point different clients to different license files.

Having complex requirements for software distribution is a common problem (Hemmerich 2000). It is an area that people are constantly trying to improve. Before trying to solve the problem yourself, look at the past work in conference proceedings and journals for inspiration. Someone may have solved your exact problem already.

23.2.4 Handling Second-Class Citizens

Software depots also need to handle off-beat operating systems that may exist on the network. These hosts, often referred to as "second-class citizens," are OSs that do not receive the full support prescribed for first-class citizens (see Section 1.1), but exist on your network and require minimal support. The support that second-class citizens receive might simply be the allocation of an IP address and a few other simple configuration parameters to get the device up and running.

The software depot required for second-class citizen OSs tends to be minimal: applications required for the special purpose of that machine, possibly compilers, and the tools required by the SAs. We explicitly recommend against trying to provide every package available in the full depots. It would be a huge effort for little gain.

It is important to have a written policy on second-class citizen OSs. Indicate the level of support to be expected and areas in which customers are expected to provide their own support. If there is a small software depot, the policy should specify a minimal set of packages customers should expect to find in the depot.

We recommend a few groups of tools that should be included in a small depot. Install the tools needed for the purpose of the machine. For example, if this machine is for porting software to that OS, install the appropriate compiler tool chain. If the host is for running a particular application or service, install the required software for that. The tools required for SA processes (automated and otherwise) should also be installed. These include inventory collectors, log rotators, backups, software depot updates, debugging tools, and so on. Finally, every company has a short list of convenience tools that can be provided for your own benefit. This includes the command-line version of the corporate phone number lookup software, minimal email ("send only") configurations, and so on.

---

[3]We recommend centralizing license servers, but we include this example because we often find that for political reasons they are not centralized.

❖ **A Toolchain**   A *developers toolchain* is a term meaning the specific software required to build software. In some environments, this might involve software from various vendors or sources. This usually includes build tools (such as `make` and `autoconf`), compilers, assemblers, linkers, interpreters, debuggers, source code control systems (RCS, CVS, ClearCase, SourceSafe), and various homegrown utilities that are involved in the development process. The term *chain* refers to the fact that one tool often leads to the next, such as the compile, assemble, link sequence.

23.3   Conclusion

In this chapter, we have discussed software depots. Software depots are an organized way of providing software packages to many hosts, though having a good organization is even useful for a single host. A good software depot provides a ubiquitous set of tools that become as much a part of the culture of your customers as the network itself.

Historically, Windows and UNIX depots tend to be very different. Windows depots tend to be repositories of software to be installed, and UNIX depots tend to be repositories of software used in real time from the depot.

Sites should have a written policy regarding various depot issues: how and by whom packages get installed, what systems receive the services of the depot, how requests and support issues are handled, and so on.

We described simple depots for both UNIX and Windows environments, showing that policy and organization are key and that an extremely powerful depot can be created with very little software. There are many Open Source packages for maintaining depots, and thus we recommend against creating one from scratch. Find one that you like and modify it to suit your needs.

Although the purpose of a software depot is to provide the same software to many hosts, eventually you will receive requests to have customizations for particular hosts or groups of hosts. We discussed the most common kinds of requests and some simple solutions.

Exercises

1. Describe the software depot used in your current environment, its benefits, and its deficiencies. If you do not have a depot, describe where software is currently installed and the pros and cons of adopting one.

2. What are the policies for your software depot? If you do not have any policies or do not have a depot, develop a set of policies for a depot at your site. Justify the policy decisions made in your depot policy.

3. In the UNIX example (Section 23.1.6), what happens to `perl` modules and other add-on packages? How would you handle this situation?

4. Compare your current software depot to one of the samples described in this chapter. How is it better or worse?

5. If you are at a small site that does not require a complicated software depot, describe what kind of simple software depot you do have. At what point will you have grown to require a more complicated depot? What might that look like? How will you convert to this new system?

6. Develop a set of codes for each of the OSs and the various versions of each OS in use at your location akin to what was used in Section 23.1.6. Explain and justify your decisions.

Chapter 24

Service Monitoring

Monitoring is an important component of providing a reliable, professional service. The two primary types of monitoring are real-time monitoring and historical monitoring. Each has a very different purpose. As discussed in Section 3.1.13, monitoring is a basic component of building a service and meeting the service levels that are expected or required of that service.

A useful business axiom goes, "if you can't measure it, you can't manage it." In the field of system administration, this translates to "if you aren't measuring it, you aren't managing it."

Monitoring is essential for any well-run site, but it is a project that can keep increasing in scope. This chapter should help you anticipate and prepare for that. We look at what the basics of a monitoring system are and then discuss the numerous ways that you can improve your monitoring system.

For some sites, such as sites providing a service over the Internet, comprehensive monitoring is a business requirement. These sites need to monitor everything to make sure that they don't lose revenue because of an outage that goes unnoticed. E-commerce sites will probably need to implement everything presented in this chapter.

24.1   The Basics

There are several motivations for systems monitoring. It can be used to rapidly detect and fix problems, identify the source of problems, predict and avoid future problems, and provide data on SAs' achievements. There are two primary ways to monitor systems. The first is gathering historical data related to availability and usage. The other is real-time monitoring to ensure that SAs are notified of failures.

Historical availability monitoring is used for recording long-term uptime statistics. This has two components: collecting the data and viewing the data. The results of historical monitoring are conclusions such as "The web service was up 99.99 percent of the time last year, up from the previous year's 99.9 percent statistic." Utilization data is used for capacity planning. For example, you might view a graph of bandwidth utilization for an Internet connection that has been gathered for the last year. The graph might visually depict a growth rate that indicates the pipe will be full four months from now.

Real-time monitoring alerts the SA team of a failure as soon as it happens. There are two components: a monitoring component that notices failures and an alerting component that alerts someone to the failure. There is no point in a system knowing that something has gone down unless it alerts someone to the problem. The goal is for the SA team to notice outages before customers do. This results in shorter outages and problems being fixed before customers notice, along with building the team's reputation for maintaining high-quality service.

Typically, the two different types of monitoring are performed by different systems. The tasks that are involved in each type of monitoring are very different. After reading this chapter, you should have a good idea of how they differ and what to look for in the software that you choose for each task.

But, before we continue, a word of warning: Monitoring uses network bandwidth. Within a local area network, it is not usually a significant percentage. However, over low-bandwidth (usually long-distance) connections, it can use up a significant percentage of the bandwidth, causing performance to suffer. Make sure that you know how much bandwidth your monitoring is using. A rule of thumb is that it should not exceed 1 percent of the available bandwidth. Try to optimize your monitoring system so that it is easy on low-bandwidth connections. Consider putting monitoring stations at the remote locations with a small amount of communication back to the main site, or primarily using a trap-based system in which the devices notify the monitoring system when there is a failure, rather than a polling-based system in which the monitoring system checks status periodically.

24.1.1 Historical Data

Historical data collection refers to polling systems at predefined intervals to gather utilization or statistical data from various components of the system and to check how well services that the system provides are working. The information gathered is stored and typically used to produce graphs of the system's performance over time or to detect or isolate a minor problem that occurred in the past.

Historical data collection is often introduced at a site because the SAs find themselves wondering if they need to upgrade a network, add more memory to a server, or get more CPU power. They might be wondering when they will need to order more disks for a group that consumes space rapidly, or when they will need to add extra capacity to the backup system. To answer these questions, they realize that they need to monitor the systems in question and gather utilization data over a period of time so that they can see the trends and the peaks in usage. There are many other uses for historical data, such as usage-based billing, anomaly detection (see Section 7.1.4) and presenting data to the customer base or management (see Chapter 26).

Historical data can consume a lot of disk space, especially if the data is not condensed or expired. However, limiting disk space consumption by condensing the data or expiring it affects the level of detail or historical perspective you can provide. Bear this trade-off in mind as you are looking for a system for your historical data collection. Expired data can be written to a backup storage device before it is deleted, but retrieval becomes a greater effort. How you intend to use the data that you gather from the historical monitoring will help to determine what level of detail you need to keep and for how long. For example, if you are using the data for usage-based billing and you bill monthly, you will want to keep complete details for a few months, in case there is a query. You may then archive the data and expire the online detailed data but save the graphs to provide online access for your customers to reference. Alternatively, if you are just using the graphs internally for observing trends and predicting capacity needs, you might want a system that keeps complete data for the last 48 hours, reasonably detailed information for the last two weeks, somewhat less detailed information for the last two months, and very condensed data for the previous two years, with everything older than two years being discarded. Consider what you are going to use the data for and how much space you can use when deciding on how much to condense the data. Ideally, the amount of condensing that the system does and the expiration time of the data should be configurable.

Another thing that you need to consider in choosing your monitoring system is how it gathers its data. Typically, a system that performs historical data collection will want to poll the systems that it monitors at regular intervals. Ideally, the polling interval should be configurable. The polling mechanism should be able to use a standard form of communication such as SNMPv2. It should be able to use the usual IP mechanisms, such as ICMP echoes (pings) and opening TCP connections on any port, sending some specific data down that connection and checking the response that is received using pattern matching. It is also useful to have a monitoring system that records latency information, or how long a transaction took. The latency correlates well to the end-users' experiences. Having a service that responds very slowly is practically the same as having one that doesn't respond at all. The monitoring system should support as many other polling mechanisms as possible, preferably incorporating a mechanism to feed in data from any source and parse the results from that query. The ability to add your own tests is important, especially in highly customized environments. On the other hand, a multitude of predefined tests is also valuable, so that you do not need to write everything from scratch.

The output that you generally want from this type of monitoring system is graphs that have clear units along each axis. You can use the graphs to see what the usage trends are or to notice problems such as sudden, unexpected peaks or drops in usage. You can use the graphs to predict when you need to add capacity of any sort and as an aid in the budget process, which is discussed in more detail in Chapter 29. A graph is also a convenient form of documentation to pass up the management chain. It clearly illustrates your point, and your managers will appreciate you having solid data to support your request for more bandwidth, memory, disk space, or whatever it is that you need.

24.1.2   Real-Time Monitoring

Real-time monitoring involves a combination of polling systems to check status and watching error messages that systems send to the monitoring system to check for problems. Real-time monitoring usually involves both checking for outages and checking whether subsystems exceed preset threshold values. Real-time monitoring also requires an associated alerting system to notify SAs of problems because this is its primary purpose.

A real-time monitoring system stores little or no historical data. Usually, it will store the previous result of each query and the length of time since the last status change. Sometimes, it will store running averages or high and low watermarks, but it rarely stores more than that. The storage requirements are minimal. Unlike historical monitoring, which is used for proactive system administration, real-time monitoring is used to improve reactive system administration.

A real-time monitoring system tells you when hosts are down, a service is not responding, or some other problem has arisen. A real-time monitoring system should be able to monitor everything you can think of that can indicate a problem. It should be able both to poll systems and applications for status and to receive alerts directly from those systems if they detect a problem at any time. As with historical monitoring, it should be able to use standard mechanisms such as SNMPv2 polling, SNMPv2 traps, ICMP pings, and TCP, as well as provide a mechanism for incorporating other forms of monitoring.

It also should be capable of sending alerts to multiple recipients using a variety of different mechanisms, such as email, paging, telephone, and opening trouble tickets. Alerts should go to multiple recipients because an alert that is sent to one person could fail if that person's pager or phone has died or if the person is busy or distracted with something else.

When evaluating a monitoring system, look at the things that it can monitor natively to see how well it matches your needs. You should be considering monitoring both availability and capacity. *Availability monitoring* means detecting failures of hosts, applications, network devices, other devices, network interfaces, or connections of any kind. *Capacity monitoring* means detecting when some component of your infrastructure becomes, or is about to become, overloaded. For example, that component could be CPU, memory, disk space, swap, backup device, network or other data connection, remote access device, number of processes, available ports, application limitations, or the number of users on a system. As with historical monitoring systems, it is important that the system be flexible and permit the creation of your own test modules. It is preferable that a system can use the same modules for both real-time and historical monitoring.

The most important components of a real-time monitoring system are the notification mechanism and the processes that your site puts into place for dealing with the notifications or alerts.

Alerting

When implementing a real-time monitoring system, you care less about the monitoring than the alerting. There is no point in special software knowing that something has failed or is overloaded unless it tells a human about it or does something about it and makes a note of it for a human to look at later. In the next section we will discuss monitoring systems that actively try to fix failures. For now, let's just consider problem alerts.

Look at the alerting mechanism. It should not depend on any components of the system that is being monitored. If a service or part of the network can fail and cause alerts to fail, that is a bad situation. Email is a popular alerting mechanism, but it should not be the only one. The service can fail and can have long delays. Alerting needs to happen quickly. Also consider whether the alerting mechanism can be monitored by third parties. Wireless communication such as paging is susceptible to third-party

monitoring. At a minimum, do not send sensitive information, such as passwords over these channels, and consider whether or not information such as
`backbone-router is down for 45 minutes` is proprietary information.

Whatever monitoring system you use, you need to have a policy that
describes how the alerts are handled. The policy needs to answer some fundamental questions before you can implement real-time monitoring. How
many people do the alerts go to? Do alerts go to the helpdesk or to the individuals who look after the components that are having problems, or some
combination of the two? How do the recipients of the alerts coordinate their
work, so that everyone knows who is handling each problem and they don't
get in each other's way? If problems persist beyond some predetermined
length of time, do you want to escalate the problem? If so, what is the escalation path? How often do you want to be informed of a problem, and
does that depend on what the problem is? How do you want to be informed
of the problem? What is the severity of each problem? Can the severity be
used as a way to determine the policy on how the problem is handled? Your
monitoring and alerting system must be able to implement your policy.

When choosing a real-time monitoring system, look at what your policy
says about how you want it to alert you of problems, and how often. For
example, if you implement an early-warning mechanism for capacity problems, you may want it to open a trouble ticket with an appropriate priority
in your existing helpdesk system. You probably also want it to do so only
when the value being monitored changes from acceptable to unacceptable,
as opposed to every time that it registers as unacceptable (which could be
every few minutes), though you may want it to update the existing ticket
when it detects that the problem still exists after some configurable interval.
On the other hand, if the monitoring system detects an outage, particularly
of a critical component, you probably want it to actively page someone who
is on call. You may even want it to continue paging that person every time
it detects that the error condition still exists, with information on how long
the condition has existed. You may want the notifications to become more
frequent or less frequent as the problem persists. Your monitoring system
should be flexible in the forms of alerting that it uses, and it should allow
you to use different alerting mechanisms for different types of problems.

You also need to consider the error messages that the system gives.
They must be clear and easy to understand. If recipients of an alert need
to look up information or call another person to translate the error message into something they understand, then the message is not clear enough.
For example, an error message that says `SNMP query to 10.10.10.1 for
1.2.3.4.5.6.7.8.9.10 failed` is not as clear as `Interface Hssi4/0/0 on
wan-router-1 is down`. Equally, `Connect to port 80 on 10.10.20.20
failed` is not as clear as `Web server on www-20 is not responding`.
However, the message must not make assumptions that may be wrong.

For example, if the message said `Web server on www-20 is not running`, rather than that it was not responding, an SA might check and see that it was running, and assume that it was a false alert, rather than checking to see if it might be hung or failing to respond for some other reason.

I'm Hot! I'm Wet!

One night, very early in the morning, a couple's phone rang. The wife woke up and answered, to hear a sultry female voice saying, "I'm hot. I'm wet." Putting it down as a prank call, she hung up. Thirty minutes later, it repeated. After the fourth call, the husband finally woke up and took the call and bolted from his bed.

It was the alarm system in his machine room. The HVAC had broken down, spilling water under the floor. This was the alerting system calling him. The vendor hadn't told him how the alert happened, just that he should put his phone number in a particular configuration file. Test your alerting system, and inform those who might encounter it in your stead.

Another component of the policy and procedures that your monitoring and alerting system should implement is the escalation policy that describes how long each problem should be permitted to persist before it is escalated to another person, typically a manager. The escalation policy ensures that even if the person who is receiving the alert is on vacation or doesn't respond, the issue will be passed on to someone else. The escalation policy needs to describe various escalation paths for different categories of alerts.

Case Study: Escalation Procedure

One homegrown system had a particularly sophisticated escalation procedure. The system could be configured with a responsibility grid that mapped services to responsible entities. The entities could be a person or group of people. The system could be configured with vacation schedules, so it knew whom not to alert. If a problem persisted, the system could walk up a responsibility chain, paging increasingly senior staff. Each type of service (email, web, DNS, and so on) had its own configuration, and particular systems (the CEO's web server, the e-commerce web site, and so on) could be marked as critical, in which case the escalations happened faster. Each service had a default responsible entity, but this could be overridden for particular systems that had special requirements. All of this led to an extremely effective alerting service.

You may also want to be able to acknowledge an urgent alarm so that it stops sending alerts for a given period, until it is manually cleared, until the problem clears, or some combination of those, depending on the policy. This is similar to the snooze button on an alarm clock. The acknowledgement is an indication that you are actively working on the problem and relieves you of the annoyance of constant paging while you are trying to fix the problem. Without this feature, it is tempting to turn off an alarm, which leads to forgetting to fix the problem, or worse, forgetting to reset the alarm.

Active Monitoring Systems

An active monitoring system is one that processes the problems it detects and actively fixes the ones that it knows how to deal with. For example, an active monitoring system might reset a modem port that it detects is in a strange state, or it might remove a modem from a modem pool if it could not be fixed by a reset.

Active monitoring systems can be useful up to a point. Although they respond more quickly than a human can, they have limitations. In general, an active monitoring system can only implement a temporary fix. It won't detect and permanently fix the root of a problem, which is what really needs to happen (as discussed in Chapter 5). An active monitoring system also needs to make sure that it reports what it is doing and opens a trouble ticket for the permanent fix. However, it may be more difficult for the SAs to diagnose the real source of the problem when a temporary fix has been applied. The SAs also need to make sure that they don't get lazy and not bother to permanently fix the problems that the active monitoring system has identified. If the SAs just automate temporary fixes through an active monitoring system, entropy will set in and the system as a whole will become less reliable.

Active monitoring systems also have a limit to the problems they can solve, even temporarily. Some problems that the system may detect but cannot fix are caused by a physical failure, such as a printer running out of ink or paper, or being switched off or disconnected. If it doesn't accurately diagnose the source of the problem and tries to fix it through software commands, it may cause more problems than it solves. Other problems may require complex debugging, and it is not feasible to expect an automated system to be able to correctly diagnose all such problems. In particular, problems that require debugging on multiple hosts and pieces of networking equipment, such as slow file transfers between two hosts on a quiescent network, are currently beyond the abilities of all the automated systems we know.

It is a good idea to limit what an automated system can do, in any case. From a security point of view, if the automated system has privileged access to all or most machines, it is very vulnerable to exploitation. The focus in writing such a system is always utility rather than security, and active monitoring systems are large, complex programs that have privileged access to some machines; thus there will be security holes to exploit. They are also interesting targets because of the level of network-wide privileged access they have. An active monitoring system is not something that you want to have on an unprotected network. From a reliability perspective, the more that this program is permitted to do on your network, the greater is the calamity that can befall you if it goes awry.

24.2 The Icing

Once you have basic monitoring in place and start scaling it up to monitor more devices, you will want to make the monitoring system more accessible to other SAs, so that all the SAs in the company are able to maintain their own device lists. You will also start noticing the things that it doesn't catch and want to start monitoring entire transactions from beginning to end. In other words, instead of just checking that the mail machine is up and accepting SMTP connections, you might want to check that it can actually deliver a mail message. You also may want to see how long the transactions take to complete.

You, your team, and your management ultimately will want to monitor more and more items until you are monitoring, essentially, everything. We will look at ways to ease scaling. Another enhancement that you may want to add in the future is device discovery, so that you know when new devices are added to the network.

24.2.1 Accessibility

Typically, a monitoring system is set up by one or two SAs, who become familiar with every detail of it. They are the only ones who know how to add new things to monitor, so they also become the ones to do all the additions and changes. Initially, this may not involve much work, but with time the monitoring system will become more popular and the workload will increase.

As the monitoring system becomes more established and stable, it is important to make it accessible to the group as a whole. Any of the SAs should be able to add something to the list of things that are monitored, rather than having to submit a request to a particular SA who will be busy with other tasks.

Making the monitoring system accessible requires good documentation. Some forms of monitoring may require finding a piece of information that is not normally used in the course of day-to-day administration, such as the SNMP MIB for a component of the system. The documentation should tell the SA what information he will need and how to find it, as well as how to put that information into the monitoring configuration. If there are choices such as how often the item should be queried, what values correspond to what alert state, problem prioritization, what graphs to draw, or how to define an escalation path, those must all be clearly documented as well. This is a situation in which documenting the preferred defaults is key.

It is frustrating for both the SAs who set up the system and the rest of the SAs in the group if all requests for additional monitoring have to go through one or two people. If the system is not accessible to the whole group, it will not be used as extensively and the group will not benefit as much from it.

24.2.2   Pervasive Monitoring

Ultimately, it is nice to be able to monitor everything, or at least everything beyond the desktops. This is particularly important for sites that depend on extremely high availability, such as e-commerce sites. If adding systems and services to monitor is a task that is performed manually, it will be forgotten or omitted on occasion. To really make monitoring pervasive throughout your service, it should be incorporated into the installation process.

For example, if you build many identical machines to provide a service, you should be using an automated installation process, as described in Chapter 1. If you are building machines this way, you could incorporate adding the machine to the monitoring system as part of that build process. Alternatively, you could install something on the machine that detects when it has been deployed in its final location (if you stage the machines through a protected build network) and provide a way for it to notify the monitoring system that it is alive and what it needs to have monitored.

Pervasive monitoring is important for some sites. Being sure that you are in fact monitoring everything requires some degree of automation.

24.2.3   Device Discovery

It can also be useful to have a monitoring system that detects when devices are added to the network. Such a system is useful at sites that need pervasive monitoring because it should detect any devices that fell through the cracks and failed to be added to the monitoring system through some other means. It can also be useful simply to know that a device was added and when that happened. If the device is causing a problem on the network, for example, that knowledge can save hours of debugging time.

24.2.4 End-to-End Tests

End-to-end testing means testing entire transactions with the monitoring system acting as a customer of the service and checking to see if its entire transaction completes successfully. An end-to-end test might be relatively simple, such as sending email through a mail server or requesting particular web pages that cause database queries and checking the content that is returned. It might be a more complex test that simulates all the steps that a customer would make to purchase something on your e-commerce site.

Case Study: Mailping

At AT&T (and later Lucent) John Bagley and Jim Witthoff developed the mailping facility. It relays email messages ("mailpings") off mail servers and measures the time it takes to find its way back to the mailping machine. At one point, it monitored over 80 email servers, including both UNIX and MS-Exchange SMTP gateways. It provides several web tools to display the delivery time data for a given day or for a given server over a specified period. In addition to historical data collection, it includes a mechanism for generating alerts if a particular message has not been delivered after a certain threshold. The ability to have end-to-end monitoring of the mail transport within their company permitted them to not only respond to problems quickly, but also develop metrics that let them improve the service over time. Some commercial monitoring systems now offer this facility.

Once you start monitoring extensively, you will see problems that your monitoring system fails to catch. For example, if you are providing an e-commerce service over the Internet, a sequence of events has to complete successfully for your customer to be able to complete a transaction. Your monitoring system may show that everything is up and working, but an end-user may still experience a problem in executing a complete transaction.

The transaction may rely on things that you haven't thought of monitoring or that are very difficult to monitor. For example, if the transaction relies on sending an email complete properly, something may be wrong with your mail server configuration, preventing it from sending mail even though it answers on the SMTP port. Or a bug in the application could cause it to loop, fail, or generate garbage at some point in the process. Or the database could be missing some tables. Any number of things could go wrong without being detected by your monitoring system.

The best way to ensure that the service your customers want to use is up and functioning properly is to emulate a customer and check if the transaction completes successfully. In the example of an e-commerce site, build a test case that requests pages in the order that a customer would and check the content of the page that is returned at each stage to make sure that the appropriate data and links are there. Check the database to ensure that the transaction has been recorded in the appropriate place. Perform a credit card authorization check and make sure that it completes successfully. Send email and make sure that it actually arrives. Step through every part of the process as the customer would do, and make sure that everything is as expected at each step.

This end-to-end testing can uncover problems that might otherwise go unnoticed until a customer calls to complain. In an e-commerce environment, failing to notice a problem for a while can be very costly. There is a large and growing market of commercial monitoring systems, many of which are focused on the particular needs of e-commerce customer space.

24.2.5 Application Response Time Monitoring

The other sort of extended monitoring that can be very useful in both corporate and e-commerce environments is application response time monitoring. Every component of a system can be operational, but if the system is too slow, your customers will not be happy. In an e-commerce environment, this means that you will lose business. In a corporate environment, it will lead to a loss of productivity and numerous calls about the network being slow or perhaps a system or application being slow. In either case, unless you are monitoring the application response time, it will probably take quite a while to figure out why your customers are unhappy, by which time your reputation may have suffered heavy damage.

It is much better to devise a way to monitor the application response time as it appears to the end-user of the application. It is then useful to have both a historical chart and some sort of a threshold alert for the response time. Application response time is typically an extension of the end-to-end testing discussed previously.

24.2.6 Scaling

Once you start monitoring some things and see how useful the monitoring is, you will want to monitor more aspects of your site. Increasing the number of things to be monitored introduces scaling problems. All monitoring systems have problems as you scale them. Simply gathering all the data that needs to be checked every five minutes is time consuming. It can reach a point where the monitoring system is still trying to collect and process the data from one run when the next round of data collection begins.

Systems doing historical monitoring usually need to do extra processing to condense the data that they store. Some devices may take a while to respond to the information requested, and the system usually can only handle a limited number of open requests at a time. All of this can lead to scaling problems as the system monitors more objects.

Case Study: Scaling Problems

WebTV Networks used multi-router traffic grapher (MRTG) (Oetiker 1998a) to monitor their network equipment and provide historical graphs. As their network grew, they discovered that a monitoring run would start before the previous one was finished. The machine had to do a lot of data processing as part of each run. They looked into the problem, and one of the network operations staff decided to write a "next generation" of MRTG that would not need to do as much processing per run. The package that arose from that work is Cricket (Allen 1999).

When scaling a monitoring system to thousands of entities around a large network, you can find that network links become clogged just from the monitoring traffic. To solve this problem, some monitoring systems have remote probes that collect data and only send summaries back to the master station. If these are strategically placed around the network, they can greatly reduce the amount of network traffic generated. The master station stores the data and makes it available to the SAs. The master station also holds the master configuration and distributes that to the remote monitoring stations. This model scales much further than a single monitoring station or multiple unrelated monitoring stations.

Real-time monitoring systems also have scaling problems. When such a system is watching many aspects of many devices, there will always be some things that are "red," indicating some form of outage requiring attention. To scale the system appropriately, the SAs must be able to tell at a glance which of the "red" issues is the "reddest" and having the most impact. Essentially, the problem is that a monitoring system typically only has a few states to indicate the condition of the monitored item. Often there are only three: "green," "yellow," and "red." Monitoring many things requires a finer granularity. For example, a very granular priority system could be built in, and the reporting system could display the problems in a priority-ordered list.

Another problem often experienced is that an outage of a (nonredundant) network component between the monitoring system and objects that are being monitored can cause a huge flood of failures to show up in the monitoring system, when there is in fact only one failure. The flood of alerts can hide the real cause of the problem and cause the people receiving the alerts to panic. Ideally, a monitoring system should have a concept of dependency chains. The dependency chain for an object that the system is watching lists the other outages that will cause this object to show up as experiencing an outage as well. The monitoring system should then use the dependency chain to alter its alerting. For example, rather than sending 50 pager alerts, it could send one that says "multiple failures: root cause ..." and list only the highest outage in the chain, not the outages that are downstream. On a graphical display, it should show the outages along with their dependency chains in an appropriate tree structure so that the root is clearly visible. This is not a trivial feature to implement or maintain, and it is unlikely to be available in every monitoring system. If you do not have an error roll-up feature like this in your monitoring system, you may be able to implement something similar through having multiple remote monitoring stations, particularly in a WAN environment, with the central monitoring system alerting the SAs when it fails to receive a report from the remote monitoring systems, and otherwise alerting them of the problems that the remote systems found. Alternatively, you should train your staff on the situation and keep up-to-date dependency maps available for them to reference when flooded with alerts.

Another problem with scaling a real-time monitoring system relates to how the problems are handled. If multiple people all try to solve the same problem in an uncoordinated way, not knowing that others are working on it, they may make the problem worse. At the very least, some time will be wasted. In addition, they will get in each other's way and confuse each other as to what is happening on the system. The monitoring system should have some way to enable an SA to "claim" a problem, so that other SAs know someone is working on it and whom to go to if they want to help out. This may be done through the trouble ticket system and procedures surrounding the assignment of a problem before an SA begins work on it.

24.3 Conclusion

In this chapter, we discussed monitoring in its two different incarnations: historical data gathering and real-time monitoring and alerting. They are quite different from each other in what each involves and what each is useful for, yet you need to consider some of the same problems with both.

Historical availability monitoring and data collection means tracking availability and usage of systems in order to graph and analyze the data later. It involves gathering, storing, and condensing lots of data. Historical data collection requires lots of disk space, databases, and processing. It is useful for capacity planning, budget justification, customer billing, providing an overview of what is happening at a site when a problem is detected, and anomaly detection.

Real-time monitoring involves polling systems to check their state and watching for problem notifications from built-in system monitors. Real-time monitoring is generally combined with an alerting system. This combination is used to detect problems and notify the SAs of them (almost) as soon as they happen. It is a tool for providing better service and for detecting the root of a problem. It gives more precise information than a customer-oriented problem report, such as "I can't download my mail."

Both types of monitoring are required tools at an e-commerce site because the customers are so much more distant and fickle—they don't really care if you know about or fix the problem, because they can just go to another site. Monitoring is a useful tool in any well-run site in both its forms.

Both forms of monitoring have problems when it comes to scaling, and splitting the monitoring system into several data gatherers and one central master is the best method in both cases. Real-time monitoring has scaling problems involving prioritization and response to alerts in an appropriate, timely, and coordinated manner.

As your monitoring system becomes more sophisticated, you will want to consider implementing end-to-end testing and application response time testing so that you know exactly what the end-user is experiencing and whether that is acceptable. You also may want to consider ways to ensure that everything is monitored appropriately, particularly in a service provider environment. To do so, you can look at ways to add a new system to the monitoring list when it is built. You may also look at ways to detect when new devices have been added to the network, but not to the monitoring system.

Monitoring is a very useful tool. It is also a project that will increase in scope as it is implemented. Knowing the ways that the system will need to grow will help you select the right monitoring systems at the beginning of the project, scale them, and add functionality to them as needed during their lifetime.

Exercises

1. How do you currently monitor systems for which you are responsible? If you do not have a formal monitoring system, have you automated any of your ad hoc monitoring?

2. Have you implemented active monitoring for anything in your environment? If so, how well does it work? Does it ever prevent you from finding the root cause of a problem? Explain why or why not.

3. What systems would you add to a monitoring system if you had it and why? What aspects of those systems would you monitor?

4. If you already have a monitoring system, in what ways could you improve it?

5. What features that were discussed in this chapter are most important to you in selecting a monitoring system for your site and why?

6. What, if any, other features that we did not discuss are important to you and why?

7. Investigate freely available historical data monitoring systems. Which one do you think would suit your environment best and why?

8. Investigate commercial historical data monitoring systems. Which one do you think would suit your environment best and why?

9. If you had to choose between the free and commercial historical data monitoring systems that you selected in the previous questions, which would you pick for your site and why? What, if any, features do you feel it lacks?

10. Investigate freely available real-time monitoring systems. Which one do you think would suit your environment best and why?

11. Investigate commercial real-time monitoring systems. Which one do you think would suit your environment best and why?

12. If you had to choose between the free and commercial real-time monitoring systems that you selected in the previous questions, which would you pick for your site and why? What, if any, features do you feel it is lacking?

13. How many items (machines, network devices, applications, and so on) do you think a monitoring system at your site would need to scale to in the next three years? What would you need to meet that demand?

14. Are there any advantages or disadvantages to using the same package for both types of monitoring, if that is possible?

PART IV

Management

Chapter 25

Organizational Structures

Factors in the success of system administrators (SAs) at any institution include how they fit into the organization and how their team is structured. This chapter examines some of the issues that every site should consider in building the system administration team. It covers what we have seen in a variety of companies and how the various organizational structures have affected those companies. It concludes with some sample organizational structures for various sites.

One of the areas over which the organizational structure has a strong influence is communication. The structure of the organization defines the primary communication paths among the SAs, as well as between the SAs and their customers.[1] Both sets of communication are key to the SA team's success. The SAs at a site need to cooperate in order to build a solid, coherent computing infrastructure for the rest of the company to use. However, they must do so in a way that meets the needs of the customers and provides them with solid support and good customer service.

---

[1] Communications between SAs and their managers are also critical and can make or break a team. This is covered in detail in Chapters 28 and 29.

Management and individuals should work hard to avoid an "us and them" attitude regardless of how the organization is structured. Some organizational structures can foster that attitude more than others, but poor communication channels are always at the heart of such problems.

25.1 The Basics

Creating an effective system administration organization free of conflicts both with the customer base and internally is a difficult challenge. Sizing and funding the SA function appropriately so that the team can provide good service levels without seeming a financial burden to the company is another tricky area. We also will examine the effects the management chain can have on that issue.

The ideal SA team is one that can provide the right level of service at the smallest possible cost. Part of providing good service to your company is keeping your costs as low as possible without adversely affecting service levels. To do that, you need to have the right SAs with the right set of skills doing the right jobs. Throwing more people into the SA team doesn't help as much as getting the right people into the SA team. A good SA team has a comprehensive set of technical skills and is staffed with people who have good communication skills and work well with others.

Small SA groups need well-rounded SAs with broad skill sets. The larger SA groups need to be divided into different functional areas. The functions that should be provided by a central group and those that are better served by small distributed teams of SAs are identified. The centralized versus decentralized models for system administration teams are explained, along with the advantages and disadvantages of each approach.

25.1.1 Sizing

Sizing a system administration team appropriately is an important but difficult task. If the team is too small, it will be ineffective, and the rest of the company will suffer through unreliable infrastructure and poor customer service. If it is too large, the company will incur unnecessary costs, and communication among the SAs will be harder to do well. In practice, system administration teams are more often understaffed than overstaffed. It is unusual, though not unheard of, to see an overstaffed system administration team. Overstaffing typically is related to not having the right set of skills in the organization. If the SA team is having trouble supporting the customers and providing the level of service and reliability that is required, simply adding more people may not be the answer. Adding the right

Fill in the *approximate* percentage of time spent on each category.
Please make sure they add up to 100 percent.

	Percentage		Quantity
Customer/desktop support		Number of customers	
Customer server support		Number of customer servers	
Infrastructure support		Number of infrastructure machines	

Figure 25.1: Short form for gathering approximate numbers
for prediction of growth rate

set of skills through new people, training, or consultants could be the right
answer.

When deciding on the size of the system administration team, the management of the organization should take into account several factors. These
include the number and variety of people in the company, the number and
variety of machines in the company, the complexity of the environment, the
type of work that the company does, the service levels required by different
groups, and how mission-critical the various computer services are.

It is a good idea to survey the SAs to find out approximately how much
time each of them is spending supporting the customers in each group, the
machines in each group, and the central infrastructure machines. Ideally,
your trouble-ticket system should be able to give you this information for
a given period quite quickly. If it cannot, you can have each SA to fill out
with approximate numbers a short form such as the one in Figure 25.1. This
information will provide a basis for deriving a growth rate for the SA team
that should keep the service levels approximately constant. It should also
give insight into areas that consume a lot of SA time and allow you to look
for ways to reduce support overhead.

Case Study: *High Support Costs*

When Synopsys did a survey of where the SAs were spending their time, the managers discovered that SAs were spending a lot of time supporting old, ailing equipment that also had high maintenance contract costs. Replacing the equipment with
new, faster hardware would yield continuing savings in machine room space and
labor. They used this information to persuade the group that owned the equipment
to retire it and replace it with new machines. This enabled the SAs to use their time
more effectively and provide better customer service.

There is no magic customer-to-SA ratio that works for every company. The most obvious and most often used factor in determining the size of the SA group is the number of customers the SA team needs to support. This doesn't work well because different customers have different needs. For example, a university campus has a huge number of people using the equipment, but most of them are not very time intensive to support because they are not using the machines all day every day, they are reasonably tolerant of small outages, and they are generally not doing work that requires pushing the machines to their limits. However, other customers, such as hardware designers and gene sequencing groups, can put quite a strain on the machines and the network. They also often run long jobs that require high availability and are intolerant of outages. In other environments where the customer base is not composed of people in high-tech industry, support calls can take on more of a user-interface and environment training slant, which increases the number of SAs needed to provide adequate support. A typical ratio may be 20:1. In a corporate research environment where most people do most of their work on computers, the ratio can be from 20:1 to 60:1, depending on the type of work and service levels that customers need. A typical software development environment in a high-tech company requires a ratio of about 50:1. Universities typically have ratios that are in the vicinity of 500:1 or 1,000:1, depending on how many students they serve. All organizations should have at least two SAs, or they should have some way of providing suitable cover for their one SA if that person is ill or on vacation.

Machines themselves also require support time, independent of explicit customer requests. Servers require regular backups, software and OS upgrades and patches, monitoring, and hardware upgrades and maintenance. Some of this can be optimized through techniques discussed elsewhere in this book, but there is still significant server maintenance time. If desktops are easily replaceable clones of each other, they also require support time, though it is minimal because you can just swap out a broken machine.

In any reasonably large organization, there will be some people who spend their time primarily maintaining infrastructure services, such as email, printing, the network, authentication, and name service. Companies that provide e-commerce or other critical web-based services to their customers will also require a team to maintain the relevant systems.

All of these areas must be taken into account when sizing the organization. Customer-to-SA ratios are tempting, but they only tell half the story. Gather real data from your organization to see where SAs are spending their time. Use it to look for places where automation and process can be improved and to find services or systems that you may not want to support any more. Define SLAs with your customers and use them to help size the SA team appropriately.

25.1.2 Cost Centers

Money is at the center of everything in every business. How and by whom system administration is funded is central to the success or failure of the system administration team.

The primary reason that the system administration function is generally understaffed is that it is viewed as a "cost center" rather than a "profit center." Simply put, it does not bring in money, it is just overhead. Thus, to maximize profits, you must minimize overhead costs, which generally leads to restricting the size and growth of the system administration team.

Case Study: *Controlling Costs*

A midsize software company growing by about 30 percent annually was trying to control costs, so it restricted the growth of the budget for the SA team. The management of the SA team knew that the team was suffering and that there would be more problems in the future, but it needed a way to quantify this and express it to the upper management of the company.

They performed a study to determine where the budget was being spent and highlighted factors that they could not control in their expenditure. For example, they derived per-person and per-server support costs. However, they could not control the number of people that other groups hired or the number of servers that other groups bought, so they could not control their budget for those costs. If the budget did not keep pace with those costs, service levels would drop.

The most significant factor was how maintenance contracts were handled. After the first year, maintenance contract fees for machines under contract were billed to the central SA group, not to the departments that bought and owned the machines. Based on past trends, they calculated their budget growth rate and determined that in five years, the entire system administration budget would be consumed by maintenance contracts alone. There would be no money left even for salaries. Last one out, turn off the lights (and sign the maintenance contract)!

Once the SA management was able to quantify and explain their budget problems, the CFO and his team devised a new funding model to fix the problems by making each department responsible for the system administration costs that it incurred.

You must be able to explain and justify the money that is spent on system administration if you are to avoid being underfunded.

It is difficult to show how the system administration team is saving the company money when everything is running smoothly. Unfortunately, it is easier to demonstrate where the company is losing money by understaffing system administration after the infrastructure and support has deteriorated to the point that people working in the profit centers are losing significant amounts of time through computer and network problems. If a company reaches this stage, however, it is almost impossible to recover completely. The trust and cooperation of the customer base will have been lost, and that is very difficult to regain.

You want to avoid reaching this state, which means figuring out a funding model that works and then justifying it. You need to be able to answer the following questions: Who pays? How does it scale? And what do they get for their money?

How the funding model is designed also has an impact on the organizational structure because the people who are paying typically want significant control. Generally, SAs are either paid for directly by business units and report into the business units or they are centrally funded by the company and form their own business unit. These are the *decentralized* and *centralized* models, respectively. It is not uncommon to see companies switch from one model to the other and back again every few years because both models have strengths and weaknesses.

When a company changes from one model to the other, it is always stressful for the SAs. It is important for the management of the company to have frank, open meetings with the SAs. The SAs need to hear management acknowledge the strengths of the existing structure and the problems that the group will face in maintaining those strengths. The SAs also need to be told frankly what the weaknesses with the current structure are and how the new structure should address those weaknesses. They should be given a chance to voice their concerns, ask questions, and suggest solutions. They may have valuable insights for management on how their existing strengths can be preserved. If the SAs are genuinely involved in the process, it has a much higher chance of success. Representatives from the customer groups also should be involved in the process. It needs to be a team effort to succeed.

The primary motivation for the decentralized model is to give the individual departments better or more customized service through having a stronger relationship with their SAs and more control over the work that they do. The primary motivation for centralizing system administration is to control costs through tracking costs centrally and then reducing them by eliminating redundancy and taking advantage of economies of scale.

When a company moves to a central system administration organization, it looks for standardization and reduced duplication of services. However, the individual departments will be sensitive about losing their control and highly customized services. They will be sensitive to the smallest failure or drop in performance after centralization and will be slow to trust the central group. Rather than work with the central group to try and fix the problems, they may even hire their own rogue SAs to provide the support they used to have, defeating the purpose of the centralization process and hiding the true system administration costs the company is incurring.

Changing from one model to the other is difficult. It is hard on both the SAs and their customers. It is much better to get it right the first time or to work on incremental improvements, instead of hoping that a radical shift will fix all the problems without introducing new ones.

Funding the SA team should be decentralized to a large degree, or it will become a black hole on the books into which vast sums of money seem to disappear. Decentralizing the funding can make the business units aware of the cost of maintaining old equipment and of other time sinks. It can also enable each business unit to still control its level of support and have a different level than other business units. If they want better support, they should encourage the SA assigned to them to automate tasks or put forward the funding to hire more SAs. However, when a business unit has only one SA, doubling that may seem a prohibitively large jump.

Given a time analysis of the SAs' work and any predefined SLAs, it is possible to produce a funding model in which each business unit pays a per-person and per-server fee based on its chosen service level. This fee incorporates the infrastructure cost needed to support those people and machines, as well as the direct costs. This approach decentralizes the cost, while having an added benefit that the business unit does not have to increase its SA head-count by whole units. It does require rigorous procedures to ensure that groups who are paying for higher service levels receive what they pay for.

Ideally, the beneficiaries of the services should pay directly for the services they receive. Systems based around a "tax" are open to abuse, with people trying to get as much as possible out of the services they are paying for, which can ultimately increase costs. However, cost tracking and billing can add so much overhead that it is actually cheaper to endure a little service abuse. A hybrid method, in which charges are rolled up to a higher level or groups exceeding certain limits incur additional charges, may be workable. For example, you might divide the cost of providing remote access proportionately across divisions rather than provide bills down to the level of single customers. Groups that exceed a predefined per-person level are also charged for the excess.

Naturally, for budget planning and control reasons, the managers want to either know in advance what the costs will be or at least have a good estimate. That way, they can make sure that they don't run over budget by having unexpectedly high system administration costs.

25.1.3   Management Chain

The management chain can have considerable influence on how the system administration organization is run. Sometimes, particularly in fast-paced companies, it comes under the chief technical officer (CTO), who is also in charge of the engineering and research and development organizations. Other times it is grouped with the facilities function and reports through the chief operating officer (COO) or through the chief financial officer (CFO). These have different implications.

When the system administration function reports through the CTO or the engineering organization, there are several beneficial effects and some potential problems. The most demanding customers are typically in that organization, so they have a closer relationship with the SAs. The group generally is quite well funded because they are part of a profit center that can directly see the results of their investment in system administration. However, other parts of the company may suffer because the people setting the priorities for the SAs will be biased toward the projects for the engineering group. As the company grows, the engineering function will be split into several business units, each with their own vice president. By this time, the system administration function will either be split into many different groups supporting different business units, or it will report to some other part of the company because it will not be a part of a single "engineering" hierarchy.

In relation to other reporting structures, such as through the COO or CFO, the system administration function is a cost center and tends to receive less money. The people that the SA team reports through usually have only the vaguest understanding of what the group does and what costs are involved. However, the COO or CFO typically has a broader view of the company as a whole and so will usually be more even-handed in allocating system administration resources. This reporting structure benefits from a strong management team that can communicate well with upper management to explain the budget, responsibilities, and priorities of the team. It can be advantageous to report through the CFO, because if the budget requirements of the SA team can be properly explained and justified, the CFO is in a position to determine the best way to have the company pay for the group.

A simple way to express this is that if the information technology (IT) organization reports to the CFO, the company may view IT as a cost that must be reduced. If your CIO reports to your CTO, then the company may view IT as something to invest in to increase profits, or the CTO may see it unnecessary in a high-tech company and decide that everyone can just look after their own machines. Equally, if SA groups report directly into the business units who fund them, then the business units will usually invest as much into IT as they need, though quality may be uneven across the company. Every reporting structure has strengths and weaknesses. There is no one right answer for every organization. The strengths and weaknesses also depend on the views and personalities of the people involved.

The SA managers need to be aware of how their reporting structure affects the SA team and should capitalize on the strengths while mitigating the weaknesses inherent in that reporting structure.

25.1.4 Appropriate Skills

When building an SA team, the hiring managers need to assemble a well-rounded team with a variety of skill sets and roles. The different roles that SAs can take on are discussed in more detail in Appendix A.

The duties of the SAs can be divided into four primary categories. Some SAs need to provide *maintenance* and *customer support,* which includes the helpdesk (as described in Chapter 15), server maintenance, second-tier helpdesk support, and the SAs who support a particular group of customers on a day-to-day basis.

Some SAs need to be involved in *deployment* of new services. These implementers should be dedicated to their current projects so that they are not affected by urgent customer requests that can push the project completion date back.

SAs implement and deploy new service architectures that are developed by the *design* team. The design team is composed of systems *architects* who investigate new technologies and design and prototype new services for the customers and other SAs. The design team must keep in touch with customers' needs through the other SA teams, and they are responsible for making sure that new services are planned and built in advance of when the customers need them.

If you have separate teams of SAs responsible for networks, databases, security, and so on, each of these groups must have staff who cover the range of categories that SAs encompass. There must be people to design, deploy, and maintain each supported area.

An SA team also benefits greatly from *senior generalists* who understand, in depth, how all or most of the different components work and interact with each other. These SAs are able to solve complex, end-to-end problems that may elude SAs who specialize in only one or two areas. These SAs are often referred to as *integrators* because they can integrate different technologies effectively to produce the best possible systems and services.

Overlap often occurs between the different categories, particularly in smaller companies where one or two SAs need to fulfill all roles to some degree. In larger companies, the roles are typically separated. Junior SAs are often hired to work at the helpdesk. As they gain experience, they can move into second-tier support positions and later into deployment roles, day-to-day business unit support roles, or infrastructure maintenance roles. The most senior SAs typically fill the design and senior generalist roles.

In larger companies, finding ways to give the SAs a chance to spend some time in other roles, working with other teams, gives them growth and mentoring opportunities and helps to educate the rest of the team on their experiences and insights.

Rotating all the SAs through the helpdesk can give them valuable insight into the most common problems, some of which they may be able to fix permanently. It can also provide training opportunities for the junior SAs and faster call resolution for some more complicated calls. Helpdesk personnel can be rotated out of the helpdesk to give them a break and to enable them to spend a week being mentored through more senior work with customers or implementers.

Similarly, having implementers become involved in direct customer support should give them feedback on customers' needs and how well their services are performing. Involving them in design work should provide them with extra challenges and can help get their feedback to the designers.

SAs in roles that do not normally require much customer contact, such as server maintenance, design, and implementation roles, can lose touch with the customers' needs. Rotating them through roles that require a lot of customer contact can keep them in touch with the company's direction.

25.1.5   Infrastructure Teams

When a company grows, it should have some people who are dedicated to infrastructure support. An infrastructure team will look after centralized services such as authentication, printing, email, name service, calendar service, networking, remote access, directory services, and security. They also will be generally responsible for automated services for the SAs who are providing customer support, such as the automatic loading, configuration, and patching of new machines described in Chapter 1.

The infrastructure team must be a cohesive unit, even if it is spread over multiple locations. The company's infrastructure should be consistent and interoperable among all the sites. If different groups are running different pieces of the infrastructure, they may fail to agree on the protocols and interfaces between the components with adverse results.

Case Study: Distributed Network Support

A large, multinational computer manufacturing company implemented distributed management of networks and computers. Responsibilities were split between different IT groups so that the central IT department handled the WAN, remote sites had a local SA, while each department at headquarters had its own IT group to handle system and network administration. One of the primary reasons for the distributed management model was that the tools for remote domain administration were not available. These tools are more commonplace today.

In the early days with 20 sites, it seemed simple enough to merely give each site a subdomain, a class C network, and provide the SAs with tools to easily generate zone files. However, when the company had 200 sites with different administrators wanting to manage their subdomains slightly differently, whenever an administrator left the company, the SA team had a training problem. In addition, many disputes went unresolved because, in some cases, the management chains of the two disputing sides only intersected at the CEO level. There was no one who could reasonably be expected to arbitrate and decide what should be done.

Having so many subdomains also increased the amount of work the SAs had to do any time someone moved to a different department. Their mailboxes had to be moved; mail aliases, internal mailing lists, and NIS maps had to be changed; the various modem pool authentication servers needed updating; and so on. With a proper, centrally managed system, only the mailbox might have to be moved, with a single corresponding mail alias change. With so many changes needed, things were inevitably missed and mistakes were made.

The lack of a central system administration management structure was also expensive for the company in other ways. In particular, the numerous different system administration groups were unable to agree on a network architecture or even on what network hardware to use. In the end, overlapping networks were built with lots of duplication, using a variety of hardware. As a result, they had to use the most basic (and therefore most commonly supported) routing protocol, which was RIPv1 at the time, so that all the networks could actually talk to each other. However, some incompatibilities between some of the vendors' implementations of RIP resulted in traffic between some networks getting dropped. The network that resulted from this unarbitrated, decentralized process was unreliable and unsupportable. But no one had the authority to remedy the source of their problems. On the contrary, each department continued to fund its own administration team and adamantly defended its territory.

Many years later, when all the tools for centralizing network management, name space control, network addressing, and many other aspects of site maintenance were available, the company still conformed to the distributed administration model.

Modern computing infrastructures rely heavily on the network and network services. Most of what SAs and customers do is rooted in the network. If the network or network services architecture is badly implemented, it increases the SAs' workloads dramatically. Network design and implementation must be a cooperative effort, and, where it cannot be, standard "border" protocols must be used as the interface between the different groups.

In the case of security, the security of the company as a whole is only as secure as the weakest link. If different groups have different standards and policies, it will be impossible to know how good the company's security really is.

Email is part of the company's interface to its customers and the rest of the world and look consistent and professional and be reliable and easy to debug. This means having standard email addresses,[2] and having a few mail relays that concentrate outbound mail and distribute inbound mail to a reasonable number of mail delivery hosts. It also means correctly configuring any machine that will send mail, so that it uses the correct mail relays. All of this requires cooperation between infrastructure teams across the globe.

Each piece of infrastructure has its own particular ways in which it must be built and supported as a coherent unit. All infrastructure services fall into disarray when different parts of them are managed by different groups who do not cooperate with each other. Organizationally, this means that it is advisable to create an infrastructure group and plan for its growth as needed. When other regions need their own infrastructure SAs, those SAs should report to the central infrastructure managers rather than to regional SA managers.

25.1.6   Customer Support

Customer support is a key part of the system administration function. Customer support means making sure that customers can work effectively. That, in turn, means being part of the solution for all their computing needs. Customer support generally works best in a more distributed model, in contrast to infrastructure support.

Having dedicated customer support personnel helps align your response time with your customers' expectations. As will be discussed in the next chapter (specifically Section 26.1.3), having personnel dedicated to quickly responding to short requests and passing larger requests on to "back office" personnel matches response time with customer expectations.

Customers like to know who their support people are. They build a relationship with a person and become familiar with that person's way of working and communication style. They feel more comfortable in asking that person for help. They can be more confident that their SA will know the context of what they are doing and what services the department uses and how, and that the SA will know what assumptions can be made about the customer and the environment.

We mentioned earlier that choosing between centralized and decentralized models for the system administration organization has an impact on

---

[2]A standard email address is one in which everything looks like it comes from foo.com, for example, rather than each person's individual desktop name appearing on the outside.

customer support and the relationships between the SAs and between the customers and the SAs.

In the decentralized model, where each department or group has its own small SA team, communication with the customers is typically strong, whereas communication between the SAs is generally weak. The customers will have a more familiar relationship with their SAs but will ultimately suffer because of the lack of communication between the SAs. For example, if the SAs' efforts are not well coordinated, many tasks may not be automated; there will not be consistent machines, OSs, patch levels, and applications across the company; and some services that should be centralized may be implemented multiple times. All of these will result in inefficiency and lack of reliability that will ultimately be detrimental to the service the customers receive.

In the centralized model, communication between the SAs is generally strong and communication with the customer base is weak. The centralized model can lead to an "us and them" attitude on both sides. On the other hand, that is balanced by the infrastructure generally being stronger and the site being more consistent and robust. However, customers will probably feel they are not getting the attention they need, and projects for individual departments may be delayed unacceptably in favor of infrastructure projects or projects for other departments. Each department will suffer from not having its own SA paying attention to its specific needs.

A centralized support model can result in customers talking to a different person each time they place a support call. Because the SAs all support so many people, the SA who responds to a support call may not know the department well and probably won't know the customer. This is not a support model that satisfies customers. A team of at most five SAs should support a customer group. Customers want to know their SAs and have confidence that the SAs are familiar with the department's setup and requirements. If a customer-visible SA team is larger than about five, divide the team so that each half of the team supports one half of that customer group. Another approach is to look at ways to reduce the number of SAs who provide direct customer support to that group by having some SAs work behind the scenes.

Some companies use hybrid models, in which each department or business unit has some dedicated SAs who report to the centralized system administration organization. This model is not perfect either because some business unit SAs may be more vocal than others, causing some departments' needs not to be addressed properly by the automation and standardization performed centrally on behalf of the business units. Hybrid models have a lot of potential, but they can also introduce the worst features of both centralized and decentralized models.

Whichever model you use, be aware of its weaknesses and do what you can to mitigate them.

25.1.7   Helpdesk

The helpdesk function is one that works best when centralized. Customers want one phone number, email address, and web page for support requests. They don't want to know which particular department owns a given problem, nor do they want to risk their request getting lost between departments because the one that received it doesn't know who should resolve it.

Large companies need well-coordinated regional helpdesks with each reasonably large campus having its own. With multiple helpdesks, escalation procedures and call hand-off procedures become critical because some calls will cross regional boundaries. Large companies need to find the right balance between a tightly controlled centralized helpdesk that can handle all calls and smaller distributed ones that cannot handle all the calls but can provide a friendlier, more personal face on the system administration organization. Chapter 15 discusses creation and management of helpdesks in detail.

25.1.8   Outsourcing

Outsourcing the system administration function can seem an appealing option to some companies because system administration is not usually considered a "core competency" of the company. If system administration is not a key part of the company's business, the company may prefer to outsource the entire area to an outsource contract company. That way, they only have to negotiate a contract and not worry about SA recruiting, compensation packages, retention, and all the other issues that are part of having employees.

For some companies, outsourcing makes sense. If a company is fairly small and has basic computing needs, negotiating a contract is easier than trying to hire an SA when the company has nobody who can evaluate the SA's skill level or performance. If the company is not satisfied with the outsourcing company, it can renegotiate the contract or take the more difficult route of replacing that company with a new one. It is not as easy to change or terminate an employment contract.

Some companies rely heavily on highly available computer systems for revenue-generating work. Others need to move rapidly with changing technology. In these situations, outsourcing has several disadvantages. In complex environments, it is not easy to switch out one SA team for another without suffering a significant amount of degraded service and outages while the new team becomes familiar with the site. In environments where high availability is important, contracts based on an SLA that stipulates high availability will be very expensive. If the contract does not provide for high availability, it probably will not be achieved because the contractors do not have a stake in the company, and their company will control the hours that the contractors work because they will want to bill for overtime. It is also difficult to get an outsourcing company that will move the customer site along the cutting edge of technology because it is difficult to do so and still maintain service levels. Arguably, system administration should be one of the "core competencies" of a high-tech company.

Security is another sensitive subject in the area of outsourcing. If security is important to a company, particularly in the areas of information protection and handling customer-confidential information, the legal department will need strict confidentiality agreements and assurances regarding what companies the security contractors work for before, during, and after their work at this company. If a security breach can result in loss of customer confidence, or otherwise severely affect the company's revenue stream, then the security function should be one of the company's "core competencies." In-house security staff have a stake in the company's success and failure, whereas the outsourcing company's liability will be limited in their contracts.

In companies that have a revenue-generating Internet presence or an e-commerce site, the SA function of maintaining this site is one of the core functions of the company. As a result, most companies are unwilling to outsource this area of their business. They want the people responsible for maintaining high availability on their Internet sites to have a personal stake in their success or failure. For companies that receive only a small amount of revenue from their Internet presence and do not otherwise rely on high-availability computer systems, staffing the SA team for round-the-clock coverage can be prohibitively expensive, with outsourcing proving a more financially attractive option.

Many companies outsource their Internet presence to some degree by putting their Internet service machines into a co-location (co-lo) center. The main advantage of a co-lo is that the service provider has redundant high-bandwidth Internet connections and highly redundant power and cooling facilities that are prohibitively expensive for most companies to afford on their own. Co-location has definite economies of scale. Some high-end outsourcing companies also support the machines and the applications running on them. Others might have someone available to power-cycle a given machine on request. As with other forms of outsourcing, it is important to have service levels defined in the contract, with financial penalties if they are not met. The service levels should include guaranteed bandwidth, response times on service calls, power and cooling, uptime, physical security and network availability guarantees.

Outsourcing is a sensitive subject, on which many people have strong views. We have tried to present some of the pros and cons of outsourcing in different situations. Ultimately, it is a business decision that is largely out of the hands of the SAs and their managers. (More discussion of the topic is in Section 14.2.2.)

25.2   The Icing

The icing on a system administration organization is the ability to use consultants and contractors to help your team grow and build new services and infrastructure well, while still maintaining service levels. Used in the right way, consultants and contractors can give in-house staff opportunities to grow and gain experience. Used in the wrong way, they can offend, dishearten, and alienate the SA team.

We distinguish between consultants and contractors by their skill level and the work they perform. A consultant brings significant new and in-depth skills to the table, usually for a specific project. A contractor brings skills that the company may already have and performs tasks that the SA group already performs.

25.2.1   Consultants and Contractors

Consultants who are experts in their fields can be useful temporary additions to a system administration team. A consultant should be engaged for a specific project, such as designing and building a new service that needs to scale rapidly to support the whole company, in which in-house SAs may not currently have experience.

A successful relationship with a consultant will involve the SAs, particularly architects and implementers, in the project on which the consultant is working. The consultant should be willing to share ideas, brainstorm, and generally work with the team and should not dictate to them. A good consultant can bring necessary expertise and experience to a new endeavor, resulting in a better design and increased knowledge for the in-house SAs.

On the other hand, it is not good for the morale and success of an SA team to bring in consultants for the new and interesting projects while the in-house SAs deal with the day-to-day support and maintenance. The new service will not be as well supported as it would be if the in-house SAs were involved and understood the design. It may also not take into account local quirks or be as well integrated with other systems as it would be if local knowledge were used in the design. The in-house SAs will not get the opportunity to grow and learn new skills and will become dissatisfied with their positions, resulting in high turnover and unsatisfactory levels of customer support.

If new projects need to be implemented, but the in-house SAs do not have time to participate, contractors should be brought in to back-fill for the in-house SAs' day-to-day tasks, not necessarily to implement the new service.

The project will usually be more successful in terms of budget, features, and on-going support and maintenance if the in-house SAs are involved, rather than giving it entirely to an outside team. Helping the SAs to participate in new projects through relieving their day-to-day workload will also lead to a stronger, happier SA team.

Rotating the in-house SAs who participate in the interesting projects so that all the SAs have a chance to be involved in a project also strengthens the team.

25.3 Sample Organizational Structures

How do the different roles and responsibilities fit into companies of different sizes? How does being an e-commerce site change the organization of the SA function? We describe what the system administration organization should look like in small, medium, and large companies and an e-commerce site. For these examples, a small company is typically between 20 and 100 employees, a medium company is between 1,000 and 3,000 employees, and a large company is over 20,000 employees.

25.3.1 Small Company

A small company will have one or two SAs, who are expected to cover all the bases between them. There will be no formal helpdesk. They will be involved in customer support and infrastructure maintenance. However, usually only one of them will be involved in designing and implementing new services as they are required. As request volume grows, usually right around the 20-employee mark, a helpdesk ticket system is useful for time management and ensures that requests don't get "lost."

As a small company moves beyond 100 employees and starts growing into a mid-size company, its system administration organization will be formed. This intermediate time is when the big decisions about how to organize and fund system administration need to be made by the company's senior management. The formal helpdesk will be formed during the transitional stages, and initially it will be staffed by a rotation of SAs in customer support roles.

25.3.2 Medium Company

In a mid-size company, the SAs start to specialize a bit more. A helpdesk should have been formed before the company reached the 1,000-employee mark and should have dedicated staff. The helpdesk will be expected to solve reasonably complex problems. SAs in customer support roles may still rotate through the helpdesk to augment the dedicated staff. Some SAs will specialize in a specific OS. Others will take on networking or security, initially as part-time responsibilities and later, as the company grows, as full-time positions. The architects generally will also be implementers, and ideally they should be capable of solving end-to-end problems involving several different technologies. Customer support personnel also can be included in the design and implementation projects through designating days for project work and days for customer support work.

25.3.3   Large Company

A large company will have a high degree of specialization among the SA team. It will have a well-staffed helpdesk with a clearly defined second-tier support team for the more difficult problems. It will have small customer support teams dedicated to different departments or business units. It will have a central infrastructure support group and a central security team. It will have at least one architect for each technology area and teams of implementers for each area. It may have regional SA organizations, or SA organizations dedicated to subsidiaries or large business divisions. These SA organizations will need formal communication paths to coordinate their work and clearly defined areas of responsibility. They should all be covered by the same company policies, if possible.

25.3.4   E-commerce Site

An e-commerce site is different from other sites in that it has two different sets of computers, networks, and services that require different levels of availability and are governed by different sets of priorities. A problem with a revenue-generating Internet service will always take precedence over an internal customer support call because the former results in the company losing money directly, whereas the latter is only indirectly linked to the revenue stream.

To avoid this conflict of interest, a company with a large e-commerce site needs two separate SA teams. One team supports only the Internet presence, and the other supports only the corporate systems. There should be a clean separation between the equipment used for each entity because they have different availability requirements and different functions. Sites where parts of the Internet service rely on parts of the corporate infrastructure inevitably run into problems. A clean separation is also more readily maintained if different SA groups are in charge of each area.

The composition of the corporate SA team depends on the size of the company, as described above. The composition of the Internet service is somewhat different. It may have a helpdesk that is part of the customer

support organization.[3] Although that helpdesk may have second-tier support to which calls are escalated, there will not be small internal customer
support teams that serve each department. There will only be SAs who
are responsible for the support and maintenance of the Internet service and
architects and implementers who design and deploy enhancements to the
service and scale the service to meet customer demand.

25.3.5 Universities and Non-Profit Organizations

It is important for non-profit organizations to watch and take control of
ongoing costs. Typically they have very limited budgets, so it is vital that all
the money that is available for computing is used properly with organizations
and departments working together with everyone's best interest in mind. It
is easier to control costs when services are centralized. However, universities
often have small fiefdoms built around the funding that individual research
groups or professors receive. It is in the best interests of the university or
non-profit organization to centralize as much as possible and to work as a
team. To do so requires strong leadership from the head of the organization
and good service from the central SA team.

Case Study: *Use Limited Resources Wisely*

Here's an example of what can happen if there is no budget for centralized services.
A department in a university had a limited amount of money to spend on equipment. Several research groups within the department received additional money
for equipment from their research projects. Equipment that was retired from use in
a research group was given to the department to help support the undergraduate
and infrastructure needs. The department had some glaring needs that it had been
unable to fund. The backup system was only able to accommodate the machines
that were used by the undergraduates. There was no backup service for research
computers. The servers that provided email, printing, software depot, and home
directory services for the department were two unreliable machines that were designed to be desktop workstations and were 7 years old.

   However, there was no coordination within the department on how best to
spend the money from research contracts. One professor had enough money from a
research project to buy four or five high-end PCs with plenty of disk space, monitors,
and suitable graphics cards. Instead, he decided to buy two of the most expensive
PCs possible with hardware that was not needed and an additional processor that
could not be used by the computational code that ran on the machine, because the

---

[3]A helpdesk that supports external customers of the company, as opposed to the internal
customers of the corporate SA team.

code was not able to run in parallel. Both PCs were given to one PhD student, who already had a high-end computer. They were largely unused. No machines were handed down to the department, and no consideration was given to purchasing a backup server for the research community in the department.

Each professor was entitled to spend his own money, and none of them were willing to spend it on something that would benefit people outside their group in addition to their own group. Instead, money was blatantly wasted, and the whole department suffered. Ultimately, the head of department was responsible for failing to motivate the professors in the department to work as a team.

25.4   Conclusion

The size and cost of the system administration team is an area that is often closely watched. Where the system administration organization reports into at the vice-presidential level can also have considerable impact on those two areas. A company typically wants to optimize its spending on system administration so that it has the smallest budget possible without adversely affecting other people in the company. The system administration team in general, and its managers in particular, have a responsibility to help the company to strike the right balance. Optimizing the SA team to have the right mix of skills and positions within the team is one of the ways in which the system administration organization can help. Providing data on how and why other groups' spending affects the SA group's spending helps, as does suggesting and participating in funding models that make other departments more directly responsible for the system administration costs incurred, thus making the cost/benefit analysis for the profit centers more accurate.

Another hot area for the system administration organization is the debate on centralized versus decentralized system administration. Infrastructure functions need to be centralized to provide a smoothly running, reliable service. Other than the helpdesk function, the more direct customer support roles can benefit from being less centralized, but there are many pitfalls to avoid in doing so. Communication levels between the SAs need to be maintained at a high level, the different teams need to cooperate, and dispute resolution between different groups should happen at a lower level in the management chain than the CEO.

Consultants and contractors can be used effectively as short-term resources to advance particular projects that would otherwise have to wait. However, they should be used in such a way as to give the permanent SAs the opportunity to get involved in these interesting projects, learn, and advance their skills. Using only short-term resources to build systems for the permanent SAs to support is not a recipe for success.

As companies grow, the SAs tend to become more specialized, focusing on particular areas, rather than being expected to solve everything. They face problems of scale in all areas that do not arise in smaller companies. There often is more pressure to keep up with new technologies. Larger companies need architects for the different technology areas to look at the big picture and steer the group in the right direction. A large company also benefits significantly from having some senior generalists to solve difficult end-to-end problems.

Companies that provide a significant service over the Internet primarily differ from other companies in that they need two separate SA teams to maintain the two separate pieces of infrastructure. The team supporting the Internet service also needs a different mix of skills than that of a typical internal system administration support team.

Exercises

1. Is your system administration team centralized or decentralized?

2. Are there parts of your system administration team that are decentralized that might work more effectively if they were centralized? What problems do you think centralizing those groups would solve? What problems might it create?

3. Are there parts of your system administration team that are centralized that might work more effectively if they were decentralized? What problems do you think decentralizing those groups would solve? What problems might it create?

4. In what ways have consultants or contractors been employed effectively by your organization?

5. In what ways have consultants or contractors been employed ineffectively by your organization? How would you change what was done to make the relationship succeed and meet its goals?

6. How is your system administration organization funded? What are the problems with your current funding model, and what are the benefits? Can you think of ways that it might be improved? What data would you need to present to upper management to get your ideas approved?

7. What are the relationships between the different components of your system administration organization? Can you think of ways to get SAs involved in other areas periodically? What advantages and disadvantages would the team experience from implementing that idea?

Chapter 26

Perception and Visibility

System administration, when done correctly, is like good theater: The audience sees a wonderful show and never realizes how many months of planning were required to create the show nor how much backstage work was happening during the performance. The majority of the work required for any performance is invisible to the audience. There is good reason why SAs refer to the work they do as "behind the scenes." Even so, the audience appreciates and values the show *more* if they understand what went into creating the production. They are more invested in the success of the theater if they feel some kind of relationship to its people.

Perception is how people see you; it is a measure of quality. *Visibility* is how much people see of you; it is a measure of quantity. This chapter is about how customers see you and how to improve their perception of you. You are a great person,[1] and we hope that this chapter will help you shine.

A customer's perception of you is their reality of you. If you are working hard but aren't perceived that way, people will assume you are not. If they do not know you exist, then you don't exist. If they know you exist, but have a

---

[1] Our publisher assures us that this book will only be read by quality people like yourself.

vacuum of information about what you are doing, they will assume the worst. That's reality.

Many SAs feel that perception and visibility isn't their job, or that they have no control over how people perceive them, or that this is all just a hunk of baloney, and real SAs are only concerned with technical problems. They feel that if they do the technical part of their jobs well, then they will be perceived well and will be visible. Thus we've made an effort to make our examples as real and down-to-earth as possible.

26.1   The Basics

This section is about perception. We've already established that you are a quality individual. Do people perceive you accurately? The basics of this chapter deal with improving how you are perceived and establishing your positive visibility. Every interaction with others is an opportunity to improve how you are perceived. The first impression that you make with customers dominates all future interactions with them. You must have a positive attitude about the people you support because they will perceive you by your attitude.

Customers perceive the efficiency of the work you do not by how hard you work, but by how soon their requests are completed. Therefore we will discuss a technique that lets you match your priorities to customer expectations of completion time. We will end this section with a discussion of what we call being a "system advocate"—that is, being proactive in meeting the needs of customers.

You are responsible for whether you are perceived positively or negatively. Take responsibility for improving how you are perceived. Nobody else will do it for you.

These are the key elements every SA must master to achieve positive visibility. Some of these are more appropriate for management to initiate, but others must be done on the personal level. After this section, we will discuss techniques SAs can use to increase the amount of visibility they receive.

26.1.1   A Good First Impression

It is important to make a good first impression with your customers. If you get off on the wrong foot, it is difficult to regain their trust. On the other hand, if you make a good first impression, the occasional mistake will be looked at as a fluke.

Try to remember back to grade school on the first day of the school year, in particular. The kid who got in trouble that day was assumed to be "the bad kid" for the rest of the year. He was watched closely, was rarely trusted, and never got the benefit of the doubt. If anything went wrong, he was accused. On the other hand, some students were on their best behavior the first week of school. They went out of their way to be especially nice to the teacher. For the rest of the year, they could get away with occasional infractions or ask for and receive permission to bend the rules.

Think of a good first impression as a "goodwill bank account." Every good thing you do goes into an account, and you can survive one bad thing for every five (maybe ten) good things in the account. Making a good first impression starts that bank account with a positive balance.

If your first interaction with a customer is at an appointment, there are many things you can do to make a good first impression: Be on time or early, polite, friendly, and willing to listen. Humans are visual beings, so appearance and facial expression are two things people notice first. Smile. Pay attention to what you wear. Being "well dressed" has different definitions at different companies—a suit is respected at some, mocked at others.

Chromatically Different Hair

Dressing in a way that gives a positive first impression means different things at different companies. An SA we know wears baggy overalls and dyes her hair bright pink (the current "rave fashion"). She's quite a sight! For a while she was an SA at a major company in Silicon Valley. When she was assigned to directly support a web farm for a small group of people, they were extremely respectful of and enthusiastic about her. When expressing their enthusiasm, they often mentioned her hair. One day a peer told her that the reason she had gained such quick acceptance by the customers was that they figured that anyone who dressed that way and got away with it must be technically excellent.

The First Time I Met You

Tom ran into someone he hadn't seen for five years. The person casually recalled, "I still remember the silly t-shirt you were wearing the first time I met you!" First impressions are lasting impressions. Every day is a day you can potentially make a first impression.

What you wear on your face is also important. A nonexasperated, unruffled exterior is the greatest asset an SA can have. Smile now and then, or people will remember you as "the grumpy one."

You have an existing "installed base" of reputation with your current customers, but it is extremely important to make a good first impression with each new person who is hired. Eventually these "new people" will be the majority of your customers. Making a good first impression on new hires begins before their first day at work. You need to make sure that when they arrive they will find their computer is already in their office, it is configured, their accounts are created, and everything is working properly.

On a person's first day, he can be nervous and afraid of his new surroundings. Having everything set up gives him a warm and invited feeling that not only affects his impression of the SAs, but of the entire company. The SAs have an opportunity to establish a reputation for being organized, competent, and having the customer's needs in mind.

Businesses are realizing that a new hire's first day sets the tone for the employee's entire time with the company. A person arriving for the first day of work usually is highly motivated. To maintain this motivation the person must be productive right away. Every day that the person is delayed from being productive reduces motivation. If you want high performance, make sure new employees can get started right away.

Slow PC Delivery

A programmer in New Jersey told us that when she started working at a large insurance company, she didn't receive a computer for her first month there. This may be acceptable for nontechnical jobs, but she was a programmer! Members of her group were curious why this upset her because this was the status quo for PC deployment in their division. She was paid to do nothing for the first month, and everyone considered this "normal." This was a waste of company resources. The fact that fellow employees had grown accustomed to such slow response indicates that the SAs of this company had been doing an unimpressive job for a long time.

To ensure that people have what they need on their first day, you should establish a process with the cooperation of other administrative personnel, often outside of the system administration team. Secretaries usually have a checklist of arrangements to make for all new hires. It is key to make sure that computing needs are on that checklist: finding out what kind of computer the person needs, procuring the computer, arranging their network jacks, finding out what their preferred login name is, determining what internal mailing lists they need to be on, finding out what software they need, getting the accounts created, and so on. If there is a standard desktop computer configuration, then preconfigured machines should be on hand and ready to be deployed. If there is no standard configuration, there has to be a process where the new hire is contacted weeks in advance to arrange for the proper equipment to be ordered, installed, and tested.

On the employee's first day, the friendliest member of your SA team should visit the person to do some kind of in-person orientation, answer questions, and personally deliver a printed "welcome to our network" guide. The orientation process puts a face to the SA team. This is comforting to the customer. Customers don't like faceless organizations. It is easier to get angry at a person whom you have never met. The orientation is an investment that pays off with an improved relationship in the future.

Case Study: Everyone Gets an Orientation Session

If the SAs don't visit new hires to give them an orientation, someone else will. One company felt that doing such an orientation was a waste of time for the SAs and assumed it would be an annoyance to new employees. What happened instead is that a peer employee would end up briefing the person about how to log in and during the process take time to bad-mouth the SA team or recount the last unplanned system outage. It was a long time before the SA team realized this was happening and even longer before they could turn the situation around.

26.1.2 Attitude, Perception, and Customers

How people perceive you is directly related to the attitude you project. It is important to have a positive attitude because people pick up on your attitude very quickly.

The number one attitude problem among SAs is a blatant disrespect for the people whom they are hired to serve. It is surprising how often we remind SAs that their users are not "lusers" or "pests with requests." They are the reason SAs have jobs. SAs are there to serve but, more importantly, to advocate for these people. The SAs and the computer users are all on the same team.

We advocate that SAs stop using the term "users" and replace it with the term "customers" (Smallwood 1992). This becomes a reminder that they are in a service industry, supporting the needs of these people instead of "pests" who make requests all day. Doing this can change SAs' attitudes dramatically.

It is very enlightening to work as a consultant where the customers are directly paying you for your SA work and will replace you if you don't meet their needs. It helps you to realize how much better things work when you treat your "users" as customers and really listen to what they need.

Conversely, an SA can get into trouble if she adopts the attitude that "the customer is always right." That's going too far. Part of an SA's job is to (politely) say "no" when appropriate. An SA can end up doing the customer's job if she does *everything* the customer requests. Instead the SA must remember to help the customer help himself. It is a balancing act. The SA management needs to establish a clear definition of where to draw the line.

As an SA moves from customer support to higher-level roles such as system architect, the "customer" relationship often gives way to a more collaborative relationship where the SA and the customer work together as a team. As this happens, you are trying to develop a "business partners" relationship. You work together to do what is best for the company and define a "scope of work" that delineates what SAs should do and what customers should do, but the customer relationship still should remain.

We've tried to role-model this language throughout this book. We've always referred to the people whom we serve as "customers," only using the term "user" when we mean someone who uses a particular device or service.

Another attitude problem SAs can develop is becoming frustrated by the fact that customers do nothing but bring them problems. SAs can develop resentment toward customers that makes them want to avoid them or moan every time customers come to SAs' offices. This is a bad thing. We hear comments such as, "Oh great! Here comes another problem." This is an ironic situation because your job as an SA is to fix problems. If you get frustrated by the constant flood of problems, maybe you need a vacation (see Section 27.2.2). When you return, you can ponder the reality that being a SA means that people come to you to fix problems. A more positive attitude is to address every "problem" as a puzzle.

Related to that situation is the attitude, "All my users are stupid," or "Why do these people always call the help line with dumb questions?" Our reply: They wouldn't be calling if they knew the answer; and you wouldn't have been hired if you didn't know more about this than they do. "My users are idiots! They barely know anything about computers!" Our reply: They know enough to work for a company that is smart enough to hire someone like you who can answer their questions, and they know a lot more about their own areas of expertise than you do. You should occasionally create opportunities to interact with your customers in which they won't be coming to you with problems. Take the initiative to visit them occasionally. We'll have more suggestions later in this chapter.

Venting About Customers

An SA lost the respect of his customers and was later removed after an incident in which he loudly complained about them in the company cafeteria. His complaint was that although they were brilliant in topics outside of computers, he felt their approach to computers was idiotic. He complained about them to no end while eating lunch and explained that he felt it was beneath him to have to help them. One mistake he made was using the word "idiots" and worse words to describe them. Another mistake he made was to misunderstand the hand signals all his coworkers were giving him to try to explain that the people he was talking about and their director were sitting at the table behind him.

If your customers frustrate you, complain in private to your manager and work on constructive solutions. Don't gripe about them in public. Venting is a much-needed form of stress release: Find the right forum for it.

You should adopt an enlightened attitude toward trouble reports. Requests from customers can be exciting challenges and opportunities to do a fantastic job, one of which you can be proud. When you integrate this attitude into your life, your customers will notice the difference in the service you provide. When replying to a customer's trouble ticket, end with a sincere note of thanks for reporting the problem: "Thank you for reporting this. It helped us fix the problem and find ways to prevent it in the future." It can make all the difference.

Your attitude shows through in everything you do.

26.1.3 Align Your Priorities with Customer Expectations

The way you prioritize your tasks influences how customers perceive your effectiveness. You can make customers a lot happier if your priorities match their expectations.[2]

Customers expect small things to happen quickly and big things to take a reasonable amount of time. The definition of "big" and "small" is their definition, which is based on their perception of your job. For example, allocating an IP address, which is perceived as taking a minute or two, should happen quickly. Installing a new computer is perceived as a bigger process, and it is reasonable to take a day or two. When a critical server is down, customers expect you to not be working on anything but handling the emergency.[3] Therefore you can make customers much happier if you prioritize requests so that emergencies are handled first, then quick requests, followed by longer requests.

---

[2] Thanks to Ralph Loura for this technique.

[3] Console servers let you perform tasks on a server's console from your desk. However, customers may get the impression that you don't care about the down machine because you aren't in the machine room. It can be useful to assure them that you are virtually working in the machine room, perhaps inviting them to look at your screen.

In a given day, you or your group may complete 100, 500, or five million requests. If you do them in the order that they arrive, your customers will not be extremely happy with your work, even though their requests were completed. Instead, you can do the same amount of work in a day, but in a different order, and customers will be delighted because their expectations were matched.

A customer will be upset if he is told his small request has to wait until you have completed a larger request, such as installing a new computer. Imagine how upset you would get if you had to wait for a one-page print job because someone was printing a 400-page report that was ahead of you in the queue. It's very similar. It is important, however, to make sure that big jobs are not postponed endlessly by small ones.

Quick requests are often easy to automate, so they become "self-serve." You can arrange for a web page that will do the task for the customer. Our example above concerned allocating an IP address for a customer. In theory, we should be using DHCP so that IP addresses are provided in real time, matching customer expectations without incurring any work on our part. However, some devices can't use DHCP; in those cases, we have to do something a little more creative. It might not be worth the effort to develop a web page that lets customers allocate their own IP addresses. Instead, you might keep a list of the next ten available IP addresses on a pad of paper on your door. People can tear off the IP address they are going to use if they print their names in the right spot so you can later update your inventory. Creative solutions such as that can be fun to invent. Sometimes, the solution is as simple as keeping the spare toner cartridges near the printer so that the time to install them is not dominated by the time to walk to a distant supply room.

In addition to using this reordering technique on the personal level, you can use it throughout an organization. You can divide the SA team so there are front-line support people who perform requests that customers expect to see done quickly. Requests that will take more time can be passed on to second-tier personnel. Senior SAs can be in charge of larger projects, such as the creation of services. This division of labor enables you to ensure that your priorities are aligned with customer expectations and shelters people who are working on long-term projects from constant interruptions (see Section 27.1.2). This may sound like something only large SA teams can afford to do, but even a team of two SAs can benefit from this technique. One SA can shield the other from interruptions in the morning and vice versa in the afternoon.

26.1.4   Be the System Advocate

Customers perceive you as being somewhere between a clerk who reactively performs menial tasks and an advocate who proactively solves their problems and lobbies for their needs. This section is about becoming an advocate, which we feel is the better position to be in.

On one end of the spectrum there is what we call a "system clerk." The system clerk is reactive rather than proactive. The clerk is told what to do on a schedule and does not participate in planning his work. The budget for the clerk often comes from nontechnical budgets. A system clerk might spend the day installing software, performing backups, creating accounts by manually entering the various commands required to do so, and so on.

On the other end of the spectrum there is what we call the "system advocate." The system advocate has a different attitude toward her job. She is proactive about her customers' technical needs, she advocates those needs to management, automates the clerical tasks that she is asked to do, and is involved in the planning process for projects that affect her. Earlier, we discussed having new customers' machines and accounts set up on the day they arrive. To achieve that goal, the SAs must be involved in the hiring process. Becoming involved is the kind of proactive step that a system advocate would take.

Between the clerk and the advocate are an infinite number of gradations. Try to be conscious of where you are and what you can do to move toward being an advocate.

Becoming an advocate is a slow evolution. It starts with just one proactive project. Being proactive is an investment that pays off in the future. It consumes time now but saves time later. It can be hard to find time for proactive work if you are having trouble just keeping your head above water. Select one thing you feel is achievable and would have a significant impact, or get your manager's suggestions. If your manager believes in the potential impact, she should be willing to reallocate some of your time to the project.

It is better to be the advocate for many reasons. It's better for your company because it means that you are aligning your priorities with those of your customers. It puts your focus on where you can best serve the people who rate and review you. It is better for you because it develops your own reputation as a "can do" person. People with such reputations have better chances during promotion opportunities. When raises are being calculated, it certainly helps to have a reputation for being the most helpful person in the group.

A large team usually will have the entire spectrum from clerks to advocates. The clerks are an important part of the team. The clerk role is where SAs get started and learn from others; they provide the advocates with useful assistance. Even the newest SA should adopt a proactive "can-do" attitude, however, and should work toward becoming an advocate. There is a big difference between a clerk being directed by SAs and one being directed by the customers. The one who is directed by SAs will be told the right way to do things and has the opportunity to learn and grow. The one who is directed by customers doesn't have the chance to learn from experts in the field and is not valued by those who direct her.

The biggest benefit comes from adopting the can-do attitude across the entire SA team. The team becomes an active, positive force for change within the organization. The team becomes valued as a whole. Many companies live and die on whether they have the right IT infrastructure to achieve their business goals. Be part of that infrastructure.

Following are some examples to illustrate the difference between how a clerk and an advocate would handle various situations.

Installing Software

You would think that installing software would be fairly straightforward, but many subprocesses are involved. A clerk, for example, might receive the software to be installed from a customer who has purchased it. The customer may have ordered it weeks ago and is anxiously awaiting its installation. Often, in this situation, something goes wrong. The customer didn't know that there is a network license server and has licensed it to his own workstation instead. This breaks the strategy of having a few, well-maintained and monitored, license servers. More often, the installation fails because of something simple that takes a long time to repair. For example, the customer was expecting the software to be installed on a machine that is overburdened and shouldn't have new applications added to it; the license is to a host that is being decommissioned soon; or the system runs out of disk space. It can take a long time to resolve such obstacles before a second installation attempt can succeed.

While the clerk is congratulating himself for accomplishing the installation after overcoming so many obstacles, the customer is complaining to the SA's boss that he had to wait weeks until the software was installed. The customer has no understanding that, for example, installing additional disk space is something that must be planned. Nor does he understand that the addition of a new license server requires more monitoring and reliability planning, and that by not leveraging the planned infrastructure, future work will require more effort for the SA team. There is no accounting for the real cost of the software, which should have included the cost of disk storage, CPU capacity, and the fact that the installation had to be performed twice. The multiweek installation effort did not match the customer's expectation of a quick install after he received the media. As discussed in Section 26.1.3, matching the customer's expectations is critical.

A system advocate would be in a position to make the process go more smoothly. The customers would have known to involve the SA in the process from the beginning. The advocate would have interviewed the customer to get a basic understanding of the purpose of the software and performed capacity planning to allocate the proper disk, CPU, and network needs.

A timetable would be agreed to by all parties involved so there would be no misunderstandings. The purchase would include the software (possibly ordered by the SA so that the licensing is correct), as well as any additional disk, CPU, or network capacity. The potential problems can be resolved in parallel with the ordering of the software.

As a result of this planning, the software is matched with the appropriate disk, CPU, and network capacity, the customer has achieved a better understanding of the SA processes, and the SA achieves a better understanding of the customer's needs. We value what we understand and devalue what we don't understand. Through this process, both sides value the other person more.

Solving a Performance Problem

A customer complains about slow system performance. A clerk might be told to upgrade the customer's machine to a faster network card because all customers assume that systems are always slow because of slow networks.[4] Little is improved after the installation, and the customer is not happy. The problem has not been properly diagnosed.

The last time Tom observed a situation like this, the server that the customer was using had a mere 10Mb Ethernet connection and upgrading to a 100Mb Ethernet card in the client's PC flooded the server, making the problem worse.

An advocate would take a more active role by observing the problem, possibly before the customer notices it, if there is a good monitoring system in place, using various tools to diagnose the problem, and proposing a few solutions. The advocate takes the time to explain the problem and the various potential solutions with enough detail that they can select the best solution together. The proposal, is presented to management by the customer, who is now capable of explaining the issues. The SA is in the room to support the customer if he stumbles. After management approves the purchase and the problem is fixed, the customer is very happy.

The result of such a team effort is a customer base that is more invested in the evolution of the network.

Simple Automation Is Fine

The advocate uses the time management advice in Chapter 27 to find the extra time needed to take on proactive projects. She also creates additional time in her day by automating her most time-consuming tasks. Automation opens doors to better ways of doing things.

---

[4] As a historical note: Before network-centric computing, all customers assumed that system slowness was always due to a lack of RAM.

The clerk might choose to put off all account creation requests until a certain day of the week, then do them all "in batch." Customers see extremely poor turnaround time. The advocate automates the task so that creating accounts is simple and she can do them on demand.

Automating a task does not have to be extremely complicated. Don't get bogged down in creating the perfect system. A simple script that assists with "the common case" may be more valuable than a large system that automates every possible aspect of a task. At one site, the procedure to configure the BOOTP server to accept a new NCD X Terminal simply output the commands the SA should type. If the commands looked right, they would cut and paste them to a shell prompt. The script was easy to write because it doesn't have to deal with asking, "Are you sure?" or odd-ball special cases. If the X Terminal required something special, the SA could use the output as the basis for the commands that were actually typed.

Manually loading a machine's OS also can be a long manual process, especially if a series of "from memory" customizations must be made. OS vendors provide tools for automating installations that also automate customizations, as discussed in Chapter 1. The advocate takes advantage of these tools, whereas the clerk continues manually loading OSs.

How to Automate Anything

The most important thing to remember when automating a process is to first do the entire process manually, then automate those steps exactly. After that, you can improvise, add new features, or make this small program part of a larger superstructure. But first you must do it yourself and automate your actual steps.

We know this from experience. We have seen many novice SAs struggle for weeks trying to automate a process, only to discover that they were trying to automate something that *they* weren't sure how to do! It's easy to get into this trap. On a theoretical level, we think we know how to do it. It sounds easy, why would automating it be difficult? Why not just start by writing code to do it? Instead, a lot of time is wasted because you don't know if you can do something until you've actually done it.

As you manually perform the process, record what you do. Actually do the process, don't just think your way through it. You are not as good as simulating a computer as a computer is. For example, if you were automating the creation of user accounts, record all the various steps as you do the process manually. Now test the account to make sure it works. You might find that you forgot something, requiring you to revise the process.

Once the steps are recorded, consider how to automate each step. Is there a command that performs that function? What happens "behind the scenes" when I click on that button? Does it modify a registry setting? Run a program? Update a file?

Now write code to automate that one step. Don't wait until all the code is written to start testing. Test each step separately before adding it to your main program. Test the main program after each step's automation is added. Finding mistakes early on is key to writing solid code. This avoids the situation in which you find that a mistake made in the first step made the rest of your code useless. Even worse is discovering that fixing a problem in the first step has ramifications to the rest of the steps. Imagine if a particular variable established in the first step now needs to be an array of variables. Now all future steps that use that variable have to be modified. What if you accidentally don't change it everywhere? What if this radically changes the algorithms used in later steps? If those steps are already coded, you will find yourself hacking the code to conform to the variable, rather than writing it cleanly the first time. For these reasons, automating and testing one step at a time will produce a better system.

The Practice of Programming by Kernighan and Pike (1999) has excellent advice on such incremental development and testing of software. Bentley's *Programming Pearls* (1999) is an excellent book to read next if you find yourself developing more complicated algorithms.

26.2   The Icing

The previous parts of this chapter dealt with improving how you are perceived. The next level is to increase your visibility. We were talking about quality, now we are talking about quantity.

The SA's *visibility paradox* is that SAs are only noticed if something breaks. Achieving consecutive months of 100 percent uptime takes a huge amount of behind-the-scenes work and dedication. Management may get the impression that the SAs aren't needed because they do not see the work required. Then a server crashes every hour until a controller is replaced. Suddenly, the SA is valuable. He is the hero. He is important. This is not a good position to be in because people get the impression that the SAs do nothing 95 percent of the time because they don't see the important, back-office work the SAs do.

One alternative is to maintain an unstable system so that the SAs are always needed and noticed. That is a bad idea. A better idea is to find subtle ways to make sure that the customers understand the value of what the SAs do.

You are responsible for the amount of visibility you receive. Take responsibility for achieving it. Nobody else will promote you except yourself.

None of these techniques should be attempted if you aren't providing good service to your customers. The keystone of good visibility is to already be doing good work. There is no point in advertising a bad product.

26.2.1   The System Status Web Page

A good way to be visible to your customers is to provide a web page that lists the status of your network. SAs should be able to easily update the status message so that when there are outages, they can easily list them. When there are no outages, the system should state so. The status should be time/date stamped so that people understand how current the information is. The page should have information about how to report problems, links to your monitoring systems, a schedule of planned outages, and news about recent major changes.

Most people start a web browser at least once a day. If the default web page (at least as delivered) is your status page, then there is an opportunity to be in their field of vision quite often. Because customers can change their browser's default page, it is important to include content that is useful to the customers on a daily basis so that they do not change the default. Links to local weather, news, and corporate services can discourage people from switching.

A status web page sends a message that you care. If there is an outage being reported, it tells the customers that you are working on the problem and reduces the number of redundant phone calls complaining about the interruption.

A status message should be simple and assure people that the problem is being looked into. "Server `sinclair` is down, we're working on it." In the absence of this information, people often assume you are out to lunch, ignoring the problem, or ignorant of the problem. Taking ten seconds to give the status creates the positive visibility you desire.

As customers become accustomed to checking this URL, there will be fewer interruptions while you try to fix the problem. There is nothing worse than being delayed from working on a problem because you are busy answering phone calls from customers who want to help by reporting the problem. People will not develop the habit of checking this URL until you consistently update it.

This can be a simple web page or it can be as complicated as a web portal that delivers other news and features. Commercial and free portal software has a range of features and complexity.

Low-tech solutions also work well. One site simply put a whiteboard at the entrance to the machine room, and SAs wrote status messages there. If a method gets the message across, it is a good solution. This approach only works well in smaller environments where the machine room is convenient to the customers.

26.2.2 Management Meetings

Although being visible to all customers is useful, a more targeted approach is also valid. A regularly scheduled one-on-one meeting with the head of each customer group can be very valuable. Often, each SA is aligned with one or two customer groups. A 30-minute meeting every two weeks with the manager of each group can keep him aware as to the projects being done for his people. The manager can stay abreast of what kind of work is being requested by his staff and help prioritize those projects. You will occasionally find the manager eliminating certain requests. The secondary purpose of such meetings should be to educate the manager regarding infrastructure changes being made that, while invisible to them, are being done to improve the network. This process goes a long way in shedding light on the invisible.

26.2.3 Physical Visibility

When considering your visibility, consider your physical visibility. Where you sit may cause you to be out of sight and out of mind. If your office is hidden behind a physical barrier, you are projecting an image of being inaccessible and unfriendly. If your office is in everyone's view, you are under the microscope. Every break you take will be seen as slacking off. People will not understand that an SA's job involves bursts of activity and inactivity.

It is good to find a balance between being physically visible and invisible. A strategic way of managing this is to have a good mix of visibility within your team. People responsible for directly interfacing with customers and doing customer care should be more visible, whereas back office programmers and architects should be less visible.

26.2.4 Town Meetings

Another way of increasing your positive visibility is to host regularly scheduled meetings open to all customers. Such meetings can be an excellent forum for bi-directional feedback. They can also be a disaster if you are unprepared. Planning is essential.

Some organizations have yearly "town hall" meetings. These usually include a high-level manager presenting a "state of the network" address that reviews the last year's accomplishments and the next year's challenges. This is usually a slide presentation. One way to communicate that your SA team has division of labor and structure is to have different area heads present briefly on their domains, rather than one person doing the entire presentation. Question-and-answer sessions should follow each presentation. Meetings like this can drag on forever if not planned properly. It is important to have all speakers meet to plan how long each will talk and what each will say. Have a script that is reviewed by all speakers! Make sure there is little redundancy and that everyone adheres to the schedule. Have an M.C. whose role is to introduce people and to signal people when their time is up.

Some organizations host monthly or quarterly meetings. These "user group" meetings often are half entertainment (to draw people in) and half bi-directional communication. The first half may be a demo or speaker. You might have a vendor come talk about something exciting, such as a future product roadmap or to introduce a new product. Avoid sales presentations. SAs might present an interesting new tool to the customers and spark interest by presenting plans for major network upgrades, information on hot topics such as how to avoid spam, and so on. This is an excellent forum to present a dress rehearsal for paper presentations that SAs may be doing at future conferences, such as LISA. Doing this also communicates to the customers that the SA staff is receiving external professional acknowledgement of their good work. The second half is a bi-directional feedback session, such as a question-and-answer forum or a facilitated discussion on a particular issue. These meetings are also an opportunity to announce scheduled changes and explain why they are needed. Following is the format used by one organization for their quarterly user group meeting.

1. *Welcome* (2 minutes): Welcome the group and thank them for attending. It is a good idea to have the agenda written on a whiteboard so people know what to expect.

2. *Introductions* (5 minutes): The attendees introduce themselves.

3. *Feedback* (20 minutes): Getting feedback from the customers is part art and part science. You want people to focus on their needs, rather than on how those needs should be met. Consider taking a class on meeting facilitation if you feel weak in this area. Ask open-ended questions, for example, "If one thing could be improved, it would be..." "The single best part of our computing environment is..." "The single worst part of our computing environment is..." "My job would be easier if..."

   Keep a log of what participants suggest. A huge pad of paper on an easel is best, so everyone can see what is being recorded. Don't write full sentences, just key phrases such as, "faster install new C++ releases" or "add CPUs `server5`." Once a page is filled, tape it to the wall and go to the next page.

   Do not reject or explain away any requests. Just record what people say. To get the best responses, people must feel they are safe. People do not feel safe—and will stop talking—if every suggestion is answered with your reason why that "just isn't possible" or "we can't afford it." However, be clear that recording an idea does not guarantee it will be implemented.

Be careful of permitting one talkative person to dominate the meeting. If this happens, you might want to use phrases such as, "Let's hear from the people in the room who have not spoken yet," or in extreme cases, you can go around the room having each person answer the question in sequence, without permitting others to interrupt.

Don't get stuck in an infinite loop. If you hit your time limit, cut off discussion politely and move on. People have busy schedules and need to get back to work.

4. *Review* (10 minutes): Review what you've recorded by reading the items out loud. Consider reviewing these lists with your management afterward to prioritize (and reject) tasks.

5. *Show and tell* (30 minutes): This is the main attraction. People want to be entertained, which means different things to different people. The best way to entertain technical people is to have them learn something new. Nontechnical people might want to learn about some mysterious part of the system. Ask a vendor to present information on a product, have an internal person present some information about something he does or has found useful, or you might want to focus on a new feature of your network. This may be a good time to explain a big change that is coming soon or describe your network topology or some aspect of the system that you find customers often don't understand.

6. *Meeting review* (5 minutes): Have each person in turn say how they felt the meeting went (less than one sentence each). For large groups, it can be better to have people say a single word, or to just raise their hands if they want to comment.

7. *Closing* (2 minutes): First, ask for a show of hands to indicate if they thought the meeting was useful. Remind them that you are available if people want to drop by and discuss the issues further. Then (and this is important), thank people for taking time out of their busy schedules.

26.2.5 Newsletters

Many large system administration organizations produce a monthly or quarterly newsletter. Sometimes, these are excellent and useful to the customers, but mostly we find that they are ignored or backfire by sending a message that your team is more concerned with PR than solving problems.

We feel that if you must have a newsletter, it should be simple and useful. A simple layout, preferably simple ASCII email. The content should be useful to the intended audience, possibly including frequently asked questions or an "ask the SAs" column that selects one question per issue to explain in detail.

If you have hired a full-time person to do nothing but produce the newsletter, you don't have a simple newsletter.

26.2.6   Mail to All Customers

Before major changes, such as those that might be implemented in a maintenance window as discussed in Chapter 12, send a brief email to all customers telling them about the outage and what improvements they will experience afterwards. Sending useful mass email is an art. Make it very brief and to the point. The most important information should be in the first two sentences. Most people will only read that far. Extra information for those who are interested should be contained in a few additional, brief paragraphs. For example, a good mass email about system maintenance might read as follows:

```
Printing in Buildings 1 and 2 will not work on Saturday, June 24
between 8 AM and 11 AM because of essential system maintenance.
    If this is a problem, please let John Smith know at extension
54321 as soon as possible.
    The printing servers in those buildings are approaching the end
of their useful lives, and we anticipate that they will become
less reliable in a few months. We are replacing them with new
hardware now, so that we don't suffer from reliability problems
in the future. If you have further questions, please contact us
by email at print-team@company.com.
```

On the other hand, an email sent to all customers that is wordier, like a traditional letter, is less useful. The following, for example, does not get the important point across quickly:

```
Dear all,
To serve you better, the system administration team monitors all
components of the system. We endeavor to anticipate problems and
to fix them before they arise. To do so, we need to occasionally
schedule outages of some component of the system in order to
perform maintenance. We do our best to schedule the maintenance
at a time that will not adversely affect any urgent work in
other parts of the company.
    We have identified a potential problem with the print servers
in Buildings 1 and 2. We anticipate that those print servers
will become less reliable in a few months' time and will then
cause problems printing in those buildings. Because of this, we
have scheduled some time on Saturday, June 24 between 8 AM and
11 AM to replace those servers with new, reliable machines.
Because of that, you will be unable to print in Buildings 1
and 2 during those hours.
```

If the timing of this maintenance window will interfere with
some urgent work, please let us know as soon as possible and we
will reschedule it for another time. John Smith, at extension
54321, is the person to contact about scheduling issues.

As always, we are happy to answer any questions that you might
have about this maintenance work. Questions can be addressed
directly to the people working on this project by sending email
to print-team@company.com. All other questions should be
addressed to helpdesk@company.com as usual.

Thank you for your cooperation with our ongoing maintenance
program.
The SA Team

Such email should always include two ways of contacting the SAs if there
are questions or if someone has an issue with what is being announced.
It is critical that this contact information be accurate. We've seen many
complaints from people who received such a notice but for various reasons
weren't able to contact the author. It is important that the different contact methods are two different means (email and phone, fax and phone,
and so on), not just, for example, two email addresses. Be sure that you
aren't telling people, "If you're email isn't working, please send email to our
helpdesk to have your problem fixed."

Mass email should only be used occasionally and for important changes.
Too much mass email or mass email that is too wordy wastes everyone's time
and will be seen as a nuisance.

26.2.7 Lunch

Breaking bread with customers is an excellent way to stay visible. Eating
lunch with different customers every day or even once a week is a great way
to stay in touch in a way that is friendly and nonintrusive.

Free Lunch
Tommy Reingold at Bell Labs watches the serial numbers on the trouble
tickets that are generated. The creator of every 10,000th ticket is taken out
to lunch. He pays for the lunch out of pocket because of the value he gets
out of the experience. It's a simple, inexpensive thing to do that helps build
the reputation of the SA team as being fun and interesting. This "contest"
isn't advertised, which makes it even more of a surprise to customers when
they win. It can be fun to watch people send an extra ticket or two to try
to increase their chances of winning.

26.3   Conclusion

Perception and visibility should not be left to be managed by fate. Take an active role in managing both. Unmanaged, they will be a disaster. As we become conscious of these concepts, we quickly find many ways to improve them.

Perception is about quality, how people perceive you. Creating a good first impression is a technical issue that requires much planning. Establishing the processes by which new customers have their computers and all accounts the day they arrive requires coordination between many different people. It is important that new customers receive some kind of orientation to welcome them to the network, as well as some kind of "getting started" documentation.

We find that referring to "users" as "customers" changes how we treat them. It focuses our attention on the fact that we serve them. It is important to treat your customers with respect. There is no such thing as a "stupid" question.

We discussed a little queuing theory technique for reordering the requests that you receive, so that their completion time is aligned with the expected completion time.

We discussed the "system advocate" philosophy of system administration. A system advocate is a proactive SA who takes the initiative to solve problems before they happen. Transforming a clerical role to a proactive system advocacy role is a change in attitude and working style that can dramatically improve the service you provide to your customers. It isn't easy—it requires hard work and an investment in time now for a payoff later.

Visibility is about quantity—how much people see of you. We discussed many ways to increase your visibility. Creating a system status web page puts you in front of customers' eyes daily. Meetings with management help them understand what you do and help you maintain focus on their highest priorities. The office locations of every member in your team affects your team's visibility. People who are "customer facing" should be in the more visible locations. Different types of open meetings can be held, including town hall and user group meetings. Newsletters are often produced by SA groups but rarely read by customers. They are a lot of work to produce and just too easy to ignore. Having lunch and social functions with customers is a simple way to maintain interaction.

Taking control of your perception and visibility is required to manage your and your team's personal positive visibility. Managing these things effectively enhances your ability to work well with your customers, increases your opportunities to serve your customers better, and has great potential to enhance your career.

Exercises

1. What is the first impression you make on your new customers? Is it positive or negative? What can you do to improve this?

2. Ask three customers what they remember about the first time they interacted with your SA team. What did you learn from this?

3. At your site, who gives new hires their first-day orientation?

4. Do the members of your team use the term "user" or "customer?" What behavior do you role-model for others?

5. When you need to vent about a customer, whom do you talk to and where?

6. Select ten typical customer requests, and estimate your customer expectations for how long they should take to be completed. Poll three customers for their expectations. How did you do? What did you learn?

7. In what way does your organizational structure benefit or hurt attempts to match customer expectations of completion time? How could this be improved? What do you do on the personal level in this regard, and what can you do to improve?

8. On a scale of one (clerk) to seven (advocate), where are you? Why do you say so? How did you decide on your rating? What steps can you take to move toward advocate?

9. Do you experience the system administrator's visibility paradox mentioned in Section 26.2? Give some examples. What can you do to turn this situation around?

10. Which of these projects would have the biggest positive impact on your organization's visibility: a system status web page, regular meetings with key managers, reorganizing the location of your and your team's offices, town hall meetings, user meetings, a newsletter, or having lunch occasionally with your customers?

11. Does your group produce a newsletter for their customers? Poll five customers on whether they read it and what they find useful if they do. What did you learn?

12. Who on your team is best qualified to host a user meeting?

13. Discuss with your manager this question: What needs the most improvement: your perception or your visibility? What about your team?

Chapter 27

Being Happy

This chapter is about being a happy system administrator (SA). Happiness means different things to different people. A happy SA deals well with stress and an endless incoming workload, looks forward to going to work each day, and has a positive relationship with customers, coworkers, and managers. Happiness is feeling sufficiently in control of your work life and having a good social and family life. It means feeling like you're accomplishing something and deriving satisfaction from your job. It means getting along well with the people you work with, as well as the management above you.

Just as happiness means different things to different people, various techniques in this chapter may appeal more to different readers. Mostly, we've tried to list what has worked for us. For example, there are hundreds of books on time management, but here we try to list the 10 percent of such books that applies to issues SAs face. If you think time management books are 90 percent junk, then hopefully we've covered the remaining 10 percent for you here.

The happy SAs we've met have certain common habits: good personal skills, communication skills, self-psychology, and techniques for managing their manager. We use the word *habits* because people do them unconsciously, like they might tap their fingers when they hear a song on the radio. These behaviors come naturally to some people, but they need to be learned by others. Books, lectures, classes, conferences, and even training camps teach most of these techniques. It's pretty amazing that happiness comes from a set of skills that can be developed through practice!

Making a habit of a technique isn't easy. Don't expect immediate success. If you try again and again, it will become easier and easier. A common rule of thumb is that a habit can be learned if you perform the behavior for a month. Start today.

The goal of this chapter is to give you a taste of these skills and techniques and then refer you to resources for a more complete explanation.

27.1 The Basics

The basics involve being organized and being able to communicate well. Good follow-through is an important goal; it comes from being organized and requires good time management. Professional development is important, too. These basic skills are a platform on which you can build a successful career.

27.1.1 Organizing for Excellent Follow-Through

Follow-through means completing what you commited to do. One common habit among happy SAs is that they stay organized by maintaining a written or electronic organizer (personal digital assistant, or PDA) that records their to-do lists and appointment calendar. These go a long way to ensuring follow-through. Nothing is more frustrating to customers than dropped requests and appointments. You will be happier if you develop the respect that comes from having a reputation for excellent follow-through. This is one of the reasons that we put so much emphasis on using trouble-ticket tracking software throughout this book. Such software assures us that promises are not forgotten.

Your brain only has so much storage space, so don't overload it with items that are better recorded in your organizer. Albert Einstein is rumored to have been so concerned about making sure that 100 percent of his brain was used for physics that he didn't "waste" it on silly things such as what to wear (he had seven outfits, all the same—one for each day of the week) or his home address and phone number (he kept them written on a card in his wallet). When people asked him for his phone number he advised them to look it up in the phone book. He didn't memorize it.

Your memory is imperfect. Your organizer, on the other hand, will not accidentally drop an action item or reverse two appointments. You should have a single organizer, so that all this information is in one place. This is better than having a million pieces of paper taped to your monitor. Combine your work and social calendars so that conflicts don't arise. You wouldn't want to miss that important birthday or anniversary or a meeting with a customer. Maintaining separate calendars at home and at work is asking for trouble. They will become out of sync.

A combined organizer should include your social events, anniversaries, doctor's appointments, non-work-related to-do items, and reminders of regular events, such as the dates for your next annual physical and your car's next inspection. Use your organizer to remind yourself of regular, repeating events. Include reminders to take breaks, to do something nice for yourself, and to compliment your significant others. Use your organizer to record the names of movies that you want to see so the next time you are at a video rental store you aren't frustrated trying to remember that great movie that coworkers recommended. None of these things should be lost in a mess of notes taped to your desk or in your messy and imperfect brain.

Case Study: Dynamic To-Do Lists

In an attempt to achieve perfect follow-through, Tom maintains a to-do list on each page of a page-per-day calendar. He lists little things and big things. He begins each day by copying the items that remained incomplete from yesterday's page to today's page. Hopefully that is only a couple items. Already on the page are items that he previously committed to doing that day. Then he adds anything else that comes to mind. He then reads the list and tags each item that absolutely has to be done today. After those are completed and crossed off, he works on the remainder of the list. Copying the list each day forces him to spend some time planning his day. It also gives him incentive to not let an item slip, because he will have to copy it more often. It gives him a sense of accomplishment when he sees how much he completed the previous day. Although this sounds tedious, it is quite effective and leaves him with a stack of past to-do lists he can refer to in the event that he needs to see the history of action on an item. There are software packages, PDAs, and even web-based portals that automate this process, but Tom prefers to do it manually. It keeps him in touch with what he's doing and forces him to carry a physical binder that is large enough to carry a small folder, pens, and sheets of paper that are big enough to freely draw diagrams. Tom draws a lot of diagrams in his work. The system, although not perfect, works for him.

Having a system, no matter what system that is, is better than having no system at all. We believe this so strongly that we encourage employers to pay for the PDAs (or old-fashioned paper organizers) used by employees, even if they are used for maintaining both social and work information. We're not concerned with which system you use, but we are concerned if you aren't using any system.

Once you have been maintaining your organizer for a while, you will find that you can focus and concentrate better. You can focus better on what you are doing when you aren't also trying to remember what you are doing next, what you have to do next week, and whether that customer meeting is next Wednesday or the Wednesday after that. It's as if you can purposely forget things after you have recorded them in your organizer. Each morning you can review today's items to refresh your memory and set your focus for the day. Let your organizer work for you; don't duplicate its work.

27.1.2   Time Management

Time management is about using time wisely. Rather than increasing productivity by working more hours, you can do more in the same amount of time through a number of techniques and a little planning.

The phrase "work smarter, not harder" can't be more true. Customers don't see how hard you work. They see what you accomplish. Align yourself with this bit of reality. Anybody can work hard, and we're sure that all the readers of this book do. Successful SAs focus on results achieved not on effort expended.

Time Management Is Hard for SAs

Time management is extremely difficult for SAs because an SA's job is typically interrupt-driven. Being interrupt-driven means that people (or other external events) interrupt you with requests. This means that rather than working on your high-priority goals, you are spending time responding to other people's requests, which are based on their priorities. Imagine trying to drive a bus from New Jersey to San Francisco if you stopped the bus every time a passenger asked you to. You might never actually get to your destination! Although it is valuable and interesting to have stopped at those locations, your job was to get the bus and the passengers to San Francisco. A critical step toward good time management for SAs is to break away from being interrupt-driven.

You can break the cycle. You can split your day, perhaps working on projects in the morning and responding to requests in the afternoon. If customers know that this is your work cycle, they will respect that and only bother you in the mornings for emergencies. If they don't, you can politely record their request and tell them that you will get to it in the afternoon. Alternatively, you can trade with a coworker so someone is always taking care of interrupts. Or you can simply arrive extremely early in the morning, when others aren't around to interrupt you.

When you are interrupted, you can deflect the interruption by writing the request into your personal to-do list and tell the person that you will get to the request later. Sometimes, you are in a place where you do not have the means to write down a request. For example, you are walking through the lobby when Cindy Lou interrupts you with a request. In this case, it can be useful to explicitly state, "I'm not going to remember your request because I can't write it down right now. Could you please send me email?" People will appreciate the honesty if you do not sound rude or indignant. It is easy to come off sounding rude in this situation, so we recommend being extra nice. If a trouble-ticket system such as the ones mentioned in Section 15.1.7 is used to drive your to-do list, it can be effective to ask the person to submit a ticket. It trains customers to use the channels that were set up just for them. It can be effective to show customers you are taking them seriously by listening to them and telling them specifically how to phrase the request in the ticket system. You might say, "Could you create a ticket that says, 'Fix the DNS problem on server 5, John[1] knows what I mean.'" The customer will appreciate not having to spend so much time composing the message. The key to a good deflection is to not be perceived as rude, and help the customer get help.

Goal-setting

A common time management problem is that you feel as though you are spinning your wheels—working hard month after month, but not getting anywhere. You are spending so much time mopping the floor that you don't have time to fix the leak. You can break this cycle only by changing your behavior. We suggest *goal-setting*. Take some time to set goals for the next month. Write down everything that comes to mind, in any order. Then prioritize them and eliminate the low-priority items. Plan what smaller steps are required to meet the remaining goals. Prioritize the tasks that will bring you closer to those goals, and stop doing the things that won't.

Planning a year in advance may seem like writing science fiction, especially if you are in an environment where things are changing rapidly. You might think it is unreasonable to plan more than six months in advance at a start-up, but don't pressure yourself to only have hard "business" goals. Even at a start-up where quarterly goals aren't precise, you can have long-term goals: Fix or replace the four least reliable servers, be on time for meetings more often than not, meet monthly growth plans on time, force yourself to take time for yourself, get a promotion, accrue a down-payment on a house.

One useful technique is to spend an hour on the first day of the month reviewing your accomplishments from the last month to see how they got you closer to your bigger goals. Then plan what you want to accomplish in the next month, possibly revising your one-year goals. You can begin each

---

[1] Only if your name is John.

week by reviewing your status. This has the effect of keeping your goals in the front of your mind. How many times have you gotten close to a deadline and thought, "Gosh, I can't believe I forgot to work on that!" Trust the process. It works!

Daily Planning

Again, planning is the key to successful time management. You should begin each day reviewing your to-do list, prioritizing items, and fitting them into your schedule for the day. This is a five-minute investment with a huge payoff.

Case Study: Putting It All Together

Speaking of early mornings, Tom finds that he can get more work done in the first hour of the day than the rest of the day combined, because there are no interruptions. People don't interrupt him because they are aren't in yet or are too busy checking their email, preparing for the day, and so on. He used to spend his first hour reading email and visiting the various web sites (Adams 2000) he visits once per day. However, one day he realized that it would be better to use this most productive hour for something more, well, productive. Instead, he starts off by checking his monitoring system for any red alerts and then his email box for messages tagged "urgent," but then resists the temptation to read the other messages.[2] He invests five minutes planning his day: First he reviews, edits, and prioritizes his to-do items, possibly moving some items to tomorrow's list if there won't be time for them. He then schedules his day with a granularity of one hour. He blocks out time for meetings that he must attend. He blocks out a couple of hours for interrupt-driven tasks. He blocks out the remaining hours for his top-priority projects. The remainder of this first hour is spent working on his single highest-priority item. He even ignores phone calls. This first hour ensures him that this most important project gets at least some attention every day. His most productive hour is spent on his most important tasks. He doesn't do this every day, but he always wishes he had. When he skips this step important tasks get forgotten, appointments are missed, and schedules slip.

Chopping your day into one-hour increments may not be right for you. Half-hour increments might be better or might totally stress you out. Half-day increments might be better for you. Experiment a little and discover what works best.

---

[2]Actually his monitoring system and email system send urgent messages to his pager so that he can avoid that step entirely.

Although the first hour of the day may be extremely productive because of the lack of interruptions, you are likely to find another time of the day that is extremely productive because of your biological clock. Some people find their most productive hour is in the midafternoon, or 6 PM, or even 2 AM. There is no rhyme or reason to it, it's just the way they are built. Whatever it may be, plan your schedule around this. Schedule the work that requires the most thought, attention to detail, or energy during that hour. Your most productive hour might not be when you expect it. It might also change as you grow older, sort of the same way that your sleep patterns change as you grow older. The only way to find your productivity peaks is to slow down, listen to your body, and pay attention.

After reading the previous case study we bet you think Tom is a "morning person." Amazingly, he isn't. Starting the day by working out a schedule wakes him up to the reality of what he needs to do that day. He finds the first hour so productive because of the lack of interruptions, not because his biological clock makes mornings a good time for him to work. His peak hour is 7 PM at night, especially if he had dinner at 5 PM.

Touch All Paper Once

Time management books will also recommend a couple of other techniques that bear repeating here because they are useful to SAs.

One technique is "touch every piece of paper only once." Process each piece of mail completely, rather than sorting it into piles to process later. As you touch each item, examine it and decide if you are going to: throw it away without being read, read it and throw it away, deal with it and then throw it away, respond to it and then throw it away, or file it. Sometimes, dealing with an item means recording it in your to-do list. Other times, you can write your response in the margin and send it back to the party who sent it. The worst thing you can do is read it, then put it in a pile to be dealt with later: this means you will have read it twice, which is a waste of time. Remember that everything you file creates more work when you go to clean your files or makes the effort of maintaining the file a larger task. File as little as possible. When in doubt: throw it out.[3] If it was really important and you later find that you need it, you can contact the source for a new copy.

---

[3]Non-SAs might place such items in a "throw out in 30 days" folder that is emptied once a month. However, we find that SAs don't receive important items on paper. SAs receive important information electronically. Paper notifications that SAs receive tend to be from the nontechnical people in our company that only want to bother us with useless information, such as the fact that repairs will be made to the second floor restroom and people should use the third floor restroom in the meantime. We believe that the SAs reading this book are smart enough to go to the third floor on their own when they see the second floor bathrooms are being repaired.

Email can be treated the same way. If you read each item and then keep it to process later, you are effectively doubling the amount of email you process. Instead, read and delete it, file it, paste it into your to-do system (and delete the original), or forward it to someone else (and delete the original). If you never delete email because you fear that you might need the message some day, configure your system to archive every message you receive in a "archive folder." You can then delete email without fear because you know you can refer to the archive. This archive can be rotated like log files, only retaining the last few months of email to conserve disk space.

Even better than doing all of this yourself is to have an automated system do it for you. UNIX systems are known for having some excellent mail-processing utilities, such as `procmail` (van den Berg 1990). Tom lives by the phrase, "If you aren't using `procmail`, you're working too hard." Systems such as `procmail` allow you to set up filters to presort your email based on various criteria. Tom has a folder for each mailing list he is on and uses `procmail` to filter messages from mailing lists to the appropriate folder. This keeps his mailbox relatively clean (see below). If he doesn't find time to read a particular mailing list for an entire week, he simply deletes the folder's contents: if it was earth-shattering news he would have heard about it elsewhere or would have seen the fireball personally as it shattered the earth. Filters also have the ability to call other software: `procmail` sends a copy of email to Tom's pager if it comes from his boss, has the word "urgent" in the Subject:, or mentions the word "lunch." This ensures that his three top priorities receive immediate attention, yet he does not need to continually check for new email. Tom also uses filters to archive all incoming email to a folder named after the current year and month. A cron job runs on the first day of every month that compresses the archives that are more than three months old. Every now and then he burns these archives into a CD-ROM and deletes any that are older than one year. This balances his need for a permanent record with his desire not to waste disk space.

Staying Focused

Time management books talk a lot about staying focused. A common tip is that messy desks are full of distractions that make it difficult for the brain to focus. Extending that to computer users means also keeping a clean email box and a clean computer graphical user interface (GUI) desktop. The more icons on the screen, the more visual distractions that are present to make your mind wander. Instead, virtual screens can greatly help maintain focus by only showing the information on which you want to be focused. It may sound radical, but you also might disable any systems that let you know when you have new email and instead set aside a couple of small blocks of time each day during which you read email. Email can become one of the interruptions that prevents you from getting your job done.

Daily Tasks

If something must be done today, do it first. That ensures that it gets done. If there is a task that you have to repeat *every* day, then schedule it for early in the day.

Case Study: Schedule Daily Tasks Efficiently

Tom used to have to change backup tapes every day. It took about 15 minutes if everything went right and an hour if it didn't. His plan, which didn't work well, was to start changing the tapes at 5:30 PM, so he could leave by 6:00 PM. If he started at 5:30 PM but the task only took 15 minutes, he would then waste another 15 minutes because he didn't want to start a new project right before he would have to leave. That would waste more than an hour a week. If he had been deeply involved in a project and lost track of time, he would find himself starting to change tapes when he was already late for whatever he was doing after work. He'd be late, stressed because he was late, angry while changing tapes because now he was going to be even later, and arrive at his afterwork function stressed and unhappy. He tried changing them first thing in the morning, but that conflicted with his attempt to use that first hour for his most important tasks. Finally he settled on changing tapes immediately after lunch. This worked well and became somewhat of a ritual that got him back into work mode. If something has to be done every day, don't schedule it for the end of the day.

Precompile Decisions

It is more efficient to make a decision once, rather than over and over again. This is why compiled languages tend to be faster than interpreted languages. Think about what a compiler's optimizer does: It spends a little extra time now to save time in the future. For example, if a variable is added to a constant, the optimizer will eliminate this calculation if it determines that the constant is zero. An interpreter, on the other hand, can't do such an optimization because it would take longer to check if the constant is zero before every addition than it would to just do the addition. You can precompile your decisions the same way. Decide to do something once and retain that decision. When you are breaking your old habit, your mind might start to try to make the decision from scratch. Instead, distract your brain by replacing those thoughts with a mantra that represents your precompiled decision. Here are some mantras that worked for us.

Change Tapes M-W-F: In Section 21.1.6, we discussed a backup system that required a lot of daily thinking to decide if tapes should be changed. Instead, it was decided that time was more valuable than blank tapes, and tapes were simply changed on certain days whether it was necessary or not.

Take the Organizer: Tom was always trying to decide if he should take his organizer with him. It was obvious that it should be taken to meetings, but would he need it while working in a customer's office? He found that every time he was leaving his office he was delaying himself to consider whether he would need his organizer. If he didn't take it, but later needed it, he would revert back to writing notes on tiny slips of paper that would invariably get lost. He also found himself losing his organizer, always finding it later in some office that he had visited to help a customer. When going home at night, he'd pause to decide if he should bring it home. If he left it at the office, he'd invariably end up needing it at home. If he did bring it home, the next morning he'd often forget it at home because he would not remember if he had brought it home the previous night. The solution to all of these problems was to precompile this decision: "Tom will always bring his organizer with him wherever he goes." As a result, he always had it when he needed it, whether he was in the office or at home. He never reverted to notes on slips of paper. It never got left at home because when he left for work he knew it should be with him. He no longer lost it because he developed the habit of making sure he had it with him whenever he left a room. He was more focused because his brain didn't need to sidetrack to make an unrelated decision about his organizer every time he sprang into action. He saved time because he wasn't wasting it deciding the same issue over and over.

Sooner Is Better Than Later: Our final example helps prevent procrastination. For smaller tasks, we suggest that "sooner is better than later." For example, Tom would often procrastinate on small items because if it is small, he could do it "any time." However, "any time" would rarely arrive. For example, when driving home late at night, he would notice that his car was low on gas. He'd decide that he could do it on the way to work the next day, especially if he could remember to leave a little early. As luck would have it, he would be late the next day, and needing to get gas would make him even later. After adopting this mantra he would get gas at night when he realized he was in need. There are many similar situations in the life of an SA: Place the order now, make the phone call now, start the process now, and so on. When you start to debate with yourself about whether it is the right time to do these tasks, remind yourself that, "sooner is better than later."

These precompiled decisions work well for us. You should take time to consider which decisions you find yourself making over and over again and select one or two to precompile. You will lose a little flexibility, but you will gain a lot of other benefits. The mantras you develop will be specific to your lifestyle, dress, or possibly even gender. One woman's style of dress made it difficult to always carry an organizer. Instead she always keeps a single sheet of paper in her handbag on which to scribble notes. Her mantra was "when I sit down at my computer, I will transfer the notes from my sheet." Whatever works for your situation is just fine.

Find Free Time

Free time is hiding all over the place, but you have to look hard to find it. You can also create free time by getting rid of time wasters. Here are some easy places to look for spare time.

- Most businesses have a "light" time of the year. Software shops with a new release every four months usually have a three- to four-week "slow period" after each release. You might have spare time then, or that may be the busy time for you as you get things ready for the customers' busy periods. You may find that during their busy periods nobody bothers you.
- Eliminate rather than automate. As SAs, we tend to accumulate things and then spend a lot of time managing what we've accumulated. We think we're improving our situation when we find better ways to manage our accumulated time wasters and often forget that we would save even more time by having a smaller list of things to manage in the first place.
- Stop reading Usenet Newsgroups. Period.
- Remove yourself from the two busiest mailing lists you are on. Repeat this once a month.
- Take advantage of mail-filtering software such as `procmail`.
- Take advantage of the early morning: Come in an hour earlier.
- Shorten your commute to work by avoiding rush-hour traffic. Work odd hours. Determine your body's "alertness hours," and change your schedule accordingly.
- Have your boss send you to a one-day time management class.
- Invest in training workshops or books that will enable you to automate tasks (write code) in less time. If you don't know `perl` and `make`, learn them today.
- Hold weekly or monthly meetings with your chief customer (a manager or department head) to set priorities and eliminate superfluous items.
- Hire an assistant. A part-time assistant to take care of some of the clerical (tactical) tasks can free you for more important (strategic) duties and can be a great way to train someone to be an SA. Possible candidates: a local high school student, a technically inclined secretary, the person who covers for you when you are away, a summer

intern, or an interested programmer. Students are particularly useful because they are inexpensive and are looking for ways to gain experience.

Dealing with People Who Lack Time Management Skills

Sometimes, you find yourself dealing with people who lack good time management skills, and their ineffectiveness affects your ability to get your job done. We recommend three steps. The last one is quite extreme.

The first step is to coach these individuals. Help them see what is wrong with their processes, and encourage them to get help. Do this tactfully. People hate to be told that they are wrong; lead them to realize it themselves. Ask if there is any way that you could help them get this done faster.

The second step is to work with their management. However, sometimes those first two steps are not possible, for example, you are only dealing with this person for a short time or the person is in a different part of your company (or a different company!) and it would be inappropriate and presumptuous to try to coach them.

The third step is to be used only as a last resort. Find a way to manage their time. For example, your project is delayed because you are waiting for something to be completed by someone else. This person never gets around to your request because he is being interrupt-driven. In this case, make sure you are the highest-priority interrupt. If you have to, stand in his office until your request is complete. Ironically this is exactly what you should *not* let anyone do to you. However, it's obvious that the person you are dealing with in this situation hasn't read this chapter. Don't let someone drowning in bad time management drag you down with them. (If you notice people are doing this technique to you, maybe you need to reread this entire chapter.)

Dealing with Slow Bureaucrats

There are many techniques for dealing with slow bureaucrats. We'd like to point out our two favorites. The first technique is to befriend them. These people typically deal with an endless stream of faceless people who are angry and impatient. Be one of the pleasant people they talk with today. Give them a pleasant change of pace by being the opposite of the last ten people with whom they've dealt. They will work harder for you. Talk with them about things that might interest them, which may be entirely boring to you. Talk as if you've been friends forever (but be sincere). Ask them how their day is going and offer sympathy when they tell you how overloaded they are. If talking via phone, ask how the weather is in their area. To really get on their good side say something such as, "Can you believe that latest decision by our CEO/president?" Although this may sound like a waste of time that slows you down, it's an investment that pays off in better service.

Our other technique works when you have to deal with the same person over and over. When a bureaucrat tells us that a request takes multiple weeks to complete, we often back off and conserve the number of requests that we give them so as to not overload them. That just delays our own projects! Instead, do the opposite: give them hundreds of requests at once. Rather than taking longer to complete, large requests usually get escalated to managers who have the authority to streamline processes, cut corners, or make special exceptions. For example if each request requires individual approval, the manager will find a way to classify some or all of the requests as "generic" and push those through all at once. A bureaucrat's job is to maintain processes that they themselves do not set and therefore can not optimize. If the problem is the process, doing something unusual makes your request break out of that process. Then it is something they (or their managers) do control and thus can create a more efficient process.

Time Management Training

Time management training can be a small investment with a big payoff. It is very inexpensive compared with the potential productivity gain. Many internal corporate education centers offer one- and two-day time management classes. Take advantage of these internal courses, especially if your department pays for these with "internal dollars" instead of real cash. Most classes teach dozens of techniques, and each student finds a different subset of them useful. Enter such training with an open mind.

This section is only a brief introduction to time management techniques. Self-help books (see Lakein 1996, MacKenzie 1997) can help you develop the techniques listed above, plus much more. When you manage your time well, you get satisfaction from your sense of being in control of your working hours, and you are more productive. This makes you a happier SA.

27.1.3 Communication Skills

Communication problems are at the heart of all problems. Learning to communicate well is crucial to being happy and successful in your job and in your personal life.

All problems can be viewed as communication problems. Two people in an office that don't like each other simply haven't taken responsibility for learning how to communicate despite their disagreements. You shouldn't have to like someone to work with them. You just need to be able to communicate.

Technical issues are communication issues: A dead disk on a server is only a *problem* if no one communicated that an outage would be unacceptable or if the communication was not listened to and acted on (for example, RAID should have been used to make the system survive single-disk failures).

Four Categories of Problems

Problems in life generally fall into one of four categories: my problems, your problems, our problems, and other people's problems. Each can be helped by a different set of communication skills.

1. *My Problems:* When I have a problem, I need to make sure I'm being heard. We will discuss a technique called "I statements."
2. *Your Problems:* When you bring a problem to me, I need to make sure I'm hearing you properly so that I can take appropriate action or help you troubleshoot. We will discuss a technique known as "active listening."
3. *Our Problems:* When you and I have a common problem, we need to be able to communicate with each other so that we can agree on a problem definition and action plan. If we have to present this information to others, more communication skills are required, such as presentation skills and "I statements." This situation will require all the communication skills we describe in this section.
4. *Other People's Problems:* When other people have problems, I have to use discipline and not get involved. People spend a lot of time worrying about other people's problems. Instead, they should be focused on their own concerns. The communication skill required here is the discipline of minding your own business.

I Statements

I statements are a tool to help you make your point and also communicate the feelings you have. The value of an "I statement" is that it lets you get the issue off your chest in such a way that others can do something constructive about what you have said. You have given them a fixable problem statement. What happens as a result is usually positive. When we make our needs known, the universe tends to take care of us.

The general form is "I feel [*emotion*] when you [*action*]." It makes people aware of the effect of their actions. This is much more effective than just telling someone that you don't like a particular behavior.

An "I statement" expresses soft emotions rather than hard emotions. Soft emotions are emotions of sadness or fear. Hard emotions are emotions of anger. It is said that underlying every hard emotion is a soft emotion. So, before you express your "I statement," figure out what the soft emotion is and express *that*. Those hearing anger will become defensive, and they will not hear you as well. Hearing fear or sadness makes people want to care for you and help solve your problem. Here are some sample "I statements."

- I feel hurt when you criticize me instead of my work.
- I feel unvalued when you credit my boss with the work that I did.
- I feel very happy that you completed the project on time.

- I feel frustrated when you demand reliability but won't fund the changes I recommend.
- I feel disappointed when I receive complaints from customers saying that you don't meet your commitments.
- I feel untrusted when you install web-censoring software on our gateway.

Active Listening

Listening is more important than talking. That's why we have twice as many ears as mouths. Active listening is a technique that ensures complete communication. We will discuss three tools: mirroring, summary, and reflection statements.

Mirroring. You wouldn't trust a file transfer protocol that sent packets but never received any kind of acknowledgment that the packets had properly arrived. However, most people talk and never verify whether they are understood. Most people listen and assume that what they heard, and how they interpreted it, is what the speaker intended. Most people treat conversations as two uni-directional packet streams. We can do better.

Active listening techniques are used by the listener. When the listener hears something, he seeks to understand what was said before he replies to it. Instead of replying with his next statement, he takes the time to *mirror* back what he just heard with an accurate but shorter statement. It's like verifying a packet checksum before you use the data.

The speaker might say, "People are complaining that the file server is slow." The listener, while tempted to offer a solution, replies, "So you are saying that several people are complaining about the file server speed?" The speaker then sends an acknowledgment or negative acknowledgment: "Actually, Mark got a single complaint and passed it along."

Now the listener understands the situation much better. Mark forwarded a complaint about slow file server performance. Although all such complaints should be verified before they are fixed (see Section 16.2.3), Mark's technical competence can indicate whether the complaint has been filtered for validity already. Also, we now know that this information has been relayed twice, which indicates that information loss is occurring. Your reaction to this complete information is much different, and more focused, than a typical reaction to the original statement.

Your interpretation of what someone said is based on your upbringing and experiences, which are completely unique to each person. The more diverse your organization is, the more important mirroring becomes. The more you deal with people from other parts of the country or other parts of the world, the more likely it is that the person you are speaking to has a different basis for semantic interpretation.

Don't Trust Your Ears

Tom was in an organization that was struggling with only 10 people, but had a promise of hiring 40 more people at the next round of funding, for a total of 50 people. The funding arrived but was less than expected, and the CEO told the team, "We'll have to make some changes because we will have a smaller team in the next year." The CEO meant that the 50-person goal was reduced, but everyone in the room thought he meant the current team of 10 would be reduced. Both interpretations are semantically valid but active listening helped clear the confusion. Someone mirrored his statement by saying, "So I hear you saying we're reducing our group rather than hiring new people." The CEO immediately realized that he was misunderstood and was able to clarify what he meant.

To sound like you aren't challenging the person, it is useful to begin a "mirror" statements with "I hear you saying that . . . ." Once you understand the speaker, you can react to what you've heard. If everyone on your team uses that same phrase, it can become a quiet signal that active listening is being attempted and that you are trying to understand the person in earnest. This can be really useful, or it can become a running joke. Either way, consider it "team building."

Case Study: "Say Again?"

Standardizing on certain phrases sounds silly but can be useful. A small team worked in a noisy environment and often couldn't hear each other very well. This problem was made worse by the fact that listeners asking, "What?" sometimes sounded like they were challenging the speakers, who then became defensive and reexplained what they had just said instead of simply repeating it. The listener would become frustrated because they simply wanted the last statement repeated. They established the protocol of saying, "Say again?" to mean "please repeat that, I didn't hear you," so that it was no longer confused with "Are you nuts? Prove it!" An outsider listening to them saying "Say again?" all the time might have found it humorous to watch, but this protocol worked well for them.

Summary Statements.   Summary statements are when you pause the conversation to list the points made so far. A summary statement is a form of mirroring, but it covers more material. It is often useful after a person has completed several long points and you want to make sure you heard everything and heard everything correctly. Sometimes, summary statements are used when you feel people would benefit from hearing what they just said. Sometimes, hearing someone else say a summary of what you've just said can be enlightening, especially if the person reframes the statements a little differently. Summary statements are also vital toward the end of a meeting to make sure everyone leaves with an understanding of what's happened and what will happen next.

A summary statement should list the points in short, pithy statements. If people correct your summary, take the time to process clarifications and then repeat the summary statement. Sometimes, boiling down a person's thoughts helps the person solve his problem.

A sample summary statement would be: "Let me summarize what I've heard so far. You are upset at the way John treats you. He berates you at meetings. He disagrees with the decisions you make. He takes credit for the work you do. This is making you very upset." A statement such as that tells the person that he is being heard and lets him verify that you didn't miss any of the key points.

Grouping the issues reframes them and draws out underlying issues that might need to be solved before the surface ones can be dealt with effectively. Reframing a summary might sound like this: "Let me summarize what I've heard so far. Two of your points seem to be problems resulting from lack of funding: we're short on staff and we are dealing with underpowered servers that we can't afford to upgrade. On the other hand, four of your points are related to a lack of training: Josh is hitting the wall in his AIX knowledge, Mary doesn't understand the debugging tools we have, Larry hasn't learned `Python`, and Sue hasn't transitioned to MagentaSoft yet."

At the end of a meeting, a summary statement might sound like this: "To summarize: The problem is slow server performance. Customers are complaining. We've eliminated the possibility of an overloaded LAN or hot spots on the volumes. Sarah will check with the programmers to see if their algorithms work well over a high-latency WAN. Margaret will find two clients and verify that they themselves aren't overloaded. We will revisit this next week." This lets everyone verify that they all agreed to the same thing. It can be useful to email such summaries to all the participants as a permanent record of the action plan and agreements.

Reflection. Reflection is a technique to assure people that they are being heard. This is particularly important when the person is overcome by emotions. The secret to dealing with angry people is to immediately do something to acknowledge their emotions. You must deal with their emotions before you can deal with resolving their complaints. This calms them down. Then you can begin to deal with the problem in a more rational manner.

The technique that we use here is referred to as *reflection*. This is where you blurt out the name of the emotion you see coming from the person. It sounds simple and bizarre, but it is very effective.[4]

Suppose someone came to your office and yelled, "I'm sick of the way the network is so damn unreliable!" The best response is to reply, "Wow! You are really upset about this!" This is much better than becoming defensive.

First the person realizes that he has been heard. This is half the battle. Most of the frustration he is feeling is from the simple fact that he doesn't feel like he is being heard. It takes a lot of courage for him to come to you with a complaint. Maybe there have been other times that he was upset about something but didn't come to you. When he is in front of you and you acknowledge months of frustration instead of denying it or becoming defensive, this will calm him considerably.

Next, he will realize how he must look. People often get so enraged that they don't realize how angry they look. Reflection subtly tells him what he looks like, which can embarrass him slightly, but will also help him regain composure.

Now he will start to collect himself. He may reply, "Darn right I'm upset!" This tells you that reflection has worked, because he is inadvertently using the mirroring technique discussed earlier. You can show openness to resolving the problem by saying something such as, "So sit down and we'll talk about it." At this point, he should calm down and you can productively discuss the problem.

If not, draw on your active listening skills (mirroring and summary statements) to discuss the emotional side of the issue. We can't stress enough that technical issues can't be solved until you've effectively responded to the emotional side of the issue.

Once he has calmed down, be ready with your mirroring and summary statements to address the technical issue.

27.1.4   Constant Professional Development

Professional development means receiving the training required to maintain and improve your skills, and it also means associating yourself with the professional organizations of your field.

There may be professions that don't change much and don't require keeping up with the latest technology and techniques. However, system administration isn't one of them.

---

[4] . . . and we promise that you will feel silly the first time you try it . . . .

There are two reasons for learning new skills: it helps in your career and it's fun. It is our experience that SAs tend to rank "learning new things" high on their list of fun things. Never turn down the opportunity to learn.

Reading can keep you up-to-date with new technology. There is a constant flow of new books, magazines, and trade and academic journals. We also recommend that you subscribe to the trade journal of the industry that you serve, so that you are familiar with the industry trends that concern your customers.

One-day workshops and training programs serve a different purpose than week-long conferences. One-day seminars tend to be tactical: focused on a particular technology or skill. Week-long conferences are strategic: offering opportunities to discuss broader topics, to network, to build community, and to further the craft of system administration as a respected profession. Week-long conferences have a powerful effect, providing a much-needed opportunity to relax, and they provide a supportive environment where you can take a step back from your day-to-day work and consider the big picture. Attendees return to their job brimming with new ideas and vision; refreshed, motivated, and with a new outlook.

Although this book does not endorse particular products, we can't hold back our enthusiasm for the USENIX (The Advanced Computing Systems Association) and SAGE (The System Administrators Guild) organizations. We get a lot of value from the USENIX Annual Technical Conference, Security Symposium, and LISA (Large Installation System Administration) conferences. There are many ways to become involved in these international groups, in addition to the various local chapters. Volunteering with these groups, writing papers, submitting articles to their newsletters, helping plan conferences, and speaking at their meetings can go a long way toward developing your reputation and career.

27.1.5 Staying Technical

We often hear SAs complain, "They're trying to turn me into a manager, but I want to stay technical!" and ask for advice about how not to be promoted.

If this is your situation there are a couple of things to remember. First of all, if your manager is trying to promote you to management he means it as a compliment. Don't be offended. Although some SAs have negative opinions of managers, managers tend to think management is a good position. Maybe he is seeing great potential for you. Take the suggestion seriously and consider it for a while. Maybe it is right for you. Do, however, remember that becoming a manager does mean giving up technical responsibilities; don't feel that you'll be able to retain your technical duties and adopt new responsibilities.

Some SAs slowly slide into management, adopting slightly increasing management responsibilities over time. Suddenly, they realize they are managers and don't want to be.

To prevent this, you must be aware of what kind of tasks you are adopting. If you want to stay technical, it is important to discuss this with your boss. Establish that there is a difference between being the "technical lead" of a group and being "manager" of a group. Come to agreement on where the line is drawn: a litmus test, so to speak. Then you can both be aware of the issue. For example, a "technical lead" is part of the technical process of architecting and deploying a new system. "Management" tasks usually involve budgets, salary and performance reviews, and other HR issues.

We'll discuss more about career management in Section 27.2.3.

27.2   The Icing

Now that you can manage yourself, your time, and your career, these skills can combine to create some higher-level skills such as the basics of negotiation, a little philosophy about loving your job, and managing your manager.

27.2.1   Learn to Negotiate

SAs need good negotiation skills because they are often dealing with vendors, dealing with customers, or negotiating salary and compensation. Negotiation is the art of getting what you want. It requires all the communication skills of the previous section and then some.

Work Toward the Win-Win
It is important to work toward a win-win situation. That is, negotiate toward an agreement that makes both parties successful. It is useless to negotiate vendors to a price so low that they cannot afford to give you good service or to be negotiated down to the point that you are not getting what you want. A win-lose situation is where you win and the other person loses. This is the second-best situation. Lose-lose and lose-win situations are left as an exercise for the reader.

Recognize the Situation
The first step in negotiation is to recognize that you are in a negotiating situation. It may sound strange, but countless times we've heard people sign a contract yet later say things such as, "I should have asked for more money." or "Maybe they were willing to negotiate." This means that the person didn't pause to consider whether they should be in negotiating mode. It's always polite to say the magical incantation, "Is that negotiable?" when

talking with customers, vendors, tech support personnel, auto dealers, and even parents.

When your team is in a negotiating situation, communicate this fact to the entire team. Call a meeting and explain what's happening. Knowledge is power, so make sure the team knows what information should not be leaked.

Case Study: *Prepare the Team and Prevent Mistakes*

An investment firm learned that the high-tech start-up they were talking to needed the funding by a certain date. They leveraged this to their benefit. How did the investment firm learn this information? Members of the start-up freely gave out the information because nobody had told them not to provide the information. This could have been prevented if the start-up members had been assembled and told the strategy, in particular which information to protect. There are ways to communicate urgency without losing leverage. They could also have designated a "point person" to communicate on particular sensitive points; other team members could refer information seekers to that person.

You also have to be conscious of the power dynamic. Who is the requestor? Who is the requestee? Who holds the power in the negotiation? If you are in the power seat, then you can control the negotiation. If they are in the power seat, you must be much better prepared to defend your requests. The requestor is not always the person lacking power, nor is the person receiving the request automatically in power. The power dynamic is not static. It can change unexpectedly.

Power Can Shift

Tom was negotiating with a vendor who was in the power seat because Tom's company had such a large legacy investment in the vendor's product and couldn't change vendors easily. However, one of their salespeople let it slip that if they didn't book the sale by the end of the week, it would be counted toward the next year's sales quota. Now Tom was in the power position. He knew that they would rather receive their commission on this year's balance sheet. When the salespeople wouldn't reduce their price, he introduced issues that would delay the contract being signed, but promised that roadblocks would be cleared and the contract would be signed before the end of the week if he got the product at the price he wanted. They caved.

Plan Your Negotiations

Planning is important. Sit down with the people who will be on your side and decide what you hope to gain: which of those things you are willing to negotiate away, which are medium priority, and items you can't live without. Decide what elements need to be kept secret, and how such issues will be contained. Discuss the power dynamic and how that affects the strategy. Script how the meeting will be conducted, what you are going to say, and what your reaction will be if they bring up certain issues.

It is important to know what you are asking for in specific terms. Nebulous requests can delay negotiations needlessly.

Case Study: *Know Who a Vendor's Competition Is*

In the early 1990s, Sun Microsystems and HP were at war for the workstation market. An SA found himself working at a company that used workstations from both companies. He found it useful to put a Sun poster on his office wall and drink coffee from a Sun coffee mug when HP salespeople would visit him and the reverse when Sun salespeople visited. It was a subtle reminder that he could go elsewhere.

Case Study: *Do Your Homework*

There can be a big payoff if you do your homework, especially if the other side hasn't done any. When Tom meets with vendors to renew a yearly maintenance contract, he always brings a stack of printouts, each page being a trouble ticket that the vendor did not handle well. On each one are handwritten notes from the staff person involved describing what happened. Although the mishandled tickets are always a minority, it isn't Tom's fault that the vendor never arrives with data to show this. The vendor is instead humbled by the physical depiction of their mistakes and more willing to negotiate. At key points in the negotiations, Tom picks a page, reads the note out loud, frowns, and sits quietly until the vendor responds with another concession. None of this would be so effective if vendors would only do their homework and arrive with statistics about what a good job they do on the majority of the service requests.

Other Techniques Require Rehearsal

Before some difficult price negotiations, Tom made his team rehearse the situation in which Tom would be angry enough to walk out of the room for a couple minutes. His team was to act nervous, be silent for a minute, then tell the salespeople, "We've *never* seen him so unhappy with a vendor." They then fidgeted nervously in their chairs until Tom returned. Practice makes perfect.

These last two examples involved hardball tactics that rarely should be used. They hurt the relationship between you and the other party. This will burn you in the future. As we said earlier, it is better to strive for a win-win situation. Each negotiation is an opportunity to develop a positive relationship. The future payoff is immeasurable. There is only one time when such tactics should be used, and that is when you will never have to negotiate with that person again (Koren and Goodman 1992).

The last two examples were exactly that situation: After the negotiations, that salesperson was "out of the loop" until the contracts were up for renewal. They were multi-year maintenance contracts, virtually guaranteeing that years from now, when the renewals were being negotiated, a different salesperson would be involved. Quarterly updates to the contracts were done through a customer service hotline whose staff had no visibility to the harshness of the prior negotiations. The salesperson that Tom normally dealt with for hardware purchases was not involved in the maintenance contract negotiations, and therefore no bridges were burned there. Finally, Tom knew that he was leaving that position and therefore would not be involved in the next renewal negotiation. If bridges were burned, his successor could use another famous technique: blame the predecessor to get on the good side of a vendor. "Oh, *he* was a jerk, but *I'm* the nice guy. So let's begin this relationship with a fresh start." This trick only works once. If you are a harsh negotiator too often, people will eventually stop dealing with you.

Variety is good, too, as we see in the next example.

Case Study: Use a Variety of Techniques

Tom was in awe at one person's success when negotiating by always being so impossible to deal with that people always gave in to her. However, soon Tom realized that this was her only technique and sadly watched her career have problems as she burned too many bridges. People avoided dealing with her all together. She became isolated. If you play with fire, you will get burned.

Format of a Negotiation Meeting

The general format for an effective negotiating meeting is to define the terms, get agreement on the common ground, and then work on the more difficult parts. It sets a positive tone early on to resolve the easy issues. If something thought to be easy starts to take a long time, table it until later. Often, you will get to the end of the list of issues only to discover that there is very little disagreement or that the one item that you disagree on can be dropped. Commonly, you will discover that both people are actually on the same side, in which case the negotiation should be more along the lines of agreement seeking and making commitments.

Salary (and Other) Negotiation Tips

These tips relate to making requests and offers. They are particularly useful during salary negotiations, but apply to all negotiations.

Ask for What You Honestly, Honestly Want: Don't negotiate against yourself. Some people start off with a reduced request because they are embarrassed by asking for what they want, feel guilty that they want so much, or think their opponent will think it is unreasonable and will refuse to continue. Don't be silly! Reducing the request is your opponent's job, not yours. Don't do their job for them. You'll get more respect if you are honest about asking for what you want. You'll be surprised at how many times the request is accepted. Your job is to ask. Their job is to agree or disagree. Do *your* job.

After You Make a Request or Offer, Close Your Mouth: You also shouldn't negotiate against yourself when making a request or offer. People make the mistake of stating a proposal, getting nervous at the silence they hear, and immediately make a concession to sweeten the deal. Your job is to make the offer or request; their job is to accept or reject it. Sometimes, people are silent because they need time to think or because they are hoping to make you nervous so that you will upgrade your offer without even being asked. If silence makes you nervous, fill your mind by repeating the phrase, "The next person to talk is the loser." Give things time and wait for their response.

Don't Reveal Your Strategy to Your Opponent: Although you shouldn't be paranoid, you also shouldn't reveal your strategy to your opponent. Don't reveal how low or high you are willing to go, just the offer you are making at that point. If an agent (real-estate agent, recruiter, head hunter, or other such agent) is negotiating on your behalf, the person really represents whoever is paying him. It is always acceptable to directly ask an agent, "Who pays your commission in this situation?" You don't want to be surprised to find out that it is you! If he won't tell you who pays him, then he is not being ethical. Being told, "Oh don't worry, you don't have to pay a thing" means that he is being paid by your opponent. If he is paid by your opponent, he is an extension of your opponent and you should only reveal what you would reveal to your opponent. He may say that he represents you, but if he receives a commission from the employer, landlord, or whomever, then he "represents your position" to the other side, but he is acting in your opponent's best interest. Therefore if he asks how high (or low) you are willing to go, address him like you would your opponent: Only reveal your current offer. If he demands to know your low and high range so he "can negotiate on your behalf," give him an artificial range.[5]

Always Refuse a First Offer: Every *first offer* has built into it some room for movement in case it is rejected. Therefore always reject the first offer. This recommendation is demonstrated in the 1995 film *Clueless* (Heckerling 1995). This trick only works once. Don't automatically think that if they sweetened the offer once, they can do it again. If they aren't willing to budge, put your tail between your legs and accept the first offer. This is a risky technique, use with caution.

Silence as a Negotiating Tool

As mentioned previously, being quiet is a critical negotiating skill. Silence from your opponent may simply mean she is thinking, has nothing to say, or is trying to make you nervous. Most people get nervous when they hear silence during a negotiation. They respond by offering concessions that haven't even been requested. Another important time to be silent is when you get to an agreement. We've seen two sides finally get to an agreement, only to have them ruined by someone bringing up new issues. You've got what you were asking for, so shut up!

Be Careful What You Say

A woman was moving to a different division for an opportunity that gave her a raise and a promotion. Her new boss told her what the new salary would be and then asked, "Would you like it to be more?" She replied, "Yes." She was dumbfounded that anyone would ask such a silly question. Is there any other answer she could logically give? He should have simply waited for her to sign the paper, and only offer more money if she rejected the offer. Now that he had offered to increase her salary and she agreed, he had no recourse other than to increase the offer on the spot. She later commented that she wouldn't hire someone that answered "no" to such a question. To her it would be like failing an IQ test. She also mentioned that she wouldn't let anyone that asked such a question work for her. They might trade the family's last cow for magic beans.

---

[5]Speaking of not revealing your strategy: We would like you to know that we haven't revealed all of our secrets, so don't try to use any of these techniques against us. We have countertechniques. Really!

Although all of these negotiating techniques have worked for us, we're not high-powered negotiation experts. Luckily, some real experts have written books on the topic. Often, books are specialized for a particular profession or situation. There is no negotiating book specifically for SAs, but *The Haggler's Handbook* (Koren and Goodman 1992) is a very good general-purpose book and has the benefit of being one tip per page. You can read one page per day when getting dressed in the morning; in a matter of weeks you will be a much better negotiator.

27.2.2   Loving Your Job

The happy SAs that we've met love their jobs. This isn't an accident. They didn't fall into jobs that they love; they worked in many jobs in many types of companies and started to realize what they liked and didn't like. They then could become more focused when job hunting. It can take years, even decades, to figure out what motivates you to love your job and find a job that provides those qualities, but it is something to think about as your career evolves.

Do What You Love to Do

The 1999 film *Office Space* (Judge 1999) makes an interesting point. Imagine that you've won the lottery and don't have to work anymore. What would you do to fill your time? Your answer is what you should be doing as a career. If you would spend your days rebuilding old cars, become an auto mechanic. Maybe you are an SA because you would spend your time playing with computers. What are the aspects of computing that you enjoy so much? Consider integrating those things into your career.

Motivation

Being motivated about your job is no accident. Satisfying, long-term motivators are different for different people. Money motivates people, but only in the short term. We find it doesn't sustain motivation very well. Some people are motivated by the good feeling that they receive after they have helped someone. It sounds simple, but helping people is habit-forming. The good feeling you get from knowing you've helped someone is so powerful that once you've had a taste of it you crave it even more. You want to return to that good feeling, so helping people becomes even more important and you strive to help even more people (Dickens, Glazer, and O'Donoghue 1988).

The compliments we receive are habit-forming in the same way. A compliment propels us forward. Imagine every compliment you get from your boss propelling you, motivating you to continue to achieve great things.

The problem is that those compliments take a long path between your ear and the part of the brain that *accepts the compliment*. Somewhere in that path is a minefield known as your *critical inner voice*. Sometimes, that voice reaches up, grabs that compliment mid-air, and pours toxic waste on it. Then that compliment is tainted. By the time it reaches its destination, the toxic waste has corrupted the compliment into something that hurts you or at least is a no-op. Thus, instead of a stream of incoming compliments that propel you, you have a stream of negatives that sap your energy.

For some people, this critical inner voice is a small, manageable little beast. For some, it is a loud, bellowing giant. Therapy can help manage that giant by helping you deal with the source of the problem, be it an overly critical parent, an overbearing significant other, or shame.

Shame comes from feeling bad about something and holding those feelings inside rather than letting them out. We often feel that personal problems should stay at home and not be discussed at work, but bottling up these problems can be unhealthy and wreck your productivity. Suppose one of your parents is ill, and you haven't shared this or how it makes you feel with your coworkers. The positive feedback you receive should make you feel good and motivate you, but instead the toxic shame of, for example, feeling that you aren't visiting your ill parent enough, negates the compliment, for example "Oh, they wouldn't have given me that compliment if they knew what a terrible daughter I am."

Therefore it is important to accept compliments. When we deflect compliments, we do a disservice to ourselves. We tend to reply to a compliment with, "Oh, it wasn't a big deal" or "I did a small part; Margaret really did all the work." If someone is being polite enough to compliment you, then be polite enough to accept the darn compliment! If you aren't sure what to say, a simple, "Thank you!" will suffice.

Shame can take other forms. Fears of racism, sexism, or homophobia can hold us back from reaching our full potential. You might invalidate compliments you receive if you feel your manager is biased against your sex, race, religion, sexual orientation, or gender identity. You can turn these issues around by discussing these fears with your coworkers and working to gain a better understanding and appreciation for your differences. If your corporate culture discourages openness about personal issues, you may find it useful to at least open up privately to someone such as your boss or a close coworker.

An Unsafe Workplace Is an Unproductive Workplace

A bisexual SA lost a week's worth of productivity because he overheard a coworker in the next cubicle saying that "queers should all be killed." Would it be safe for him to walk to his car after work if this coworker found out he was bisexual? Would the coworker sabotage his work? Every time he tried to work, the memory of his coworker's words distracted him. The next day he brought up this issue to his boss, who refused to talk with the coworker or move the SA's cubicle. Eventually, the SA left the company. The manager could have saved the cost of recruiting and training a new staff person if he had taken the time to make it clear to the coworker that such comments are inappropriate in the workplace and that their company valued people by the quality of their work, not by their race, sexual orientation, gender, or other nonwork issues. The manager could have also explained that the diversity of the group was what made it strong.

Happiness

Cognitive theorists believe that being happy or sad is not driven by whether good or bad things are happening to us, but by how we react to what is happening around us. How can this be? Again we return to the concept of the critical inner voice. Some people can shut down that voice when they need to; others pay too much attention to it.

For example, suppose a tree falls on someone's house. You might think that is a bad thing, but others might not. One person might think, "Of course it fell on my house; I don't deserve a safe home." On the other hand, someone else might think, "I'm glad nobody got hurt!" and look forward to the opportunity to redecorate once the repairs are complete!

The opposite situation can also be true. You typically would think that getting a raise would be a good thing. However, for some it might introduce a big barrel of worries: "I'm already working as hard as I can; now they'll expect even more! I'm doomed to fail." The first part of *The Feeling Good Handbook* (Burns 1999a) gives further examples.

A little insecurity is normal and healthy. It keeps us out of harm's way and encourages us to "measure twice, cut once." However, too much can cause problems.

Luckily, you can retrain yourself. The first step is to recognize that this critical inner voice exists. We can be so accustomed to it that we believe it without pausing to evaluate what it is saying. Once you have recognized that it is speaking, pause to think about what it is saying. Consider the source. Is it simply doubting everything? Is it viewing the world as black and white? Is it repeating negative things you were told by outsiders?

Case Study: Consider the Source

One SA had a major breakthrough when he realized that his critical inner voice was always saying negative things that his hypercritical mother had said to him when he was young. In fact, the voice sounded like his mother's voice! He realized

> that these thoughts were just echoes of the extreme negativity he had received as a child. They were not useful bits of advice. He set out to develop the habit of ignoring those thoughts until they disappeared. It worked!

Retraining yourself is not easy, but it can be done successfully. Many people choose to do it with the help and guidance of a therapist. Others do it on their own. Burns (1999a) includes a large number of techniques and a useful guide to selecting the ones that are right for you. Take advantage of the confidential Employee Assistance Program (EAP) that your employer provides as part of their mental health benefits package.

Good Boss/Bad Boss

Your manager affects your ability to love your job more than the kind of work you do. *A bad job with a great boss is better than a great job with a bad boss.* Let's use this analogy: Suppose your job was the best, most fantastic job in the world. For example, suppose you were being paid to eat chocolate all day. If your boss was a jerk, you would still hate your job. On the other hand, if you had a terrible job, a great boss would find a way to make it enjoyable. Our personal experience is that most people leave their job not because they don't enjoy their work, but because they didn't like their boss.

Accepting Criticism

In addition to accepting compliments well, it is important to take criticism well. Everyone receives criticism now and then. Some people interpret all comments as criticism; others let the smallest criticism wreck their self-esteem. That's not good. However, if you take criticism positively, it can help you change your behavior so that you improve yourself. Criticism is a good thing: It prevents us from repeating mistakes. Imagine how terrible it would be if we went through life making the same mistake over and over again! Rather than accepting criticism with disdain for the critic, it is healthier to thank the person for his honesty and think about what you can do better in the future.

It is important to distinguish between constructive and nonconstructive criticism. Nonconstructive criticism hurts feelings without helping the situation. Be careful of the nonconstructive criticism you give yourself: Don't "should" yourself to death. "Should" is a scolding word, and when we think to ourselves "Oh, I *should* have done such and such," you are scolding yourself about something you can't control: the past. It is much better to replace "I should have" with "next time I will."

Your Support Structure

Everyone needs a support structure. Everyone needs someone to talk with now and then. Your support structure is the network of people you can go to when you need to talk about a problem. Having different people you can go to for advice on office politics, technical advice, and general life advice is very important when you feel you are over your head. It takes time to develop these relationships. Sometimes, the right person is your spouse or significant other, a friend, a coworker or manager, or even an email list of people who share a common interest.

Ask for Help with Personal Problems

It is important to ask for help. We find that SAs tend not to be very good at seeking help for personal problems and instead are prone to letting a problem build up until they feel like exploding.

Maybe it is related to some "macho" culture of being self-sufficient. Maybe because SAs solve problems before their customers notice them, they expect other people to read their minds when they themselves have problems. Maybe it's because SAs are expected to solve technical problems on their own, and they try to carry that into their personal lives. Even when they do "reach out" for technical help, it is often to nonhuman resources: web pages, FAQs, and manuals. Even asking for help on electronic mailing lists has an air of not talking about your problems face to face.

Successful people know that it is not a weakness to ask for help. In fact, people respect someone who takes responsibility for getting help. It creates less of a burden on others to deal with a problem when it is small, rather than when it has escalated into a large emergency. Most importantly, problems are solved quicker when many people work on them. Share the wealth! Friends help other friends. It's like a bank account: you make a deposit when you help your friends, and you shouldn't feel bad about making a withdrawal every now and then.

Should Have Asked for Help

Everything would have been better if one SA had asked for help. He was going to present a paper at a very large SA conference. When he didn't show up at the designated time (15 minutes before his presentation), the coordinators went through a lot of pain to reorder the other speakers. He did show up just moments before he was to speak, when the session chair was introducing the next speaker. She continued with the reordered schedule because she didn't know whether the speaker who had just arrived was ready to present his talk. He was late because he had only brought overhead transparencies, rather than his laptop with the presentation on it. Before the conference he had checked that this would suffice. However, earlier that day, he had asked a technician at the conference whether it was possible to use transparencies, because everyone else was using laptops. The technician was unaware of that equipment and erroneously told him that it was not possible to use overhead transparencies. Instead of asking one of the conference coordinators for help, he got permission from his boss to rent a laptop for a large sum of money. The rented laptop only ran Windows, and his presentation had been written under Linux, so he then spent several hours retyping the presentation into Windows, while his boss made the presentation available over the Internet in case he could find someone with a Linux laptop that he could borrow. Had he asked for help, the coordinators would have been able to show him and the technician the transparency equipment or would have been easily able to find a Linux laptop for him to use. Instead, he created a lot of stress for himself and others and spent a large amount of money to procure a temporary laptop. He should have asked for help.

We have other similar anecdotes that involve other personal issues such as finance, health, relationship and family problems, and even drug and alcohol abuse. In every case, the person's friends wished they had been called upon sooner. That's what friends are for.

Balance Work and Personal Life

Finding balance between work and personal time is important to mental health. Although it can be gratifying to be a hardcore techie who works day and night, eventually burnout will become a problem. Taking time for yourself is key. Taking breaks during the day, getting regular sleep, having a social life outside of work, and not working yourself to death are all critical habits to develop.

Treat your significant other with the respect he or she deserves. Many SAs work so many hours that their significant others become "technology widows." That shows little respect for them. Family time[6] is important time; take time for them. Schedule it in your datebook. Give them the thanks and admiration they deserve. Put pictures of them on your desk, so you are always reminded that you do it for them (Crittenden 1995). The most valuable thing you can give your family is time. Nobody's last words have ever been, "I wish I had spent more time at the office."

Respecting your body is also important. Listen to your body. If you are tired, go to sleep. If you are hungry, eat. If you aren't feeling well, help your

---

[6]By "family" we mean a very wide definition. Single people have families too. Some people have chosen families rather than biological ones (Small 1993).

body repair itself. It's ironic that we often meet people who take care of immense networks, but don't know how to take care of their own bodies.

Your employer gives you vacation time. Take it—the company doesn't give it to you because they're nice people, they give it to you because if they don't, you will burn out and then be completely useless to them. Long ago, employers discovered that vacations benefit both the employer and the employee.

You don't do yourself or your company a favor by skipping vacations. Many times we've heard from people who prided themselves for not having taken a vacation in years. We hear things such as, "The company can't live without me" and claims that skipping vacations shows your dedication. Actually, the opposite is true. If you don't disappear for a week or two once a year, there is no way to discover if your job is documented properly or that your fall-back coverage is properly trained. It is better to learn what coverage is missing during a vacation that you return from, rather than when you quit or, heaven forbid, get hit by a truck.

Awards Wall

Finally, we have one more recommendation to maintaining positive self-esteem and loving your job. Maintain an "accomplishment wall." This is a place where you post all of the positive feedback you receive: A note from a customer that says thanks, awards you have received, and so on. Make sure these are in a place that you see every day, so that you have a constant reminder of the positive things you've done. If you are the team leader, you might consider having such a wall for all the team's accomplishments located in a place that the entire team will see.

> ❖ **Electronic Accomplishment Wall**   Much positive feedback is received via email. We recommend that you save every "thank you" you receive in an email folder named "feathers,"[7] because they are the feathers in your cap. When you write your yearly accomplishments list, you can review this folder to make sure you didn't forget anything. On days that you are depressed or things aren't going well, pop open this folder and feel the love. Sounds silly? Prove us wrong by trying it.

27.2.3   Managing Your Manager

Let's discuss a little "boss philosophy" first. Your boss has a job to do. Her performance is measured by whether certain goals are achieved. These goals

---

[7]Thanks to Tommy Reingold for this name.

are too big for any one person to complete alone. That's why you exist. Your assignment is to do a bunch of tasks that equal a small fraction of your boss' goal. Your fraction, plus the fractions of all your coworkers, should complete that goal. Some people think of their job as the tasks they are assigned. That's not true. Your job is to make your boss a success. Amazingly, your boss is in the same situation. She has been assigned a small fraction of what her boss needs to accomplish. Her boss' boss and up the chain all the way to the head of your organization are in this situation. When everyone does their little fractions, they all total up to one big success.

Why should you care about your boss' success? Firstly, a successful boss gets promoted. An ethical boss will take you along with her. Secondly, a manager has a limited amount of time and energy. She is going to expend that time and energy on the people who are most likely to help her succeed. To manage your boss, you are going to need her time and energy. Obviously, a manager is going to respect the wishes of a star performer more than a slacker.

Managing is about steering the boat that other people are rowing. Turning the rudder points the boat in the right direction, but someone else has to do the work to get you to your destination. You may think that it is your boss' job to manage you, but the reverse is also true. You must manage your boss; steer her toward what will make you happy.

Case Study: Pleasing the Visionary

An SA joined a university to fix a crumbling, unstable heterogeneous network. The network needed the very basics of upgrades: quality wiring, modern switches and routers, uniform OS configuration, and so on. However, the Dean thought himself to be quite a visionary and wasn't interested in projects with such little flair. He wanted futuristic projects that would bring status like desktop video and virtual reality systems. None of those projects could possibly happen until the basic upgrades were done. The SA couldn't get any of the fundamental problems fixed until he started explaining them to the Dean as the steps required to achieve his futuristic goals. He explained to the Dean that he was going to make him a success, and these were the steps along the way to that goal.

Now we can talk about managing your boss.

The first part of managing your boss is to make your needs known. Managers can't read your mind, so don't get upset when they don't guess what you want. On the other hand, you also are not the only thing on your manager's mind. Respect that by not going overboard and pestering her. Strike a balance.

One need you should communicate, perhaps once or twice a year, is your career goal. This doesn't have to be a 20-page document supporting the reasons for your request, but it should not be simply mentioned in passing, either.

Steer Promotions to You

Tom claims that he never received a promotion for which he didn't directly ask. In college, he was a student operator at the university computer center. One day he walked to the director's office and stated, "I want you to know that I want to be one of the student managers here, and I'll do what it takes to get there." At the end of the school year, he was told that if he worked hard and was on his best behavior for the entire summer, then he would receive the promotion before the new school year. He worked hard and was on his best behavior and received the promotion.[8] History repeated itself in his future jobs.

Putting an idea in a manager's ear means that the next time the manager comes to the right situation, you will be a potential candidate. A good manager will immediately start coaching you to groom you into that position, testing the waters, and watching to see if you show promise to successfully fulfill the role you have requested. The manager can structure your tasks and training in the right direction.

Don't do this if you don't have a specific career goal or are unsure about your goals. At most companies, it is unacceptable to be without goals. You might communicate a technical skill you want to develop. If you want to stay where you are, be sure to let your boss know that you are happy as is!

Another steering technique is to let your boss help you with time management. When you have a completely overloaded schedule with no end in sight, let your boss set your priorities. Don't bring a complaint about being overloaded. Managers receive complaints all day long, and they don't want another one. Instead, bring your to-do list annotated with how long each item should take to complete. Explain that the total time for these projects is more than your eight-hour day (or 40-hour week) and ask for help prioritizing the list.

A typical manager will have several positive reactions. First of all, it's quite a compliment that you are seeking the manager's wisdom. Second, it makes the manager happy, because after a day of receiving selfish request after selfish request, you have come to her with a message that says, "I want

---

[8]It helped that he had a great boss.

to meet your top goals, tell me what they are." This can be very refreshing! Lastly, this gives your manager a real view into what kind of work you do. Your manager may notice tasks that should be completely eliminated or may reduce your load by delegating tasks to other people in your team. Maybe that other team member made the manager aware that he wanted more of a particular kind of assignment, and this is your boss' opportunity to give it to him.

Finally, we'd like to discuss the concept of *upward delegation,* or delegating action items to your boss. Certain tasks are appropriate for upward delegation and others are not. Your manager should be concerned with steering the boat, not rowing it. Don't upward delegate busywork. However, upward delegation is appropriate for anything that you feel you don't have the authority to do. Creating an action item for your boss is most appropriate when that action item will leverage the manager's authority to make other action items go away. For example, it would be inappropriate to tell customers that you don't want to help them. However, it is appropriate to delegate to your boss the assignment of talking to a customer's manager about the scope of work that your group does and that the customer is not to make certain requests in the future. If your boss is successful, managerial authority will have been used to save time for many people in your team.

Use Your Boss' Power When Needed
A group of SAs responsible for deploying PCs was missing deadlines because of an increase in custom configuration requests. These special requests required extremely large amounts of time. It turned out that many of these requests were not work-related. One request was for a MIDI card, something that was not required for the person's job. Another request was to create a dual-boot PC on which one of the partitions would be an OS that was not officially supported, but had better games available for it. The SAs delegated to their boss the assignment to talk with the customers' director and deal with the situation. He explained that the SAs were not being paid to help with the staff's hobbies or children's entertainment. The manager was able to use his authority to save time for an entire team of SAs.

Although such a request is always appropriate to upward delegate, others may be in more of a gray area—for example, telling a manager that a presentation would be better received if she did it herself. Such a request is much more likely to be accepted if it is made soon after you have received a compliment about achieving a large milestone. You might keep a mental list of items you want to ask for and pull out the most important one when you receive a compliment. It's difficult for a manager to turn down a *reasonable* request made immediately after thanking you for saving the company more money than you make in a year.

27.3   Further Reading

The habits listed in this chapter are difficult to develop. Books can help, as can workshops. Expect to be a little frustrated when you begin, but assure yourself that things will get easier as time goes on. One day you'll notice that you've mastered the habit without realizing it.

Communication skills, negotiating, and follow-through are often the topics of books for salespeople. It can be useful to read such books and apply what you learn to your career. The classic books *The One Minute Sales Person* by Spencer Johnson (1991) and *The One Minute Manager* by D. Kenneth Blanchard (1993) are full of advice that can be applied to SAs.

There are many excellent books on getting organized and setting goals. Two of them include Morgenstern's *Organizing from the Inside Out* (1998) and McGee-Cooper's *Time Management for Unmanageable People* (1994).

If you've never read a self-help book, it's difficult to imagine that a stack of paper with writing on it can solve your problems. Let us lessen that skepticism right here. Self-help books are great! However, let's be realistic: Only you can change you: books only offer suggestions, advice, and new ways of looking at what you've been seeing all along. Not every book is going to be the right one for you. Maybe the way the author addresses the subject, the particular problems the book addresses, or the writing style isn't the right match for you. That is why you can find a dozen self-help books on any given topic, each with a different style to appeal to different people. We also recommend that you think critically about advice being offered before you try it. Be suspicious of any book that professes to fix all of your problems (if it seems too good to be true, it probably is), requires no work (all behavior modification requires work), or encourages you to sell the techniques to others (if it really worked, it wouldn't need a pyramid scheme to sell it). We have tried to recommend timeless classics that have been on the market for a long time; books that have developed solid reputations for being effective. If you still doubt the usefulness of self-help books, put down the one you're reading right now.

27.4   Conclusion

It is important to be happy. It is important to be successful. These concepts are interrelated.

Successful people have excellent follow-through and focus, achieved by maintaining written or electronic to-do lists and calendars. This prevents them from dropping action items or missing appointments and deadlines.

Time management is a discipline that helps you accomplish your highest-priority goals. It is difficult for SAs to manage their time because there is so much temptation to be interrupt-driven. SAs must set goals if they are to achieve them. Planning your day is a good way to stay on track. Reading email efficiently can cut your mail processing time in half. Staying focused requires discipline also. If something is the highest priority, stay focused on it until it is done. Fill the wait time with your other priorities. Finding free time is a matter of eliminating the time wasters, not managing them better or doing them more efficiently.

We discussed communication skills such as "I statements" to make yourself heard, mirroring to confirm you understand people, reflecting to deal with emotional people, and summary statements to verify that members of a group are in sync with each other. These skills help us deal with the four kinds of problems in the world: mine, yours, ours, and other people's. These communication skills are useful in your work, but they also are key to your social life. In fact, they are the skills that are taught in marriage counseling. We hope that reading that section improves your relationships inside and outside of work.

Negotiation is about asking for what you want and striving for win-win situations. You should be aware of the power dynamic and how to shift it if you are not in a position of power.

Professional development is especially important in this constantly changing high-tech field. One-day tutorials tend to be tactical, while week-long conferences tend to be strategic. Both are useful and important.

We want you to love your job and be happy with your job. That means maintaining good mental health, balancing stress, handling criticism, and taking care of yourself. You don't do anyone a favor by skipping vacations.

Managing your boss is a component of ensuring your happiness. This involves paying attention to her priorities so that she will pay attention to yours. Make your needs known. Attend to your manager's success. It is appropriate to delegate to your boss action items that leverage her authority to solve problems for many people who work for her.

The average person spends the majority of his waking hours at work. You deserve to be happy when you are there.

Exercises

1. Imagine that you've won the lottery and no longer have to work. What would you do? Why aren't you doing it now? How could you be doing it now?

2. What do you do to ensure good follow-through?

3. What percent of your day is interrupt-driven? What can you do to reduce the interrupt-driven nature of your job?

4. What are your goals for the next month, year, and five years?

5. How do you spend the first hour of your day? What can you do to make that hour more productive?

6. How do you manage your email? What strategy do you implement in your email filtering?

7. What time management training is available to you?

8. What tasks do you have to do every day or every week? When do you do them?

9. Name three low-priority items you can eliminate from your to-do list.

10. Name three time wasters you can eliminate.

11. What types of communication or interpersonal skills training is available to you?

12. How confident are you in your negotiation skills? How much negotiating do you have to do? How could you improve your skills?

13. Describe your last negotiation and what you could have done to improve it.

14. What are your primary outlets for professional development? What support do you receive from your employer for this?

15. Are you an optimist or a pessimist? Give two examples.

16. How accepting is your workplace to being open about your personal life? If your workplace does not condone this, who can you go to for support when you need it? Is your workplace safe?

17. Describe your support network.

18. When was your last vacation? Did you read your work email account during it? If you did, was it really a vacation? Do you promise not to read email on your next vacation?

19. Spend 15 minutes creating your awards wall.

20. Are your priorities in alignment with those of your boss? How do you know? How do you ensure that they are?

21. What is the next promotion you want? Who knows that this is your goal?

22. When someone is standing in your office until you complete something they asked you to do, are they doing what is recommended in Section 27.1.2?

23. Describe the last time you needed to use upward delegation. How did your manager react? What will you do in the future to improve this?

24. What's your favorite self-help book?

Chapter 28

A Guide for Technical Managers

A technical manager is someone who understands system administration work in depth. She knows what is involved in running a site and working with customers. She probably used to be a senior SA, but has now taken on a supervisory role. She probably is still involved at some level in the technical aspects of running the site, too. Her role includes mentoring more junior SAs and helping them to develop both their technical and interpersonal skills. Her technical staff look to her to deal with red tape or roadblocks they may come across in the course of their work, so that they can focus on the technical issues.

The technical manager also interacts with nontechnical managers in her management chain and throughout the rest of the company. She is expected to be able to communicate well with both nontechnical managers and her technical staff. She acts as a buffer and an interpreter between the two sets of people.

28.1 The Basics

To be a successful technical manager, you need to understand how to work with both nontechnical managers and your technical staff. Your technical staff will consider that the way you deal with them is of utmost importance.

If you fail to make them feel appreciated or to help them when they need you, the group will fall apart. If you fail to work well with the nontechnical managers in the company, you will not be able to set realistic goals, deadlines, and budgets for your group, and you will not be able to project a good image of your group to the company. These problems also will adversely affect your group.

In this section, we will look at how to work with both your technical staff and the nontechnical managers in the company. We will look at some of your responsibilities as a technical manager and prepare you for some of the decisions you will have to make in that position.

28.1.1   Responsibilities

A technical manager has responsibilities to her staff, the company, and herself. She must keep her team's morale high and to support them in what they do. She should take care of developing their careers and helping them improve their technical skills. She needs to provide vision to the group, keeping them focused on the direction they are going. She has a responsibility toward the company to keep her group performing well and within budget. She must manage all of this while keeping herself sane and without falling completely behind on technology. She also must keep track of what her employees are doing without getting in their way.

Team Morale

The primary responsibility of a technical manager is to keep her team's morale high. If their morale is high, they will be motivated to take on even the most arduous tasks, they will enjoy their work, they will work as a team, staff turnover will be low, and hiring new staff will be easy. However, when morale is low, their productivity will go down and turnover will increase. It will also be harder to hire new staff, because the interview candidates will sense the low morale in the group and not want to be a part of it. Many groups have neither high nor low morale. They are somewhere in between, and the behavior of the team members also is somewhere in between. They are not willing to try to perform miracles on a daily basis, but neither are they leaving in droves. If the technical manager performs her job well, the team's morale should be high. Section 29.1.1 discusses morale issues in more detail.

Removing Roadblocks

The next most important responsibility to your staff is to restart processes that have broken down and to remove roadblocks that are preventing work from getting done. In other words, grease the wheels.

There are a couple of ways to revive a process. Sometimes, people aren't communicating, and you can connect the right two people. Sometimes, decisions aren't being made, often because people feel they aren't sure of the proper direction, they don't feel empowered, or they are stuck in an "infinite loop" debating issues. You can intervene and recommunicate your vision, empower them to make the best decision, or communicate priorities to end the debate. These are all communication issues. It's your job to resolve them.

Being a good listener is important because problems often solve themselves when you simply listen to the people involved. For example, projects may be stalled because people aren't sure what to do and, in fact, neither are you. However, you can intervene and listen to people describe the situation. Making people explain a problem to a third party (you) forces them to think through the problem carefully. The solution usually becomes obvious, even if you didn't understand what they said. It is best to have them discuss the issue until the solution becomes apparent either to them or to you.

Removing roadblocks usually involves taking on the nontechnical, bureaucratic tasks so your staff has more time to focus on what they were hired to do: detailed technical tasks. For example, you might clarify a policy, offer to reply to management if they are reluctant to fund a project, purchase a time-saving tool, or empower people to say or do something they weren't sure if they should do.

New technical managers often complain that they feel like they aren't getting anything done because they are used to having tangible results (machines installed, lines of code written), but their new role is more "soft issues." You might find yourself busy all day connecting people, removing roadblocks left and right, and enabling people to get things done, but not have anything tangible to show for it. However, that is the nature of your job.

Rewards

Technical managers must reward their staff. Rewards are very powerful. However, they also can be misapplied with disastrous results. A good book on managing people can give you a complete guide, but here we would like to highlight a couple of points.

Take the time to find out what motivates each person in your group. What is a reward to one person is punishment for others. Everyone is different. Pay attention to what each person in your group considers to be a reward. Keep notes in your PDA if it will help you remember. Publicly congratulating individuals for a job well done in front of their peers can be a hugely satisfying reward to some. An introvert might find that to be a painful experience. Patting someone on the shoulder and saying "good job" can be a powerful reward to some. Others may find that highly intimidating and others may find it insufficient. One powerful reward for SAs is being given new assignments that are interesting to them. Each person finds different things to be "interesting." Take notice of the types of assignments each staff person seems to enjoy doing. Usually these will be the assignments that they do first when they are left to set their own priorities. You can also ask people what projects they like to do.

Reward the behavior you want to encourage. Never reward negative behavior. For example, if a staff member seeks your attention, but goes about getting it by sending email to you and your entire staff, don't respond to the email. That would be encouraging negative behavior. Instead, respond when the person uses a proper communication channel. Although this will take a long time to produce the desired outcome, it will have a much more lasting result. Again you must remember that different people find different actions to be a reward (or a punishment).

Punishing negative behavior is a last resort. Punishing negative behavior is less effective than rewarding positive behavior. Think about when you were young and your parents punished you for doing something. Didn't it make you want to do that even more? The punishment also got you the attention you were craving, which means it was rewarding you.

If you must respond to negative behavior, do so in a way that doesn't reward the behavior. Returning to our email example, politely reply that such comments should be brought directly to your attention. If your reply fulfills the person's request, you are training him to repeat the behavior in the future. If he was simply starved for attention, you have rewarded his technique by giving him the attention he craved.

People should be expected to do what is in their job description. They receive a paycheck for doing that work. You should not back down on that point. Going beyond the call of duty, however, deserves to be rewarded with perks and bonuses. Confusing these two concepts can be a disaster. If you give a bonus or perk to people for doing their jobs, they will expect bonuses just for doing what they are paid to do. Soon there will be a sense of entitlement in the group.

Case Study: Bonuses Are for Special Deeds

A company distributed fake money ("Lucky Bucks") to staff members that were doing particularly good work. Lucky Bucks could be redeemed for prizes. Managers would hand out Lucky Bucks when nearly any task was completed. This was rewarding people for doing the things their job description entailed. As a result, the staff became annoyed when they had to do anything without receiving a specific reward. The management had accidentally trained the staff to think that they should receive special celebrations for just plain doing their job. The staff became unmanageable. When the Lucky Bucks program was ended the management had to spend years bringing back an appropriate work ethic. The management should have used discipline in handing out Lucky Bucks and only rewarded behavior that was extra special. In hindsight, they learned that if a program's goal was to encourage one thing, it should reward that one thing and nothing else.

Case Study: *Special Achievements Deserve Bonuses*

When Bell Labs was split between AT&T and Lucent, the SAs went through a lot of extra work to split the network on time. They received token bonuses when the project was complete (Limoncelli et al. 1997). This is an example of a properly administered bonus. Such a large project was atypical and out of the scope of their job descriptions. The bonus was well received.

If they had been hired specifically to split the network, a reward only would have been appropriate if it was rewarding an unexpected success, such as early completion.

Keeping Track of the Group

The technical manager is responsible to the company for keeping the group on track and knowing what her staff is doing. Some technical managers will use weekly or monthly reports as a way to keep track of what everyone is doing. Others will have regular one-on-one, face-to-face meetings with each staff member. If you arrange regular meetings, make sure that you don't schedule them more often than you can manage. Arranging meetings and constantly canceling them or showing up late is very annoying and demoralizing for your staff. It is better to arrange one meeting once a month that you always attend than to arrange one every week and only show up to one or two of them a month. Meetings provide a good opportunity for dialogue that wouldn't otherwise occur. The manager can immediately address some concerns or answer some questions that an employee might not put in a report. If a manager does ask for reports, she must make sure that she sets aside time to both read them and respond to any issues raised in them. It is irritating and demoralizing for employees to have to interrupt their work to write a report that no one reads. It is also a waste of the company's resources.

Brief, periodic reports can be useful for the technical manager to refer to when she needs to see if her team can take on a new project or explain why they don't have time to do something. However, there may be other ways to get that information, such as through the call tracking system.

Case Study: Automated Reports

A technical manager at a mid-size software company got automatic daily reports on what his staff were doing by programming the call tracking software to let him know which calls his team members updated each day and how much time they had spent on each of those calls. He was always able to discuss what his staff were doing at a moment's notice.

Another technical manager at a consulting company programmed the billing system to send him a list first thing in the morning of the hours that each of the consultants he was responsible for had billed the previous day. He always knew who was going to be low on hours for the week, and when someone had stayed up all night working, even if they were at a remote customer site.

Another technical manager wrote scripts to page him with calls in the call tracking system that had not been updated in 24 hours, in addition to the above daily reports. He worked in an Internet service company, where the calls were all customer problems rather than long-term maintenance projects.

Finding out what your staff are up to without interrupting their work for status reports is often preferable to periodic reports. However, it does rely on discipline on the part of the staff to regularly update their calls or enter their billing hours, for example. If they do not update their calls, that is also good information for the manager. It is then a good idea for the manager to find out why they haven't. There is a good chance that there is a problem with those employees. They may be overloaded, they may have low morale, or they may just have bad work habits. In any case, the manager should talk with them.

Group meetings are also a useful way to keep track of what's happening and provide a forum to let everyone know what everyone else is doing. It is important for the group to stay in touch with each others' work so that they can give input on other projects and know when another project may influence theirs.

It is also important for the manager to track her group's metrics. Somewhere in her management chain, the technical manager reports to a nontechnical manager. It is important for her to be able to demonstrate familiarity with and proper understanding and analysis of her department's metrics to build consensus with executive staff. No matter how important the technical manager thinks metrics are to her, the reality is that part of her job is to know her team's data better than anyone else so that she can communicate effectively with executive staff.

Support

The technical manager plays a supporting role for her team, aiding them in their work through handling bureaucratic tasks and supporting them in their interactions with the rest of the company. She should support them in the work they do. She should accept blame for failures that the group is responsible for, deflect the blame away from the team members, and not seek to assign fault to individuals while expecting the team to do better the next time. The responsible individual should privately receive a warning, rather than learn of the manager's dissatisfaction months later during performance reviews. On the other hand, she should make sure that the individuals in the team are recognized and rewarded for their successes, rather than taking the praise herself. The technical manager should be able to derive satisfaction from seeing that her staff are content and successful rather than from receiving praise for their accomplishments.

Another way that the technical manager supports her staff in their work is by taking responsibility for contract negotiations and bureaucratic tasks. This includes jobs such as getting maintenance contracts approved and renewed, dealing with nondisclosure agreements (NDAs), and negotiating with vendors and the purchasing department when necessary. The manager usually has the authority to sign contracts on behalf of the company, whereas the technical staff usually do not. She is also expected to be a better negotiator than her staff. By doing these tasks, she allows her team to concentrate on the technical tasks that they specialize in and enjoy, and she relieves them of the tedium of bureaucratic overhead. If she has employees who are interested in learning these skills, she should mentor them and give them the opportunity to relieve her of some of this work.

She should also support her team when they need to enforce company policy. At times, a policy may seem inconvenient to an SA's customer. The policy was implemented for a reason, and not enforcing it will ultimately be to the company's disadvantage. If the SAs are put into the position of saying "no" to their customers, they can seem unhelpful. If the "no" comes from someone of higher authority, it will be accepted more readily. Either way, it takes the onus off the SA. If it seems to be appropriate to have the policy modified, the manager should facilitate the effort herself or help her staff facilitate it.

Case Study: Enforcing the Policy

One technical manager was known for telling staff, "Your job is to say 'no.' My job is to make it stick." If a customer pushed back about enforcing a policy, the SAs would explain to the customer why the policy existed and would help the customer achieve their end goal, which usually could be done via a different path that wouldn't violate any policies. However, if the customer still pushed back, the SAs could count on their manager to take on the task of explaining why the policy was in place and why it was going to be enforced. This let the SAs stay focused on their technical tasks rather than dealing with what was essentially a business issue.

Case Study: Let Me Be the Bad Guy

Another manager helped his SAs get through bureaucratic messes by letting himself be portrayed as the bad guy. This manager often told his staff, "Explain it to the customer, and if they don't like it, blame me! Make me the bad guy!" This gave the SAs a tool they could use to deflect anger and save face. SAs would say to someone, "I understand your plight, but my boss won't let me, and you know how strict he is." Enough SAs used this excuse that eventually word spread. Corporate bureaucrats didn't want to have to face this mystery manager and reacted quickly to any requests from the group. Yet they never actually dealt with him directly.

The technique can be successful as long as it isn't overused. However, it works better when the customer in question is another staff member at the same level as the SA or below. If the staff member is at the same level as the SA manager or higher, we recommend that the SA escalates to his manager and lets her deal with the problem directly and then escalate to her manager if necessary. If the manager gets a reputation as someone who is impossible to work with, it can be bad for her career.

Standing by a Policy Need Not Be Humorless

Standing up for your SA team can also be done with a sense of humor. The following email was sent to users of a particular network after a series of outages.

```
From: Head of the SA Team
To: Users of this network
Subject: Network theft problem

   This is a quick note to enlist your support on a serious
issue that involves all of us.
   We are seeing an increasing rate of theft on our network. At
least once a week, the computer support team is diverted for an
hour or two to track a case of network theft.
```

In all cases, we have identified the person who perpetrated the theft, and, shockingly enough, in each case it has been one of our colleagues within the department! What is even more shocking is that once confronted, the person often shows no remorse and has little concern for the impact the actions have had on peers.

What am I talking about?

It has become a common practice for people to steal an IP address without registering it. They install a PC, workstation, or printer and simply use an address they ''think'' is not used. Later on, when SAs are allocating addresses for a new device, we discover a conflicting IP address already in use on the network.

This creates hours of wasted time each week for computing support and affects users as a result of systems being down. We have had cases recently in which people have used addresses already in use by critical servers, printers, other people's PCs, and the like.

This has the same effect as if someone walked up to another person's PC when no one was around and pulled the network connection out of the back of it. That person is affected, and the computing staff loses hours tracking the culprit diverting them from REAL work.

Please obtain an IP address from the computing team BEFORE installing any new device on the network. Your coworkers will thank you.

Thanks

P.S. If you are working in a lab where you have a need to dynamically install and remove systems, we can arrange to assign you a block of IP addresses that you can cycle through or even arrange a custom DHCP configuration just for you.

Feel free to craft your own similar message using this one as a base. In fact, this message was originally written by Ralph Loura and has been reused by many groups since.

Vision Leader

The technical manager is also responsible for having a vision for the group. She needs to know where the group is going and what their goal is. Setting an appropriate vision for the group requires being in touch with the direction of the company as a whole and figuring out how the group can help the company reach its goals. She should remind the group of the vision to help keep them focused. The vision should be a long-term vision and should have some shorter milestones on the way so that the SAs can see the progress they are making toward the group's vision. The milestones might be annual or quarterly goals for the group. She needs to keep the vision consistent, because employees need to feel their role is stable. SAs hate to feel that they are heading for point A one day and point B the next, especially when points A and B are in completely different directions. Because of day-to-day issues that arise, there are times when a short-term decision may seem contrary to what she previously told the staff. She should know how to explain how something that appears to be a shift in direction is actually fulfilling a long-term goal.

Case Study: Explain Decisions That Appear Contrary to Direction

A technical manager of customer support organization had a staff of eight customer support engineers (CSEs) supporting more than 180 customers and more than 200 technology and channel partners. The software product that they were supporting was so complex that it took at least four months to get a CSE up to speed. The manager enforced the rule that partners who called for support on their own installations got lower priority than customers or partners calling on behalf of a customer. A week after he had started enforcing this direction, he found out that the company was negotiating a huge partnership deal and that calls from this potential partner should be made higher priority. He needed to communicate this message to his group without making them feel the group's direction had changed.

First, he told the group that this potential partner did not take priority over customers in production who were down, because that was a decision the executive staff would accept and understand. Then he explained that although customers are more important than partners, this particular partner was prepared to sign a deal that would allow them to be on-site with dozens of customers. The more that the partner learned up front, the more calls they would be able to handle at customer sites and the less they would rely on the CSEs in the future. This would ultimately give all customers better support. The CSEs understood the decision in context. It made a short-term exception to the group's vision that they did not feel was contradictory.

Unless the company is floundering and changing its direction all the time, tying your group's direction to the company's direction should make sure that your vision can stay stable and consistent over time. In floundering companies, maintaining what is perceived as a locally stable vision can shelter the SA team from the morale-killing corporate instability. However, the manager should balance the need for sheltering the team with the need to keep her employees informed if it looks like the company is going to sink. Part of managing their careers is helping them to move on at the right time.

Coaching

The technical manager is also responsible for coaching her team. She needs to help them develop professionally and technically. A good coach needs infinite patience. People learn in different ways and at different speeds, but most people will not learn well or quickly if the person coaching them lets her frustration show. Coaching means taking the time to explain what to do and why and being there when they need help. It means watching them make their own mistakes and helping them to learn from them, without making them feel like a bad person. It means making time for them. Typically the junior SAs are the ones who need the most coaching. With practice, you can learn to give successively more difficult tasks to people to develop their skills, letting them fail, but encouraging them to continue. If they don't fail occasionally, you aren't increasing the difficulty fast enough.

A big part of coaching is delegation. System administration is about controlling machines and networks, but delegation is about letting go of control and letting others be in control. They are opposing skills, and therefore many SAs need extra help learning to delegate.

When giving protégés successively more difficult tasks, you have to let them fail and be supportive without getting angry. Here's a tip for you if you feel yourself getting angry in these situations: remember that if they knew what they were doing, they would be doing it without your coaching. You are there to help them with the problems. Otherwise, you are like an auto mechanic who complains that people only bring broken cars to his shop.

Let People Learn from Mistakes

Once Tom was coaching two engineers who were going to upgrade a link between two routers from 10Mb Ethernet to 100Mb FastEthernet. The two routers were in different parts of the building. He asked them to go to the server rooms and pantomime the change (see Section 11.2.5) to make sure all the right connectors were available. He had done this in front of them during previous projects. They laughed at Tom for making this suggestion, and Tom had a feeling that they weren't actually going to do it. When the maintenance window arrived, they discovered that their fiber patch cord had the wrong type of connector. The maintenance window had to be rescheduled.

Tom could have gone behind their backs and done the checking himself. He also could have marched them down to the room to do the tests. Either would have been insulting and bad for morale. Instead, he checked to make sure that the project wasn't critical and could be delayed by a week or so without affecting other projects if something went wrong. The two technicians were adults and knew how to learn from mistakes. He noticed that on future projects they pantomimed such changes without being asked.

When we get angry at someone who is learning, it is often because we feel we are perfect, and it can be very frustrating to deal with people who aren't. We know we're perfect: we know the process, we're good at it, and we've even developed some interesting little refinements that make the process go well. It is difficult and frustrating to watch someone without all of our experience stumble through the process. What we need to remember is that it took a long time for us to become perfect, and we need to let them take their time becoming perfect, too. It will take them longer to become perfect than it did for us, because we're so perfect, but they *will* get there some day. Remember this any time you forget to be humble.

Sometimes, no matter how hard you try, you will find yourself coaching someone who just doesn't seem to "get it." Try to understand where his confusion lies and how he is thinking, and then approach your teaching from that point of view. Always try your best and assume that you have a communication problem that you need to resolve, rather than giving up or getting frustrated. Occasionally, you will come across someone who learns a lot more slowly than you would like. Adjust your expectations accordingly, but don't stop trying. He will pick up more as time goes on.

Technical Development

The technical manager is responsible for ensuring that her senior SAs also get to develop their technical skills and keep up with technological advances. She achieves this in several ways. She delegates large and complex tasks to them that she would otherwise have been more directly involved with herself. She makes sure that they attend relevant conferences and encourages them to write papers and otherwise participate in those conferences and other outside technical groups. Some companies allocate a certain amount of money and time[1] per person for professional development. The technical manager is responsible for ensuring that her management understands the value of professional development and that they fund it appropriately.

The technical manager should also work with her employees to make sure that they get the most out of that money and that they share what they learn with the rest of the group. She should make sure that the group or department has a comprehensive library of technical books for her team to reference. She should also find opportunities to get her senior SAs involved in projects in other areas that they are interested in, to help them broaden their areas of expertise.

Career Paths

Career planning is often talked about but rarely done. A career path meeting is a time for the manager to listen to the employee talk about where the

---

[1] It is reasonable for an SA to expect about 40 hours of professional development a year.

employee wants to be five years from now. The manager must then consider how these desires can fit into the skills and roles that she requires in the group. Only then can she and the employee discuss what short-term and long-term objectives will meet those goals. The manager may learn that nobody in her current team wants to be in certain roles and therefore identifies roles that must be developed within the group or sought when hiring the next team member.

To do career planning right, technical managers should allocate an entire hour once a year with every member of their staff to focus solely on this topic. It should not be the same meeting that includes the yearly performance review, as that praise (or reprimand) should not be diluted. The performance review meeting is for the manager to communicate to the employee. The career path meeting should focus on the manager listening to the employee.

This meeting is a learning experience for the manager, who might get some surprises: The introvert of the group actually wants to become the team leader or the team leader wants to be coached to be your successor. You might learn that someone is utterly bored and wants to change roles completely. It is easier to retrain someone than to hire an outsider, so these change requests should be encouraged. It also results in a cross-trained team.

Most people, especially younger people, don't know what their career path should be. The technical manager should make suggestions only after employees have exhausted their ideas of where they could go. Typical suggestions are along obvious paths: junior SAs to become intermediate and then senior SAs. She should help them to become proficient at what they do and then gradually increase the scope of their jobs so that they gain experience and proficiency in more areas. For intermediate SAs, she should watch as they develop, see what gaps they have in their expertise, and encourage them to fill those gaps. As they become more senior, she may want to encourage them to specialize in particular areas of interest.

Senior SAs are the most likely to suffer a career crisis. They have worked hard to reach this position, but now what should their goals be? For some, the answer is to encourage them to become more recognized and involved in the field. They should work toward advancing the profession of system administration by getting involved in organizing conferences, as well as presenting at them; or by working with organizations, such as the IETF, to play a part in the specification and design of future technologies. Others may want to get a taste of management to see if that is a direction they might want to pursue. Give them the opportunity to manage some projects, supervise and mentor some more junior SAs, choose and manage contractors to help with particular projects, get involved in the budget process, and participate in cross-functional committee meetings on behalf of the group.

Budget

A technical manager is also responsible for her group's budget. She prepares a realistic annual budget request, including salary increases and bonuses, new staff, the costs of supporting the existing systems, scaling existing systems to meet the growth of the company, improving areas that are performing below the required service level, upgrading systems that will need upgrading, and funding the new projects that are required to keep the company moving with the times at an appropriate pace.

Once she has been given a budget for her group, which may be less than what she requested, she is responsible for making sure that her group remains within budget while achieving what they need to achieve. If the budget is significantly below what was requested, she needs to identify the tasks that cannot be done while working to obtain additional funds.

Stay in Touch with Technology

A technical manager also has a responsibility to herself and to her staff to stay knowledgeable about new technology. She is the technical guide, mentor, and vision leader for the group. If she loses touch with new technologies, she will not be effective in setting an appropriate vision for her staff and leading them toward it. Nor will she be as effective in coaching her staff and helping them to develop technically. She may even resist the introduction of new technologies because she is unfamiliar with them and does not feel comfortable moving the company in that direction.

28.1.2   Working with Nontechnical Managers

A technical manager should be able to work well with the nontechnical managers in her management chain and in her customer base. The key components of a successful relationship with nontechnical management are communication and setting and meeting expectations. Use graphs and quantitative data to address issues relating to the business goals of the company and of the group. The relationships with the nontechnical managers are key to the technical manager's success and job satisfaction.

Use Analogies They Understand

A technical manager had to explain what an Ethernet switch was to a financial director of his division. This was when Ethernet switches were new, and the proposal to upgrade their entire network was going to be very expensive. He began by getting an understanding of technology the director *did* understand, which was mostly limited to telephone equipment. Therefore he explained that the network was like a phone system. Right now any two computers can only talk to each other at any given moment. All the others had to wait. The Ethernet switches, he explained, would let any two computers talk at any given moment rather than waiting. This the director could understand. The purchase was approved quickly because he found a way to communicate the value in terms the director could understand.

In general, other managers that you work with will want to know that you (and your team) can accomplish what they need when they need it. They don't want to know the technical details of what you will need to do, and they expect you to figure out the actual requirements they want met. Make sure that any deadlines you set for yourself or your team are on the pessimistic side of realistic. It is better to give pessimistic estimates and surprise people when you are early, rather than to disappoint customers by being late. However, taken to extremes, they will find you obstructive, will be unable to commit to meeting their own deadlines, and may go around you to make things happen.

Your direct management chain wants you to meet the deadlines they set for you, and to keep your customers happy. They do not want to have to deal with complaints relating to you or your team. They want to know they can delegate things to you and be sure that they will be accomplished on schedule. If you can't meet a deadline or accomplish a task for your customers or your managers, they want to know as early as possible so that they can manage the impact of a slipped schedule.

The nontechnical managers who you work with will also expect you to set direction for your group based on customer requirements. When they look for status, they want to know how you are performing in terms of the requirements and the goals and deadlines that were set. They generally do not want to be bombarded with technical details. However, if they do ask you to go into depth on technical points, do not be afraid to go right down into the details. If you are going too deep, they will stop you. Avoid vague generalities: Be definite and precise.

When working with your management chain, particularly on budget issues, justify what you need in terms of helping the company meet its goals or making your group meet the goals that have been set for it by the company. They will need to be kept abreast of the large-scale tasks that your group is working on so that they can answer accurately when asked by their peers and superiors. Keeping your management chain informed of what your group is doing is also important if you want to protect your group from being overburdened with extra work. If they don't know what your resources are allocated to, they may assume that it is nothing important and volunteer your group for extra projects, to the detriment of your existing commitments.

Know the Requirements

A basic expectation that nontechnical managers have of the technical staff is that they know the requirements behind the tasks they are performing.

For customer support calls, knowing the requirements means understanding the root of the problem and the time constraints, as discussed in Chapter 16. For building a new service, it means understanding the customers' needs, how the service will be used, how it needs to scale, performance requirements, the support model, financial constraints, interoperability requirements, and all the other aspects that were discussed in Chapter 3.

Knowing the requirements and bearing them in mind as you work tends to keep you and your team more focused on the specific problem at hand. It is easy for an SA to lose focus when investigating one problem causes him to find others, or when looking at ways to build a new service opens up all sorts of possibilities in other areas. This is known as *Feature Creep*. Your customers and your management chain expect you to use the requirements to direct your team's work, avoiding other interesting diversions to meet all of your goals on time. Equally, they expect you to explore other possibilities that arise, if they are in line with the requirements. Deciding what to do is a matter of keeping the big picture in mind, not just the fine details of a particular part. The technical manager is the one who is expected to keep the big picture in focus and provide direction.

Communication with your management and customers should also be based on the requirements. For example, if you are building a new service, your manager or a customer might want to know why your team is doing it one way rather than another. If you believe that your team's approach is better than what the other person proposes, use the requirements to express why. In other words, rather than saying "it's a better design," you should explain which requirements led you to choose this design rather than the other one. For example, it may be that it is easier to support your design, it interoperates with other services, it scales to the required size more cheaply or with better performance, it can be implemented in the required time scale, it uses more reliable systems, or it has more of the required features. Even if you think you are being too verbose, it is probably what they are looking for. If you are overwhelming them with information, they will stop you. Overcommunicating is better than undercommunicating. Over time, you will learn what level of information each individual prefers.

Customer requirements are a significant part of any work that an SA performs. Finding out what they are involves asking the right questions of your customers and listening to their answers, getting clarification where necessary. The process of building the list of customer requirements is an opportunity to build a cooperative relationship with the customers. It should also be used as a platform for giving the customers feedback and setting realistic expectations.

Clearly identifying the requirements and using them to direct your team's work results in faster problem resolution and better services, both of which lead to happier customers and happier managers.

28.1.3 Working with Your Employees

A technical manager's employees are a significant part of her job. She needs to keep their morale high and keep them happy to be working for her. She also needs to encourage them to perform well in their jobs and make sure that they know what is expected of them.

Be a Good Role Model

A manager influences the behavior of her group by the way that she acts toward others, including her employees. If she is short-tempered and irritable, her employees will behave in a similar manner toward their customers. If she doesn't seem to care about her job, her group will mirror that in a lack of concern for its customers. However, if she treats her employees well, they will be attentive to their customers' needs. If she goes out of her way to help others, her employees will do the same.

The technical manager should take care to exhibit the behavior she would like her group to emulate. Lead by example, and your group will follow. She should see her employees as her primary customers and try to keep them happy. If they are happy, there is a much higher chance that they will keep their customers happy. If the group's customers are happy, then her managers will be happy (with her, at least).

Treat Your Employees with Respect

Treating employees well is a key part of maintaining morale and loyalty. One way for a manager to show appreciation for her employees is to be aware of each group member's hire date and do something on their anniversaries. Something small that celebrates each person spending another year at the company makes them feel appreciated.

Another way for a technical manager to let her staff know that they are appreciated is to publicly acknowledge them when they do good work. Her compliments should be specific, sincere, and timely. Vague, belated, or insincere compliments can be demotivators. Excellent work that involved effort beyond the normal call of duty should be rewarded with at least a small bonus.[2]

---

[2]Recognition and being made to feel important and valued are bigger motivators than money. However, lack of promised (or unrealistically expected) money is always a demotivator. Using money as an incentive can create an expectation that you can't maintain.

Recognition Is Important

A friend of Christine's worked at Xerox PARC during a turbulent period. Morale in the SA group was very low. Both managers of the group quit, and he was left as the "acting manager." He had no budget for providing incentives. He spoke to the company cafeteria manager and asked if he could give away a free lunch once a week to someone in his group, with the cafeteria charging the cost back to his department. The way that things worked in Xerox, internal money that didn't result in anyone receiving cash didn't count against the budget and so was essentially free. He then explained to his staff that each week at their staff meeting, they would recognize someone who had gone above and beyond the call of duty. He couldn't afford anything fancy, but he printed up little "certificates" with gold stars on them, and gave away the free lunches. It was a huge hit. Morale improved, despite the fact that the cafeteria food wasn't even all that good. The recognition and the token reward was enough.

If an employee fails in a particular task, he will usually know that he has done so. If it is not too serious a failure, take him aside and tell him not to worry about it and that everyone makes mistakes. Permit him to consider his failure in peace and to think about what he could have done differently. If is was serious, reprimand him, but be sure to do so in private. It is important to have a short conversation not long after the incident so that the employee does not brood over the mistake for too long and blow it out of proportion. Take the heat from the customers or your management on his behalf. He will know that you are aware of his error and will appreciate what you are doing. He will be determined not to put you in that position again if he can help it.

However, sometimes people make mistakes and don't realize it. Some people don't have the same standards as you, and you need to explain to them that they've actually failed. Some people are convinced that nothing is ever their fault. You need to explain clearly to them that they are at fault. Only by understanding and appreciating their mistakes will they be able to improve.

When you reprimand someone, it should be done face to face and be timely and specific about the behavior that needs to be changed. Reprimands should never be done in public. If you reprimand an employee in public in order to make a public example of him, you are showing a lack of respect toward those who work for you, and it will demotivate the entire team. That lack of respect will be mirrored back at you and may be reflected in your staff not treating their customers with respect either.

A manager should respect her staff by keeping them informed about important events that are happening within the group and the company. It is important to strike a balance in doing so, however. It can be destructive and distracting to know every potential change when most of them don't happen. Significant news may need to be presented in the right way, so that it does not cause undue concern. However, it should be presented in a timely manner once it is certain. When a manager doesn't trust her employees to react in a calm, responsible manner to events in the company, she is showing them disrespect.

Lack of Information

At a small consulting company, the senior management were so paranoid about releasing any information to the employees that could be construed as bad news that they insisted on doing it themselves and refused to let the technical managers inform their staff. This led to a lot of dissatisfaction among the technical managers and the staff alike. In one incident, one of the first five employees of the company only found out that a key member of the company was leaving through a companywide email news bulletin sent out by one of the founders. The newsletter mentioned the departure in an off-hand manner in the last paragraph. The employee was (understandably) so upset by the incident that from then on his manager and a couple of others went against the management's instructions to the contrary and kept certain employees properly informed.

A manager should listen to her staff. They need to be able to discuss things that are on their minds. If they have a problem with a customer, a co-worker, or a vendor, or even have a personal problem, they should be able to talk to her about it. She needs to be available to her employees. She should always make them feel that their needs are important to her, even if she has other pressing work. Keeping the group working effectively will accomplish more than she can accomplish on her own. However, she also needs to find time to do her own work, without making her group feel neglected. Scheduled weekly meetings with each employee can go a long way toward reducing the number of times that she is interrupted during the rest of the week. These meetings don't need to be elaborate or long. They just give the manager a chance to ask how things are going and if she can help with anything. It gives the employee a chance to mention anything he thinks she might want to know about, without feeling like he's making a big issue over it by making an appointment or interrupting her work to tell her. It should also make the employee more comfortable with the manager and generally improve the relationship. On occasions when she has a particularly tight deadline, a good way of ensuring that she is still in touch with important issues, but is not involved in the lesser ones, is to let her staff know that she has a deadline and to say that she will be closeting herself away but wants them to interrupt her if they need her help.

A technical manager generally likes to be quite involved with her staff and their projects. She is interested in how they are solving the problems they face and in the new technologies that they are bringing into the company. However, she needs to be careful that her interest and her knowledge of how to solve many of the problems that they might be facing for the first time does not lead to micro-managing her staff. Micro-management is irritating to the SAs and demonstrates a lack of faith in their ability to solve the problems. You need to have faith in your staff. Encourage them to communicate with you on their progress and let you know when they would like to talk about the problems that they encounter, but do not look for progress reports several times a day or continually ask, for example, if they have completed this task or spoken to that person yet. Respect their ability to do their jobs well, and give them the space to do so.

It is important for a technical manager not only to believe in her staff, but to demonstrate to them that she believes in their ability to do whatever jobs she gives them. She should believe in them until they consistently give her reason not to. They should not have to prove themselves worthy of her trust; they should have it automatically until they show themselves to be unworthy of it.

Be Positive

One component of maintaining high morale in a group is to be positive about the group's abilities and direction. A technical manager should let her staff know that she believes in them and will do what she has to do to get them what they need to be successful. She should never harp on how great things were in the past, either with this group or elsewhere; instead, she should look forward to a bright future.

If she is a new manager brought in to manage a group that she has been told by her management is failing in one way or another, she should not show that she believes they are failing. She should be positive, and she should talk to the people in the group to understand their impressions of the group. She should not start changing things until she understands why things are the way they are and can determine what is good and bad. Gratuitous change indicates that she thinks they are doing everything wrong. However, she does need to address the problem reasonably quickly, whether it be real or just how the group is perceived. If she fails to do so, she will lose the support of her management, without which she will be an ineffectual advocate for her group.

New Director

A system administration organization of 75 people got a new director. The director was told by his management that the group he was taking on was dysfunctional and did not work as a team. Although the group did have problems, it also had a very strong team spirit. The director gave a speech on his first day about how he was going to build a team and how all the people at his previous company had loved working for him and cried when he left. The SAs left the meeting feeling that they were all going to lose their jobs to people from his old company and doubting their working relationships with other parts of the group. He also left them doubting his ability to run the group because he apparently was out of touch with the group's biggest asset: its team spirit.

Give Clear Direction

A technical manager needs to make sure that everyone in the group understands the division of responsibilities within the group and that they each take care of their own areas. She should make sure that each person is only working on the things that he is assigned to do and not working on other projects unless or until she asks him to, or at least agrees to it. She should let her people know that they if they take responsibility for meeting their deadlines and keeping their customers happy, she will take care of the things she is responsible for and will not feel obliged to micro-manage them.

She needs to be clear about what she expects of them. If they frequently do not give her what she is looking for, she is probably not explaining herself clearly. If she believes that she is explaining herself clearly but is still not getting the results that she wants, she should ask the employee to explain back to her in detail what it is that the employee thinks she wants. This can lead to a useful dialog if there is a misunderstanding. If there is no misunderstanding, at least she knows that there is a problem and can deal with it directly.

Don't assume that you are communicating well just because you know exactly what you want. It is not always obvious to others. Some managers don't realize that they are not explaining what they want clearly enough. They use what is sometimes called the "bring me a rock" management technique. The manager says to the employee "Bring me a rock." The employee dutifully brings her a "rock." She says "No, no! Not that rock! I wanted a *rock*!" The employee searches for a different rock, and so on, until he finally stumbles on the particular kind of rock that his manager wants. Over time, the employee usually learns what the manager is looking for when she asks for a rock, but only if the manager is consistent about the types of "rocks" that she likes. The rock may be a style of writing, a way of laying out project proposals, a budget request, a project design specification, a service implementation, or a solution to a customer's problem. It is anything that the manager asks for but does not describe or explain adequately. Working for a manager who uses the bring-me-a-rock technique can be very frustrating. It usually leads to high employee turnover.

28.1.4   Decisions

Certain decisions usually fall to the technical manager to make. These include group staffing decisions and prioritizing and allocating tasks to the group members. The technical manager also often has to decide whether to buy a product to solve a particular problem or to build the solution in-house.

Roles and Responsibilities

The technical manager should consider the responsibilities of her group and the talents of the people in it when she is hiring new staff, as well as when she is allocating projects or areas of responsibility to the various team members.

When hiring, she should look for gaps that need to be filled in terms of skillsets and personality types. Appendix A looks at the different roles that SAs can play. A technical manager should try to make sure that she has a good balance in the roles relevant to her area of responsibility. Chapter 30 discusses how to hire people who will work well in your environment.

Given the mix of people in her group, the technical manager should distribute the work load appropriately. When doing so, she must consider her people's talents, experience, and career growth. She needs to give them tasks that they are capable of handling, tasks that will stretch their skills and help them grow, and enough variety to keep the work interesting.

Priorities

The technical manager also must decide the group's priorities and negotiate them with her management and her customers. In making those decisions, she should consider the importance or impact of a project and the amount of time and effort required to accomplish it. She should prioritize the items that will make the biggest impact over all others as depicted in Figure 28.1.

It is easy to understand why you should put a high priority on doing projects that require little effort but would result in a big impact. It is easy to understand why the lowest priority is given to the other extreme, projects that require a large effort, yet will only have a small impact.

The question becomes whether priorities 2 and 3 should be swapped. We claim that your priority should be on the biggest impact, rather than the least effort. Otherwise, you will be distracted by easy projects that have very little benefit. It requires discipline to avoid these. They are inviting because of the potential for instant gratification; they will be accomplishments. You

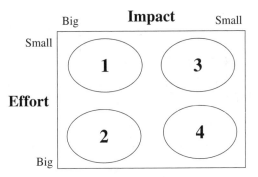

Figure 28.1: Setting priorities based on impact. (The numbers indicate the order in which tasks should be done.)

can spend months avoiding the high-impact projects by filling your day with "one more little task" that you want to do because it would be "so easy." This is one way that big projects get delayed. The technical manager must steer her team away from this trap.

Typically, if you have accurately understood the impact of and effort involved in each task, your management will support you in your decision. Your customers may or may not agree with where you rated their projects because they may be biased against projects that aren't directly helping them. However, the projects of theirs that you rated as having a big impact should be the most important things on which their group depends.

Case Study: Bigger Impact, Better Results

A company had two systems that weren't under change management. After a while, this lack of change management became a maintenance nightmare. It was chaos. Management decided to convert both systems to use the company's standard change management procedures. Which should be converted first?

Consider the effort required: Project A would be the easier system to convert because the team that put it together already used a fairly clean process that just needed to be improved to meet corporate standards. Project B would be difficult to convert because they had a more chaotic process. Based on the effort required, some people would do Project A first.

Now let's consider the impact of the two conversions. Project A's unofficial, but somewhat formal, processes kept it running fairly well. Moving it to the corporate standard for change management wouldn't have a very large impact. On the other hand, Project B's lack of formal processes resulted in a constant stream of problems and failures. Change management would help it greatly. It would free up four engineers to work on other projects, rather than having them spend day after day chasing problems. That would have a large, positive impact on the small company.

Initially they had planned on converting Project A first: The path of least resistance. However, following the "bigger impact" method helped them decide to start with Project B. After both conversions were complete the team was glad they had made this decision.

Buy Versus Build

A technical manager is often faced with the "buy versus build" decision. Should she buy a product or assign team members to write the software themselves? This decision really encompasses a continuum that includes buy, integrate, glue, or build, as follows:

Buy a complete canned solution: Complete solutions exist in many industries, usually mature product spaces such as word processing applications.

Integrate or customize a product into the environment: Larger applications require customization and configuration. An accounting system needs large amounts of customization to match your business needs. Helpdesk software needs to be configured to understand what products are being supported, who is being supported, and other workflow issues. If a system is completely configurable, small sites may find such customization to be as difficult as writing a system from scratch. Often, only large environments can benefit from highly configurable systems. Buying a system that is more configurable than the site needs often wastes time.

Glue together several products: Often, the solution a site needs doesn't exist, but smaller systems can be combined to build a complete solution. The key is that some coding will be required to connect the components. The team's job becomes gluing them together. For example, rarely do different OSs handle user accounts the same way, but they can reference some kind of database. A site might deploy a SQL database and create the glue that lets each OS authenticate from it. NT systems might create and delete accounts as they are added and deleted from the database. UNIX systems might generate their /etc/passwd files from dumps of the SQL tables or via stored SQL procedures (Finke 2000). Certain combinations of glued products become so commonplace that vendors spring up to provide preconfigured packages to fill the gap. They can usually provide additional value or higher performance through expert customization. Auspex did this after seeing so many sites creating dedicated file servers out of UNIX boxes. They provided network/NFS hardware accelerators with NFS and CIFS (Common Internet File System) software and NIS for authentication. Mirapoint provided an integrated mail system after seeing so many people glue together mail servers out of a UNIX box, POP3 (Post Office Protocol 3) (Myers and Rose 1996) and Internet Message Access Protocol version 4 (IMAP4) (Crispin 1996) software, and an MTA (Mail Transport Agent) such as Sendmail.

Build the solution from scratch: The highest level of customization comes from this method. The technical manager and her team must go the entire route of gathering requirements, designing the architecture, implementation, testing, and deployment.

There are positive and negative aspects to each choice. One end of the scale—buy—generally is believed to involve less work, have a faster "time to availability," and offer a lower cost in terms of human resources. On the other hand, these solutions are "one size fits all," less customized, and may have a steep learning curve. Support can be a positive and a negative thing: A commercial product (or commercial support for an Open Source product) will have a phone number that can be called when one has a question. On the other hand, it may be several long product cycles before bugs are fixed, if they are not considered urgent enough for a patch.

Building a solution from scratch has pros and cons, too. The solution is built to solve the exact problems that the group faces. It will fit with the existing environment, platforms, and methods. The cost is in time rather than in capital expense, which can be important in environments with little money to spend but a lot of people. Universities in particular often lean toward building systems from scratch because of their tight budgets and nearly endless supply of cheap labor. Another benefit of custom solutions is that they sometimes turn into products, or reseller/OEM deals are made, or the authors gain fame through publishing their work either on the Internet or at conferences such as LISA. The pride of creating original software can motivate the team.

Support after the initial team has gone away is a separate issue. Custom solutions can become a support nightmare after the programmers have left the group or graduated. On the other hand, commercial software vendors tend to continue to support the current versions of their applications until the company is bought by a competitor or goes bankrupt.

There are positive and negative points on both sides, so how does the technical manager make this decision? She must look at how she values what each method brings.

We already discussed that the prime reason for buying a solution is the faster time to availability. The prime reason for building a solution in-house is the ability to get features that aren't available externally. She must take an introspective look at why those features are required. Forgoing commercial software for a minor reason, personal biases, or antivendor feelings is just plain wrong. On the other hand, sometimes a required feature is not available elsewhere because nobody has thought of it before. Developing a system in-house is worthwhile if you will receive value that commercial systems could not provide. This may lead to a competitive advantage.

Case Study: Building a Competitive Advantage

A manufacturer of Pentium-compatible CPUs was able to beat Intel's own ship date for a particular speed of processor because they had developed a batch scheduling system in-house that let them easily do large volumes of compute-intensive work. When the chip was announced, they attributed their success to this custom solution; they couldn't have achieved this with commercial batch schedulers available at the time.

A competitive advantage typically does not last long in our fast-paced computer industry. That should be taken into account as part of the decision process. A few months of being ahead of the game is often enough to gain a significant commercial advantage, though.

Advantages Are Short-Term
At the USENIX Large Installation System Administration (LISA) conference one year, someone asked, "What's the incentive to submit a paper to LISA when it means that our competitors will then be able to learn our secret weapon?" Someone from the above-mentioned chip company stood up and explained that they were permitted to publish a description of the batch-processing system because they knew that by the time the LISA conference rolled around (six months after the paper was submitted and a year after the chip had shipped), the competition would already have caught up and would be using such a system.

Custom solutions are common when an idea is new enough that commercial solutions are not yet available. However the technical manager must pay attention to emerging commercial products and learn to acknowledge when a custom solution has been surpassed by one. For example, when UNIX was new, it was considered interesting and innovative to write yet another system for managing backups. Now, however, this is considered a "solved problem" for small sites and too complicated to build in-house for large sites.

Although the ability to gain original features is appealing, it is generally a good idea for the technical manager not to assume that the site's needs are very specialized, and instead seek out commercial packages to see what's available. She will at least learn of features she may not otherwise have thought of, but may want to integrate or avoid. Along with reviewing the current popular products, she should also review the proceedings of SA conferences, particularly the USENIX and LISA conferences.[3]

When commercial packages are used, it can be valuable for the technical manager or a senior member of the team to partner with the vendor to influence development decisions toward the new features that her site most needs. In cutting-edge environments, it can be useful to say things such as, "If we need this feature this year, all your other customers will need it next year." Large companies can use their financial muscle to influence such decisions. However, when a partnership is created, it is important to clearly define who owns the ideas; there may be intellectual property issues to consider.

The "buy versus build" decision is one that comes up often, and yet there is no universal right answer. It comes down to issues of time, level of customization, and availability of features. As an industry matures, there are more commercial options. But the satisfaction of implementing your own brilliant idea cannot be overstated.

28.2 The Icing

So, your group is now running smoothly, you have made the decisions you need to make, and you have all your responsibilities under control. What's next? We suggest some ways to make your team stronger. But more importantly, now that you have figured out how to keep your staff, management, and customers all happy, it's time to spare some thought for yourself. Work on your own career growth. Think about whether there is something that you can do to give yourself a bit of extra job satisfaction.

28.2.1 Make Your Team Even Stronger

Consider ways to make the team stronger. Encourage teamwork and give employees an opportunity to learn by getting them to collaborate on larger projects. Get them to write conference papers together. Organize fun social events and include their families. Something like a "pot luck" dinner in a park, to which everyone brings something for the group to eat, can improve their job satisfaction and relationships with others in the group. However, make sure that some people aren't left out of these events because of on-call

---

[3]Available at `http://www.usenix.org/`.

support obligations or other work-related reasons. If someone is left out, he starts to feel isolated, unimportant, and not part of the team.

The longer people stay with the group and the less turnover there is, the more they will feel part of the team and the more likely they are to stick with it through hard times. Figure out ways to retain your employees. Just as important as employee retention is hiring the right people. Make sure that the people you hire are good team fits. One bad fit can have a very bad effect on a group.

28.2.2   Sell Your Department to Senior Management

Make sure that senior management knows what your group does and how they benefit the company. The more visible your group is, and particularly the more visibly successful your group is, the more chance you have of getting the resources to help your staff do their jobs and reward them for their work. Make sure that senior managers know about your group's contributions to major projects around the company. If someone works crazy hours to ensure that a demonstration at a conference or to a customer works flawlessly, make sure the person gets credit and recognition for it. When your group introduces new services or upgrades an existing service, make sure senior managers understand how it improves others' efficiency and saves the company money. Chapter 26 details ways to make the group's successes visible. It is vital to the ongoing success of the group that senior management recognizes the group as an asset to the company.

28.2.3   Work on Your Own Career Growth

Having helped everyone who works for you, spare a thought for yourself. Make sure that you get the recognition that you deserve for your own accomplishments, as well as the reflected glory of your group's successes. Learn about the company's business so that you can relate better to your group's customers and make better decisions about which requests should take priority. Learn about business management so that you can relate better to the nontechnical managers in your management chain. Understand what they are looking for and why, so that you can meet their needs, and they will gain confidence in you and your team.

28.2.4   Do Something You Enjoy

Last but not least, consider how to keep yourself satisfied in the role of technical manager. Find a way to give yourself a task that you will enjoy as a break from your normal routine. For most technical managers, this means taking on some low-profile, low-urgency technical projects. A bit of technical work will provide a nice break from your other tasks, and it will help to keep you in touch with technology and the sorts of tasks that your staff perform day to day. Don't take on too much, however. Doing some technical work is the icing on the cake, but everything else must take priority.

28.3 Conclusion

The position of a technical manager is that of a person who is expected to be both a senior SA and a manager. As a senior SA, she mentors more junior members of her group and acts as a technical resource for the group. As a manager, she needs to manage the budget, deal with contracts, and work with her managers and customers to try to keep everyone happy and her group going in the same direction as the rest of the company.

She is a role model and vision leader for her employees. She is the person to whom her management looks for information on what the SAs are doing. She is the person the customers' managers talk to for negotiating schedules and resource allocations for their projects.

Her primary responsibility is to keep her staff's morale high. To do that she needs to treat them with respect and reward them for good work. She needs to keep them informed but not overwhelm them with ever-changing whims of other groups. She needs to support her team and protect them from the wrath of disappointed customers, but also help them to improve in the future. She needs to promote their technical development and steer them along their career paths.

She is also required to make some decisions on behalf of the group. She needs to decide on the division of responsibilities within the group. She needs to recognize when she needs more staff and decide what roles the new staff members need to fill for the group. She also has to decide whether they should buy commercial solutions to solve particular problems or whether her staff should build the solution themselves.

She also needs to take care of herself. She should make time for herself and do something that she enjoys, such as taking on a low-priority technical project that she can work on as a break from everything else.

People new to management might be interested in *The One Minute Manager* by D. Kenneth Blanchard (1993) and a related book, *The One Minute Manager Meets the Monkey* by William Oncken, Jr., and Hal Burrows (Oncken et al. 1991). Both are short but extremely useful books.

Exercises

1. What attitude do you role model for the rest of your team to emulate?

2. Who was the best technical manager you ever had and why? What faults did that person have?

3. Who was the worst technical manager you ever had and why? What assets did that person have as your manager?

4. If you are a technical manager, what do you think you are doing well? What areas do you think you could improve?

5. Describe a group you worked in that had high morale. What factors do you think contributed to the high morale?

6. Describe a group you worked in that had low morale. What factors do you think contributed to the low morale?

7. Describe a situation in which the morale in the group you were working in dropped significantly. What factors do you think precipitated the fall in morale?

8. What do you do to let your staff know that you appreciate their work?

9. What are you doing to help your staff's technical development? Is technical development adequately funded for your group?

10. Describe your relationship with your (nontechnical) manager. What were (or are) the primary difficulties you needed to overcome to make it a successful working relationship?

11. What kinds of rewards are given in your group? Based on the discussion in Section 28.1.1, are they being properly administered? What are the positive or negative results of these bonuses or perks?

12. What do you consider your primary responsibilities?

13. Describe a situation in which you had to make the "buy versus build" decision and you chose to "buy." Why did you make that choice? With hindsight, was it the right choice?

14. Describe a situation in which you had to make the "buy versus build" decision and you chose to "build." Why did you make that choice? With hindsight, was it the right choice?

15. Describe the division of responsibilities in your group. Is there anything that you think should be changed?

16. What do you do to treat yourself and keep enjoying your work?

Chapter 29

A Guide for Nontechnical Managers

This chapter looks at the relationship between nontechnical managers and the senior technical staff in the system administration organization. It examines the relationship between the SA staff and their management chain, as well as the relationships between the managers of the customer base and the senior technical SA staff. In particular, this chapter is geared for the nontechnical manager to which the system administration organization reports.

Both the SAs and the managers have certain expectations of and responsibilities to each other. To form a good relationship, both parties must understand what those expectations and responsibilities are and how to meet them. Good relationships are based on mutual respect and good communication. This chapter includes techniques that encourage both.

This chapter does not look at system administration organizational structures, the strengths and weaknesses of the centralized and decentralized models, or how they affect the team. Those issues are also of interest to the nontechnical manager and are covered in Chapters 14 and 25.

29.1   The Basics

The primary goal of the nontechnical manager in a technical system administration organization is to keep morale high. When morale is high, the technical staff will do whatever is needed of them, even if it involves constant heroics and late nights. When morale drops, they will be no longer willing to put everything into a job that they find depressing and unrewarding. The relationship between the technical organization and its management is a key part of the technical staff's morale.

All relationships are founded on communication, and the relationships that nontechnical managers have with the senior technical staff are no exception. We will look at ways how the nontechnical manager can help to improve communication with the technical staff. We will look at both interpersonal communication and the role that staff meetings can play.

Providing SAs with opportunities to participate in professional development activities, such as conferences and training courses, is a necessary part of increasing their job satisfaction. SAs need to keep in touch with ever-changing technologies, and they typically enjoy doing so.

To work well together, the SA team and their manager need to have a shared vision. He should expect his senior technical staff to provide a one-year vision for each of their areas of expertise. He should give them the information and direction they require to create such a plan. He should use this information in his budget process and involve senior SAs throughout the entire budget and planning process. He should keep them in the loop on the decision-making process. Doing so can be a beneficial experience for everyone. It helps the SAs understand the direction of the company and makes them feel involved and invested in the outcome.

29.1.1   Morale

System administration is often very stressful. There can be an ever-increasing stack of work, clashing deadlines, some irate customers, lots of little crises, and occasional big emergencies. SAs need to spend time communicating with others, yet the stack of work is telling them to work continuously. This high-stress work life makes SAs very sensitive to the atmosphere at work and to feeling under-appreciated. A good nontechnical manager should figure out how to guide the group with a light hand and prevent outside influences from disturbing their workflow or upsetting morale.

The nontechnical manager should hand his staff problems, not solutions. The senior technical staff expect to be given high-level direction by their nontechnical managers, to be trusted to achieve those goals, and to give periodic progress reports. Micro-management of projects distracts, slows down, and demoralizes SAs, as it does other technical staff. They also expect their managers to assist in clearing any roadblocks they may encounter in trying to meet their goals and to fight for adequate funding so that the SAs can complete their projects and achieve the service levels expected of them. The nontechnical manager should also aim to act as a filter and a buffer for the technical staff to screen them from the stress of knowing all the things that might happen but don't, while giving them enough advance warning of the projects that do happen.

The manager is the enabler. He enables his employees to do their jobs, while keeping the worst of the politics out of their way. A nontechnical manager should never try to make or direct technical decisions. When he has to override a technical decision for political reasons, he should explain to his people what the reasons were and why he did it or they will resent him and morale will plummet.

An uncertain future can completely destroy morale. Why work when you may lose your job? Why do a complete solution (with good documentation, reliability engineering, and so on) when you think the group will not be around in a couple of months? Why do any long-term planning when the long-term plan for the group keeps changing? In a large company, rumors of reorganizations, layoffs, changes, and shuffles are constant. It is the nontechnical manager's job to be the shield that prevents these rumors from getting to the SA team. He should keep those potential changes in mind and inform senior staff members when a change looks probable. But he should only make it general knowledge after the decision has been made. Even if he is the person who must consider these potential corporate improvements, he must project an image of a solid future or employees will leave left and right. It is important, however, not to give false or misleading assurances, or the staff will not trust him.

Case Study: Uncertainty Is Bad for Morale

A new manager didn't realize the importance of projecting a solid future and discussed every rumored change with his senior SAs. Every thought and notion about budget cuts, increases, shuffles, and reorganizations was discussed with the senior SAs. Soon, everyone in the group was convinced that management was out to kill their group, planned to downsize the company, was unhappy with them, and so on. Why would management be proposing these changes if they weren't unhappy with the team? The reality is that it is management's job to always be thinking in terms of making changes that benefit the company. The previous managers had dealt with the same issues, but hadn't exposed the SA team to any but the most likely situations. Thus what the SA team saw was years of feeling like they had a solid and predictable future, but now a year of constant threats of change. In reality, the changes actually happened at the same rate, but the perception was that there was less certainty of their future. SAs started leaving the team one by one. When certain senior SAs left, upper management panicked and had to educate the manager about the effect he was having.

This is not to say that management should make major decisions in a vacuum, without the consultation of the senior SAs, but a balance must be achieved.

The SA team needs to know that they can count on their manager for support. If he does not establish this reputation, they will leave for a company where they can get that support.

Support the Team

A manager sent a clear message to his team. An SA repairing one hard drive on a workstation accidentally reformatted a different drive on the machine. The data that had been deleted was data that had been collected in the field over the last two years and was not being backed up—two years' data that could not be regenerated. Realizing that the situation could spin out of control, the manager took the SA (who was nearly suicidal with fear) out of the loop immediately. He met with the customers, explained what had happened, and took responsibility for the team's mistake. The customers were appropriately angry at the situation, but the manager stood up for his team. Having data on a workstation was against policy: all data was to be kept on the servers where backups were done. The disks had been attached to the workstation years ago and only with the agreement that the customers acknowledged that the data wouldn't be backed up, and thus should only be used for temporary files and as a workspace. The SA's manager agreed to pay the full cost of a disk repair service, even though they would charge a high fee whether they were successful or not (they weren't). The customers were not happy, but they respected the manager for sticking up for his team (the fact that he was built like a football player may have helped here). The SA was not publicly punished for what he had done. The week of living in fear for his job was certainly punishment enough, and we can assume that the SA's yearly performance review was to be affected by this. The manager knew that the SA had learned his lesson and never talked about the incident except to say, "I'm sure you've learned a lot from this and will be more careful in the future."

The manager's actions spoke louder than words: Honest mistakes are part of the job, and his staff will receive his support if they work hard, are careful, and own up to their mistakes.

29.1.2   Communication

Technical staff often can experience a language problem when talking to people who are not familiar with their area of expertise. This problem can lead to a breakdown in communication. Typically, the technical staff will develop the habit of using vague generalities that mask the details rather than give details that may mean little to the listener. The senior technical staff should be coached to learn the language of their nontechnical managers and customers and to use that language in their conversations with their managers and customers. That language is based on the requirements behind the work that the technical staff are doing. The SAs should know the requirements that govern their work, base their decisions around those requirements, and discuss the project's progress in relation to those requirements.

29.1.3 Staff Meetings

Formal staff meetings between SAs and their nontechnical manager help to keep the SAs in touch with what is happening in their group and within the company as a whole. Such quarterly meetings can be an opportunity for the manager to communicate the direction that he wants the group to move, yet empower them to decide how to meet those goals. These meetings require planning. He should meet with the senior SAs and script how the meeting should go. Just as he may not understand the SAs' technical jargon, they have an equally difficult time understanding "management speak" and management's perspective. It is critical to review with a senior SA how various ideas will be presented so that they are understood and, more importantly, so that negative triggers are avoided. A bold statement that is meant to be empowering can be a disastrous demoralizing announcement when interpreted by SA ears. Discussing the outline (or "script") for the meeting with an SA will avoid that problem.

Rehearse Executive Visits to Avoid Disasters

A company vice president once met with the SA team with the intention of showing his support for the group. The meeting went very well until his last comment, when he unwittingly stepped into an area of hot debate. Whereas the previous 45 minutes had gone swimmingly, the last 15 minutes were spent deflecting anger about the topic. The VP didn't think the topic was significant and didn't realize how emotional it was for the team. He ended up looking like he didn't care about the SAs. The meeting was such a disaster that the senior SAs called a team meeting later that day to try to recover from the damage done. They were not successful, and it took weeks to recover from the meeting. In that time, both a senior and a junior SA left the group. All of this could have been avoided if the VP had met with the senior SAs beforehand. Tom's high school drama teacher always used to say, "Never do anything in performance you haven't done in rehearsal." The VP would have benefited greatly from that advice.

The nontechnical manager also should encourage the team to have regular, weekly meetings to maintain cohesion on technical issues. These meetings should function as opportunities for SAs to seek help from others, or to become involved in projects or standards on which others in the group are working. These meetings can be a valuable way to keep the group united, involved, and happy.

SAs, like most people, want to know what is going on around them at work and to participate at least a little in projects that affect, or simply interest, them. Because many SAs, particularly those in direct customer support roles, spend most of their time working with customers rather than other SAs, they can feel isolated from the SA team. It is important to make them a part of the team and to involve them in the direction that the SA group takes in new technologies and standards. Regular staff meetings are a good way for SA managers to keep their teams unified and informed. These meetings enable team members to find out what others are working on, what issues or projects others anticipate, and where they can look for feedback on certain ideas or help with problems. The staff meeting should keep the SAs up-to-date with anything important that is happening elsewhere in the company. It can be used as a forum for regularly reminding SAs of important policies, procedures that should be followed, or internal standards.

These meetings are also useful because they may be one of the few times that front-line support people interact with back-line support or engineering. It is common at these meetings for back-line support to learn of systemic problems that they need to solve for the front-line personnel. It is also an opportunity for senior technical leads to educate the rest of the group on technical issues.

Case Study: Use Staff Meetings for Knowledge Transfer

One SA team that has weekly meetings includes a 20-minute segment during which a senior SA explains some technical aspect of how their enterprise works. This gives senior SAs experience with presenting information and cross-trains the entire group on technical issues.

29.1.4   Look for One-Year Plans

An SA's work is by nature composed of lots of small tasks and a few large ones. As a result, it is easy for an SA to lose sight of the big picture of what is happening in the company and the corresponding direction that her own work should take. Drawing up one-year plans periodically can help to bring the big picture back into focus. It also helps the SA's manager and customers to plan better for the coming year.

Nontechnical managers should expect their senior technical staff to have a vision of the direction in which the company's computing environment is heading. The senior technical staff should anticipate new service requirements and necessary upgrades and should be thinking of ways to optimize SA tasks or otherwise improve service. A senior SA should always be looking at least a year ahead and planning the projects for the coming year so that they are evenly spaced out rather than all needed at once.

Of course, unexpected projects, such as a merger or acquisition, will always crop up, but the wise senior SA will be expecting the unexpected and will have leeway in her project schedule to accommodate those situations.

The nontechnical manager should require the senior technical staff to have a one-year plan and to keep him apprised of it. It gives him the opportunity to figure out what, if any, money is available for those SA projects. It also gives him a chance to find the funding for the projects from groups who have an interest in seeing them succeed.

29.1.5   Technical Staff and the Budget Process

Even better than the senior SAs having a one-year plan is involving the senior SAs in the budget process. Senior SAs should be able to build a detailed expenditure plan for the coming year using their one-year plan, their knowledge of day-to-day maintenance and growth issues, time scales for implementing projects, and staff availability.

Involving the senior SAs in the budget process gives them a forum for expressing their vision for their areas. It helps the manager to build a better budget by making him aware of all the projects, growth, and maintenance expenditures that the senior SAs foresee, rather than being surprised by them when an SA suddenly needs to spend money on something critical.

It gives the SAs an opportunity to explain what they need and why and to have some control over the funding in their areas. It also gives them some insight into one aspect of management, which may be helpful for those SAs who are interested in becoming managers.

Include Technical Staff in the Budget Process

A manager of the infrastructure team at Synopsys included the architect for each technology area in his budget process. When budget time was approaching, he asked his architects to build a list of projects and ongoing growth and maintenance work that they would like their groups to accomplish in the coming financial year. They had to prioritize that list. For each item, they had to estimate capital and noncapital expenditure and head count that would be required to meet that goal. They had to divide that expenditure into the quarters of the fiscal year in which they anticipated it would be spent. He also told them to draw a line through the list. Items above the line had to happen, items below the line would be good things to accomplish, but were not critical.

He took these lists and used them to compile his own prioritized list, grouping some individual items into a single line item and then drawing the line where he believed it should be. He also added salary and other information that only he had access to or responsibility for. That list was given to the director of the group, who compiled his list from all of his sources, and so on.

The manager discussed his compiled list with all the architects, using it as a vehicle to keep the architects of the different areas in touch with what the other infrastructure areas were doing. As the budget process progressed, he kept the architects informed of the progress of the list and their line items. This level of involvement helped the architects to see a bigger picture of what was happening in the company and to understand why some budget items received funding and others did not. It also gave the architects a plan to follow for the coming year and let them decide, before problems could arise, how to cope without things that they felt were critical but which did not get funded.

The quarter-by-quarter budget should be used to check the group's progress against its goals. Putting this information onto a budget spreadsheet and making it available to everyone helps people to see what is going on in other areas. If something unexpected arises during the year, the managers can use the spreadsheet to figure out how to find the funding for it.

At some companies, it is important to spend the allocated money in the early part of the year because the budget can get cut during the year, taking away most or all of the unspent money. In companies such as this, the SAs should plan to spend the latter part of the year working on projects that do not require new equipment or that use equipment that was bought earlier in the year.

Some companies also automatically deduct a certain amount from every budget request. For example, the senior managers might look at the list of projects from the SA group that they believe are reasonable and then deduct 25 percent from the requested amount. This approach to budgets is cultural within the company, and so everyone who knows about it then pads the budget by that amount to make sure that they get the amount they need. In such a company, it is important to recognize that budget cutting and padding go on. The nontechnical manager should make sure that he understands what the group's real needs are and should make sure that he does the right thing to meet those needs. If necessary, he should add in some projects that he can justify, but that the group can manage without.

Once the budget has been decided on and allocated to the group, it is important that the nontechnical manager delegates the responsibility for completing the funded tasks and the authority for spending the budget to the technical manager. If the technical manager is given the responsibility, but not the authority, to spend the budget, she will become frustrated and eventually leave. Nothing is more demeaning than to be given the responsibility for something without the authority required to achieve the goal.

29.1.6 Professional Development

Providing SAs with professional development opportunities is one of the key ways of increasing their job satisfaction. It benefits the company to keep them up-to-date on the latest technologies and methods for solving problems that they face in their day-to-day work. It also benefits the company to improve the SAs' skills and to keep them up-to-date with developments in, and the direction of, the industry. Professional development includes attending relevant conferences, taking appropriate courses, and having well-stocked bookshelves. The nontechnical manager of the SA team should make sure that each employee has some funding available to use for professional development.

Managers should encourage the technical staff to attend conferences and courses to improve their skills. They should be conscious of the different value proposition of one-day workshops versus week-long conferences. One-day workshops and training programs tend to be tactical, focusing on a particular technology or skill. Week-long conferences are strategic, offering opportunities to discuss broader topics.

Attending conferences enables the SA to keep in touch with the industry through formal presentations, vendor exhibitions, and simply talking to peers from many different backgrounds to learn from their experiences. The benefits of the so-called "hallway track" at conferences, where attendees share problems and ideas, cannot be overemphasized. A conference or training course is very intensive, but it also gives SAs some distance and perspective on their work, which can also help with sticky problems. Training should be off-site so that it is not interrupted. Ideally, both conferences and training should be out of town to give the SAs a chance to concentrate on professional development undisturbed. They should even be able to turn off their cell-phones and pagers during sessions.

Junior SAs often benefit more from attending taught courses than conferences. Some specialized taught courses can also be useful to senior SAs. In addition to the content of the course, it enables the senior SA to dedicate uninterrupted time (that they would otherwise be unable to find) to thinking about a particular technology in depth.

Many system administration tasks require an in-depth understanding of a protocol or how a particular technology works. It is impossible for an SA to keep all the details of every protocol and technology in his head, so he needs to have access to a good reference library at all times. Each SA should own the books that he uses most often, and, ideally, the company should also have a large collection of system administration books available for reference.

We like to see companies allocate an allowance for each employee to spend on professional development each year. It covers some conferences, courses, and book purchasing for each SA. This approach ensures that all SAs can benefit from a development opportunity. Get the SAs involved in choosing how they want to use their allocation and encourage them to make use of it. Professional development is in everybody's best interests, and positive encouragement makes the SAs feel appreciated and a valuable part of the company.

Professional development is also discussed in Section 27.1.4.

29.2   The Icing

When the basics of good relationships with the technical staff are covered, the nontechnical manager can consider a couple of things to get those relationships moving along even more smoothly. Rather than just developing a detailed one-year plan, the technical manager should encourage the technical staff to sketch out a five-year plan, too. He should consider how to incorporate their five-year plans into the annual budget process to ensure that the funds they need for their projects arrive when they need them.

The technical manager should also set up relationships between each customer-oriented technical staff member and one of their customers who can act as a single point of contact for the whole group. He should have the SA schedule regular meetings with that person to track hot topics and have the customer representative assist the SA in prioritizing tasks for the customer group and resolving priority clashes between people in the group.

The nontechnical manager also should try to learn about what the technical staff in his group do. He does not need to become an expert in those technical fields, but an understanding of their work will help communication with staff and customers.

29.2.1   Have a Five-Year Vision

In Chapter 3, we mentioned that when an SA builds a service, she should try to build it so that it will last for three to five years. The corollary is that she will need to upgrade services about once every three to five years. Somehow rebuilding and upgrading services needs to fit in between all the other projects that she has to do, and she still needs to have time for day-to-day maintenance and customer support.

Planning SA projects five years out is a good way to make sure that they all happen at reasonable times. Five years out? "But we don't know what's going to happen next week!" Actually there are many long-term issues to be concerned with. Network technology tends to change enough to require new wiring every 5 to 10 years. The fast server they installed this year will be the slowest server in five years, if the machine still exists. Long-term strategies that plan on machines being replaced or upgraded at certain intervals should be reconsidered based on how the technology is evolving. Upgrades should be performed before the service starts falling apart. In many workplaces, it can sometimes take a few years of looking for budget allocation for a particular new service or upgrade before it is approved. Starting to ask for the money before the team really needs it can be a good way to make sure the projects happen at a reasonable time. Obviously, the group needs the five-year plan if the nontechnical manager is to look for money ahead of time. Be careful not to allocate the money before it can reasonably be used, however, or you risk losing it and not getting the budget for other projects in the future.

Case Study: Time Budget Requests Well

The senior network administrator at Synopsys had project scheduling and budget requests down to a fine art. He became good at predicting how many years he would need to request a budget for a particular item before it was allocated. He could predict how many times his management team would put a given project "below the line" before they would get worried by how long they had been refusing this new service or upgrade and put it above the line. He planned projects and started looking for money for them far enough in advance so that he was always able to do the projects at the right time.

The nontechnical manager should take the five-year plan for each group, plus his knowledge of the budget process, and prepare senior management for the upcoming projects, rather than each senior technical person trying to do so.

Another aspect of the five-year plan is having technical staff who are able to predict what new, up-and-coming technologies your company will want to use in the future, when the technologies will be mature enough to use, and when the customer demand for them will warrant the investment. Senior managers and customers will learn of a new technology and want to know when the company is going to provide that service. It is essential for the architects to stay on top of the new technologies and their maturities, so that they can help answer those questions sensibly and completely when asked. If an architect is unsure or can't give a good answer to the question, then the group may be pressured to deploy the technology before it is sufficiently reliable and supportable. On the other hand, the SAs gain a lot of credibility and can ease the pressure for the new technology if their manager is able to answer such questions with: "We expect the technology to have developed to the point where it will be useful and stable enough for our purposes in 18 months, and we have tentatively scheduled an evaluation project for that time. We will be looking for the resources for that evaluation project in our next year's budget." If he does give an answer like that, he will need to be able to substantiate the time claim and explain why the team believes it is not ready for the company's use just yet. The architect should be involved in the conversation so that she can provide the details that the manager needs.

Start-up and e-commerce companies may find it impossible to plan five years down the road if the company itself has only been around for a short time. However, in this situation the SAs are most likely much closer to the CEO and the vision of how the company will evolve. This can make it even easier to have a "vision" for the future than, say, at a large company where the SAs are buried five levels of management away from any kind of corporate strategic planning. If the company strategy is to be purchased by a bigger company, your five-year plan is not to invest too heavily in long-term infrastructure. If the strategy is to expand by opening sales offices around the world, then the group's plans can center around the different needs that such an environment would create (for example, building a WAN and a Network Operations Center). Even an amorphous vision of the future can give the team better direction than no plan at all.

29.2.2 Meetings with Single Point of Contact

In many places in this book, we emphasize communication between the SAs and their customers. Having regularly scheduled meetings with a single point of contact on the customers' team to track hot issues is a good way to formalize some of the communication. It does not replace the project-related, support-call related, or other ad hoc conversations that the SA has with her customers; instead, it adds to them. The manager of the system administration organization should push the customer organizations into designating a single point of contact and making these meetings happen.

These scheduled meetings act as a focal point for both the SA and her customers. Before each meeting, both people should take some time on their own and with colleagues on their respective teams to consider what projects, maintenance, or problems the other party should know about. In the meetings, the status of previous issues should be tracked, and new topics should be discussed and added to the list. The SA can also use the list to prioritize tasks with the customer and to set realistic goals for new projects.

These meetings provide the customers with a valuable insight into what their SAs are working on. They give the customers status information on large projects and help them to understand why some of their jobs might be completed later than they would like. It allows someone in the customers' department to use his knowledge of his group's work to set priorities. The people in the group who have conflicting deadlines have to decide among themselves what their priorities are and communicate that to the SAs through their point of contact. This prioritization technique should result in the right decisions being made for the company, gives the responsibility for making those decisions to the right people, and sets the expectations for the customers from the outset. When SAs are forced to prioritize tasks without feedback from someone who is ultimately in charge of all the projects that rely on those tasks, they can make the wrong decisions, or end up trying to accomplish everything in an impossible time-frame.

The meetings actually save SAs' and the customers' time by avoiding frequent "status check" emails and conversations for the myriad tasks that the SAs are working on. The customers know what to expect and when to expect it, and they can quickly get a status update from their single point of contact or possibly through a web page, if the SAs track status there. The meetings are also a trust- and confidence-building exercise. No one likes throwing tasks into a black hole and hoping that they will be completed—or worse, expecting that they won't be.

Case Study: Weekly Meetings with Customers Save Time

One senior SA reluctantly began having weekly meetings with each department head in the cluster of groups that he supported. Initially the meetings took an hour, but eventually turned into short, 15-minute status updates as things settled down. When a large change was coming or if there was a problem, the meetings would increase in length until the issue was resolved. The meetings helped keep the SA focused on what was important to the customers, yet also helped educate the customers about things that were important to the SA (taking a little longer on certain projects to make sure they would scale or could be better supported, and so on). The result was that customer satisfaction increased dramatically because they felt the SAs were listening to them. The SA was happier in his job because he was receiving positive feedback. One day the SA told the person that had encouraged him to have these meetings that he was sorry he had resisted them. "I have the same work load and I'm doing the same amount of work, yet the customers are much happier and I'm much happier. Mathematically that doesn't make sense! It's magic!" Yes, it is.

Sometimes, customers will resist these meetings. Some will totally reject the idea. In time, they will hear from their peers how useful the meetings are for them and change their mind. Alternatively, you may choose other ways to increase communication with them. A department head once rejected the suggestion and said, "I'm happy with what you do. If something is wrong, don't I complain?" In fact, that person had a very good sense of what his own time management needs were and was very good about bringing issues to the SA rather than letting them smolder. Some people like the push model; some people like the pull model.

Not everyone can realistically have a single point of contact, however. SAs who are responsible for company-wide infrastructure, for example, can't expect one person in the company to be able to identify everyone's needs or mediate in their priority negotiations. These SAs should gather all the infrastructure-related issues from the SAs who serve the customer base more directly. They will need to do their own prioritization with the help of their management. In sensitive cases, they can bring together the single points of contact from the groups with conflicting requirements and look for them to come to some resolution. The manager of the system administration organization should also be available to help with such issues.

29.2.3   Understand the Technical Staff's Work

A nontechnical manager should make his best effort to understand what his technical staff does. He does not need to become an expert in the field, but rather should understand and appreciate what tasks they undertake and what is involved in the things that he and their customers request of them.[1] He will be better able to communicate with the technical staff and the group's customers if he understands what his staff does. Customers expect a certain level of knowledge from the nontechnical manager in charge of the group. He should try not to disappoint them because it will reflect on his group. He will also be better able to represent the group's budget needs to

---

[1] This book might be a good place to start for a nontechnical manager who wants to understand what SAs do!

senior management and better able to negotiate with senior managers and customers on behalf of the group, if he understands his employees' jobs. He will make better decisions with this knowledge. The team will be happier with the way he represents them and will also appreciate any effort he makes to understand what they do.

Learning Helps

One manager found himself managing a group of technical people whose jobs entailed things that he had never been involved with before. He had a good relationship with them, but it noticeably improved when he did some reading about their jobs and demonstrated this new understanding to them.

29.3   Conclusion

A successful working relationship between nontechnical managers and the senior technical SA staff is built around communication and mutual respect. The nontechnical manager's job is to maintain morale by shielding the SA team from political issues and supporting them by going to bat for them in both good times and bad. Managers should keep SAs in the loop about what is happening in the company, particularly the areas that relate to the SAs' work, but without speculating on every rumor. Formal meetings between the technical staff and their manager, and each SA and her customers' single point of contact, are good ways to stay in touch.

Advance planning through one-year and five-year plans gives managers and customers confidence in the SAs and valuable insight into the work that they do. It also gives the managers the opportunity to look for budget allocations for the projects that the SAs foresee, rather than having to veto the projects regularly because of lack of funding. Involving the senior SAs in the budget process gives them insight into the way it works, which can aid their planning and give them good experience.

Exercises

1. What is your group's one-year plan? How well does the budget match it? How can you improve upon that?

2. How has your company invested in the professional development of the SA staff in the last three years? How do you think it should progress in the coming years?

3. What conferences would your technical staff like to attend? How can you distribute conference attendance fairly without jeopardizing your SA coverage during those conferences?

4. If you have regular staff meetings, do you keep your staff informed and cover the topics your team is interested in? How would you improve the meetings? If you don't have regular meetings, what would you use as an agenda for setting them up and how often would you hold them?

5. Get your senior staff to sketch out a five-year plan. How much do you think each of the projects on that list will cost?

6. Based on the five-year plan and what you know of your budget process, when will you start looking for funding for each project?

7. Look at each of the customer organizations. Who would be the ideal single point of contact for your SAs in each organization? If you do not already have a single point of contact scheme set up, try setting up a test relationship and arranging regular status meetings between the appropriate SA and the single point of contact.

8. Section 29.1.1 contained an anecdote that involved defending the SA team even though a disastrous mistake had been made. Relate a similar situation that you have been in or describe what you would have done if you were the manager in the anecdote.

Chapter 30

Hiring System Administrators

This chapter looks at hiring system administrators (SAs). It focuses on areas that are different in some way from hiring other staff. These are the things that the system administration staff and managers need to know. Everything else should be taken care of by the HR department.

This chapter does not cover areas of hiring that are generic and apply across the board. For example, it does not cover compensation packages, on-call compensation, overtime pay, compensation (comp) time, or traditional incentive schemes such as stock options, hiring bonuses, and performance bonuses. It doesn't look at how location, lifestyle, working from home, facilities for remote work, or training and conferences can factor into the hiring process.

It does cover the basics of how to recruit and interview SAs and how to retain SAs. It also looks at some things a company can do to stand out as a fun company for which to work.

30.1 The Basics

The hiring process can be simplified into two stages. The first stage is to identify the people whom you want to hire. The second stage is to persuade them that they want to work for you.

The first stage, identifying whom you want to hire, is in many ways the most complicated. To determine if you want to hire someone, you must first know what you want the new hire to do and how skilled the person needs to be. Then you need to recruit appropriate candidates to get resumes from interested, qualified SAs. Then you need to pick the interview team and make sure they are briefed appropriately on the interview process and determine who is tasked with finding out what information. The interviewers need to know how to interview the candidates in the particular areas of interest and how to treat the candidate during the interview process.

The second stage, persuading the candidate to work for you, actually overlaps a little with the first. The most important part of recruiting the candidate is doing the interview process well. The interviewers should show the best of the company and the position to the candidate, and the experience should make him want to work there. The timing also needs to be right; move quickly for the right candidates. We will end with tips on how to avoid hiring by retaining staff.

30.1.1   Job Description

Although time consuming, it is worthwhile to write a job description specific to every position. A written job description is a communication tool. Writing it is a catalyst that encourages team members to express their visions for the position, resolve differences, and settle on a clear definition. Once written, it communicates to potential candidates what the job is about. During the interview, it communicates a focus to the interviewers. When having to decide between two similarly qualified candidates, the job description serves to focus the decision makers on what is being sought.

There are two competing philosophies related to filling an open position. One is called *hire the skill.* That means look for someone with the exact skills specified in the job description. Years later you intend to find this person doing the exact same job he was hired to do, without variation. The other philosophy is called *hire the person.* That means look for quality people and hire them, even if their specific skills only overlap what's listed in the job description. If you "hire the person," you are hiring them for their intelligence, creativity, and imagination, even if they lack some of the specific credentials associated with their job. These people may surprise you by changing a job so dramatically that the effort required is much less and the results are much better. They may do this through the elimination of unnecessary tasks, automating mundane tasks, and finding publicly available resources that accomplish the task. It is easier to "hire the person" when you have many open positions, each requiring a different set of skills. If the first quality person you find has a few skills from each job description, you can redefine the position around that person. The next person you look for should have the remaining skills.

We tend to find ourselves mostly hiring senior-level SAs in such large quantities that we almost exclusively "hire the person." We only recommend "hiring the skill" in specific strategic instances.

Case Study: "Hire the Skill" Only Strategically

One SA team "hired the person" for certain roles and "hired the skill" for others. For example, the senior SAs were expected to find creative solutions for the problems at hand. For those positions, they "hired the person." On the other hand, they had a league of technicians that deployed new PCs. They only needed to start automated procedures to load the OS and then deliver the fully configured computers to the right office. For that role, they found that "hiring the skill" worked best.

The hire-the-person strategy only works within limits. Make sure you actually have something for the person to do. One Silicon Valley computer company had a strategy of hiring people because they were great, on the assumption that they would find projects on their own and do wonderful things. However, many of these people just became lost, felt unwanted, and became extremely unhappy. Such a strategy works well for hiring researchers doing transformational work, but not when hiring SAs. Make sure they have a job description and just give them room to breathe.

Some candidates want to be very clear about what their job will be so that they can decide whether it is something they want to do and will enable them to advance their career goals. These candidates will reject an offer of a job when they are unclear as to what they will be doing. Other candidates want to know if there is flexibility in the job, so that they can gain experience in a variety of different areas. In both cases, the interviewers need to know what the job entails and where it can be flexible, so that both sides know whether the candidate will be suited to the job. Be flexible if there are multiple positions available. Some candidates may be perfect for part of one job and part of another. To be flexible, the interviewers should be aware of all of the requirements in all of the open job descriptions, so that they can talk to the candidate about other possibilities, if appropriate.

So, the first step in the hiring process is to determine why you need a new person and what it is that the person will be doing. Figure out what gaps you have in your organization. Chapter 25 describes organizational structures and how to build a well-rounded team. This should help you decide whom they should be working with and what skill-sets they should have to complement the existing team's skills. Then think about what roles you want the new employee to take on, as described in Appendix A. This should give you an idea of the personality type and the soft skills for which you are searching. From this list of requirements, figure out which are essential and which are desired. You now have a basis for the job description.

30.1.2   Skill Level

After building the basic job description, you should have a reasonable idea of the skill level required for the position. Map your notion of what you need to the SAGE skill levels described in their booklet *Job Descriptions for System Administrators* (Darmohray 1993). This is becoming the standard way of communicating such things in job descriptions, advertisements, and resumes.

The skill level of the person you hire has economic implications. Some organizations believe in hiring the lowest possible skill for first- and second-tier support to save money. The theory is that the position that they need the most of should be filled by dumb, inexpensive, and, if you'll excuse the expression, little more than trained monkeys. Other organizations have a different philosophy, which is to hire people who are smart and highly motivated and are on the verge of being overqualified for the position. These people will be bored with the repetitive tasks and will eliminate them by instituting automation or recommending process changes that will continually improve the organization. In essence, these people will gladly put themselves out of a job because they know that their motivation will lead to other positions in the organization.

A talented, motivated SA who verges on being overqualified is worth more than two unmotivated, unskilled SAs who are hired to just make up the numbers. The ideal candidate for the more junior position is bright, interested, and has recently entered the field. If you invest in people like this and give them opportunities to learn and do more, they will rapidly rise in skill levels, giving you ideal candidates for promotion into more senior positions that can be harder to fill. If you are lucky enough to hire people like this, make sure that their salaries and bonuses keep pace with their rising skill levels, even if it means pushing through special raises outside review periods. These people are valuable and hard to replace, and they will be hired away by another company if you do not keep pace. Giving them extra raises outside of review periods also builds loyalty for the long term.

30.1.3   Recruiting

Once you have decided what position you are trying to fill and what skill level you are looking for, you need to find appropriate candidates for the job. The best candidates are usually found through personal recommendations from members of the SA team or customers. A recommendation from a customer will usually lead to a candidate who is good at all aspects of the job, including customer interaction and follow-through.

System administration conferences are also good places to recruit candidates. It may be possible to do some interviewing at the conference, and it is also possible for the candidates to talk to members of the SA team to find out what they are like and what it is like to work at the company. SAs who attend these conferences are often good candidates because they are keeping up with what is happening in the field and are interested in learning.

Use technology if you want to attract people who appreciate technology. Several places on the Internet are designed exclusively for job posting, especially mailing lists and web sites. The company's own web site should advertise available positions. Some head-hunters who specialize in SA recruiting may have a useful database of SAs and the types of jobs that interest them. In our experience, technological methods are better than old-fashioned newspaper advertisements and signs in the window.

One problem that often arises in hiring SAs is that the HR staff does not really understand SA resumes or SA job descriptions the way SAs do. Excellent resumes often get rejected by HR before they are even seen by the SA team because the HR person does not recognize the resume as being good. This is particularly true if the company uses a computerized resume scanning and processing system. They typically code for keywords and are fine if you want to "hire the skill" but not if you want to "hire the person" (Darmohray 2001). The best way to make sure that good resumes do not get discarded is to have one HR person assigned to hiring SAs and to have SAs and SA managers team up with her to gain an understanding of how to identify good and bad resumes, what is relevant for one position or another, and so on. Eventually, the HR person should be able to go through the resumes and pick out all the good ones. The HR person will tend to focus on key words to look for, such as certifications, particular technologies, products, and brand names. We've had to explain terminology, such as the fact that IRIX, Solaris, and AIX all mean "UNIX." We've found it useful to give copies of the SAGE booklet (Darmohray 1993) to HR personnel. Once trained, the SA managers can let her do her job in peace and have confidence that they are not missing out on good candidates. The best recruiting campaign in the world will fail if the resumes do not get past the HR department. Reward the HR person whom you have trained when he succeeds. Make sure he is the first person in his department to receive computer upgrades. Make all the other HR staff want to be the next to be trained.

Sometimes, a recruiter or someone from HR is the first person to talk to the candidate and does a phone screen. It is important to make sure that this first contact goes well. A recruiter who knows what to look for in the resume should also know how to perform a phone screen.

Bad Phone-Screening Alienates a Candidate

A large software company phone-screened a candidate for a software development vacancy. The candidate had a research degree in computer science and some software development experience. The HR person who performed the phone-screen asked the candidate to rate her programming skills against the other people that she had worked with in the research group. She tried to explain that everyone in the group was good at programming, but that the ability to understand and solve the problems was the more important and relevant skill. Her interviewer didn't seem to understand what she was saying. At the end of the interview, the interviewer told her that it was interesting talking to her and that he had never spoken to a computer scientist (as opposed to a programmer) before. The candidate decided right then that there was no way she wanted to work for that company. Various recruiters and managers called her trying to persuade her that she was interested in the job several times after she told them that she was not interested in pursuing the job. They also displayed some corporate arrogance. Even after she told them she had accepted another job, they couldn't understand why she was not interested because *they* were interested in continuing to interview her. This attitude confirmed her decision not to work for that company.

If your company has an in-house recruiter, an education process should be instituted. The best recruiting campaign in the world will fail if potential candidates think your recruiter is an idiot.

30.1.4   Timing Is Everything

In hiring, timing is everything. Sometimes positions open up just after an excellent candidate has taken a position elsewhere, or the perfect candidate becomes available right after the job has been offered to someone else. Sometimes, the timing mismatch is unavoidable, but other times a company's inability to move quickly costs the company the chance of hiring the best candidates.

When trying to attract SAs into a company that is meant to be a high-tech, fun company, the company needs to be able to move quickly and make hiring decisions quickly. If a company delays too long in making its decision or has a long, drawn out interviewing process, the best candidates already will have accepted offers somewhere else. Some companies even write the offer letter before the candidate arrives, particularly if the candidate is being flown in from far away. The offer can be made on the spot, and the candidate can stay for an extra day or two to look at housing and schools if he wants.

A balance must be found between interviewing lots of candidates to find the best ones and moving quickly when a potentially suitable candidate is identified. Moving too slowly can result in losing the candidate to another company, but moving too quickly can result in hiring the wrong person.

Don't Rush a Hiring Decision

A mid-size software company needed to hire a network administrator to develop network tools. The team interviewed a candidate who was reasonably well qualified, but his experience was on different hardware. He already had an offer from another company. They knew that they had to make a decision quickly, but they were not sure about his skills or his team fit. They wanted to do another round of interviewing, but there was not enough time. They decided to offer him the job for fear that they would not get a better candidate and would regret losing the opportunity. He accepted the offer, and unfortunately he did not work out well in that position or with the team. The team was stuck with the bad decision that was made under time pressure. Given more time and another round of interviews, they may have decided against hiring him. Hiring a new employee is a long-term commitment; it pays to take the time to get the right person. If the person is genuinely interested, he will ask the other company for more time to make a decision, and they should give it to him for fear of losing him by forcing his hand. All parties should take the time they need and give the others that benefit.

Strike While the Iron's Hot

A Silicon Valley start-up went bankrupt and had to let all its employees go on a Friday morning. One of the people who was let go was a well-known SA. Several companies rushed to employ him. Over the course of the following week, he had first- and second-round interviews with a few companies, and at the end of the week he had several offers and made his decision. One of the companies that he decided against did not have the right people interview him and had not trained the employees well in the art of interviewing, because they unintentionally told him why he should not work there. Another company that was very interested in hiring him was unable to move as quickly as the others and failed to have him even interview with the necessary people before the end of the week.

To get good, well-known SAs, it is important to move very quickly. Slow companies lose—timing is everything.

30.1.5   Team Considerations

It is important to make sure that the person you are hiring will fit into the team. One aspect of this is making sure that there aren't any serious personality clashes. A personality clash can lead to people not enjoying their work and using their energy in a negative way that lowers morale in the team. Chapter 29 explains more about why low morale is bad for the team. The SAGE booklet, *Hiring System Administrators* (Phillips and LeFebvre 1998), contains an excellent discussion on the psychology of hiring and how every new person that joins the group changes the team dynamic.

Sometimes, the decision is difficult because there may not be any obvious personality clashes, but the candidate has a different style from the rest of the team. This is where careful consideration of the job description before trying to interview candidates should help. The candidate's style of working may be something that the team is lacking and, as a result, all the interviewers will be aware that it is a desirable quality.

The Dilbert® Check

One group always asked candidates to "relate the story line of your favorite Dilbert strip" as a way to see if the person would fit into their fun-loving culture. There was no "right answer," but a lot was learned from which strip the candidate selected. Sometimes it revealed the kind of coworker they didn't like to be with, which character they related to the most, or what their current job's work environment was like. Most important, it revealed whether the person could tell a joke. Nobody would be rejected solely on the basis of not being a Dilbert fan; however, it is interesting to note that there was one time they hired a candidate who had never heard of Dilbert and by some amazing coincidence the person didn't work out and was encouraged to find work elsewhere. We are not recommending that someone shouldn't be hired just because they haven't heard of Dilbert, just that they need special mentoring and a small budget to purchase the latest Scott Adams book.

The Other Dilbert® Check

One candidate always made a point of looking at the cartoons pinned outside the offices and cubicles of the company at which he was interviewing. People tend to find cartoons funnier when they resonate with what happens at their own company. Looking at the cartoons people liked gave him a good insight into what it was really like to work at the company.

Know What You Are Looking For

A mid-size company was trying to hire a second person for the security team. The system administration organization was a young, dynamic, fast-paced, fast-growing team. The security SA's manager gave her the responsibility for choosing the right partner for the security team. However, the manager did not provide direction or advice on what was lacking in the organization. She interviewed one candidate who was well qualified, but she decided against hiring him because she was unsure of the team fit. He was a steady, reliable worker who always carefully researched and considered all the options, whereas the rest of the SA team was made up of people who made quick decisions that were almost always good, but occasionally had negative repercussions. She was not sure how well he would get on in that environment. In retrospect, she realized that he was the ideal candidate, precisely because of his difference in style.

Another aspect of team diversity relates to cultural and ethnic diversity. Diversity in a team can be managed to garner excellent results. Everyone on a team brings their own history and background, and these differences enrich a team. It's one of the ways that a group can make better decisions than a lone person. We all grow up with different experiences based on our level of wealth, ethnic culture, stability, and myriad other issues. These experiences affect our thought processes; that is, we all think differently because of them. If we all had the same life experiences and thought the same way, we'd be redundant! Instead, it is possible to manage diversity as your strong suit.

Three Different Backgrounds

Three SAs who worked together had very different upbringings. One had strict, religious parents who gave her a structured upbringing. Therefore structure gave her comfort and security; everything had to be documented in detail before she could move forward. The other was kicked out of his house as a teenager when his parents found out that he was gay. He had to learn to survive on his own; he resisted structure and valued self-reliance. Another had been brought up in a very unstructured household that moved around the country a lot. He craved structure, but expected unanticipated change. As a result, all three had relatively predictable work-habits and design styles. Because they saw these differences as having many tools in their toolbox, it made for powerful results. Any design had to have enough structure to satisfy the first person, each component had to be self-reliant enough to satisfy the second person, and the system had to be able to deal with change well enough to satisfy the third. When documentation needed to be written, they knew who would see to its completion. This situation could have been a disaster if it had led to disagreements, but instead it was managed to be their strength!

A manager must create an environment that supports and celebrates diversity rather than trying to fit everyone into the same "box." Role-model the behavior of having a willingness to listen and understand. Challenge the group to understand each other and find "best of both worlds" solutions.

Four World Views

Tom once interviewed the highest-performing engineering team in his division to find the secret of their success. One of the engineers pointed out that the four of them each came from very different religious backgrounds, each of which represented a different world view. He felt that this was their biggest strength. One's deity was inside us all, one's looked down on everyone with a mindful eye, another was at the center of everything, and another was out of reach to all but a very few. The world views were reflected in how they addressed engineering problems. Although they all had different world views, they all agreed that none was the right world view for every engineering problem. Instead, they each could perform his own analysis of a problem using very different philosophies. When they came together to share their results, they had a very thorough analysis. The discussions that resulted helped each member gain a deeper understanding of the problem because each person tended to find different issues and solutions. Once they all saw eye-to-eye, they could design a solution that took the best aspects from each of their analyses.

There is another aspect of the team picture that is no less important— that is, mentoring and providing opportunities for growth for the junior members of the team. Junior SAs need to be mentored, and they also need to be given the opportunity to grow rapidly and demonstrate their talent, especially in their first SA job. It can be very worthwhile to take a risk on hiring a junior SA who seems to have potential if an appropriate mentor is available. Never hire junior SAs into positions where they will not get properly mentored and trained on a day-to-day basis. People hired into positions like this will not enjoy their work and often will make mistakes that other people have to correct. Hiring juniors into an SA role, giving them super-user access, and insufficient mentoring is a recipe for disaster, and they are likely to create more work for others rather than relieve the work load.

Make Sure Junior SAs Have Mentors

An ISP start-up split their system administration organization into two parts to avoid a conflict in priorities. One team looked after the Internet service, and the other looked after the corporate systems and networks. Senior SAs kept transferring from the corporate team to the service team, and at one point only a couple of junior SAs were left on the corporate team. The senior SAs on the service team answered questions and helped out when they could, but their priority was maintaining the service. One day, the root partition on the corporate mail server filled up. The junior SA who found the problem went looking for help from the senior SAs, but they were all heavily involved in some important work on the service and couldn't spare much time. She decided that the best thing to do was to find some large files that probably weren't used very much, move them to another disk partition, and create links to them from the original location. Unfortunately, she chose the shared libraries, not knowing what they were or the effect that moving them would have.

When she moved the libraries, she discovered that she could not make links to them because that command no longer worked. As she tried to figure out what was wrong, she discovered that none of the commands she tried worked. She decided to try rebooting the system to see if that fixed the problem. Of course, the system was unable to boot without the shared libraries, which made things worse. She ended up taking the mail server and another system apart in the computer room to try to boot the machine and recover it to a working state. As luck would have it, when she was in the middle of this operation, with computer parts strewn all over the floor, a TV crew that was doing a feature on the company came through the computer room and decided that she made for interesting footage. This added even more stress and embarrassment to an already awful situation.

Eventually, when the corporate mail server had been down for several hours and senior management was expressing their displeasure, one of the senior SAs on the service team was able to break away and help her to fix the problem. He also took the time to explain what the shared libraries were and why they were so critical. If she had a mentor who was able to spend time with her and help her through problems such as this, the situation would have been resolved quickly without a huge outage and embarrassing TV footage.

30.1.6 Select the Interview Team

An important part of the hiring process is the interviewing process. The interviewers need to work as a team to find out if the person has the necessary technical and soft skills and is a team fit. This is another situation in which the job description plays an important part. What exactly are the skills that the candidate is supposed to have? Divide the desired skills up into small, related sets and assign one set of desired skills to each interviewer. Select the interviewers based on their ability to interview for, and rate the candidates on, a particular set of skills. Some people are better at interviewing than others. If you are doing a lot of hiring, make sure that they don't get totally swamped with first-round interviews. Consider saving them for the second round. Make sure that all the interviewers are aware of what skills they are interviewing for and what skills other people are interviewing for, so that there is minimal duplication and everything is covered. Only really critical skills should be assigned to more than one person. If two people are assigned to interview for the same skill, make sure that they ask different questions. Make sure that all the interviewers understand that all areas will be covered properly by someone, so that they are all comfortable in their team role.

In the case in which there are many openings, have the interview team cover the skills required across all the jobs. It will probably take a while to fill all the positions. As more positions are filled, the search can be narrowed and the skills needed restricted to cover the gaps that remain in the SA team's skill-set. If there are many positions, describe them all to the candidate and, if appropriate, express willingness to have some cross-over between the positions. Find out what positions the candidate finds the most interesting and appropriate for her skills.

Both the candidates and the team members will want to know with whom they will be working. It is vital that the candidates spend time during the interview process with the person who will be their manager and the people with whom they will work most closely. Give the candidate the opportunity to meet as many people in the team as possible, without making the interview process overwhelming and exhausting. Consider adding a customer to the interview team (this benefits the candidate and your relationship with your customers). Bring the candidate to lunch with two or three SAs, and give her a chance to relax by not asking her questions, just talking about something interesting, giving her a chance to join in if and when she feels like it. This gives her an opportunity to get to know some of her potential coworkers in a more relaxed environment, which should help her to decide whether she wants to work with your team. One common mistake is to ignore the person at lunch. Make sure that you try to keep the candidate involved in the conversation. Ask open-ended questions to encourage her to converse with the group.

30.1.7   Interview Process

The most important point that all interviewers need to remember is to respect the candidate. The candidate should always leave feeling like the interview was worthwhile and the people that he spoke to were the sort of people with whom he would like to work. He should have the impression that interviewing him was the most important thing on the interviewers' minds. Remember, you want the candidates to want to work with you. You want them to tell their friends that your company looks like a great place to work. They need to leave the building with their self-respect intact and liking the company. Other ways to show respect include the following:

Be Prompt for Your Interview, Don't Leave the Candidate Waiting: The candidate has given up a lot of his time to come to the interview; don't make him feel that it was a waste of time.

Before Meeting the Candidate, Turn OFF All Radios, Pagers, and Cell Phones: Your company will survive for an hour without you, even if it doesn't feel that way. You don't want the candidate to feel like the site is in such a bad way that he will never have a moment's peace. Nor do you want to waste precious interviewing time worrying about, or dealing with, problems at the site.

Show Interest in the Candidate: Did he have a hard time finding the place? Was the traffic bad? How is he finding the interviews so far? Would he like a drink or a quick break?

Make Sure Everyone Is Asking Different Questions: It shows the candidate that the group communicates and works well as a team. It shows that thought and preparation went into the interview process. Answering the same questions over and over is a waste of time for the candidate. Asking different questions also gives the interviewers a broader view of the candidate when they compare notes later.

Don't Set Out to Prove You Know More: The point of the interview is to find out how much the candidate knows, not to demonstrate your own brilliance or to try to catch him on some insignificant little detail that most SAs will never come across in their careers.

Ease the Candidate into It: Start with relatively easy questions to give him a chance to build confidence and gradually make them more difficult. This process will give you a good idea of the candidate's skill level and gives the candidate a chance to demonstrate his true skills, rather than succumbing to nerves and forgetting everything. It is in both parties' interests for the candidate to show his true skill level.

Don't Prolong the Agony: When you find the candidate's limits in one area, back off and try to find his limits in another area. Give him a chance to build up confidence before probing his limits.

Try to Identify Your Concerns as You Go: If you are unsure how he would respond in a certain situation, it is best to realize that during the interview when you have a chance to direct your questions to validate or disprove your concerns.

Take Care of the Candidate

An Internet start-up interviewed a senior SA who had been personally recommended and recruited by the two most senior SAs on staff. The interview time was 6 PM to 10 PM. The employees of the start-up were working late nights all the time and always ordered take-out dinners from nearby restaurants. During one of the interviews, someone asked the interviewer what he wanted for dinner but did not ask the candidate, who also had not eaten. The next interviewer brought in his dinner and proceeded to eat it in front of the candidate, without thinking to ask if she wanted anything. The same thing happened during the second round of interviews. She was offered the job, and they were surprised when she turned it down. In the ensuing months, she talked to many people about the awful interview process, and came across others who had undergone similar experiences and also turned the company down.

Successful interviewing requires preparation, practice, and coordination. Record your thoughts on the interview and the candidate as soon as you come out of the interview. Doing so gives you the freshest, most accurate picture of the candidate when the team gets together to decide whom to hire. It also gives you the opportunity to think about concerns that you may not have probed in the interview and to ask a later interviewer to direct some questioning toward those concerns.

One of the biggest mistakes that companies make is to "sell the company" only after they've asked enough questions to determine that the candidate is qualified for the job. They feel that anything else is wasting time with people who aren't going to be hired. As a result, qualified candidates walk away from an interview thinking "what a boring company!" or possibly "what a bunch of jerks!" Instead, start each interview by explaining what a great company you have and why you personally like the company. This starts them off feeling eager to join; it relaxes them and makes the interview go smoother. It also puts you in better light. If they aren't qualified for the position, they might have friends who are, and you want them to be telling all their friends about your wonderful company. Also, an unqualified person may be qualified later in her career, and it would be a shame if you've turned her off to your company by one bad interview.

30.1.8 Technical Interviewing

Some interviewers must interview the candidates for their technical skills. This task can prove to be a challenge in a field as broad as system administration. However, the job description should provide a basis for an approach to the technical interviewing. It should identify whether the person needs specific technical skills and experience or more general problem-solving skills, for example. Technical interviewing for an architect position should identify design skills, rather than intimate knowledge of the latest hardware from a particular vendor.

The interviewers must pitch the interview questions at the right level. Architects should be presented with an architectural problem and asked to discuss the problems they see and how they would go about solving them. For senior SAs, the interviewer should pick an area of technical expertise that they both have in common and dig deep. Check for problem-solving skills and the ability to explain what he is doing, in addition to being able to do the tasks. Intermediate SAs should have a reasonable breadth of experience, problem-solving skills, and the ability to explain what they are doing. Junior SAs should demonstrate that they have tried to understand what they were doing and how things worked beyond what their specific job required. Look for junior SAs who pay attention to detail and are methodical. When interviewing SAs with no previous experience, look for someone who has an interest in computers and in how things in general work. Have they written computer games or taken their home PCs apart?

When looking for problem-solving skills, it can be informative to see if the candidate understands how things other than computers work. Ask them to explain how a couple of everyday items work, such as an internal combustion engine or a flush toilet. Find out what else the candidate fixes. Does she fix electrical appliances that break, or blocked sinks, or furniture? Does she know how to change the oil in her car, or do any small jobs on it? Some people feel that the ability to read sheet music demonstrates logical, methodical thinking and good problem-solving skills. Come up with imaginative ways to figure out how the candidate thinks. Ask them why manhole covers are round.

It is always good to look at candidates' past experiences and get their thoughts on them. For example, asking what accomplishment they are most proud of and why can give you a good idea of what they are capable of and what they see as difficult challenges to overcome. Ask them about situations they have been in that they wish they had handled differently, and what they would have done differently in hindsight and why. You want to know that they can learn from their mistakes. Ask the candidates to describe a big mess that they have had to clean up, how it came into existence, how they fixed it, and what constraints they had to work under to fix it. The candidates will enjoy telling their stories, and this should provide insight into how the candidates think and work. Ask them to tell you about a big project they have had to work on alone or in a team. If you are interested in a particular skill, ask the candidates about a problem that needed solving in that area. Ask them about a tricky problem you have encountered in that area and see how they would have approached it. Most of all, just get them talking about real-life experiences. It's easier and more interesting for them, and gives you a better idea of what they are capable of than dry, "how does this work" questions.

Don't ask "trivia" questions—questions with one highly specific, correct answer. People can forget that kind of thing when under stress. If their job requires them to know which pin on a V.35 interface is used to transmit data, they can look it up when they have the job. General questions help you understand more about candidates than trivia.

> ❖ **Asking Candidates to Rate Their Own Skills**   Asking candidates to rate their own skills can help indicate their level of self-confidence, but little else. You don't know their basis for comparison. Some people are brought up being taught to always downplay their skills. A hiring manager once nearly lost a candidate who said she didn't know much about Macintoshes. It turned out that she used one eight hours a day and was supporting four applications for her department. But she didn't know how to program one. Ask people to describe their experience instead.

30.1.9   Nontechnical Interviewing

For nontechnical interviewing, it can be particularly useful to take a course on interview techniques. There are several approaches to interviewing. One that works well in our experience is behavioral interviewing, which looks at past behavior to predict future actions. This technique can also be used for technical interviewing. Questions are phrased something like: "Think of a time when.... Describe the situation to me, and tell me what you did." Do it in such a way that it is clear that you won't fault the candidate for this situation having arisen and that you just want to know how he handled it. For example, you might say to an SA candidate "We have all experienced times when things have become really busy and something has fallen through the cracks or has been delayed. Think of a time when this happened to you. Describe the situation to me, and tell me how you handled it. What did you learn from the experience?" Ask about both good and bad things. For example, ask about the best project that the candidate worked on, and why he felt it was the best, and then ask about the worst one. Ask about the person's best and worst manager to find out what he likes and dislikes in a manager and what his working style is. This technique works better than an approach that asks the candidate how she *would* deal with a particular situation, because it is often easier for people to see how they should behave when asked in such an academic fashion. However, when these situations arise, there are other pressures and other factors that result in different behavior. Behavioral interviewing looks at how the candidate actually behaved in real-life situations.

The nontechnical interviews are used to evaluate the candidate's soft skills. They should be used to find out how the person works in a team environment, how he relates to customers, how he organizes his time, whether he needs lots of direction or just a little, whether he likes a narrow job description or the opportunity to work in lots of areas, and so on. Typically, there are no right or wrong answers to these questions. The interviewing team needs to hear the answers to decide if the person fits into the team, fits the particular position, or perhaps is more suited to another position.

For example, a company might interview a candidate who is very bright, but is someone who completes 80 percent of the task and then loses interest because all of the difficult problems have been solved. If this person can be teamed up with someone else who enjoys taking tasks to completion and will enjoy learning from the other person, then he would be a good hire. However, if there is no one to pair with this person, then he probably is not a good choice.

Try to find out what the candidate's work habits are. If he stays in touch with technology by reading mailing lists and news groups and by surfing the web, does he do so to the detriment of his other work, or does he find the right balance? The interviewer should get a good idea of the candidate's approach by chatting about how he keeps up with technology and what mailing lists he reads. Some people waste phenomenal amounts of time keeping up with the latest technology and lots of mailing lists. They can be fun and interesting to talk to, but frustrating to work with if they don't get much real work done.

Gauge the candidate's interest in computers. If computers are the focus of his life and are his only pastime, then he will burn out at some point. He may work long hours because he enjoys the work so much, but that is not healthy or a recipe for long-term success. He may also spend a large part of his time in the office playing with fun technology that has nothing to do with his work. Because he works such long hours and spends all of his time with computers, it will be hard for him to figure out how much real work he is doing and how much he is just playing around. On the other hand, some candidates may be surprisingly computer-averse. They may not want to touch or see a computer outside of working hours. These people generally lead a sustainable lifestyle and will not burn out (they may have already had that experience), but they are less likely to be happy working lots of long hours. However, they are also more likely to be productive all of the hours that they do work. They are also less likely to be the first to hear about a new technology or to try it and suggest introducing it. Ideally, the candidate should have a balance between these two extremes. But there are jobs that are suited to people at either end of the scale. Again, the interviewers need to know what they are looking for in the candidate.

30.1.10   Sell the Position

Beyond finding out which candidates the team wants to work with, the interview is also the time to persuade candidates that they want to work for the company. The first step on that path is to respect the candidates and make sure the interview process does not waste their time or leave them feeling humiliated, as discussed in Section 30.1.7. The people whom the candidates meet during the interview process should represent the best of the team. They should be people with whom the candidates will want to work.

The position itself is also important. Find out what the candidate is looking for and figure out if you can offer that in this position. Does the candidate want to work in a specific area of system administration, or does she want to be able to work with many different aspects? Let the candidate know if the position can be made into what she wants it to be. Each interviewer should think about all the things they find positive about the company and the group and share those with the candidates.

Companies such as Internet commerce sites, ISPs, and SA consulting companies can make the most of the fact that the SA function is part of the core business of the company, and so it is (or should be) well funded and viewed as a profit center rather than a cost center. We have always found it more enjoyable to work for companies that look to SAs as valuable resources that must be invested in, rather than "overhead" that must be reduced.

30.1.11   Employee Retention

Once you have hired a good employee, you want the person to stick around for the long term. What motivates SAs to remain at a company is different for different people, but there are some areas that cover most people.

At the time of writing, there is a high demand for SAs and salaries are rapidly inflating. Although salary is important, because no one wants to feel exploited, offering the highest salaries does not necessarily retain employees. Salaries should be competitive, but it is more important for the SAs to be happy in their work.

One of the secrets to retaining SAs is to keep their jobs interesting. If there are tedious, repetitive tasks that some SAs have to do over and over, get someone to automate those tasks. The person who is doing the automation will enjoy it, the SAs who no longer have to do the repetitive task will appreciate it, and efficiency will be improved.

As with most people, SAs like recognition for working hard and doing a good job. Performance bonuses are one way to recognize employees, but simply thanking them in group meetings for the work they are doing can work just as well.

Appreciation and Enjoyment Are Key

A consulting company that had many excellent SAs was going through a turbulent period and losing a lot of staff. One SA who left commented that the senior management of the company had no idea what motivated people. Most of those who left were well paid and all were offered a pay increase to stay. But as this departing employee put it: "People work for money; people work hard for appreciation; but people work the hardest when they love what they do. People are recognized as "the best" when they love what they do, where they do it, and who they do it for."

Good SAs enjoy working with other good SAs. SAs like to see important infrastructure projects funded and like to be a part of building good infrastructure. SAs like to feel like they are a part of the company, rather than an unimportant, often ignored appendage. They like to have a good relationship with the people with whom they work closely, who generally are their customers. Although most SAs thrive on being busy, most do not enjoy being overloaded to the point where they are unable to meet customer expectations. SAs are often not the most communicative employees, but they like to be kept informed and expect their managers to notice when they are overloaded or when they pull off great feats. SAs also want to have the opportunity to advance their careers; they will move on if they know they will stagnate where they are.

SAs also like "fun stuff." Fast connections to home, high-end laptops, and the opportunity to work with new technologies help to keep the appeal of the work environment high. Finding opportunities for SAs to work from home can also help retain them.

The final element in keeping most SAs happy is their direct manager. Some people like a friendly relationship with their manager; others just like clear lines of management and the knowledge that their manager has faith in them and will support them in what they do. Chapters 28 and 29 examine the roles of technical and nontechnical managers in detail. People take jobs because of money, but people leave jobs because of bad managers. As discussed in Section 27.2.2, it's not what you do, but whom you do it for.

30.2   The Icing

Once a company has mastered the basics of hiring SAs, the final thing to consider is how to make the company stand out as somewhere that SAs will want to work. This section looks at some ways to get noticed.

30.2.1   Get Noticed

Employing some nontraditional incentives that are fun and different can help to get the company noticed and enhance its reputation as a fun place to work. For example, one company gave all interview candidates a Palm Pilot at the interview. Another company had informal group outings to a nearby roller-coaster park, and the company bought season tickets for those who were interested. Another company had the latest video games and game controllers in rooms in a few buildings around the campus. Senior SAs and some managers in another company developed a tradition of playing multi-player computer games one night a week. Others arrange sports or games leagues within the company or against other companies. Although most of these activities are not of universal interest, they are interesting to enough people that they distinguish the company as being a fun place to work, which can help attract even employees who are not interested in the activity that is offered.

Other, work-oriented schemes can help to distinguish the company in a positive way. There are several local SA organizations, for example, that have regular meetings that need to be hosted somewhere. Hosting the local SAGE group or just regular talks on a topic of interest to SAs one evening a month makes the company more attractive to SAs. Encouraging SAs to write and present papers and tutorials at conferences also demonstrates that the company is a good place for SAs to work and gets the company's name known in the SA field.

Ultimately, the aim is to get the company noticed and considered to be a fun place to work and a place that values its SAs. Be creative!

30.3   Conclusion

The secret to hiring is good planning and follow-through. Hiring SAs starts with a good job description. The job description helps to define the skill level that is required and the soft skills that are needed, and it helps to direct the interviewers' questioning toward relevant topics. It is also used for recruiting appropriate candidates. The best way to recruit good candidates is through personal recommendations from customers and staff. Other ways that are oriented toward technologically minded people are also good.

The skill level of the person hired has financial implications, and companies should be aware of the hidden costs of hiring underqualified staff with lower salary requirements. The interview process should give the candidate the opportunity to meet the key people whom she will be working with, if hired. The interviewers should represent the company at its best. They should respect the candidate and make sure that the interview experience is pleasant. The technical and soft skills that are required for the job should be divided among the interviewers, and they should all know how to interview for their assigned skills. They should give the candidate a chance to shine by easing her into the questioning and letting her build confidence. This chapter looked at ways to assess problem-solving skills and design skills. Soft skills are just as important as technical skills. Interviewing courses can be very helpful for suggesting ways to accurately assess these skills in the candidates.

Once the right candidate has been identified, she must be persuaded that she wants to take the job. This process starts with the very first contact the candidate has with the company. The candidate must have felt respected and well-treated throughout the interview process. Trying to recruit someone who has been offended in the interview process is pointless. The compensation package is a part of wooing the candidate, but so are the positive aspects of working for the group, such as a cool staff or being well-funded. Having a reputation as a fun place to work or a place that values SAs can help enormously in hiring the right employees.

After people have been hired, they should be retained. Interviewing is a costly process.

For further reading on this topic, we highly recommend Strata Rose Chalup's article on the topic of technical interviews (Chalup 2000). This should be required reading for anyone conducting technical interviews.

Exercises

1. Write a detailed job description for an open position in your group or for a position for which you would like to be able to hire someone.

2. Does your company hire people above, below, or at the skill level required for a position? Illustrate your answer with some examples.

3. Who in your group is good at interviewing and who is not good at it? Why?

4. What roles do you think are missing from your team?

5. How diverse is your team? What could you do to recruit members who have different ethnic and cultural backgrounds than the people currently employed?

6. Who would be able to act as a mentor for a junior SA, if your group was to hire one?

7. Are there junior SAs in your group who are not mentored? If so, what good and bad experiences has the junior SA had as a result of the lack of mentoring?

8. How have you made the interview process pleasant for a candidate in the past?

9. How have you made the interview process unpleasant for a candidate in the past? Why did that happen? What can be done to prevent that from happening again?

10. Write a job description for someone who would have the skills you feel are lacking in your team.

11. What technical questions would you ask of a candidate for the position for which you wrote a job description (above)?

12. What nontechnical questions would you ask of a candidate for that position?

13. What are the best things about working in your current company?

14. What are the worst things about working in your current company?

15. What motivates you to stay at your current company?

16. If you needed to start looking for a job tomorrow, where would you want to work and why?

17. How well does your company do at retaining employees? What do you think the reason for this is?

18. What do you think your company does or could do to stand out as a good place to work?

Chapter 31

Firing System Administrators

This chapter is about how to remove fellow SAs from your site because they've been fired. Our wish is that you never need to use the information in this chapter. The reality is that everyone will need to use this information someday. You may not be a manager saddled with the responsibility of deciding to fire someone, but you may be the SA that must deal with the consequences.

This chapter is not about why someone should be fired. We can't help you there. It is instead about the technical tasks that must be performed when it happens. In fact, you might say that this chapter begins after the management decision has been made to fire the person, and you must remove their access from the network.

Removing SAs' access against their will is a unique situation. SAs have privileged access to the systems and are likely to have access to all systems. They may know the system better than you do because they built it. On the other hand, the techniques in this chapter can also be used when dealing with an SA who is leaving a company on good terms. Whether people are leaving on good or bad terms, the potential for the situation to turn ugly makes them a liability to the company's computer infrastructure.

Large companies usually have procedures for removing access when someone leaves. Small- and mid-size companies may have ad hoc procedures.

Hopefully, this chapter can serve as a starting point if you need to establish a termination procedure.

31.1   The Basics

From an SA perspective, the basic process of firing someone boils down to these issues[1]:

Follow Your Corporate HR Policy: The Most Important Rule.

Remove Physical Access: "Can he get into the building?"

Remove Remote Access: "Can he remotely access our network?"

Remove Service Access: "Have access rights to applications been withdrawn?"

Have Fewer Access Databases: The fewer points of control, the easier it is to lock someone out.

In this section, we will discuss each of the areas in detail and follow up with anecdotes that show how they have been addressed in some real-life situations.

31.1.1   Follow Your Corporate HR Policy

The single most important rule is that you must follow the policies of your company with regard to firing people. These policies are written by people who understand the complex legal rules around employee termination. They are the experts, not you. They have guidelines around what to say, what not to say, how to do it, how not to do it. Usually, this is such a rare and delicate event that someone from HR holds your hand through it.

HR might recommend any number of techniques from calling the employee at home and telling the person not to come into work again to something as confrontational as two security guards and someone from HR meeting the employee at his cubicle and informing him that his personal effects will be shipped to him, as the security guards escort him out of the building.

31.1.2   Remove Physical Access

Physical access means, quite simply, "Make sure the person can't get in the building." Usually, this is the function of HR or corporate security. For example, HR should already have a procedure for retrieving the employee's ID badge, which is checked by guards at the building entrance. If card-key

---

[1] This model is an extension of the one described in a paper titled "Adverse Terminations Procedures" by Matthew F. Ringel and Tom Limoncelli (Ringel and Limoncelli 1999).

access is used, the card-key system must be programmed to deny access to that card-key regardless of whether the card-key has been returned. Keys to any rooms must be retrieved or locks changed. Combination locks, safe combinations, and so on must be changed. Is there a barn, maintenance shed, shack, outhouse, dog house, or annex that has network connectivity? Check them too. Because physical instruments such as doors and keys have been around longer than computers, most companies usually have good procedures related to them already. Follow them. Very small companies might not have any kind of identification badge or similar system in place. In that case, have the receptionist and other employees been notified of what to do if they see this person in or near the building?

You must also schedule time for the SA to return any equipment that he may have at home. Any computers that are returned are suspect. The disks should be erased to prevent virus transmission.

31.1.3 Remove Remote Access

Remote access refers to the many ways someone might get into the networks. These include, but are not limited to, modem pools, ISDN lines, xDSL, inbound connections through a firewall, and VPN service. Access to all of these systems must be disabled. This can be difficult if each of them is run by a different team or has a different access control system.

31.1.4 Remove Service Access

Service access refers to the applications and services that are inside the network. Each of these services usually has a password. Examples include POP3/IMAP4 (Myers and Rose 1996, Crispin 1996), servers, database servers, UNIX servers (each with their own `/etc/passwd` file to be checked, or a global NIS or Kerberos database to be checked), NT Domain logins, SMB servers (NT File Server), and so on.

Discussion

The issues introduced so far relate to actions that are taken when someone is actively being removed. Logistically speaking, each issue can be assigned to a separate subteam: Managers can take care of the HR processes, corporate security ensures physical access is removed, the remote access administrators have their tasks, and the SAs can focus on removing service access.

The process described so far is tolerant to some mistakes. Access is divided into three tiers: physical, remote, and service. Mistakes can be made in one tier and access is still prevented. If, for example, a login on a particular service hasn't been disabled, but the person can't enter the building physically or get in via remote access, he can't get to the account to cause any damage.

This process is not theoretical. It is based on the best current practices of the companies we have interviewed. The names have been changed, but these anecdotes are real.

Firing the Boss

A large manufacturing company had to "suspend, pending investigation" the manager of a team of SAs. This person had administrative access to all the systems in his domain and had access to the network via every remote access method that the system administration group provided.

Without the accused manager knowing, a meeting was called by the accused manager's director, with the lead SA and corporate security. The corporate security officer explained the situation and the action plan. The lead SA was to change all the "root" (privileged account) passwords that evening, and in the morning the director would meet with the system administration group (without their manager) to inform them of the situation. They would be told to suspend all access to the systems. If something could not be suspended, access would be deleted. The system administration group was split into subteams based on remote and service access.

The lead SA spent the evening changing the "root" password on every system. In the morning, all the SAs were brought into a closed meeting and the situation was explained to them. The physical access aspects were taken care of by corporate security. The system administration team was assigned the remote and service access issues. They brainstormed on each issue separately, which helped them maintain focus. All changes were logged and logs were turned over to the lead SA.

There was one problem where, to make a long story short, if he had a photographic memory, he could have leveraged a form of remote access to gain access to the network. It was going to take a couple days to rectify this problem, and nothing could make that happen any faster. Even so, the risk of that happening was considered to be low and the system administration team was confident that physical and service access had been completely removed and logs could be monitored for intrusions. In other words, they were confident that doing a complete job on two of the tiers would compensate for being incomplete on the third tier.

During the investigation, the accused manager resigned. The logs of what access had been removed were useful as a check list of what access had been suspended and now needed to be deleted.

The process worked very effectively. There was increased efficiency from splitting into teams. The potential problem with remote access was compensated by effectively removing all other access.

Removal at an Academic Institution

Academic entities tend to be very astute about termination procedures, as they often have batches of terminated accounts at the end of every academic year. The university setting is a good example of how "practice makes perfect." However, this anecdote involves someone with privileged access to many machines.

At a large state university, a long-time operator with "root" access to all UNIX systems was to be terminated. After some discussion, it was decided to use the following procedure: A small team was assembled to list all the access she had and how to disable each, including card-key and host access. When the designated time arrived, she was told that her boss needed to speak with her in his office. Her office and her boss's office were in opposite parts of the building and the trip would take at least ten minutes. By the time she reached her boss's office, all of her accounts had been disabled.

Because this was a public university, they were not able to eliminate physical access to the building, but card-key changes prevented her from gaining direct physical access to sensitive machines. Remote access could not be disabled because the large university did not use a firewall. Access to a PC lab was similar to access from the Internet in that it was considered an untrusted network. Because the operator had access that was so extremely pervasive, the only way to ensure complete coverage was to have all the senior SAs involved in removing all *service* access.

Amicably Leaving a Company

An SA at a small software development company announced he was leaving and offered one month's notice to help the company transition. The SA was actually involved in interviewing a replacement. All responsibilities had been transitioned the day before the termination date. On his last day, the SA walked into his boss' office and became **root** in a window on his workstation. While the boss watched, he disabled his own regular login. He then issued the commands to change the password of various routers and let his boss enter the new password. He then repeated this for a few other "system accounts." Finally, he issued the command to activate their "change root password on all systems" procedure and let his boss enter the new password. The boss was shocked that the soon-to-be ex-employee was doing such a complete job of transitioning duties and deleting himself from the system. Finally the SA put his card-key and physical keys on the boss desk and left the building. About two weeks later, the ex-employee remembered that he had forgotten to change the password on a particular nonprivileged system account on a machine that had a modem directly attached to it. The ex-employee reports that he confirmed with former coworkers that the ex-employer didn't disable the account until he notified them of the error.

With one exception, the termination was complete. However, the exception crossed the remote and service tiers because the account (service access) was on a host that was directly connected to the outside world (remote access). Also, it was unsafe for the new passwords to be set in front of the exiting employee, who could have been watching the keyboard. The employee also could have recorded the new passwords as they were being set. The garden-variety `script` command on UNIX does not record nonechoed input (such as passwords), but there are plenty of keyboard capturing utilities that do, on all OSs.

The company took a risk by not disabling access as soon as notice was given. However, it was a reasonable risk to take considering that it was not an adverse termination.

31.1.5   Fewer Access Databases

In terms of what SA tasks must be completed, disabling access is all about updating access databases that specify who may do what: Password files, RADIUS lists, network connections, and ACLs are all access databases. There is less work to do if there are fewer of these databases. Therefore system architects should always attempt to design systems with as few such databases as possible.

Part of the process involves brainstorming to try to remember all the ways in which access must be disabled. This process can be aided by having a good inventory and mechanisms to control the global environment based on updates to the database as described in Section 6.2.2.

31.2   The Icing

Now that we have covered the basics, there are certain operational policies that make the process smoother and reduce risk.

31.2.1   A Single Authentication Database

Although having fewer access databases is a benefit, having all services authenticated off one database brings about a new paradigm. This is easy to do if all services are controlled by handheld authenticators (HHA) that access the same database.

In the first case study (Section 31.1.4), access to many services (VPNs, in-bound telnet through the firewall, root access, and so on) were controlled by a single HHA system. Disabling the manager's record in the HHA database resulted in immediately disabling many different services at the same time.

This does not relieve SAs from deleting the person from the individual services' configuration files. An HHA system provides authentication information, not authority. That is, it tells the service who is knocking at the door, not whether they should be let in. That decision is left to the local service. For example, an HHA-based replacement for the UNIX `/bin/su` command would query the HHA server to find out who entered the command, but the software normally has a local configuration file that indicates who may become `root`. With the HHA disabled, nobody will ever authenticate to that user, but this does not make a username listed in that configuration file a moot point. Processes are not killed; `cron, at`, and other automated systems may continue to run. Eventually all references to the person must be removed or deleted.

Having all of those local configuration files and access databases centralized into a single database is the next advancement that we are looking forward to. LDAP, Kerberos, NDS, and other technologies bring us closer to that goal.

31.2.2 Monitoring System File Changes

If someone suspects he may be fired, he may create a back door (a way to get into the system that others do not know about) or plant a logic bomb (software that causes damage once he has gone). Ideally, you can take a snapshot of all software before the person becomes suspicious and compare it to the running system on a regular basis. However, that is time consuming, requires a lot of storage, and would easily tip off the person that something is about to happen.

However, no suspicions can be raised if such a thing is always done. Programs that checksum system files and report changes are commonly found. The earliest to achieve popularity is named "Tripwire." If this process is an automated system that is used regularly to notice external intruders, system failures, or other problems, it will be much easier to use it without raising suspicion. However, care must be taken to make sure that that person being fired doesn't update the database so that his changes aren't noticed.

Such a system is an excellent measure to detect any kind of intrusions. However, it is time consuming to process all the false-positives. The issue becomes scaling it to many machines.

31.3   Conclusion

Firing SAs isn't fun or easy, but sometimes it has to happen.

The basics are very simple: The most important rule is to follow the policies of your HR department. They are the experts, and you are supporting their process. There are three tiers of access that must be removed: Physical access, remote access, and service access. The primary benefit of the three-tier model is that it provides a structured approach (versus ad hoc), and it is tolerant to mistakes made at any one level. Architectures that seek to minimize the number of access databases and a well-maintained inventory ease the process considerably.

In creating a checklist for all the manners of access to be disabled, one might begin with the "new hire" procedure as a starting point: Whatever is done for a new hire must be undone for a termination. Although no checklist is complete, we have assembled several checklists of things to disable in the event of termination:

Physical Access: Change combination locks, change all applicable safe combinations, doors with keys should have locks changed (even if keys are returned). Remove access for all buildings (for example, remote locations, shacks, utility buildings).

Have Ex-Employee Surrender: Keys, card-keys, badges, HHAs, PDAs (Pilot, Newton, and so on), and any company-owned equipment that they have at home (computers, hubs, routers, and so on).

Remote Access: Modem pools, ISDN pool, VPN servers, in-bound network access (that is, `ssh`, `telnet`, `rlogin`) cable modem access, xDSL X.25 access.

Service Access: Database servers, NIS domains, NT domains, superuser access (IDs such as `root` and `Administrator`), Netnews (IDs such as `news`, `usenet`, and `uucp`), password files, RADIUS servers.

The Icing is a set of design and operational factors that better prepare a site for the unlikely but important tasks. The fewer the administrative databases, the easier the task will be, but if they are all tied to a single authentication database, the entire process becomes much simpler. Regularly maintained file checksum histories provide a way to detect and prevent back doors and logic bombs.

Dividing the process into HR policy plus physical, remote, and service access brings clarity to the process. The process can be explained easily. The staff can be divided into a physical team, a remote team, and a service team. Each team can then work with total clarity because they only have one task.

This process works best when one can leverage the infrastructure that should be in any system. A solid security infrastructure keeps the wrong people out. Having a single (or few) administrative databases, such as a well-implemented HHA architecture, makes disabling all access from a central place a snap. Properly documented environments and well-maintained inventory improve one's ability to disable all access quickly. Routine Tripwire runs and system monitoring processes are some of the automation that may already be in place at a site. The better the infrastructure is, the easier this process becomes.

The process described in this chapter handles the extreme case of terminating an SA but is also a useful model to consider when anyone leaves a company, simply leaves your domain of support, or when an SA changes jobs within a company and should no longer have privileged access to the systems she previously administered. We don't cover those topics directly. We felt that it would be more interesting to cover one extreme case and leave the others as an exercise to the reader.

Our discussion of this topic has been restricted to the technical side of the process. The nontechnical side, the human side, is equally important. You are changing this person's life in a very profound way. They have bills to pay, family to support, and a life to live. Corporate policies range from "get them out the door immediately" to "we're laying you off in six months." There are potential problems with both, but from our point of view, the latter not only works best but shows trust and respect. The trust and respect issue is not so much for the benefit of the person being laid off, but for the benefit of those remaining.

Exercises

1. When people are fired, does HR know whom to contact in the IT organization to have their access disabled?

2. In your current environment, what must be disabled if you were to be fired? Outside of checking individual hosts for local accounts, how many individual administrative systems did you have to touch?

3. What improvements to your system could make it easier to disable your access when you are fired?

4. A system like Tripwire causes periodic points of filesystem I/O. How does that affect the planning and deployment of such a system? How is this different for a file server, an e-commerce server, and a database server?

Epilogue

We began this book asking for a concise definition of "system administration." Now we're no closer to an answer. If anything, we've broadened the definition. Rather than building a crisper definition of system administration, we've discussed customer support, repair, operations, architecture definition, deployment, disaster planning, and even management skills. System administration is an extremely broad field and no simple definition can cover it all.

We hope you've learned a lot from reading this book. We've certainly learned a lot by writing it. Having to put into words things that had become second-nature has required us to undergo a high degree of self-examination. Writing down such things has forced us to think hard about everything we do, every habit we've developed. The peer-review process stands us naked in front of our mentors and comrades to receive criticism of our fundamental beliefs. We're better for writing this book, and we hope you are better for reading it. We hope some day you write a book and enjoy the same exhilaration.

The most exciting part of this book has been to record, in such a permanent form, the rants and anecdotes that we have accumulated over our careers. We respond to certain technical and nontechnical issues by getting on our soapboxes to expound our opinions. These monologues are refined every time we repeat them, until we find ourselves repeating them word for word, over and over again. We can honestly say that this book includes every tubthumping rant either of us blurt out with Pavlovian predictability. With a little bit of luck, these rants will stand the test of time. This book also captures every useful anecdote in our library of experience. Each anecdote teaches an important lesson or two. We can rest assured that these anecdotes will not be lost, and we can safely look forward to all the new anecdotes we will accrue in the future.

System administration is a culture. Every culture has its anecdotes, myths, and stories. It is how we pass our history to new generations and propagate the lessons and values that are important to us. We learn best from hearing our culture's stories and anecdotes. We enrich the culture every time we share a new one.

We'd like to share with you one final anecdote.

A Concise Definition

A facility had several researchers from a variety of universities visiting for the summer. That autumn, after they left, the SAs had to decommission their computers and clean the large room they had been sharing. The SAs found a scrap of paper that had been taped near the phone. It simply said, "Makes things work," followed by the phone number of the SAs.

It was absolutely the highest compliment they had ever received.

The Many Roles of a System Administrator

This appendix is heavy on philosophy. If that turns you off, you can skip it, but we think it will help you think about your place in the universe, or at least your role within your company, organization, or SA team. Examining your own role within an organization helps you focus, which helps you do a better job. It can give you a long-term perspective of your career. That helps you make the big career decisions necessary for having a happy and successful life.

This can also give your organization a framework for thinking about what roles they want you to play. Each of these roles in some way affects your organization. This is by no means a complete list; however, it is a very good starting point. You should use this to consider what roles are missing in your organization and perhaps to start on a quest to fill them.

It is interesting to think about which and how many of these roles you are asked to play as your career moves forward. It can help you plan your career. Some entry-level SAs are asked to play single roles and grow into more roles as they gain experience. Sometimes, you start out flooded with many roles and specialize as time goes on.

A small site may require its single SA to take on all roles. As the organization grows, certain roles can be transferred to newly hired SAs. Sometimes, you discover you don't enjoy a particular role and look to avoid it when you change jobs. Thinking about these roles may also help guide your career with respect to what kind of companies you decide to work for: Small companies tend to require people to fill multiple roles, larger companies tend to require people to specialize, and mega-corporations have people so specialized that it can seem bizarre to outsiders. Technology companies respect and reward those who play the role of pushing for new technology, whereas other companies often discourage too much change.

A.1   Common Roles

Within a company, there are many roles. Some are more critical than others; some are good and some are bad. Here we list many common roles, the value they provide to the company, how those people derive satisfaction from the job, and what customers tend to expect from them.

A.1.1   The Installer

Some people view an SA as the person who installs "stuff." This is one of the roles that customers see most often, and therefore it is most often associated with the career of system administration. The customer rarely sees the other, possibly more critical positions, such as the people that design the infrastructure.

The value to the company that installers provide is their ability to follow through and see that the job gets done. They are often the final and most critical link in the deployment chain.

When installation is being done on a large scale, the item that is being installed is usually preconfigured at some central location. Installers are trained on the specific situations they are expected to see and have a second-tier resource to call on if they come across an unexpected situation. In that case, the kind of person who makes a good installer is one who enjoys meeting and helping the customers and gets satisfaction from doing the same task well many times over. On the other hand, in smaller deployments, the installer is often expected to be a higher-skilled person because more unexpected situations will be encountered.

When you are the installer, you are the public "face" of the organization, it is important to be friendly and polite. People will assume the entire organization acts the same way that you do.

A.1.2   The Repair Person

Things break. Some people view an SA as a repair person. Just as people call a dishwasher repair person when their dishwasher breaks, they call a computer repair person when their computer breaks. SAs also repair bigger and sometimes more nebulous things such as "the Internet" and "the network." Whether the real problem is simply a broken cable or a much larger problem is of little interest to the customer.

The value that repair people provide to a company is when technological problems stall a business, the repair person brings the company back to life.

Repair people receive satisfaction from knowing they've helped someone and enjoy the challenge of a good puzzle or mystery.

When you are the repair person, customers want to know that you are concerned with their problems. They want to feel like their problems are the most important problems in the world.

A.1.3   The Maintainer

The maintainer is the person who maintains systems that have been previously built. They're very good at following the instructions presented to them, either in a written manual or through training. They do not seek to improve the system, instead, they are willing to maintain it as it is.

The value provided to the company by the maintainers is that they bring stability to our environment. These are not the people who are going to break things trying to improve them, replace them, or spend all day reading magazines about new things to install. Once companies spend money to install something, they need it to be stable long enough to pay for itself before it is replaced with something newer.

Maintainers receive satisfaction from knowing that their work is part of the big picture that keeps the organization working. They tend to be glad that they aren't the people who have to figure out how to design and install the next generation of systems and may even have disdain for those who wish to replace their stable system with something new.

When you are the maintainer, customers want two opposing things: They want to know that you are maintaining the stability of their world, and they want you to be flexible when they seek customizations.

A.1.4   The Problem Preventer

A role that is invisible to most customers is the problem preventer. This is the person who looks for problems and fixes them before the problem becomes visible. This is the behind-the-scenes planning and preventive maintenance that prevents problems in the future. A good problem preventer collects metrics to find trends, but also has an ear to the ground to know what future problems may arise.

The value provided to the company by the problem preventer is that averting problems is less costly than fixing problems when they happen.

Problem preventers receive satisfaction from knowing that their work prevented problems that no one even knows could have happened. It is a private joy. They enjoy thinking in the longer term rather than getting immediate satisfaction from solving an emergency.

Typical customers do not know that this person exists, but their management does. They expect this person to have priorities that are the same as theirs.

A.1.5   The Hero

The SA can be the hero who saves the day. Like the firefighter who pulls people out of a burning building, the hero receives adulation and praise. The network was down, but now it is up. The demo wasn't going to be ready, but the SA worked all weekend to bring the network to that part of the building. Heroes get satisfaction out of their jobs from the praise they receive after the fact.

The value a hero provides to the company is huge: Management always rewards a hero. Ironically, the person who prevents problems receives little visibility, though their contribution may be as or more valuable.

Heroes receive satisfaction knowing that they hold the key to some knowledge that the company could not live without. The hero role is not one that promotes a healthy nonwork life. Heroes give up nights, weekends, and vacations, often with no notice. Their personal life takes second priority. Eventually, heroes burn out and become martyrs, unless management finds some way to help them manage their stress.

Customers expect the hero to be anywhere at any time. Customers would prefer the hero was the only person they dealt with, because this dashing superstar has become someone on whom they can rely. However, customers need to learn that if they get what they want, the hero will burn out. New heroes take a while to find.

A.1.6   The Infrastructure Builder

A corporate network depends on a lot of infrastructure: DNS, directories, databases, scripts, switches, and so on. None of this is seen by the typical customer, except when an outage is explained after the fact and they hear mysterious phrases like "it was a problem with the DNS server."

The larger the company is, the more valuable infrastructure people become. A good infrastructure is like a solid base on which a house can be built. You can build a house on a shaky base and adjust for it with more complicated and costly house designs, but in the long run it is cheaper to have started with a solid base. A tiny company has almost no infrastructure. Larger companies get benefits from amortizing the cost of a quality infrastructure over larger and larger customer bases. When small companies grow to become large companies, often what makes this go smoothly is having had the foresight to employ SAs who "think big" about infrastructure.

Infrastructure builders are the kind of people who get satisfaction out of doing long-term planning, taking existing systems and improving them, scaling large systems into humongous systems, and overhauling legacy systems and replacing them with newer systems. They are proud of their ability to not only build extremely huge systems, but coordinate elegant ways to transition to them.

When you are the infrastructure builder, you have two groups of customers. There is the general customer population who wants the computer infrastructure to be reliable and wants new infrastructure to be deployed yesterday. Your other customers are the SAs whose systems sit on top of the infrastructure you are building. They want documentation and an infrastructure that is reliable and easy for them to understand, and they want it *now,* because when you miss a deadline it makes their projects late too.

A.1.7   The Policywriter

Policies are the backbone of IT. They communicate the wishes of the top corporate officials and dictate how things should be done, tell when they should be done, and explain why they are done. SAs are often asked to write policies on behalf of management. Social problems can not be solved by technology. Some social problems only can be solved by written policy.

The value to the company that the policy creators provide is that they solve some problems and prevent new ones. Policies are a communication tool. As a company grows, communication becomes more difficult and more important.

Policywriters gain satisfaction from knowing that their knowledge, skills, and personal experiences contributed to a policy that improved an organization. They also enjoy being the facilitator who is able to obtain buy-in from many different communities.

When you are the policywriter, customers expect you to seek their input. This should be done at the beginning of the process. It disempowers people to ask for their opinion after the major decisions have been made. Your willingness to listen will be appreciated.

A.1.8   The System Clerk

System clerks are SAs with very little power or decision-making responsibilities. They are given instructions to be followed, such as "create an account for Fred" and "allocate an IP address." If the clerk works as an assistant to a higher-level SA, this can be a fine arrangement. In fact, it is an excellent way to start a career. However, we have seen system clerks that report to nontechnical management, who get frustrated when the clerk is not able to tackle things outside his normal duties.

The value provided to the company comes from performing the tasks that would otherwise distract senior SAs from more specialized tasks and providing coverage for SAs when they are away. A system clerk is also an excellent candidate to fill a more senior SA position as it opens. He already knows the environment and the hiring manager knows his personality. However, if the environment has no senior SAs, the value provided is often that of a scapegoat for a bad computing environment, when the real problem is management's lack of understanding about how to manage technology.

The clerk receives satisfaction from a job well done, from learning new skills, and from looking forward to the excellent growth path ahead of him.

When you are the clerk, customers want their requests to be performed immediately, whether that is reasonable or not. Chapter 26 has more information about dealing with this situation.

Case Study: Site with Only System Clerks

A site needs a balance of senior-level SAs and clerks. There once was a site that had only system clerks. Their training included rudimentary UNIX skills: perform backups, create accounts, allocate IP addresses and IP subnets, install new software, and add new hosts. They fell victim to the "we can always add one more" syndrome: New allocations were blindly made as requested, with no overall plan for increasing capacity. For example, a new host would be added to a subnet without any network capacity planning. This worked for a while, but eventually it led to overloaded subnets. Customers complained of slow networks, but the clerks did not have the network engineering skills to fix the problem. Customers solved this problem themselves by requesting private subnets to gain their own private dedicated local bandwidth. The clerks would happily allocate a new IP subnet, and users would connect it to the rest of the network via a routing-enabled workstation with two NICs. These interconnections were unreliable because hosts route packets slowly, especially when they become overloaded. The more overloaded the main networks became, the more dedicated subnets that were created. Eventually, much of the slowness of the network was caused by the slow interconnections between these private pools of bandwidth. Compute servers also suffered from the same lack of capacity planning. The customers installed their own compute servers, even though the performance problems they were trying to work around were most likely related to the slow host-based routing. These new, fast servers overpowered the 10Mb network, particularly because they were often an order of magnitude faster than the hosts doing the routing. By the time the organization hired a senior-level

SA, the network was a swamp of unreliable subnets, badly configured compute servers, and antique file servers. They had 50 subnets for about 500 users. It took nearly two years to clean up the mess and modernize the network.

A.1.9 The Lab Technician

The lab technician is an SA for a lab filled with highly specialized equipment. For example, in a chemical research firm, the lab technician may be responsible for a small network that connects all the scopes and monitoring devices. At a telecommunications manufacturer, the lab technician may maintain all the equipment in a protocol interoperability room where they have one of every version of a product, the competition's products, and a suite of traffic generators. The lab technician is responsible for installing new equipment, integrating systems together for ad hoc projects,[1] and being able to understand enough of her customers' specialties to translate their needs into the tasks she must perform. The lab technician usually has a small network or group of networks that connect to the main corporate network and depend on the main corporate network for most services; if she is smart, she also makes friends in the corporate services area to pick their brains for technical knowledge.

Lab technicians provide value to the company by letting the researchers focus on designing the experiments rather than executing them. They also add value by being a walking knowledge base of technical information.

The lab technician derives satisfaction from getting an experiment or demo successfully completed on time. However, if she does not get direct congratulations from the researchers that she serves, she may grow resentful. Lab technicians need to remember that their researchers are grateful, whether they express it or not. Researchers will maintain technician motivation and retain them longer if the technicians are included in recognition ceremonies, awards, dinners, and so on.

When you are the lab technician, customers want to know that something can be done, not how it will be done. They want their requirements met, though it is your responsibility to draw out of them what those requirements are. Active listening skills can greatly help in this area.

A.1.10 The Product Finder

The product finder is the person who reads every technology magazine and review so that when someone asks, "Is there a software package that

---

[1] In most labs they are all ad hoc.

compresses widgets?" the product finder can not only recommend a list of widget compressors, but can also recommend ways to determine which is the most appropriate for the particular application. If he doesn't know off-hand where to find such a product, he knows where to look for one.

The value provided to the company by the product finder is his ability to always have "just read a review about that kind of thing." Managers should not watch this kind of person closely, because they will be appalled to discover that he spends half his work day surfing the web and reading magazines. They must weigh that against the time that this person saves for everyone else.

Product finders receive satisfaction from being the person with all the right resources. They can be annoying to others in the group, even those they help, because everyone would like to have the time to surf the web and keep in touch, but most people (necessarily) have other priorities.

When you are the product finder, customers want summaries rather than details. If you provide them with every detail that you've learned on the subject in a long rambling story that takes hours to read, they will shy away from you. Be concise.

A.1.11 The Solution Designer

A key role for SAs in a company is that of the solution designers. They hear there is a problem, and shortly thereafter they have a solution that is better than anyone would have expected. This may solve a small issue such as installing an e-fax server to make it easier to send faxes, or it may resolve a large issue such as creating an electronic version of a process that is currently processed on paper. They are different than the product finder, because they are more likely to build something from scratch or to integrate some smaller packages.

The value provided to the company by solution designers is that they grease the wheels of the company by removing roadblocks and simplifying bureaucratic processes.

The solution designer receives satisfaction from knowing that her solutions are used, because usage indicates that people like it.

When you are the solution designer, customers want to see their aspect of the problem solved, not what you may perceive as the problem nor what would actually save the company money. For example, in an environment where expense reports are faxed to headquarters (HQ), you might create a way for the data to be entered electronically so that HQ doesn't have to retype all the data. However, your customers aren't helped by saving time at HQ; they just want the preparation to be made easier. That would be solved with a better user interface or a system that could download their corporate credit card bill off the service provider's web site. Your customers wouldn't even care if the output was then e-faxed to HQ for manual re-entry.

A.1.12 The Ad Hoc Solution Finder

The ad hoc solution finder is someone who, on an emergency basis, can create a solution to a seemingly impossible problem. This is the person who magically, yet securely, gets network connectivity to the moon for your big demo to the moon men. These people may know more about the tools than the average person who uses the tools, possibly from dissecting them. This is different than the hero, because the hero usually puts out fires (fixes problems), whereas this person builds solutions.

The value provided to the company by ad hoc solution finders is that they find solutions that cover for the fact that technology is not as flexible as some special situations require or that your corporate network has weaknesses that you have not invested in fixing. The former is a situation that gets better over time. The latter indicates a lack of proper technology management.

The ad hoc solution finder receives satisfaction from saving the day. Like the role of hero, the ad hoc solution finder can get burned out if their services are needed too often.

When you are the ad hoc solution finder, customers want miracles to happen and don't want to be reminded that the emergency could have been prevented through better planning by the company, which is rarely their fault.

A.1.13 The Unrequested Solution Person

Some SAs find themselves providing solutions that weren't requested. This can be a good thing and a bad thing. One SA was rewarded for installing a paperless fax system for his users that wasn't requested but soon became a major productivity enhancement. It was based on free software and used their existing modem pool, so the tangible cost was zero. This same SA was once reprimanded for spending too much time on "self-directed projects" and was encouraged to focus on his assigned tasks.

The value provided to the company by this role is they are usually close to their customers and positioned to see needs that upper management wouldn't see or understand. They may also be more in tune to new products that their less-technical customers may not be aware of.

Individuals in this role receive satisfaction from discovering that their guesses of what might be useful turn out to be correct.

When you are in this role, customers want you to guess correctly what will or won't be useful to them; talking with them regularly at appropriate times is critical. They will be concerned that these new projects don't interfere with your assigned project's deadlines, especially when that would result in them missing their deadlines. Management will be concerned about the cost of your time and of any tangible costs, especially when an unrequested new service does not get used.

A.1.14   The On-Call Expert

The on-call expert is always available to give advice. This is a person who has established herself as knowledgeable in all or most aspects of the system. Sometimes, the on-call expert has a narrow focus; other times she is an all-around expert.

The value provided to the company by this role is that people have someone to call when they need advice: whether someone needs to know an exact answer or simply a good starting point for research.

The on-call expert receives satisfaction from helping people and from the ego trip that is inherent to the role. Because technology changes quickly, she requires time to maintain her knowledge, whether that is time spent reading magazines, networking at conferences, or experimenting with new products.

When you are the expert, you must remember to help people help themselves, otherwise you will find yourself overcommitted.

A.1.15   The Educator

The educator spends his time teaching customers to use the services available. The educator may stop by to fix a problem with a printer, but he stays to teach the customer how to better use the spreadsheet software. He also finds himself writing most of the user documentation.

The educator is valuable to the company because his work results in people working more efficiently with the tools they have. The educator has close interactions with customers and therefore learns what problems people are having. He becomes a resource for finding out what the customers need.

The educator receives satisfaction from knowing that his documentation is used and appreciated and from knowing that people work better because of his efforts.

When you are the educator, customers want you to understand their jobs, how they work, and, most importantly, what it is in their tools that they find confusing. They want documentation that answers the questions they have, not what the developers think is important.

A.1.16   The Policy Enforcer

The policy enforcer is the person responsible for saying "no" when someone wants to do something that is against policy. He is also the person that shuts down violators. The policy enforcer depends on two tools equally: policies and management support. Policies must be written and published for all to see. If the policies are not written, enforcement will be inconsistent because he will have to make up the rules as he goes along and his peers may enforce different ideas of what is right and wrong. The second tool is management support. The policy has no teeth if management bends the rules every time someone requests an exception. Often, the enforcer has the authority to disconnect a network jack if the violation is creating a global problem and the violator cannot be contacted in a reasonable amount of time. If the management does not support the enforcer's decision, the enforcer can't do his job. If management approves a security policy but then permits an exception after the enforcer says "no," the enforcer loses authority and the will or reason to continue.

The value provided to the company by the policy enforcer is by giving people a reason to follow the policies that management decided were best for the company. If management constantly makes exceptions, the policy isn't very good, the management agreed to policies they didn't understand, or the management isn't doing their job. A manager shouldn't sign off on a policy and then continually sign off on requests for exceptions.

The policy enforcer receives satisfaction from knowing that he is actively trying to keep the company following the direction set by the management and from being chartered to steamroller through the site ensuring compliance.

When you are the policy enforcer, customers want to get their jobs done and don't understand why so many roadblocks (policies) are preventing them from doing that. Rather than saying "no," it can be more useful to help them by understanding what they are trying to achieve and helping them reach that goal and stay within policy. If you do not like to be in this role, but feel there is no way to escape it, you might consider assertiveness training or books such as *When I Say No I Feel Guilty* by Manuel J. Smith (1975, 2000).

A Policy with Exceptions

A site had a security policy that created a lot of extra work for anyone who wanted to abide by it. For a web site to be accessible from outside the firewall, the site had to be replicated on the outside, rather than by poking a hole in the firewall to let outsiders access the internal host. This replicated site could not make connections back into the company. If it needed access to an internal service (such as a database), that service also had to be replicated. Making a service completely self-sufficient was very difficult. Therefore, when the enforcer rejected a request, the employee would cry to management and an exception would be granted. Eventually, enough holes were poked in the firewall that the policy didn't mean anything. The policy enforcer proposed a revision to the policy that simply reflected management's behavior: Holes would be poked if the cost of replication would exceed a certain number of hours of work. Management was in a furor at the proposal because it was against their beliefs in how they wanted security to be done. When the enforcer pointed out all the exceptions they had made, they understood his point. Although old exceptions were grandfathered, management was much better at supporting the policy enforcer after the revision. If management wasn't going to support the policy, the enforcer shouldn't have to either.

A.1.17   The Disaster Worrier

Someone in the group should be worried about things going wrong. When a solution is being proposed, this person asks, "What is the failure mode?" Of course, the disaster worrier can't drive all decisions, or projects will never be completed or will be over budget. This person needs to be balanced by an optimist. However, without someone keeping an eye out for potential disasters, a team can create a house of cards.

The value provided to the company by the disaster worrier is not felt directly, except in times of emergency. Half the system is failing, but the other half keeps working because of controls put in place. General system robustness can be the result of this person.

This person receives satisfaction from safety and stability.

When you are in this role, others around you may get tired of your constant push for belts and suspenders. It is important to pick your battles rather than have an opinion at every turn. Nobody likes to hear laments like, "That wouldn't have failed if people had listened to me" or "Next time you won't be so quick to ignore me!" It may be better to share responsibility rather than place blame and refer to future improvement rather than gloat about your expertise: "In the future, we need to write scripts that handle disk-full situations." Gentle one-on-one coaching is more effective than public bemoaning.

A.1.18   The Careful Planner

The careful planner is the person who takes the time to plan each step of the project in which she is involved. She builds good test plans and is never flustered when things go wrong, because she has already figured out what to do.

The value provided to the company by the careful planner is that she completes important tasks reliably and flawlessly.

This person derives satisfaction from completing a task and knowing that it is really finished and watching the first customers use it without a hitch. She takes pride in her work.

When you are in this role, others come to rely on your work being flawless. You are often given the tasks that cannot afford to fail. Continue to work as you always did and don't let the importance of the tasks weigh you down. Be aware that your meticulous work takes time and others are always in a hurry and may get agitated watching you work. Make sure that you develop a talent for predicting how long you will need to complete a task. You don't want to be seen as someone who couldn't meet a deadline if it walked up and introduced itself.

A.1.19   The Capacity Planner

The capacity planner is the person who makes the system scale as it grows. This person notices when things are getting full, running out, or becoming overloaded. Good capacity planners pay attention to utilization patterns and are in tune with business changes that may affect them. Great capacity planners install systems that do this monitoring automatically and produce graphs that predict when capacity will run out. Vendors can help capacity planners by documenting data that they would find useful such as how much RAM and disk space is required as a function of the number of users.

The value provided to the company by this role is that traffic jams are prevented. This is another role that goes unnoticed if the job is done properly. This person also helps the company fix the problem the right way (too many times we've seen departments trying to speed up a server by adding more RAM, when the real problem was an overloaded network connection).

The capacity planner receives satisfaction from knowing that problems are prevented, that people heed their warnings, and from finding the real source of problems when they might be perceived as originating elsewhere.

When you are the capacity planner, customers want you to have accurate data and solutions that won't cost any money. It is your job to justify costs. As always, explaining things in the customer's language is critical.

A.1.20   The Budget Administrator

The budget administrator is the SA who keeps tabs on how much money is left in the budget and helps write the budget for next year. This person knows what the money is meant to be spent on and when it is meant to be spent and figures out ways to make the budget stretch further.

The value provided to the company by the budget administrator is that SA expenses are kept under control, the tasks that need doing are funded (within reason) even if they are unexpected, and management can perform financial planning based on reliable figures for the coming year.

The budget administrator receives satisfaction from staying within budget and yet managing to fund extra, important projects that were not budgeted for.

When you are the budget administrator, customers want you to stay in budget, to prepare a good budget plan for the next year, to accurately evaluate what the most important projects are, to make sure that all the critical tasks have funding, and to show how the money they let you spend is benefiting them.

A.1.21   The Customer's Advocate

The customer's advocate is the person who can help a person speak up for her needs. He is the translator and lobbyist positioned between the customer and her management. The advocate doesn't just recommend a solution, he coaches the customer on how to sell the idea to her boss and stands by during the presentation in case she needs help.

The value provided to the company by the advocate is to help the customers get through red tape, language barriers, and get what they need.

The advocate receives satisfaction from knowing he has helped someone. He also knows that by interfacing with management he is able to put his SA team in a good light and perform the role of the helpful facilitator. Often, you help a customer get what she needs by working the system, rather than going around it, which is especially valuable if you also created the system.

When you are the advocate, customers want you to understand them before you start suggesting solutions. They want you to understand their technical needs, as well as soft issues such as schedule and budget.

A.1.22   The Technocrat

The technocrat is the advocate for new technology. When a system needs to be repaired or replaced, he puts more value in the new system because it is new, even if it still has bugs. He disdains those that seek comfort in old systems that may be "good enough." The disaster worrier can provide good counterbalance to the technocrat.

The value provided to the company by the technocrat is that he prevents the company from becoming technically stagnant.

The technocrat receives satisfaction from being surrounded by the latest new technology (dare we say, "new-toy" syndrome?).

When you are the technocrat, customers want you to focus on the value proposition rather than that newer is better.

A.1.23   The Salesperson

The salesperson can be selling a couple different types of items. She may be selling a particular policy, new service, or proposal. She may be selling the SA team itself, either to upper management or to the customers. A salesperson is concerned with finding the needs of customers and then convincing them that what she has to sell meets those needs. New services are easier to "sell" if the customers were involved in the specification and selection process.

The value provided to the company by the salesperson is that she makes the SA team's job easier. A great system that is never accepted by the customers is not useful to the company. A great policy that saves the company money is not helpful if the customers work around it because they don't understand the benefits.

The salesperson receives short-term satisfaction from "making the sale," but for real, lasting satisfaction, the salesperson must develop a relationship with the customers and find herself feeling like she truly helps the customers in a meaningful way.

When you are the salesperson, customers want to have their needs understood and appreciated. They want to be talked with, not to.

A.1.24   The Vendor Liaison

The vendor liaison maintains a relationship with one or more vendors. She may know a vendor's product line better than anyone else the in the group and is privy to upcoming products. She is a resource for the other SAs, thus saving calls to the salesperson.

The value provided to the company by the vendor liaison is in having someone who understands and is dedicated to the company's needs dealing with a vendor. Having a single point of contact saves resources.

The vendor liaison receives satisfaction from being the expert that everyone respects, from being the "first to know" about vendor news, and from the free lunches and shirts she receives.

When you are the vendor liaison, customers want you to be all-knowing about the vendor, open minded about competing vendors, and a harsh negotiator when getting prices.

A.1.25   The Visionary

The visionary is the person in the group who looks at the big picture and has a vision of where the group should go.

The value provided to the company by the visionary is that he keeps the group focused on what's next.

The visionary receives satisfaction when he looks back over the years and sees that in the long term he really did make a difference. All those incremental improvements accumulated and met major goals.

When you are the visionary, customers want to know what's happening next and may not be too concerned with the long term. Your team's reputation for being able to execute a plan affects your ability to sell your vision to the customers.

A.1.26   The Mother

The mother is the SA who nurtures the customers. It's difficult to explain except through example. One SA spent her mornings walking through the halls, stopping by each person's office to see how things were. She would fix small problems and note the bigger problems for the afternoon. She would answer many user-interface questions that a customer might have felt were "too small" to ask the helpdesk. The customers were making a big paradigm change (from X Terminals to PCs running X Terminal emulators), and this mothering was exactly what they needed. In her morning walks, she would answer hundreds of questions and resolve dozens of problems that would otherwise have been tickets submitted to the helpdesk. The customers got very used to this level of service and soon came to rely on her morning visits as part of what kept them productive.

The value provided to the company by the mother is a high degree of hand-holding, which can be critical at particular times (times of great change) or with particular customer groups (nontechnical customers). The personal contact also ensures a more precise understanding of the customers' needs.

The mother receives satisfaction from the personal relationships she develops with her customers. When you are the mother, customers want to know that their immediate needs are being met and will put less emphasis on the long-term strategy.

You must remember to keep an eye on the future and not get too absorbed in the present.

A.1.27   The Monitor

The monitor is the watch-dog who notices how well things are running. Sometimes, the monitor uses low-tech methods: He uses the same services that his customers use. Although the SAs may have a private file server, this person stores his files on the file server that the customers use, so he can "feel their pain." As this person becomes more sophisticated, he automates his monitoring, but then he watches the monitoring system's output and takes the time to fix things rather than just clear the alarms.

The value provided to the company by the monitor is that problems are noticed before customers start complaining. This can give the perception of a trouble-free network.

The monitor receives satisfaction from being the first to notice a problem, from knowing that he's working on fixing a problem before customers report it, and knowing that problems are prevented by monitoring capacity issues.

When you are the monitor, customers most likely don't know you exist. If they did, they would want your testing to simulate their real workloads (end-to-end testing). For example, it isn't good enough to know that a mail server is up. You must test that a message can be submitted, relayed, delivered, and read.

A.1.28   The Facilitator

The facilitator is a person in the group with excellent communication skills. He tends to turn impromptu discussions into decision-making meetings. He is often asked to run meetings, especially large meetings in which keeping focus can be difficult.

The facilitator adds value by making processes run smoother. He may not take on a lot of action items, but he gets groups of people to agree to what needs to be done and who is going to do it. He keeps meetings efficient and fun.

The facilitator receives satisfaction from seeing people come to agreement on goals and taking initiative to see the goals completed.

When you are the facilitator, the other members on your team want you to facilitate all their discussions. It is important to coach other people into being facilitators and create an environment where everyone has good communication skills.

A.1.29   The Customer/SA

Sometimes, a customer is also an SA. Sometimes, this is because a customer has certain responsibilities that require privileged access or because the customer used to be an SA and retains some of those responsibilities.

The value provided to the company by the customer/SA is that when other SAs are on vacation, this person can fill in. In fact, in situations in which there is only a single SA, it is useful to coach one of the customers on daily operational issues, so he can provide vacation coverage. Having an additional person who can change backup tapes, create user accounts, and solve the top 10 most frequent problems can be very useful.

The customer/SA receives satisfaction from the role if he holds SAs (or super-user access) in high esteem. Alternatively, he may receive some kind of "combat pay" for being cross-trained.

When you are the customer/SA, the main SA team wants to know that you aren't interfering with their plans, are following the right procedures, and are upholding the same ethical practices as they are. The other customers want to know that you will be able to keep things running when called upon to do so.

A.1.30   Customer Support

The customer support SA is a person who views his job as being centered on the human customer making the request, rather than the technical processes that he is involved with. He views his job as helping customers with the system, which is quite static. Major changes to the system come from external forces, such as a systems programming group.

The customer support SA is valuable to the company because he is the human interface to the full SA team. Most customers never see any "back line" support.

The customer support SA receives satisfaction from the personal relationships that he develops and the satisfaction of knowing that he has helped a real live human.

When you are the customer support SA, customers want their issues dealt with on their schedules. If they perceive the situation to be an emergency, they expect you to stop everything and help them.

A.1.31   The Policy Navigator

The policy navigator understands the rules and regulations of the bureaucracy and can help others navigate through or around them. The navigator can help someone get through a process or work around a policy without violating it.

The value provided to the SA team by this role is that she can get things done faster when having to deal with "the system," and, when needed, she is the expert in working around the system without getting into hot water.

The policy navigator receives satisfaction from knowing that her connections and knowledge have contributed to a project.

When you are the policy navigator, your customers want things to get done, regardless of whether you stay within the system. This can put you in a difficult situation when it seems to the customer that it is easier to violate policy or work around the system.

A.2   Negative Roles

The following sections describe some negative roles that you want to avoid.

A.2.1   The Bleeding Edger

Sometimes an SA can be so excited by new technology that he seeks to unleash it on the customers before it is ready. Rather than being on the leading edge, he keeps the company on the bleeding edge. The phrase "bleeding edge" comes from the fact that the customers always seem to be enduring the pain of new services that are still buggy.

A.2.2   Technology Staller

The counter-balance to the bleeding edger is the person who stalls on the use of any new technology. This person is risk-averse. Sometimes she has a favorite excuse, such as not being satisfied with the back-out plan. She is happy with the current OS release, the current OS distribution, the current brand of computers, amount of bandwidth, and type of network topology. The staller doesn't see the lack of technology refresh and the problems that it has created. Ironically, this person used to be on the cutting edge, but has now become stuck in a rut. She may have been the person who eschewed the mainframes and adopted UNIX or laughed at the workstation users who wouldn't adopt PCs. However cutting-edge she once was, she has found something she is comfortable with and now has become the person she used to mock years ago.

A.2.3   The SA Who Cried Wolf

This person is worried about things that aren't happening or are unlikely to happen. Much of system administration is about managing risks. Although we can take acceptable risks, this person thinks all risks are unacceptable. This person slows projects from getting off the ground. He predicts doom or failure constantly without hard facts to back it up. Sometimes he is just uncomfortable with anything he isn't in control of or about which he isn't educated. Sometimes, this person will waste a lot of time working on problems that aren't even on your radar and ignore more pressing problems. The biggest danger with this person is that when he is correct he will be ignored.

A.2.4   The Cowboy

The cowboy is the SA who rushes into fixing systems or implementing new services without proper planning, thinking through the consequences, or a back-out plan. He does not bother to ask his manager beforehand or to check with the customers. He does not test his work properly to verify that it is working and goes home without telling anyone what he has done. He sees himself as talented and fast-working, and thinks that others try to put too much red tape in his way and that they are inappreciative of his talents. He doesn't document anything and "knows" that he is invaluable to the company.

The Cowboy

A mid-size computing hardware manufacturer had a cowboy in a senior SA position. His management had brought in a consulting group to rearchitect the network and to build a transition plan from the old network to the new one. The plan was agreed upon, the equipment was ordered, a schedule was laid out and agreed upon with the customers, and test plans were being built with the customers. The day that the new equipment arrived, the cowboy stayed late and ripped out the old network equipment and installed the new gear. He did not use the new architecture, he ignored all the components of the transition plan that were to solve other problems in the process of the transition, and he did not do much, if any, testing. The next day when people returned to work, many of them found that they had no network connection. Those affected included the CEO, the entire customer support department, the cowboy's management chain, and many of the engineers. The helpdesk and the rest of the SA group had no idea what had happened because he had not told anyone, and he didn't bother arriving until much later in the day. He was still proud of what he had done and unrepentant because he viewed the transition plan and test plan as a big waste of time and money. He enjoyed showing that he could do it on his own in a few hours, when the consultants were taking so much time over it. He was oblivious to the cost of the major outage that he had caused and the damage he had inflicted on the SA group's reputation.

A.2.5 Slaves, Scapegoats, or Janitors

Sometimes, SAs are in the role of being slaves, scapegoats, or janitors. Slaves are expected to do tasks without question, even if they might be able to suggest better processes if they were told the big picture. Sometimes, others use SAs as scapegoats. All bad things that happen are blamed on the SAs. The SAs are blamed for a project being late, even if the customers weren't communicating their needs. Sometimes, SAs are thought of as janitors— people who aren't valuable to the company's direct business, but are unskilled workers who are purely the overhead. All three of these roles are problems with management not understanding the purpose of SAs in their own organization. However, it is the SA's responsibility to fix these problems by increasing communication and working on their team's visibility within the organization.

A.3   Team Roles

Within an SA team, there are some roles that, with the exception of the martyr, should be a part of every team.

A.3.1   The End-to-End Expert

The end-to-end expert is the person who understands the technology being used from the lowest to the highest levels. She is the person who is critical for solving obscure problems, as well as major outages. Obscure problems usually are the result of multiple simultaneous failures or strange interactions between different areas, and they require expertise in all areas to be able to solve them. Major outages affect multiple subsystems and require a deep understanding of the overall architecture to pinpoint the real problem.

A.3.2   The Outsider

During a prolonged outage, sometimes the people working on the problem get the SA equivalent of writer's block. They're going in circles, unable to make a significant improvement in the situation. The role that is most useful here is the outsider. The outsider brings a fresh viewpoint to the situation. By making everyone explain what has happened so far, people often realize the solution. Sometimes, the role of this person is to encourage the people to seek outside help or escalate the problem to higher authorities or to vendor support. Other times, this person's role is to simply recognize that it is time to give up: There is a back-out plan and it should be implemented.

A.3.3   The Level-Minded Person

Another role is the person who decides at what level to solve a particular problem. People always tend to think that problems can be solved at their own level. Technicians think they need to work harder. Programmers think they need to introduce new software to fix the problem. However, another role is the person who has an understanding of all the levels, including management. After weeks of trying to solve a problem, this is the person who suggests that it would be less expensive and possibly more effective to simply get a higher level of management to announce that a certain practice is not allowed. It may be better to find the first manager up the organization chart who outranks the two bickering customers and give the problem to her to solve. This is also the person most likely to quote the old Internet adage: "Technology can't solve social problems," then seek a policy change.

A.3.4   The Martyr

The martyr is the person who feels resentment for carrying the torch when he feels that nobody else has as much work as he does. Unable to understand why nobody else works the long hours that he does and unhappy with his lack of social life or financial success, this person bemoans the problems of the world. This can happen as a result of burnout or low self-esteem. Burnout happens when a person does not balance work with recreation. Sadly, in today's fast-paced, modern culture, some people grow up not learning the importance of relaxation. They feel they are always "at work." This extreme work ethic may be the secret to their success, but it is not a sustainable success because it leads to burnout. Once burnt, working harder only makes the situation worse. Self-esteem is something we learn (or don't learn) when we are young that dictates our happiness. Cognitive theorists believe that our mental state (are we happy or sad?) is not a sign of whether good or bad things are happening to us, but is a sign of how we react to what is happening to us (Burns 1999b). We can even be unhappy in response to good events if our self-esteem has been damaged to the point that no matter what happens, we feel worthless. This can happen when we turn around good news and events and change them into things to worry about: "He liked my work on that project! What if I can't meet those expectations every time? What if my coworkers become jealous and resent me?" There are therapies designed to help people in this situation (Burns 1999a).

A.3.5   Doers of Repetitive Tasks

Some personality types lend themselves to doing repetitive tasks. These people should be valued because they solve immediate problems. This book can't stress enough the importance of automation, but some tasks either can't be automated (such as physically delivering new machines) or are not repeated enough to make it cost effective to be automated. This role is an important one for the team. This person can offload repetitive tasks from higher-skilled people. These smaller tasks are often excellent training for higher level tasks.

A.3.6   The Social Director

The social director is the person who boosts team spirit by remembering people's birthdays, anniversaries, and other excuses to have the group celebrate. Getting people to relate to each other in a nonwork context can build team cohesion. The key to success in this position is to make sure that people don't feel imposed upon and to make sure you don't overdo it and risk the boss considering you a time-waster.

Monthly Birthday Lunch
One SA team had a policy of going out to lunch once a month. The people whose birthday was that month didn't have to pay and were responsible for coordinating the next month's lunch. It was a valuable team-building tradition. Because of a couple of factors, the tradition stopped for a year. To restart the process, the team held a lunch for anyone who had a birthday in the last 12 months, and the boss paid the entire bill.

A.3.7   Mr. Break Time

During an emergency situation, it is key to have someone who notices when people are becoming exhausted and encourages them to take a break. People may feel that the task is too important to stop working on it, but this person realizes that nothing is getting done and a break might refresh people. Tom is known to disappear and return with pizzas and drinks. Often, by walking away from a problem, people can take the time to think through the problem and come up with better solutions.

There are other roles that exist in an SA team, but we feel the preceding ones deserve highlighting.

A.4   Conclusion

We hope that as you read this appendix you found one or more of these paragraphs to be like looking into a mirror and seeing yourself for the very first time. Now you can be conscious of what motivates you and how you fit into your team.

This may help you realize that you play many roles in your organization and may play a special role on your team. You wear many hats. As you wear each hat, you can be conscious of the value you should be providing to the company, what motivates you, and what customers expect from you.

Maybe you learned something good or bad about yourself. Maybe you learned something new about yourself or validated feelings that you already had. It may convince you to seek personal improvement in an area of your life. The next time you consider a career change, you might spend more time thinking about the roles you like to be in or the roles that match your skills and compare those with to the roles you will be asked to play in the new position. Don't be worried if you feel that every role appeals to you. Maybe that is your destiny in life, or maybe as you gain more experience and learn you will find new clarity in your feelings about these things.

Maybe this appendix made you realize that your organization is in dire need of one of the roles described here. Maybe you've noticed something missing from your SA team. Maybe you should try to take on that role more often, encourage others to take on that role, or look for those skills the next time you hire someone. You may realize that your organization has too many people in a particular role, which indicates that you need balance. Maybe this appendix helped you notice that a certain person is fulfilling a negative role and needs coaching to change.

Maybe this appendix made you realize that people on your team all play too many roles, or don't play enough roles, or the roles aren't balanced.

Most of all, we hope that this part of the book helped you understand the people on your team who are not like you. Now you can appreciate the value they bring to the team. A strong team includes people with different skills and from various backgrounds; each brings something unique to the table. Those differences do not divide a team, but make it stronger. For that to happen, the team must be conscious of the differences and take time to value them rather than run from them.

Exercises

1. What roles do you see yourself in? (Don't be humble.) Do you want to remain in these roles? What roles are you not in that appeal to you?

2. What roles did you see yourself in early in your career? How is that different from the roles you are in now?

3. What roles do you see yourself fulfilling in the future?

4. What personal changes would you like to make so that you can better serve in your role or move into new roles?

5. What roles do you not like? Why? How are they different from the roles you are currently fulfilling?

6. For each person on your team, determine which roles they portray. If you feel it wouldn't destroy your friendship, have them do the same thing and share each other's lists. How much did the therapy bills cost?

7. Psychologists and managers know that other people cannot be changed; they need to see the need for change themselves and decide how to make the change on their own. Did this chapter make you realize that someone on your team is fulfilling a negative role and needs to make some personal changes? How might you help that person see the need for change? Is that person you?

8. What roles are missing from your team? How can you develop those roles in your team?

9. This appendix does not contain a complete list of roles. What roles do you feel should be added to this list? How are they valuable to the organization or team, or in what ways are they negative roles? What are the motivators for these roles? What do customers expect from them?

What to Do When ...

In this appendix we pull together the various elements from the rest of the book to show you how they can be used to deal with everyday situations or solve common questions SAs and managers often have.

B.1 I'm Building a Site from Scratch

- Think about the organizational structure you need—Chapter 25.
- Plan your namespaces carefully—Chapter 6.
- Build a rock-solid data center—Chapter 17.
- Build a rock-solid network—Chapter 18.
- Build services that will scale—Chapter 3.
- Build a software depot, or at least plan a small directory hierarchy that can grow into a software depot—Chapter 23.
- Establish your initial core application services:
  - email—Chapter 19
  - DNS, DHCP—Section 1.1.3
  - file service, backups—Chapter 21
  - printing—Chapter 20
  - remote access—Chapter 22

B.2   My Small Site Is Growing

- Have you grown to the point that you need a helpdesk?—Chapter 15.
- Have you grown to the point that you need a network operations center dedicated to monitoring—Chapter 24—and coordinating network operations?
- Think about your organization and whom you need to hire—Chapter 25.
- Make sure you are monitoring services for capacity as well as availability so that you can predict when to scale them—Chapter 24.
- Be ready for an influx of new employees—See B.19, B.20, B.21.

B.3   My Large Site Is Going Global

- Design your WAN architecture—Chapter 18.
- Make sure your helpdesk really is 24×7. Look at ways to leverage SAs in other time zones—Chapter 15.
- Architect services to take account of long-distance links (usually lower bandwidth and less reliable)—Chapter 3.
- Qualify applications for use over high-latency links—Section 3.1.2.

B.4   Services Are Being Replaced

- Be conscious of the process—Chapter 11.
- Manage your DHCP lease times to aide the transition—Section 1.1.4.
- Don't hardcode server names into configurations, hardcode aliases that move with the service—Section 3.1.6.
- Manage your DNS time-to-live values to switch to new servers—Section 13.2.1.

B.5   Moving a Data Center

- You need to have a scheduled maintenance window, unless everything is fully redundant and you can move one half of a redundant pair and then the other—Chapter 12.
- Make sure the new data center is properly designed—Chapter 17.
- Back up every file system of any machine before it is moved.
- Perform a "firedrill" on your data backup system—Section 21.2.1.
- Develop test cases before you move and test, test, test everything after the move is complete—Chapter 11.

- Label every cable before it is disconnected—Section 17.1.7.
- Establish minimal services (redundant hardware) at a new location with new equipment, then move everything else.
- Test the new environment (networking, power, UPS, HVAC, and so on) before the move begins—Section 17.1.4.
- Perform a dress rehearsal—Section 11.2.5.

B.6 Lots of People Are Moving Their Office

- Work with facilities to allocate just one "move day" each week.
- Establish a procedure and a form that will get you all the information you need about each person who is moving (what equipment they have, how many network connections, telephone connections, special needs). Have SAs check out nonstandard equipment in advance and make notes.
- Connect and test network connections ahead of time.
- Have customers power down their machines before the move and put all cables, mice, keyboards, and other bits that might get lost into a marked box.
- Brainstorm all the ways that some of the work can be done by the people moving. Be careful to assess their skill level—maybe certain people shouldn't do anything themselves.
- Have a moving company actually move the equipment and have a designated SA move team do the unpacking, reconnecting, and testing. Take care in selecting the movers—there are some good companies out there, but there are also a lot of bad ones.
- Train the helpdesk to check with customers who report problems to see if they have just moved and didn't have the problem before the move; then, pass those requests to the move team rather than the usual escalation path.
- Formalizing the process, limiting it to one day a week, doing the prep work, and having a move team makes it go more smoothly with less downtime for the customers and less move-related problems for the SAs to check out.

B.7 Dealing With Mergers and Aquisitions

- If you are the CEO, you should involve your CIO before the merger is even announced.
- If you are an SA, try to find out who at the other company actually has the authority to make "the big decisions."

- Start a dialog with the SAs at the other company. Understand their support structure, service levels, network architecture, security model, and policies. Determine what the new model is going to look like.
- Have at least one initial face-to-face meeting with the SAs at the other company. It's easier to get angry at someone you haven't met, which should be avoided.
- Move on to technical details. Are there namespace conflicts?—Chapter 6. How are you going to resolve them?
- Adopt the best processes of the two companies—don't blindly select the processes of the bigger company.
- Be sensitive to cultural differences between the two groups. Diverse opinions can be a good thing if people can learn to respect each other—Sections 30.1.5 and 27.2.2.
- Make sure both SA teams have a high-level overview diagram of both networks, as well as a detailed map of each site's LAN—Chapter 18.
- What should the new network architecture look like?—Chapter 18. How will the two networks be connected? Are some remote offices likely to merge with each other? What does the new security model or security perimeter look like?—Chapter 7.
- Ask senior management about corporate identity issues. Do the corporate identities need to merge or stay separate? What implications does this have on the email infrastructure—Chapter 19—and Internet-facing services?
- Are there any customers or business partners of either company who will be sensitive to the merger, and/or want their intellectual property protected from the other company?—Chapter 7.
- Compare the policies mentioned in Chapter 7, looking in particular for differences in privacy policy, security policy, and how each interconnect with business partners.
- Check router tables of both companies and verify that the IP address space in use doesn't overlap. (This is particularly a problem if you both use RFC1918 address space [Lear et al. 1994, Rekhler et al. 1996].)
- Consider putting a firewall between the two companies until both have compatible security policies—Chapter 7.

B.8   A Machine Keeps Crashing!

- Establish a temporary workaround. Communicate to customers that it is temporary.
- Find the real cause—Chapter 4.
- Fix the real cause, not the symptoms—Chapter 5.
- Replace the system—Chapter 11.

- If the root cause is hardware, buy better hardware—Chapter 2.
- If the root cause is environmental, provide a better physical environment for your hardware—Chapter 17.
- Provide your SAs better training on diagnostic tools—Chapter 4.

B.9 Which Tools Should I Purchase for My SA Team?

- A laptop with network diagnostic tools such as network sniffer, DHCP client in verbose mode, encrypted telnet/ssh client, tftpserver, and so on. Also provide both wired and wireless Ethernet—Section 17.1.10.
- A library of the standard reference books for the technologies they are involved in—Sections 28.1.1, 29.1.6, and bibliography.
- A set of screwdrivers in all the sizes computers use. Find a way to deal with the fact that people will borrow the most common screwdriver and not return it—Section 17.1.12. Either buy many of that one tool, or do as one site did: buy each SA 10 small screwdriver sets. When SAs asked to borrow a tool, they were told, "You can't borrow my tools but here is a complete set as a gift so you don't have to bother me again."
- High-speed connectivity to their home and the necessary tools so that they can telecommute.
- A portable label printer—Section 17.1.12.
- A cable tester.
- A spare PC or server for experimenting with new configurations—Section 13.2.1.
- Radios or walkie-talkies for communicating inside the building—Chapter 17 and Section 12.1.7.
- A PDA or nonelectronic organizer—Section 27.1.2.
- Membership to professional societies such as USENIX and SAGE—Section 27.1.4.
- A variety of headache medicines. It's really difficult to solve big problems when you have a headache.

B.10 Why Should I Bother Documenting Systems and Procedures

- Good documentation describes the "why" as well as the "how to."
- When you do things right and they "just work," even you will have forgotten the details when they break or need upgrading.
- You get to go on vacation—Section 27.2.2.

- You get to move on to more interesting projects rather than being stuck doing the same stuff because you are the only one who knows how it works—Section 24.2.1.
- You will get a reputation as being a real asset to the company (raises, bonuses and promotions . . . , or at least fame and fortune).

B.11   Why Should I Bother Documenting Policies

- Other people can't read your mind—Section A.1.16.
- It communicates expectations for your own team, not just your customers—Section 7.1.3 and Chapter 9.
- It's unethical to enforce a policy that isn't communicated to the people that it governs—Section 9.2.1.
- It's abusive to punish people for not reading your mind——Section A.1.16.

B.12   How Do I Identify the Fundamental Problems in My Environment?

- Look at the Basics section of each chapter.
- Survey the management chain that funds you—Chapter 25.
- Survey two or three customers that use your services—Section 26.2.2.
- Survey all customers.
- Identify what kinds of problems consume your time the most—Section 26.1.3.
- Ask the helpdesk employees what problems they see the most—Sections 15.1.6 and 25.1.4.
- Ask the people configuring the devices in the field what problems they see the most, and what customers complain about the most.
- If your architecture isn't simple enough to draw by hand on a whiteboard, maybe it's too complicated to manage—Section 18.1.2.

B.13   I Need More Money for Projects!

- Establish "the need" in the minds of your managers.
- Find out what management wants, and communicate how the projects you need money for will serve that goal.
- Become part of the budget process—Sections 28.1.1 and 29.1.5.

- Do more with less: Make sure that your staff has good time-management skills—Section 27.1.2.
- Manage your boss better—Section 27.2.3.
- Learn how your management communicates with you and communicate in a compatible way—Chapters 28 and 29.

B.14 Projects Don't Get Done!

- Make sure the people involved have good time-management skills—Section 27.1.2.
- Reduce the number of projects.
- Don't spend time on the projects that don't matter—Figure 28.1.
- Prioritize → Focus → Win.
- Outsource the highest-impact projects—Sections 14.2.2, 22.1.5, and 25.1.8.
- Hire clerical staff to take on tactical tasks (mundane work) so that you have more time for strategic tasks (vision and development), or to write code.
- Hire short-term contract programmers to write code to spec.

B.15 Customers Are Unhappy

- Make sure you make a good impression on new customers—Section 26.1.1.
- Make sure you communicate more with existing customers—Section 26.2.4 and Chapter 26.
- Create a System Status web page—Section 26.2.1.
- Create a local Enterprise Portal for your site—Section 26.2.1.

B.16 Management Is Unhappy

- Meet with them in person to listen to the complaints; *don't* try to do it via email.
- Find out your manager's priorities and adopt them as your own—Section 27.2.3.
- Be sure you know how management communicates with you and communicate in a compatible way—Chapters 28 and 29.
- Make sure people in specialized roles understand the roles—Appendix A.

B.17   SAs Are Unhappy

- Make sure their direct manager knows how to manage them well—Chapter 28.
- Make sure executive management supports the management of SAs—Chapter 29.
- Make sure SAs are taking care of themselves—Chapter 27.
- Make sure SAs are in roles that they want and understand—Appendix A.
- If SAs are overloaded, make sure they manage their time well—Section 27.1.2; or hire more people and divide the work—Chapter 30.
- Fire any SAs who may be fomenting discontent—Chapter 31.

B.18   Systems Are Too Slow

- Use your monitoring systems to establish where the bottlenecks are—Chapter 24.
- Look at performance-tuning information that is specific to each architecture so that you know what to monitor and how to do it.
- Recommend a solution based on your findings.
- Know what the real problem is before you try to fix it—Chapter 4.

B.19   There's a Big Influx of Computers

- Make sure you understand the *economic difference* between "desktop" and "server" hosts. Educate your boss or CFO about the difference or they will balk at high-priced servers—Section 2.1.3.
- Make sure you understand the *physical differences* between "desktop" and "server" hosts—Section 2.1.1.
- Establish a small number of standard hardware configurations and purchase them in bulk—Section 1.2.3.
- Make sure you have automated host installation, configuration, and updates—Chapter 1.
- Check power and HVAC capacity for your data center—Chapter 17.
- If new hosts are for new employees, see B.20.

B.20   There's a Big Influx of New Users

- If new hosts are for new employees, make sure the hiring process includes ensuring that new computers and accounts are set up before people arrive—Section 26.1.1.

- Make sure you have a stockpile of standard desktops preconfigured and ready to deploy.
- Make sure you have automated host installation, configuration, and updates—Chapter 1.
- Make sure there is proper new user documentation and that you have adequate staff to do orientation—Section 26.1.1.
- Make sure there is at least one simple game on every computer. It makes new computer users feel good about their machines if it entertains them too—less scary too.
- Check to make sure the building can withstand the increase in power utilization.

B.21   There's a Big Influx of New SAs

- Assign mentors to junior SAs—Sections 28.1.1 and 30.1.5.
- Have an orientation for each SA level to make sure they understand the key processes and policies; make sure that it is clear whom they should go to for help.
- It's essential to have documentation.
- Purchase proper reference books, both technical and "soft topics"—time management, communication, and people skills—Chapter 27.
- Give them all copies of this book.

B.22   Our SA Team Has a High Attrition Rate

- Be sure HR performs exit interviews.
- Completely lock out the SAs who leave from the systems—Chapter 31.
- Make the group aware that you are willing to listen to complaints in private.
- Have an "upward feedback session" at which your staff reviews your performance.
- Have an anonymous "upward feedback session" so that your staff can review your performance.
- Determine what you, as a manager, might be doing wrong—Chapters 28 and 29.
- Do things that increase morale: Have the team design and produce a t-shirt together—a dozen dollars spent on t-shirts can induce a morale improvement that thousands of dollars in raises can't.
- Make sure everyone in the group has read Chapter 27, but don't force it on them ... that only reduces morale.
- If everyone is leaving because of one bad apple, get rid of him or her.

B.23   Our User-Base Has a High Attrition Rate

- Make sure management signals the SA team to disable accounts, remote access, and so on in a timely manner—Chapter 31.
- Make sure exiting employees return all company-owned equipment and software they have at home.
- Take measures against theft as people leave.
- Take measures against intellectual property theft, possibly restricting remote access.

B.24   I'm New to a Group

- Before you comment, ask questions to make sure you understand the situation.
- Meet all your coworkers one-on-one.
- Meet with customers informally (lunch) and formally—Chapter 26.
- Be sure to make a good first impression, especially with customers —Section 26.1.1.
- Give credence to your coworkers when they tell you what the problems in the group are. Don't reject them out of hand.
- Don't blindly believe your coworkers when they tell you what the problems in the group are. Verify them first.

B.25   I'm the New Manager of a Group

- Meet all your employees one-on-one. Ask them what they do, what role they would like to be in, and where they see themselves in three years. The purpose of this meeting is to listen to them, not to talk.
- Establish weekly group staff meetings.
- Meet your manager and your peers one-on-one to get their views.
- From day one, show the team that you have faith in them all —Chapter 28.
- Meet with customers informally (lunch) and formally—Chapter 26.
- Ask everyone to tell you what the problems facing the group are, listen carefully to everyone, and then look at the evidence and make up your own mind.
- Before you comment, ask questions to make sure you understand the situation.

B.26 I'm Looking for a New Job

- Determine why you are looking for a new job—understand your motivation.
- Determine what role you want to play in the new group—Appendix A.
- Determine which kind of organization—Section 25.3—you enjoy working in the most.
- Meet as many of your potential future coworkers as possible to find out what the group is like—Chapter 30.
- Never accept the first offer right off the bat. The first offer is just a proposal. Negotiate!—Section 27.2.1.
- Negotiate the things that are important to you in writing (conferences, training, vacation).
- Don't work for a company that doesn't let you interview their boss or your future boss.

B.27 I Need to Hire Many New SAs Quickly

- Use as many recruiting methods as possible—organize fun events at the appropriate conferences, use online boards, get referrals from SAs and customers—Chapter 30.
- Make sure you have a good recruiter and HR contact who knows what a good SA is.
- Determine how many SAs of what level and what skills you need each to have.
- Move quickly when you get a good candidate. You can refine your search later as you get to know what skills you have hired already.

B.28 I Need to Increase Total System Reliability

- Set up monitoring to pinpoint uptime problems—Chapter 24.
- Deploy end-to-end monitoring for key applications—Section 24.2.4.
- Reduce dependencies. Nothing in the data center should rely on anything outside of the data center—Sections 3.1.7 and 12.1.7.

B.29 I Need to Decrease Costs

- Decrease costs by centralizing some services—Chapter 14.
- Are you paying high maintenance on old equipment that it would be cheaper to replace?—Section 2.1.4.

- Reduce running costs, such as remote access, through outsourcing —Chapter 22 and Section 14.2.2.
- Can you reduce the support burden through standards and/or automation?—Chapter 1.
- Can you reduce support overhead through applications training for customers, or better documentation?
- Can you distribute costs more directly to the groups that incur them, such as maintenance charges, remote access charges, special. hardware, high-bandwidth use of wide-area links?—Section 25.1.2.
- Are people not paying for the services you provide? If they say, "It's important" but aren't willing to pay for the service, then it isn't important.

B.30   I Need to Add Features

- Know the requirements—Chapter 3.
- Make sure you maintain at least existing service and availability levels.
- If altering an existing service, have a back-out plan.
- Look into building an entirely new system and cutting over rather than altering the running one.
- If it's a really big infrastructure change, consider a maintenance window—Chapter 12.
- Decentralize so that local features can be catered to.
- Test! Test! Test!
- Document! Document! Document!

B.31   It Hurts When I Do "This"

- Don't do "that."

If It Hurts, Don't Do It

A small field office of a multinational company had a visit from a new SA supporting the international field offices. The local person who performed the SA tasks when there was no SA had told him over the telephone that the network was "painful." He assumed that she meant painfully slow until he got there and got a powerful electrical shock from the 10Base-2 network. He closed the office and sent everyone home immediately while he called an electrician to trace and fix the problem.

B.32   I Need to Build Customer Confidence

- Improve follow-through—Section 27.1.1.
- Discard projects that you haven't been able to achieve until you have enough time to complete the ones you need to.
- Communicate more—Chapter 26.
- Focus on projects that matter to the customers—Figure 28.1.
- Create a good first impression on the people entering your organization—Section 26.1.1.

B.33   I Need to Build the Team's Self-Confidence

- Start with a few simple, achievable projects then involve them in more difficult projects.
- Ask them what training they feel they need, and provide it.
- Coach them. Get coaching on how to coach!

B.34   I Need to Improve the Team's Follow-Through

- Find out why they are not following through.
- Make sure your trouble-ticket system assists them in tracking customer requests—make sure it isn't just for tracking short-term requests. Be sure it isn't so cumbersome that people avoid using it—Section 15.1.7.
- Encourage team members to have a single place to list all their requests—Section 27.1.1.
- Discourage team members from trying to keep to-do lists in their heads—Section 27.1.1.
- Purchase PDAs for all team members—Section 27.1.1.

B.35   I've Been Asked to Do Something, but I'm Not Sure of the Ethics Involved

- Log all events and actions.
- Get the request in writing.
- Check for a written policy regarding the situation—Chapter 9.
- If there is no written policy, absolutely get it in writing.
- Consult with your manager, *before* doing anything.

B.36   My Dishwasher Leaves Spots on My Glasses

- Spots are usually the result of not using hot enough water rather than finding a special soap or even using a special cycle on the machine.
- Check for problems with the hot water going to your dishwasher.
- Have the temperature of your hot water adjusted.
- Before starting the dishwasher, run the water in the adjacent sink until it's hot.

B.37   I Need to Protect My Job!

- Be the best SA in the group: have positive visibility—Chapter 26.
- Document everything—policies and technical and configuration information and procedures.
- Have good follow-through.
- Help everyone as much as possible.
- Be a good mentor.
- Use your time effectively—Chapter 27.
- Automate as much as you can—Chapter 1 and Sections 5.2, 21.1.6, and 26.1.4.
- Always keep the customers' needs in mind—Sections 26.1.3 and 27.2.3.

B.38   I'm Not Sure What I Should Do Next!

- Depending on what stage you are in, certain infrastructure issues should be happening:
  - Basic services, such as email, printing, remote access, and security, need to be there from the outset.
  - Automation of common tasks, such as machine installations, configuration, maintenance, account creation, and deletion, should happen early; so should basic policies.
  - Software depot should happen a little later (but not before it is a mess).
  - Documentation should be written as things are implemented or it will never happen.
  - Monitoring needs to happen before you can think about improvements and scaling, which are issues for a more mature site.
  - Chapter 15 talks about when and how the helpdesk should come into the process.
- Get more in touch with your customers to find out what their priorities are.

- Improve your trouble-ticket system—Chapter 15.
- Review the top 10 percent of the ticket generators—Section 15.2.1.
- Adopt better revision control of configuration files—Chapter 10, particularly Section 10.1.1.

B.39   There's Never Enough Time to Get Work Done!

- Read the time management section—Section 27.1.2.
- Take a time-management class—Section 27.1.2.
- Use a Console Server so that you aren't spending so much time running back and forth to the machine room—Sections 17.1.10 and 2.1.8 and 12.1.7.

Acronyms

ACL	Access Control List
AICPA	American Institute of Certified Public Accountants
ATM	Asynchronous Transfer Mode
ATS	Automatic Transfer Switch
AUP	Acceptable Use Policy
BGP	Border Gateway Protocol
BOOTP	Boot Protocol
CAD	Computer-Aided Design
CAP	Columbia Appletalk Protocol
CEO	Chief Executive Officer
CERT	Computer Emergency Response Team
CFO	Chief Financial Officer
CGI	Common Gateway Interface
CIAC	Computer Incident Advisory Capability
CIFS	Common Internet File System
CIO	Chief Information Officer
Co-lo	Co-location Center
COO	Chief Operating Officer
CPU	Central Processing Unit
CSE	Computer Support Engineer

CSU/DSU	channel service unit/data service unit
CTO	Chief Technology Officer
CVS	Concurrent Versions System
DHCP	Dynamic Host Configuration Protocol
DLT	Digital Linear Tape
DNA	deoxyribonucleic acid
DNS	Domain Name Service
DoS	Denial of Service
EAP	Employee Assistance Program
EDA	Electronic Design Automation
EIA/TIA	Electronic Industry Association/Telecommunications Industry Association
EIGRP	Enhanced Interior Gateway Routing Protocol
ESD	Electrostatic Discharge
ETR	Estimated Time to Repair
ETSI	European Telecommunication Standards Institute
FAQ	Frequently Asked Question
FCC	Federal Communications Commission
FDDI	Fiber-Distributed Data Interface
FTP	File Transfer Protocol
GUI	graphical user interface
HHA	handheld authentication
HTTP	HyperText Transfer Protocol
HVAC	heating, ventilation, and air-conditioning
I/O	Input/Output
ICMP	Internet Control Message Protocol
IDF	Intermediate Distribution Frame
IDS	Intrusion Detection System
IETF	Internet Engineering Task Force
IMAP	Internet Access Message Protocol
IP	intellectual property
IP	Internet Protocol
IS	information systems
ISDN	Integrated Service Digital Network
ISP	Internet Service Provider
IT	information technology
KVM	Keyboard, Video, and Mouse
LAN	local area network
LDAP	Lightweight Directory Access Protocol
LISA	Large Installation System Association
LPD	Line Printer Daemon Protocol
MAC	media access control
MDF	main distribution frame
MIB	Management Information Base

MIDI	musical instrument digital interface
MIL-SPEC	U.S. military specifications
MONET	Multiwavelength Optical Network
MPEG	Moving Picture Experts Group
MPLS	Multi Protocol Label Switching
MRTG	multi-router traffic graphic
MS-SMS	Microsoft's System Management Service
MTP	Mail Transfer Protocol
MTTR	mean time to repair
MUA	mail user agent
MX	Mail eXchanger
NAS	Network Attached Storage
NCDI	Network Computing Devices, Inc.
NDA	Non-Disclosure Agreement
NEBS	Network Equipment Building System
NFS	Network File System
NIC	Network Interface Card (PC Ethernet network card)
NIS	Network Information Service
NOC	Network Operations Center
OEM	original equipment manufacturer
OLTP	On-line Transaction Processing
OS	operating system
OSI	Open Systems Interconnection
OSPF	Open Shortest Path First
OTP	one-time password
PARIS	Programmable Automatic Remote Installation Service
PC	personal computer
PDA	personal digital assistant
PDU	power distribution unit
PIN	personal identification number
POP	Post Office Protocol
POPI	Protection of Proprietary Information
POP3	Post Office Protocol 3
PR	public relations
QA	quality assurance
QoS	quality of service
RAID	Redundant Array of Independent Disks
RAM	random access memory
RAS	remote access server
RCS	Revision Control System
RFC	Request for Comments
RIP	Routing Information Protocol
RPC	Remote Procedure Call
RTT	Round Trip Time

SA   system administrator
SAGE   System Administrators Guild
SAN   Storage Area Network
SANS   System Administration, Networking, and Security
SAS   Statement of Auditing Standards
SCCS   Source Code Control System
SCM   Software Configuration Management
SCP   Session Control Protocol
SEC   Securities and Exchange Commission
SID   Security ID
SLA   service level agreement
SMB   Server Message Block
SME   subject matter expert
SMTP   Simple Mail Transfer Protocol
SNMP   Simple Network Management Protocol
SONET   Synchronous Optical Network
SQL   Structured Query Language
SSH   Secure SHell
STP   Spanning Tree Protocol
SUID   Set User ID
TCP   Transmission Control Protocol
TFTP   Trivial File Transfer Protocol
TTL   time to live
UID   user identification
UPS   uninterruptible power supply
VLANs   virtual LANs
VPN   virtual private network
VRRP   Virtual Router Redundancy Protocol
WAN   wide area network

Bibliography

[Abrahams 1997] Marc Abrahams. *The Best of Annals of Improbable Research.* New York: W.H. Freeman, 1997 (ISBN: 0716730944).

[Adams 2000] Scott Adams. *The Dilbert Principle.* London: PanMacmillan/Boxtree (ISBN: 0752272209)—http://www.Dilbert.com.

[Albitz et al. 1998] Paul Albitz, Cricket Liu, and Mike Loukides (Eds.). *DNS and BIND.* Sebastapol, CA: O'Reilly & Associates, September (ISBN: 1565925122).

[Allen 1999] Jeff R. Allen. Driving by the rear-view mirror: Managing a network with Cricket. In *Proceedings First Conference on Network Administration (NETA '99),* Santa Clara, April 7–10, pp. 1–10. USENIX.

[Allman and Amos 1985] Eric Allman and Miriam Amos. Sendmail revisited. In *Proceedings USENIX Conference,* Portland, OR, Summer, pp. 547–555. USENIX.

[Anonymous 1997] Anonymous. The backhoe, natural enemy of the network administrator, July—http://www.23.com/backhoe/.

[Archer 1993] Barrie Archer. Towards a POSIX standard for software administration. In *Proceedings Systems Administration (LISA VII) Conference.* Monterey, November 1–5, pp. 67–79. USENIX.

[Beck 1999] R. Beck. Dealing with public Ethernet jacks—switches, gateways and authentication. In *Proceedings of the Thirteenth Systems Administration Conference LISA (SAGE/USENIX),* p. 149.

[Bent 1993] Wilson H. Bent, Jr. System administration as a user interface: An extended metaphor. In *Proceedings Systems Administration (LISA VII) Conference,* Monterey, November 1–5, pp. 209–212. USENIX.

[Bentley 1999] Jon L. Bentley. *Programming Pearls, Second Edition.* Reading, MA: Addison-Wesley (ISBN: 0201657880).

[Berkowitz 1998] Howard C. Berkowitz. *Designing Addressing Architectures for Routing and Switching:* Indianapolis, IN: Macmillan Technical Publishing (ISBN: 1578700590).

[Berkowitz 1999] Howard C. Berkowitz. *Designing Routing and Switching Architectures.* Indianapolis, IN: Macmillan Technical Publishing (ISBN: 1578700604).

[Berliner 1990] Brian Berliner. CVS II: Parallelizing software development. In *USENIX Conference Proceedings,* Washington, January 22–26, pp. 341–352. USENIX.

[Bernstein 1997] D. J. Bernstein. VERP: Variable envelope return paths, February 1997—http://crypto/proto/verptxt.

[Black 1999] Darryl P. Black. *Building Switched Networks: Multilayer Switching, QoS, IP Multicast, Network Policy, and Service Level Agreements.* Reading, MA: Addison-Wesley (ISBN: 0201379538).

[Black 2000] Uyless D. Black. *IP Routing Protocols: RIP, OSPF, BGP, PNNI and Cisco Routing Protocols.* Upper Saddle River, NJ: Prentice Hall (ISBN: 0130142484).

[Black 2001] Uyless D. Black. *MPLS and Label Switching Networks.* Upper Saddle River, NJ: Prentice Hall (ISBN: 0130158232).

[Blanchard 1993] Kenneth H. Blanchard. *The One Minute Manager.* New York: Berkley Publishing Group (ISBN: 0425098478).

[Bolinger 1995] D. Bolinger. *Applying RCS and SCCS.* Sebastapol, CA: O'Reilly and Associates (ISBN: 1565921178).

[Braden 1989] R. T. Braden. RFC1123: Requirements for Internet hosts—application and support, October. See also STD0003. Updates RFC0822 [Crocker 1982]. Updated by RFC2181 [Elz/Bush 1997]. Status: STANDARD.

[Brutlag 2000] Jake D. Brutlag. Aberrant behavior detection in time series for network monitoring. In *Fourteenth Systems Administration Conference (LISA '00),* New Orleans, December 3–8. USENIX.

[Burgess 1995] Mark Burgess. A site configuration engine. *Computing Systems,* 8(3): 309–337.

[Burgess 2000] Mark Burgess. *Principles of Network and System Administration.* New York: John Wiley & Sons (ISBN: 0471823031).

[Burns 1999a] David D. Burns. *The Feeling Good Handbook.* New York: Avon (ISBN: 0452281326).

[Burns 1999b] David D. Burns. *Feeling Good: The New Mood Therapy.* New York: Avon (ISBN: 0380810336).

[Chalup 2000] Strata Rose Chalup. Technical interviews. *USENIX ;login:,* 25(8): 52–61.

[Chalup et al. 1998] Strata Rose Chalup, Christine Hogan, Greg Kulosa, Bryan McDonald, and Bryan Stansell. Drinking from the fire(walls) hose: Another approach to very large mailing lists. *In Proceedings Twelfth Systems Administration Conference (LISA '98),* Boston, December 6–11, p. 317. USENIX.

[Chapman 1992] D. Brent Chapman. Majordomo: How I manage 17 mailing lists without answering "request" mail. In *Proceedings Systems Administration (LISA VI) Conference,* Long Beach, October 19–23, pp. 135–143. USENIX.

[Chapman and Andrade 1997] Robert B. Chapman and Kathleen R. Andrade. *Insourcing After the Outsourcing: MIS Survival Guide.* New York: AMACOM (ISBN: 0814403867).

[Cheswick and Bellovin 1994] William R. Cheswick and Steven M. Bellovin. *Firewalls and Internet Security: Repelling the Wiley Hacker.* Reading, MA: Addison-Wesley (ISBN: 0201633574).

[Colyer and Wong 1992] Wallace Colyer and Walter Wong. Depot: A tool for managing software environments. In *Proceedings Systems Administration (LISA VI) Conference,* Long Beach, October 19–23, pp. 153–162. USENIX.

[Comer 2000] Douglas Comer. *Internetworking with TCP/IP, Vol. I: Principles, Protocols and Architecture.* Upper Saddle River, NJ: Prentice Hall (ISBN: 0130183806).

[Crichton 1993] Michael Crichton. *Jurassic Park* (film).

[Crispin 1996] M. Crispin. RFC2060: Internet Message Access Protocol, version 4rev1, December. Obsoletes RFC1730. Status: PROPOSED STANDARD.

[Crittenden 1995] Jennifer Crittenden. *The Simpsons*—Episode 2F10, "And Maggie Makes Three" (January)—http://www.snpp.com/episodes/2F10.html.

[Crocker 1982] D. Crocker. RFC822: Standard for the format of ARPA Internet text messages, August. *See also* STD0011. Obsoletes RFC0733. Updated by RFC1123 [Braden 1989], RFC1138, RFC1148, RFC1327, RFC2156. Status: STANDARD.

[Curtin 1999a] Matt Curtin. Electronic snake oil. *USENIX ;login:,* 24(2): 31–38.

[Curtin 1999b] Matt Curtin. Snake Oil Warning Signs: Encryption Software to Avoid, April—http://www.interhack.net/people/cmcurtin/snake-oil-faq.html.

[Dagenais et al. 1993] Michel Dagenais, Stephane Boucher, Robert Grin-Lajoie, Pierre Laplante, Pierre Mailhot, and Centre de Recherche Informatique de Montreal. LUDE: A distributed software library. In *Proceedings Systems Administration (LISA VII) Conference,* Monterey, November 1–5, pp. 25–32. USENIX.

[Darmohray 1993] Tina Darmohray (Ed.). Job Descriptions for System Administrators. USENIX for SAGE, *Short Topics in System Administration #1,* the System Administrator's Guild, October (ISBN: 188044657X).

[Darmohray 2001] Tina Darmohray. Radio buttons and resumes, *USENIX ;login* 26(3), June 2001.

[Davis et al. 1996] C. Davis, P. Vixie, T. Goodwin, and I. Dickinson. RFC1876: A means for expressing location information in the domain name system, January. Updates RFC1034, RFC1035. Status: EXPERIMENTAL.

[Della Maggiora et al. 2000] Paul L. Della Maggiora, Christopher E. Elliott, James M. Thompson, Robert L. Pavone Jr., and Kent J. Phelps. *Performance and Fault Management.* Indianapolis, IN: Cisco Press (ISBN: 1578701805).

[Denning 1999] Dorothy E. Denning. *Information Warfare and Security.* Reading, MA: Addison-Wesley, 1999 (ISBN: 0201433036).

[Dickens, Glazer, and O'Donoghue 1988] Charles Dickens, Mitch Glazer, and Michael O'Donoghue. *Scrooged* (film).

[Dijker 1999] Barbara L. Dijker. Round and round we go. *USENIX ;login:,* 24(2): 8.

[Dodge 1999] John Dodge. Maybe Ascend should have bought Lucent. *ZD-Net eWeek,* January—http://www.zdnet.com/eweek/stories/general/0,11011,385015,00.html.

[Drzyzgula 2000] Robert Drzyzgula. Designing a data center instrumentation system. In *Proceedings Fourteenth Systems Administration Conference (LISA '00),* New Orleans, December 3–8. USENIX.

[Elz and Bush 1996] R. Elz and R. Bush. RFC 1982: Serial number arithmetic, August 1996. Updates RFC1034, RFC1035. Status: PROPOSED STANDARD.

[Elz and Bush 1997] R. Elz and R. Bush. RFC2181: Clarifications to the DNS specification, July. Updates RFC1034, RFC1035, RFC1123. Status: PROPOSED STANDARD.

[Epps, Bailey, and Glatz 1999] Alan Epps, Dr. Glenn Bailey, and Douglas Glatz. NFS and SMB data sharing within a heterogeneous environment: A real world study. *In Proceedings Second Large Installation System Administration of Windows NT Conference,* Seattle, July 14–17, pp. 37–42. USENIX.

[Evard 1997] Remy Evard. An analysis of UNIX system configuration. In *Proceedings Eleventh Systems Administration Conference (LISA '97)*, San Diego, October 26–31, p. 179. USENIX.

[Farrow 1997] Rik Farrow. Software review: SSH for windows. USENIX ;login:, 22(2): 76, April 1997.

[Feit 1999] Sidnie Feit. *Wide Area High Speed Networks*. Reading, MA: Pearson Higher Education (ISBN: 1578701147).

[Fine and Romig 1990] Thomas A. Fine and Steven M. Romig. A console server. In *LISA IV Conference Proceedings,* Colorado Springs, October 18–19, pp. 97–100. USENIX.

[Finke 1994a] Jon Finke. Automating printing configuration. In *LISA VIII Conference Proceedings*, San Diego, September 19–23, pp. 175–183. USENIX.

[Finke 1994b] Jon Finke. Monitoring usage of workstations with a relational database. In *LISA VIII Conference Proceedings,* San Diego, September 19–23, pp. 149–157. USENIX.

[Finke 1995] Jon Finke. SQL 2 html: Automatic generation of HTML database schemas. In *Proceedings Ninth Systems Administration Conference (LISA '95)*, Monterey, September 17–22, pp. 133–138. USENIX.

[Finke 1996] Jon Finke. Institute whitepages as a system Administration problem. In *Proceedings Tenth Systems Administration Conference (LISA '96)* Chicago, September 29–October 4, pp. 233–240. USENIX.

[Finke 1997] Jon Finke. Automation of site configuration management. In *Proceedings Eleventh Systems Administration Conference (LISA '97)*, San Diego, October 26–31, p. 155. USENIX.

[Finke 2000] Jon Finke. An improved approach for generating configuration files from a database. In *Proceedings of the Fourteenth Systems Administration Conference LISA* (SAGE/USENIX), p. 29.

[Fulmer 2000] Kenneth L. Fulmer. *Business Continuity Planning: A Step-by-Step Guide with Planning Forms*. Brookfield, CT: Rothstein Associates (ISBN: 0964164817).

[Fulmer and Levine 1998] Robert Fulmer and Alex Levine. Autoinstall for NT: Complete NT installation over the network. In *Proceedings Large Installation System Administration of Windows NT Conference,* Seattle, August 5–8, p. 27. USENIX.

[Furlani and Osel 1996] John L. Furlani and Peter W. Osel. Abstract yourself with modules. In *Proceedings Tenth Systems Administration Conference (LISA '96)*, Chicago, September 29–October 4, pp. 193–203. USENIX.

[Garfinkel 1994] Simson Garfinkel. *PGP: Pretty Good Privacy*. Sebastapol, CA: O'Reilly and Associates (ISBN: 1565920988).

[Garfinkel and Spafford 1996] Simson Garfinkel and Gene Spafford. *Practical UNIX and Internet Security*. Sebastapol, CA: O'Reilly and Associates (ISBN: 1565921488).

[Garfinkel and Spafford 1997] Simson Garfinkel and Gene Spafford. *Web Security and Commerce*. Sebastapol, CA: O'Reilly and Associates (ISBN: 1565922697).

[Gay and Essinger 2000] Charles L. Gay and James Essinger. *Inside Outsourcing*. Nicholas Brealey (ISBN: 1857882040).

[Glickstein 1996] Bob Glickstein. GNU stow—http://www.gnu.org/software/stow/stow.html.

[Group Staff Outsource 1996] Group Staff Outsource. *Outsourcing*. Indianapolis, IN: South-Western Publishing (ISBN: 0538847514).

[Guichard and Pepelnjak 2000] Jim Guichard and Ivan Pepelnjak. *MPLS and VPN Architectures: A Practical Guide to Understanding, Designing and Deploying MPLS and MPLS-Enabled VPNs*. Indianapolis, IN: Cisco Press (ISBN: 1587050021).

[Guth and Radosevich 1998] Rob Guth and Lynda Radosevich. IBM crosses the olympic finish line. *InfoWorld*, February—http://archive.infoworld.com/cgi-bin/displayArchive.pl?/98/06/e01-06.79%.htm.

[Halabi and McPherson 2000] Sam Halabi and Danny McPherson. Internet Routing Architectures. Indianapolis, IN: Cisco Press (ISBN: 157870233X).

[Harlander 1994] Dr. Magnus Harlander. Central system Administration in a heterogeneous UNIX environment: GeNUAdmin. In *LISA VIII Conference Proceedings*, San Diego, September 19–23, pp. 1–8. USENIX.

[Harris and Stansell 2000] David Harris and Bryan Stansell. Finding time to do it all. *USENIX ;login:*, 25(6): http://www.conserver.com/consoles/.

[Heckerling 1995] Amy Heckerling. *Clueless* (film).

[Heiss 1999] Jason Heiss. Enterprise rollouts with Jumpstart. In *Proceedings Thirteenth Systems Administration Conference (LISA '99)*, Seattle, November 7–12. USENIX.

[Hemmerich 2000] Chris Hemmerich. Automating request-based software distribution. In *Proceedings Fourteenth Systems Administration Conference (LISA '00)*, New Orleans, December 3–8. USENIX.

[Horowitz and Lunt 1997] M. Horowitz and S. Lunt. RFC2228: FTP security extensions, October. Updates RFC0959. Status: PROPOSED STANDARD.

[Houle 1996] Bill Houle. Majorcool: A web interface to majordomo. In *Proceedings Tenth Systems Administration Conference (LISA'96)*, Chicago, September 29–October 4, pp. 145–153. USENIX.

[Hume 1988] Andrew Hume. The file motel—an incremental backup system for UNIX. In *USENIX Conference Proceedings*, San Francisco, Summer, pp. 61–72. USENIX.

[Hunt and Watanabe 1993] Tim Hunter and Scott Watanabe. Guerrilla system administration: Scaling small group Systems Administration to a larger installed base. In *Proceedings Systems Administration (LISA VII) Conference,* Monterey, November 1–5, pp. 99–105. USENIX.

[Jennings and Passaro 1999] Robert W. Jennings and John Passaro. *Make It Big in the $100 Billion Outsource Contracting Industry*. Westfield Press (ISBN: 096543110X).

[Johnson 1991] Spencer Johnson. *The One Minute Sales Person*. New York: Avon Books (ISBN: 0380716038).

[Judge 1999] Mike Judge. *Office Space* (film).

[Kantor and Lapsley 1986] B. Kantor and P. Lapsley. RFC977: Network news transfer protocol: A proposed standard for the stream-based transmission of news, February. Status: PROPOSED STANDARD.

[Katcher 1999] Jeff Katcher. NetApp Tech Report 3070: Scalable Infrastructure for Internet Business—http://www.netapp.com/tech_library/3070.html.

[Keagy 2000] Scott Keagy. *Integrating Voice and Data Networks*. Indianapolis, IN: Cisco Press (ISBN: 1578701961).

[Kercheval 1999] Berry Kercheval. *DHCP: A Guide to Dynamic TCP/IP Network Configuration*. Englewood Cliffs, NJ: Prentice Hall (ISBN: 0130997218).

[Kernighan and Pike 1999] Brian W. Kernighan and Rob Pike. *The Practice of Programming*. Reading, MA: Addison-Wesley (ISBN: 020161586X).

[Knight et al. 1998] S. Knight, D. Weaver, D. Whipple, R. Hinden, D. Mitzel, P. Hunt, P. Higginson, M. Shand, and A. Lindem. RFC2338: Virtual Router Redundancy Protocol, April. Status: PROPOSED STANDARD.

[Koren and Goodman 1992] Leonard Koren and Peter Goodman. *The Haggler's Handbook: One Hour to Negotiating Power*. New York: W.W. Norton (ISBN: 0393309207).

[Kovacich 1998] Gerald Kovacich. *The Information Systems Security Officer's Guide: Establishing and Managing an Information Protection Program*. Boston: Butterworth-Heinenmann (ISBN: 0750698969).

[Kubicki 1992] Carol Kubicki. Customer satisfaction metrics and measurement. In *Proceedings Systems Administration (LISA VI) Conference*, Long Beach, October 19–23, pp. 63–68. USENIX.

[Kubicki 1993] Carol Kubicki. The system administration maturity model—SAMM. In *Proceedings Systems Administration (LISA VII) Conference*, Monterey, November 1–5, pp. 213–225. USENIX.

[Kuong 2000] Javier F. Kuong. *Application Service Provisioning*. Management Advisory Publications (ISBN: 0940706490).

[Lakein 1996] Alan Lakein. *How to Get Control of Your Time and Your Life*. New York: New American Library (ISBN: 0451167724).

[Lear et al. 1994] E. Lear, E. Fair, D. Crocker, and T. Kessler. RFC1627: Network 10 considered harmful (some practices shouldn't be codified), June. Made obsolete by BCP0005, RFC1918 [Rekhter et al 1996]. Status: INFORMATIONAL.

[Leber 1998] Jody Leber. *Windows NT Backup and Restore*. Sebastapol, CA: O'Reilly & Associates (ISBN: 1565922727).

[Lee 1999] Donald C. Lee. *Enhanced IP Services for Cisco Networks: A Practical Resource for Deploying Quality of Service, Security, IP Routing, and VPN Services*. Indianapolis, IN: Cisco Press (ISBN: 1578701066).

[Lemon and Droms 1999] Ted Lemon and Ralph E. Droms. *The DHCP Handbook: Understanding, Deploying, and Managing Automated Configuration Services*. Reading, MA: Pearson Higher Education (ISBN: 1578701376).

[Levitt 1997] Alan M. Levitt. *Disaster Planning and Recovery: A Guide for Facilities Professionals*. New York: John Wiley & Sons (ISBN: 0471142050).

[Levy 2001] Elias Levy. Bugtraq—http://www.securityfocus.com/frames/?content=/ forums/bugtraq/intro.html%.

[Libes 1990] D. Libes. RFC1178: Choosing a name for your computer, August. *See also* FYI0005. Status: INFORMATIONAL.

[Limoncelli 1998] Thomas A. Limoncelli. Please quit. *USENIX ;login:* 23(5): 38.

[Limoncelli 1999] Thomas A. Limoncelli. Deconstructing user requests and the nine step model. In *Proceedings of the Thirteenth Systems Administration conference LISA* (SAGE/USENIX), p. 35.

[Limoncelli et al. 1998] Thomas A. Limoncelli, Robert Fulmer, Thomas Reingold, Alex Levine, and Ralph Loura. Providing reliable NT desktop services by avoiding NT server. In *Proceedings Large Installation System Administration of Windows NT Conference,* Seattle, August 5–8, p. 75. USENIX.

[Limoncelli and Hogan 2001] Thomas A. Limoncelli and Christine Hogan. *Principles of Network and System Administration.* Boston: Addison-Wesley (ISBN: 0201702711).

[Limoncelli et al. 1997] Thomas A. Limoncelli, Tom Reingold, Ravi Narayan, and Ralph Loura. Creating a Network for Lucent Bell Labs Research South. In *Proceedings Eleventh Systems Administration Conference (LISA '97),* San Diego, October 26–31, p. 123. USENIX.

[Lions 1996] John Lions. *Lions' Commentary on UNIX, Sixth Edition,* with Source Code. Menlo Park, CA: Peer-to-Peer Communications (ISBN: 1573980137).

[Liu 2001] Cricket Liu. The Ties that BIND: Using BIND Name Servers with Windows 2000. *Linux Magazine,* March—http://www.linux-mag.com/2001-03/toc.html.

[Locke et al. 2000] Christopher Locke, Rick Levine, Doc Searls, and David Weinberger. The Cluetrain Manifesto: *The End of Business as Usual.* Boston: Perseus Press (ISBN: 0738202444).

[MacKenzie 1997] R. Alec MacKenzie. *The Time Trap.* New York: AMACOM (ISBN: 081447926X).

[Maniago 1987] Pierette Maniago. Consulting via mail at Andrew. In *Large Installation System Administrators Workshop Proceedings,* Philadelphia, April 9–10, pp. 22–23. USENIX.

[Marcus 1999] J. Scott Marcus. *Designing Wide Area Networks and Internetworks: A Practical Guide.* Reading, MA: Addison-Wesley (ISBN: 0201695847).

[Mauro and McDougall 2000] Jim Mauro and Richard McDougall. *Solaris Internals: Core Kernel Architecture.* Upper Saddle River, NJ: Prentice Hall PTR/Sun MicroSystems Press (ISBN: 0130224960).

[McGee-Cooper 1994] Ann McGee-Cooper. *Time Management for Unmanageable People.* New York: Bantam/Doubleday (ISBN: 0553370715).

[McKusick, Bostic, and Karels 1996] Marshall Kirk McKusick, Keith Bostic, and Michael J. Karels (Eds.). *The Design and Implementation of the 4.4BSD Operating System.* Reading, MA: Addison-Wesley (ISBN: 0201549794).

[McLaughlin 1990] L. McLaughlin, III. RFC1179: Line Printer Daemon Protocol, August. Status: INFORMATIONAL.

[McNutt 1993] Dinah McNutt. Role-based system administration or who, what, where, and how. In *Proceedings Systems Administration (LISA VII) Conference,* Monterey, November 1–5, pp. 107–112. USENIX.

[Menter 1993] E. Scott Menter. Managing the mission critical environment. In *Proceedings Systems Administration (LISA VII) Conference,* Monterey, November 1–5, pp. 81–86. USENIX.

[Miller and Davis 2000] Arthur R. Miller and Micheal H. Davis. *Intellectual Property, Patents, Trademarks and Copyright in a Nutshell.* Belmont, CA: West/Wadsworth (ISBN: 0314235191).

[Miller and Donnini 2000] Allan Miller and Alex Donnini. Relieving the burden of system administration support through support automation. In *Proceedings Fourteenth Systems Administration Conference (LISA '00),* New Orleans, December 3–8. USENIX.

[Miller and Morris 1996] Mark Miller and Joe Morris. Centralized administration of distributed firewalls. In *Proceedings Tenth Systems Administration Conference (LISA '96),* Chicago, September 29–October 4, pp. 19–23. USENIX.

[Mogul and Postel 1985] J. C. Mogul and J. Postel. RFC950: Internet Standard Subnetting Procedure, August. Updates RFC0792. *See also* STD0005. Status: STANDARD.

[Moran and Lyon 1993] Joe Moran and Bob Lyon. The restore-o-mounter: The file motel revisited. In *USENIX Conference Proceedings,* Cincinnati, Summer, pp. 45–58. USENIX.

[Morgenstern 1998] Julie Morgenstern. *Organizing from the Inside Out: The Foolproof System for Organizing Your Home, Your Office and Your Life.* Dallas: Owl Publishing (ISBN: 0805056491).

[Moy 2000] John T. Moy. *OSPF: Anatomy of an Internet Routing Protocol.* Reading, MA: Addison-Wesley (ISBN: 0201634724).

[Myers and Rose 1996] J. Myers and M. Rose. RFC1939: Post Office Protocol, version 3, May. *See also* STD0053. Obsoletes RFC1725. Updated by RFC1957, RFC2449. Status: STANDARD.

[Mylott 1995] Thomas R. Mylott, III. *Computer Outsourcing: Managing the Transfer of Information Systems.* Englewood Cliffs, NJ: Prentice Hall (ISBN: 013127614X).

[Neumann 1997] Peter Neumann. *Computer-Related Risks.* Reading, MA: Addison-Wesley (ISBN: 020155805X).

[Niksic 1998] Hrvoje Niksic. GNU wget—http://www.gnu.org/software/wget/wget.html.

[Norberg and Russell 2000] Stefan Norberg and Deborah Russell. *Securing Windows NT/2000 Servers for the Internet: a Checklist for System Administrators.* Sebastapol, CA: O'Reilly and Associates (ISBN: 1565927680).

[Northcutt 1999] Stephen Northcutt. G4.1—Computer Security Incident Handling: Step-by-Step. Bethesda, MD: SANS Institute, February (ISBN: 0967299217).

[Oetiker 1998a] Tobias Oetiker. MRTG—the Multi Router Traffic Grapher. In *Proceedings Twelfth Systems Administration Conference (LISA '98),* Boston, December 6–11, p. 141. USENIX.

[Oetiker 1998b] Tobias Oetiker. SEPP—software installation and sharing system. In *Proceedings Twelfth Systems Administration Conference (LISA '98),* Boston, December 6–11, p. 253. USENIX.

[Oncken et al. 1991] William Oncken, Jr., et al. *The One Minute Manager Meets the Monkey*. Palatine, IL: Quill (ISBN: 0688103804).

[Ondishko 1989] Denise Ondishko. Administration of department machines by a central group. In *USENIX Conference Proceedings*, Baltimore, Summer, pp. 73–82. USENIX.

[Oppliger 2000] Ralf Oppliger. *Secure Messaging with PGP and S/MIME*. Norwood, MA: Artech House (ISBN: 158053161X).

[Osterman 2000] Michael Osterman. The Impact of Effective Storage Technology on Exchange TCO, January—http://www.cnilive.com/docs_pub/html/stor00.html.

[Peacock and Giuffrida 1988] Don Peacock and Mark Giuffrida. Big Brother: A network services expert. In *USENIX Conference Proceedings,* San Francisco, Summer, pp. 393–398. USENIX.

[Pepelnjak 2000] Ivan Pepelnjak. *EIGRP Network Design Solutions*. Indianapolis, IN: Cisco Press (ISBN: 1578701651).

[Perlman 2000] Radia Perlman. *Interconnections, Second Edition: Bridges, Routers, Switches, and Internetworking Protocols*. Boston: Addison-Wesley (ISBN: 0201634481).

[Phillips and LeFebvre 1998] Gretchen Phillips and William LeFebvre. Hiring System Administrators. USENIX for SAGE, Short Topics in System Administration #5—the System Administrator's Guild (ISBN: 1880446383).

[Pildush 2000] Galina Diker Pildush. *Cisco ATM Solution: Master ATM Implementation of Cisco Networks*. Indianapolis, IN: Cisco Press (ISBN: 1578702135).

[Postel 1981] J. Postel. RFC792: Internet Control Message Protocol, September. Obsoletes RFC0777. Updated by RFC0950 [Mogul and Postel 1985]. *See also* STD0005. Status: STANDARD.

[Postel and Reynolds 1985] J. Postel and J. K. Reynolds. RFC959: File Transfer Protocol, October. Obsoletes RFC0765. Updated by RFC2228 [Horowitz and Lunt 1997]. Status: STANDARD.

[Powell and Mason 1995] Patrick Powell and Justin Mason. LPRng—an enhanced printer spooler system. In *Proceedings Ninth Systems Administration Conference (LISA '95),* Monterey, September 17–22, pp. 13–24. USENIX.

[Powers and Russell 1993] Dr. Paul Powers and Deborah Russell. *Love Your Job!* Sebastapol, CA: O'Reilly and Associates (ISBN: 1565920368).

[Preston 1999] W. Curtis Preston. *UNIX Backup and Recovery*. Sebastapol, CA: O'Reilly & Associates (ISBN: 1565926420).

[Rekhter et al. 1996] Y. Rekhter, B. Moskowitz, D. Karrenberg, G. J. de Groot, and E. Lear. RFC1918: Address allocation for private Internets, February. *See also* BCP0005. Obsoletes RFC1627, RFC1597. Status: BEST CURRENT PRACTICE.

[Ressman and Valdés 2000] David Ressman and John Valdés. Use of cfengine for automated multiplatform software and patch distribution. In *Proceedings Fourteenth Systems Administration Conference (LISA '00),* New Orleans, December 3–8. USENIX.

[Rigney et al. 1997] C. Rigney, A. Rubens, W. Simpson, and S. Willens. RFC2138: Remote authentication dial in user service (RADIUS), April. Obsoletes RFC2058. Status: PROPOSED STANDARD.

[Ringel and Limoncelli 1999] Matt F. Ringel and Thomas A. Limoncelli. Adverse termination procedures or how to fire a system administrator. In *Proceedings of the Thirteenth Systems Administration Conference LISA* (SAGE/USENIX), p. 45.

[Rothery and Robertson 1995] Brian Rothery and Ian Robertson. *The Truth about Outsourcing.* Burlington, VT: Ashgate Publishing Company (ISBN: 0566075156).

[Schafer 1992a] Peg Schafer. bbn-public—contributions from the user community. In *Proceedings Systems Administration (LISA VI) Conference,* Long Beach, October 19–23, pp. 211–213. USENIX.

[Schafer 1992b] Peg Schafer. Is centralized system administration the answer? In *Proceedings Systems Administration (LISA VI) Conference,* Long Beach, October 19–23, pp. 55–61. USENIX.

[Schreider 1998] Tari Schreider. *Encyclopedia of Disaster Recovery, Security and Risk Management.* Duluth, GA: Crucible Publishing Works (ISBN: 0966272900).

[Schwartz, Cottrell, and Dart 1994] Karl L. Schwartz, Les Cottrell, and Marty Dart. Adventures in the evolution of a high-bandwidth network for central servers. In *LISA VIII Conference Proceedings,* San Diego, September 19–23, pp. 159–166. USENIX.

[Shapiro and Allman 1999] Gregory Neil Shapiro and Eric Allman. Sendmail evolution: 8.10 and beyond. In *Proceedings FREENIX Track: 1999 USENIX Annual Technical Conference,* Monterey, June 6–11, pp. 149–158. USENIX.

[Sheldon and Cox 2000] Tom Sheldon and Phil Cox (Eds.). *Windows 2000 Security Handbook.* New York: McGraw-Hill (ISBN: 0072124334).

[Small 1993] Fred Small. *Everything possible,* November. In particular, the title song.

[Smallwood 1992] Kevin Smallwood. SAGE views: Whither the customer? *USENIX ;login:,* 17(5): 15–16.

[Smith 1975] Manuel J. Smith. *When I Say No, I Feel Guilty.* New York: Bantam (ISBN: 0553263900).

[Smith 2000] Manuel J. Smith. *When I Say No I Feel Guilty, Vol. II: For Managers and Executives.* A Train Press (ISBN: 0970299605).

[Snyder et al. 1986] Garth Snyder, Todd Miller, et al. sudo—http://www.courtesan.com/sudo.

[Spurgeon 2000] Charles E. Spurgeon. *Ethernet: The Definitive Guide.* Sebastapol, CA: O'Reilly and Associates (ISBN: 1565926609).

[Stern 1991] Hal Stern. Managing NFS and NIS. Sebastapol, CA: O'Reilly and Associates, Inc., 1991 (ISBN: 0937175757).

[Stevens 1994] W. Richard Stevens. *TCP/IP Illustrated, Volume 1: The Protocols.* Reading, MA: Addison-Wesley (ISBN: 0201633469).

[Stewart 1999] John W. Stewart. *BGP4: Inter-Domain Routing in the Internet.* Reading, MA: Addison-Wesley (ISBN: 0201379511).

[Thomas 1998a] Thomas M. Thomas. OSPF Network Design Solutions. Indianapolis, IN: Cisco Press, December 1998 (ISBN: 1578700469).

[Thorpe 1998b] Christopher Thorpe. SSU: Extending SSH for secure root administration. In *Proceedings Twelfth Systems Administration Conference (LISA '98),* Boston, December 6–11, p. 27. USENIX.

[Valian and Watson 1999] Peter Valian and Todd K. Watson. NetReg: An automated DHCP registration system. In *Proceedings Thirteenth Systems Administration Conference (LISA '99)*, Seattle, November 7–12. USENIX.

[van den Berg 1990] Stephen R. van den Berg. procmail—http://www.procmail.org.

[Van Epp and Baines 1992] Peter Van Epp and Bill Baines. Dropping the mainframe without crushing the users: Mainframe to distributed UNIX in nine months. In *Proceedings Systems Administration (LISA VI) Conference,* Long Beach, October 19–23, pp. 39–53. USENIX.

[Vegesna 2001] Srinivas Vegesna. *IP Quality of Service.* Indianapolis, IN: Cisco Press (ISBN: 1578701163).

[Viega et al. 1998] John Viega, Barry Warsaw, and Ken Manheimer. Mailman: The GNU mailing list manager. In *Proceedings Twelfth Systems Administration Conference (LISA '98),* Boston, December 6–11, p. 309. USENIX.

[Vincent——] Jesse Vincent. "Request Tracker" http://www.fsck.com/projects/rt/.

[Williams 1998] Oakie D. Williams. *Outsourcing: A CIO's Perspective.* Boca Raton, FL: CRC Press/St. Lucie Press (ISBN: 1574442163).

[Williamson 2000] Beau Williamson. Developing IP Multicast Networks: The Definitive Guide to Designing and Deploying Cisco IP Multicast Networks. Indianapolis, IN: Cisco Press, January 2000 (ISBN: 1578700779).

[Wood 1999] Charles C. Wood. *Information Security Policies Made Easy.* Houston: Baseline Software/PentaSafe (ISBN: 1881585069).

[Yeong, Howes, and Kille 1995] W. Yeong, T. Howes, and S. Kille. RFC1777: Lightweight Directory Access Protocol, March. Obsoletes RFC1487. Status: DRAFT STANDARD.

[Ylonen 1996] Tatu Ylonen. SSH—secure login connections over the Internet. In *Proceedings Sixth USENIX Security Symposium,* San Jose, July 22–25, pp. 37–42. USENIX.

[Zwicky et al. 1990] Elizabeth D. Zwicky, Steve Simmons, and Ron Dalton. Policy as a system administration tool. In *LISA IV Conference Proceedings,* Colorado Springs, October 18–19, pp. 115–124. USENIX.

[Zwicky et al. 2000] Elizabeth D. Zwicky, D. Brent Chapman, and Simon Cooper. *Building Internet Firewalls.* Sebastapol, CA: O'Reilly and Associates (ISBN: 1565928717).

Index

Sys•tems
Ad•min•is•tra•tor

n. One who performs systems administration functions as a primary responsibility of their employment.

http://www.sage.org

SAGE is The System Administrators Guild, the premiere international professional organization dedicated to the support of system administrators and the advance of systems administration as a profession. SAGE seeks to:

■ **Strengthen the Community** — SAGE works for the benefit of the sysadmin community by establishing standards of professional excellence and recognizing those who achieve it, developing guidelines for improving technical and managerial capabilities of its members and promoting activities that support the community and profession.

■ **Provide Learning Resources** — SAGE offers many educational, technical and professional resources that teach the skills critical to systems administrators working in rapidly changing technical environments.

■ **Share Knowledge** — Learning through experience has been a hallmark of the SAGE experience. SAGE provides the forum where system administrators can discuss, compare, commiserate and resolve common issues and concerns.

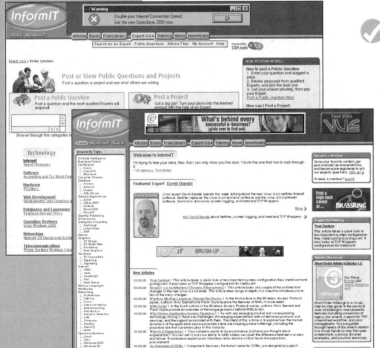